National Intelligencer Newspaper Abstracts 1851

Joan M. Dixon

HERITAGE BOOKS
2008

HERITAGE BOOKS
AN IMPRINT OF HERITAGE BOOKS, INC.

Books, CDs, and more—Worldwide

For our listing of thousands of titles see our website
at
www.HeritageBooks.com

Published 2008 by
HERITAGE BOOKS, INC.
Publishing Division
100 Railroad Ave. #104
Westminster, Maryland 21157

Copyright © 2008 Joan M. Dixon

All rights reserved. No part of this book may be reproduced or transmitted in any form or by any means, electronic or mechanical, including photocopying, recording or by any information storage and retrieval system without written permission from the author, except for the inclusion of brief quotations in a review.

International Standard Book Numbers
Paperbound: 978-0-7884-4569-9
Clothbound: 978-0-7884-7650-1

NATIONAL INTELLIGENCER NEWSPAPER WASHINGTON, D C 1851

TABLE OF CONTENTS

Daily National Intelligencer, Washington, D C, 1851: pg 1

Baker's Chocolate: 89
Biography of John Sevier: 442
Biography of Wm Wirt: 60
California-Cmte of Vigilance: 307-309
Capt Kidd adventures: 511
Centennial Anniversary of Georgetown: 400-402
Claims against Mexico-awards: 178-182

Commencements: Columbian College: 302
               Georgetown College: 318-319
               Howard Univ: 306
               Nat'l Med College, D C: 122
               Visitation Academy, Gtwn: 323-324
               Washington Seminary: 300

Court Martial trial of Brig Gen Geo Talcott: 248; 295
Death of Cmdor Jas Barron: 189
Death of Gen Geo M Brooke: 133
Death of Polowaski: 245
Explosion of the frig Donna Maria II: 75-76
Executed Patriots: 359
General Orders-War Dept: 9; 126-128; 248; 287-291; 317-318; 423; 500-502
Hungarian emigrants: 393-394; 445
Invaders of Cuba: 431-432
Kosciusko trial: 240; 253-254
Letter from Daniel Webster: 110
Licenses issued in Washington: 98-109; 164-172; 458-462
Life of Cmdor Jacob Jones: 211
Life of Constantine Anthoine Beelen: 27
Lopez forces: 372-373
Loss of ship Ivanhoe: 155

Maryland Agricultural Society: 451-452
Military Academy Cadets: 149

Murder of Catharine Day: 211; 311; 350
Murder of Wm Cosden family: 93
National Library destroyed: 542
Naval Academy candidates: 237
Oak Hill Cemetery: 215; 427

Officers of the: brig Porpoise: 79
                        ship Cyane: 440
                        ship Saint Lawrence: 76
                        sloop of war Germantown: 174
                        sloop of war John Adams: 194
                        sloop of war Vandalia: 444
                        steamboat Yanke: 174
                        steamer Saranac: 40
                        steamer Susquehanna: 242

Original letter of Daniel Boone: 506
Prisoners-Habana/Havana: 378; 407-409
Relic of the Revolution: 347
Remains of Admr Paul Jones: 254; 509
Sale of estate of Michael Hillegas: 112
Sale of Washington real estate for taxes: 285-286
Steamer Dacotah/Dakotah disaster: 352; 355
Steamer James Jackson disaster: 410
Steamer Ohio disaster: 222
Surgeons-U S Navy: 81
U S Coast Survey personnel: 74-75
Visit to Old Braintree: 322
West Point graduates: 278

Index: pg 549

PREFACE
Daily National Intelligencer Newspaper Abstracts
1851
Joan M Dixon

The National Intelligencer & Washington Advertiser is hereafter the Daily National Intelligencer. It was the first newspaper printed in Washington, D C; Samuel H Smith, the originator. The same was transferred to Jos Gales, jr on Aug 31, 1810; on Nov 1, 1812, the paper was under the firm of Jos Gales, sr, & Wm W Seaton. The Library of Congress has microfilm of the paper from the first issue of Oct 31, 1800 thru Jan 8, 1870, the final paper. The Evening Star Newspaper of Jan 10, 1870 reports: The Intelligencer is discontinued; the proprietor, Mr Alex Delmar, says that having lost several thousand dollars, & being in poor health, he has resolved to discontinue its publication.

Included in the abstracts are advertisements; appointments by the President; Hse o/Rep petitions; passed Acts; legal notices; marriages; deaths; mscl notices; social events; tax sales; military promotions; court cases; deaths by accident; prisoners; & maritime information-crews. Items or events which might be a clue as to the location, age or relationship of an individual are copied

No attempt has been made to correct the spelling. Due to the length of some articles, it was necessary to present only the highlights of same. Chancery and Equity records are copied as written.

The index contains all surnames and *tracts of lands/places*. **Maritime vessels** are found under barge, boat, brig, frig, schn'r, ship, sloop, steamboat, tugboat, yacht or vessel.

ABBREVIATIONS:

AA CO	ANNE ARUNDEL COUNTY
CO	COMPANY/COUNTY
CMDER	COMMANDER
CMDOR	COMMODOR
D C	DISTRICT OF COLUMBIA
ELIZ	ELIZABETH
ELIZA	ELIZA
MONTG CO	MONTGOMERY COUNTY
PG CO	PRINCE GEORGE'S CO
WASH	WASHINGTON
WASH, D C	WASHINGTON, DISTRICT OF COLUMBIA

BOOKS IN THE NATIONAL INTELLIGENCER NEWSPAPER SERIES: 1800-1805/1806-1810/1811-1813/1814-1817/1818-1820/1821-1823/1824-1826/1827-1829/1830-1831/1832-1833/1834-1835/1836-1837/1838-1839/1840/1841/1842/1843/1844/1845/1845/1847/1848/1849/1850/1851/1852/ SPECIAL CIVIL WARS 2 VOLS, 1861-1865

Dedicated to special cousin "Dick"
Richard Earl Barber: b Feb 1927-Wash; d Oct 1993-Md
Married on Aug 28, 1959-Md to
Adelaide Hock Bell: b Oct 1927; d Aug 1999-Md

DAILY NATIONAL INTELLIGENCER NEWSPAPER
WASHINGTON, D C
1851

WED JAN 1, 1851
Senate: 1-Ptn of Robt J Cox for a pension: who states he was placed on the pension roll in Jan, 1850, in consequence of wounds received which rendered him totally unable. He obtained his certificate of discharge from Gen Quitman in 1847. His ptn asks that he may receive a pension from the time of his discharge up to the time he was put on the pension roll: referred to the Cmte on Pensions. 2-Memorial of Josiah Snow & A Bangs, & associates, asking a donation or subscription on the part of the U S for a telegraph line from Mississippi river to Calif: referred to the Cmte on the Post Ofc & Post Roads. 3-Ptn of Jas L Gage, a gentleman of very high intelligence, & a learned machinist, desires a contract for collecting together & repairing the useless public arms of the U S: referred to the Cmte on Military Affairs. 4-Memorial of Henry Williams & others, owners of the brig **Nimrod**, asking to be indemnified for the loss of said brig, unjustly seized & sold under the erroneous allegation that the timber on board was cut on the Gov't lands: referred to the Cmte of Claims. 5-Ptn of Nancy Wright, widow of Jas Wright, late an ofcr in the revenue cutter service, asking to be allowed a pension. Her husband was an engineer on board the U S steamship **McLane** during the Mexican war, & he died of disease contracted by exposure in the public service: referred to the Cmte on Pensions. 6-Cmte on Public Lands: memorial of D Pollock, in behalf of the heirs of Wm Harper, submitted an adverse report: ordered to be printed. Same cmte: claim of Chas Melrose, for the correction of an error in the location of the bounty land warrants, with a bill for his relief: ordered to a second reading. 7-Claim of the widow of Brevet Col Kneas Mackay, late of the quartermaster's dept of the U S army, for a pension: referred to the Cmte on Pensions. 8-Cmte on Military Affairs: memorial of Maria M Alexander, only heir of Geo Madison, asking remuneration for sacrifices & services during the war of the Revolution: asked to be discharged from the further consideration of the ptn & that it be referred to the Cmte on Revolutionary Claims. 8-Cmte on Indian Affairs: memorial of the legal reps of Wm Armstrong, late acting Superintendent of the Western Territory, bill for their relief: ordered to a second reading. 9-Cmte of Claims: memorial of Jas Robertson, asking indemnity for certain injuries inflicted on him by an ofcr of the U S Senate: asked to be discharged from the further consideration of the same.

U S District Court, Springfield, Ill, Dec 18: Chas Emery, alias Chas Baker, was found guilty of robbing the mail, Feb, Apr, May, & Jul last. Sentenced to 6 years in the penitentiary.

Jas Waters froze to death during a storm on Mon week, near North Adams, Mass. He was about 30 years old, & leaves a wife & 2 children. He was a temperance man.

Planter's Advocate, published at Macon, Noxubee Co, Miss: on Dec 8, Mr Jonathan Henkle & Mr Adams, of that county, were reclining on the side of a hill, when they were attacked by a large eagle which fastened its talons in the breast of Mr Henkle. A fight ensued between the men & the eagle, & they succeeded in capturing it alive. Mr Henkle received a slight wound in the breast. The eagle is said to be very large.

On Mon, as Jas Fleming, son of Mr John Fleming, hackdriver, was returning to his father's house, on 4½ st, near Md ave, when he was knocked down & robbed. His personal injury is very serious. He was robbed of 2 to 3 weeks' earnings.

This is to give notice that, whereas the subscriber assigned to Saml Ward, of N Y C, trustee, for the benefit of Lucy L Ward, his wife, one-fourth part of his right in Montgomery's Vertical Tubular Steam Boiler," secured by letter patent dated Dec 26, 1845; & also one-fourth part of his right in Montgomery's Safety Guard," secured by patent dated Sep 22, 1845; Whereas, by instrument of writing dated Oct 1, 1849, [to be found on record,] the same Saml & Lucy L Ward covenanted to secure a note of hand of the same Saml Ward for $3,700, with interest, to be paid out of the first proceeds of said fourth part interest in said patent right, & also to be secured by a mortgage on a plantation in Texas, which said mortgage, though often requested, the same Saml Ward & Lucy L Ward, have refused to give: & as there are large sums now due to the subscriber from them, proceeds of said patent right agreed to be secured to said subscriber. Now this is to caution the public against the purchase from Saml & Lucy L Ward, or any agent of theirs, the said interest in said patent, as they have utterly failed to comply with any of the terms which said assignment was made to them. –Jas Montgomery

By order of distrain for ground rent due to Wm M Maddox by A Wilson & L Hass, I will expose at public sale, on Jan 7, sundry goods & chattels. H R Maryman, Bailiff

Criminal Court-Wash. 1-Jury recommended mercy to prisoner Horsed Mediperis. 2-Henry Young sentenced to 3 years in the penitentiary for grand larceny. 3-Chew Dorsey, free negro, guilty of larceny: sentenced to 18 months in the penitentiary. 4-Ellen Lindsley, free negress: sentenced to 6 years in the penitentiary for theft. 5-Wm Brown, free negro, old offender, sentenced to 1 year in the penitentiary for petit larceny. 6-Mary Frances Wheeler, free negress, sentenced to 1 year in the penitentiary for grand larceny. 7-Jas Proctor, free negro, sentenced to 2 years in the penitentiary for grand larceny. 8-Jas Digges, free negro, old offender, acquitted of petit larceny. 9-Peyton Harris, free negro, acquitted of petit larceny. 10-Peyton Harris, freed negro, acquitted of petit larceny.

For rent: 2 story frame house on Md ave, between 6th & 7th sts. Apply to Owen Leddy, on 7th st, or H Leddy, corner of 11th & I sts. –M F Gannon

THU JAN 2, 1851
Postmaster Gen est'd the following new Post Ofcs for week ending Dec 28, 1850.

Ofc	County, State	Postmaster
S Brookfield	Madison, N Y	Joshua D Clarke
Centre Valley	Otsego, N Y	Oliver P Thrall
Libson Centre	St Lawrence, N Y	John McBride
Fort Washington	PG Co, Md	Orlando B Wilcox
Focht's Forge	Schuylkill, Pa	Abraham Focht
Levi	Jackson, Ohio	John Kennedy
Boyd's Tavern	Albemarle, Val	A J Shepherd
Cedar Grove	Kaufman, Texas	W Gibbard
Marshall	Marshall, Ia	Moses F Barnett
Wild Cat	Carroll, Ia	Elias L Hall
Taylor's Corner	De Kalb, Ia	B F Kendall
Yellow River	Marshall, Ia	B F Kendall
Cedar Grove	Breckenridge, Ky	Isaac Atkinson
Centre Point	Knox, Ill	Zimri Pond
Goshen Prairie	Mercer, Mo	Thos Ballen
Pacific City	Lewis, Or	Jas D Holman

Names Changed: Hawkin's, Sullivan Co, N Y, changed to Fremont.
Tompkinsville, Chas Co, Md, charged to Harris' Lot.
Green Oak Centre, Livingston Co, Mich, changed to Warnerville.
Dentonville, Hanover Co, Va, changed to Rockville.
Skinnersville, Wash Co, N C, changed to Leo.
Alfred, Henderson, Texas, changed to Athens.
Talladega, Jefferson Co, Ark, changed to Lehi.
Chickasaw Crossing, Jackson Co, Ark, changed to Augusta.
Tanner's Creek, Dearborn Co, Ind, changed to Guilford.
Lamar, Marion Co, Tenn, changed to Fairview.
Elizabeth, Andrew Co, Mo, changed to Boston.

The undersigned, lately of the Aracen's Head, N Y, & formerly of the Alhambra, Richmond, Va, have fitted up the elegant Restaurant lately erected by the Messrs Brown, at 6th & C st, & will be open from 11 till 1 o'clock. Dinner, suppers & dishes of all kinds sent to private families, & oysters pickled to order.
–Russell W Allen

Orphans Court of Wash Co, D C. Letters testamentary on the personal estate of Jas Williams, late of said county, deceased. –Wm B Todd, J H Wailes, execs

Mrd: on Dec 19, in Rockingham Co, by Rev Mr Dodson, Hon David S Reid, Govn'r elect of N C, to Miss Henrietta W, daughter of the Hon Thos Settle

John McCormick, of Montgomery, Ala, was accidentally drowned on Dec 24, when his skiff was upset. He was recently editor of the Montgomery Advertiser.

FRI JAN 3, 1851
Senate: 1-Ptn of Eliz Butler, heir & child of a Revolutionary soldier, asking to be allowed a pension: referred to the Cmte on Pensions. 2-Ptn of Dr Chas Richardson, of Balt, who states that he has discovered the cause of potato rot: he prays for appropriation to enable him to make more thorough examination into the matter. He has also invented a new mode of ventilation applicable to ships, jails, & hospitals, calculated to prevent disease. Referred to the Cmte on Naval Affairs. 3-Memorial of Henny R F Capron, widow of a gallant ofcr of the army who was killed in Mexico during the war with that republic, asking that the half pay granted her may be continued for life: referred to the Cmte on Pensions. 4-Memorial of Maria L Walker, daughter & heir of John Tayloe Griffin, asking compensation for the services of her father as commissary in the war of the Revolution, & also indemnity for losses sustained & the reimbursement of money advanced for the use of the U S during said war: referred to the Cmte on Revolutionary Claims. 5-Memorial of F Andrews, asking to be allowed extra pay & bounty for his services as an Affairs.

Criminal Court-Wash. 1-John Ford, free negro, not guilty for petit larceny. 2-John Winders, free negro, guilty of assault & bettery. 3-David Rawlings, free negro, guilty of petit larceny, & sentenced to 4 months in jail. 4-Aaron Talbot & Danl Chase, free negro lads, guilty of petit larceny & sentenced each to 4 months in jail.

Was killed in Phil city, on Dec 22, by the falling from the cars, Henry Hoeke, a native of Germany, but for the last 12 years a respected citizen of this place, aged about 45 years. His funeral is on Sunday, at 2 o'clock, from his late residence near the Navy Yard.

Mrd: on Jan 1, by Rev Mr Chenowith, of Balt, Mr John E Buckington, of Wash, to Miss Mgt E Ashton, of Balt.

Died: Jan 1, suddenly, at her residence at Oatland, near Brookeville, in Montg Co, Md, Margaret D Bowie, in her 47th year, sister of the Hon R J Bowie, of the House of Reps.

SAT JAN 4, 1851
Orphans Court of Wash Co, D C. In the case of John F Ennis, adm of Rev Jos Vanhorsigh, deceased, the adm & Court have appointed Jan 28, for the settlement of the estate, with the assets in hand. –Edw N Roach, Reg/o will.

Senate: 1-Memorial of A J Williamson, a 1st Lt of the 3rd Infty, asking to be indemnified for his baggage & equipage, lost by the destruction of a transport vessel on board of which he was embarked in charge of a detachment of recruits for the army: referred to the Cmte of Claims. 2-Bill for the relief of Hubert H Booley: passed. 3-Bill for the relief of Ira Day, of Vt: passed.

House of Reps: 1-Bills recommended that they pass: Relief of: Monmouth B Hart, Joel Kelly, & Wm Close, securities for the late Benj F Hart, a purser in the U S Navy. Relief of Thos Ryder, a British subject. Relief of Eleanor Davidson; of Jos Johnson; of Capt Wm Duerson, of Ind; of the legal reps of Bernard Todd, deceased; of John Deamit; of Andrew Smith; of Polly Carver, excx of Nathan Carver; of John Poe, of Louisville, Ky; of Edmund Dexter, of Cincinnati; of Adolphus Meier & Co, of St Louis; of Andrew Smith. A pension to Sarah A Bush. Bill to provide for the payment of certain moneys to the legal reps of Conrad Ten Eyck, late marshal of the District of Michigan, deceased. Bill to compensate Wm Woodbridge & Henry Chipman, for services in adjusting titles to lands in Michigan, & for other purposes. Bill to compensate & reimburse the owners & crew of the whaling ship **Chandler Price** the losses & expenses incurred in ransoming the crew of the ship **Columbia**. Bill granting a pension to Mary Pike, widow of Ezra Pike, deceased, was increased from $44.12 to $54.76. Bill for the relief of Thos R Saunders was amended, so as to make the pension commence in Jan, 1850, instead of in 1848. Bill to increase the pension of Henry Click, of Cocke Co, Tenn, was amended so as to make said increase commence in 1850, instead of 1848. Bill for the relief of Geo S Clafflin, was amended by making the pension begin in 1850, instead of 1849. Bill for the relief of Wm Sparks was amended by making his pension commence in 1850, instead of 1847. 2-The following bills were objected to, & lie over: bill of Geo W Billings: relief of Hery La Reintree; relief of the heirs of Lt Col Henry Miller; relief of Anthony Walton Bayard; relief of Thos Coats; relief of Parmelia Slavin, late wife of John Blue, deceased; relief of Geo Keller; relief of Geo G Bishop, & the legal reps of John Arnold, deceased. 3-The resolution to pay J W Nye $525 for damages claimed under a contract with the Postmaster of the House of Reps, was objected to. 4-Bills objected to: relief of: the heirs of Geo B Reed, deceased: of the legal reps of Benj Fry, deceased; of Mrs Susan C Randall; of the heirs of Nicholas Lacharce & others; & of Thos Wishart. Payment of a debt due to the heirs of Antoine Peltier: objected to.

Died: on Jan 3, after a long & painful illness, Mrs Mgt Coleman, in her 47th year. Her funeral will be from her late residence, south B st, Capitol Hill, Sunday, at 2 o'clock.

Died: on Jan 3, Eliz Donnelly, wife of Jas Donnelly, late of N Y, aged 23 years. Her funeral will take place on Sunday, at 3 o'clock, from her late residence, 12th & C st, Island.

Died: on Jan 2, Patrick Boyle, aged 75 years. His funeral will take place from the residence of C Gautier, 11th st, near Pa ave, this morning, at 9 o'clock.

MON JAN 6, 1851
Household & kitchen furniture at auction: on Jan 8, at the late residence of Jas Williams, deceased. -A Green, auctioneer

Ladies Hair-dressing: Mr Eugene Betout, late hair-dresser to the Duchess of Mecklenburg, lately arrived from Paris, is now in Washington. Apply to Mrs Delarue, Pa ave, between 12th & 13th sts.

Dissolution of the copartnership existing under the firm of H W Blunt & Co, by mutal consent. –B Forrest, H W Blunt [H W Blunt will continue the Grocery business, Gtwn.]

House of Reps: 1-Ptn of Isaac C Lockwood, praying for relief on account of the failure of title to land conveyed by the U S. 2-Ptn of Saml W Brady, a soldier in the Mexican war, asking for a pension for a wound or injury. 3-Memorial of Richd McClure, late postmaster at Wheeling, Va, asking for a fair adjustment of his accounts as postmaster. 4-Ptn of J M Brown & others, citizens of Bloomfield, Turnbull Co, Ohio, praying Congress to repeal the fugitive slave law. 5-Ptn of Robt White, an invalid pensioner, of Preble Co, Ohio, praying for an increase of his pension.

The inauguration of E Louis Lowe, Govn'r elect of Md, will take place today at Annapolis, Md.

Edw Clemens & Thos Read, found guilty of piracy & murder, committed on the high seas in Jan last, near the Island of Trinidad, were on Mon last brought into the Richmond, Va Court to receive their sentence. They will suffer death by hanging, on Jan 31.

Mrd: on Jan 2, by Rev Mr Gorsuch, Cobinton O West, of Greigsville, Preston Co, Va, to Miss Atharia Barker, of Wash.

Mrd: Jan 2, in Wash City, by Rev Mr Lanahan, J Fenwick Young, of this District, to Miss Nora Carroll Livingston, youngest daughter of the late Hon Robt Le Roy Livingston, of the State of N Y.

Mrd: on Jan 1, by Rev Mr Chenowith, of Balt, Mr John E Buckingham, of Wash, to Miss Mgt J Ashton, of Balt.

Mrd: on Dec 24, at *Esperance Plantation*, La, by Rev W O Preston, Benj W Frazier, jr, to Caroline E, daughter of Dr J H Loughborough.

Mrd: on Dec 10, at **Mount Oak**, by Rev Owen Thackara, Robt Bowie, of Cedar Hill, to Eleanor B Magruder, eldest daughter of John B Mullikin, all of PG Co, Md.

Died: on Jan 3, at Gtwn, D C, Chas E Eckle, aged 68 years, an old & respectable citizen of Gtwn.

Died: on Nov 1, 1850, at Marysville, Yuba Co, Calif, Wm H Dietz, of Wash City. He had been a resident of this place for 14 years, & full of hope & enterprise, influenced by a noble ambition to provide for a family endeared to him, he left this city for the new empire just annexed to the U S. He was there arrested by the hand of death, cut down in the prime of life far away from home & kindred; but his widow & children have the consolation of knowing that he received in his last moments attentions not bestowed on all who have died in that land.

Died: on Jan 3, in Gtwn, D C, in his 7th year, Franklin Blake, son of Wm A & Goorvina Gordon.

The Hon Bowen Whiting died at his residence in Geneva, N Y, on Sunday week, aged 63 years. His decease was sudden & quite unexpected to himself, though not entirely so to his friends. He has been a resident of that part of the country 30 years or more.

Edwin Croswell, who has been for many years the senior editor of the Albany Argus, has sold his interest to Mr Jas J Johnson, who has been book-keeper there for a long time. It will now be conducted by Messrs Sherman Croswell, Shaw, & Johnson. –N Y Courier

Orphans Court of Wash Co, D C. Letters of administration on the personal estate of Jas Mount, late of said county, deceased. –Sarah Ann Mount, admx

City Item: on Thu last, Mr John Hutchinson, an elderly & respectable citizen, residing near Mr Stone's farm, north of Wash City, was attacked. This murderous assault & robbery was made by a negro, who, after knocking Mr Hutchinson down with a slung stone, cut him in the throat with a knife & rifled his pockets. Mr Hutchinson was dangerously wounded. [Jan 7th newspaper: Mr Hutchinson identified a colored man named Sandy Sprigg as the perpetrator of the robbery. He was immediately committed.] [Jan 14th newspaper: Sandy Sprigg found guilty.]

TUE JAN 7, 1851
$5 reward for return of a strayed black mare. –Benj Williamson, 10th & G st.

Reasonable reward for recovery of runaway colored woman, Theresa, a slave. She has been hired to Mr Brenner, & is supposed to be yet in Wash City. –Robt Hall

Criminal Court-Wash: Sat. 1-Caroline Johnson, alias Lewis, not guilty of grand larceny. 2-Jas Butler, free negro, sentenced to 2 weeks in the county jail for assault & battery. 3-Lucy Wheeler, Jane Robinson, & Maria Robinson, guilty of riot & assault, & each fined $1 & costs. The accused had been in jail for some weeks before they were sentenced. 4-Geo Payne, convicted of assault & battery, sentenced to 2 weeks in the county jail. 5-Saml Hall, alias Geo King, alias Jas Hall, alias Jos Able, a white boy 16 years of age, was found guilty of forgery in 3 cases.

Senate: 1-House bills referred to the Cmte on Pensions: relief of: Eleanor Davidson; of Jos Johnson; of John M Rosbury; of Thos R Saunders; of Wm Sparks; of Warren Raymond; of Geo S Claflin. Also, pension to Sarah A Bush; pension to Mary Pike, widow of Ezra Pike; & pension of Henry Click, of Cocke Co, Tenn. 2-House bills referred to the Cmte of Claims: relief of Monmouth B Hart, Joel Kelly, & Wm Close, securities for the late Benj Hart, a purser in the U S Navy. Relief of: Polly Carver, excx of Nathan Carver; of John Poe, of Louisville, Ky; of Capt Wm Duerson, of Ind; of the legal reps of Bernard Todd, deceased. 3-House bills referred to the Cmte on Commerce: relief of Edmund Dexter, of Cincinnati; of Adolphus Meier & Co, of St Louis; & act to compensate & reimburse the owners & crew of the whaling ship **Chandler Price** the losses & expenses incurred in ransoming the crew of the ship **Columbia**. 4-House bills referred to the Cmte on the Judiciary: to provide certain moneys to the legal reps of Conrad Ten Eyck, late marshal of the Dist of Mich, deceased. 5-Act to provide compensation to Wm Woodbridge & Henry Chipman, for services in adjusting titles to lands in Mich, & for other purposes. 6-Act for the relief of Sarah Duncan, widow of Silas Duncan, late master commandant in the U S Navy: referred to the Cmte on Naval Affairs. 7-Act for the relief of Thos Rider, a British subject: referred to the Cmte on Foreign Relations. 8-Act for the relief of John Deammit: referred to the Cmte on the Post Ofc & Post Roads. 9-Memorial of Milo Sutliff & Levi H Case, asking that the amount of money lost by then in consequence of the seizure & condemnation of certain wool for an alleged violation of the revenue laws, may be refunded: referred to the Cmte on Finance. 10-Memorial from Jas W Finch, asking compensation for a vessel lost in the service of the U S: referred to the Cmte of Claims. 11-Memorial of Hartwell Carser & his associates, asking that a charter be granted them for the construction of a railroad to the Pacific Ocean: referred to the Cmte on Roads & Canals. 12-Ptn of Ezekiel Brown, asking a pension: referred to the Cmte on Pensions. 13-Ptn of Wm Boardman & others, citizens of New Haven Co, asking an amendment of the patent laws: ordered to lie on the table. 14-Ptn of David Feller, asking an increase of pension: referred to the Cmte on Pensions.

Valuable property at auction: on Jan 16, property known as Mr J K Boyd's: fronting on Pa ave, near 11th st. Also a splendid 3 story brick bldg fronting on 11th st, near Pa ave. The above property is sold subject to a deed of trust held by D Clagett.
-A Green, auct

Official: Gen Orders, #48. War Dept, Adj Gen Ofc, Wash, Dec 31, 1850. Board of Ofcrs to assemble in Wash City on Jan 15, 1851, to revise the uniform dress of the U S army.

Bvt Col E A Hitchcock, 3rd Infty
Bvt Col C F Smith, 2nd Artl
Bvt Col G Wright, 4th Infty
Col G A McCall, Inspec Gen
Bvt Lt Col P St G Cooke, 2nd Dragoons

Bvt Lt Col J H Eaton, 3rd Infty
Bvt Maj R S Garnett, 7th Infty
Bvt Maj F O Wyse, 3rd Artl
Bvt Maj H C Wayne, Assist Quartermaster

By order of the Sec of War: R Jones, Adj Gen

Millard Fillmore recognizes Bartholomew Watts, who has been appointed Vice Consul of Brazil for the port & district of New Orleans, in Louisiana. Jan 3, 1851

Commission on Claims against Mexico: 1-Memorial of Thos O Larkin & Talbert H Green, claiming for supplies furnished to the Mexican troops in Calif before Jul 6, 1846: received. 2-Memorial of Alpheus B Thompson, claiming for detention in person, & otherwise, in Calif from 1833 to 1837, & for consequent losses & charges: received. 3-Memorial of Wm S Underhill, for himself & as assignee of Wm McKinley, claiming for 15 days' hire of brig **Spy**, in the revolt of Yucatan, in 1843: received. 4-Memorial of Jos B Eaton, for himself, Saml Parsons, & Wm Richardson, joint owners of ship **Sterling** & her cargo, claiming for moneys & property advanced to the Mexican Gov't in Calif, in 1843: received. 5-Memorial of Volney Ostrander, a passenger on board the schnr **Julius Caesar**, claiming for imprisonment of person & loss of property: received.. 6-Memorial of Fred'k Bange, & Albert Southmayd, joint owners of schnr **Caroline** & her cargo, claiming for losses consequent on her seizure at Matamoros, in 1846: received. 7-Memorial of Jas L Rudolph, claiming for his expulsion from Reynosa on Apr 9, 1846: received. 8-Memorial of Wm Richardson, claiming to recover the balance of proceeds of the brig **Mary**, sold at Tampico, in 1837, to pay a fine on her: received. 9-Memorial of Rufus K Turnage, for seizure as passenger on board the schnr **Martha**, in Galveston bay, in 1835, & subsequently imprisonment & losses: received.

Mrd: on Dec 31, at St Peter's Church, Capitol Hill, by Rev Mr Lenahan, Mr J A C Iardella to Miss Mgt A Bulger, both of Wash City.

The undersigned, a graduate, will open, on Jan 13, in the room over West Market, an English, Classical, & Mathematical School. French & Spanish will also be taught if desired. –Archibald Roane

WED JAN 8, 1851
Household & kitchen furniture at auction: on Jan 8, at the residence of Col McClelland, on 6th st, between D & E sts. –C W Boteler, auct

Postmaster Gen est'd the following new Post Ofcs for week ending Jan 4, 1851.

Ofc	County, State	Postmaster
Jonesville	Crittenden, Vt	Bertran N Jones
West Bolton	Chittenden, Vt	Franklin D Colton
Underhill Centre	Chittenden, Vt	B M Burbank
Eagleville	Tolland, Conn	E B Hibbard
W Willington	Tolland, Conn	Darius Starr, jr
Mount Kisco	West Chester, N Y	Jas Hall
Tradesville	West Chester, N Y	Walter Cox
Suspen Bridge	Niagara, N Y	John T Collier
North Potsdam	St Lawrence, N Y	Rollin Ashley
Cherryville	Hunterdon, N J	Wm Large
Mississinawa	Darke, Ohio	Wm H Light
Lottridge	Athens, Ohio	Edw Lawrence
Silver Run	Meigs, Ohio	Eli Ripley
Free Mile	Brown, Ohio	Saml Pettit
Seal	Wyandott, Ohio	Jas F Wadsworth
Veto	Washington, Ohio	Benj E Gorham
Huff's	Athens, Ohio	Isaac B Dudrey
Dukes	Purnam, Ohio	Jas Jackson
Butlerville	Butler, Ala	Henry S Staggers
Black Jack	De Soto Parish, La	Robt Hall
Routh's Point	Concordia Parish, La	J Routh Williams
Mineral Springs	Bexar, Texas	Jno Sutherland
Centreville	Leon, Texas	Wm B Johnston, jr
Stover	Dallas, Ark	Josiah Stover
Cross Roads	Franklin, Ark	Stephen H Chism
Relf's Bluff	Drew, Ark	Wm C Norton
Gravel Ridge	Bradley, Ark	A B Coward
War Eagle	Madison, Ark	M Roberson
Chambersville	Dallas, Ark	___ Bass
Jatton	Grant, Ia	Wm Jetton
Stips' Hill	Franklin, Ia	Robt A Ward
Sharp's Mills	Harrison, Ia	Everett Carver
Auburn	Cannon, Tenn	Abner N Fisher
Lebanus	Robertson, Tenn	Wm R Sadler
Weaver's Mill	Kenton, Ky	Geo A Yates
Anderson	Clark, Ill	Jas B Anderson
Clifton	Jefferson, Mo	Joshua Herrington
Abingdon	Jefferson, Iowa	Shelton Morris
New Buda	Decatur, Iowa	Ladislaus Ujhazi
Brookville	Jefferson, Iowa	Wilkins Warwick
Swan River	Benton, Minne	Wm A Aitkin

Names Changed: Leesburgh, Cumberland Co, N J, changed to Dorchester.
Checkered House, Oswego Co, N Y, changed to Kasoag.
Masonville, Daviess Co, Ky, changed to Fillmore.

Mrd: on Jan 6, by Rev Mr Donelan, Hon Ransom Halloway, member of the House of Reps for the 8th Congressional District of N Y, to Miss Eliza Genevieve Waring, daughter of the late Col Waring, of Mount Pleasant, PG Co, Md.

Died: on Dec 6, in Cambridge, Mass, Mrs Martha Homans, aged 84, relict of Benj Homans, formerly Chief Clerk in the Navy Dept.

The ship **Silas Leonard**, which arrived at Boston from New Orleans on Jan 4, landed at *Fort Independence* Companies B & D of the 3rd Infty, U S army, Maj Thomas, commanding. Nine of the soldiers & 2 of the crew died on the passage of cholera.

The Portuguese frig **Dona Maria** blew up off Macao on the anniversary of the birthday of the Consort of the Queen of Portugal. All the ofcrs, men, & others on board, including some of the ofcrs of the U S ship **Marion**, except 1 ofcr & 15 men, perished.

Wash Corp: 1-Ptn from D J Bishop, for the remission of a fine: referred to the Cmte of Claims. 2-Bill for the relief of Guy Graham: referred to the Cmte of Claims. 3-Act for the relief of Mary Ann & Abigail McWinn: passed.

Senate: 1-Ordered that Jacob Willcox have leave to withdraw his petition & papers. 2-Mr Felch gave notice of his intention to ask leave to introduce a bill for the relief of Wm A Richmond. 3-Ptn of Lt John W Davidson, praying that he may not be obliged to refund $218.47, [funds of the Commissary dept,] which was stolen from him by soldiers of the U S army at Los Angeles, Calif, whilst he was performing the duties of Assist Quartermaster & Commissary at that post. 4-Ptn of Moses Wright, praying Congress to grant him a pension for disease incurred in the war of 1812. 5-Ptn of Mrs Nancy Heaggard, heir-at-law of Wm Grimes, deceased, praying an allowance of interest on money heretofore paid for the Revolutionary services of her father.

John Brisbin, [Dem] has been elected to Congress from the Luzerne district of Pa, to fill the vacancy in the House of Reps, caused by the death of the Hon Chester Butler.

Ambrose C Kingsland was inducted into the ofc as Mayor of N Y C on Mon.

Orphans Court of Wash Co, D C. In the case of Susan E Gordon & David Gordon, adms of Geo Fisher, deceased, the adms & Court have appointed Jan 28 next for the final settlement of the said estate. —Edw N Roach, Reg/o wills

Commission on Claims against Mexico: 1-Two memorials of John A Robinson, severally claiming for illegal exactions & seizure of goods at Guaymas, Texas, in 1843 & 1844, & for a forced loan exacted from him at Hernesillo, while exiled there in 1846: claims allowed: amount to be awarded subject to the future action of the Board. 2-Memorial of John Haggerty, Thos E Davis, & Alex'r H Dana, claiming for the destruction of certain bldgs & merchandise in New Washington, Texas, by the Mexican army invasion of 1836: claim was not allowed. 3-Memorial of Robt M Forbes & John A Parker, claiming for losses by the destruction of property in the invasion of Texas in 1836: claim rejected. 4-Memorial of Robt J Clow, filed on Aug 22 last: rejected. 5-Memorial of Nathan Barkley, adm of B B Boling, deceased; that of the same, adm of S Barker, deceased; that of the same, adm of Alex'r C Dugill, deceased: all rejected.

For sale: lot G in square 533, fronting on Indiana ave, with a 3 story brick house thereon. –S S Williams

THU JAN 9, 1851
Ofcr W Barnaclo, having been deputed by the Marshal to arrest Hillary Hutchins, against whom a bench warrant had been issued, proceeded to Gtwn where Hutchins resided to make arrest. Hutchins knocked him down and beat him about the face & head, & made his escape. Dr May said Barnaclo was severely injured though not dangerously. [Jan 10th newspaper: Hutchins was arrested yesterday at Monocacy, by ofcr Cox.] [Feb 3rd newspaper: Hutchins sentenced to 8 months in jail; & one week for an assault on a citizen of Gtwn.]

Criminal Court-Wash-Wed. Fred'k Rickman, charged with grand larceny, was found guilty & sentenced to 2 years in the penitentiary.

Gen Tom Thumb, one of the wonders of the age, arrived in Wash City this morning & held his first levee at Union Hall.

Public sale of valuable property: by deed of trust from John H Brunning, dated May 24, 1849, recorded in liber J A S #5, folios 97 thru 99, land records of Wash Co, D C.

Sale on Feb 7, of lot 3 in square 527, in Wash City, commencing on 4th st, with a 2 story frame house. –Richd Wallach, trustee -C W Boteler, auct

Sale: by order to distrain, one frame bldg, seized & taken, & will be sold to satisfy ground rent due in arrears by R H Stewart to W W Corcoran, for the east half of lot 23, in square A. Sale on Jan 18, upon the premises. –J L Henshaw, Deputy Marshal

Lt Wm P McArthur, of the U S Navy, & lately attached to the coast survey, died at Panama on Dec 23. He was an excellent ofcr, highly esteemed by all who knew him.

The U S storeship **Fredonia**, Lt Commandant F A Neville, arrived at N Y on Monday, from San Francisco via Valparaiso. She brings home the remains of Passed Midshipman Tenant McLanahan, who was killed at San Jose, Calif, during the Mexican war.

Rev Jos R Wilson, of Wash Co, Pa, son of the late Judge Wilson, of Steubenville, Ohio, has recently been selected to fill the chair of Chemistry & Natural Sciences, in Hampden Sydney College, Prince Edw Co, Va . But a young man, he is a ripe scholar.

Senate: 1-Bill for the relief of Wm A Richmond: referred to the Cmte on Indian Affairs. 2-Ptn of Wm H Prentiss, asking additional compensation as assistant messenger in the Dept of State: referred to the Cmte of Claims. 3-Ptn of Jas Robertson, of N Y, Editor of the Truth, requesting the appointment of a select cmte to consider the claim which he has frequently presented to the Senate, arising out of alleged injuries occasioned by his arrest & imprisonment in Dec, 1849. 4-Memorial of Chas S Jackson, asking certain allowances as deputy inspector & marker at Phil, rejected on the settlement of his accounts: referred to the Cmte on Commerce 5-Ptn of Albert Fitz, asking compensation for his services as special agent to the West Indies in 1841: referred to the Cmte on Foreign. Relations. 6-Ptn of Sarah E Chase, widow of Capt Leslie Chase, have leave to withdraw her documents on the files of the Senate. 7-Cmte of Claims: memorial of Jas Dunning, asking that interest might be allowed on an amount due under a contract, submitted a report in writing, which was ordered to be printed, with a bill for his relief, which was ordered to a second reading.

Mrd: on Jan 4, by Rev Mr Morgan, Mr Wm G Bishop, of N Y, to Miss Emeline, youngest daughter of Danl Pierce, of Wash City.

Mrd: on Dec 31, by Rev Mr Lanahan, M P Mohun to Miss Rosella A Brawner, both of Wash City.

Died: on Jan 7, Jabez Gore, an assist clerk in the ofc of the House of Reps: in his 40th year of his age. He was esteemed by his associates for his excellent traits of character.

Died: Jan 6, at her residence, in PG Co, Md, Mrs Charlotte Cox, wife of Wm Cox, sr, in her 75th year.

Household & kitchen furniture at auction: on Jan 15, at the house occupied by Mrs F M Foster, at 9th & Pa ave. -Dyer & McGuire, aucts

FRI JAN 10, 1851
Household & kitchen furniture at auction: Jan 13, at the U S Hotel, Pa ave, between 3rd & 4½ sts, all the furniture of the establishment belonging to E H Fuller.
-A Green, auct

Senate: 1-Ordered that Arnold Naudaine have leave to withdraw his petition & papers. 2-Cmte on Pensions: asked to be discharged from the further consideration of the ptn of Wm Blake: agreed to. Same cmte: asked to be discharged from the further consideration of the ptn of Jas H Robinson for an increase of pension: discharged accordingly. Same cmte: asked to be discharged from the further consideration of the ptn of Michl R Boos, for a pension on account of services in the army during the last war with Great Britian: discharged accordingly. Same cmte: claim of Saml Wilson, a Revolutionary soldier: ordered to be printed. Same cmte: ptn of Meribah Chandler, widow of a Revolutionary soldier, asking arrears of pension: ordered to be printed. Same cmte: asked to be discharged from the further consideration of the ptn of the inhabitants of Cayuga Co, N Y, in behalf of Mary Ingersol: which was agreed to. Same cmte: asked to be discharged from the further consideration of the ptn of Mary Kirkpatrick, asking a pension for the services of her husband during the Revolutionary war: which was agreed to. 3-Cmte on Commerce: memorial of Thos B Livingston, consul of the U S at the port of Halifax, Nova Scotia, asking to be allowed a salary; adverse report on the same. 4-Cmte on Public Lands: memorial of Mgt Gray, widow of Capt Robt Gray, the discoverer of the Columbia river: passed to a 2nd reading. 5-Cmte on Pensions: ptn of Sarah Crandall, widow of a soldier of the Revolution, asking a pension: passed to a 2nd reading. Same cmte: ptn of Jas Wormsley, a soldier of the Revolution, asking a pension: ordered to a 2nd reading. Same cmte: ptn of citizens of Cayuga Co, N Y, asking that Phoebe Morris may be allowed a pension, submitted an adverse report on the same. Same cmte: bill for the relief of Sarah D Mackay: asked for immediate consideration.

St Mary's Co Court, Court of Equity, Dec term, 1850. Levi Nutwell vs Ann Edwards & others. The bill states that Levi Nutwell, cmplnt, Ann Edwards, Richd Johnson, Raphael Johnson, Catharine Drury, John Jarboe, Wm Jarboe, Geo Jarboe, Mary Jarboe, & Eliz Jarboe, are seized as tenants in common in certain real estate in said county; that the widow's dower & one undivided tenth part of said real estate belongs to the cmplnt in this cause; that one undivided tenth part of said real estate belongs to each of the above parties, dfndnts. The bill states that it will be to the advantage of the said parties to sell the real estate, & divide the proceeds among the parties aforesaid; that Eliz Jarboe is an infant under the age of 21 years; & that the said Catharine Drury, Richd Johnson, Raphael Johnson, & Ann Edwards are residents of the State of Ky. –Peter W Crain -Wm T Maddox, Clerk St Mary's Co Court

Mrd: on Jan 9, in Christ Church, Wash, by Rev Mr Hodges, John B Sprigg to Miss Martha R Stansbury, all of the District of Columbia.

Commission on Claims against Mexico: 1-Claim of Volney Ostrander was adjudged valid. So was that of Geo W Van Stavoren, for 17 boxes of chewing tobacco, seized at Vera Cruz in 1839, as prohibited, but never legally condemned. Also, that of Chas Stillman, for his expulsion for his residence & business at Matamoros, under Gen Ampudia's order of Apr 11, 1846.

Intelligence received of the death of at Panama, on Dec 23 last, of Lt Com Wm P McArthur, U S Navy, assistant in the Coast Survey. He was prostrated by an attack of a fever of the malignant type, contracted while preparing his vessel for sea, but persisted in volunteering for the charge of the hydrographic party on the western coast. A subsequent relapse did not abate his determination to enter as a pioneer upon this arduous service. An attack of dysentery prostrated him completely. His remains were consigned to a foreign soil, to be brought, let us hope, to his country, where all his affections centered.

SAT JAN 11, 1851
Commission on Claims against Mexico: 1-Memorial of Wm Richardson, claiming to recover the excess of proceeds of sale of the brig **Mary** beyond the amount of the fine to pay which she was sold at Tampico in 1837: Board made an award in favor of the claim, reserving the amount for future action. 2-Memorial of Rufus K Turnage: the Board made an award in favor of the claim, under the usual reservation as to the amount.

Criminal Court: 1-Jo Allemander found guilty of stealing silver articles the property of W G Eliot, jr. He was afterwards found guilty of stealing silver articles the property of W O Dayton. Jos Brown, an accomplice, was found guilty of aiding in the robbery of Mr Eliot. The prisoner pleaded guilty. Each prisoner was sentenced to 10 years in the penitentiary for their offences.

Mrd: Jan 9, by Rev Mr Bennett, Mr Archibald Roane, of Texas, to Miss Ruth Allen, of Wash City.

Mrd: on Thu last, by Rev Mr Slattery, Patrick McManus to Miss Ellen Smith, all of Wash City.

Mrd: on Jan 9, in Gtwn, D C, by Rev T Myers, Mr Robt A B Moorman, of Fancy Hill, Va, to Miss Annie M, 3rd daughter of Jos Libbey, of the former place.

Mrd: on Jan 9, at the Episcopal Theological Seminary, Fairfax Co, Va, by Rev Mr Lockwood, Miss Louisa Virginia Macrae, of Fairfax, to Mr Albert G Gardiner, of Alexandria Co.

Mrd: on Jan 8, in Balt, by Rev Dr Johns, Lt Edmund Lanier, of the U S Navy, to Mary, daughter of Dr N R Smith.

Died: on Jan 10, Capt Wm P Mathews, formerly of Balt, Md, & late a clerk in the Treasury Dept, leaving a deeply afflicted family to mourn their sad bereavement. His funeral will be from his late residence on 9th st, near F, on Sun, at 2 o'clock.

Died: on Jan 9, Mrs Avarilla M Vermillion, aged 36 years. Her funeral will be at the residence of her brother-in-law, Alex Provest, Pa ave, between 9th & 10th sts, today at 11 A M.

For rent: the whole of the 2nd & 3rd stories of that large & excellent Brick House on the s e corner of Pa ave & 13th sts. Apply to the subscriber, Jos Wimsatt.

Orphans Court of Wash Co, D C. Letters of administration, with the will annexed, on the personal estate of Alfred R Dawson, late of said county, deceased. –Nicholas Dorsey, adm w a. [Accounts against the above estate may be left with Mr John F Coyle, who will forward them to the administrator.]

To whom it may concern: Alex'r Norris, late of Taliaferro Co, Ga, but formerly of Md, died in 1832, leaving a will which contains this clause: "Item 2nd: I give & bequeath to my brothers' & sisters' children, also to my dear wife's brothers' & sisters; children, an equal share of what property remains in her hands after her death, with the exception of the first named tract of land." The testator's said wife, Rebecca Norris, formerly Rebecca Moore, is now also dead, & an estate of a value somewhat above $15,000 remain for division among the persons described in the above clause. No division can be made until the number of legatees is ascertained, & no payment made until his or her identity is established. Each legatee is interested in furnishing all the possible information concerning himself & all the rest, to the subscriber, at Crawfordville, Ga. –Wm B Moore, adm, with the will annexed, of Alex'r Norris, deceased.

The case of Henry Long, claimed as a fugitive slave by his master, residing at Richmond, Va , which has been for some days past on hearing at N Y, first before a Com'r, & afterwards before the District Court, in which Judge Judson, of Conn, presided, has been decided by the Judge in favor of the claim of the master. The Marshal provided a sufficient force to convey the fugitive back to Va..

Valuable bldg lots at public auction: by deed of trust from John B Hillary, dated Dec 12, 1846, recorded in Liber W B 132, folios 57 thru 59, in the land records of Wash Co, D C: on Jan 20, all of square 394, in Wash City. –Chas McNamee, trustee -John Martin & Co aucts

For rent: double house on corner of 13th & H sts. Inquire at Mr Reed's Grocery, 14th & F sts.

MON JAN 13, 1850
The Hon Chas Augustus Murray, 2nd son of the late Earl of Dunmore, & nephew of the Duke of Hamilton, was married in Scotland to Miss Eliz Wadsworth, only daughter of the late Mr Wadsworth, of Genesee, N Y, on the 14th of last month.

The remains of Stephen Girard, at Phil, were exhumed on Sat last, preparatory to their final interment in the grounds of Girard College.

Criminal Court-Wash-Sat. Mary Mason, free negress, convicted the second time of theft, was sentenced to 1 year in the penitentiary.

Died: on Jan 11, in her 5th year, of disease of the brain, Eliza B Watkins, daughter of Geo S & Caroline Watkins, of Wash City.

Orphans' Court Sale: Jan 16, all the household & kitchen furniture of the late Mrs Eliz A Farrall, deceased, on *English Hill*. –J W Beck, adm W a -McDevitt & Robinson, aucts

Trustees' sale of houses & lot: by deed of trust from Francis Selden, dated Dec 28, 1844, recorded in Liber W B 427, folios 524 thru 526, & a decree of the Circuit Court of Wash Co, D C, made in the cause wherein Freeman Black is cmplnt, & Francis Selden & Anna Rosetta Hoban & others, heirs at law of Jas Hoban, deceased, are dfndnts: public sale on Jan 31, 1851, on the premises, of lot 2 in square 247, with the bldgs thereon, on L st north, between 13th & 14th sts, a rapidly improving part of Wash City. –Chas S Wallach, trustee –C W Boteler, auct

Orphans Court of Wash Co, D C. Letters of administration, with will annexed, on the personal estate of Eliz A Farrall, late of said county, deceased.
-J W Beck, adm, w a

TUE JAN 14, 1851
Mrd: on Jan 7, in Frederick, by Rev Mr Mulledy, John J McCollam, of Wash City, to Miss Drucilla Balderston, of the former place.

Senate: 1-Ptn from Mgt Rapole, widow of a soldier of the Revolution, asking to be allowed a pension: referred to the Cmte on Pensions. 2-Ptn from the residents of Niagara Co, N Y, in behalf of the claim of Stephen Warren to indemnity for losses sustained during the late war with Great Britain: referred to the Cmte of Claims.

Mrs A T McCormick, 7th & E sts, has a vacant front room suitable for a single gentleman, if application be made early. Gentlemen wishing their meals only can also be accommodated.

Appointments by the Pres: 1-Jas S Calhoun, of Ga, to be Govn'r of the Territory of New Mexico. 2-Thos Nelson, of N Y, to be Chief Justice of the Supreme Court of the U S for the Territory of Oregon, in place of Wm P Bryant, resigned.
3-Abram M Fridley, of N Y, to be Winnebago Indian Agent.
4-Consul: Robt R Gatton, of Md, at Mazatlan, in place of John Parrott, resigned.
Wm H Kelly, of Mass, for Tahiti & the Independent Society Islands.
Edw A Saunders, of N Y, at Buenos Ayres, in place of Jos Graham, removed.
Edw McCall, of Pa, at Lima, in place of Stanhope Prevost, resigned.
John S Gilmer, of Md, at Bahia, in place of Wm T Purnell, resigned.
Edw Ely, of Pa, at Bombay.

Died: on Jan 3, at *Mount Pleasant*, [the residence of the Rev E L Childs,] Chas Co, Md, in her 20th year, Bettie M, consort of Francis Price, & daughter of the late Noble Barnes.

Among the strangers we note Mr Edmund Lafayette, of France, grandson of the venerated Marquis de Lafayette. He is here the guest of his friend & fellow school-fellow, Fred'k Skinner, on Capitol Hill.

Sale of stock of fancy good, ornamental hair-work, millinery, & furnishing articles, on Jan 20. We shall sell the entire stock in the store occupied by John H Gibbs. -Dyer & McGuire, aucts

Valuable city property for sale, belonging to the estate of John McClelland: 2 brick houses on 13th st, 2 stories, basement, & garret, brick stables & walls. Also, 7 bldg lots on I st, between 12th & 13th sts. Inquire of the subscriber, on N Y ave, between 13th & 14th sts, or corner of 10th & E sts. –John McClelland

WED JAN 15, 1851
Criminal Court-Wash-Tue. 1-Thomas, alias Tom Taylor, free negro, on old offender, was found guilty of stealing 4 reams of paper, the property of the U S: sentenced to 3 years in the penitentiary. 2-Sandy Sprigg, free negro, guilty of an assault with intent to kill John Hutchinson, was sentenced yesterday. His wife had made an appeal for mercy. Judge Crawford said, in view of Spriggs bad character, & of having been convicted serveral years ago with intent to kill Geo Milburn, he was bound to inflict the longest term of imprisonment prescribed by law: 8 years at labor in the penitentiary.

Commission on Claims against Mexico: 1-Claim of Wm S Underhill, in his own right & as assignee of Wm McKinley, for 15 days' hire of brig **Spy**, by Mexican Commissary Genr'l, in the revolt of Yucatan, in 1843, was adjudged valid, with the usual reservation as to the amount awarded.

Millard Fillmore, Pres of the U S, recognizes J L Roger, who has been appointed Vice consul for the Pontifical States at Charleston, S C. -Jan 11, 1851

Wash Corp: 1-Act for the relief of John Dove: referred to the Cmte on Improvements. 2-Act for the relief of C Buckingham: passed. 3-Bill for the relief of Mary Ann & Abigail McMinn: referred to the Cmte on Improvements. 4-Cmte of Claims: asked to be discharged from the further consideration of the ptn of S Parish, on the ground that the cmte had no jurisdiction in the case. 5-Cmte on Improvements: claim of John A Sauer: passed. 6-Ptn of Jas Hollidge, for permission to keep certain streets enclosed: referred to the Cmte on Police.

Postmaster Gen has est'd the following new Post Ofcs for week ending Jan 11, 1851.

Ofc	County, State	Postmaster
Rangeley	Franklin, Maine	John Haley
North Sedgwick	Hancock, Maine	Reuben H Gray
West Hampden	Penobscot, Maine	Josiah Wiswell
Charles River Village	Norfolk, Mass	Josiah Newell
Warrenville	Somerset, N J	Danl Cory
Brandywine Springs	Newcastle, Del	Wm Callen, jr
Birdsboro'	Berks, Pa	Geo Krabb
State Line	Franklin, Pa	John Rearich
Calvin	Huntingdon, Pa	Benj F Glasgow
West Spring Creek	Warren, Pa	Nathl Wood
Campbellsville	Sullivan, Pa	John Campbell
Kingston Centre	Delaware, Ohio	Jas N Stark
Groveland	Fulton, Ohio	E S Hanson
Torch	Athens, Ohio	Nicholas Baker
Fillmore	Washington, Ohio	Alex McGirr
Rush	Shiawassee, Mich	Lewis Hart
Hoodsville	Marion, Va	Alfred Hood
Greenbrier Run	Doddridge, Va	Ezra F Randolph
Spruce Hill	Highland, Va	Amos E Campbell
Strode	Culpeper, Va	Philip G Smith
Britton's Neck	Marion District, S C	Geo W Woodbery
Ariel	Marion District, S C	J N Stevenson
Tabernacle	Marion District, S C	C D Rowell
Angley's Branch	Barnwell District, S C	Jno H Ha ley
Level	Richland District, S C	Jere Entyminger
Gilchrist's Bridge	Marion District, S C	D Gilchrist
Countsville	Lexington District, S C	J H Counts
Bluff Spring	Talladega, Ala	Stephen P Steed
Dark Corner	De Soto, Miss	J P Neims
Harding's Point	Mississippi, Ark	Thos M Harding

Baker's Springs	Polk, Ark	Joel A Hall
Cornine	Union, Ark	Wm Jameson
Twleve Mile	Cass, Ia	Stephen Martin
Maysvlle	Huntington, Ia	John Turner
Webster	Wayne, Ia	Allen Teagle
Notre Dame	St Joseph, Ia	Edw Sorin
Terryville	Carroll, Tenn	John B Terry
Hinklesburg	Oldham, Ky	Richd Glore
Atlas	Pike, Ill	Jere G Adams
Four Mile Prairie	Fayette, Ill	Austin F Morey
Empier	Whitesides, Ill	Orlando C Stolp
Saverton	Rawls, Mo	D B Lindsley
North Janesville	Rock, Wis	John Russell
Wyslusing	Grant, Wis	John M Otis
Sussex	Wankesha, Wis	Richd Cooling

Names Changed: Olive Green, Delaware Co, Ohio, changed to Porter.
Hart Springs, Sussex Co, Va , changed to Blackwater.
Thomas, Marion Co, Fla, changed to Lake Griffin.
Jackson, Lawrence Co, Ark, changed to Spring River.
White Creek, Bartholomew Co, Ind, changed to Mount Healthy.
Red Bridge, Hawkins Co, Tenn, changed to Mooresburg.
Harmony Landing, Oldham Co, Ky, changed to Goshen.

Commission on Claims against Mexico: 1-Claim of Wm S Underhill, in his own right & as assignee of Wm McKinley, for 15 days' hire of brig **Spy**, by Mexican Commissary Genr'l, in the revolt of Yucatan, in 1843, was adjudged valid, with the usual reservation as to the amount awarded.

The Hon Saml Bell, who died at his residence in Chester, N H, on Dec 23, at the advanced age of 81 years, was born at Londonderry, N H, in Feb, 1770, & was a descendant of one of the families of Scotch Presbyterian emigrants from the vicinity of the city of the same name in Ireland, by whom that part of the State was settled. He was educated at the Univ of Dartmouth, & entered the profession of the law, having pursued his studies under the elder Judge Saml Dana. He held the ofc of Govn'r of N H from 1819 to 1823, & that of U S Senator from 1823 to 1835.

Orphans Court of Wash Co, D C. Letters of administration on personal estate of David English, late of said county, deceased. –Richd Henderson, R M English, adms Communications addressed to either of the administrators, Hall Town, Jefferson Co, Va , will be promptly attended to.

Mrs Bailey, renowned for her patriotism in furnishing means for prosecuting the battles of the Revolution, was burnt to death a few days since in her residence in Groton, opposite New London. She was upwards of 90 years of age.

Addison Gilmore, Pres of the Western Railroad, [Mass] & head of the banking house of Gilmore, Blake, & Ward, died suddenly on Fri in Watertown, of a disease of the heart. He attended a ball, & had just completed a dance & sat down by the side of his wife, when he fell forward & expired. He was 48 years old.

Senate: 1-Memorial of Thos Ritchie, representing that he is a party interested in the contract of Wm A Belt, to execute certain classes of printing of Congress, & praying that he may be released from his contract, & that other prices may be substituted: referred to the Cmte on Printing. 2-Cmte on Finance: asked to be discharged from the further consideration of the memorial of John M Sewall: which was agreed to.

Mrd: in Norfolk, in St Paul's Church, by Rev Mr Jackson, Lt Col R E De Russey, U S Army, to Miss Helen A Maxwell, of that city. [No marriage date given-current item.]

Mrd: on Jan 12, by Rev Mr Moore, Mr Geo H Kendrick, of Wash, to Miss Virginia Bridwell, of Va, daughter of Timothy Bridwell.

Died: on Jan 13, in her 16th year, Victoria, only daughter of Capt Jos Smoot, U S Navy. Her funeral is today at 1 o'clock, from the residence of her father, #3 Franklin Row.

Died: yesterday, in Wash City, Miss Ellen Adams, late of Emmittsburg, Md, of typhoid fever, in her 22nd year. Her sickness was brief, & she died fully resigned to the will of her Saviour. Her funeral is tomorrow, from the residence of Mr Gustavus A Clarke, from the City Hall, at 3½ P M.

Died: on Jan 2, at Blockley Hospital, near Phil, Danl W Davis, son of Barnabas Davis, of this place, aged 41 years.

THU JAN 16, 1851
Senate: 1-Ptn from Jeremiah H Winney, citizen of N Y, asking to be allowed an increase of pension: referred to the Cmte on Pensions.

Criminal Court: 1-The trial of Mary Benedict alias Lawson, on an indictment of willful & corrupt perjury: verdict tomorrow. She is a neatly dressed white woman, & resides in Alexandria, Va . [Jan 17th newspaper: prisoner guilty & sentenced to 4 years in the Penitentiary.]

A man who gave his name as Magness, who said he came from Richmond, was arrested on Tuesday on the charge of attempting to pick the pocket of John Friddel, of Gtwn, aged about 24 years.

Household & kitchen furniture at auction: on Jan 18, by order of the Orphans Court of Wash Co, D C: the personal effects of A R Dowson, deceased. Sale in front of the Auction Store. -A Green, auctioneer

For sale: 3 story brick house on Pa ave, near 6th st. –R Cruit, on the premises.

For sale: splendid Country Seat, 1½ miles from the city, on the Balt Pike, adjoining the property of Jos Gales & H L Chapin, containing 65 acres, with a new dwlg of 2 stories & 1½ story-6 rooms in all. –John A Bartruff, or apply to John F Callan, E & 7th sts.

Assignee's sale of the extensive & unique variety of curious, rare, & useful books, London stationery, engravings, drawing materials, belonging to the estate of the late Wm A Colman, contained at 304 Bradway, upstairs. –S Colman, agent

Fatal affray at Macon, Geo, on Sun week, between Mr Wills H Hughes, one of the deputy sheriffs of that county, & Thos Knight, jr, which resulted in the death of Hughes, from a pistol shot discharged by his antagonist, who was arrested & committed to prison. Mr Hughes is the person who lately went to Boston in quest of a fugitive slave, & Mr Knight is the brother of the one who accompanied him.

On Jan 1 a mulatto man was apprehended as a fugitive, & as he was being taken to the calaboose, he drew a pistol & shot Mr John R Chester, the Recorder of the city, killing him instantly. The negro was taken to jail; but the people assembled in an hour, under great excitement, & hung him to a tree. This occurred lately at Memphis.

Mrd: Jan 14, by Rev Mr Gossage, Wm Cammack, jr, to Mgt E Taylor, all of Wash City.

Mrd: on Jul 15, by Rev Mr Gilliss, Capt Wm H Hull to Miss Nannie J, daughter of Col Jas J Randolph, all of Wash City.

Died: yesterday, in Wash City, in her 20th year, Mary Ann Sage, daughter of Mr G A Sage, after an illness of but a few days. Her funeral is tomorrow at 10 o'clock, from her father's residence, corner of 3rd & East Capitol sts.

Mrs Offley, centre house, **Gadsby's row**, corner of Pa ave & I st, has several furnished rooms to rent, with board.

Notice: the subscriber had just received delivery of Virgina Lump Coal. It will be sold cheap. Apply at the Lumber, Lime & Coal Yard on 1st st, near the Capitol. –John Purdy

The Tuscaloosa [Ala] Monitor announces the death of Maj Hardin Perkins, one of the oldest & most respectable citizens of that place, & largely identified with the history of Alabama. At the time of his death he was a Rep from Tuscaloosa Co. A native of Tenn, he removed in early manhood to Alabama, & died at his residence in Tuscaloosa on Dec 31, aged about 59 years.

By virtue of an execution to me directed, I will expose to public sale, on Jan 22: 1 board shop & 5 pump logs, in Wash Co, D C, on 14th st, between Mr Burch's stable & the bridge, taken under execution as the property of Jesse Lee, to satisfy a debt due to John Purdy, & will be sold by me on said day. –D C Waters, Constable

FRI JAN 17, 1851
Senate: 1-Memorial from John Ryle & other inhabitants of Paterson, N J, silk manufacturers, dyers, & others, interest in the silk trade of the U S: regarding the unjust operation of the tariff of 1846 upon their branch of business: referred to the Cmte on Finance. 2-Ptn of Mr John Jas Flournoy, a citizen of Ga, who suggests the Gov't should reserve some of the richest portions of the mining districts in Calif to be worked by its own hands: referred to the Cmte on Finance. 3-Ptn of Jan Jones, formerly wife of Hezekiah Douglass, deceased, asking compensation for the transportation of troops by her late husband during the Florida war: referred to the Cmte of Claims. 4-Order that Arris Crosby have leave to withdraw his ptn & papers. 5-Additional document in relation to the claim of Wm Neins, for an extension of his patent: referred to the Cmte on Patents & the Patent Ofc. 6-Cmte on Military Affairs: memorial of John S Knox, asking indemnity for losses occasioned by explosion of ordnance stores, asked to be discharged from the further consideration of the same: agreed to. Same cmte ptn of Pamela Preswick, in behalf of herself & other heirs of Wm Wigton, for services during the late war with Great Britain, asked to be discharged from the further consideration of the same: agreed to. Same cmte: ptn of Marie Mason, asking arrears of pay due her husband, Maj Milo Mason, asked to be discharged from the further consideration of the same: agreed to. 7-Cmte on the Post Ofc & Post Roads: bill for the relief of John Dearmit, recommended its passage.

It is affirmed that negotiations for a marriage between the Emperor of Austria & the Princess Sidonia of Saxony have been brought to a conclusion, & it will be celebrated next May with great splendor. The Princess is only 17 & very beautiful. Her father, the Prince John, brother of the reigning King, is, owing to the latter having no offspring, next heir to the throne. –Eng Paper

Mr John B Guthrie has been elected Mayor of the city of Pittsburg, to supersede the present eccentric incumbent, [Mayor Barker,] who was honored with an election to this important ofc while confined in prison for a misdemeanor. The people soon repented of their folly, & would before now have reversed their own decision if opportunity had offered.

The Phil American of a day or 2 ago chronicled the decease of Thos Birch, an old & well known artist of that city. He died at the ripe age of 72. He produced a very large number of pictures, which are scattered over the U S, & many of them highly treasured.

Commission on Claims against Mexico: 1-Memorial of Edw M Robinson, exc of Jos Flemming, deceased, who was surviving partner of Wm A Marshall, in the firm of Flemming & Marshall, claiming to recover amount of duties illegally exacted at Tampico, in 1839-1940, was ordered to be received. 2-Memorial of Lewis H Pollock, claiming for illegal imprisonment & for destruction of property at San Francisco & Santa Barbara, in 1840: same was allowed; the amount to be awarded subject to the future action of the Board. 3-Memorial of Jas Johnson, claiming for losses by robberies & revolutions in Mexico, & for personal outrages in 1832 & 1841, was submitted, examined, & suspended. Board took the claim up again for consideration, & found the claim invalid, & it was rejected. 4-Memorial of Andrew Fenton, claiming for demurrage on the brig **Ada Eliza**, at Lerma, in 1843, & for loss of chain cable, with proofs & documents in support of the same: not a valid claim against the Republic of Mexico: rejected accordingly. 5-Memorial of Jas S Thayer, adm of Jas Trest, & of Fred'k E Radcliff, adm of Augustus Radcliff, claiming severally a moiety of expenses paid in the discharge of the ofc of Mexican Vice consul for N Y, 1831 thru 1834: ordered to be received.

Appointments by the Pres: the Justices of the Peace for Wash Co, D C: Benj K Morsell, Nicholas B Van Zandt, David Saunders, Benj B French, & Robt H Clements, Wash; Robt White, Gtwn.

Mrd: on Jan 16, by Rev John J Murray, Wm Clabaugh, of Gtwn, to Eliz Cissel, daughter of Thos Cissel, of Wash.

Died: on Jan 15, at Gloucester, N J, Mr Joshua A Folansbee, aged 52.

Died: on Jan 15, in Wash City, of scarlet fever, aged 5 years, James, son of B J Barbour, of Orange Co, Va , & grandson of the late Gov Jas Barbour.

Died: on Nov 24, 1850, at his residence, near the town of Opelousas, La, the Hon Geo King, aged 82 years. The deceased was a native of Stafford Co, Va , removed to Ky in 1784, & thence to New Orleans in 1795. For 36 years he discharged the onerous & responsible duties of Parish Judge, in the Parish of his last residence. The deceased was the father of Judge King, late of the bench of the Supreme Court of Louisiana. [Jan 22nd newspaper: Geo King became one of Gen Wayne's captains; ten of my best years were passed as his neighbor; 45 years have passed since I first met this man, in all the vigor of manhood. Peace to his sacred remains; they rest in the same earth with those of my first wife. Wm Darby, Wash, Jan 18, 1851.]

By virtue of a warrant of distrain from Mrs Hope Thomas against J Roberts, for ground rent on lot 18 in square 348, on 11th st, at D: I have seized & levied on 2 old brick houses, on said lot, & shall offer the same, for cash, at public auction, on Feb 19, to satisfy said distrain. –Robt R Hazard, Bailiff for H Thomas

Com'r sale of real estate: by virtue of a decree pronounced by his honor, Judge Tyler, of the Circuit Court of Alexandria Co, at its Jun term, 1850: public auction at Ball's Cross Road's, near the premises, on Feb 17, that beautiful tract of land of which John Biddle Chapman died seized, situated in Alexandria Co, Va , containing about 453 to 460 acres. Jos H Bradley, Christopher Neale, com'rs -Geo White, auct

$3 reward for lost Newfoundland Dog, to S A Wainwright, on G st, between 19th & 20th sts.

Criminal Court-Wash. The Court took up the case of Francis Camper, charged with the willful murder of Martan Ragan, on Aug 12. Jurors sworn: Messrs Zephaniah Jones, Jas Murray, Jas H Birch, G W Stroud, Wm Douglass, John B Harrison, Harrison Craig, W Van Reswick, Jacob Small, Peter Hepburn, Jacob A Bender, & Thos H Langley. Thos E Williams occupied the stand for nearly 3 hours. [Jan 18th newspaper: witnesses who testified: John McMullin, Dr Morgan, Dr Stone, Ezekiel Young, jr, A E L Keese, H J Schadd, Alex'r Tate, & J A W Clarvoe.] [Jan 20th newspaper: witnesses who testified: the Mayor, the Marshal of the District, ofcrs Handy, Wollard, Cox, & Barnaclo; & Mrs Moran, with whom the prisoner boarded at the time of the alleged murder.] [Jan 21st newspaper: witnesses who testified on the part of the prosecution: Michl Ragan, Mgt Ragan, John Conner, Alex'r Tate, Thos Woodward, Walter Lenox, John M Mullen, & B K Morsell. For the defence: Wm A Boss, W Kerr, John Hodgson, Jas Turtin, & Barney Brown. [Jan 22nd newspaper: testified for the defence: John Burns, Jas Moran, & Thos C Donn.] [Jan 27th newspaper: on Fri night the jury returned a verdict against the prisoner for manslaughter, which will subject him to imprisonment in the penitentiary for a term not exceeding 8 years.

SAT JAN 18, 1851
Commission on Claims against Mexico: 1-Memorial of Wm Bevan, owner of the schnr **Vigilant**, claiming for her seizure & confiscation by the Mexican authorities in 1843: ordered to be received. 2-Memorial of Wm S Messervey, claiming for losses consequent on his expulsion from Chihuahua, in 1846, which was rejected on Mar 18, 1850, as not conforming to rules, & which was re-filed as amended on Nov 20 last, was ordered to be received.

Mrd: on Jan 16, at the First Presbyterian Church, by Rev Dr Lawrie, Hon Geo C King, of Newport, R I, to Miss Eliz C Seaver, daughter of Jonathan Seaver, of this District.

Lt Col Patrick Henry Galt, U S Army, died at Phil on Sunday last. He was a native of Wmsburg, Va , & entered the army in 1814, during a period of war. He served with distinguished reputation in Gen Scott's army in Mexico, participating in all the heroic & brilliant achievements of that ever memorable campaign. –Norfolk Herald

Senate: 1-Cmte on Pensions: asked to be discharged from the further consideration of the ptn of Grace Denny Sergeant: agreed to. Same cmte: asked to be discharged from the further consideration of the ptn of Nancy C Van Rensselaer, widow of Lt Col Henry K Van Rensselaer, [asking an increase of her pension:] agreed to. Same cmte: asked to be discharged from the further consideration of the ptn of Wm H Ferguson: agreed to. Same cmte: bill for the relief of Saml Dewey: recommended that it do not pass. Same cmte: memorial of Evelina Porter, widow of the late Cmdor David Porter, asking that a bill may be passed granting her a 5 years pension, submitted an adverse report in writing, which was ordered to the printed. Same cmte: asked to be discharged from the further consideration of the ptn of ptn of Thos Flanagan, asking a pension for the loss of an eye from a wound: which was agreed to. 2-Ptn of Cornelius Vanderbilt, of N Y C, who states that he has been 30 years past extensively engaged in the business of bldg & running steam vessels. He makes a proposal to the Govn't which is in entire conformity with his known liberality of character. He proposes to build 6 steamers of the largest burden, for the purpose of navigating between N Y & Chagres, & between San Francisco & Panama. He proposes that the U S shall have the privilege of purchasing these steamers at their cost in the event of any war, or threatened war, making it desirable to add to the armament of the U S upon the ocean. He also proposes to carry the mail, whenever the Gov't desires it, at $30,000 per annum for each steamer, which is much less than the sum now paid: referred to the Cmte on Finance. 3-Additonal documents relating to the claim of Capt Hiram Paulding, U S Navy: referred to the Cmte on Naval Affairs.

Died: on Jan 16, in Wash City, after a painful & protracted illness, Mrs Amand Greeves, in her 35th year, wife of John Greeves & daughter of Robt Boyd. She leaves a numerous circle of relatives & friends to mourn her loss. Her funeral is this afternoon, at 3 o'clock, from her father's residence, on 7th st.

Trustee's sale of real estate: on Feb 10, by deed of trust recorded in Liber W B 138, folios 188 thru 191, in the land records for Wash Co, D C: sale of all the lots, pieces, or parcels of ground owned or claimed by Thos Y Conley & Azariah Fuller, situated in square 60, believed to be lot 1; that part of lot 2 which was conveyed by Scholfield to Evans on Jan 28, 1797; & lots 3, 5, & 6, in said square. Also, lots 6, 8, 11, & 12, in square 61, with 2 good dwlgs thereon, one brick & one frame. –H Naylor, trustee -A Green, auctioneer

MON JAN 20, 1851
House of Reps: 1-Bill for the relief of A Baudouin & A D Roberts, of N Y C: laid aside, with a recommendation that it do not pass. 2-Bill for the relief of Sayles J Bowen: recommended that it do pass. 3-Bill for the relief of Darl Steenroad: Mr Bowlin moved to amend the bill by striking out the sum of $4,905, the amount allowed in the bill, & inserting the sum of $2,000. Mr Daniel moved to amend the amendment by striking out the $2,000 & inserting $2,500: which was disagreed to. The amemdment of Mr Bowlin was agreed to. The Bill was then laid aside with the recommendation that it do not pass. 4-Bill for the relief of Wm J Price: recommended that it do not pass. 5-Bill for the relief of Robt Davidson: recommended that it do pass. 6-Bill for the relief of Christopher H Pin: recommended that it do pass. 7-Pt of Majors Ringland, Logan, & others, ofcrs & soldiers of the war of 1812, for additional bounty land, in consideration of special services rendered by them at a critical period of the campaign, & gratefully acknowledged by Gen Harrison in the Gen Order discharging said ofcrs & soldiers.

D W Hopkins, the sheriff of St Clair Co, Ill, & by virtue of that ofc collector of the State & county revenue, has been detected in a defalcation to the amount of $17,000, perhaps more, & left for parts unknown.

Harrisburg Republican: Maj John Maupin, merchant of Wmsburg, Va, died by his own hand. He was a brother to the editor of the Republican to whom he had greatly endeared himself by many acts of kindness. No cause is assigned for the suicidal act, which has plunged the family in the deepest grief. Maj Maupin was a native of Rockingham Co, but resided in Wmsburg many years.

Hon Jos B Anthony died at his residence in the borough of Wmsport, Pa, Fri last, of an affection of the heart, aged about 50 years. He was President Judge of the Judicial Dist.

Obit: Constantine Anthoine Beelen, died at his residence in Pittsburg, Pa, on Dec 18, in his 84th year. He came to this country with his father & mother, the Baron & Baroness de Beelen de Bertholf, the former of whom was appointed by the Emperor of Austria, Joseph the Second, to proceed to the U S in a public capacity, soon after the peace of '83, & in that capacity resided with his lady in Phil for a considerable time. Difficulties prevented his return home, whereupon they remained in this country, & died here. They were buried at a beautiful chapel in the interior of this State, erected by the Baron at his own expense. The son went to Pittsburgh at an early age, where he married & passed his life. Had he chosen to return to Austria later in life he would have inherited the title & a portion of the estates of his father, but he preferred remaining in America. He had several descendants, one of whom, a daughter, married Wm A Simpson, of Pittsburgh. His memory will long be cherished by those to whom he was known. –Phil Inquirer

Mrd: on Jan 10, in Nashville, Tenn, by Rev Mr Tomes, Thos Plater, formerly of Wash, to Miss Sarah B Buchanan, of Nashville, Tenn.

Died: on Jan 18, of Quinsy, at the residence of her grandson, John L Wirt, on Capitol Hill, north side, Mrs Eliz McCardle, aged 87 years, a devout Christian, & member of the Roman Catholic Church. She was one of the early settlers & oldest inhabitants of Wash City. Her funeral is today at 3 o'clock, from the residence of J L Wirt.

Died: on Jan 18, in Gtwn, after a lingering illness, Mrs Mary Lutz, in her 72nd year, wife of the late John Lutz.

Mr & Mrs Hlasco: Dancing Academy, at the Saloon of Temperance Hall, E st, will be opened on Jan 21. Mr Hlasco is instructor at Mrs Phelps' Patapsco Institute, Ellicott's Mills, Mrs Gibson's Ingleside Academy, Mr & Mrs Archer's, & at Mr & Mrs Streeter's Academies.

Rev Alex M Cowan, agent of the Ky colonization society, left Louisville on Mon last for New Orleans, with 50 emigrants from Ky. The vessel to take them to Liberia is to sail today, Jan 20.

TUE JAN 21, 1851
For rent, & possession immediately, a 3 story brick house on K st, between 25th & 26th sts, near Gtwn, adjoining the residence of John Davison. Apply to Saml Smoot, opposite.

Suitable reward for return of gold spectacles lost. –Alex'r McIntire, Firemen's Ins Co.

Mr John B Guthrie has been elected Mayor of the city of Pittsburg, to supersede the present eccentric incumbent, [Mayor Barker,] who was honored with an election to this important ofc while confined in prison for a misdemeanor. The people soon repented of their folly, & would before now have reversed their own decision if opportunity had offered.

Commission on Claims against Mexico: 1-Memorial of Christian Alby, claiming for seizure & imprisonment in Calif in 1839, & for losses consequent: ordered to be received. 2-Memorial of Jas Macgregor, adm of Wally & Donaldson, claiming for violation of charter, stopping of their cotton mill at Tampico in 1836, & consequent losses: ordered to be received. 3-Memorial of Geo Lafler, Peter Lafler, & Thomaso Paroles de Walley, admx of Saml Walley, claiming for explusion from Tampico on Jun 12, 1846, & for consequent stoppage of business & loss of property: ordered to be received.

Senate: 1-Ptn from Bethiah Black, daughter of a Revolutionary Ofcr, asking to be allowed a pension in consideration of the services of her father: referred to the Cmte on Pensions. 2-Ptn from David P Weeks, asking arrears of pension: referred to the Cmte on Pensions. 3-Ptn of S Griffin, asking a pension on account of the services of her former husband, Thos Kibby, as a musician in the marine corps: referred to the Cmte on Pensions. 4-Memorial of Hans Nelson, alias Kunsten, asking to be allowed a pension for his services during the Revolutionary war: referred to the Cmte on Pensions. 5-Memorial of Jos Valliere D'Hauterive, asking that the U S court of the district of Arkansas may be authorized to adjudicate his claim to a tract of land granted by the Govn'r Genr'l of Louisiana to said D'Hauterive in 1792: referred to the Cmte on Public Lands. 6-Ptn of Sarah R Jenks, widow of Geo J Jenks, of Phil, who states that her husband was the owner of a ship **James**, & that in the war of 1812 that ship with its cargo was seized by the Spanish authorities in Florida, & the whole was lost to the owner. The claim was submitted to the com'rs in Florida, & was allowed by them, but has never been allowed here. Ptn was referred to the Cmte of Claims. 7-Ordered that Gilbert Vrooman, heir-at-law of Peter Vrooman, deceased, have leave to withdraw his ptn & papers. 8-Ordered that John Rossberry have leave to withdraw his ptn & papers. 9-Ordered that Richd T Merrick have leave to withdraw his ptn & papers. 10-Ordered that the ptn & papers in the case of Clement & Bryan, on the files of the Senate, be referred to the Cmte on the Judiciary. 11-Cmte of Claims: bill for the relief of the legal reps of Bernard Todd, deceased: recommended its passage. 12-Cmte on the Post Ofc & the Post Roads, submitted an adverse report on the memorial of F W Johnson: ordered to be printed. Same cmte: memorial of Robt Jamison & Benj Williamson, asking compensation for their service in carrying the mail: ordered to a second reading. 13-Cmte on the Library: directs the distribution of the works of Alex'r Hamilton & other purposes: passed to a 2nd reading.

Died: on Jan 20, Julian Montandon, in his 67th year. His funeral is tomorrow at 3 o'clock, from his late residence on Pa ave, between 12th & 13th sts.

WED JAN 22, 1851
Mrd: on Jan 16, at the F st Presbyterian Church, by Rev Dr Laurie, Hon Geo C King, of Newport, R I, to Miss Eliz C Seaver, daughter of Jonathan Seaver, of this District.

Obit-the numerous friends of the late Mrs Sarah Virginia Darrell, wife of Mr Wm Darrell, of the Gen Post Ofc, cannot permit her to pass from their sight without recording their grief at her departure. Vacant is her seat in her Family, & in the Church which she loved. [No death date given-recent item.]

From Calif: 1-Among the deaths at Calif are Jas Letcher, of Lexington, Va; Louis Ellis, of Wash, D C; & Mr R C Matlack, of Balt. 2-The military under Col Rogers at Placerville had been disbanded.

Colonization Society: 34th Anniversary was held last night in the First Presbyterian Church. Since the last annual meeting, four of the Vice Presidents have died, viz: John Kerr, M C, of Natchez, Miss; Hon Jonathan Hyde, of Bath, Maine; Rev C C Cuyler, D D, of Phil, Pa; & John McDonogh, of New Orleans.

Postmaster Gen est'd the following new Post Ofcs for week ending Jan 18, 1851.

Ofc	County, State	Postmaster
Larone	Somerset, Maine	Tilly Emery
North Clarendon	Rutland, Vt	Henry T Brown
Marion	Hartford, Ct	Thos M Beecher
N'th Leominster	Worcester, Mass	Wm F Howe
Conklin Centre	Broome, N Y	Z Blakeslee
Glenmore	Oneida, N Y	Wm N Larabee
Newtonville	Albany, N Y	H H Dodge
Ewing's Neck	Cumberland, N J	Joel S Robinson
Fisherville	Dauphin, Pa	Abel Wise
Nottingham	Harrison, Ohio	Isaac Shields
Eurek's Neck	Greene, Ohio	Wm C Howell
North Cannon	Kent, Mich	Jas W Werd
Steele's Landing	Ottawa, Mich	Reuben Reynolds
Fillmore	Randolph, Va	Saml Dinkle
Dornicktown	Monongalia, Va	Wm Hale
Bloomingdale	Cabell, Va	Wm F Dusenberry
Legal Law	York District, S C	John L Carroll
Ashland	Forsyth, Ga	Nimrod Cross
Vernon	Washington, Fla	Stephen J Roche
Lawrenceport	Lawrence, Ia	Geo N Steele
Buffalo	White, Ia	Jonathan Slayter
Bloomingport	Randolph, Ia	Jos P Boyd
Vale Mills	Giles, Tenn	Danl Guthrie
Orland	Cook, Ill	Alanson St Clair
Bee Ridge	Knox, Mo	Garrard Snell
Ashton	Clark, Mo	Geo W Powell
Garden grove	Decatur, Iowa	O N Kellogg
Willamette Forks	Linn, Ohio	Wm Spore

Names Changed: Woodville, Laurens District, S C, changed to Palmetto.
Oldham, Crittenden Co, Ark, changed to Greenock.
De Bastrop, Drew Co, Ark, changed to Holly Point.

Five women, Sarah Wood, Ann Kelly, Jane Wilson, Mary McCready, & Hanna Mowers, with several accomplices, were arrested in N Y on Fri on a charge of passing counterfeit money. Benj Drake is supposed to belong to the same gang.

Senate: 1-Memorial of David Winslow, of Portland, Maine, a contractor, asking to be relieved from a judgment obtained against him by the U S, in consequence of the war with Mexico & the famine in Ireland having raised the price of beef to an extent far beyond what could have been calculated upon at the time he made his contract: referred to the Cmte of Claims. 2-Memorial of Nicholas Gevelot, asking compensation for the construction of a small model of an equestrian statue of Gen Geo Washington: referred to the Cmte on the Library. 3-Ptn & papers of Wm H Shover, on the files of the Senate: be referred to the Cmte on Military Affairs. 4-Cmte on Finance: asked to be discharged from the further consideration of the memorial of Thos M Hope, & that it be referred to the Cmte of Claims. Same cmte: asked to be discharged from the further consideration of the ptn of John Jas Flournoy, of Ga. 5-Cmte of Claims: memorial of Robt D Sewall, exc of Robt Sewall, deceased, asking indemnity for certain property destroyed by the enemy during the late war with Great Britain: ordered to a 2nd reading. 6-Bill for the relief of Wm P Greene: referred to the Cmte of Claims.

THU JAN 23, 1851
Died: yesterday, Mrs Jane C Richards, aged 25 years, wife of Alfred Richards, formerly of Chas Co, Md. Her funeral is today, at 3 o'clock, from her late residence, on N st, between 1st & South Capitol st, Wash.

Cuban trials at New Orleans. Opening of the U S Circuit Court at New Orleans on Jan 10, Judge McCaleb overruled the objections of Gen Henderson to the admission of evidence going to show that an expedition was made from the U S to Cuba, [that fact not being distinctly alleged in the indictment,] & the Court proceed with the examination of witnesses. Letter produced by the D A pending the trial: Letter to the Hon John M Clayton, Sec of State, Wash: Ofc of the U S Atty. Eastern District of Louisiana, New Orleans, Jun 23, 1850. I report to you that the Grand Jury of this district yesterday preferred indictments, for the violation of the act of Apr 20, 1818, against the following persons: Narclace Lopez, L J Sigur, Donahue Augustin, John A Quintmen, Colesworth Pinckney Smith, John Henderson, J L O'Sullivan, Theodore O'Hara, John A Pickett, J R Hayden, Chatham R Wheat, Thos Theodore Hawkins, W H Bell, M J Bunce, Peter Smith, & ___ Gonzales. –Logan Hunt, U S Atty

We learn that the residence of Bishop Meade, in Clarke Co, Va, was accidentally destroyed by fire a few days ago. His valuable library was saved.

John Vanhooser lives in Jefferson Co, Tenn, & he voted for Gen Washington for the Presidency. He is in the 122nd year of his age. Until recently, the Knoxville [Tenn] Register tells us, he was in the habit of walking 5 or 6 miles, without fatigue. He is a German by birth, but emigrated to this country about 100 years since. He was in several of the most important battles of the Revolution. Recently one of his daughters, age 80 years, paid him a visit & found him in his usual health.

Senate: 1-Ptn from Jas Stoddard, praying for compensation for his services & the use of a wagon & horses pressed in the service of the U S during the last war with Great Britain. He asks for an allowance of bounty land or for a pension. Referred to the Cmte on Pensions. 2-Memorial of Wm R Shoemaker, military storekeeper at Santa Fe, New Mexico, setting forth the utter inadequacy of the pay allowed to reimburse his necessary & unavoidable expenses, asking an increase of his pay, & compensation for extra services while performing the duty of commissary: referred to the Cmte on MilitaryAffairs. 3-Memorial of Jesse McKinley, asking that his treatise on phonotype may be printed in common type, with the Declaration of Independence annexed in the phonotypic alphabet: referred to the Cmte on Printing. 4-Memorial of the heirs of Jas Bell, asking the reimbursement of money advanced & supplies furnished to Gov't during the Revolutionary war. The memorial prays that a proviso to a former act which was passed, authorizing a settlement of the accounts of Jas Bell, may be repealed, which proviso limits the amount to be paid to $5,000, when on the settlement of accounts $27,000 was found due to him. The memorial asks for the repeal of the provico that the balance may be paid to his heirs: referred to the Cmte of Claims. 5-Cmte on Naval Affairs: memorial of John O Means, asking to be allowed compensation for his services as acting purser in the navy: passed to a second reading.

House of Reps: 1-Cmte on Revolutionary Claims: adverse reports on the ptns of Wm Straber et al, heirs of Peter Straber, deceased; Saml Jack, one of the heirs of Matthew Jack, deceased; & Saml T Cooper. Same cmte: discharged from the further consideration of the ptns of Wm Randall, heir of Richd R Randall, Mrs Sarah Mandeville, & of the heirs of Lt Fred Von Weissenfels, & they were laid on the table. Same cmte: adverse report on the ptn of Henry Dygert, heir of Peter Dygert, & it was laid on the table. 2-Cmte on the Judiciary: discharged from the further consideration of the ptns of N N Barmon, & David Brenton: laid on the table. 3-Cmte on Private Land Claims: bill to enable Jacob Banta to locate 2 Revolutionary bounty land certificates: bill was recommitted. Same cmte: act to confirm the sale of school lands made to J B Gregoire & P Gregoire, in La: committed.

FRI JAN 24, 1851
Saml Hamilton, the senior Purser in the U S Navy, died at his residence in Talbot Co, Md, on Sat last, at the advanced age of 73 years. He was the purser of the brig **Lawrence**, the vessel bearing the pennant of the gallant Perry in his memorable action on the Lakes. He served with the Cmdor himself at the last gun fired from the brig, & was desperately wounded by the discharge from the enemy which dismantled the gun & left the vessel powerless.

Among the deaths at San Francisco, is that of Mr Henry Howison, of this city, who went to Calif to seek his fortune, but has found there, with too many others, an untimely grave. Mr Howison has left a family behind him.

Senate: 1-Cmte on Pensions: ptn of Wm Tell Zollickoffer, asking to be allowed a pension for services during the Mexican war: rejected. Same cmte: bill for the relief of Avery Downer: recommended that it do not pass. Same cmte: asked to be discharged from the further consideration of the ptn of Ann Dodd, widow of a Revolutionary soldier: which was agreed to. Same cmte: asked to be discharged from the further consideration of the ptn of Jas Tarrant: which was agreed to. Same cmte: bill for the relief of John B Barton, & the other surviving children of the late Gen Wm Barton: ordered to a second reading. Same cmte: asked to be discharged from the further consideration of the ptn of Anna McLean, widow of an ofcr that died in service, asking to be allowed a pension: which was agree to. Same cmte: asked to be discharged from the further consideration of the ptn of John Hamilton, asking bounty land for services during the Mexican war: which was agreed to. 2-Memorial of Richd Nickerson, asking confirmation of the title of a certain tract of land entered by said Nickerson: referred to the Cmte on Public Lands.

Official: information has been received at the Dept of State from Amos B Corwine, U S Consul at Panama, of the death, within his Consular district, of Dr Williams, a citizen of the U S. Mr Corwine states that the partner in trade & friends of Dr Williams proceeded to Calif with his effects, a few hours after his death & burial, & that he was unable to ascertain his Christian name & place of residence.

Mrd: on Jan 23, in Christ Church, by Rev Mr Hough, Mr Robt H Broom to Miss Maria Meehan, all of Wash City.

Died: on Jan 22, at the residence of her uncle, Col J Brooks, near Washington, Eliz A Brooks, aged 19 years. Her funeral is this morning at 11 o'clock.

Died: on Jan 21, at her residence in Indian town, near Port Tobacco, Chas Co, Md, Mrs Jno D Freeman, aged 46 years, leaving an affectionate husband & 7 children to mourn her loss.

Died: on Jan 23, after a long & severe illness, Mrs Ann Maria Maryman, in her 31st year. The deceased has left a disconsolate husband & children to mourn her irreparable loss. Her funeral is today at 10 o'clock, at her late residence on East Capitol st, Capitol Hill.

Died: on Jan 23, after a short illness, Hamilton, son of Jas B & Mary C Phillips, aged 1 year, 11 months & 12 days. His funeral is this afternoon, at 1 o'clock, corner of 6th & H sts.

The subscriber forwarns all person from receiving a promissory note given by him May 8, 1848, to Mgt Burns, for $60 with interest; which not is alleged to have been mislaid or lost, & for which he has this day given full satisfaction.
–Robt P Dodge, Gtwn

House of Reps: 1-Ptn of Henry O McEnery, John H Durkgrave, & J B Felhiol, praying for an act to grant them compensation for locating military bounty land warrants & Choctaw Indian land scrip. 2-Memorial of John A Ragan, praying Congress to take into consideration his plan of improving the Lakes of the U S.

Marshal's sale: by 2 writs of fieri facias: public sale on Feb 20, in Wash City, of square 720 & 721, to be sold to satisfy judgments 169 & 170 to Oct, 1850, Geo Watterston & Robt Brown, adms of Robt Kedglie vs Jas Crutchett.
–Richd Wallach, Marshal D C

By writ of fieri facias, I have levied on sundry goods & chattels, [mostly furniture] the property of Wm Pressey, to be sold on Jan 30, to satisfy an execution in favor of Wm Coale, use of Thos M & B Milburn. Terms cash. –J A Ratcliff, Constable

By writ of venditioni exponas, I have levied on lots 9 & 10, in square 544, on the Island in Wash City, as the property of Jos Martini, & will sell the same on Jan 27, to pay & satisfy judgments due Nathl Carusi, Jas A Ratcliffe, & Wm McConnell. Terms cash. Wm Coal, Constable
+
By 3 writs of fiera facias, I have seized & levied on lots 9 & 10 in square 544, on the island of the city of Wash, as the goods & chattels, lands & tenements, rights & credits of Jos Martini, & shall sell the same on Feb 24, to pay & satisfy judgments in favor of Mrs M A W Radcliffe, J T Lenman & J A Lenman, trading under the firm of Lenman & Brother, & W B Todd. Terms cash. –A E L Reese, Constable

SAT JAN 25, 1851
Senate: 1-Memorial of John A Dix & John A Bolles, sureties of the late Paymaster R S Dix, asking that certain credits may be allowed in the settlement of the accounts of said Dix: referred to the Cmte on Military Affairs. 2-Memorial from C Stoddart & his associates, asking that a contract may be entered into with them to carry the mails in steamers from Norfolk to Gibraltar, touching at certain ports in the Mediterranean: referred to the Cmte on the Post Ofc & Post Roads. 3-Memorial of Wm P Green, asking compensation for his services as a custom-house ofcr at Providence, R I: referred to the Cmte on Commerce: recommended its passage. 4-Memorial of Sarah Gardenier, widow of Capt J R B Gardenier, of the U S army, asking to be allowed a pension & bounty land: referred to the Cmte on Pensions. 5-Memorial from J H Smith, U S Consul at Beyrout, asking that his consulate may be made a consulate general, & that the salary appertaining to the ofc may be increased: referred to the Cmte on Commerce. 6-Cmte on Pensions: ptn of Harriet R F Capron, widow of an ofcr of the army who was killed in Mexico, praying that the half-pay granted her may be continued for life: passed to a second reading. Same cmte: bill for the relief of Wm Slocum, of N Y: recommended that it do not pass. Same cmte: bill granting a pension to Mary Pike, widow of Ezra Pike: recommended that it do not pass. 7-Bill for the relief of John B Barton & the other children of the late Gen W Barton,

Passed. 8-Bill for the relief of Eliz Jones, & other children, if any, of John Carr, a Revolutionary pensioner, the amount of pension ascertained to have been due to Carr at his death: the amount to be paid to be computed at $8 per month from May 18, 1818 to Jun 7, 1831. [He served in Col Gibson's regt, which was not a continental regt, & was not therefore embraced in the act of Mar, 1818, which act applied only to the continental establishment. Although originally Col Gibson's regt was a State regt, by an act of Va Assembly, was transfered to the continental establishment, as a substitute for the 9th Va continental regt, which had been annihilated at the battle of Germantown.] Bill ordered to be engrossed for a 3rd reading. 9-Bill for the relief of Thompson Hutchison: proposes to pay Thompson Hutchison, son of Thos Hutchison, who was late a Revolutionary pensioner of the U S, & who was in error striken off the pension roll in 1818, the amount of pension which would have been due him at his death in Feb, 1835: the amount to be computed from Jul 24, 1818, the date of his pension certificate, to Feb 1, 1835, at the rate of $8 per month. Bill engrossed for a 3rd reading. 10-Bill granting a pension to Eliz Monroe, widow of Thos J C Monroe, late of the U S army, for 5 years, to commence from Jan 1, 1848, a pension, payable semi-annually, equal to one-half the payment which her late husband was entitled to at the time of his death. Bill engrossed for a 3rd reading. 11-Bill for the relief of Jos Watson: to cause a full release & acquittances of the claim of the U S against Watson, as one of the sureties of Henry Ashton, late marshal of D C: & provides that the property in the District, held in trust for the payment of the claim, be conveyed to his legal reps free & discharged from such incumbrance. This individual discharged certain duties in the Territory of Michigan, for which he received no compensation. Shortly after that event, the marshal became insolvent & suits were instituted against his sureties. The heirs of Jos Watson became responsible for the amount of $1,300. They executed to the U S a deed of trust on all the property they possess. The most of them are females. The late Sec of the Treas suspended the collection of the amount. Bill was engrossed for a 3rd reading. 12-Bill for the relief of Thos Rhodes: to pay him $3,175.11 in full satisfaction for the expenses incurred by him in opening & constructing a road from Mobile to Pascagoula Bay, for the transportation of mail in 1828, in pursuance of an implied authority & contract from the Postmast Gen. Bill engrossed for a 3rd reading. 13-Bill for the relief of the legal reps of Joshua Kennedy, deceased: to pay the legal reps $6.500, in full compensation for the destruction of his property by the Creek Indians in 1813. Cmte think the bill ought to pass.

Millard Fillmore, Pres of the U S, recognizes Theophile De Rutte, who has been appointed Consul of Switzerland, at San Francisco, Calif. Jan 22, 1851

Household & kitchen furniture at auction: on Jan 27, at the store of Wm Marshall, Pa ave, between 6th & 7th sts, large assortment of clothing. -A Green, auctioneer

Saml Ward King, formerly Govn'r of R I, died recently in Providence, after a slow & lingering illness.

Rev Walter Colton died at his residence in Phil on Jan 22, after a protracted illness, alleged to have been a complication of disease induced by his services in Calif, & by exposures on his return. He was appointed to a chaplaincy in the navy under Gen Jackson, & distinguished himself as the author of several literary productions. He leaves a widow & a son, & a numerous circle of family connexions, to mourn his loss.

Commission on Claims against Mexico: 1-Memorials submitted, examined, & suspended: of Anthony Day, Wm H Sumner, & Geo Curtis, trustees of the Galveston Bay & Texas Land Co, claiming for losses by violation of contracts with Burnette, Travals, & Vehlein. That of Dr John Chas Beale, claiming for the destruction of his property by the Mexican army in 1835.

Mrd: on Jan 23, at Brentwood, near Wash, by Rev Mr Pyne, Lt Carlile Patterson, U S Navy, to Eliza Worthington, daughter of the Hon Jos Pearson.

House of Reps: 1-There being no objection to the following bills, they were laid aside to be reported to the House-relief of: the heirs of Semoice, a friendly Creek Indian; relief of Saml Smith, Linn McGhee, & Semoice, Creek Indians; also act for the relief of Susan Marlow. Bills for the relief of: heirs-at-law of Col David Hopkins. Relief of:

Wm Hawkins	Josiah P Pilcher
Adlen & Williams	Eli Darling
Edmund L Du Barry	Jas F Green
John Morrison	Geo C Thomas
Mary Kirby Smith	Wm B Edwards
Adam Garlock	Isaac Cook & others
Maj E H Fitzgerald	Virginia Woollen Co
Manosh D Robison	Securities of Robt S Moore
Dunning R McNair	

Legal reps of Robt S Burroughs & Stephen Hopkins
Malvina Cruzat, widow of Manuel Cruzat, late navy agent at New Orleans
Gustavus A De Russey, late an acting purser in the navy
Adjustment of accounts of John D Colmesnil, Pres of the Ohio & Miss Mail Line Co
Pension to Asel Wilkinson
Compensation to Jas W Low & others, for the capture of the British private armed schnr **Ann**, during the late war with Great Britain.
The following bills were objected to: Relief of:
The grandchildren of Maj Gen Baron De Kalb.
Of the heirs of Capt Saml Ranson, an ofcr of the Revolutionary war, killed at the battle of Wyoming

Heirs of Jos Savage	David Myerle
Heirs of Dennis Purcell	Jas W Wilkins
Ezra Chapman	Peter Frost

Mary W Thompson
Hamilton Carroll
Geo Armstrong
Thos Crown
John Ozias
Wm Speiden
Rebecca Winn
John Hogan
Maurice K Simons
John H Piatt, deceased
Emily Stone
Capt Lewis Warrington & others
B M Bouton, Harriet F Fisher, & Geo Wright
Stephen Colwell, of Phil adm with the will annexed of Wm T Smith, deceased, late of Phil, merchant, in behalf of the distributees to said estate.
Pension to Alice Markland
Resolution to pay Chas J Ingersoll the same per diem, pay, & mileage that is allowed to members from the commencement of the 26th Congress to Jan 16, 1840
Bill to incorporate the German Roman Catholic St Joseph's Benevolent Society
Bills laid aside to be reported to the House: Relief of:
Rebecca Freeman, widow of Pearson Freeman

Thos Flanagan
Jonas D Platt
Wm Gove
Lot Davis

Fielding G Brown
Isaac Cobb
Martha Dameron
Wm Lynch

Jas Mains
Isaac Downs
Gardner Herring
Slvanus Blodgett

Pension to Benj Cressey
2-Bill for the relief of Alanson Pool was amended to allow him merely a pension, instead of a pension & bounty land warrant, as provided in the bill. 3-Bill for the relief of Chas S Mathews, Chas Wood, & Jas Hall, was amended reducing the sum named from $12,119.47 to $11,500. 4-Bill for the relief of the adms of Oliver Lee, deceased, was amended by striking out the interest named therein. 5-<u>Bills with the recommendation that they do pass</u>: relief of Edmund L Du Barry; relief of the heirs-at-law of Col David Hopkins; relief of Alanson Pool & of Fielding G Brown. 5-Bill for the relief of Charlotte Lynch, the bill for the relief of A Boudouin & A D Roberts, of N Y C, & the bill for the relief of Danl Deenrod, were objected to, & they lie ever under the rule. 6-Bills read a 3rd time & passed: Relief of: Andrew Smith; Sayles J Bowen; Wm J Price; C H Pix; & Robt Davidson. 7-Ptn of John Edgecomb & Wm Davis for the benefit of the bounty land act passed Sep 28, 1850. Also, ptn of John Edgecomb for remuneration for loss of clothes & property, occasioned by the voluntary destruction of the U S ship **Adams** in 1814. 8-Ptn of Danl Winslow for relief from a contract to furnish beef for the U S navy.

MON JAN 27, 1851
Wash City Ordinance: 1-Relief of C Buckingham: pay him the sum of $191.82, balance due for continuing the water-pipes across Pa ave. 2-Relief of Reuben Brown: fine imposed for a violation of the law to buying & selling in market-houses at market-hours, is remitted: provided he pay the costs of prosecution.

Mrd: on Jan 19, at Cape Island, N J, by Rev J M Church, Mr Richd R Thompson, late of Wash City, to Miss Anna S Hand, of the former place.

Senate: 1-Document presented in relation to the claim of Talbot H Greene, containing a certificate of the amount due by the U S Gov't to Greene, as per receipt of Lt Col J C Fremont, for articles delivered the Calif btln, Monterey, Nov 16, 1846, for $10,855.16: referred to the Cmte on Military Affairs. 2-Memorial of Henry Smith, a Cherokee Indian, asking for certain land to which was entitled under the treaty of 1835 with that tribe: referred to the Cmte on Indian Affairs. 3-Memorial of Thos Kinney, asking that the bounty land law of Sep 28, 1850, may be modified: ordered to lie on the table. 4-Ptn of Simeon Geron, asking to be allowed compensation for certain services performed by him as an express rider during the late war with Mexico: referred to the Cmte on Military Affairs. 5-Cmte on Pensions: ptn of the heirs of Nathan King, submitted an adverse report on the same. 6-Cmte on Military Affairs: memorial of Wm Vance & Brothers, asking to be reimbursed certain sums paid by them for volunteers marching to their place of rendezvous, asked to be discharged from the further consideration of the same: which was agreed to. 7-Cmte of Claims: bill for the relief of Mannouth B Hart, Joel Kelly, & Wm Close, sureties for the late Benj F Hart, a purser in the U S Navy: recommended its passage. 8-Cmte of Claims: memorial of Wm G Buckner, exc of John J Bulde, deceased: adverse report on the same. Same cmte: ptn of Bryan Callaghan: passed to a second reading. 9-Bill introduced to provide for the just settlement of the account of John C Berg, late an assistant paymaster in the U S army: referred to the Cmte on Military Affairs. 10-Bills passed: Relief of: Thos Rhodes; Nathl Champ & others; Thompson Hutchison; & Eliz Jones, & the other children of John Carr.

Danl Brown, a citizen of Brownsville, Pa, was caught in one of the circular saws belonging to the Plank Road Co, & had both his legs cut entire off. He died immediately.

Two sons of the Rev Asher Moore, at Hightstown, N J, aged 9 & 11 years, while playing upon some ice which covered a pond of water, on Thursday fell through, & were drowned.

Wash Corp: 1-Ptn of Geo Hill & others for the opening of O & P sts north, from North Capitol st to 5th st west: referred to the Cmte on Police. 2-Ptn of Wm Jones & others, praying for the improvement of 8th st, from M to R I ave: referred to the Cmte on Improvements. 3-Ptn of Jas B Greenwell & others, for improvement of D st, from 3rd to 1st sts: referred to the Cmte on Improvements. 4-Resolution to authorize the Mayor to investigate claim of John A Sauer: passed.

Died: on Jan 25, in Wash City, at the residence of her son, Mr John L Clubb, Mrs Eliz Clubb, in her 70th year. Her funeral will take place today at 2 o'clock.

Died: on Jan 21, in Princeton, N J, Dr J Irwin Dunn, formerly of Wash City. [+Dr Jeremiah Dunn, Mayor of Princeton, on his return from Trenton Thu last, was thrown from his sulkey, 6 miles from Princeton, & killed.]

TUE JAN 28, 1851

Senate: 1-Memorial from Evelina Porter, widow of Com David Porter, asking Congress to grant her such reasonable sum as may prove their proper appreciation of the services, suffering, & sacrifices of her late husband: referred to the Cmte on Naval Affairs. 2-Mr Bright gave notice of his intention to introduce a bill for the relief of Franklin Hardin. 3-Act for the relief of Jasper A Malthy: referred to the Cmte on Public Lands. 4-Act for the relief of Wm J Price: referred to the Cmte on Public Lands. 5-Act for the relief of Jas W Low & others: referred to the Cmte on Commerce. 6-Bills referred to the Cmte on Naval Affairs: Relief of-Eli Darling; Gustavus A De Russy, late an acting purser in the navy; sureties of Robt S Moore, deceased, late a purser in the U S navy; & pension to Asel Wilkinson. 7-Bills referred to the Cmte on the Judiciary-Relief of Andrew Smith; & relief of C H Pix. 8-Act for the relief of Dunning R McNair: referred to the Cmte on the Post Ofc & Post Roads. 9-Bills referred to the Cmte on Military Affairs-Relief of-Wm Hankins; Alden & Williams; & Josiah P Pilcher. 10-Bills referred to the Cmte on Pensions: Relief of-Mary Kirby Smith; John Morrison; Adam Garlock; Alanson Pool; Wm B Edwards; Geo C Thomas; & Jas F Green. 11-Bills referred to the Cmte of Claims: Relief of-Sayles J Bowen; Maj E H Fitzgerald; Manoah D Robinson; adms of Oliver Lee, deceased; legal reps of Robt S Burrough & of Stephen Hopkins; Malvina Crusat; & Isaac Cook & others. 12-Bills referred to the Cmte on Private Lands: Relief of-Robt Davidson; & heirs of Semoice, a friendly Creek Indian. 13-Act to further amend an act approved Jul 2, 1836, for the relief of Saml Smith, Lynn Macghee, & Semoice, Creek Indians, & also an act passed Jul 2, 1836, for the relief of Susan Marlow. 14-Act to amend an act entitled An act for the relief of Fred'k Durvine, approved Aug 14, 1848. 15-Ptn of Geo E Baker, assist marshal of Kings Co, N Y, asking additional compensation for his services in taking the 7th census: referred to the Cmte of Claims. 16-Memorial of Danl Ravenel & John Ravenel, excx of Saml Prioleau, jr, deceased, asking indemnity for property destroyed during the Revolutionary war: referred to the Cmte on Revolutionary Claims. 17-Memorial of A W Burns, late paymaster in the U S army, asking that his accounts may be so adjusted as to allow him the balance found against him in final settlement: referred to the Cmte on Military Affairs. 18-Memorial of Robt M Hamilton, Consul at Montevideo, asking compensation for diplomatic services rendered: referred to the Cmte on Foreign Affairs. 19-Ordered that the ptn & papers of David Hutter on the files of the Senate be referred to the Cmte on Indian Affairs. 20-Cmte of the Whole: bill proposed to constitute Jas Giddings, Wm H Gunnell, Edw Hall, Christopher F Brown, Stanislaus Murray, & David A Hall, & their present & future associates, a body politic & corporate in the Dist of Columbia, by the name & style of the Union Gas Light Co, with a capital stock not exceeding $100,000 in share of $50. Bill engrossed for a 3rd reading.

Appointments by the Pres: 1-Alex'r M Ross, of N Y, to be U S Consul at St Catharine's. 2-Gideon S Holmes, of Mass, to be U S Consul at the Cape of Good Hope.

Yesterday, Stephen Bennet, alias Bill Baker, was brought into the U S District Court on a habeas corpus. It was alleged by the claimant, Edw B Gallup, that the respondent, Bennet, absconded from his employment at Havre de Grace, Md, some 3 years ago. He was arrested in Columbia, Pa, on Thu, by ofcr Snyder, of Balt, assisted by ofcr Hinblink, of Lancaster. The respondent was identified by persons to whom he had been hired by his master, Mr Gallup. He was remanded to the custody of the Marshal. –Phil Inq, 1/25

The U S war steamer **Saranac**, the flag-ship of the Home Squadron, has sailed from Norfolk for the West Indies. List of her ofcrs: Cmdor, Foxhall A Parker, Capt, Josiah Tatnall; Lts, Thos W Brent, Overton Carr, Wm B May, Geo Wells; Acting Master, Albert N Smith; Purser, John J Jones; Surgeon, Ninian Pinckney; Passed Assist Surgeon, Maurius Duvall; Lt of Marines, Jas H Jones; Cmdor's Sec, Leroy Parker; Passed Midshipmen, Wm F Spicer; J Posey Hall, Jos A Sewall; Capt's Clerk, Chas Francis; Purser's Clerk, ___ Reardon; Midshipmen, Danl L Braine, Jas H Rowan, jr; Chief Engineer, Wm W W Wood; 1st Assist Engineer, Michl Quinn; 2nd Assist Engineers, _____ _____, [copied as written,] J W Parks; 3rd Assist Engineers, Wm F Lynch, D J Mapes, T A Jackson, Francis C Dale; Boatswain, John Crosby; Gunner, Thos Robinson; Carpenter, Chas Boardman; Sailmaker, Jas Frazer; Passenger, Robt M Walsh, Special Agent to St Domingo.

Mrd: on Jan 21, at Newark, N J, by Rev Saml J Southard, Wm H Heiss, of Phil, to Miss Harriet Whaley, only daughter of Thos Whaley, deceased, of N Y.

Died: on Mar 7 last, in Stockton, Calif, Dr Jas Washington Parsons, only son of Mr Bernard Parsons, of Wash City, in his 46th year. The deceased was a resident citizen of Guayaquil, South America, for a number of years, & lately of the former place.

WED JAN 29, 1851
Senate: 1-Memorial of the widow & heirs of John Hood, deceased, asking the donation of a section of land in lieu of land to which the said Hood claimed the right of pre-emption: referred to the Cmte on Public Lands. 2-Memorial of Isaac D Marks, asking that the instalments due the Mexican Gov't, under the treaty of Guadalupe Hidalgo, may be paid at N Y C, agreeably to an arrangement which he proposes to carry into effect: referred to the Cmte on Finance. 3-Cmte of Claims: memorial of Don B Juan Domercq, asking indemnity for certain losses sustained, submitted a report in writing, which was ordered to be printed, accompanied by a bill for the relief of Don B Juan Domercq, a Spanish subject, which was ordered to a 2nd reading.

House of Reps: 1-Memorial of Geo E Baker, an assistant marshal of Kings Co, N Y, asking additional compensation for services in taking the census. 2-Ptn of Wm Stevenson, of Saco, Maine, for a pension. 3-Ptn of Wm M Meek & 80 other citizens of Adams Co, Ohio, praying relief of Lindsay Gosett, a citizen of that county.

Postmaster Gen est'd the following new Post Ofcs for week ending Jan 25, 1851.

Ofc	County, State	Postmaster
Winter Harbor	Hancock, Maine	Timothy Stewart
South Sangerville	Piscataquis, Maine	Moses Gilman
Bakersville	Litchfield, Ct	Anthony Baker
East Hampton Lake	Middlesex, Ct	M W Comstock
Hecla Works	Oneida, N Y	Ralph B Shelley
Sullivanville	Chemung, N Y	Edw Wing
Franklin Falls	Franklin, N Y	John Stearns
Sparta	Livingston, N Y	John McNair
Edinburgh	Mercer, N J	Richd R Rogers
Van Hiseville	Mercer, N J	Abram Van Hise
Dutch Neck	Mercer, N J	John S Robins
Chipana	Newcastle, Del	Wm B McCrone
Freeland	Baltimore, Md	Jas F Gemmill
Clearsville	Bedford, Pa	John L Grove
Warfordsburgh	Fulton, Pa	Jas L Stevens
Leesport	Berks, Pa	Geo W Althouse
Little Gap	Carbon, Pa	Jos J Albright
Paradise Valley	Monroe, Pa	David Edinger
Rousseau	Morgan, Ohio	Jas Sopher
Maple Grove	Knox, Ohio	Richd Roberts
Fallassburgh	Kent, Mich	John M Waters
Aquia	Stafford, Va	Geo H Cockrell
Randolph Macon College	Mecklenburg, Va	David Duncan
Pliny	Putnam, Va	M P Brow
Toomsborough	Wilkinson, Ga	W F Sandford
Winfield	Columbia, Ga	V M Barnes
Stow's Ferry	Tallapoosa, Ala	Joel Stow
Mount Isabel	De Soto, Miss	L W Stewart
Mustang	Lavacca, Texas	Maryland Jones
Fitz Henry	Conway, Ark	Thos W Venable
Hale's Mills	Fentress, Ten	J D Hale
McHargue's Mills	Knox, Ky	Wm McHargues
Winona	Trimble, Ky	Jas H Turner
Hitesville	Coles, Ill	Huston H Pinnell
Logan	Laclede, Mo	John McElvoy
Haydensville	Calif	J C Higginbotham

Names Changed: 1-Townsend, Lincoln Co, Maine, changed to Southport. 2-East Thomaston, Lincoln Co, Maine, to Rockland. 3-Sparta, Livingston Co, N Y, to North Sparta. 4-Brakeleyville, Monroe Co, Pa, to Analomink. 5-Lindsay's Turn Out, Albemarle Co, Va, to Bentiroglis. 6-Buffalo Run, Monroe Co, Va, to Mouth of Indian.

Circuit Court of Wash Co, D C-in Chancery. Amelia J Young, by her next friend, Nicholas Callan, cmplnt, against John Hunter, Nathl C Hunter, Fred'k A Hunter, Thos J Hunter, Laura V Hunter, Adelaide White & Robt White her husband, Mgt Eskridge & Chas Eskridge her husband, heirs at law of John C Hunter, deceased, & Henry N Young. Bill: the dfndnt, Henry N Young, by several deeds recited in said bill, conveyed certain real & personal estate to the said John C Hunter, in trust for the sole & separate use of the said cmplnt; that the said John C Hunter is now deceased, leaving the above named dfndnts. The bill alleges that the said several dfndnts have no real interest in the said property, & prays that some other person should be appointed by the Court as trustee in the place & stead of the said John C Hunter, deceased. And it being suggested to the Court that the said Nathl, Fred'k A, Thos J Hunter, & Mgt Eskridge & Chas G Eskridge, her husband, reside & are out of the District of Columbia, it is by the Court, Dec 16, 1850, ordered that said dfndnts do, on or before the first Mon of Jun next, appear in Court, either in person or by solicitor, & show cause, if any they have, why the said cmplnt should not have relief as prayed. –Jno A Smith, Clerk

Commission on Claims against Mexico: 1-Memorial of Wm L Scott, claiming for seizure of $6,000 in specie at Chihuahua in 1830, & that of Isaac D Marks, claiming for damages by expulsion from Matamoros in Aug, 1845, & for 10 months thereafter, were ordered to be received. 2-Memorial of Stewart Newell, claiming for damages by non-fulfilment of contracts with the Provisional Gov't of Gen Canales, assumed by Gen Arista, on its submission in 1840, & that of Wm C H Waddell & others, claiming for damages by dispersion of their colonies on Beale's Grant, in Texas, at the approach of the Mexican army in 1835-6, were submitted, examined, & suspended.

Mrd: Jan 28, by Rev P B O'Flannigan, Andrew Goddard to Miss Maria C Goldsborough, both of Gtwn, D C.

Mrd: Jan 28, by Rev Mr Edwards, John E Huddleston, of PG Co, Md, to Miss M L Warring, of Wash City.

Mrd: on Jan 16, at Cincinnati, by Rev Mr Nicholson, Solomon W Roberts, of Phil, Chief Engineer of the Ohio & Pa Railroad, to Anna S, daughter of R H Rickey, of Cincinnati.

Mrd: on Jan 23, at Alexandria, by Rev Mr Danforth, Wm P Gunnell, M D, of Fairfax C H, to Miss Martha A Lindsley, of Alexandria.

Died: yesterday, in Wash City, Mrs Priscilla Dodson, in her 72nd year, relict of the late Capt Jos Dodson, of Cambridge, Eastern Shore of Md. She died in the full triumphs of the Christian faith, in which she had lived for nearly 60 years. Her funeral is tomorrow, at 11 o'clock, from the residence of her daughter, Mrs Adams.

Died: Jan 28, at his residence, 3rd st, Gtwn, D C, in his 42nd year, Mr Richd E Cropley. His funeral is this afternoon, at 3 o'clock.

Died: on Jan 17, at Buffalo, N Y, Mrs Catharine B Peter, wife of Jas F Peter, & 2nd daughter of Jas J Baldwin, of that city, aged 26 years.

THU JAN 30, 1851
House of Reps: 1-Cmte on Indian Affairs: Act for the relief of Lewis A Thomas & Thos Rogers: recommended that it do not pass, the claim having been heretofore paid: laid on the table. Same cmte: act for the relief of H J McClintock, Harrison McGill, & Mansfield Carter: committed. Same cmte: joint resolution for the relief of John H Horn: passed. Same cmte: bill for the benefit of Mary Woodbury & Eliz Odell: committed. Same cmte: adverse report on the ptn of Alex'r Ray, guardian of the children of Templin W Ross: laid on the table. 2-Ptn of John J Combs, asking the bounty land to which his father was entitled as a soldier during the last war with Great Britain: referred to the Cmte on the Territories. 3-Cmte on the Judiciary: bill for the relief of C H Pix: recommended its passage. Same cmte: bill for the relief of Andrew Smith: recommended its passage. 4-Cmte on Foreign Relations: bill for the release of Lt Com Wm D Porter, U S Navy: passed to a second reading. 5-Cmte on Indian Affairs: adverse reports on the ptns of E D McKinny, R J McElhany, & N R Smith, sureties of Saml H Burch; of Peter Randon, rep of John Randon, deceased; & of the reps of Wm Armstrong, deceased: all laid on the table. Same cmte: discharged from the further consideration of the ptn of A B Dawson: laid on the table. Same cmte: act for the relief of Theodore E Elliott: committed.

The telegraph reports a dreadful case of murder & suicide at Penfield, near Rochester, on Sunday. The murderer was John Everett; his victim, Sarah Sharpe, his sister-in-law. Their bodies were found a few yards from a house where Miss Sharpe had been visiting, both with their throats cut.

Very early on Tue, Mr Wm Wilson of Wash City, victualler, lost his stable, slaughter-house, & 2 valuable horses, by fire. His residence & premises are n e of the Capitol.

Commission on Claims against Mexico: 1-Memorial of John C Jones, claiming for losses & detention of the brig **Loriot**: same was allowed: amount to be awarded subject to the future action of the Board. 2-Memorial of Alpheus B Thompson, claiming as supercargo of the brig **Loriot**, for his detention in Calif, from 1833 to 1837: same to be allowed; the amount to be awarded subject to the future action of the Board. 3-Memorial of Wm Bevan, principal owner of the schnr **Vigilant**: rejected. 4-Memorials of Wm H Sumner & of Nathl Richards, severally claiming for losses by violation of contract with Burnett, Zavala, & Vehlein: suspended.

Chas McKean died very suddenly yesterday in the upper story of Ward's bldg, corner of 2nd st & Pa ave.

Criminal Court-Wash-Tue: 1-Hilleary Hutchins, alias Fowler, [a man measuring 6 feet 3 inches, & very stout made,] was found guilty of an aggravated assault on Wm H Barnaclo, a bailiff of the Court. Also, aggravated assault upon ofcr Glasco, while in the discharge of his duty. 2-Nace Bell, free negro: guilty of hog stealing. 3-Geo Fesnot acquitted for stealing 44 cabbages. 4-Saml Tinkler, Saml Bacon, J Huff, & G Lamb were tried for rioting: all found guilty except Lamb, who was acquitted. [Jan 31st newspaper: Tinkler, Bacon, & Huff, each sentenced to 3 months in the county jail, & to pay $1 & costs. John Thomas, a free negro, an old offender, convicted of stealing turkeys, was sentenced to 3 years at labor in the penitentiary.]

Mrd: on Jan 27, by Rev Mr Lanahan, Wm E Hutchinson to Miss Ann Catharine Harrison, all of Wash City.

Mr Audubon, the distinguished Ornithologist died on Mon at Minniesland, his country seat, on the North River, near N Y C, at the advanced age of between 70 & 80 years.

At the first election under the Pittsburgh charter, Maj Ebenezer Denny was elected Mayor. He was born at Carlisle, Pa, in 1758. A brother of his father was killed at Quebec, under Montgomery. His mother had 2 brothers in the army; one of them, Maj Parker, was an ofcr of influence & distinction. Her father was a wealthy farmer, who left everything to his sons, [the custom in those days.] Ebenezer Denny, at age 14, was the bearer of dispatches to the Commandant at **Fort Pitt**, in 1772. At 18, he was a volunteer on board a letter of marque & reprisal, which sailed from Phil. Off Trinidad he was promoted to the command of the quarter deck; & on his return was appointed ensign in the Pa line of the regular army. He was in the battle of Jas River, under Wayne; after the surrender of Cornwallis, he was selected by Col Richd Butler to plant the first American flag on the British parapet. He was also in Harmar's & St Clair's campaigns, & the bloody battles in which they terminated. He retired from service in 1794, & died in Pittsburgh in 1821.

FRI JAN 31, 1851
Died: on Jan 30, suddenly, Mrs Mary Holland, in her 69th year, relict of Edw Holland. Her funeral is on Sat at 2 o'clock, from her late residence, 11th & G sts.

Commission on Claims against Mexico: 1-Memorial of Peter L Laguerenna, for himself & as survivor partner of the trading firm of Laguerenna & Bourdel, claiming for losses sustained by the sacking of the Parian, in the city of Mexico, during the insurrection of Dec, 1828: suspended. 2-Memorial of Anthony Dey: suspended. 3-Memorial of Nathl Lord: suspended. 4-Memorial of Paul Rankert: suspended.

Wash Corp: 1-Cmte of Claims: bill for the relief of Alex'r Mahon: reported without amendment. 2-Bill for the relief of Jas Brown: passed. 3-Cmte of Claims: act for the relief of D J Bishop: passed. 4-Ptn from A N Clements for remission of a fine: referred to the Cmte of Claims. 5-Ptn from Edw Chapman, exc of Mary Chapman, asking that the interest paid by him on a paving tax may be reduced: referred to the Cmte of Claims. 6-Nominated by the Mayor for the Board of Health:
Dr R Johnson & Chas Calvert-1st Ward
Dr T Miller & John H Riley-2nd Ward
Dr J C Hall & W P Young-3rd Ward
Dr T B J Frye & G C Grammer-4th Ward
Dr J B Gardiner & Wm P Ferguson-5th Ward
Dr Noble Young & Jas Crandell-6th Ward
Wm B Randolph & Saml Byington-7th Ward
Which nominations were considered & confirmed.

Senate: 1-Additional document presented in the case of Thos M Hope, late U S marshal for the district of Ill: referred to the Cmte of Claims. 2-Memorial of John W Whipple, adm of Jos H Whipple, late a captain in the U S army, asking that his accounts may be settled: referred to the Cmte of Claims. 3-Memorial of Jane Irwin, the daughter & only heir of Col Jared Irwin, asking that she may be allowed a pension, in consideration of the services of her father, & indemnity for losses sustained by him during the Revolutionary war: referred to the Cmte of Claims. 4-Cmte on Military Affairs: asked to be discharged from the further consideration of the ptn of Gustavus A Parsons: which was agreed to. Same cmte: asked to be discharged from the further consideration of the ptn of Jas W Simmons, stating that his salary as military storekeeper at Calif is inadequate: agreed to. Same cmte: asked to be discharged from the further consideration of the ptn of Jas C Wilson, a clerk in the ofc of the Chief Engineer: agreed to. Same cmte: asked to be discharged from the further consideration of the ptn of Geo C Hutter; memorial of F Andrews; & memorial of Angeline B N Cooke, widow of Col Wm G Cooke: which were agreed to. 5-Cmte of Claims: memorial of the heirs of Harman Blannerhasset, asking to be indemnified for injuries done to the estate on an island in Ohio, & destroyed after having been taken in possession by order of the Gov't: bill for the relief of Harman Blennerhasset, deceased: ordered to a second reading. 6-Cmte on Pensions: adverse report on the ptn of Saml D Davis: ordered to be printed. Same cmte: memorial of Mary F B Levely, widow of Capt Henry Levely, asking arrears of pension: bill for her relief passed to a 2nd reading. Same cmte: ptn of Lavina Taylor, widow of the late Isaac Taylor, of the U S army, asking that the same pension may be allowed to her as to the widows of volunteers: passed to a 2nd reading. Same cmte: ptn of Nancy Wright, widow of Jas Wright, late an ofcr in the revenue service, asking to be allowed a pension; bill for her relief passed to a 2nd reading.

Mr Jas S Wadsworth, who is a passenger on board the missing steamer **Atlantic**, is one of the wealthiest men in the State of N Y. A letter from his sister in England, Mrs Murray, states that she parted with him on board the **Atlantic**.

Buffalo, Jan 30. The steamboat **John Adams**, from New Orleans bound for Cincinnati, was sunk on yesterday near Greenville, in 5 minutes after she struck; the cabin parted from her hull & broken her in two. Over 100 lives were lost, including all the deck hands & 2 of the firemen. All the Cabin passengers escaped.

J B & A Tate have received a lot of cheap & desirable goods: puffs, caps, veils, edgings, nets, kid gloves, & sleeves & cuffs. King's Cheap Lace Store, between 10th & 11th sts, on Pa ave.

A Naval Court Martial for the trial of Cmder Marston for the loss of the sloop-of-war **Yorktown**, assembled on board the ship **Pennsylvania** on Mon. It is composed of: Cmdor Geisinger, Pres: Capts Dulany, Forrest, Cmders Farragut, Dornin, Upshur, & G Adams, members. Thos C Tabb, Judge Advocate. Lt Chas C Barton will also be tried by the Court. –Norfolk Beacon

SAT FEB 1, 1851
The Hon David S Kaufman, a Rep in Congress from Texas, died yesterday at his lodgings at the U S Hotel, of an affection of the heart. His wife & child were with him.

Senate: 1-Ptn from John R Pritchard, asking to have his pension increased: referred to the Cmte on Pensions. 2-Ptn of Herrick Aiken, asking an extension of his patent for a saw-set: referred to the Cmte on Patents & the Patent Ofc. 3-On motion of Mr Dodge, of Iowa, It was ordered that Robt Grignon have leave to withdraw his ptn & papers. 4-Cmte on Pensions: ptn of Sallie T Floyd, widow of Lt Col R Floyd, who resigned in consequence of disease contracted in service, asking a pension: ordered to a 2nd reading. Same cmte: act for the relief of Warren Raymond, with a recommendation that it do not pass. Same cmte: act for the relief of John M Rosbury; act for the relief of Geo S Claflin; act for the relief of Thos R Saunders; act for the relief of Wm Sparks; act granting a pension to Sarah A Bush: with a recommendation that they do not pass. 5-Cmte on Naval Affairs: House bill for the relief of Gustavus De Russy, late an acting purser in the navy, with a recommendation that it pass. Same cmte: House bill for the relief of the securities of Robt S Moore, deceased, late a purser in the U S Navy, with a recommendation that it pass. 6-Cmte on Post Ofcs: memorial of Jos Snow, A Banks, & their associates, with a bill granting the right of way for, & to aid in the construction of, a line of telegraph from the Mississippi river to the Pacific Ocean: ordered to a 2nd reading. 7-Cmte on Pensions: referred the documents relating to the claim of Mrs Emilie Hooe, widow of Capt Alex'r S Hooe: passed to a 2nd reading.

The Gov't schnr **Wm A Graham**, Passed Midshipman Jos Fry commanding, is at Algiers, opposite to New Orleans, preparing to sail for Key West. It is attached to the coast survey, & proceeds on that duty to Key West, where she will take on board the distinguished naturalist, Prof Agassie, who is making an exploration of the coral reefs.

Dunbar, who cruelly murdered his two step-brothers in the expectation of becoming the heir to their property, was hung at Albany yesterday. He confessed his guilt, & the justice of the sentence.

Mrs Martha Myers, the last survivor of the massacre of Wyoming, died at Kingston, Luzerne Co, Pa, on the 4th ult, aged 89. Her father, Thos Bennet, was one of the 40 white men who built the stockade called **Forty Fort**.

Mrd: on Jan 29, by Rev Mr Tinkle, Mr Francis T Herst to Miss Caroline C Arny, both of Gtwn.

Died: on Jan 31, Mrs Mary Magdalen, consort of Jacob Seufferle, in her 63rd year, a native of Wurtemburg, Germany, & for the last 16 years a resident of Wash City. Her funeral is tomorrow at 3 o'clock, from her late residence.

Died: on Jan 31, John Laurence, in his 64th year. His funeral is today at 2 o'clock, from his late residence, corner of Fayette & 2nd sts, Gtwn.

Died: on Jan 31, Wm D Talley, in his 62nd year. His funeral is Sat at 11 o'clock, from his late residence on 11th st.

$5 reward for recovery of a Black Cloth Sack Overcoat, with a velvet collar, & a red morocco pocket case of surgical instruments, stolen from the ofc of Dr S W Everett, Lane & Tucker's bldg, Pa ave, Wash.

Criminal Court: the U S vs Edw Thecker, tried on an assault at Gtwn on a colored female, the jury, unable to make a verdict, were discharged. 2-John J Johnson & Saml Spaulding were tried yesterday for riot & acquitted.

Household & kitchen furniture at auction: on Mar 1, at the residence of the late Mrs Madison, by order of the Orphans Court of Wash Co, D C. Among the articles are portraits by Stuart, Trumball, & others. -Dyer & McGuire, aucts

Household & kitchen furniture at auction: on Feb 5, at the corner of East Capitol st & 2nd sts east, near the residence of B B French. -A Green, auctioneer

Rock Hill Female Academy, Fauquier Co, Va, will commence on Feb 19, 1851. For particulars address E Milligan, Auburn, Fauquier Co, Va.

MON FEB 3, 1851

Senate: 1-Ptn of Phoebe Glover, asking a pension in consideration of the services of her father during the war of the Revolution, & the services of her son during the war of 1812 with Great Britain: referred to the Cmte on Pensions. 2-Ptn of Saml Lake, asking such amendment of the bounty land law as will secure 160 acres of land to all those who served in the war of 1812: referred to the Cmte on Public Lands.
3-Documents submitted in relation to the claim of John C Bergh for per centage on disbursements of extra pay to volunteers, under the act of Aug 12, 1848, in the war with Mexico: referred to the Cmte on Military Affairs. 4-Memorial of Wm P McArthur & other ofcrs of the army engaged in the coast survey in Calif & Oregon, soliciting an increase of their compensation: referred to the Cmte on Naval Affairs.
5-Ptn of Israel Johnson, asking compensation for services performed under the direction of U S Indian agents: referred to the Cmte on Indian Affairs.
6-Announcement of the death of the Hon David S Kaufman, a member of the House from the State of Texas. He died in Wash City, yesterday, at his lodging, surrounded by an affectionate family. He was born in Cumberland Co, Pa, in 1813, & educated at Nassau Hall, Princeton, N J. His funeral will be Monday, at 12 o'clock. [His children at present are too young to be aware of the loss they have sustained.]

Mellen Davis, residing in Natick, was run down & killed upon the Worcester railroad on Mon. He leaves a wife & 6 children.

Marshal's sale: by writ of fieri facias, on Feb 28, in front of the Court-house door of said county, the following: all that tract or parcel of land in said county, upon Rock Creek, being part of the tract of land called *Peter's Mill Seat*, as the same was patented by the late Robt Peter, deceased, of Md, in or about 1801, so far as apply to the said parcel intended to be conveyed by a deed from Geo W Peter to Abner C Peirce, dated Mar 27, 1848, the whole now divided into 2 parts by the Wash & Rockville Turnpike road; divided from the remainder of the said tract now belonging to Richd Butt, containing 366½ acs, excepting the parcels called *Fellowship*, *addition to Fellowship*, & *new addition*; seized & levied upon as the property of Abner C Peirce, & sold to satisfy judicials 113, to Oct term, 1850, in favor of Saml E Tyson & Rachel his wife. –Richd Wallach, Mrshl-D C

Land warrant 66,252, Mexican War, issued Oct 1, 1848, in the name & favor of Gideon A Strange, has been lost through transmission of mail, or stolen or destroyed; application has been made for a re-issue. –Gideon A Strange, Union Mills, Fluvanna Co, Va

Valuable improved property for sale: by deed of trust: at Pa ave & 17th sts: with the bldgs & improvements to the said undivided half, as described in a deed of trust from Jas Williams & Eliza R Williams to Robt Cruitt, recorded in Liber W B 102, folios 123 thru 127, of the land records of Wash Co, D C. –Robt Cruitt, trustee
-Dyer & McGuire, aucts

Commission on Claims against Mexico: 1-Memorial of Lucius H Armstrong & Jas Jackson, claiming for losses in consequence of expulsion from Tampico, in May, 1846, & for the detention of brig **Foam**: ordered to be received. 2-Memorial of Michl Dougherty, part owner & master of schnr **Louisiana**, claiming for her seizure at Sota La Marina, in 1825, for his imprisonment, & for consequent damages: ordered to be received. 3-Memorial of Wm S Henry, Arietta L his wife, & others, in relation to the claim of Richd S Coxe, trustee of the Union land Co: ordered to be placed with other papers for further consideration. 4-Memorial of Wm H Martin, praying that the award to be made by the Board for the losses sustained by Thos Powell in the capture of the schnr **Louisiana**, as set forth in the memorials of John Powell & of the New Orleans canal & banking company, may be made in his favor, for the reasons set forth in his memorial: ordered to be filed with the papers in those cases. 5-Memorials: of Thos O Larkin; of Jos B Eaton; of Benj T Reed; of the joint claim of Thos O Larkin & Talbot H Green, copartners: claims were allowed: amount to be awarded subject to the future action of the Board. 6-Memorial of Peter Laguerenne, for himself & as surviving partner of the late trading firm of Borie & Laguerenne: same was rejected. 7-Memorial of Jos W Henry: submitted. 8-Memorial of Stephen Whitney, claiming for losses by prohibition to settle colonists in Texas: suspended for further consideration. 8-Memorial of Geo Griswold, Stephen Whitney, John Haggerty, & others, claiming for losses prohibition to settle colonists in Texas: suspended for further consideration. 9-Memorial of Geo Griswold & the excs of Nathl L Griswold, deceased, claiming for losses by prohibition to settle colonists in Texas: ordered to be suspended. 10-Memorial of Chas Callaghan, claiming for injuries sustained by the detention of the brig **Ann** at Vera Cruz, in 1839: rejected. 11-Memorial of Alex'r M Bouton & Mathew Armstrong, claiming for the value of the cargo of the schnr **Rebecca Eliza**, seized at Tampico in 1829: said memorial not received. 12-Letter from Mr Chas Callaghan, preferring, as the rep of Mrs St Angelo, a claim for a further award in addition to that made by the Commission in 1839: ordered to be put on file.

Dr A B Boone, of Duncansville, S C, was accidentally killed on Jan 23, while riding on horseback near his residence. His horse took fright & dashed his rider against a tree, fracturing his skull, & causing almost instant death.

Orphans Court of Wash Co, D C. Letters of administration on the personal estate of Jas E W Thompson, late of said county, deceased. –Geo Savage, John D Clark, adms

Orphans Court of Wash Co, D C. Letters of administration on the personal estate of Eleanor Dunlop, late of said county, deceased. –Geo W Dunlop, adm

Criminal Court-Wash-Sat. 1-Geo Krouse & Randolph Robinson, convicted of an assault, were sentenced to be imprisoned 2 months in the county jail.

On Sat ofcrs Handy & Wollard arrested H B Allison, about 40 years of age, who is charged with robbing Mr McKinger, at Richmond, Va , on Fri, of his pocket book containing several hundred dollars.

TUE FEB 4, 1851
The funeral of the Hon David S Kaufman, late Rep from Texas, was held on Sat: burial in Congressional Cemetery, Wash.

Conn Courant: letter from Bristol, Conn describes a scene such as has rarely been witnessed. Capt Jesse Gaylord, of that town, was attending the funeral of Mrs Johnson, & assisting in the ceremony. Another man & himself lowered the coffin into the grave, & Gaylord fell back, & did not speak afterwards. He was quite dead. Apoplexy was supposed to be the cause of his death.

Died: on Jan 21, in N Y C, Alex'r Gardiner, Clerk of the U S Circuit Court, & U S Com'r, in N Y C, & brother-in-law of Ex-Pres Tyler. He was in his 31st year.

Died: on Feb 1, in Chas Co, Md, at the residence of his father, Col Theodore Mudd, after a lingering & painful illness, Robt Ignatius Mudd, in his 16th year.

Stonington, Conn, Jan 30, 1851. The 17 year old daughter of Rev Mr Gonsalves, the esteemed Lutheran missionary, whose field of love is in N Y C, but whose residence is in this town, died when she fell backwards, & struck her head on a stone.
–Corr Balt Sun

House for sale on N J ave: a 3 story brick house. Inquire of Jas G Coombe.

Household & kitchen furniture at auction: on Feb 6, at the residence of Allen A Hall, on *Union Row*, on F st, between 6th & 7th sts. –C W Boteler, auct

WED FEB 5, 1851
Geo Robinett died suddenly at the North American Hotel, N Y, on Sat, from medicine improperly administered. E J Lathan undertook to relieve Robinett of his thirst of drinking 6 gallons of water daily. A post morten found lobelia had been administered & Latham was committed to the Tombs for examination.
–Journal of Commerce

The Eastern Mails brings news of the death of Hon Benj W Crowninshield, of Mass, who died in Boston, the place of his residence, on Monday last. He was appointed by Pres Madison to the ofc of Sec of the Navy, nearly 40 years ago, from Dec, 1814 until 1818, when he resigned. [Feb 6th newspaper: Mr Crowninshield was in his 80th year. He had long been afflicted with a disease of the heart. –Boston Courier]

Senate: 1-Memorial from A G Benson in relation to the settlement of his accounts: referred to the Cmte on Naval Affairs. 2-Memorial of Wm E Woodbridge, asking an appropriation to test, by experiments with guns of heavy caliber, an improvement in gunnery invented by him: referred to the Cmte on Military Affairs. 3-Ptn of Jos Beckwith, a Revolutionary soldier, asking to be allowed a pension in consideration of his services: referred to the Cmte on Pensions. 4-Cmte on Pensions: asking to be discharged from the further consideration of the ptn of Lazarus Knapp, the relief asked having been granted at the Pension Ofc: agreed to. 5-Ptn of the legal reps of Jos Ford, deceased, an ofcr in the Revolutionary war, asking a pension: referred to the Cmte on Public Lands. 6-Cmte of Claims: bill for the relief of Oliver Lee, recommended its passage. 7-Cmte on Private Land Claims: house bill 201, being an act further to amend an act approved Jul 2, 1836, for the relief of Saml Smith, Lynn Macghee, & Semoice, Creek Indians, & also an act passed Jul 2, 1836, for the relief of Susan Marlow: recommended its passage. 8-House bill 200 for the relief of the heirs of Semoice, a friendly Indian: recommended its passage. 9-Cmte of Claims: bill of Richd Mackall, asking indemnity for property destroyed by the enemy during the war of 1812: ordered to a 2nd reading. 10-Cmte on Military Affairs: memorial of Dr Thos M Morton, asking to be recognized as surgeon for Col Doniphan's regt, instead of assisting surgeon, reported that the prayer of the petitioner be rejected. 11-Cmte of Claims: bill for the relief of Capt Wm Duerson, of Indiana: recommended it do not pass. 12-Memorial from John R Simonson & others, assist marshals for taking the 7th census in King's Co, N Y, asking additional compensation: referred to the Cmte of Claims.

Trustee's sale of negro man, Prymus, horse, cart, & dray, property of Wm Mills, to secure H R Maryman. –B K Morsell, trustee -McDevitt & Robinson, aucts

Orphans Court of Wash Co, D C. Letters of administration on the personal estate of Wm Hammack, late of said county, deceased. –John Robinson, adm [By order of the Orphans Court of Wash Co, D C, on Sat next, I shall sell all the carpenter's tools of Wm Hammack, deceased. –John Robinson, adm -McDevitt & Robinson, aucts]

Died: on Feb 1, at Wheeling, Va , Mrs Mary Ellen, consort of Mr Thos Wheat, aged 66 years.

Auction on Thursday next, at the store lately occupied by Mr Chas Eckle, on Bridge st, Gtwn. -Bernard & Buckey, aucts

For rent: 2 story brick house on Md ave, between 6th & 7th sts. Apply to Owen Leddy, on 7th st, or to H Leddy, 11th & I sts. –M F Gannon

Mrd: on Jan 29, 1851, at Milton, Delaware, by Rev John L McKim, John E Parker, of Gtwn, Delaware, to Miss Eliza E, eldest daughter of Dr Wm W Wolfe, of the former place.

Postmaster Gen est'd the following new Post Ofcs for week ending Feb 1, 1851.

Ofc	County, State	Postmaster
Genie	Strafford, N H	C S Whitehouse
Lakeland	Suffolk, N Y	Edgar F Peck
Rural Hill	Jefferson, N Y	Philo Hungerford
Webb's Mills	Chemung, N Y	J V Mapes
East Shelby	Orleans, N Y	Edmund Fuller, jr
Fillmore	Monmouth, N J	Wm Jackson
Cookstown	Burlington, N J	Jos M Reeves
Gumborough	Sussex, Del	S N Hearn
Shanksville	Somerset, Pa	Josiah Brank
Saltlick	Fayette, Pa	A Cooper
Kessler's	Northampton, Pa	Philip Kessler
Leonixville	Susquehanna, Pa	S D Tompkins
Key Stone	Perry, Pa	H Foulke
Ariel	Wayne, Pa	Wm L Lesher
Bosserman's Mills	Perry, Pa	Geo Merkel
Moss Side	Alleghany, Pa	Archibald McLees
Woodland	Clearfield, Pa	F P Hutxthal
Monroeville	Alleghany, Pa	Joel Monroe
Dunkinsville	Adams, Ohio	Jno Chambers
Saltpetre	Washington, Ohio	David Hendershot
West Barre	Fulton, Ohio	Amos Taft
Tymochtes	Wyandott, Ohio	Jas H Williams
Sebewa	Ionia, Mich	Benj D Weld
Pine Creek	Calhoun, Mich	Jas Winters
Cheat River Depot	Preston, Va	Patrick O'Conner
Alto	Louisa, Va	Jno Swift
Pleasant Hills	Fayette, Va	Philip Blume
Waterloo	Fauquier, Va	Jno Ambler
Rusk	Surry, N C	Pleasant B Roberts
Ridgeway	Fairfield District, S C	Jno N Rosborough
Caledonia	Rusk, Texas	S P Allen
Fort Duncan	Kinney, Texas	Geo Van Ness
Southerland Springs	Bexar, Texas	Jno Southerland
La Mar	Refugio, Texas	Jas W Byrne
Round Botton	Izard, Ark	Jno Lancaster
Albany	Delaware, Ia	Thos Lewis
Crittenden	Howard, Ia	Isaac Hayworth
Williamson	Owen, Ia	Stacy R Youngman
Bloom	Rush, Ia	Geo Hittle
Warrenton	Gibson, Ia	Joshua Duncan
Cumberland	Grundy, Ten	W G Gwinn

Montrose	Smith, Ten	Wm Belcher
Laurel Fork	Bath, Ky	Jno Latham
Higginsville	Vermillion, Ill	Wm Magness
Crittenden	Daviess, Mo	Westly N Pryor
Milldam	Madison, Mo	Danl Whitener
Barton	Washington, Wis	Jno R Taylor
Georgetown	Lafayette, Wis	Asa McCollum
Denoon	Wankesha, Wis	Victor M Willard
Stoner's Prairie	Dane, Wis	Wm Vroman
Seven-mile Creek	Sauk, Wis	Chauncey B Strong
Blakesburg	Wapello, Iowa	Wm Kinder
Nodaway	Page, Iowa	Richd F Connor
Rapids	Boon, Iowa	Jno Dawson
Adamsville	Davis, Iowa	Benj Adair
Bute Creek	Marion, Oregon	Jeremiah Jack

Name Changed: Scrantonia, Luzerne Co, Pa, changed to Scranton.
North Moreland, Wyoming Co, Pa, changed to Keelersburgh.
Coal Mines, Chesterfield Co, Va, changed to Blackheth.
Centreport, Dallas Co, Ala, changed to Elm Bluff.
Hamilton, Antanga Co, Ala, changed to Calhoun.
Indian Creek, Giles Co, Tenn, changed to Benker's Hill.
Pleasant Green, Daviess Co, Ky, changed to Burtonsville.
Pulaski, Fond Du Lac Co, Wis, changed to Springvale.

Mrd: on Feb 1, in Wash City, by Rev Mr Morgan, Mr Jas Orr, of Decatur, Ala, to Miss Sarah Jane Sherman, of Saratoga Co, N Y.

Mrd: on Feb 3, in Wash City, by Rev Mr Edwards, L F Beeler, of Cumberland, Md, to Miss Amanda Fillins, of PG Co, Md.

THU FEB 6, 1851
Commission on Claims against Mexico: 1-Memorial of Richd S Coxe, trustee of Gilbert L Thompson & others, claiming for goods lost, expenses incurred, titles to land in Texas not obtained, contract for exclusive steam navigation of Trinity river violated: suspended for further consideration. That of Richd S Coxe, trustee of the Trinity Land Co, claiming for losses by prohibition to settle colonists in Texas under grants to Burnett, Zavala, & Vehlein: suspended for further consideration.
2-Memorial of Louis S Hargous, claiming for damages to the firm of L Hargous & Co, by his expulsion from Vera Cruz on May 18, 1846: suspended for further consideration. That of the same, claiming for losses by expulsion as above & by false imprisonment: suspended for further consideration. 3-Memorial of John H Mears, claiming for losses by expulsion from his mines in San Louis Potosi in Oct 1846: suspended for further consideration. 4-Memorial of Ferdinand Clark, claiming for losses by the illegal seizure of the schnr **Louisiana** at Soto la Marina in 1825:

ordered to be received. 5-Memorial of Ben Harrison, claiming for 2 impressments into the Mexican service, losses of property, & non-payment of stipulated wages: ordered to be received. 6-Memorial of John M Togno, claiming for his expulsion from the city of Mexico in Jun, 1847: rejected. 6-Memorial of Jas W Zacharie, claiming for loss by seizure & condemnation of the schnr **Susan** in 1825: rejected. 7-Memorial of Mgt P Hallet, admx of John Hallet, deceased, claiming for the intestates losses by confiscation of his goods at Goliad, Texas, in 1832: same was allowed: the amount to be awarded subject to the future action of the Board.

City Item: some reckless villain or villains broke into St Matthew's Church, in Wash City, on Tue or Wed, & stole from the altar the crucifix. The villain supposed the crucifix was of sold silver, but it was only silver plated.

Mrd: Feb 3, by Rev Dr Butler, Bickerton Saunders to Miss Nancy Barrett, both of Louisa Co, Va .

Died: on Feb 5, Mrs Susan A Sniffin, aged 37 years. Her funeral is tomorrow at 2 o'clock, from her late residence, on Garrison st, opposite the Marine Barracks.

Senate: 1-Memorial of John Carlin, asking that donations of land may be made for the purpose of establishing & supporting institutions for the care & education of the deaf & dumb in the U S: referred to the Cmte on Public Lands. 2-Memorial of Barnabas Bates, asking that a contract may be made with him & his associates for the transportation & delivery of the U S mail at a reduced rate: referred to the Cmte on the Post Ofc & Post Roads. 3-Memorial of Ann C Gray & John S Gray & others, stating that they are the reps & co-heirs of J C Gray, of the Revolutionary army, asking indemnity for losses sustained on commutation certificates: referred to the Cmte on Pensions. 4-Memorial of John Lee, asking to be reimbursed for certain expenses incurred in the improvement of a public square attached to the Capitol: referred to the Cmte of Claims. 5-Memorial from Lt Col D D Mitchell, of the Missouri volunteers, asking to be relieved from the operation of a judgment rendered against him for an act done in obedience to the orders of his commanding ofcr: referred to the Cmte on Military Affairs. 6-Cmte on Private Land Claims: bill for the relief of Robt Davidson: recommended that it do not pass. Same cmte: bill to amend an act for the relief of Fred'k Durvine, approved Aug 14, 1848: recommended its passage.

New and elegant watches, jewelry, silver ware and eyeglasses. –M W Galt & Brother, Pa ave, between 9th & 10th sts.

Mr Abbott, conductor of a freight train on the Boston & Maine railroad, was instantly killed at South Reading on Thu last, in making a misstep, & falling before the cars.

Rev Jas Wallace, D D, the distinguished Mathematician, died on Jan 15, at his residence in Lexington district, S C. He was ordained a clergyman of the Roman Catholic Church, & appointed to the chair of Mathematics in Gtwn College, D C. He removed to Columbia, S C, & was appointed Prof of Mathematics in S C College. He possessed one of the choicest & most extensive scientific libraries in the U S, which was almost entirely destroyed by the great conflagration of 1837; the remnant of which was bequeathed to the Catholic Theological Seminary of Charleston, S C. He was a resident of the State for the last 38 years.

Mr Geo Condon, of Cushing, was found on Jan 24, a sort distance from his residence, frozen to death. He went from his home in Friendship on Wed, about 6 miles, taking with him a daughter, whom he left there, & set out on his return home alone. His daughter returned home on Fri, until which time his family supposed he was in Friendship. He must have lost his road & wandered in the storm, & was overcome with exhaustion. -Thomaston [Me] Miscellany

Oysters & Game at the Empire Restaurant. –R W Allen, 6th & C sts

For rent: the neat Cottage residence on C st south, adjoining the property of Wm M Morrison, near the Smithsonian Institution. Enquire of E Brooke, 11th & B sts.

WED FEB 7, 1851
Telegraph dispatches, several days ago, mentioned the destruction of the steamer **John Adams**, on the Ohio, & the loss of over 100 passengers. Cincinnati, Feb 4: on Jan 27, the steamer **John Adams**, Capt H A Jones, bound for Cincinnati, near the head of Island 82, struck a snag or stump & sunk in 2 minutes. The ladies in the cabin were all saved. After suffering many hours in the water, they were enabled to get ashore at the plantation of Mr Carter. The boat **Peytone** came along & took passengers on board, with the exception of Capt Jones & his family, Mr Wilson, the mate, & a few others. Capt Shalcross gave the number on board as 230. The deck passengers were California, German, & Irish emigrants, going to Cincinnati. The cargo was also for Cincinnati.

Died: yesterday, at the residence of Mr J T Sullivan, of Wash City, John K Townsend, M D, of Phil, Pa.

Died: on Feb 1, Arabella Florinda Little, aged 3 months, daughter of Jas & Araminta Little.

Balt, Feb 6. A dispatch from Boston says that the persons lost in the ship **Franconia**, of Balt, were Capt John A Smith, Wm Berry, the first mate, a passenger named Thompson, a military ofcr from Nassau, N P, the steward, cook, & 4 seamen.

Commission on Claims against Mexico: 1-Joint memorial of Elisha Copeland, for himself & as one of the assignees of H Price & Co & of Wm Fowle, as one of the same assignees, claiming for an unpaid draft taken in payment for supplies furnished to the Gov't of Calif in 1825: claim is not valid against the republic of Mexico: not allowed. 2-Memorial of Henry Stevens, claiming for damages by his expulsion from Metamoros in Apr, 1846, being taken up for consideration: same was allowed: amount to be awarded subject to the future action of the Board. 3-Memorial of Burwell Green, claiming for seizure of his goods taken for more trading purposes upon the Santa Fe expedition from Texas: suspended for further consideration. The following day: memorial of Burwell Green: was by leave withdrawn. 4-Memorial of Francisco del Hoys, atty for Captana Noguens, administrator with the will annexed of Francisco Arenas, Geo R Bowden submitted, as of counsel in the claims, his motion for leave to withdraw the exemplified & substitute a notarial copy of the will of Arenas, & to withdraw the original memorial, in order to file another more formal. Same was agreed to.

Mrd: on Feb 6, in Wash City, by Rev S A Roszell, Royal A Miller to Miss Susan E Perrie, all of Wash City.

House of Reps: 1-Ptn of Oliver Herrick, a captain in the army of 1812, for an increase of pension. 2-Cmte on Military Affairs: bill for the relief of Mrs Mgt Hetzel, widow & administratrix of A R Hetzel, late assist quartermaster in the U S army: committed. Same cmte: bill to procide for the payment of the companies of Capts Price, Bush, & Suarez, for military service in Florida; a bill for the relief of the legal reps of Antonio Pacheco, & a bill for the relief of Giles W Ellis: committed. 3-Ptn of J G Tuthill, Richd Gelston, & Chas Woodhull, assistant marshals of Suffolk Co, N Y, to take the census, asking further compensation for their services.

Senate: 1-Cmte on Pensions: asked to be discharged from the further consideration of the ptn of David Linn: on the ground of insufficiency of proof to warrant his name being placed on the pension roll: which was agreed to. Same cmte: asked to be discharged from the further consideration of the memorial of the heirs of Andrew D Crosby, late a purser in the U S Navy: agreed to. 2-Cmte on Printing: memorial of John Carlin: reported against printing the same: which was agreed to. 3-Cmte on Pensions: bill for the relief of Mary Kirby: recommended its passage. Same cmte: bill for the relief of Alanson Pool: recommended its passage. Same cmte: bill for the relief of John Morrison: recommended its passage. Same cmte: bill for the relief of Adam Garlock: recommended its passage.

THU FEB 8, 1851
Died: on the 6th proximo, in Wash City, of consumption, Mrs Anna M Adams, of New Haven, Conn, wife of C B Adams, of the Treasury Dept. Her remains have been taken North for interment.

Wash City Ordinances: 1-Act for the relief of John Dove: to be paid $80 for a flag footway laid across H st north. 2-Act for the relief of Wm B Wilson: to pay him $47.08, the balance due him for laying a flag footway across Pa ave & 9th st. 3-Act for the relief of Jas Brown: to pay him $2, same having been paid erroneously by Brown for a dog tax.

Senate: 1-Ptn of John Baneff, asking that he may be allowed bounty land in consideration of the services of his father during the last war with Great Britain: referred to the Cmte on Pensions. 2-Memorial of R E House & others, asking for the superiority of their printing telegraph over all others, in Europe or American & assuring Congress that no man whose name is not appended to the memorial has any shadow of right to contract for or promise the use of House's telegraph upon the route to the Pacific: referred to the Cmte on Patents & the Patent Ofc.

Commission on Claims against Mexico: 1-Memorial of Jos Henry: claiming, for his arrest at Chihuahua, on Jan 2, 1847, for 50 days' imprisonment & consequent losses: claim is not valid against the Republic of Mexico: not allowed. 2-Memorial of Chas Danforth, surviving partner of Godwin, Clark & Co, claiming for damages on contract with the Mexican Gov't in 1831: same was allowed; the amount to be awarded subject to the further action of the Board. 3-Two memorials of John Parrott, claiming severally for the acquestration of his goods at Mazatlan in 1845, & for the seizure of the cargo of the brig **Matador**, in 1845: allowed accordingly; the amount to be awarded subject to the future action of the Board. 4-Memorial of Mrs Hannah Ulrick, claiming for the rent of 2 rooms in which were lodged, from the death of Mr Martinez till the arrival of Mr Almonte, the archives & furniture of the Mexican Legation: same was allowed: amount to be awarded subject to the future action of the Board.

The funeral of John K Townsend, M D, late of Phil, will take place from the residence of John T Sullivan, on 7th st, this morning, at 11 o'clock.

Mrd: on Feb 6, at the Church of the Epiphany, by Rev John W French, Mr Alex'r H Brown, of Md, & Miss Mary J Murray, daughter of the late A B Murray, of Balt.

Mrd: on Feb 6, in Christ's Church, by Rev Mr Hodges, John T Phelps to Sarah Eliz Kidwell, all of Wash City.

For rent: the house #6, *Union Row*, F st, just vacated by Allen A Hall. Apply at the Republic ofc, 9th st.

Stray calf came to the subscriber some weeks ago, which the owner can have by describing the same, proving property & paying charges. Inquire of Martin Loxmann, corner of North Capitol & H sts.

MON FEB 10, 1851

Senate: 1-Cmte of Claims: memorial of Ernest Eude, Clement Dubamel, & Jos Derlis, asking compensation for a vessel destroyed; submitted an adverse report, which was ordered to be printed. 2-Memorial from the biscuit manufacturers in N Y C, remonstrating against the extension of Wm R Nevin's patent for a biscuit machine: referred to the Cmte on Patents & the Patent Ofc.

Died: on Feb 8, in Wash City, Eleanor D, daughter of Andrew & Ann Rothwell, in her 17th year. Her funeral is this morning at 11 o'clock, from her father's residence.

Died: yesterday, Miss Hanna Wood, a native of Phil. Her funeral will take place on Tue, at 3 o'clock, from the residence of her brother-in-law, Richd Cruit, on Pa ave, between 4½ & 6th sts.

Died: Feb 8, in Gtwn, D C, Mrs Sarah Rebecca Collins, daughter of Capt Tucker, of West River, Anne Arundel Co, Md, & wife of Jos Henry Collins.

Died: Feb 4, at the residence of his father, in Warrenton, Va, Dr Richd H Moore, in his 31st year.

Died: on Feb 8, in Wash City, James, infant son of James & Susan Jack, aged 28 days.

Herr Reyninger, the wire-walker, was lately killed at Baton Rouge, La, by falling from the wires, in attempting to walk from the tower of the State capitol.

Gen Hinton, who has been confined in the Columbus [Ohio] jail, being indicted for robbing the mail, has been released on bail in the sum of $15,000.

Household & kitchen furniture at auction: on Feb 12, at the residence & boarding-house of Mrs Pierce, on Pa ave, between 1st & 2nd sts. -A Green, auctioneer

At Phil, last week, Chas J Chamberlain, the proprietor of a drug shop, & Wm McFadden, his clerk, were indicted for involuntary manslaughter, in causing the death of Miss Neil, by putting up morphine instead of quinine, ordered in a prescription. It was established that Chamberlain was not in the city at the time of the transaction, & was acquitted. McFadden pleaded guilty. Sentence suspended for the present.

Valuable tract of land containing 2,300 acres, lying in Hardy Co, Va, at auction: on Feb 27, it being the land purchased by Addison Murdock, deceased, of Leonard M Deakens & John Hoye, excs of Wm Deakens, & lying on the North Branch of the Potomac river, in said county, beginning at Mineral Spring, well known as the *Big Elk Lick Spring*. -A Green, auctioneer

TUE FEB 11, 1851

Pacific News, under date of Yuba City, Dec 18: 1-Bernard B Light, of Hedgeville, Va, was frozen to death a few miles north of Downieville. The snow was about a foot deep at the time. 2-The cholera has been very fatal at Santa Babara. In many cases whole families became extinct. 3-The schnr **Patuxent**, on Gov't service, was lost on Nov 20th in Trinidad Bay. About 14 days previous one of her boats was capsized at the mouth of Klamath river, & 3 lives lost, namely, Lt Woodward, Phenix Davis, a passenger, & a seaman named Edwards.

Senate: 1-Mr Pearce presented the credentials of the Hon Thos G Pratt, elected a Senator by the Legislature of the State of Md for 6 years, from & after Mar 4 next: which were read. 2-Cmte on Pensions: ptn of Mary Smith Whetmore, widow of an ofcr of the army, asked a pension: adverse report on the same. Same cmte: ptn of Hester L Henry, widow of Wm Henry, asking a pension, in consideration of the services of her husband: adverse report on the same. Same cmte: ptn of S G Green: made an adverse report on the same. Same cmte: ptn of Abraham L Knickerbocker, asking to be allowed a pension for injuries received whilst engaged in the U S service at the arsenal at Watervleit: adverse report in writing. Same cmte: ptn of Edith Farns, widow of Edmund Farns, asking to be allowed full pension under the act of 1838: made an adverse report in writing. Same cmte: ptn of Wm C Harrison, asking a pension for the loss of an eye while employed in the revenue service: made an adverse report on the same. Same cmte: asked to be discharged from the further consideration of the ptn of Absalom Hughes: which was agreed to. Same cmte: asked to be discharged from the further consideration of the ptn of Parkerson Hocker, asking a pension for services in the Florida war, & that the petitioner have leave to withdraw his papers: which was agreed to. 3-Cmte on Revolutionary Claims: ptn of the heirs of Jas Bell: ordered to a second reading. 4-Cmte on Public Lands: House bill for the relief of Jasper A Maltby: recommended that it do not pass. Same cmte: memorial of Robt Butler, late surveyor general of Florida, asking additional compensation & the reimbursement of certain expenses: adverse report in writing on the same. 5-Memorial presented from John L Hayes, asking to be allowed for rent paid by him while a clerk in the U S courts for the district of N H, for rooms in which he kept the records & papers of the courts: referred to the Cmte of Claims. 6-Ptn of Betsey S Warren, asking to be allowed a pension, in consideration of the services of her father, Gen Jos Spencer, in the Revolutionary war: referred to the Cmte on Pensions. 7-Memorial of Alert Root & others, asking a postponement for the present of the bill for the amendment of the patent laws: ordered to lie on the table.

Balt, Feb 10. Mr Jas Wilson, of the firm of Wm Wilson & Sons, one of our oldest, most opulent, & respected merchants, died at his residence here this morning. He was a gentleman of the old school, & one in whose long career no blemish could be found.

The biography of Wm Wirt, by John P Kennedy, has recalled to my memory a lamentable fact connected with his death. At the death of this distinguished orator & jurist some of his legal friends proposed to erect a monument over his body, in the Congressional Burying-ground in Wash City. This consent was obtained, & on Feb 20, 1834, the remains of Wirt were laid in the receiving vault of the cemetery. The rule adopted by the Vestry of Christ's Church, who have the management of this cemetery, limits the retention of bodies in the receiving vaults to one month. The time for Wirt's remains to remain there was extended from time to time, & finally, in Jan 20, 1835, it was deposited in the humble grave where it now reposes, between those of Gen Jacob Brown & Judge Philip Barbour. No stone marks the spot. A broken shaft covers the body of Gen Brown, erected by Congress. Why has the grave of Wirt been so long & so strangely neglected? What has become of the funds collected for his monument? The ofcrs of the navy have erected a fine monument in honor of the brave & gallant young men who fell off Tripoli, & the ofcrs of the medical staff one to the memory of Dr Lovell, formerly Surgeon General of the army, alike honorable to the living & the dead. If the members of the legal profession, although they promised to do so, as well as to contribute funds for the erection of a monument to Chief Justice Marshall, in the same cemetery, still neglect this duty, it is to be hoped that Congress will do something to honor the memory of both those great & illustrious men. -W

Died: on Feb 8, Fannie Ellen, daughter of Thos J & Mary A Galt, aged 2 years & 4 months.

Died: on Feb 9, in Gtwn, D C, Charles Burnett, son of Thos A & Sarah A Lazenby, aged 16 months.

Commission on Claims against Mexico: 1-Memorial of Christian Alby, claiming for seizure & imprisonment in Calif in 1839, & for losses: claim is valid against the Republic of Mexico: allowed accordingly: the amount to be awarded subject to the future action of the Board. 2-Memorial of Asmus C Bredell, claiming for seizures & pillage, of schnr **Lodi**, & her cargo, at Corpus Christi, in 1838: claim is not valid against the Republic of Mexico: same was not allowed. 3-Memorial of Jas L Rudolph, claiming for expulsion from Reynosa on Apr 9, 1846: claim is valid, & allowed accordingly: the amount to be awarded subject to the future action of the Board.

Obit-died: on Jan 30, at Cincinnati, Thos Worthington King, 2nd son of the late Edw King, in his 32nd year. A native of Ohio, he was educated at Harvard Univ, where he was graduated in 1840. He entered the counting-house of the late Richd Alsop, of Phil, &, after several years, in voyages to South America & China, & a short residence in New Orleans, he entered into mercantile business at Cincinnati in 1845.

Balt, Feb 10. Mr Jas Wilson, of the firm of Wm Wilson & Sons, one of our oldest, most opulent, & respected merchants, died at his residence here this morning. He was a gentleman of the old school, & one in whose long career no blemish could be found.

Died: on Jan 24, after a short & severe illness, at the residence of Mrs Sarah C Waring, his mother-in-law, in PG Co, Md, Dr Richd H Clagett, aged 42. The deceased had been compelled, from feeble health, to with draw from the practice of his profession for some time before his death. He has left a widow & son to grieve him, & a large circle of attached connexions & friends.

Died: on Jan 31, the aged & venerable Dr McWhir. He was an Irishman by birth, emigrated to this country about 1783, & settled at Alexandria, Va, where he taught for several years. He thence removed to Georgia, with a view to take charge of the Richmond Co Academy, but finally settled at Sunbury, as teacher & preacher. Whilst at Alexandria, he was often the inmate of Gen Washington's house, at **Mount Vernon**, & was also the instructor of two of the General's nephews. He died at Mr Roswell King's, in Liberty Co, in his 92nd year. –Savannah Republican

Venison Hams, pickled York River Oysters, & Va Old Hams, selected by that well-known caterer Capt W Claiborne, more familiarly known as the Old Commodore, put up by the Cmdor's lady. –Elexius Simms, corner of F & 13th sts.

WED FEB 12, 1851

Senate: 1-Memorial from Wm B Tucker & others, inventors & interested in inventions: report the state of the patent laws as they now exist: ordered to lie on the table. 2-Memorial of Richd Eldward, late deputy postmaster at Natchez, asking to be allowed certain items which had been rejected in the settlement of his accounts by the Post Ofc Dept: referred to the Cmte on the Post Ofc & Post Roads. 3-Memorial of Bela M Hughes, late receiver of public moneys at Plattsburg, Miss, asking to be allowed additional compensation for locating military bounty land warrants: ordered to lie on the table. 4-Additional documents presented in relation to the claim of Margaret Drew, for a negro that escaped from the service of a quartermaster in the army: referred to the Cmte of Claims. 5-Memorial of Jas B Moore & his associates, asking that a contract may be entered into with them for the establishment of a line of mail steamers from Calif or Oregon to China: referred to the Cmte on the Post Ofc & Post Roads. 6-Ptn from Elijah Murray, asking an appropriation may be made for the construction of a marine railway on an improved plan invented by him: referred to the Cmte on Naval Affairs. 7-Ptn of Sarah Anne Watson, widow of the late Col W H Watson, asking that her pension may be continued during her natural life: referred to the Cmte on Pensions. 8-Memorial of Isaac Adams, asking an extension of the patents granted him for improvement in printing process: referred to the Cmte on Patents & the Patent Ofc. 9-Memorial of Geo Morris, who was a soldier in the war of 1812: he represents that he was captured at the battle of River Raisin, with the troops engaged in that action; that after the battle he was taken by the Indians to the region near Lake Superior, & kept at the western termination of that lake, & in that quarter, going to & fro, as the Indians migrated about, until 1816, 3 or 4 years after the battle. When he obtained his liberty, it being purchased by some persons near Detroit, & returned to Ky, he found that most of his ofcrs had been killed or had died, so that it was impossible for him to obtain the pay to which he was entitled. He represents that when young & active he cared very little about his pay, but as he has grown old & has a large family of children, he thinks that, in consequence of his long detention among the Indians, growing out of his service for the U S, Congress ought to pay something for those sufferings & services: referred to the Cmte of Claims. 10-Ordered that leave be granted to withdraw the papers of Wm Johnson & G Kidwell. 11-Cmte of Claims: bill for the relief of Isaac Cook: reported back without amendment. Same cmte: memorial of Saml Boots, asking the payment of a balance of salary claimed to be due him as a clerk in the Treasury ofcr: recommended that the petition be rejected. Same cmte: memorial of Tobias Purrington, a clerk in the Comptroller's ofc, asking an increase of compensation: recommended that the prayer not be granted. Same cmte: ptn of John McAvoy, with a bill for his relief: passed to a 2nd reading. 12-Cmte on Military Affairs: asked to be discharged from the further consideration of the memorial of Wm Wood, in behalf of himself, & a company of riflement, asking to be placed on the same footing in regard to bounty land as the volunteers in the war with Mexico: discharged accordingly. Same cmte: asked to be discharged from the further consideration of the memorial of Wm H Payne, in behalf of himself & a company of Florida volunteers, asking compensation for their services in the Florida war: discharged accordingly. Same cmte: asked to be discharged from the further consideration of the memorial of S L Sparkman & John Parker, captains of rangers during the late difficulties with the Florida Indians, asking remuneration for their services & losses: discharged accordingly. Same cmte: asked to be discharged from the further consideration of the ptn of Wm R Shoemaker, military storekeeper at Santa Fe, New Mexico, asking an increase of pay for his services while performing the duty of commissary: discharged accordingly. 13-Cmte of Claims: ptn of Richd G Dove, asking compensation for his services as assistant messenger in the 3rd Auditor's ofc: ordered to be printed. Same cmte: memorial of Thos M Hope, asking to be reimbursed for moneys paid out by him as U S marshal: recommended it be rejected. Same cmte: asked to be discharged from the further consideration of the ptn of Nicholas M Kerr: discharged accordingly. 14-Cmte on Military Affairs: to inquire into establishing a Western armory at Paducah, Ky. Communication from Messrs W F Norton & Jas Larmon: amount of business done in dry goods, hardware, groceries in 1850: about $600,000. –Jas Larmon, W E Norton Communication from H W Hurt & H W Brown: how many houses were built in Paducah in 1850: not less than 400, all white men; white labor can be had at anytime to meet any demand. Mr J D Allard stated that he resided in Ill on the Ohio above Paducah about 10 years; that he moved to this place in 1849; that he cultivates a large farm in Ill, opposite Paducah, & he hires hands in Paducah to cultivate his farm. Mr U C P Pool makes a similar statement. Mr W A Lee & L

W Rawleigh stated they are boat builders, residing in Paducah; in 1850 not less than 100 ship carpenters & men were employed at that business; that not less than 65 steamboats were built & repaired at Paducah in 1850. At least $300,000 was paid out.

It is worth a walk from any part of Wash City to the new <u>Railroad Depot</u>, to take a view of the improvements now in progress under the direction & auspices of the Balt & Wash Railroad Co. The engine house is of brick, in the form of a hexagon, 62 feet in diameter, & 24 feet high to the eaves. The car house is 340½ feet, the roof is to project 8 feet on each side. The main bldg, of which the foundation is now being laid, will front 119 feet on N J ave: in the tower will be a clock & bell. The bldgs are now being erected under the direction of Mr J H McMachen, of Balt, superintendent. Mr M G Emery, of Wash City, executed the granite work, the blue rock foundation, & the brown stone. Mr Saml Hevner is the bricklayer. In 6 or 8 months all the bldgs will be completed.

Postmaster Gen has est'd the following new Post Ofcs for week ending Feb 8, 1851.

Ofc	County, State	Postmaster
N Sedgwick	Hancock, Me	Ephraim Closson
S Bradford	Orange, Vt	Henry W Bayley
S Ryegate	Caledonia, Vt	Chas Stewart
S Manchester	Hartford, Ct	Ward Cheney
M Washington	Berkshire, Mass	Horace W Lamson
Tottenville	Richmond, N Y	John Totten
W Onondaga	Onondaga, N Y	Myron Clift
Red Jacket	Erie, N Y	Asa Whittemore
Ogden	Monroe, N Y	Geo C Howard
Marshfield	Erie, N Y	John Potter
East Eden	Erie, N Y	Simeon Clark
Mount Olive	St Mary's, Md	Henry Goodrich
Robisonville	Beford, Pa	Wm Robison
Shehola	Pike, Pa	Dewitt C King
Texas	Lycoming, Pa	Wm Foote
Yiohagany	Westmoreland, Pa	Alex'r Fulton
New Freedom	York, Pa	E W Free
Pike Valley	Potter, Pa	Calvin Catrick
Vogansville	Lancaster, Pa	Mark S Graff
Cambridge	Lancaster, Pa	John W Irwin
S Hermitage	Lancaster, Pa	John McGill
Decaturville	Washington, Ohio	Philip Shrader, jr
Doylestown	Paulding, Ohio	Danl Ridemour
North Union	Washington, Ohio	Joel Gilbert
Wheat Ridge	Adams, Ohio	W B Brown

Tully	Van Wert, Ohio	John Lair
Brennersville	Preble, Ohio	Philip Riechard
Peck's Run	Barbour, Va	W H Browning
Hargrove's Tavern	Nansemond, Va	Jas Hargrove
Lake Comfort	Hyde, N C	Reuben Benson
Danbury	Stokes, N C	Ferdinand Dalton
Little River Depot	Richland Dist, S C	Thos R Center
Calk's Ferry	Lexington, S C	W W Holeman
Rocky Well	Lexington, S C	G J Hooks
Beech Island	Edgefield, S C	Thos M Foster
Hope Station	Lexington, S C	H J Epting
Tiger	Rabun, Ga	Harris Cannon
Woodville	Green, Ga	W H Scovell
Tallokas	Loundes, Ga	P O Wing
Copano	Refugio, Texas	Walter Lambert
Iron Wood Bluff	Itawamba, Miss	Henry W Stegall
Leighton's	Yalla Busha, Miss	John T Leigh
Sylamore	Izard, Ark	Tobias Sudulph
Kinderhook	Pike, Ia	Jas Madison
Fruit Hill	Vigo, Ia	John Bell
North Bend	Lawrence, Ten	Geo A Potts
Stanton	Bracken, Ky	Saml Hedges
Green's Store	Scott, Ky	Geo Mallory
George's Creek	Lawrence, Ky	Reuben Burgess
Fulton Centre	Fulton, Ill	Wm K Nichols
Millard	Walworth, Wis	Hiram Taylor
Fremont	Brown, Wis	Ira Sumner

Names Changed: North Sedgwick, Hancock Co, Maine, changed to West Sedgwick. East Eden, Hancock Co, Maine, changed to Salisbury Cove.
Round Hill, Smith Co, Texas, changed to Canton.
Dunlap's Prairie, Cook Co, Ill, changed to Leyden.
Patch Grove, Grant Co, Wis, changed to Ursine.

Mrd: last evening, in Wash City, by Rev Jos White, Mr John Clapham, U S Navy, to Miss Ann M Barber, of Fauquier Co, Va .

Mrd: on Feb 9, by Rev Mr Marks, Mr Wm Venable to Miss Mary Edelin, of PG Co, Md.

Mrd: on Feb 9, by Rev O B Brown, Mr Milton Clark to Mrs Susan Beardsley.

Died: on Feb 2, at Piqua, Ohio, of erysipelas, in her 35th year, Mrs Catherine B, wife of the Rev C W Fitch, of that place, & daughter of the late Thos C Wright, of Gtwn, D C.

Lt Col S H Long, Topographical Engineer: Louisville, Jan 29, 1847. Offers remarks on the port of Paducah, "expressive of my conviction of its eligibility as a commercial depot."

John Rady, charged with a murderous assault upon Messrs Wharton & Todd several months ago, was brought to Wash City on Sat by ofcrs Cox & Hilton, who arrested the prisoner at Salem, Roanoke Co, Va. Rady is safely lodged in jail.

For sale: splendid country seat, 2 miles from the Capitol, on the Balt Turnpike: contains 30 acres, more or less. Call on me at Mr Edw Fenwick's, adjoining. It adjoins the property of Col Wm Hickey, & John Macduel. It has no bldgs on it. —Jos Thos Fenwick

Beautiful residence in view of the City of Wash for sale: ***Evermay***, the residence of the late Lewis Grant Davidson, on the extreme right of the Heights of Gtwn: the dwlg house is of brick, 2 stories high, with neatly finished garrets, with wing for kitchen, servants' room, pantry; stables, carriage house, cow shed, dairy, gardener's house, & other ofcs, all of brick, attached. The lot covers an area of 20 acres & more, & is divided from Kalorama, the former residence of Joel Barlow & of the late Col Bomford by Rock Creek. The house faces the south. It is now occupied by the Hon H Bosch Spencer, Minister from Belgium. Also, a farm of 723 acres in Montg Co, Md, now occupied by Robt G Davidson; upon which is a valuable stone quarry, now worked by Mr Offutt. Also, lots in Beall's addition to Gtwn, viz: parts of lots 173 & 174, fronting 90 feet on Green st & 100 feet on Olive st; part of lots 15 & 16 fronting 40 feet on Wash st; lots 107 & 110, each fronting 60 feet on Beall st, with the houses thereon. And 1,500 acres of land in Hardy Co, Va, on Abraham's creek, about 20 miles distant from ***Merefield***. Apply to the subscriber in Gtwn, or to Saml G Davidson, atty at law, Wash. -W Redin, Trustee & atty for the heirs

Account of the blowing up of the Portuguese frig **Dona Maria II**, at Macao, China, Oct 29: of 224 men, 188 perished in the explosion, amongst whom were her Cmder, 5 Lts, 1 Midshipman, & Assist Surgeon, & the Purser. The cause of the explosion is a mystery. Ofcrs & crew of the U S frig **Marion** are highly spoken of for their services in rescuing 10 men from the water or from the burning hull. [Letter dated U S ship **Marion**: Macao, Nov 8, 1850: to his Excellency Antonio Joze de Miranda, Sec of Gov't: I accept the congratulations of the honorable Council upon the escape of the **Marion** from danger, which has the greater weight as coming from those who suffered so secerely from the calamity which occasioned such danger. —W M Glendy, Cmder]

THU FEB 13, 1851

Balt, Feb 12. Govn'r Lowe has offered the appointment of Atty Gen of Md, to fill the vacancy caused by the death of Mr Richardson, to Robt J Brent, formerly of Wash.

Wash Corp: 1-Bill for the relief of Wm Dowling: passed. 2-Cmte of Claims: bill for the relief of J S Reed: passed. 3-Ptn from Chas Wilkes & others, owners of property on North Capitol & B & C sts north, in relation to grading of said streets: referred to the Cmte on Improvements. 4-Bill for the relief of John Fletcher: passed.

For sale or rent, the Farm called *Summer Hill*, adjoining the estate of the late Gen Alex Hunter, in Alexandria Co, Va, containing 150 acres. –Louisa Hunter

Died: yesterday, Albert A, infant son of Jas & Mary Williamson, aged 8 months. His funeral is this evening at 3 o'clock, from the residence of its parents, Capitol Hill.

House of Reps: 1-Memorial of Alice S Dowlin, widow of Florence Dowlin, asking compensation for injuries received by her husband in the service of the U S.

Senate: 1-Memorial of Jos Bryan & Geo N Sanders was presented, asking that a contract may be entered into with them for the establishment of a line of war steamers to the coast of Africa & Southern Europe, for the purpose of carrying the mails, promoting commerce, the colonization of free negroes, & the suppression of the slave trade. 2-Memorial from Jos Rodney Croskey, late American Consul at Cowes, in the Isle of Wight, in the year 1844, asking to be reimbursed $1,000 for extraordinary expenses incurred by him in supporting the dignity of the country: referred to the Cmte on Naval Affairs. 3-Memorial of Amelia Dumas & Louisa Dumas, excx of Abigail Dumas, asking indemnity for injuries done to their property by the capture of a vessel & cargo by French privateer in 1803, & carried into the Island of St Jago de Cuba & sold: referred to the Cmte on Commerce. 4-Ptn of Hannah Webb, asking to be allowed an increase of pension: referred to the Cmte on Pensions. 5-Cmte on Commerce: bill for the compensation of Jas W Low & others, for the capture of the British private armed vessel **Ann**, during the late war with Great Britain: recommended its passage. 6-Cmte on Military Affairs: recommended that the bill to provide for the just settlements of the accounts of Jno C Bergh, late an assist paymaster in the U S army: recommended that it do not pass. Same cmte: memorial of A W Burns, assist paymaster, asking to be allowed a balance found against him in the settlement of his accounts, submitted an adverse report: which was ordered to be printed.

Mrd: on Feb 11, in Christ Church, Wash, by Rev Mr Hodges, Andrew F Beedle to Miss Emma Hodge, all of Wash City.

Mrd: on Feb 11, in Wash City, by Rev Wm Matthews, Jos N Young to Joanna Frances, daughter of Maj Parke G Howle, U S M C.

Mrd: on Feb 5, in Charlestown, Jefferson Co, Va , by Rev Dudly Tyng, Mr P C Little, of Gtwn, D C, to Miss Julia Roberts, formerly of Massachusetts.

Mrd: on Tue last, by Rev C A David, Edw Magruder, of PG Co, Md, to Laura E, daughter of Thos Wilson, of Montg Co, Md.

The following from the San Francisco Herald of Dec 16 last, gives account of the death of Lt R S Woodward, of the Revenue service, formerly of Gtwn, D C, but recently of New Haven, Conn, where he married, & now leaves an amiable wife & 2 children, as well as a large number of relatives & friends in each place. Lt Woodward, who sailed from this port Oct 25 in the schnr **Patuxent**, on a Gov't survey, was upset in a boat at the mouth of the Klamath, Nov 5, & drowned, with 2 others-P Davis, a passenger, & J Edwards, a seaman. Nov 28th the **Patuxent** drove from her anchors before a southeaster, in Trinidad, &, going ashore, became a total wreck.

FRI FEB 14, 1851
Mrd: on Feb 13, at St Patrick's Church, Wash, by Rev Mr Slattery, Jas Wm Norton to Miss Lucretia Harper, of Montg Co, Md.

Died: on Feb 7, at his farm, in Chas Co, Md, W Bruce Wilson, aged 52 years, 2nd son of the late Jas Wilson, of Alexandria.

Knight, who some time since killed Hughes in Macon, Ga, has been found guilty of manslaughter, & sentenced to 4 years in the penitentiary.

Commission on Claims against Mexico: 1-On motion of Col Paine, ordered that the case of Geo W Van Stavoren, claiming for illegal seizure of tobacco at Vera Cruz in 1839, be again taken up for consideration, in consequence of certain testimony, bearing on said claim, being sent to the Board from the Dept of State since the opinion in relation thereto to which the Board came to on the 8th of Jan last.

By 3 writs of venditioni exponas, I have levied on all the right, title, interest, & estate of Jos Martini, in & unto lots 9 & 10, in square 544, in Wash City, & will offer the same for sale on Mar 16, in front of the premises, corner of 4½ & M st, [Island,] to pay & satisfy judgments in favor of Nathl Carusi, Wm McCormick, & Jas A Ratcliffe. Terms cash. -Wm Coale, Constable

Meeting of the stockholders of the steamboat **Phenix** will be held at the ofc of the Company, in Alexandria, on Feb 17, at 11 o'clock. –S Shinn, Treasurer

Senate: 1-Ptn from Saml Lawrence, asking to be allowed compensation for his services as acting gunner in the U S navy: referred to the Cmte on Naval Affairs. 2-Memorial from Thos Thruston, owner of the schnr **Wanderer**, asking the passage of a law by which he can be enabled to receive $136.80, due to him as fishing bounty: referred to the Cmte on Commerce. 2-Memorial of Chas Goodyear, in relation to his patent for certain improvements in the preparation of India rubber for manufacturing purposes: referred to the Cmte on Patents & the Patent Ofc. 3-Memorial of E Mickle & Co, asking the refunding of certain duties on goods imported by them into Calif in 1849: revered to the Cmte on Finance. 4-Ptn of Eliza Ann Kendall, widow of Capt Henry Kendall, who was killed in Mexico, asked that the pension she now receives may be continued during her natural life: referred to the Cmte on Pensions. 5-Ordered that Hugh C Davis have leave to withdraw his petition & papers. 6-Cmte on Military Affairs: asked to be discharged from the further consideration of the memorial of Wm E Woodbridge, asking an appropriation to test by experiments with guns of heavy caliber an implement in gunnery invented by him: discharged accordingly. Same cmte: asked to be discharged from the further consideration of the memorial of T P Shaffner, asking the establishment of military posts from the frontier of Missousi to Santa Fe, for the protection of a line of telegraphs which he proposes to establish: discharged accordingly. 7-Cmte on Military Affairs: memorial of Chas W Carroll, asking redress for injuries suffered in consequence of his arrest & detention on an alleged false charge of being a deserter from the recruits enlisted for the army, submitted an elaborate report: ptn be rejected. Same cmte: ptn of E P Hale for bounty land, 3 months' pay, & transportation for services as assist surgeon in the 2nd regt of Tenn volunteers in the Mexican war: adverse to the prayer of the petitioner. Same cmte: memorial of Dr H R Robards, for payment due him as surgeon in the army during the Mexican war: adverse report to the prayer of the petitioner. 8-Cmte on Pensions: bill for the relief of Wm B Edwards: reported back without amendment. Same cmte: bill for the relief of Geo C Thomas: recommended that the bill do not pass. Same cmte: bill for the relief of Jas F Green: recommended that it do not pass. Same cmte: ptn of Francis E Baden: passed to a 2nd reading. Same cmte: ptn of Davis Tucker, a soldier in the last war with Great Britain, asking arrears of pension: adverse to the prayer of the petitioner. Same cmte: ptn of Asenath M Elliot, widow of Capt E G Elliot, of the U S army, asking a pension: adverse report to the prayer of the petitioner. Same cmte: ptn of Emily C B Thompson, widow of Cmdor Chas Thompson, deceased, asking that her pension may be increased & continued during her life: adverse report to the prayer of the petitioner. 9-Cmte on Naval Affairs: bill for the relief of Eli Darling: reported back without amendment.

Constable's sale of city lots: by writ of fieri facias, at the suit of Jos Boulanger, against Jos Marteni: sale of lots 9 & 10 in square 544; & by virtue of a writ of venditioni exponas, on Mar 20 next, on the premises, corner of M st south & 4th st, said lots at public auction. –John S Hutchins, Constable

For rent: 2 story brick house on the corner of Md ave & 12th st west. Inquire of Mr Thos Wells, the present occupant, or of Edw Mattingly, near the Navy Yard.

SAT FEB 15, 1851
Mrd: on Feb 13, at St Mary's Church, by Rev Mr Alig, Mr Jos Meyer, of Rockville, Md, to Jane Welch, of Wash City.

Mrd: on Feb 9, by Rev Mr Alig, Mr Michl O'Conner to Miss Mary O'Conner.

Mrd: on Jan 2, by Rev Mr Alig, Patrick Fitzgerald to Miss Ellen Collins.

Mrd: on Nov 25, by Rev Mr Alig, Mr Peter Schaefer to Miss Mary Catharine Schlattman.

Mrd: on Nov 29, by Rev Mr Alig, Edw Corridan to Honora Leehy.

Died: on Feb 14, in Wash City, in his 83rd year, Thos H Gilliss, late & for many years Chief Clerk in the 4th Auditor's Ofc. His funeral will take place from the Church of the Ascension, on Sunday next, at 2 p m.

MON FEB 17, 1851
Household & kitchen furniture at auction: on Feb 19, at the residence of Chas F Stansbury, on 12th st, between B & C sts. --C W Boteler, auct

Senate: 1-Memorial from the legal reps of John Forbes, asking the execution of the 9th article of the treaty of 1819 between the U S & Spain: referred to the Cmte on the Judiciary. 2-Mr Whitcomb presented joint resolutions of the Legislature of Indiana in relation to the claim of Francis Vigo: referred to the Cmte on Revolutionary Claims. 3-Memorial of Michl Nasa, a guard of the penitentiary in the District of Columbia, asking additional compensation for the time he was employed on other duty in the penitentiary: referred to the Cmte of Claims. 4-Cmte on Pensions: bill for the relief of Jos B Ward: ask its immediate consideration. Ward was a sgt in the volunteers in the late war with Mexico, who lost one of his arms, & has the other so mutilated & disabled as to be of but little, if any service to him, on account of a wound in the hand. To be put on the roll of pensions, at the rate of $20 per month, commencing on Mar 9, 1847, & to continue during his natural life. Mr Jones feels it should be a greater sum. Same cmte: the name of Isaac Watts Griffith, late a sgt in the army of the U S, to be placed on the roll of invalid pensions at the rate of $16 per month, commencing on Oct 28, 1747, to continue during his natural life, in lieu of the pension to which he is now entitled by law. Griffith lost his right arm while in the battle at Churubusco, in Mexico, & whilst he was leading his men into the thickest of the fight, & which he continued to do after the wound was afflicted until constrained to go off by the loss of blood, & the order of his superiors.

Circuit Court of Wash Co, D C-in Chancery. Wm B Kibby & others vs Clement Hill & others. Ratify sale of the certain part of lot 6 in square 461, in Wash City, fronting on 7th st, with improvements, to John D McPherson, for $2,425. –Jno A Smith, clerk

Maj Auguste Davezac died in N Y C on Sat, after a short illness of 36 hours.

Cmder John Marston, who was recently tried by a Naval Court Martial for the loss of the U S sloop-of-war **Yorktown**, has been fully & honorable acquitted.

Mrd: on Feb 13, at St Matthew's Church, by Rev J B Donelan, Mr Thos A Dodd, of Norfolk, Va , to Miss Amanda A Norris, of Wash City.

Mrd: on Jan 30, in Christ Church, Balt, by Rev Dr Johns, John H Smoot, of Gtwn, D C, to Julia, daughter of Col Danl Duvall, late of Fred'k Co, Md.

Mrd: Jan 29, by Rev D A Tyng, Lawson Botts to Bettie, youngest daughter of Jas L Ranson, all of Jefferson Co, Va .

Mrd: on Feb 13, in Balt, by Rev Mr Foley, Wm D Williams to Mary Ann Beers.

Died: on Feb 4, at Pensacola Navy Yard, Mary L, wife of Lt Wm D Hurst, U S N, & 3rd daughter of the late Col John M Gamble, U S M C.

Died: on Feb 15, after a short but painful illness, Kate, youngest daughter of Thos & Matilda Bayne. Her funeral is today, at 2 o'clock, from the residence of her parents near the Navy Yard.

Missing Vessel. The barque **Victor**, Clark, from Liverpool, has arrived at Balt. She has had a passage of over 90 days & uneasiness was felt for her safety.

Geo Pharoah, convicted at Westchester, Pa, of the murder of Miss Sharpless, school teacher, was on Wed sentenced by Judge Chapman, who was very impressive in his remarks previous to pronouncing sentence of death, but the culprit listened to him with the utmost composure. He has since confessed the crime, & that his object was to obtain the watch she had about her person. [Sentence not given.]

House of Reps: 1-Ptn of Chas G Fairman, an assist marshal of Chemung Co, N Y, & 57 citizens of said county, for an increase of compensation for census duties.

TUE FEB 18, 1851
Frankfort Commonwealth: tragedy near Owenton, which resulted in the death of both parties, Abner Estes & is brother-in-law B Estes, both leaving wives & children. A quarrel resulted in Abner being shot 3 times, & the other was mortally stabbed.

Senate: 1-Ptn from Jos W Edwards, asking a pension for service performed in the N Y militia during the last war with Great Britian: referred to the Cmte on Pensions. 2-Memorial from D L Milliken, Wm Milliken, J H Haines, & other residents of Burnham, Waldo Co, Maine, asking the repeal or modification of the fugitive slave law: referred to the Cmte on the Judiciary. 2-Cmte on Private Land Claims: ptn of the heirs of Jos Reynes: adverse to the prayer of the petitioner. 3-Cmte on Pensions: to inquire into the justice & expediency of so amending the act for the relief of Charlotte Lynch, sole surviving child of the late Lt Col Ebenezer Gray, of the Connecticut line of the Revolutionary army as to provide for the payment of an equal share of the amount granted by said act to Charlotte Lynch to the children of her deceased brother, Saml Gray, as being equally with the said Charlotte Lynch reps of the said Lt Col Ebenezer Gray, & entitled to succeed to his rights 4-Resolution for the relief of Lewis Kossuth & his associates, exiles from Hungary: passed to a 2nd reading. 5-Mr Davis, of Mass, gave notice of his intention to ask leave to introduce a bill for the relief of Caroline L Eustis. 6-Mr Clemens gave notice of his intention to ask leave to introduce a bill to authorize the issuance of a land patent to Britain Franks.

On Sat last Fred'k Wilkins, a waiter at Young's Cornhill Coffee-house, Boston, was arrested by a U S Marshal under a warrant issued on the complaint of Mr John DeBree, purser in the U S Navy, of Norfolk, Va, charging Wilkins with being a fugitive slave. He was taken before Geo T Curtis, the U S Com'r, & the complaint & other documents relating to the case were read. Wilkins was ordered into the custody of Marshal Devens, & the court-room was cleared of the spectators, who were principally colored people. A crowd of several hundred negroes & a few whites gathered around the bldg, rushed in, & seized the prisoner, & hurried him off up Court st toward Belknap st, to Negro Hill, where many colored people reside. Whether he has been recovered we have not heard. [Feb 20th newspaper: Boston, Feb 15, 1851: I have this day arrested the within named Shadrack. Examination was held in the U S court room: depositions read: of Wm Robertson, that he knew Shadrack as a slave of Mrs Hutchins; that he was afterwards sold at a sheriff's sale to John Higgins, who sold him to John DeBre, the present owner; also, that of Wm Marcus, setting forth that he knew Shadrack, & had seen him in Boston, where he stated that he had ran away from Mr De Bree, & asked the deponent to carry a letter to Va for him. There were present, as volunteer counsel for Shadrack, S E Sewell, Ellis G Loring, Chas List, Richd Morris, Richd H Dana, jr, & Chas G Davis. P Riley, U S Deputy Marshal]

A little son of Mr Jacob Wickard, of Cumberland, Md, aged 16 months, died on Fri last when the mother had taken the tea-kettle off & placed it on the front plate of the stove, & resumed her domestic duties. The child inhaled the steam from the spout of the kettle. He lingered until Sat, when death relieved his sufferings.

To let: the store part of the House on Bridge st, Gtwn, so long occupied by the late Chas F Eckel, as a Watchmaker's & Jewelry shop. Apply to M Adler, agent.

For sale or rent: one of those beautiful 3 story & attic brick houses on 12th st, near N Y ave. The house is just finished, with all the modern improvements. Inquire of Mr B W Reed, 14th & F sts, or W H Clampitt, at his shop, 13th & G sts.

House for rent: large 2 story frame house at 5th & H sts, having a stable, carriage-house, a large garden, & pump of water in the yard. Inquire of J H Wailes, at the Capitol.

The Trustees of the Newbern Academy wish to engage the services of a gentleman qualified to discharge the duties of Principal in their Academy. Address John R Donnell, Pres of the Board of Trustees, Newbern, N C.

Commission on Claims against Mexico: 1-Memorial of Jas W Zacharie, claiming for damaged done by shot from the city of Vera Cruz to the schnr **Scott**, off the castle: claim is not valid against the Republic of Mexico: same was not allowed. The Board proceeded to the consideration of a motion & argument on the part of Jas W Zacharie, claimant in the case of the schnr **Susan**, decided by this Board on Feb 3; & after due examination, came to an opinion that there was not ground for reversing the judgement of the Board. 2-Memorial of Lucius H Armstrong, & Jas Jackson: same was allowed accordingly: amount to be awarded subject to the future action of the Board. 3-Memorial of Geo W Van Stavoren: allowed accordingly: the amount to be awarded subject to the future action of the Board. 4-Memorials of Sanforth Kidder, claiming for destruction of his goods at Brasos Santiago, in 1836, for seizure of his flat-boat, & consequent injuries in 1846, & for a forced loan at Matamoros in 1836: the first claim is not valid against the Republic of Mexico, & not allowed. The 2nd & 3rd are valid claims, & allowed accordingly: the amount to be awarded subject to the future action of the Board.

WED FEB 19, 1851
Wash Corp: 1-Bill for the relief of Frances Jardello's heirs was concurred in. 2-Ptn of of Jas H Blake, praying the payment of certain lottery ticket: read twice.

Senate: 1-Additional documents in relation to the claim of Thos Butler: referred to the Cmte of Claims. 2-Additional documents relating to the memorial of Isaac Adams, for an extension of a patent: referred to the Cmte on Patents & the Patent Ofc. 3-Cmte of Claims: bill for the relief of the legal reps of Robt S Burrough & Stephen Hopkins: recommended its passage. 4-House bill passed for the relief of the widow of the late Col Wm Gray, in which they request the concurrence of the Senate. 5-Bill passed for the relief of the legal reps of the late Gen Walter K Armistead, of the U S army.

House of Reps: 1-Ptn from Catherine Williams, of Monticello, Ohio, asking indemnity for French spoliations prior to 1800. 2-Ptn of Thos Brooke, of Delaware Co, Pa, for a pension as an invalid volunteer. 3-Ptn of the excs of Lt Stephen Clapp, Mass line, for commutation pay.

Sale of household furniture & paintings, on Mar 1, 1851, by order of the Orphans Court of Wash Co, D C: at the residence of the late Mrs Madison. An original portrait of Washington, by Stuart. An original portrait of John Adams, by Trumbull, [pronounced by the late J Q Adams among the best portraits of his father ever taken.] Original portraits of Jefferson, by Stuart; of Jas Madison, by Stuart; & of Mrs Madison, by Stuart. An original portrait of Jas Monroe, by Vanderlyn. Christ & his 2 Disciples, 7 by 12, by Carlo Sprout. -J C McGuire, adm -Dyer & McGuire. aucts

Died: on Feb 13, at her residence, *Corbin Hill*, Essex Co, Va , after a long & painful illness, Mrs Eliz Yerby, wife of A Oscar Yerby, in her 28th year.

Mr Venable, one of the Reps in Congress from N C, has been called home by a dispatch communicating the dangerous illness of his daughter.

Albany, Feb 16. Breaking up of the ice: Wm H Tysdell & Robt Elder were drowned when the ice broke as they were crossing. It continues firm at Catskill & Kingston.

Postmaster Gen est'd the following new Post Ofcs for week ending Feb 15, 1851.

Ofc	County, State	Postmaster
North Raymond	Cumberland, Me	Wm Small
North Union	Lincoln, Me	Saml Stone
North Acton	York, Me	Asa Sweet
Monroe Centre	Waldo, Me	Saml White, jr
Laysville	New London, Ct	S E W Johnson
Cabaltville	Middlesex, Ct	Chas F Rich
East Scott	Cortland, N Y	Alvin Kellogg
Cedar Lake	Herkimer, N Y	Anson Rider
Nepevan	West Chester, N Y	N W Tompkins
Fly Creek	Otsego, N Y	Ceylon North
Garrison's	Putnam, N Y	John Garrison
East Parish	Oswego, N Y	Guy D Comstock
Sand's Mills	West Chester, N Y	Job Sands
Weston	Steuben, N Y	L Compton
Williamstown	Camden, N J	Henry Tice
Turtleville	Union, Pa	M H Taggart
Hector	Potter, Pa	Jos Sunderlin
Stembersville	Monroe, Pa	Danl Stember
Dry Valley	Union, Pa	Jos Metman
Long Valley	Monroe, Pa	Jacob Kresge

Sabinsville	Tioga, Pa	Chas P Douglas
Chestnut Ridge	Union, Pa	Saml R Baum
Dry Fork	Hamilton, Ohio	Wm Morgan
Cranberry Prairie	Mercer, Ohio	John Simison
West Newton	Allen, Ohio	John M Shields
Leipsic	Putnam, Ohio	Robt J Lawrey
Butternut Ridge	Sandusky, Ohio	Wm E Lay
Riga	Lenawee, Mich	Roswell W Knight
Canicello	Rockbridge, Va	A N Bell
Meredith's Tavern	Monongalia, Va	Wm Meredith
Amittsville	Monongalia, Va	Jas Amitt
Peach Tree	Cherokee, N C	John R Suddreth
Selkirk	Marion dist, S C	Neill Alford
White Pond	Barnwell dist, S C	J B Armstrong
Palmetto	Pontotoc, Miss	John A Boyd
Desrayauxville	Rapides Parish, La	Jules Desrayaux
Unionville	Cass, Texas	John B Thompson
Hamburgh	Ashley, Ark	M C Trammell
Sandy Ridge	Steuben, Ia	Jas A Segur
Carpenter's Creek	Jasper, Ia	Jos Downing
Alder Creek	Dubois, Ia	S W Postlethwaite
Fitch	Cass, Ia	M Tucker
Bogus Run	Starke, Ia	Danl G Hathaway
Nicholon's Mill	Jefferson, Ten	A M Nicholson
Bluff Springs	Gibson, Ten	J E Merrick
Huntsville	Scott, Ten	Calvin Looper
Fillmore	Andrew, Mo	Wm Snuffin
Troy	Davis, Iowa	Henry W Briggs
Coonville	Pottawatamie, Iowa	L F Coon

Names Changed:
New Durham Centre, Strafford Co, N H, changed to Downing's Mills.
Rockhill, Bucks Co, Pa, changed to Hagersville.
Section Ten, Van Wert Co, Ohio, changed to Delphos.
Bentivoglis, Albemarle Co, Va , changed to Bentivoglio.
Cedar Spring Asylum, Spartansburg district, S C, changed to Old Cedar Springs.
Hodgesville, Itawamba Co, Miss, changed to Marietta.

List of superintendents, assistants, & sub-assistants of the U S Coast Survey, engaged in field operations, with their compensation.
Superintendent, A D Bache: $4,500
Edmund Blunt: $3,500   J Farley: $2,000
F H Girdes: $2,500   R D Cutts: $2,000
Wm M Boyce: $2,300   H L Whiting: $1,800

J S Williams: $1,600
J B Gluck: $1,600
J J Hassler: $1,500
S C Walker: $1,500
J E Hilyard: $1,400
W E Greenwell: $1,000
Sub-Assistants:
H Adams: $600
J M Wampler: $600
Geo W Dean: $600
A M Harrison: $600

S A Gilbert: $1,000
L F Pontalis: $1,000
Chas P Bolles: $1,000
Geo D Wise: $1,000
Geo Davidson: $1,000

John Seib: $600
A S Wadsworth: $600
S A Wainwright: $600

Artificer: Thos McDonnel: $750
Computers, draughtsman, & recorders engaged in preparing work for publications.
Theo W Warner: $1,200
E Nulty: $1,000
A Schott: $600
Geo Rumpf: $600
Draughtsmen:
W M C Fairfax: $1,600
M F McClery: $1,400
Jos Welch: $1,200
Chas Mahon: $1,000
Wm Luce: $600
A Bouchke: $600
Recorders & copyists:
F Whyte: $600
___ Lee: $600
W Hay: $500
Disbursing Agent: S Hein: $2,500
Engineers:
S Sirbert: $2,000
F Dankworth: $1,500
A Kolle: $1,300
Geo McCoy: $1,300
Jno Knight: $1,200
A O Lawson: $1,000

W S Walker: $500
J C Tennant: $500
H Ober: $400

F J Rickets: $600
John Lambert: $600
A Fornaro: $500
W H Donoho: $400
W Forsyth: $400

C B Moss: $480
___ Elliott: $400
___ Cruickshank: $400
Clerk: A T Langton: $600

W Smith: $720
E F Woodward: $780
S T Pettit: $500
R T Knight: $400
Thos Donoho: $250

U S ship **Marion**: Typa Anchorage, Oct 31, 1850. I owe to the ofcrs & crew of this ship, to report their noble conduct on the occasion of the blowing up of the Portuguese frig **Donna Maria II**, lying within one cable's length of us, on Oct 29. No confusion took place-all orders were promptly obeyed. The boats were manned by volunteers, & were commanded by Acting Lts Aulick & Wilkes, & the Boatswain, Mr Burdett. Act Lt Aulick volunteered to return & extinguish the fire, but another explosion occurred, & the attempt was forbidden. Purser White & the

Governor, Mr Stocking, stood by to drown the magazine, & when their services were no longer required there, Mr White volunteered for any other duty. Midshipman Laughlin & Mr Macauley [Capt's Clerk] were on deck the whole time, & did all they could do. Mr Marcello [Sailmaker] & Mr Underwood [Purser's Steward] stood by the shell room. Dr Lockwood, Acting Master Jones, Lt of Marines Broome, Passed Midshipman Whiting, & Mr Rustic, [Carpenter,] who were on shore at the time, promptly repaired on board & were ready for any emergency. I am sorry to report that one of our men, Chas Jenkins, [seaman,] who was a boat-keeper at the time of the explosion, was severely wounded by a bolt. Very respectfully, your obedient servant, A M Pennock, Lt & Exec ofcr To Cmder Wm M Glendy, Cmdng U S ship **Marion** [Feb 24th newspaper: Letter of an Ofcr of the **Marion** to his family in Wash City, dated Nov 25, 1850, Anchorage, Macao. Too much cannot be said in praise of the coolness & promptitude of Mr Pennock, the 1st Lt, [the captain was on shore,] at the first moment of the explosion; the crew behaved admirably.]

THU FEB 20, 1851
House of Reps: 1-Bill for the relief of the heirs of Anthony T Willis: committed. 2-Bill for the relief of Geo P Smith: committed. 3-Cmte on Military Affairs: bill for the relief of Geo Talcott, brevet brig general & colonel of ordnance: committed. Same cmte: bill for the relief of the legal reps of the late Gen Walker K Armistead, of the U S army, reported back without amendment. Same cmte: bill to pay to Capt Augustus Bushell a balance due him for his services as lt-col in the Mexican war: committed. Same cmte: asked to be discharged from the further consideration of the ptn of Capt Sherman, of the U S army, & also from the further consideration of the ptn of ofcrs of the Georgia battalion: ordered to lie on the table.

The U S ship **St Lawrence**, Capt Joshua R Sands, sailed from N Y on Tue for Southampton, with the articles for exhibition at the World's Fair. List of her ofcrs: Cmder, Joshua R Sands; 1st Lt, Chas S Boggs; Surgeon, L B Hunter; Purser, S P Todd; 2nd Lt E G Parrot; 3rd Lt L B Avery; 4th Lt G H Preble; 5th Lt J K Duer; Master, B N Westcott; Marine Ofcr, R B Caldwell; Assist Surgeon, Jas F Harrison; Passed Midshipman, Jas F Monroe; Midshipmen, John G Sproston, R R Reese, Jos Tiffe, Wm T Glassell, Henry Erben, J Bruce; Capt's Clerk, C S Livingston; Purser's Clerk, Jas Todd; Boatswain, Jno Bates; Carpenter, Danl Jones; Sailmaker, Robt Hunter; Gunner, Wm Arnold; & 300 seamen & marines. Passengers: C F Stansbury, Gov't Agent; W L Long, naval storekeeper for Spezzia; D G Ford, clerk to storekeeper.

Household & kitchen furniture at auction: on Feb 24, next door to the residence of Mr Scrivener, near the Capitol gate, at the residence of a gentleman declining housekeeping. -A Green, auctioneer

Mrd: on Feb 19, at Lake Drummond, N C, Benj F Wilkins, of Wash City, to Miss Emma Jane Bingham, of Portsmouth, Va .

Mrd: on Feb 18, in Balt, at St Alphonsus Church, by Rev A Schmid, C S S R, V L Erney, of York, Pa, to Miss Catharine Matilda Smith, of Wash City, formerly of Adams Co, Pa.

Died: on Feb 18, Margaret, daughter of Thos & Margaret Robbins, aged 10 years. Her funeral is this afternoon, between 2 & 3 o'clock, corner of 12th st & Mass ave.

The Celebrated Hungarian Vocalist, Herr Krauss, is to favor our citizens with a concert on Sat evening next.

American citizen, Mr Arden, the attaché of the American embassy at Berlin, who was on his way to Paris with dispatches, was killed on Jan 23 in a dreadful accident on the Cologne & Minden railway, between Brackwede & Gutterslocke, at a spot where repairs were going on. The train descending an incline went off the rails & plunged over an embankment.

Lost, the Silver-head of a Cane with the name of V L Erney, Balt, Mar 9th engraved on it. A liberal reward will be given for its recovery if left at this ofc.

Senate: 1-Additional documents submitted in relation to the claim of Jane Irwin, daughter of & heir of Jared Irwin: referred to the Cmte on Pensions. 2-Ordered that Earnest Eude, Clement Duhammel, & Jos Derbis have leave to withdraw their papers. 3-Cmte on Indian Affairs: resolution for the relief of John H Horne: recommended its passage. 4-Cmte on Pensions: asked to be discharged from the further consideration of the memorial of Mary Morris Foote, & that it be referred to the Cmte of Claims: which was agreed to. 5-Cmte on Foreign Relations: asked to be discharged from the further consideration of the memorial of A P Brittingham, asking compensation for a vessel seized & condemned by the Mexican authorities in 1835: discharged accordingly.

FRI FEB 20, 1851
Senate: 1-Memorial of the children & heirs-at-law of Nathl Hobbs, asking the reimbursement of moneys advanced by their father to induce the enlistment of men during the Revolutionary war: referred to the Cmte on Revolutionary Claims. 2-Ptn of Abner Hancock, asking arrears of pension: referred to the Cmte on Pensions. 3-Memorial of Amos Kendall & John E Kendall, asking the payment of their claims against the Western Cherokees: referred to the Cmte on Indian Affairs. 4-Cmte on Public Lands: Act to enable Jacob Banta to locate 2 Revolutionary military land certificates: recommended its passage. 5-Cmte on Pensions: bill for the relief of Wm Brown: passed to a 2nd reading. Same cmte: bill for the relief of Chas Taylor: passed to a 2nd reading. Same cmte: adverse report on the ptn of Francis Fowler, asking a pension or other pecuniary aid. Same cmte: adverse report on the ptn of Sarah Ladd, asking a pension. Same cmte: adverse to the prayer of Rebecca Bright, widow of Jacob Bright, who was killed in the public service. Adverse on the

ground that her husband was neither by enlistment or appointment attached to either the army or navy, but simply an employe, & the cmte cannot sanction the policy of extending the pensions laws to such cases. 6-Cmte on Pensions: bill of relief for Chambers C Mullin, a soldier in the late war with Mexico, asking an increase of pension: passed to a 2nd reading. Same cmte: bill for the relief of Mary W Ketchum, widow of Thos Ketchum, asking to be allowed a pension: passed to a 2nd reading. Same cmte: ptn of John B White, asking that a certain amount of invalid money may be refunded, submitted a report, which was ordered to be printed, accompanied by a bill for the relief of the heirs of Robt White: passed to a 2nd reading. [John B White & Robt White as copied.] Same cmte: adverse report on the ptn of Hector St John Beetley, asking to be allowed arrears of pensions. Same cmte: adverse report on the ptn of Eleaxar Williams, asking a pension for services rendered during the war with Great Britian. Same cmte: adverse report on the ptn of Mary Ann C Berger, widow of the late John Thos Berger, 1st engineer of the U S transport Secretary Walker, during the war with Mexico, asking to be allowed a pension. Same cmte: asked to be discharged from the further consideration of making certain amendments to the act for the relief of Charlotte Lynch: which was agreed to. Same cmte: asked to be discharged from the further consideration of the memorial of the widow & children of Saml Gray, reps & co-heirs of Ebenezer Gray: which was agreed to.

By writ of fieri facias: public sale of one first-rate Guitar, seized & taken as the property of John Hill, to satisfy a judgment & execution in favor of John Chaner. Sale to take place in front of the Centre Market. Terms cash.
–J A Ratcliff, Constable

By writ of fieri facias: at the suit of Chas H Van Patten, against the goods & chattels of Mrs Mary Ann Pierce: I have seized 3 beds, to be offered for sale in front of the Centre Market-house, Wash City, on Mar 1. –H R Maryman, Constable

Oregon: The <u>first steamboat</u> ever built in Oregon was launched at Milwaukee on Christmas Day. During the festivities Capt F Morse, of the schnr **Merchantman**, was killed by the explosion of a gun, discharged by him when the vessel started from her ways.

Maj Richd Pollard, of Albemarle Co, Va, died in Wash City at Willard's Hotel, on Wed, of pneumonia. He had been ill but a few days. He was here with his daughter, on a brief visit. The deceased was formerly charge d'affaires to the republic of Chili. He was the brother-in-law of Mr Rives, our Minister to Paris; & his connexions in Va, as well as his numerous friends elsewhere, will deeply mourn his loss. His remains are to be conveyed to Richmond, & thence to the family burial-place at Oak Ridge, in Nelson Co. -Union

Hon Walter Booth, of Conn, has been called home suddenly from his seat in the House of Reps, by news of the severe illness of a member of his family. –Union

The U S brig **Porpoise** was at Monrovia Dec 16, bound on a cruise to leeward-all well. Her ofcrs are: Jas L Lardner, Lt Commandant; Reginald Fairfax, 1st Lt; J M Brooke, Acting Master; C W Woolley, Passed Midshipman; J G Heilman, Midshipman; J J Brownlee, Passed Assist Surgeon; J C Eldridge, Purser, J Z Forney, Capt's Clerk.

A charge of stabbing was made on Wed before Justice Morsell against John T Powers, residing on Md ave. Powers stabbed Washington O Berry in a rencontre on Tuesday. Dr Eliot, attending physician, is of opinion that Mr Berry, who is severely wounded, will recover from the injuries he received.

SAT FEB 22, 1851

Commission on Claims against Mexico: 1-Memorial of Jas S Thayer, adm of Jas Treat, deceased, & that of Fred'k E Radcliff, adm of Augustus Radcliff, deceased, severally claiming a moiety of expenses paid in the discharge of the ofc of Mexican Vice Consul in N Y from 1831 thru 1834: claims are valid, & the same were allowed accordingly: the amount to be awarded subject to the future action of the Board. 2-In the claim of Elisha Copeland & others, decided on the 5th current, Mr Fletcher Webster, as of counsel for the claimants, made as a motion for leave to introduce fresh testimony, & for a re-opening of the case thereto. 3-Memorial of Henry May, adm of Wm A Slacum, deceased, claiming for unpaid treasury notes of the State of Sonora, taken in payment for a cargo of goods sold to a merchant: claim is not valid against the Republic of Mexico: same was not allowed.

The N Y Independent gives an account of an ancient church in Lancaster Co, Va, which is almost as old as the dilapidated structure at Yorktown, but is yet perfectly sound. It was built by John Carter, as an Episcopal house of worship, above 200 years ago, & externally has scarcely begun to show the marks of time. The pews & doors have been re-constructed, the only repairs that have been made on the church. –Zion's Herald

Obit-died: the late venerable Thos H Grimes, one of the oldest & most respected citizens of Wash City, & the Church of which he was a member. He was born in Somerset Co, Md, in Dec 1768; in 1798 received the appointment of Chief Clerk to the Navy Accountant, as he was then called, now the 4th Auditor of the Treasury. He removed to Wash with the Gov't, in 1800, & continued in the same ofc until June of last year, when the infirmities of his great age compelled him to resign. He died in the midst of his children, relatives, & friends. –C M B

Mrd: on Feb 20, by Rev Mr Hodges, Thos Thornley to Miss Martha E McComb, all of Wash.

Died: on Feb 19, at Willard's Hotel, Maj Richd Pollard, of Alta Vista, Albemarle Co, Va. The remains of Maj Pollard have been removed to the family burial place at Oak Ridge, Nelson Co, Va.

Died: on Feb 20, Dr John P Vantine, aged 44 years. His funeral is today, at 3 o'clock, from his late residence, 13½ st.

Died: on Feb 20, Francis William, son of W H & Catharine Thomas, aged 18 months. His funeral is today at 3 o'clock, from the residence of Mr Levi Pumphrey, on C st.

Died: on Feb 20, at Phil, aged 23 years, Mary Kate, wife of Jas R Smith, & eldest daughter of W G W White, of Wash City.

Died: on Feb 2, at Lyme, Conn, Miss Susan Mitchel, aged 82 years. Also, on Feb 4, Miss Desire Mitchel, aged 87 years. The above were members of a very aged & singular family of 5 persons, whose united ages amount to 403 years, viz: Desire, aged 87; Saml, 84; Susan, 82; John & Louis, twins, 75 each; they were children of John Mitchel, who died in 1818, aged 87 years. The mother died in 1776, 75 years of age. This singular family have always lived on the same place where their father & grandfather lives; they have remained single, & lived bachelor & maiden lives, have been a very happy & peaceable family, without a known enemy, & have always enjoyed good health. –Saybrook Mirror

House of Reps: 1-Bill for the relief of A Baudouin & A D Roberts, of New Orleans: passed. 2-Adjustment of the accounts of John D Colmesnil: passed. 3-Bill for the relief of Danl Steenrod: recommended that it do not pass. 4-Cmte on Invalid Pensions: bills for the relief of Rebecca Freeman; of Thos Flanagan; of Jonas D Platt; of Wm Gove; of Benj Creasey; of Lot Davis; of Fielding G Brown; of Isaac Cobb; of Martha Dameron; of Wm Lynch; of Jas Mains; of Isaac Downs; of Gardner Herring; & of Sylvanus Blodget. 5-Bill for the relief of the heirs of Col David A Hopkins: claim was based upon money advanced by the claimant to the Gov't during the Revolution: pending consideration of the Bill.

Valuable Jefferson farm for sale: contains 141½ acres: belonging to the late Mrs Mary Good, with the improvements & privileges, being the same which was purchased from Jos M Brown & wife, situated on the turnpike leading from Charlestown to Smithfield. There is a good stone dwlg on the farm, a good well, & the use of Mrs Engle's fine spring. Also, will be sold the 10 acres of land purchased by Jacob Good from Wm T Washington & wife. It adjoins the other tract. –Wm T Daugherty, exc of the last will & testament of Mary Good, deceased. The personal property of Mrs Mary Good, deceased, will be sold the same day at the same place.

The Sec of War received yesterday the afflicting intelligence of the death of his brother, F B Conrad, a distinguished member of the New Orleans Bar, who died on Feb 11.

In PG Co Court, sitting as a Court of Equity. Alpheus Beall & Jane Beall his wife, et al, vs Florida Walker. This suit is to procure a decree for the sale of the real estate of Nathan Walker, late of said county, deceased. Nathan died intestate, seized & possessed of certain real estate situated in said county, leaving the following heirs & legal reps, viz: Jane Beall, Mary Beall, Catharine Beall, Jonathan T Walker, Henry Walker, Chas Walker, Eliz Beck, Saml Walker, who has departed this life intestate & without issue; & Nathan Walker, who has also departed this life intestate, leaving Florida Walker, of the State of Florida, his only child, an infant under the age of 21 years; that the said Florica resides out of the State of Md, & that it will be for her interest & advantage, & that of all parties concerned, that the said real estate should be sold, & the proceeds distributed among them. Absent dfndnt to appear in this court in person, or by guardian, on or before the 2nd Mon in Jul next. –A C Magruder, C J -John B Brooke, Clerk

MON FEB 24, 1851

Assist Surgeons in the Navy, examined by the Medical Board recently convened at the Navy Asylum, Phil, have been found qualified for promotion, & passed. 1-Robt S Maccoun, Passed Assist Surgeon, to rank next after Passed Assist Surgeon Richd McSherry. 2-Wm A Harris, Passed Assist Surgeon, to rank next after Passed Assist Surgeon Robt E Wall. 3-Passed Assist Surgeon Henry O Mayo, to rank next after Passed Assist Surgeon Wm A Harris. Of the candidates examined for admission into the service as Assist Surgeons, the following have been found qualified:

1-Saml F Cowes
2-Jacob S Dungan
3-Geo Peck
4-Chas F Fahs
5-Jenks H Otis
6-Fred'k Horner, jr
7-Jas B Whiting
8-Randolph Harrison
9-W E Wysham
1-Albert Shriver
11-T Le P Cronmiller
12-E Drayton
13-W L Nichol
14-J C Coleman
15-J P Hopkins
16-R H Cowman

House of Reps: 1-The House proceeded to the consideration of the bill for the relief of Col David A Hopkins objection was made: motion could not be entertained at this time. 2-Ptn of Mary Young, for compensation for services of her father, Wm Liggert, in the Revolutionary war.

Trustee's sale of valuable real estate: by decree of the Circuit Court of Md: public sale on Mar 18, of all that part of the land now in the possession of Mrs Norah Digges, being part of **Chillum Castle Manor**, in PG Co, containing 230 acres. Apply for information to D C Digges, atty at law, Upper Marlborough; to Geo A Digges, residing near the premises, or to the subscriber in Balt. –R S Steuart

Senate: 1-Referred to the Cmte of Claims: act for the relief of Chas S Mathews, Chas Wood, & Jas Hall; also for the relief of A Baudouin & A D Roberts, of New Orleans. 2-Bills referred to the Cmte on Naval Affairs: relief of Wm Gove; of Benj Cressey; & of Lot Davis. 3-Bills referred to the Cmte on Pensions-relief of: Rebecca Freeman; Thos Flanagan; Jonas D Platt, Fielding G Brown; Isaac Cobb; Martha Dameron; Wm Lynch; Jas Mains; Isaac Downs; Gardner Herring; & of Sylvanus Blodget.

U S Patent Ofc, Feb 22, 1851. Ptn of Moses Bayley, of Salisbury, Mass, praying for the extension of a patent granted to him on Jul 5, 1837, for an improvement in machinery for pressing all kind of woolen & cotton goods & all kinds of paper. –Thos Ewbank, Com'r of Patents

Mrd: on Feb 20, at St Paul's Church, Balt, by Bishop Whittingham, Dr Louis Mackall to Miss Mary J, daughter of Maj Thos Bonce, all of PG Co, Md.

Birth-night Ball: the Wash Light Infty announce they will give a Military & Civic Ball at Jackson Hall on Feb 24. No Hats or Caps will be allowed in the Ball-room. Tickets $1, to be had at McClery's & Butts' Drug Stores, Jos Shillington's, Jas Power's Cigar Store, & J O Warner's, Gtwn, & at the door, as well as of the following:
Cmte of Arrangements:

Capt Jos B Tate	W W S Kerr	Jacob Martin
Ensign J W Mead	Lt J F Tucker	Thos Luxen
L D Williams	Jos Stanley	Wm B Clark, Treas
F Mitchell	John Hutchinson	B F Beers, Sec
J De Saules	P M Dubant	

Died: on Sun, Columbia Saphronia McDuell, aged 19 years. Her funeral is on Tue, at 11 o'clock, at the Foundry Church.

Died: on Feb 23, Mr Lucian Carter Browne, a native of Gloucester Co, Va, aged 26 years. His funeral will be from the residence of his father-in-law, Mr Geo Mattingly, south F st, [Island,] on Feb 25, at 3½ o'clock.

Died: on Feb 18, at Red Hill, Granville Co, N C, Mrs Mary Grace Daniel, eldest daughter of the Hon A W Venable, in her 23rd year.

Died: at Jamaica Island, of cholera, Chas Albert, son of Dr Albert Dorman, of Wash City. [No death date given-current item.]

TUE FEB 25, 1851
Midshipman Thos H Looker, U S N, has arrived in Washington from Brazil, & brings dispatches from that Gov't to the U S.

Mrd: on Feb 20, in St Paul's Church, Balt, by Bishop Whittingham, Dr Louis Mackall to Miss Mary L, daughter of Maj Thos Bruce, all of PG Co, Md.

Died: on Feb 14, at Glen Wallace, Madison Co, Va, Michl Wallace, in his 74th year.

Senate: 1-Memorial from J G Chapman & other citizens of Md, recommending to Congress the passage of a law for the establishment of a military asylum for the benefit of invalid & disabled soldiers: referred to the Cmte on Military Affairs. 2-Memorial from Edw Thompson, Wells Cooper, & others, styling themselves "Old Defenders of Baltimore in the war of 1812," asking that land warrants may be made assignable: referred to the Cmte on Military Affairs. 3-Memorial of John Plumbe, in behalf of the settlers & miners in the city & county of Sacramento, against granting a charter to Asa Whitney, for the construction of a railroad to the Pacific: referred to the Cmte on Roads & Canals. 4-Bill for the relief of Wm B Hart, assignee of Alex'r Anderson, Saml Cobb, Jas Pickens, & of the legal reps of John B Forrester, deceased, to be paid the sum of $44,559, to indemnify him for extra expenses & losses incurred in emigrating Choctaw Indians: bill was ordered to be engrossed & read a 3rd time.

Died: on Feb 24, at Sandusky City, Ohio, Mary Powers, sister of Mrs Millard Fillmore.

Died: yesterday, in his 28th year, Robt Rose Fitzhugh, son of Saml Fitzhugh, of Wash City. His funeral is Thu at 3 o'clock, from the residence of his father, 7th & K sts.

WED FEB 26, 1851
Postmaster Gen est'd the following new Post Ofcs for week ending Feb 22, 1851:

Ofc	County, State	Postmaster
Readfield Depot	Kennebeck, Me	B F Melvin
Saundersville	Worcester, Mass	Gilbert C Taft
Morganville	Genesee, N Y	German Lathrop
New Kingstown	Cumberland, Pa	Adam H Yorger
Mevata	Jefferson, Pa	John Philliber
Williston	Potter, Pa	Lewis Warren
Saint Peter's	Chester, Pa	Jos Millard
New Mount Pleasant	Monroe, Pa	Jos Moyer
Six-Mile Run	Bedford, Pa	Aaron W Evans
Stewart's Run	Venango, Pa	Ira Copeland
Kratzersville	Union, Pa	H Hesser
Clifford	Susquehanna, Pa	John Halstead
Burtville	Potter, Pa	Seth Hackett
West Williamsfield	Ashtabula, Ohio	Herman Ticknor
W Kellogsville	Ashtabula, Ohio	Saml Moffitt
Allen Centre	Union, Ohio	Reuben Foote

Alum Run	Monroe, Ohio	Saml Hendershot
Venice	Shiswassee, Mich	Chas Wilkinson
Prairie River	Branch, Mich	Richd A Vail
Alton	Kent, Mich	Walter White
Maple Grove	Barry, Mich	Joel Hyde
True Blue	Botetourt, Va	Wm D Couch
Indian Valley	Floyd, Va	Robt Philips
Morgan's Creek	Orange, N C	Alex'r Hunter
Butlersville	Anderson dis, S C	Jas Jones
Craftsville	Elbert, Ga	Willis Craft
Yellow Creek	Tishemingo, Miss	Ballard D Dean
Wolf Bayou	Independence, Ark	John Reeves
Petit Jean	Yell, Ark	Thos N Hart
Rusk	Haywood, Ten	Ichabod Herring
Ox Bow	Putnam, Ill	Asahel Hannum
Argo	Carroll, Ill	Robt Art
Flat Rock	Crawford, Ill	Wm Mexwell
Patterson	Waye, Mo	John Kemper
Elm Woods	Saline, Mo	Moses Woodfin
Lane's Prairie	Osage, Mo	Wm L Pinnell
Blk Grove	Saline, Mo	Abraham Larsh
Blanche	Lafayette, Mo	Wm S Drummond
Sulphur Lick	Lincoln, Mo	John Gilliland
Pleasant Grove	Kenosha, Wis	Jas Fredenburgh
Westfield	Marquette, Wis	Robt Cochran
Oenca	Jefferson, Wis	Jos Crandall
Mount Sterling	Crawford, Wis	Wm T Sterling
Castle Grove	Jones, Iowa	Benajab Beardsley
Dawsonburg	Fremont, Iowa	Jacob Dawson
Oak Point	Lewis, Oregon	Alex S Abernethy

Names Changed: Golden Hill, Wyoming Co, Pa, changed to north Flat.
Pinksville, Clarion Co, Pa, changed to Rimersburgh.
True Blue, Botetourt Co, Va, changed to Old Hickory.
Montville, Wash Co, Texas, changed to Long Point.
Clay Lick, Owen Co, Ky, changed to Gratz.
Sheafer's Mills, Ohio Co, Ky, changed to Briggs' Mills.
Locust Forest, Butler Co, Ky, changed to Sugar Grove.

Senate: 1-Bill for the relief of Wm B Hart: passed.

Municipal Election in Gtwn on Mon: results for Mayor: Henry Addison: 312; Robt White: 178. In 1849 the majority is precisely the same it was at the last: Henry Addison: 314; John J Stull: 18.

Trustee's sale of valuable land in PG Co, Md: public sale at the Mill of the late Robt W Bowie, on Mar 17, all that part of the real estate of the said deceased, lying to the south of Mattaponi Branch, commonly called ***Connick's Farm***, containing about 440 acres. There are 3 large Tobacco Houses, 2 Corn Houses, & Quarters, for the use of the place. Wm H Tuck, Thos F Bowie, Trustees

+

At the same place: public sale of the residue of the real estate of the said Robt W Bowie, consisting of his Home Plantation, called ***Mattaponi***: a very fine estate, about 3 miles from Nottingham: upwards of 1,200 acres, one of which the widow's dower will be assigned, & the balance divided into 2 or more farms. The portion assigned as the dower will be sold subject to the incumbrance. -Wm H Tuck, C C Magruder, Trustees

Commission on Claims against Mexico: 1-Memorial of W F & E D Hyde & Co, claiming for part of the cargo of the Mexican schnr **Columbia**, seized at Brazoria in 1835, & condemned at Vera Cruz: claim is not valid against the Republic of Mexico: not allowed. 2-Memorial of Geo N Downs for himself & as surviving partner of John S Owen, claiming for losses by the seizure of the schnr **Sussanah**, driven into the Rio Bravo by weather 1845: ordered to be received. 3-Memorial of John Boute, claiming for violation of grants of exclusive navigation of Tabasco river, for loss of steamboat & service of boat in transporting troops: ordered to be received. 4-Memorial of Wm B Hatch, claiming for overcharge of tonnage duties, filed Feb 17, instant: ordered to be received. 5-Memorial of Saml Jobson, claiming for expulsion from the city of Vera cruz in May, 1846, filed 18th instant: ordered to be received. 6-Memorial of John A Zander, claiming for supplies furnished to the Mexican patriots in 1812: ordered to be received. 7-Memorial of Louis S Hargous: ordered to be received. 8-Memorial of Theodore Ducoing, claiming for expulsion from the city of Mexico in Jun, 1847: claim would not be valid against the Republic of Mexico: memorial was accordingly rejected. [Feb 27th newspaper: the memorial of John A Zander is not valid against the Republic of Mexico, & not allowed.]

Meeting: Metropolitan Literary Institute this evening, at 7 o'clock, at Temperance Hall. –Wm M Hull, Sec

Maryland Hams: very superior Hams for sale by J H McBlair.

Persons having claims against a balance due from the United to Archibald McKennon, late private in the Marine Corps, deceased, are notified to present them at the ofc of the 4th Auditor of the Treasury within 2 months from Feb 23, 1851.

In consequence of a recent domestic affliction the receptions at the Presidential Mansion will be discontinued.

Senate: 1-Memorial of R Grignon, asking the payment of a sum of money secured to him by a provision of treaty with the Menominee Indians: referred to the Cmte on Indian Affairs. 2-Cmte of Claims: bill for the relief of Sayles J Bowen: recommended its passage. 3-Cmte on Military Affairs: bill for the relief of the widow of the late Lt Col Wm Gray: recommended its passage. Lt Col Wm Gray, in the late war with Mexico, commanded a battalion on the western frontier. His command was a mixed one, consisting of 3 companies of mounted men & 2 companies of infty. His is dead, & his widow asks that in the settlement of his accounts there may be allowed the difference between the pay of a lt col of cavalry, & a lt col of infty, which amounts to $15 a month. Read a 3rd time & passed. 4-Cmte on Military Affairs: asked to be discharged from the further consideration of the memorial of A R Woolley, asking to be allowed his pay & emoluments from the time of his dismissal from the army, which he alleges was unlawful: discharged accordingly.

Notice: Mrs Matilda Dobbyns, having advertised for sale the Farm on which she now resides, n e of *Spring Tavern*, in Wash Co, D C, we do hereby notify all persons interested that we are legally entitled to about 28 acres of land in said Farm, & that we shall, as early as practicable, institute proceedings for the recovery of the same. -Geo H St Clair, Jas W St Clair

Handsome reward for missing old dark leather Trunk, with my name on a card nailed on one end. It was supposed to be sent up to the depot for Balt from the Powhatan boat on last Fri on the baggage wagon. On board the boat was the last I saw of it. –Geo W Rudd

THU FEB 27, 1851
Senate: 1-Ordered: Wm Carroll have leave to withdraw his petition & papers. 2-Ordered: Michl Bowden & Abigail Edgerly have leave to withdraw their petition & papers. 3-Resolved: Cmte on Pensions inquire into placing upon the pension list the name of the widow of Felix St Vrain, deceased, who was killed in the Black Hawk war of 1832. 4-Resolved, that there be paid to Richd H Weightman the sum of $2,000, as a reimbursement of expenses incurred by him, or, in lieu of mileage, caused by his journey from New Mexico to the seat of Gov't, in consequence of his election by the Legislature as a Senator, in anticipation of the admission of that Territory as a State. 5-Resolved, to inquire into allowing & paying to Fred'k Gilbert, a page of the Senate, for his services during the short session of the 30th Congress & the extra session of the same, the pay & compensation that was allowed to the other pages of the Senate. 6-Resolved, to pay Judge J F Kinney, of Iowa, $419.15, amount of his account for services rendered in the case of the contested elected between Wm Thompson & Danl F Miller: motion was not agreed to.

Died: Feb 24, Wm E E Randolph, aged about 42 years, formerly of Petersburgh, Va.

House of Reps: 1-Ptn of Euphemia Williams, who was arrested by the name of Mehala, as a fugitive slave, by order of the authorities of the U S whereby she incurred great expense, praying Congress to make an appropriation to pay the costs & expenses to which she was put by reason of such false & oppressive arrest

Wash Corp: 1-Ptn from Jas H Shreve & Harrison Taylor for remission of a fine: referred to Cmte of Claims. 2-Cmte of Claims: bill for the relief of Wm W Davis: passed. Same cmte: asked to be discharged from the further consideration of the ptn of A H Clements: discharged accordingly. Same cmte: bill for the relief of Jas Kanalay: passed. 3-Ptn of Saml Gregg, praying that certain work done on 6th st may be re-measured, & if a balance is found due to him, that it may be paid: referred to the Cmte on Claims. 4-Bill for the relief of Wm Ross: laid on the table. 5-Bill for the relief of Eliz Collison: passed. 6-Bill for the relief of Walter Linkins: passed.

FRI FEB 28, 1851

Senate: 1-Ptn from Eliz Davis, stating that she is now infirm & poor-that during the last war with Great Britain she hired vehicles for the removal of her furniture, & that after a portion of it had been placed in said vehicles it was taken out by order of a Gov't ofcr, & the vehicles forced into the service of the U S for the removal of the public records, from the city, in consequence of which she could not remove her property, & it was burnt with the house, which was Gov't property: referred to the Cmte of Claims. 2-Memoriable of Arabella J Strong, widow of & excx of Lorenzo N Clark, asking compensation for losses sustained by reason of the abrogation of a contract made between said Clark & Wm Armstrong, acting superintendent of the Western Territory: referred to the Cmte of Claims. 3-Cmte of Claims: asked to be discharged from the further consideration of the memorial of the citizens of Sacramento city, in relation to the claim of Wm Waldo, & that leave be granted to withdraw the same. 4-Cmte on Military Affairs: resolution directing a sword to be presented to the nearest male relative of Maj Saml Ringgold, late of the U S army: recommended its passage. Maj Ringgold, of the 3rd regt of artl, was slain in command of the light artl in the glorious battle of Palo Alto, the first battle in the war with Mexico. [Mr Dawson states that Capt Ridgely was perhaps as gallant as the lamented Maj Ringgold.]

Mrd: on Feb 25, in Gtwn, D C, by Rev Mr Atkinson, Warren Tilton, of Boston, to Sarah A, daughter of the late Robt Ould, of the former place.

Household & kitchen furniture at auction: on Mar 1, in the new granite front bldgs, recently erected by Mr Briscoe, west of the Centre Market. —C W Boteler, auct

Foreign Items: 1-Death in England of Col Geo Williams, M P for Aston, died aged 87, supposed to have been the last survivor of the army of Saratoga. He accompanied Lady Harriet Ackland on her memorable expedition to join her husband in captivity. [No death date given-current foreign item.]

The Newark Daily records the death, at Rockaway, N J, of Mrs Nancy Gordon, in her 90th year. She was the wife of David Gordon, who is past 92, & had she lived until Mar 17, she would have seen the 71st anniversary of her marriage to Mr Gordon. During the whole time thay lived in the same house, & have had 9 children, of whom 5 survive; 49 grandchildren, of whom 33 survive; 103 great grandchildren, of whom 74 survive; & 2 great grandchildren, both still living, making the number of their descendants, living & dead, 163, of whom 114 still survive.

SAT MAR 1, 1851
Dry Goods, useful articles, too numerous to mention: G W Yerby, Pa ave opposite the Centre Market.

An owner wanted for a wheelbarrow & iron kettle, supposed to have been stolen & left at my premises on E st. They will be restored on proof of property & payment of charges. -J H Phillips

Houses to be removed, at auction: 3 small brick & frame houses on Pa ave, near 4½ st. The houses are to be removed within 15 days after the day of sale. Terms cash. -A Green, auctoneer

Shocking Murder & Suicide. Geo Pecht, a respectable farmer, residing near Hollidaysvurg, Pa, on Feb 14, whilst laboring under a religious monomania, killed his daughter, aged 18 years, by a blow on the head, causing her death instantly, & then ran & jumped into the forebay of a saw mill, & was drowned before he could be rescued.

The body of Jas C Harrington, a man of respectable connexions, but who has for some time been a slave to intemperance, was found in Law's church, between Canterbury & Milford, Del, on Sat last. It is supposed he entered the gallery of the church to obtain shelter from the weather, & being intoxicated fell head foremost to the floor below.

Violent storm of wind & rain passed over Cambridge, Md, on Mon last, unroofing several houses, & one end of the dwlg of Dr Wm H Muse was blown in.

At Richmond, on Wed, while the public guard was firing a salute the horses attached to a buggy, containing Col Tomlin, took fright, throwing him out & slightly injuring him. The horses ran over Mr John Rutherford & Miss Betsy Coles, injuring the former slightly, but breaking the collar-bone and 2 ribs of Miss Coles, causing serious injuries.

Madame Anna Bishop's concert takes place tonight at Jackson Hall, & she is assisted by Signor Novelle, who comes heralded as a very superior vocalists; by Mr Bayley, an eminent instrumentalist; & the celebrated Mr Bochsa presides at the piano forte.

Died: yesterday, after a short illness, A B Lindsley, aged 64 years, lately of Frankfurt, Mo.

Died: on Feb 26, after a short illness, at the residence of his grandfather, Alexander Ray, Robt H, infant son of Robt H & Ellen L Leslie, aged 10 months.

Died: Feb 27, in Gtwn, D C, Mrs Eleanor Ray, in her 77th year. Friends of the family & of her son, Alex'r Ray, of Wash City, are invited to her funeral from her late residence on Gay st, today, at 4 o'clock.

Died: on Feb 15, in Baltimore, Thos Wannall, in his 68th year, formerly of Washington.

Attention, National Greys: ordered to assemble at your Armory, in full winter uniform, on Mar 3, at 9 o'clock, for parade. By order, P Eagen, O S.

Horses for sale at Thos Baker's Stables, 8th & D sts.

W Baker's: Plain, Sweet, Eagle French, & Vanilla Chocolates, Cocoa, Broma, Cocoa paster & Sticks: always on sale in any quantity, by the principal wholesale grocers in the Eastern cities: & by his agents, E D Brigham & Co, Boston; Jas M Bunce & Co, Hartford; Hussey & Murray, N Y; Geo Wait, Albany; Foster Bosworth, Troy, N Y; Grant & Stone, Phil; Thos V Brundige, Balt; Howell & Shoemaker, Gtwn, D C; Fowle & Co, Alexandria, Va; Vose Brothers, New Orleans; Kenret, McKee & Co, Cincinnati, O; Wm Bagaley & Co, Pittsburg, Pa. —Walter Baker, Dorchester, Mass

Law of the U S, passed at the 2nd Session of the 31st Congress. 1-Appropriated for the pay of the several companies & the expenses of 3 companies of Texas volunteers, called into service by requisition of Brevet Maj Gen Brooke: $236,934.34. 2-Appropriated for the pay & expense of 4 companies of volunteers, called into the service of the U S by Brevet Lt Col Washington, in New Mexico, in 1849: $135,530.20.

Orphans Court of Wash Co, D C. Letters of administration on the personal estate of Edw Brenan, late of Natchitoches, La, deceased. –J R McFaden, adm

For sale: highly improved farm, near the Rock Creek Church, the present residence of Maj Walker, containing about 108 acres: dwlg is a handsome 2 story brick bldg. Apply to Jackson & Brother, Pa ave, between 6th & 7th sts.

Newcastle, Del: Feb 28. Last night a man entered the house of Mr Crosden, at Gtwn Cross Roads, near Kent Co, Md, & shot him dead. He then went to his wife's bedchamber, who was lying sick, & shot her; also, her sister & a servant girl, wounding all dangerously. Perpetrator is unknown.

Public sale of large & very valuable real & personal estate: public sale on Apr 2, on the premises, all that real estate lying in Chas Co, Md, called **Glasvar**: contains about 1,200 acres, recently surveyed & laid off into 4 farms: has commodious barns; will be shown by Mr Murphy, who is residing upon the premises. Also, at the same time, the Village adjoining, called & known by the name of *Allen's Fresh*. It contains a storehouse, with a dwlg attached. There are also here 3 comfortable dwlgs, 2 barns & 3 shops; a Large Steam Mill, for grinding corn, wheat, etc, in good repair; & a number of slaves, of both sexes. –Geo Brent, R T Merrick, Port Tobacco, Md.

MON MAR 3, 1851

Brave pilots of N Y have perished while in the performance of their arduous duties. The pilot boat **Nettle** sent off her yawl to board the British brig **Eagle**, when it was struck by heavy sea & swamped. Joshua G Ballinger, John McOuran, & John Solan, were drowned. Mr Ballinger has left a wife & one child; Mr McOuran left a wife & 3 children.

Pittsburgh, Feb 24, 1851. Dr Sylvester Day, of the U S army died at the arsenal on Friday. He had been connected with the army for upwards of 40 years. His funeral was Saturday.

Mrd: on Feb 26, at Fred'k, Md, by Rev W N Pendleton, Chas E Trail to Miss Ariana, youngest daughter of Col John H McElfresh, all of that city.

Mrd: on Feb 25, at Martinsburg, Berkeley Co, Va, by Rev Jos H Plunkett, Jeremiah Harris, of Jefferson Co, Va, to Miss Susan Martha, daughter of Capt Chas Boarman, U S Navy.

Lightning struck the brig **Shakespeare**, on Feb 21, in latitude 39, longitude 74. John Powers, of St John's, New Brunswick, & Hugh McCannon, of Boston, aged 22, who were in the foretop at the time, were knocked off, & the former fell overboard. McCannon fell on the deck & died in 16 hours.

Died: yesterday, after a lingering illness, in his 63rd year, Ignatius Mudd, Com'r of the Public Bldgs. Mr Mudd was a native of Chas Co, Md, & for 30 years a resident of Wash City, highly esteemed by all who knew him as an honorable, intelligent, & most worthy gentleman. The remains of the deceased will be removed from his late residence, on Md ave, on Mar 4, at 3 o'clock, to St Patrick's Church, where the funeral services will be performed.

Household & kitchen furniture at auction: on Mar 12, at the residence of Alex'r Prevost, on Pa ave, between 8th & 9th sts. –C W Boteler, auct

Household & kitchen furniture at auction: on Mar 4, at the residence of the Hon Mr Holmes, on Missouri ave, between 3rd & 4½ sts. -A Green, auctioneer

Orphans Court of Wash Co, D C, Feb 25, 1851. In the case of Philip T Berry, adm of N Thos Browning, deceased: the Court & administrator have appointed Mar 25 next for settlement of said estate, with assets in the hands of said administrator, so far as the same have been collected & turned into money. —Ed N Roach, Reg/o wills

TUE MAR 4, 1851

Wash City Ordinances: 1-Act for the relief of Alex'r Mahon: fine imposed for an alleged violation of the law in relation to dogs is remitted: provided Mahon pay the cost of prosecution. 2-Act for the relief of Davis & Garrett: to pay them $54.55, the amount being due them for repairs at sundry times in & about City Hall. 3-Act for the relief of John Fletcher: the sum of $3.80 be paid him for a balance found to be due him for paving gutters. 4-Act for the relief of Eliz Collison: that the fine imposed for a violation of the law in relation to licences is remitted: provided she pay the costs of prosecution. 5-Act for the relief of Wm Dowling: sum of $233.41 to be paid to Dowling, the balance due him for flagging & paving on the north & south sides of the canal, in 7th st. 6-Act for the relief of J S Reed: fine imposed for an alleged violation in relation to nuisances, is remitted: provided Reed pay the costs of prosecution.

Criminal Court-Wash: Mar Term. Grand Jurors:

Jacob Gideon	Chas K Gardner	B K Morsell
Thos Thornley	Robt White	G C Grammer
Stephen P Franklin	Evan Lyons	Wm Bird
Wm H Campbell	Jos Bryan	Jas S Harvey
Michl Shanks	John Pickrell	Zachariah Walker
Enoch Tucker	John H King	John C Harkness
Saml Drury	Clement Woodward	Robt Clarke
John Underwood	Chas H Wiltberger	

Summoned to serve on the Petit Jury:

Jonathan T Walker	Jeremiah Hepburn	Wm J Gosler
Francis B Huggins	Geo Marbury	Wm Parker
Jacob Harshman	Michl Nash	Paul Stevens
Henry H McPherson	Thos Scrivener	Geo M Sothoron
Jas H Boss	J P Murphy	Jas O Withers
Abraham Butler	Geo Myers	Alfred Ray
John H Delaway	Alex Kibbey	Erastus M Chapin
Jabez B Rooker	Robt Clokey	John B Davidson
Jas H Durham	Richd Stoops	Peyton Randolph
John Sheahan	Wm Golding	Wm Ferguson

Augustus Haunchild, alias Augustus Honschild, was tried & found guilty yesterday of forgery.

Mrd: on Mar 3, by Rev J P Donelan, Jas R Brent, of Chas Co, Md, to Miss Anne Eliza Lindenberger, of Wash City.

Mrd: on Mar 3, in Wash City, by Rev Mr Slatterly, Mr Michl R Shyne to Miss Catharine O'Bryan.

On Sat, as Mr Jas O Wilson, a clerk in the 6th Auditor's ofc, was riding in a hackney carriage with a loaded revolver in his pocket the pistol went off, & the ball, taking an upward direction, severely cut the intestines of the sufferer. He is now in the Washington Infirmary under the care of Drs May, Miller, & Stone. His case is a critical one.

Seaman Richd Boarman, who was attached to the gunner's dept of the Wash Navy yard, fell from aloft on board the U S steamer **Alleghany** on Sun last, & was killed by the fall. The **Alleghany** left our navy yard on Sat for Norfolk, & Boarman was one of the hands who was employed to assist in taking her to that port.

Wash Corp: 1-Ptn of Wm B Wilson for balances due him for laying flag footways: referred to the Cmte in Improvements. 2-Account of Joshua Peirce was presented: for planting trees around the City Hall square: referred to the Cmte on Improvements. 3-Ptn from David A Hall in relation to planting hedge in square 515: referred to the Cmte on Improvements.

Died: on Mar 2, after a short & painful illness, Rosanna A, consort of Fred'k W DeKrafft, & daughter of the late Dr Chas A Beatty, of Gtwn, D C. Her funeral will be from her late residence, High st, Gtwn, at 4 o'clock this afternoon.

Died: at the residence of Richd Ronaldson, Phil, Ellen Duane Steedman, aged 3 years, daughter of Lt Chas Steedman, of the U S Navy. [No death date given-current item.]

WED MAR 5, 1851
Acts passed at the 2nd Session of the 31st Congress-relief of:
Charlotte Lynch   Dunning R McNair
Hubert H Booley   Fred'k Durrive, approved 8/14/1848
Wm Hardin   Adm of Maj Fred'k D Mills, deceased
Sayles J Bower   Jose D Ward & Isaac Watts Griffith
Widow of late Lt Col Wm Gray, of Ark
H H McClintock, Harrison Gill, & Mansfield Carter
Cincinnatus Trousdale & John G Connelly, of Ark
Legal reps of Robt S Burrough & of Stephen Hopkins
Legal reps of the late Gen Walker K Armistead, of the U S army
Gamaliel Taylor, late marshal of the district of Indiana, & his sureties
Adjustment of the accounts of John D Colmesnil

Boston Transcript of Sat: The 3½ year old son of Jas M Pittingill, #3 Washington Court, was mortally burnt last night by the breaking of a lamp filled with Porter's burning fluid. He was burnt from head to foot and died this morning.

Horrible murders in Kent Co, Md: on Feb 27, the family of Mr Wm Cosden, consisting chiefly of himself, his wife, Miss Cosden, his sister, on a visit, aged about 17 years; Miss Webster, his wife's sister; 2 small children, one an infant, the other a few years old & capable of talking; a white lad, a colored boy, & a negro woman, a kitchen servant, were living in peace & quiet, unsuspecting harm from any one. They were at tea when Mr Cosden turned his chair to the fire, & was deliberately shot down by some one from the yard, through the window, an ounce ball having penetrated his body. The wretches, 3 in number, immediately beat down the panels of the door with the butts of their guns & entered the room when they shot Mrs Cosden, but she made an effort & ran into the yard & was found dead, having a ball through or near the heart, & 2 stabs upon her person. They then shot dead Miss Cosden, & stabbed her twice. One of the fiends went upstairs, & found Miss Webster, a sister of Mrs Cosden, in bed, where she had been confined by sickness for 2 weeks; she implored him to spare her life; told him if money was his object, all she had was in the trunk, to take it, but spare her life. The monster deliberately raised his gun & presented it, when she raised her feeble arm to protect her person from the merciless savage; the ball tore off the greater portion of her arm, exposing the larger arteries, & forcing itself through her body; 4 slugs were found in her bed, which was set on fire by the discharge of the gun. Another of these villains repaired to the kitchen & shot down the negro woman, the ball passing through her body. The white & colored lads made their escape to Gtwn Cross Roads, a distance of 2½ miles, & gave the alarm, when the citizens immediately repaired to the place, scoured the neighborhood, but could get no clue to the murderers. Mrs Cosden & Miss Cosden were killed. Mr Cosden lived between 2 & 3 hours. He talked freely to neighbors; did not know either of the monsters; to him they were strangers. He said he did not know that he had an enemy in the world. Miss Webster is shot through the lungs & supposed mortally, & did not know the man who shot her. She described him as having black whiskers. Her clothes & money remained untouched, & plunder does not seem to have been the motive. The servant woman yet lingers-it is feared mortally wounded-& she & Miss Webster & the lads think they would know these murderers if they could see them. Mr Cosden was a young man, an excellent citizen, harmless & inoffensive, & a good farmer. He resided on the **Moody Farm**, lying on the main road from Chestertown to Phil, about midway between Gtwn Cross Roads & the Head of Sassafras, & the dwlg is about a quarter mile from the main road. Govn'r Lowe has offered a reward of $1,000 for the arrest of the murderers.

Boston Transcript of Sat: The 3½ year old son of Jas M Pittingill, #3 Washington Court, was mortally burnt last night by the breaking of a lamp filled with Porter's burning fluid. He was burnt from head to foot and died this morning.

Postmaster Gen has est'd the following new Post Ofcs for week ending Mar 1, 1851.

Ofc	County, State	Postmaster
East North Yarmouth	Cumberland, Me	Isaac S Dunn
Pittsburgh	Coos, N H	Jas Washburn
Verona Mills	Oneida, N Y	Solomon Rathburn
Bentley's Cor's	Jefferson, N Y	Elisha Bentley
Whitney's Cor's	Jefferson, N Y	Carey Z Eddy
West Berlin	Rensselaer, N Y	Ira Allen
New Lisbon	Burlington, N J	Eayre Oliphant, jr
H Clay Factory	Sussex, Del	Jas Stephens
Stillwater	Columbia, Pa	Jas McHenry
Central	Columbia, Pa	Peter Hess
Camptown	Bradford, Pa	A G Grant
Ox Bow	Wyoming, Pa	Cyrus Shaw
Henrysville	Monroe, Pa	Jas Henry
Sherman's Dale	Perry, Pa	John Lauck
Rich Creek	Logan, Va	Floyd Hinchman
Macksburg	Giles, Va	Jesse McElrath
Rose Grove	Appomattox, Va	Stephen D Davidson
Horse Creek	Lexington D, S C	David Fridell
Oak Ridge	Merriwether, Ga	Cyrus J Clower
Nochway	Randolph, Ga	Seaborn J Thomas
Brick Store	Newton, Ga	Isaac H Parker
Crawford's Cove	Saint Clair, Ala	Curtis G Benson
Newtonville	Fayette, Ala	Geo A Shelton
Alfont	Madison, Ia	H W Moulden
Nero	Henderson, Ten	Edmund Knowles
Mount Liberty	Marion, Ill	Hugh Gibson
South Bend	Lawrence, Mo	Andrew Wilson
Pilot Knob	Madison, Mo	Jos J Brady
Baley's Creek	Osage, Mo	John Harris
Greenville	Brown, Wis	Seymour How
Helenville	Jefferson, Wis	Ortgirs Bullwinkle
Pilot Groe	Lee, Iowa	Jonathan Jones
Spring Groe	Linn, Iowa	Josiah H Walton
Lacqui Parie	Dahkotah, Min T	S R Riggs
Taylor's Falls	Washington, Min T	N C D Taylor

Names Changed: 1-Cerestown, McKean Co, Pa, changed to Ceres, Alleghany Co, N Y. 2-Santa Fe, Columbia Co, Florida, changed to Collins.

At Louisville, on Sat, the tobacco manufactory of E Holbrook was destroyed by fire, & two adjoining warehouses injured. Damage stated at $20,000.

Millard Fillmore, Pres of the U S, recognizes Florentin Theodor Schmidt, of N Y who has been appointed Vice Consul of the Grand-Duchy of Baden, for the State of N Y. Also, S Morris Waln, who has been appointed Vice Consul of Austria, at Phil, Pa. -Mar 1, 1851

On Sunday evening week, Mr John Combs, one of the oldest & most respectable citizens of Frostburg, Md, locked the doors of his house & went to church with his entire family. On his return he found that the house had been broken into, & $2,140 in gold & silver, $341 in papers of various banks, & $2,600 in bonds were stolen. The robber in his haste left some of his implements behind him, which may yet lead to his direction. -Cumberlan Citizen

Mrd: on Feb 27, by Rev Mr Morgan, Everet Wroe, of Wash, to Miss Mgt E Duvall, daughter of the late Marshur Duvall, of PG Co, Md.

Mrd: on Mar 3, by Rev Mr Gillis, John W Baden, of Wash, to Mary A K Wallace, youngest daughter of the late Robt Wallace, of Montg Co, Md.

Died: on Mon, after a lingering illness, Isabel C, youngest daughter of John H & Jane C Batman. His funeral is today at 3 o'clock, from the residence of her father, on 7th st east.

Died: on Feb 17, at the residence of Miss Sarah O Hilleary, PG Co, Md, Mr Tilghman Hilleary, sr, in his 62nd year.

Circuit Court of Wash Co, D C-in Chancery. Bronaugh M Derringer, cmplnt, against Wm Choppin & au'r, dfndnts. Wm Redin, Trustee, reported sale made by him. Henry A Willard became the purchaser of a parcel of land lying near Brentwood, in this county, adjoining the lands of Mary Y Walsh, Robt Y Brent, & ___ Fenwick, containing 41 2/5 acres, for sum of $2,939.80. –John A Smith, clerk

THU MAR 6, 1851
On Fri last, Allen Clapp, formerly Steward of the Pa Hospital, died there in his 83rd year. He was a worthy member of the Society of Friends, & held the post of Steward for a quarter of a century He resigned a year or two ago, on account of the infirmities of age.

Despatch from Newcastle: Jas Fisher Clayton, the only surviving child of the Hon John M Clayton, of Delaware, died at Buena Vista, the residence of his father, on Tue, after a very short illness. He has fallen upon the very threshold of manhood. The blow will be severely felt by a parent who, but a little while since, suffered the loss in death of an elder son. With him, thus left childless in his declining days, we warmly sympathize. -North American of yesterday

For sale: a 3 story brick house at H & 17th sts. Inquire of Jas L Cathcart, 18th st.

Commission on Claims against Mexico: 1-Memorial of Nehemiah Moses & others: claiming for losses by seizure & confiscation of goods on board the schnr **Hylas**, at Tampico, in 1830: claim is not valid against the Republic of Mexico: not allowed.

Mrd: Mar 4, by Rev Mr Donelan, Richd Tonge to Miss Ellen Clark, both of Wash City.

Mrd: on Mar 4, in Annapolis, by Rev Mr Griffith, Mr Elias G Hyde to Miss Frances Ann Ridgely, all of that city.

Died: on Jan 5 last, in the city of Houston, Texas, of cholera, Dr Wm G Lewis, in his 44th year. Dr Lewis was a native of Phil, but latterly a citizen of Texas.

Died: on Mar 5, in St Louis, of consumption, Miss Mary Harriet, youngest daughter of the late Rev Alex'r McAlister, in her 19th year.

Mortality on Board: from London & Liverpool to N Y. The ship **Shannon** comes into port but little better than a floating coffin. There were 40 deaths during the voyage from ship fever, among the dead is her chief ofcr, Jas Sloan.

Family carriage, horses, & harness at auction: on Mar 6, in front of my auction store. The carriage was built by Mr Curlett, of Balt. –Wm Marshall, auct

FRI MAR 7, 1851
Laws of the U S passed at the 2nd Session of the 31st Congress: 1-Compensation to John Bryan, deputy surveyor-genr'l of Wisc & Iowa: $567.03, under contract of June 22, 1850.

Commission on Claims against Mexico: 1-Memorial of Isaac D Boyce, claiming for seizure & confiscation of tobacco, at Galveston, Apr, 1836, by the invading Mexican army, & for imprisonment: claim not valid against the Republic of Mexico: not allowed.

Venerable dignitary. Mr John Mountz, the present City Clerk of Gtwn, was elected to that ofc in 1791, & is in his 60th year of his official life. His age is now verging upon four score years, & the prospect is that he will continue in active service many years to come. The use of spectales he is wholly unacquainted, & his penmanship is as regular & handsome as it was half a century ago.

Lawrence B Taylor was on Tue re-elected Mayor of Alexandria for the ensuing year.

The barque **Osmanli**, Capt Kendrick, sailed on Tue from Boston for Smyrna, with the following missionaries: Rev D T Stoddard, of the Nestorian mission, & Mrs Stoddard, Rev Mr Rhea, of Blountville, Tenn, & Miss Whittlesey. Miss Whittlesey expects to join the Syria mission; the others are destined to the Nestorians.

Household & kitchen furniture at auction: on Mar 11, at the residence of Hon Robt C Winthrop, on C st, between 3rd & $4\frac{1}{2}$ sts. -Dyer & McGuire, aucts

Criminal Court-Wash-Thu. 1-The U S vs Warren Harris alias Warner Harris, indicted on 2 counts, one for transporting 2 slaves from the District, the other for stealing said slaves. Jury found the prisoner guilty on the first count, but recommended him to the mercy of the court. 2-Patrick Rady, indicted for arson, in setting fire to a stable & blacksmith's shop, in the occupancy of Saml Bryon, on May 27, 1850, was put on trial. Will be resumed this morning.

Death by drowning: yesterday the body of Mr Chas Webb, an actor, who was announced to perform the part of Iago last night at the Nat'l Theatre, was found in the Washington canal. Verdict of the inquest: that he was in a state of mental aberration, brought on by intemperance, & accidentally fell into the canal.

Died: on Mar 4, at Buena Vista, Newcastle Co, Delaware, after a brief but painful illness of a week, in his 28th year, Jas F Clayton, son of & only surviving child of the Hon John M Clayton, late Sec of State under Pres Taylor. Youth, health, & a warm heart, were all at once struck down by a calamity which has rendered one hearth desolate.

Died: on Mar 6, Ada Augusta, only child of Wm S & Mary A Jackson. Her funeral is Friday, at 3 o'clock, from the residence of her aunt, Mrs Howison, 9th st, between E & F sts.

Senate: 1-Mr Foote had leave to withdraw the resolution submitted by him Feb 20, to procure additional copies of the geological report of David Dale Owen. 2-Resolved, that Thos Peters is to be paid $263 for extra services performed in the retiring & folding room. 3-Papers relating to the application of John A Rogers for a pension be transmitted to the Senate, & agreed thereto.

My servant girl Jane, who was sent yesterday with a note to Mrs Miller, dressmaker, on 11th st, is missing since that time. She did not reach Mrs Miller's house. She is a mulatto, between 8 & 9 years of age. A liberal compensation will be given to discover her & bring her home. –G C Grammer, near the City Hall

Dissolution of copartnership this day by mutual consent. H M Sweeny will settle the business & continue at the old stand, Water st, Gtwn. –H M Sweeny, E Shoemaker

SAT MAR 8, 1851

Register's Ofc Wash, Feb 15, 1851. Persons who have taken out licenses during the months of Oct, Nov, & Dec, 1850.

Auction: Martin, John; Robinson, John

Billard Table: Harrison, Jos; Morse, J E

Cart:

Abbot, Jos	King, Chas
Bird, Wm	Little, Jas
Barr, Wm	Lucy, Emanuel
Boyle, John F	Martin, H
Baker, Benj	Moore, John-2
Cowling, Edw	Oxby, E J
Campbell, John F	Page, Geo
Chase, W H	Smith, Richd
Clements & Daly	Tucker, Wm
Goings, Virginia	Wood, R J
Hill, Isaac	Williamson, B
King, Z M P	

Circus: June & Co, J M

Commission: Green, Ammon; Murray & Co, S

Concert: Lind, Jenny 2 nights; Night's Serenaders

Dog:

Boak, G W	Johnson, Ellen
Boarman, S B	Knott, Geo A
Butler, M-2	Kneady, C S-2
Burch, T W	Moore, W C
Brown, T P	Oxley, E J
Bates, Wm-2	Piper, J R
Bigel, Richd	Palmer, H
Devereux, Wm	Rogers, Wm
Embrod, Jno D	Tansill, R M
Evans, Henry	Turon, Wm
Graham, J D-3	

Dray: Pumphrey, Saml

Hack:

Burrill, Jno	Beasley, Jos-3
Bush, Thos	Butler, Jas
Bowen, Jas A	Boyle, Christopher
Braxton, Nancy-2	Bell, Albert

Becket, Lemuel
Begnan, Wm
Bowen, Jas A
Ball, Griffin
Bush, Jas
Birch, Saml
Clark, Cornelius-2
Chew, Wm
Croggan, Isaac
Cowling, E-2
Clark, Thos
Cozzen, L
Corcoran, John
Davis, Jas A
Delaney, Cabel
Dant, Thos E
Dalton, Wm-2
Deltro, Thos
Davis, Jas R
Earle, Robt-4
Grimes, C W
Grathard, Saml
Golding, Singleton
Gibson, W A
Hargerty, Danl
Hartshorn, Geo
Jamison, E
Jasper, Wm
Key, Gilliss
Keizer, A

Kelcher, Jas-3
Kinsley, H
Lewis, Jno
Looby, T-2
Lowndes, H
Lee, Wm
Mason, Henry
Millins, Basil-2
Mercer, Jas
Martin, Hamilton
Masi, Vincent
Naylor, Allison-5
Page, L S
Powell, A-2
Page, L S
Pywell, R R
Ross, Danl
Smallwood, Dennis-3
Sheets, John-3
Smithson, John
Schwartze, And'w
Smith, Thos-5
Turner, Henry-3
Turner, Thos
Valentine, Wm
Von Essen, Peter
Wright, J H
Wells, Philip
Welsh, Thos

Hats & Caps:

Brown, Jas
Bear, Meir
Brawner & Co, W H
Brown, T B
Brashears, T N
Burns, Geo-2
Bayne, Thos
Colquhoun, W S
Cohen, Robt
Coyle & Son, And
Colquhoun, W S
Clark, Reuben B

Cammack, C
Duvall, Benj F
Dyer & Co, J W
Duvall, B F
Eagan & Son, Wm
Edmonston, E
Emerick, P
Freedenrick & Bro-2
Fugitt, F J
Fisher, David
Flemming, Patrick
Flemming, John-2

Fletcher, W A
Foote, And
Galligan & Son, J
Griffin, Thos B
Hyatt, R T
Harvey & Co, J S
Hoover & Sons, A
Hall, E W
Johnson & Co, T W
Janney, Henry
Knott, J H
King, Z M P
Magruder, T J
Mattingly, F
Mann, Chas
Mills, John
Maguire, John
Noyes, Wm
Ostermeyer, B
Owen & Son, E
Randall, G A W

Redstrake, W J
Rosenstock, Jos-2
Reid, A
Rugg, Jno A-2
Seldiner & Co, A
Seldner & Co
Sengstack & Clark
Sensheimer & Co, L-2
Simon, Louis
Steffan, Geo-2
Stevens, M H
Strasbinger, Ab'm
Todd, Wm B
Tucker, Frs A
Wiensenfeld & Co, L
Williams, Z
Weichmann, J C
Wilson, Jno Q
Wall, Wm-2
Young & Orem

Huckster
Adamson & Moore
Bouther, J W
Bayliss, Robt
Cole, John
Donaldson, Thos G
Donaldson, B S
Dyson, O H
Edes, W H
Fisher & Loomis
Faust, Geo
Grey, Alfred
Henry, C F
Hammond, N
Hodgkins, J
Howell, Thos
Jones, Jas
Johnson, W T-transfer
Jacob, C

Kenerly, Jas
Liesberger, H
McElfresh, Henry B
O'Neale, H
Pettit, John
Phillips, B F
Queen, E F
Richardson, C F E
Rhodes, Thos
Riley, A J
Sandford, G
Sheid, E T
Scott, Albert
Thecker, Jas
Thecker, John
Thorn, Judson H
Thompson, Jas

Indian Manners: Crossman, M L

Ins Agency: Childs, Salmon; Webb Pollard
Livery Stable: Earle, Robt

Merchandise:

Armstead, Saml
Aigler, Jacob
Aigler, Christopher
Addison & Co A
Allen, Geo F
Anderson, Garret
Alexander, John
Arnold, agent, J W
Adam, Wm
Bates, John E
Bartlett, Isaac C
Berry, Washington
Bergman, L M
Bright, Rebecca
Brenner, J A
Bayly, Wm F
Browning, P W
Brodbeck, J
Boon, John B
Bean, Geo
Brown, T B
Bohn, C
Baden & Bro, J W
Briscoe & Clarke
Butt, Saml
Brereton, J
Bastianelli & Co, T
Brown, Geo
Boteler, C W
Bird, Wm
Bower, Geo
Barnes & Mitchell
Blagden, Thos
Barber, J & C
Bishop, D J
Burnett, Enos
Briel, MIchl
Brown, Jas
Colquhoun, W S-2
Choate, W C

Cochran, G W
Caton, John
Campbell & Coyle
Choate, Wm C
Clitch, H
Clavadetscher, L
Coyle, Fitzhugh
Clements & Daly
Combs, R M
Clarke, Danl B
Carter, R W
Columbus, C
Casanave, Peter
Cox, W W
Cruit, Richd
Clarvoe, John
Clagett & Dodson
Callan, John F
Corcoran, Geo W
Clagett, Newton, May & Co
Collison, Eliz
Callahan, Jeremiah
Duckworth, Mgt
David, Richd
Duvall & Bro
Davy, Eliza
Douglass, Sam E
Dyer & Co, J W
Deveny, Chas
Dove, Wm T
Donn & Bro, J M
Delarue, M M
Davis, Jas N
DeNeale, K
Duffey, Michl
Eddy, Stephen
Entwisle, W J
Eagan & Son, Wm
Elwell, F H
Eckardt, H

Eliot, Wallace
Evans, J D
Greer, Henry
Gattenson, John
Garrettson, N
Green, Edwin
Guyton, Ophelia
Garner, Catharine
Grupe, Wm
Gray, Austin
Galt & Bro, M W
Griffin, W J
Gilman, W H
Gilman, Z D
Gardner & Co, J B
Gautier, C
Gates, G W H
Gooch, John
Harris, Eliz
Hall, John
Hazard, R R
Hatch & Co, A
Harper & Co, W
Hitz, John
Henning, Stephen
Haislip, H
Hall, J B
Hyatt, R T
Hall, R B
Huggins, Jos
Harbaugh, V
Hill, Isaac
Hinton, G W
Harvey & Co, J S
Hodgkins & Meredith
Horning, John
Handley, J
Hammack, J D
Hamersley, E H
Heard & Co
Hooe & Co, P H
Hall & Bro
Holmead, Jas B
Iardella & Bro

Johnson & Co, T W
Jones, J H
Jillard & Son, J
Jolly, John
Kelly, Wm
Knott, Geo A
King, T S
Killian, J
Keyworth, Lewis & Co
Kibbey, Wm B
Krafft, J M
Lusby, Wm
Liesberger, K
Lindsey, E
Lusby & Duvall
Lewis, Saml
Lawrence, Jas
Lenman & Bro
Letmate, C H
Lutz, Fran A
Lane, Chas H
McIntire, Alex-2
Miller, R E
Morrison, Alex
Magruder, Fielder
McPherson, H H
McCutchen, Jas
Miller, John
Moore, Jos B
McCarthy, Mary A
Miller, Jas
Moffett, Jos F
McLean & Harry
Murtagh, Mary C
Mothershead, John
Mortimer, J T
Magruder & Calvert
Moore, Douglass
McCafferty, W
McDevitt, John
Masi & Co, F
Morgan, ann C
Maxwell & Sears
Masi, S

Myers, Geo
Morrison, Wm M
Morley, Hannah L
McGregor, N M
Munch, C H
McLaughlin & Duffey
Martin & Co, Jno
Myer, Danl
Nottingham, Wm
Nairo, J W
Norbeck, Geo
Noell, Wm
Naylor, F Y
Nourse, Jas
O'Meara, W C
O'Dell, Thos F
Page, Geo
Powers, Saml E
Perry & Bro
Pearson & Co, P M
Park, W
Patterson, R S
Peaco, W H
Phillips, Jas B
Purdy, John
Pettibone, John
Purcell, Thos
Pilling, Alice
Ritchey, Hiram
Rappetti, Jos-2
Ridgely & Co
Riley, Wm R-2
Ritter, W H
Robinson, John
Radcliff & Co, J T
Steer, P J
Stone, Woodford
Schwartze, jr, A J
Skirving, Jas
Shuster & Wm, R M
Shafer & Son, Jona
Shillington, Jos

Sibley & Co, W J
Sanderson, Thos
Selthausen, F W
Stewart, Geo W
Schadd, B
Saddler, Thornton
Stewart, Wm M
Stott & Co, Saml
Savage, Geo
Savage & Co, J L
Stott & Co, C
Stevens, M H
Schmidt, F
Schad & Lang
Schlegel, F
Van Reswick, Jno
Visser, J
Voss, H H C W
Wheeler, E
Wondulick, Jno
Woodward, C
Walsh, F S
Williams, Z
Wood, Ann
White & Bro
Warriner, Chaun'y
Waters, E
Ward, Jno B
Wilner, John
Whittlesey, O
White & Sons
Whitfield, Levi
Waters, E
Winter, Wm H
Wall & Brown
Warder, Wm
Wilkins, J M
Westerfield, D
Walker, John
Wilson, John
Yerby, G W

Natural Curiosities: Haworth, W-2

Omnibus:
Davis, Jos W-6
DeNeale, K
Harrington, R H
Naylor, Allison-4

Reeside & Vanderwerken-26
Ryther, A-2
Willard, E D

Panorama: Warren B-3 weeks
Peddling: Oppenheimer, L

Retail:
Aylmer, Robt P
Ailer & Thyson
Adams, Alex
Boscoe, A
Brereton & Bro
Ball, John
Byrne, C R
Bart, J R
Buttman, J H
Berkmenn, Jno H
Brown, Robt T
Bevan, Thos
Brashears, Wm B
Brown, Jas A
Bacon & Co, Sam
Brown, Jno
Boyle, Christopher
Birth, Wm W
Brawner & Co, W H
Boyd, Robt
Byer, Henrietta
Croggon, J T S
Castell, John
Clarke, Reuben B
Curry, John
Campbell, Wm H
Campbell, Thos
Donoghue, Ellen
Dillow, Wm
Duvall, Saml
Dockman, H
Donovan, Wm
Edmondson, E A
Edwards, Le Roy

Edmondson, E A
Ellis, Henry
Fraeler, Chas
Follansbee, Jos
Frank, Jacob
Foller, Damien
Fraler, jr, Chas
Fugitt, F J
Ford, Thos G
Frazier, Jas
Fowler, Saml
Faulkner, Wm H
Fowler, Chas S
Farnham, Robt
Franklin, S P
Foster, Eliz
Funk, Nicholas
Gengenback, D
Grinder, Eleanor
Greenfield, H C
Goddard, Isaac
Green, Jas
Heitmiller, Henry
Hitz, F
Haggerty, Danl
Howell, jr, W P
Hungerford, Henry
Horsthamp, H
Hercus, Geo
Huggins, Francis B
Harvey & Co, J S
Hagerty, Wm
Hines, D
Handy, S W

Hall, Edw
Hilliard, C
Hughes, Wm
Hank, Lewis
Holmead, Anthony
Hodge, Mary
Hall, E W
Jackson, Susan
Joyce, J J
Jackson & Bro, B L
Jones, Raph'l
Johnson, John H
Kleindienst, Jno P
King, V E
Kibbey & Co, J B-2
Kough, Wm
Killmon, J T
King, Martin
Knott, J H
King, Z M P
Keley, John
Liphard, J H
Leddy, Owen
Lord, Wm
LePreux, L & A
Locheny, Hugh
Lynch, Jas
Lord, Jr, Fran B
Lloyd, Jno M
Lloyd & Co, Jas T
Laub, Eliz A
Leddy, Hugh
Lehman, Chas
Magee, P
Milstead, Thos
McPherson, W S
Martin, Jno M
Murray, Owen
Murray, Catharine
Murry, Owen
Morsell & Wilson
Marceron, P T
Murray & Semmes
Myers, Benj

McChesney, J H
Mills, Robt E
Middleton & Beall
Marceron, J L
Magee, Owen
Niegler, Jacob
Nailor, Allison
Noland, S S
O'hare, C S
Ober, S J
Otterback, jr, P
Orme, Wm
O'Leary, John
Olive, Henry
Poor, John-2
Parsons, Mary L
Pilling, Jas
Peters, J A
Pumphrey, Saml
Pett, Wm
Parker & Co, G & T
Queen, Edw T
Queen, Chas J
Quigley, Francis
Rochant, Henry
Reed, B W
Randall, G W A
Redstrake, W J
Reeves, J C
Roberts, J
Rice, E B
Roemmell, J C
Rigdon, Eliz
Ryon, Jno T
Ryon, Richd J
Redfern, Saml
Stutz, Fred'k
Shreve, John
Semmes & Bro, B I
Storm, Leonard
Sengstack & Clark
Smyth, Steuart
Sheckells, jr, Thos
Stoops, Richd

Simms, J M
Semmes, Elizius
Simms, A
Semmes & Co, J H
Semmes, T F
Simms, Edw
Sothorn, W B
Taylor, J H
Trimble, Matthew
Thompson, Robt
Thompson, Jas
Thornley, Thos
Tench, Ann
Tench, T P
Tansell, Fanny
Traverse, Elias
Talbert, Wm
Tyson, Saml E

Travers & Son, J
Thompson & Davis
Thomas, Geo
Thorn, Henry
Tate, J B & A
Taylor & Maury
Taylor, Frank
Tucker, Wm W
Upperman, W H
Waters, Theo A
Wroe, Saml
Wheatley, Geo
Wilson, Patrick
Wimsatt, R
Wirt, Jno L
Wannall, C P
Wircott, Susan

Shop:
Boulanger, J
Bully, Alex F
Burte, H
Brosnahan, C
Buckley, Timothy
Cotzenberger, J
Crane, Michl
Cuthbert, Mary A
Conlan, P
Desmond, Dennis
Davis, Jas
Douglas, John
Donohoo, John A
Fletcher, John
Fitch, Horatio S
Fitzgerald, David
Gensler, H
Greason, Wm
Hoffman, H
Hooper, Geo K
Harrison, Jos
Heisler, John
Jost, B
Kuhl, Henry

Lehman, And'w
Loobey, T
McNeal, Mark
McGraun, Jas
McNeal, M
Morse, J E
Quigley, Wm
Ready, John
Ruppel, G
Rollins, Joshua
Rollins, Washington
Riley, John
Ritter, H G
Stewart, W E
Schadd, Frans
Schadd, John
Smith, John
Schadd, B
Schadd, C
Schwearing, Fred'k
Schwartze, R
Todschinder, J A P
Thoma, Lorenzo
Thomas, Jos

Usher, John W
Williams, F H
Williams, Z

Wirt, John D
Wren, Geo W

Slut: Moore, W C

Tavern:
Adams, Notley
Adams & Butler
Benter, Wm
Benter, Wm F
Baker, Thos
Brown, T P & M
Brady, Michl
Calvert, C B
Casparis, Jas
Clements, A N
Copp, Moses
DeSaules, P A
Ehramantrout, J
Eberbach, J H
Finkman, Conrad
Foy, John
Fitzgerald
Gibson, Joshua
Gadsby, Wm
Gross, And

Golding, John
Howard, Geo T
Hancock, Andrew
Harrington, R H
Howison, Wm G
Jones, Peter
Klomann, Chas
King, Pat H
Mille, And'w
Rupp, Wm
Stutz, Geo
Sweeting, Ellen
St Clair, Geo
Talty, Michl
Thomas, John
Topham, Geo
Wingenroth, F
Wert, John
Ward, Francis
Willard, E D

Tenpin Alley:
Casparis, Jas-2
Copp, Moses

Farrar, J M-2

Theatrical: Adelphi Theatre-10
Ventriloquism: Wyman, John-4 weeks

Wagon:
Bell, Eliza
Baden & Bro, J W
Bell, D L
Blagden, Thos
Casparis, Jas
Dexter, J W
Dyer & McGuire

Leisberger, H
Lancaster, Basil
Nicholas, W B
O'Conner, Jas
Page, Geo
Spicer, Fred'k

Persons fined during months of Oct, Nov, & Dec, '50: for not having license for:
Adam, Wm: $5: selling goods
Bishop, J D: $5: selling goods
Burrell, Thos: $10: selling liquors
Barber, J & C: $5: selling goods
Brown, T P & M: $10: keeping female dog
Brown, T P & M: $5: keeping male dog
Benter, W F: $10: selling liquor on Sunday
Biggs, Perry: $10: keeping female dog
Butler, Henry: $10: keeping female dog
Coburn, John: $100: tavern
Coombs, M R: $10: selling liquor after 12 p m
Dacy, Florence: $5: selling liquor
Day, Thos: $5: dog
Fuller, E H; $10: selling liquor
Flint, C W: $10: keeping billiard table
Gibbs, Jno H: $5: selling goods
Hall, E W: $5: selling goods
Howell, Thos: $5: huckstering
Henry, C F: $10: huckstering
Howe, Walter: $5: selling goods
Harrover, W H: $5: selling goods
Jones, Jas: $10: huckstering
Knott, J H: $5: selling
Klomann, Chas: $10: selling liquor after 12 p m
King, P H: $10: selling liquor on Sunday
McClery, E J: $10: selling goods
Moore, Jno L: $10: selling liquor
McGregor, N M: $5: selling goods
Martin, Lawrence: $10: selling liquor
McLaughlin & Duffey: $5: selling goods
Nelson, J L: $40: Agency Ins Co
Orr, Sarah: $20: selling liquor
Parker, Selby: $5: selling goods
Schwartze, A: $20: hack
Sullivan, Timothy: $10: huckstering
Shadd, Fra: $10: selling liquor on Sunday
Shadd, B: $10: selling liquor on Sunday
Shadd, Fra: $10: selling liquor on Sunday
Stewart, Walter: $10: keeping billiard table
Thompson & Co, J R: $5: selling goods
Walker & Shadd: $10: selling liquor on Sunday
Walker, John: $5: selling goods
Walker & Shadd: $10: selling liquor on Sunday

The steamship **North America** arrived at N Y yesterday, from Chagres, with advices from Calif: she brings 225 passengers & $450,000 in gold dust. There had been no choice of U S Senator in Calif. The choice is now between Col Fremont & T Butler King.

Danl Mayes, formerly of Lexington, Ky, late of Jackson, Miss, has removed to New Orleans, intending to devote himself to the practice of Law. Ofc: Exchange Place, #9, Duncan's Bldgs.

Household furniture at auction: on Mar 7, at the store formerly occupied by Richd Davis, on Pa ave, between 9th & 10th sts. -Dyer & McGuire, aucts

Commission on Claims against Mexico: 1-Memorial of Jas E Brown, claiming for seizure & confiscation of the schnr **Alert** & her cargo at Tampico, in 1829: claim is valid against the Republic of Mexico, [for the vessel itself,] & was allowed: the amount to be awarded subject to the future action of the board.

For rent, **Tiber Mill**, being within the limits of Wash City, & capable of furnishing fresh meal daily. Apply to Mrs Pearson, at Brentwood, adjoining the Mill.

Criminal Court-Wash-yesterday. 1-Edw Thecker, of Gtwn, guilty of a common assault. Fined $25. 2-Nicholas Manly, guilty of assault & battery, fined $8. 3-Patrick Rady guilty of arson.

Trinity Church, the new church edifice lately erected for the Episcopalian congregation under the pastoral care of Rev C M Butler, will be opened tomorrow for religious service, but the dedication will take place at a future date.

Senate: 1-Ordered that Benj Moor & J Bankroft Woodcock have leave to withdraw their petitions & papers. 2-Ordered that Julia Ann Cossart have leave to withdraw her petition & papers. 3-Ordered that Geo W Corliss have leave to withdraw his petition & papers.

Mrd: on Feb 20, by Rev Wm B Edwards, Mr Wm P Dawson to Miss Mary Frances White, all of Wash City.

MON MAR 10, 1851
Laws of the U S passed at the 2nd Session of the 31st Congress: 1-Resolution for the relief of Louis Kossuth & his associates, exiles from Hungary: the Pres of the U S is requested to authorize the employment of some one of the public vessels which may be now cruising in the Mediterranean to receive, & convey to the U S the said Louis Kossuth & his associates in captivity.

Hon Francis L Brooke, a Judge of the Court of Appeals in Va, & formerly Pres of the Court, expired at his residence in Spotsylvania Co, on Mar 3. He had attained a very advanced age, &, for a few years preceding his demise, was infirm in health; but he possessed remarkable vigor of constitution, & preserved his mental & physical energies for an unusually long period of life. He was one of the few surviving ofcrs of the Revolutionary war, in which he served with gallantry. –Richmond Times

From Texas. 1-The Victoria Advocate reports the death of Judge Townsend Dickenson, who, it appears, was drowned in a fresh water lake about 60 miles from Corpus Christi. He formerly filled the station of Judge of the Supreme Court of Arkansas. 2-Gen Brooke had discovered that all efforts to conciliate the Camanches were unavailing, & had determined as soon as spring opened to punish them severely for their depredations.

Criminal Court-Wash-yesterday. 1-Noah C Hanson, free negro, guilty of harboring & enticing a runaway slave belonging to the Hon Mc Colcock, of Georgia.

Col Jas Tappan, a venerable citizen of Gloucester, Mass, now 84 years of age, recently addressed a letter to the Hon Danl Webster, reminding him that more than 60 years ago he [Mr Webster] was one of his pupils, when he taught school at New Salisbury. Reply:
Wash, Feb 26, 1851. I thank you for your letter, & am rejoiced to hear that you are yet among the living. I remember you perfectly well as a teacher in my infant years. I think Master Chase was my earliest schoolmaster, probably when I was 3 or 4 years old. Then came Master Tappan. You boarded at our house, & sometimes I think in the family of Mr Benj Sanburn, our neighbor, the lame man. Mr John Sanburn, son of Benj, is yet living, & is about your age. Mr John Colby, who married my eldest sister, Susannah, is also living. On the North Road is Mr Benj Hunton, & on the South Road is Mr Benj Pettingall. I think of none else among the living whom you would probably remember. I thank you again, my good old master, for your kind letter, which has awakened many sleeping recollections. –Danl Webster

$20 reward for return of stolen horse: stolen from the premises at Mount Alban, near Gtwn, D C. –A Ten Broeck

Died: on Mar 8, in Wash City, Mrs Mary Ingle, consort of Jos Ingle, deceased, formerly of Alexandria, Va, in her 71st year. Her funeral will take place from her late residence, north of the Jail, at 3 o'clock, today.

Died: on Mar 8, at the residence of his mother, on Congress st, Gtwn, Mr Jas O'Reilly, aged 32 years. His funeral is at 10 o'clock this morning.

Died: on Mar 1, in Fred'k Co, Md, William Henry, son of Jas & Sarah Eliz Owner, of Wash, D C, aged 7 months & 21 days.

Valuable 3 story brick house & lot, at 4½ & C sts, at auction: on Mar 15: the former residence of Dr Sewall, deceased. -A Green, auctioneer

Execution: Thos McLaughlin was hung at Cumberland, Md, on Fri, for the murder of his wife in Aug last-a penalty which was justly due from him for having induced a confiding woman, whom it was his duty to protect, to meet him at Cumberland, apparently with the motive of murdering her between that town & the section of the canal on which he was employed, & which purpose was accomplished in the most cruel manner. People went to witness the execution from all parts of Western Md, Va & Pa, & the Civilian says there were at least 6,000 persons present.

TUE MAR 11, 1851
The block of marble ordered by Govn'r Philip Francis Thomas as Md's contribution to the Washington Monument, is a splendid specimen of Md marble, 6 feet long & 3 feet wide, & finished in beautiful style by Messrs Baughman & Brothers, of Balt, who will forward it to Washington in the course of a few days. —Balt American

Fairmont [Va] Banner: while Mr Jas Morgan, of the mountain region of this county, was picking the flint of a loaded gun, his wife thoughtlessly approaching the muzzle, a spark ignited the powder, & the contents passed through her heart. Mr Morgan was a kind & pious husband, and has been driven almost to despair. They were members of the Methodist Episcopal Church.

Chas Co Court, Feb Term, 1851. The petition of Violetta Dent & others, for the division of the real estate whereof Priscilla E Keech, died seized. The Com'r has divided same into 5 lots; notice to be given to Alfred W Dent & Geo T Richards & Priscilla E Richards his wife, parties entitled to a proportion of said estate, & who are absent out of the State of Md: same to appear & make their election by the 3rd Mon of Jul next. —Peter W Crane, Richd H Mitchell, Clerk Chas Co Court.

Household & kitchen furniture at auction: on Mar 14, at the residence of Mrs Clarke on 4½ st. —C W Boteler, auct

Senate: 1-Ordered that Wm H Thomas have leave to withdraw his petition & papers. Same for Geo C Thomas. 2-Resolved, that the Sec of the Treasury & of War be requested to cause to be examined muster rolls, pay rolls, or other evidence, so as to ascertain the amount of rations issued under each contract made by Robt B Carter & Jas Roddey, for the supply of rations to the troops, from Jun 1, 1812, to Jun 1, 1813, & report the same to the Senate at its next session.

Criminal Court-Wash-Mon: 1-Patrick Rady, convicted of arson, to be imprisoned 2 years in the penitentiary. 2-Geo Wilson, colored boy, [an old offender,] convicted of stealing leather: sentenced to one year in the penitentiary. 3-Warren Harris alias Warner Harris: fined $300.

Wash Corp: 1-Ptn from J B Lokey, praying the payment of a balance due him for casual repairs in the 7th Ward: referred to the Cmte on Claims. 2-Ptn from Jos Smoot & others, in relation to the grade of K st, between 12th & 13th sts: referred to the Cmte on Improvements. 3-Cmte of Claims: asked to be discharged from the further consideration of the ptn of Patrick Wilson. 4-Bill for the relief of Wm W Davis: reported without an amendment. 5-Ptn of Wm Lord & others, for certain flag footways in the 4th Ward: referred to the Cmte on Improvements. 6-Ptn of John H Gleek, praying remission of a fine: referred to the Cmte of Claims. 7-Bill for the relief of Wm Ross: passed.

To let: brick house with 6 rooms, 1st Ward. I can be found on 4½ st, John T S McConchie.

Administrator's peremptory sale: estate of Michl Hillegas, deceased: 2,446½ acres of land in Sullivan Co, Pa. 1-Tract called *Austria*, surveyed in the name of Edw Reyan, containing 407¾ acres, in Fox township, Sullivan Co, [late Lycoming Co,] Pa. 2-Tract called *Silesia*, surveyed in the name of John Rhea, containing 407¾ acres; adjoining #1. 3-Tract in the name of Jas Bayard, called *Palatinate*, containing 407¾ acres, adjoining #2. 4-Tract called *Saxony*, [surveyed in the name of Andrew Hodge, sr,] containing 407¾ acres, adjoining #4. 5-Tract called *Franconia*, surveyed in the name of Andrew Hodge, jr, containing 407¾ acres, adjoining #5. 6-Tract called *Swabia*, surveyed in the name of Andrew Bayard, containing 407¾ acres, adjoining #5. Also, 8,595 acres of land in Gilmer Co, Va. 1-Tract of land surveyed Mar 7, 1850, for Henry Kuhl, of Phil, sole surviving administrator of Michl Hillegas deceased, containing 595 acres. 2-Tract surveyed for the same, Mar 6, 1850, containing 1,000 acres, on Laurel Creek. 3-Tract surveyed for the same, Oct 15, 1849, containing 1,000 acres, on Stuart's creek. 4-Tract surveyed by the same, Oct 16, 1849, containing 1,000 acres, on Stinking creek. 5-Tract surveyed by the same, Feb 23, 1850, containing 1,000 acres, on the waters of the Sand Fork of the Little Kanawha river. 6-Tract surveyed for the same, Feb 23, 1850, containing 1,000 acres, on the left hand fork of the west fork of the same river. 7-Tract surveyed for the same, Feb 20, 1850, containing 1,000 acres, partly in Gilmer & partly in Lewis Co. 8-Tract surveyed for the same, Feb 25, 1850, containing 1,000 acres, on the right hand of the Sycamore fork of Steer creek. 9-Tract surveyed for the same, Feb 27, 1850, containing 1,000 acres, on the right hand fork of the west fork of the Little Kanawha river. They will positively be sold without reserve or limitation, by order of Henry Kuhl, sole surviving administrator, with the will annexed. -M Thomas & Sons, aucts: 93 Walnut st, Phil, Pa

Celebration in Tenn on Feb 22, of the success of the Nashville & Chattanooga railroad company in tunneling the Cumberland mountain. The tunnel is 3,000 feet long, & 185 feet from the top of the mountain. About 700 ladies & gentlemen participated, passed through the tunnel, heard speeches, ate a sumptuous dinner, drank spirited toasts, & danced the night away.

Commission on Claims against Mexico: 1-Memorial of Benj Godfrey, claiming for taxes & duties illegally exacted of him at Matamoros in 1830 thru 1833: claim is not valid against the Republic of Mexico: not allowed. 2-Memorial of Benj Harrison, claiming for impressments into the Mexican service, loss of personal property, & non-payment of wages: claim is not valid against the Republic of Mexico: not allowed.

We regret to announce that Maj Wm S Henry, of the U S army, died at N Y, at the early age of 34 years. His letters from Mexico during the war, over the signature of G de L, originally purblished in the N Y Spirit of the Times were universally read & admired. Albany Argus [No death date given-current news item.]

Died: on Mar 10, of consumption, at the residence of his father, A C Brown, in the village of Bladensburg, Robt T Brown, late of Wash City. His funeral is today at 12.

$20 reward for runaway negro woman, Catharine, alias Kitty Francis.
–John P Hilton

WED MAR 12, 1851
Postmaster Gen has est'd the following new Post Ofcs for week ending Mar 8, 1851.

Ofc	County, State	Postmaster
Staffordville	Tolland, Ct	Edw G Hyde
Brier Hill	St Lawrence, N Y	David Griffin
Freehold	Greene, N Y	Egbert B Dodge
South Alden	Erie, N Y	Jas Chaddendon
North Clarkson	Monroe, N Y	John Granger
Transit	Genesee, N Y	David Coy
Beesley's Point	Cape May, N J	Jos D Chatton
Keith's X Roads	Kent, Del	Adam Finlaw
Port Blanchard	Luzerne, Pa	Sam Hodgden, jr
Glenn	McKean, Pa	Sarah Clendendon
Shade Furnace	Somerset, Pa	John Bell
Eagle Foundry	Huntingdon, Pa	Geo Keith
West Pierpont	Ashtabula, Ohio	A Gould
Leon	Ashtabula, Ohio	Mervin S Cotton
North Unionto'n	Highland, Ohio	John Gall
Oneida Mills	Carroll, Ohio	Geo Hull
Utah	Lucas, Ohio	Elijah J Woodruff
West Andover	Ashtabula, Ohio	Albert N Reed
Flippos'	Caroline, Va	Littleton Flippo
Oak Mulge	Bedford, Va	Jas M Williams
Winston	Forsyth, N C	John P Vest
Hobbysville	Spartanburg d, S C	Wm Hunter

Concordia	Bolivar, Miss	C C Herndon
Cherry Creek	Pontotoc, Miss	Nathan M Berry
Edgar	St John Bap p, La	Edgar Perret
Duvall's Bluffs	Prairie, Ark	Thos R Jett
Byrneville	Harrison, Ia	Danl K Starr
Eastville	Bath, Ky	Ephraim Goodwin
Equator	Lee, Ill	Saml Brown
Florid	Putnam, Ill	Christian Cassel
Plum	Cook, Ill	Geo F Kidder
High Blue	Jackson, Mo	Isaac Bryant
Evansville	Rock, Wis	Curtis R Bent
Cambria	Wayne, Iowa	Wm Willis

Names Changed: Valley, Mifflin Co, Pa, changed to Millroy.
Upper Hanover, Montg Co, Pa, changed to Boston.
Kelloggsville, Ashtabula Co, Ohio, changed to Monroe Centre.
West Kelloggsville, Ashtabula Co, Ohio, changed to Kellogsville.
Mundy, Genesee Co, Mich, changed to Long Lake.
Little River Depot, Richland dist, S C, changed to Littleton.
McMillan's Grove, Dupage Co, Ill, changed to Wayne Centre.

Criminal Court-Wash-Tue. 1-L Sinsheimer was acquitted of robbing W Richards of a large amount at Greason's tavern. The D A entered a nolle prosequi in the case of the U S vs Wm Greason, charged with the same offence. The dfndnt Greason was afterwards tried & found guilty of an assault upon Richards.

Orphans Court of Wash Co, D C. Letters of administration on the personal estate of Ignatius Mudd, late of Wash Co, deceased. --Mary Mudd, admx N B: Claimants will please file their claims with Stanislaus Murray.

House & lot for sale in Gtwn, on 3rd st, opposite the Convent, containing about 10 rooms. Apply to John E Neale, at the Wash City Post Ofc, or to John Carroll Brent, atty at law, 4½ st. For further particulars, apply to Richd Trunnell, Gtwn.

THU MAR 13, 1851
City Ordinances-Wash: 1-Act for the relief of Walter Linkins: to pay him $15.50 for construction of a gravel footwalk on E st, from 21st to 22nd sts. 2-Resolution relative to the erection of a wharf by Geo Page: he is permitted to proceed to fill up his new wharf on the Potomas river, in front of square 472, providing he does not intrude upon the private rights of any person.

Our esteemed townsman, John Potts, for many years a clerk in the War Dept, has been appointed by the Hon Sec Chief Clerk of that Dept.

Circuit Court of Wash Co, D C-in Chancery. Beverly W Boteler & Ellen Amelia Boteler, his wife, & Rome E Phillips, by her next friend, the said Beverly W Becker, vs Anjenetta Phillips, Sarah J Phillips & Emily V Phillips. Ratify sale by the trustee of the property name & described in the above cause on Jan 13, 1851, Wm John Aiken, being the highest bidder for the south half of said property, became the purchaser for $745, & Wm Miles, being the highest bidder for the north half of the property, became the purchaser for the sum of $730; both have complied with the terms of the sales. –John A Smith, clerk

From the Richmond Whig of Mon last: Edw Wm Johnston, of Wash, formerly of Va, has become one of the proprietors of the Whig, & will take charge of the editorial dept.

Appointments by the Pres:
Thos Butler King, to be Collector of the Revenue for the port of San Francisco.
Wm Easby, to be Com'r of Public Bldgs in Wash City, to succeed Ignatius Mudd, deceased.
John S Pendleton, of Va, to be Charge d'Affaires of the U S to the Argentine Republic.
Ogden Hoffman, jr, of San Francisco, to be Judge of the Dist Court of the U S for the northern dist of Calif.
Horace Mower, of Mich, to be an Associate Judge of the Supreme Court of the Territory of New Mexico.
John S Watts, of Indiana, to be an Associate Justice of the Supreme Court of the Territory of New Mexico.
Louis Lindner, to be U S Consul at Sonneberg, in the Ducy of Saxe Meininger Hildburghhausen, in Germany.
H Jones Brooke, of Pa, to be U S Consul at Belfast, Ireland.
Henry A Homes, of Mass, to be Assist Dragoman & Sec to Legatioon of U S in Turkey.
Saml G Brandebury, of Pa, to be Chief Justice of the Supreme Court for the Territory of Utah, in place of Jos Buffington, declined.
Jenry L Tilden, of Minnesota Territory, to be U S Marshal for Territory of Minn.
Geo G Baker, of Ohio, to be U S Consul for the port of Genoa, Sardinia.
Andrew Rothwell & Jas A Kennedy, to be Justices of the Peace in Wash Co, D C.
Thos A R Nelson, of Tenn, to be Com'r of the U S in China.
John A Bennett, to be U S Consul at Bogota, in New Grenada.
W F Boone, of Pa, to be U S Consul at Realejo, in Nicaragua.
Allen F Owen, of Georgia, to be U S Consul at Havana, in the Island of Cuba.
Saml Eckel, of Tenn, to be U S Consul at Talcahuano, in Chili.

Danl Webster speaks: It did not happen to me to be born in a log cabin, but my elder brothers & sisters were born in a log cabin, raised among the snow drifts of N H, at a period so early that when the smoke first rose from its rude chimney, & curled over the frozen hill, there was no similar evidence of a white man's habitation between it & the settlements on the rivers of Canada. Its remains still exist. I make it an annual trip; I carry my children to it to teach them the hardships endured by the generations that have gone before them. I weep to think that none of those who inhabited it are now among the living. –Home Gazette

Rev Jas C Bridgman, a missionary of the American Board at Canton, died on Dec 6 of a wound which he inflicted upon himself 5 days previously in a fit of insanity. -Boston Traveller

Prof Edw T Channing, who, for 30 years past or thereabout, has filled the chair of Rhetoric at Harvard, has resigned his professorship. He had long since determined, on reaching a certain time of life, to retire, & has fulfilled his determination.

John E Scheel, Organist, & teacher of the Piano & Vocal Music, offers again his services to the public of Washington. Please leave name at Mrs Anderson's Music Store, or with J Hilbus, or with a Zappone, teacher of languages.

Commission on Claims against Mexico: 1-Memorial of Jos Andrews, claiming for unpaid services of schnr **Mary Ann**, & her crew, in lightering & refitting the Mexican war brig **Herman**, on the coast of Florida, in 1828: claim is valid against the Republic of Mexico: same was allowed accordingly. 2-Memorial of Jonas P Levy, claiming for illegal duties exacted, iniquitous judicial decisions, in 1843, & down to 1846: claim as is laid for certain iron houses is valid against the Republic of Mexico, & that the rest is not valid. The former was allowed accordingly; the amount to be awarded subject to the future action of the Board.

Millard Fillmore, Pres of the U S, recognizes Carl Wendt, of Milwaukee, who has been appointed Consul of the Duchy of Brunswick & Luneburg, for the State of Wisconsin. -Mar 10, 1851

For rent: the house now in the occupancy of Thos Mustin, on 2nd st, between B & C sts. Inquire of Mr Mustin, on the premises, or the subscriber, Richd Dement.

To builders: having had considerable acquaintance with Mr John Ross, of Gtwn, who has had charge of the carpenter work of a dwlg house recently erected under my superintendence, it affords me great pleasure to state that I regard him as a thorough & accomplished master builder in the line of his profession, & cheerfully recommend him to any who may want a house built in a workmanlike & substantial manner. -P C Johnson

Suicide of a student in Harvard College: on Sunday night Robt Troup Paine was found dead on a sofa in his room in the college. He left a letter to his father, Dr Martin Paine, of N Y, stating that he died by his own hand, & a memorandum that he had taken 32 grains of morphine in champagne, a bottle of which, uncorked & partly empty, was found on the table. Mr Paine was 21 years old, a member of the senior class, eccentric, but amiable & much liked by his acquaintances. -Post

Household & kitchen furniture at auction: on Mar 17, at the residence & store of Timothy Buckley, on Pa ave, between 1st & 2nd sts, by deed of trust recorded in Liber J A S #17, folios 98 thru 100, of the Wash Co, D C land records. By order of Thos Young, trustee. -A Green, auctioneer

Private sale of McLeod's Schoolhouse & lot, having a front of 64 feet on 9th st. Apply to J E Kendall or Nicholas Callan, or to the subscriber. -A Green, auctioneer

Mrd: on Tue, by Rev John C Smith, Isaac H Wailes, of Wash City, to Mrs Martha Nugent, of Columbia, Pa.

Died: on Feb 21, at his residence, in Jefferson City, Mo, of pneumonia, Col Wm G Minor, formerly of Spottsylvania Co, Va, in his 45th year. Col Minor emigrated to Missouri in 1840, establishing himself at Jefferson City, entered upon the practice of his profession in the circuit of which Cole Co forms a part. During the greater part of the last 11 years he was editor of the Jefferson Inquirer.

Died: on Mar 12, Wm Thomas, in his 10th year, only son of Wm S & Ann W Dove. His funeral is this afternoon, at 4 o'clock, from the residence of his father, between 21st & 22nd sts.

Died: on Mar 7, in Wash City, Mary Gertrude Jenkins, aged 10 months & 10 days, only child of the late Leoline & Rosina L Jenkins.

FRI MAR 14, 1851
Came to my enclosures, about a month ago, 2 red cows & 2 black cows. Owners to come forward, prove property, pay charges, & take them away. Square 663.
–Wm Fraser

Oregon Spectator says that mechanics' labor is very high in Oregon, wages varying from $5 to $12 a day. Blacksmithing: Franklin Little, of Washington, D C, & Chas P Ludwig, of St Jos' Co, Mich, have recently left Oregon for the States with over $12,000 made by fair-hammering, in a little less than 10 months.

Richd Gardner, a fugitive slave owned by Miss Byers, who was arrested at Bridgewater, Beaver Co, Pa, had a hearing at Pittsburg yesterday, & was remanded to his owner.

A negro woman & her child, claimed as the property of John Perdue, of Balt Co, Md, were arrested at Columbia, Pa, on Thursday of last week, & taken to Phil for a hearing before the U S Com'r Ingraham. They ran away in 1849. The slaves were remanded to their owner, & they peacefully left Phil for their home in Md.

John G Blair, for many years past the cashier of the Farmer's Bank of Va, at Richmond, died in that city last week. He was a faithful & esteemed ofcr, & highly respected.

The Whigs of Detroit on Mar 3 elected Zachariah Chandler, their candidate for Mayor, by 312 majority over Gen John R Williams, his Democratic opponent.

Mrd: Mar 12, by Rev S A H Marks, Mr Sylvester F Gates to Miss Mary Jane Holroyd, all of Wash.

Died: on Mar 9, Mrs Eliz Burford, aged 53 years.

Died: on Thu, after a short illness, Thos Shields, aged 35 years. His funeral is on Sat at 10 o'clock, from the residence of his brother-in-law, Mr J P McKean, on 2nd, between B & C sts.

Died: on Mar 13, of croup, Amelia Jane, daughter of J T & Louisa M Quisenberry, of Wash City. Her funeral will take place at 3 o'clock today, from the residence of her parents, corner of 15th st & Mass ave.

Died: on Mar 12, Jos E Lewis, son of Washington & Rachel Lewis, in his 4th year. His funeral will take place from the residence of his parents, on Sat, at 10 o'clock.

Furnished rooms to let on 4½ st. –Eleanor Wallingsford, near Pa ave.

The wife of the chief engineer of the vessel **Atlantic** was removed to a lunatic asylum last week, having lost her reason in consequence of her belief that her husband was lost. Capt J W Rogers, the Chief Engineer of the vessel **Atlantic**, was for a number of years Capt of the mail-boat on the Potomac, which plied between Aquia Creek & Wash. We trust that his home is not destined to remain desolated by the afflication which has come upon him; but that his wife may recover her reason, when the truth of his own safety enlightens her mind. –Richmond Daily Despatch [Mar 18th newspaper: the Balt Sun states, on the authority of a gentleman intimate with the family of Mr Rogers, the engineer of the **Atlantic**, that the statement of Mrs Roger's derangement is entirely unfounded.]

For rent, a comfortable neatly furnished house in Barnum's block, Pa ave. Apply to Mrs Fleury on the premises.

Norwich, Ct, Mar 13. Mr Henry M Witter, messenger for the Norwich bank, was knocked down in the ladies' room of the Norwich & Worcester railroad depot, & robbed of $40,000. The bank has offered a $4,000 reward for the detection of the thief & the recovery of the money.

Appointments by the Pres:
Robt C Schenck, of Ohio, to be Envoy Extra & Minister Pleni to the Govn't of Brazil.
John B Kerr, of Md, to be Charge d'Affaires of the U S to the Gov't of Nicaragua.
Yelverton P King, of Ga, to be Charge d'Affaires of the U S to New Grenada.
Franklin H Clack, of Louisiana, to be Sec to the Legation of the U S in Brazil.
Saml G Goodrich, of N Y, to be U S Consul at Paris, France, in place of Robt Walsh, resigned.
John Howard Payne, to be Consul at Tunis.
Wm S Allen, of Missouri, to be Sec of the Territory of New Mexico.
Elias P West, of New Mexico, to be U S Atty for the Territory of New Mexico.
Jesse Turner, of Arkansas, to be U S Dist Atty for the western district of Arkansas.
Geo Knox, of Arkansas, to be U S Dist Atty for the western district of Arkansas.
John Jones, of New Mexico, to be U S Marshal for the Territory of New Mexico.
Collectors of the Revenue:
Thos Butler King, for the port of San Francisco.
Jesse S Hambleton, Sacramento, Calif.
Collin Wilson, Umpqua, Oregon.
Simpson P Moses, Puget's Sound, Oregon.
Wm Henry Russell, Monterey, Calif
Surveyors:
Robt Goodwin, port of Beverly, Mass.
Edw C Ward, Jacksonville, N C.
Jesse Thomas, Nashville, Tenn.
Tobias Wolfe, Memphis, Tenn.
Wm Brown, Evansville, Indiana.
Fred'k Belden, Corpus Christi, Texas.
Saml Harris, Valasco, Texas.
Geo P Newell, Pacific City, Oregon.
Alonzo Leland, Milwaukee, Oregon.
Wm M Miller, Nesqually, Oregon.
Saml Barney, Santa Barbara, Calif.
Appraiser: Geo Pendleton, San Francisco, Calif.
Appraisers at Large:
Chas Bradley, of Mass.
Mathias B Edgar, of N Y.
John S Riddle, of Pa.
Hugh W Evans, of Md.

Having seen a Notice, signed by Geo H St Clair & Jas W St Clair, stating that they hold a partial interest in the farm advertised for sale by me, I deem it proper to say that, having obtained under a decree of the Circuit Court, a full, valid, & exclusive right & title to the same, I am prepared at any time to give such title to the land as will be satisfactory to the purchaser. For further information apply to John Carroll Brent, Atty-at-Law, 4½ st. -Matilda Dobbyn

For rent: 3 story house in thorough repair, on 17th st, 1st door north of Winder's bldg. Apply to C H Winder, corner of G & 17th sts.

Public sale: on Mar 20, the well improved farm called *Cavanton*, in Alexandria Co, containing 65 acres, more or less: with a comfortable 2 story frame dwlg house, excellent water within a few yards of the door, large barn, good stables, & other out-houses. -Susan Smythie

House of the first class for sale: at G & 10th sts; stabling, carriage-house, & cow-house have been permanently built; well finished; gas pipes have been laid in the hall, parlor, saloon, & dining room. Alley is newly paved. –Jas Caden

The Lumber business carried on in the name of Jos Libbey, at Water st, Gtwn, will from this day be carried on in the name of J Libbey & Son, a partnership having been formed between them therein. –Jos Libbey, Jos Libbey, jr

SAT MAR 15, 1851
Appointment by the Pres: 1-Jas Gallier, Acting Architect for continuing the construction of the Custom House at New Orleans.

Rooms to let: south side of Pa ave, between 4½ & 6th sts. –Mrs D W Davis

Criminal Court-Wash-Wed. 1-Mary Ann Lancey was convicted of stealing under the value of $5. 2-John Magar, a county constable, found guilty of an assault & battery on a boy. 3-John Medley, found not guilty of rioting in 2 cases. Thursday: 4-Geo Borchand, found not guilty of robbing Conrad Buel of $80. 5-Washington Ingram, free negro, found guilty of an aggravated assault & battery on Kitty Dozer: fined $10 & costs. 6-John Rady, found guilty for an assault & battery with intent to kill R S Wharton & Col Payne Todd.

On Thursday Mr Thos Crown, jr, was rather seriously injured in the left hand by the accidental discharge of a revolver, which he was firing at Crown's Brick Yard, near St Patrick's burial ground. On the same afternoon, the Rev Mr Keller, of Boston, was thrown from his horse while riding with lady on Pa ave. His wounds were not serious.

Mrd: on Mar 13, by Rev Edmund C Bittinger, U S Navy, E T Chappell to Miss Hannah A Plant, both of Wash City.

Household & kitchen furniture at auction: on Mar 19, by deed of trust recorded in Liber W B 48, folios 376 thru 381, of the land records of Wash Co, D C, at the residence of Henry Jackson, on H st, between 10th & 11th sts. –Wm Hunter, Acting Trustee -A Green, auct

In Chancery: Beverly W Boteler, Rosanna E Phillips, & others, against Anjenetta Phillips, & others. By an interlocutory order of the Circuit Court of Wash Co, D C, I am directed to state the account of the Trustee in the above cause & the claims of the parties, & of the creditors of the late Overton C Phillips, deceased. Same will be given on Mar 24, at my ofc in the City Hall, Wash, 10 o'clock. –W Redin, Auditor

Died: on Mar 12, at *Ash Grove*, Fairfax Co, Va, Mr Wm Herbert, in his 65th year.

MON MAR 17, 1851
Appointments by the Pres:
Pension Ofc: Jas E Heath, of Va, to be Com'r of Pensions.
Com'rs: Jos R Ingersoll, of Pa, Arthur F Hopkins, of Ala, & Jas A Harlan, of Ky, to be Com'rs to ascertain & settle private land claims in the State of Calif.
Public Lands:
Saml D King, of D C, to be Surveyor Gen of the public lands of the State of Calif.
Alphonse Lastrapes, to be Receiver of Public Moneys at Opelousas, La, vice R Benguenel, whose term of ofc has expired.
John M Edwards, to be Receiver of Public Moneys at Kalamazoo, Mich, vice Horace Mower, resigned.
Thos W Newman, to be Register of the Land Ofc at Washington, Miss, his term of ofc having expired.
Geo Washington, to be Register of the Land Of at St Augustine, Fla, vice Wm H Simmons, whose term of ofc has expired.
Superintendents of Indian Affairs: John Drennen, of Ark, David D Mitchell, of Missouri, & Elias Murray, of Indiana, to be Superintendents for the Indian tribes east of the Rocky Mountains & north of New Mexico & Texas.
Indian Agents: Kenton Harper, Wm Wilson, Philip H Raiford, Geo Butler, John R Chenault, Thos Fitzpatrick, Luke Lea, sr, Peyton P Moore, Abram M Fridley, John S Watrous, John Owen, Asbury M Coffey, Wm J J Morrow, Thos Moseley, jr, Wm P Richardson, John E Barrow, Nathl McLean, to be agents, from & after Jun 30 next, for the Indian tribes east of the Rocky Mountains & north of New Mexico & Texas; Richd H Weightman, of New Mexico, Abraham R Woolley, of N J, John Greiner, of Ohio, & Edw H Wingfield, of Ga, to be agents for the Indians in New Mexico; Jacob H Holeman, of Ky, to be agent for the Indians in Utah; Beverly S Allen, of Tenn, to be agent for the Indians in Oregon, in place of Simeon Francis, resigned.

Annual Commencement of our Medical College was held last Sat, in the hall of the Smithsonian Institution: address delivered by Rev Dr Bacon, Pres of Columbia College, the valedictory by Dr Riley. The degree of M D was conferred upon the following students:

John C Riley, of Gtwn, D C
Jas Davidson, of Gtwn, D C
Alex'r J Semmes, Gtwn, D C
Saml Q A Burche, Wash, D C
Martin V B Bogan, Wash, D C
Henry P Howard, Texas
Henry Powers Ritter, of N Y

The honorary degree of M D was also conferred on Jos Hobbins, of London, a member of the Royal College of Surgeons of England. [Mar 19th newspaper corrections: Henry Clay Martin, of Va, should be included on the above list.]

Despatch from Camen, S C: Gen Geo McDuffie expired on Fri last, at the residence of Richd Singleton, in Sumter.

Nautical work: the Kedge Anchor, or Young Seaman's Assistant, new edition, by Wm Brady, sailingmaster, U S N-Taylor & Maury, booksellers, near 9th st.

Twenty-one hundred dollars, mostly specie, was found in a secret drawer by the appraisers of the estate of Molly Sholly, an elderly maiden recently deceased near Lebanon, Pa. That is "where the silver goes."

Criminal Court-Wash-Sat. Wm Hines charged on 5 indictments, with an assault on Jas Moran, an assault on Robt Harrison, an assault on John Medley, a riot at the Pres' House, & a riot at the Engine-house. The dfndnt was found guilty of riot at the Pres' House, & acquitted of the other cases. Hines was fined $5.

Dr J W H Lovejoy offers his professional services to the citizens of Wash. Ofc at the corner of 12th & I sts.

Edw Stith, charged with the murder of Wm Gilbert, in Cherokee Co, Ala, was arrested in this city on Sat by ofcrs Wollard & Davis. The prisoner appears to be about 50 years old; is a man of slender frame, & was the editor of a newspaper called the Cherokee Sentinel.

Miss Heaney's Academy, 4th door from the Odeon, opposite Dr Holmead's, 4½ st: will be pleased to receive several additional pupils.

U S Patent Ofc, Mar 14, 1851. Ptn of Bancroft Woodcock, formerly of Mount Pleasant, Pa, now of Wheeling, Va, praying for the extension of a patent granted to him on Jun 14, 1837, for an improvement in self-sharpening plough, for 7 years from expiration of said patent, which takes place on Jun 14, 1851.
–Thos Ewbank, Com'r of Patents

Potomac Saving Bank, 7th st, Wash City: is now open for business.
—J F Callan, Pres -T M Hanson, Cashier

TUE MAR 18, 1851
Commission on Claims against Mexico: The Sec laid before the Board the following memorials, filed since Feb 1. 1-Memorial of Danl E Smith, claiming for 1/4th part of the value of the schnr **Louisiana**: received. 2-Memorial of Elisha Riggs, claiming for non-payment of a contract for certain arms delivered to the Mexican Gov't: received. 3-Memorial of John Hayden, claiming for expulsion from Pesquieria Chica, for imprisonment, & for confiscation of goods: received. 4-Memorial of Saml St John, claiming for damages from the seizure of the schnr **Brazoria** in 1832: received. 5-Memorial of Jose Marie Caballero, claiming for certain advances made to Don Frascisco Martinez, Consul at New Orleans, for the use of the Mexican Gov't: received. 6-Memorial of Benj Burns, claiming for explusion from the City of Mexico: received. 7-Memorial of Wm Murphy, claiming for expulsion from the city of Vera Cruz on May 14, 1846, & for consequent loses: received. 8-Memorial of Walter S Cox, administrator of Jas G A McKenney, claiming for destruction of his property at Chiapas, in May, 1841: received. 9-Memorial of Theophilus Labruere, claiming for certain amounts due to him upon contracts with the Mexican Gov't: received. 10-Memorial of Wm B Cozens, claiming for goods captured in Mexico in Apr, 1846: suspended. 11-Memorial of Franklin Cooper, claiming for imprisonment, in Calif. 12-Memorial of Mary S Wetmore, admx of Alphonzo Wetmore, her husband, deceased, claiming for duties illegally exacted at Chiihuahua in 1828: suspended. 13-Memorial of Jas P Wetherell, claiming for expulsion from Chihuahua in Jan, 1846. 14-Memorial of Nathl Lord, claiming for damages sustained in the interruption of settlements under empressario contracts under Zavala & others: suspended. 15-Memorial of Alex'r J Atocha, claiming for expulsion from the republic of Mexico on Feb 26, 1845, & for losses: claim is not valid against the republic of Mexico: was not allowed. 16-Memorial of John Claiborne, administrator of Thos Hassan, claiming for the loss of the schnr **Hannah Elizabeth**, chased ashore by the Mexican vessel of war **General Bravo**, on Nov 18, 1835: claim is valid against the Republic of Mexico: same was allowed: the amount to be awarded subject to the future action of the Board. 17-Memorial of Franklin Cooper, assignee of Wm Barton: received. [This 2nd Cooper claim is different than #11.] 18-Memorial of Jas T Wethered: received. 18-Memorial of Nicholas Ricardi: suspended. 19-Memorial of Jas L Collins, claiming for losses by forced abandonment of his business in Chihuahua at the breaking out of the war: claim is not valid against the Republic of Mexico: not allowed. 20-Memorial of Isaac D Marks, claiming for duties on specie illegally exacted at Saltillo, in 1838 & 1839: claim is not valid against the Republic of Mexico: not allowed. 21-Memorial of Stewart Newell, claiming for damages by non-fulfillment of contracts with the provincial gov't of Gen Canales, assumed by Gen Arista on its submission in 1840: claim is not valid against the Republic of Mexico: not allowed. 22-The several memorials of Wm Frean, Jos M Cuculla, administrator of Simeon Cuculla, & of John

J Palmer, receiver of American insurance co, claiming for the seizure & confiscation of the American schnr **Isaac McKim**, in Mexico, in 1825: claims are not valid against the Republic of Mexico: not allowed.

For rent, a pleasant house near the War Dept, just vacated by Col Cooper: the 1st brick house from the War Dept on the north side of G st. Apply to T Drury, at his store, opposite the Seven Bldgs.

For rent: all of the house over the Clothing Store of Mr Seldiner, on Pa ave, between 4½ & 6th sts. –J M Johnson, D st, between 9th & 10th sts.

Household & kitchen furniture at auction: on Mar 20, of a family removing from the city: at the dwlg over the store of Messrs Morsell & Wilson, on Pa ave, between 6th & 7th sts. -Dyer & McGuire, aucts

Capt Henry M Shreve died at St Louis, Mo, on Mar 6. He was nearly 40 years closely identified with the commerce of the West, either in flatboat or steam navigation. During the administrations of Presidents Adams, Jackson, & Van Buren he filled the important post of U S Superintendent of Western river improvement. To him belongs the honor of demonstrating the practicability of navigating the Mississippi river with steamboats, & commanded the first steamer that ever ascended that river. Whilst the British forces were threatening New Orleans in 1814-15, he was employed by Gen Jackson in several hazardous enterprises, & during the battle of Jan 8 served one of the field pieces which destroyed the advancing column led by Gen Kean.

Household & kitchen furniture at auction: by deed of trust dated Mar 1, 1851, duly recorded: sale on Mar 21, at the residence of John H Steele, on 9th st, between G & H sts. –Chas S Wallach, Trustee -A Green, auct

Wash Corp: 1-Resolved to dismiss Mr C B Clusky as engineer of the Washington Canal. 2-Cmte on Finance: reported the resolution for the purchase of Van Derveer's map of Wash City: passed. 3-Ptn of Clark Mills for the remission of a fine: referred to the Cmte of Claims. 4-Ptn of Travers Evans for the remission of a fine: referred to the Cmte of Claims. 5-Cmte of Claims: asked to be discharged from the further consideration of the ptn of Edw Chapman, exc of Mary Chapman: discharged accordingly. 6-Cmte of Claims: asked to be discharged from the further consideration of the ptn of E W Hall: which was agreed to. 7-Cmte of Claims: bill for the relief of Wentlin Sauter: passed.

Criminal Court-Wash-Mon. 1-Addison Brown, charged with stealing chickens & turkeys, was found guilty, & sentenced to 3 years in the penitentiary. 2-Richd Bays, free negro, charged with stealing a coat, was found guilty, & sentenced to 3 years in the penitentiary.

Died: on Mar 17, of croup. Louisa Matilda, daughter of J T & Louisa Quisenberry, of Wash City. Her funeral will take place this afternoon at 3 o'clock, from the residence of her parents, corner of 15th & N sts & Mass ave.

Died: on Sunday last, at Annapolis, Alex'r Randall, jr, son of Alex'r & Catharine W Randall, after a short & painful illness, in his 2nd year.

At Rochester, N Y, on Thu last, Chas McVean, a son of David McVean, committed suicide by shooting himself through the heart. He was spending the evening at an uncle's with his wife, when suddenly he arose, kissed his wife, & drew a pistol & shot himself in the presence of all in the room. His wife immediately took a bottle of chloroform & drank it, & is now in a very dangerous state. There was some difficulty between the father & son in relation to the division of some property.

Wanted: a Teacher to teach in a high school: I will pay $500 a year & board him. Address the undersigned, Washington, Arkansas, for further particulars.
-C P Turrentine, Principal

A monument to be placed over the remains of the late Cmdor Chauncey, in the Congressional Burying Ground in Washington, has just been completed. On the front of the paneled edge is an inscription to Cmdor Chauncey, who died in Washington Jan 27, 1850, aged 67. On the right panel is an inscription to the memory of his son, Chas W, of the navy, who died at Anton Lizardo Aug 10, 1847, whil cmder of the steamer **Spitfire**. On the left panel are inscriptions, Augusta A & Catherine M, daughters of the Cmdor, the former who died in 1824, the latter in 1837; also of Edw Preble, an infant son, who died in 1842.

Household & kitchen furniture at auction: on Mar 24, at the house on the corner of 4½ & C sts, known as the former residence of Dr Sewall, deceased. -A Green, auct

Dog lost: $10 reward: -Geo E Dyer, E st, between 9th & 10th sts.

The Public are cautioned against trusting any person or persons on my account without having a written order from me. –Jos K Boyd

Wanted, at the Wash Asylum, as assistant to the Gardener of that place. Application to be made to either of the undersigned: C A Davis, The Wheeler, G H Fulmer, Com'rs.

WED MAR 19, 1851
Cuban prosecutions ended. The third trial of Gen J Henderson, accused of being concerned in the late Cuban expedition, in violation of the Neutrality Laws, resulted in a mistrial. The jury were unable to agree.

Wash Corp: 1-Cmte of Claims: act for the relief of Travers Evans: passed. 2-Ptn of Chas Lyons & Wm T Griffith for grading the alley in square 696: referred to the Cmte on Improvements. 3-Ptn from John W Shiles & others for a pavement on C st south: referred to the Cmte on Improvements. 4-Ptn of J F Clark & D Clagett for a change of grade in front of square 408: referred to the Cmte on Improvements.

Stock, farming utensils, & hay for sale on Mar 24, at the farm recently owned & occupied by Mrs H H Dyer, on the road leading to Bladensburg.
-Dyer & McGuire, aucts

Mrd: on Mar 18, by Rev Mr Woods, Mr Chas Everett, jr, to Miss Harriet Dundas, daughter of Wm H Dundas, all of Wash, D C.

Official: Gen Orders, #15: War Dept, Adj Gen Ofc, Wash, Mar 13, 1851.
Promotions & appointmens in the U S Army, made by the Pres, since the publication of Gen Orders #42, of Dec 9, 1850, & the official Army Register, Jan, 1851.
I-Promotions.
1st Regt of Artl.
1st Lt Jos A Haskin, to be Capt, Feb 22, 1851, vice Reeves, deceased, & Wayne, [Assist Quartermaster,] & McDowell, [Assist Adj Gen,] who vacate their regimental commissions. [Co D]
2nd Lt Danl M Beltzhoover, to be 1st Lt Feb 22, 1851, vice Wayne, Assist Quartermaster, who vacates his regimental commission. [Co C]
2nd Lt Otis H Tillinghast, to be 1st Lt, Feb 22, 1851, vice McDowell, assist Adj Gen, who vacates his regimental commission. [Co B]
2nd Lt Jas B Fry, to be 1st Lt, Feb 22, 1851, vice Haskins, promoted. [Co H]
Brevet 2nd Lt Adam J Slemmer, to be 2nd Lt, Feb 22, 1851, vice Beltzhoover, promoted. [Co I]
Brevet 2nd Lt Amos Beckwith, to be 2nd Lt, Feb 22, 1851, vice Fry, promoted. [Co G]
2nd Regt of Artl:
Capt Harvey Brown, of the 4th Artl, to be Major, Jan 9, 1851, vice Galt, deceased.
4th Regt of Artl:
1st Lt John P McCown, to be Capt, Jan 9, 1851, vice Brown, promoted to the 2nd Artl. [Co H]
2nd Lt Jos C Clark, jr, to be 1st Lt, Dec 11, 1850, vice Collins, resigned. [Co D]
2nd Lt Wm G Gill, to be 1st Lt, Jan 9, 1851, vice McCown, promoted. [Co M]
Brevet 2nd Lt Jacob Culbertson, to be 2nd Lt, Dec 11, 1850, vice Clark, promoted. [Co I]
Brevet 2nd Lt Oscar A Mack, of the 3rd Artl, to be 2nd Lt, Jan 9, 1851, vice Gill, promoted. [Co C]
1st Regt of Infty.
1st Lt Jas N Caldwell, to be Capt, Oct 26, 1850, vice d'Oremieuix, declined promotion. [Co A]

3rd Regt of Infty.
1st Lt Israel B Richardson, to be Capt, Mar 5, 1851, vice Henry, deceased, & Jordan, [Assist Quartermaster,] & Buel, [Assist Adj Gen,] who vacate their regimental commissions. [Co K]
2nd Lt Jas N Ward, to be 1st Lt, Mar 5, 1851, vice Jordan, Assist Quartermaster, who vacates his regimental commission. [Co A]
2nd Lt Bernard E Bee, to be 1st Lt, Mar 5, 1851, vice Buell, Assist Adj Gen, who vacates his regimental commission. [Co K]
2nd Lt Henry B Clitz, to be 1st Lt, Mar 5, 1851, vice Richardson, promoted. [Co E]
Brevet 2nd Lt Louis H Marshall, to be 2nd Lt, Mar 5, 1851, vice Ward, promoted. [Co H]
Brevet 2nd Lt John W Alley, to be 2nd Lt, Mar 5, 1851, vice Bee, promoted. [Co K]
Brevet 2nd Lt J E Maxwell, to be 2nd Lt, Mar 5, 1851, vice Clitz, promoted. [Co D]

6th Regt of Infty.
2nd Lt Ralph W Kirkham, to be 1st Lt, Jan 7, 1851, vice Morrow, deceased. [Co H]
Brevet 2nd Lt Darius D Clark, of the 2nd Infty, to be 2nd Lt, Jan 7, 1851, vice Kirkham, promoted. [Co H]

7th Regt of Infty
Brevet 2nd Lt Nicholas B Pearce, to be 2nd Lt, Mar 8, 1851, vice Sutton, resigned. [Co H]

Brevets. For gallant & meritorious services, during the war with Mexico, by & with the advice & consent of the Senate, Mar 10, 1851.
Brevet Brig Gen Bennet Riley, Lt Col 2nd Infty, [now Col 1st Infty,] to be Maj Gen by Brevet, for gallant conduct at Contreras, to date from Aug 20, 1847.
For gallant conduct at Churubusco, to date from Aug, 1847. [The day # is illegible.]
Brevet Maj Abraham C Myers, Assist Quartermaster, [Capt in the Staff,] to be Lt Col by Brevet.
Brevet Capt Oscar F Winship, Assist Adj Gen, [now Major in the Staff,] to be Major by Brevet.
Capt Wm H Gordon, 3rd Infty, to be Major by Brevet.
2nd Lt Simon B Buckner, 6th Infty, to be 1st Lt by Brevet.
Brevets-for gallant conduct at Milino del Rey. To date from Sep 8, 1847.
Brevet Col Ethan A Hitchcock, Lt Col 3rd Infty, to be Brig Gen by Brevet.
Brevet Capt Sterne H Fowler, 5th Infty, [now Capt,] to be Major by Brevet.
Brevet Capt John H Gore, 4th Infty, [now Capt,] to be Major by Brevet.
Brevet 1st Lt Simon B Buckner, 2nd Lt 6th Infty, to be Capt by Brevet.
Brevets-For gallant conduct at Chapultepec. To date from Sep 13, 1847.
Majors by Brevet.
Brevet Capt Lewis G Arnold, 2nd Artl, [now Capt.
Brevet Capt Geo W Rains, 1st Lt 4th Artl.
Brevet Capt Philip W McDonald, 1st Lt 2nd Dragoons.
Brevet Capt Edw Johnson, 1st Lt 6th Infty.
Brevet Capt Saml S Anderson, 1st Lt 2nd Artl.
Brevet Capt Geo P Andrews, 1st Lt 3rd Artl.

Captains by Brevet.
Brevet 1st Lt Innis N Palmer, 2nd Lt Mounted Riflemen.
Brevet 1st Lt Geo E Pickett, 8th Infty,[now 1st Lt.]
Brevet 1st Lt John H Lendrum, 3rd Artl, [now 1st Lt.]
Brevet 1st Lt Gustaus A DeRussy, 4th Artl, [now 1st Lt.]
Brevet 1st Lt Ulysses S Grant, 4th Infty, [now 1st Lt.]
Brevet 1st Lt Thos R McConnell, 4th Infty, [now 1st Lt.]
Brevet Lt Col Harvey Brown, Capt 4th Artl, [now Major 2nd Artl,] to be Col by Brevet, for gallant conduct at the gate of Belen, to date from Sep 13, 1847.
Brevet Maj Edw R S Canby, Assist Adj Gen, [Capt of the Staff,] to be Lt Col by Brevet, for gallant conduct at the Belen gate, to date from Sep 13, 1847.
Brevet 1st Lt Alfred Gibbs, 2nd Lt Mounted Riflemen, to be Capt by Brevet, for gallant conduct, Garita of Belen, to date from Sep 13, 1847.
Brevet Maj John H Winder, Capt 1st Artl, to be Lt Col by Brevet, for gallant conduct on entering the City of Mexico, to date from Sep 14, 1847.
1st Lt Wm T Sherman, 3rd Artl, to be Capt by Brevet, for meritorious services in Calif during the war with Mexico, to date from May 30, 1848.
II-Appointments.
Medical Dept: S Wylie Crawford, jr, of Pa, to be Assist Surgeon, Mar 10, 1851, vice Day, deceased.
Ordnance Dept: John M Comstock, of N Y, to be Paymaster & Military Storekeeper at Watervliet Arsenal, Mar 10, 1851, in place of Sanders Lansing, removed.
III-Casualties.
Resignations:
1st Lt Francis Collins, 4th Artl, Dec 11, 1850.
2nd Lt Anthony S Sutton, 7th Infty, Mar 8, 1851.
Brevet 2nd Lt Achilles Bowen, 2nd Artl, Dec 1, 1850.
Commissions vacated under the provisions of the 7th section of the act of Jun 18, 1846.
Capt Jos A Haskin, Assist Quartermaster, Feb 22, 1851, 1st Artl. [Staff commission [only] vacated.]
1st Lt Henry C W Wayne, 1st Artl,* Feb 22, 1851, Assist Quartermaster.
1st Lt Irvin McDowell, 1st Artl,* Feb 22, 1851, Assist Adj Gen.
1st Lt Thos Jordan, 3rd Infty,* Mar 5, 1851, Assist Quartermaster.
1st Lt Don Carlos Buell, 3rd Infty,* Mar 5, 1851, Assist Adj Gen
Declined: 1st Lt Theophilus d'Oremieuix, 1st Infty, promotion of Capt, Oct 26, 1850.
Deaths:
Brevet Lt Col Patrick H Galt, Major 2nd Artl, at Phil, Pa, Jan 9, 1851.
Brevet Maj Wm S Henry, Capt 3rd Infty, in N Y C, Mar 5, 1851.
Brevet Capt Alex'r Morrow, 1st Lt 6th Infty, at Fort Scott, Mo, Jan 7, 1851.
Capt Isaac S K Reeves, 1st Artl, at Flushing, N Y, Feb 22, 1851.
Assist Surgeon Sylvester Day, at Allegheny Arsenal, Pa, Feb 20, 1851.
By order: R Jones, Maj Gen *Regimental commission [only] vacated.

Wash City Ordinances: 1-Act for the relief of Wm Ross & Rebecca, his wife, for an alleged violation of law in relation to free negroes & mulattoes, is remitted and amount paid, $10, to be reimbursed to them. 2-Act for the relief of Horatio Aukward, pump contractor: sum of $6.50 be paid to him for the balance due him for making & putting in a new pump on square 688.

Postmaster Gen est'd the following new Post Ofcs for week ending Mar 15, 1851.

Ofc	County, State	Postmaster
Togus Spring	Kennebeck, Maine	Abraham S Thing
North Barrington	Strafford, H H	Darius Winkley
Ball's Pond	Fairfield, Ct	Alvah H Pearce
Centre Village	Broome, N Y	Mulford Northrup
Hessville	Montgomery, N Y	Geo Ehle
North Stockholm	St Lawrence, N Y	Stephen House
Deer Park	Suffolk, N Y	Nathan E Bassett
Munnsville	Madison, N Y	Wm E Walton
Youngsville	Sullivan, N Y	John E Spencer
Pike Pond	Sullivan, N Y	Gideon Wales
Felville	Essex, N J	Stephen B Todd
Park Hall	St Mary's, Md	John A Peake
Corinth	Belmont, O	John Smart
Cedron	Clermont, O	Z M Lansdown
Storrs	Hamilton, O	Henry F Sedam
Portage	Kalamazoo, Mich	Ebenezer Durkee
Overalls	Warren, Va	W H McCullough
Angola	Onslow, N C	Wm C Hale
East Point	De Kalb, Ga	Wm Spencer
Pond Spring	Walker, Ga	Gideon S Thomasson
Gum Creek	Dooly, Ga	Thos G Harry
Pine Borough	Marion, Fla	Willis L Crow
Cane Creek	Franklin, Ala	John D Inman
Merrilltown	Travis, Texas	Nelson Merrill
Yorktown	Dewitt, Texas	John A King
Walnut Bend	Phillips', Ark	Eli T Diamond
Bridge	St Francis, Ark	John C Johnson
Harristown	Washington, Ia	Thos W Harris
Utah	La Grange, Ia	John Merriman
St Joseph	Allen, Ia	E D Ashley
Hall's Corners	Allen, Ia	Isaac Hall
Deam	Owen, Ia	Adam Deam
Monterey	Pulaski, Ia	Peter W Demoss
Blue Grass	Fulton, Ia	H H Smith
Harlan	Allen, Ia	Wm Cutts

Aubbeenaubbee	Fulton, Ia	Jeremiah Gould
Spring Creek	Cass, Ia	Dugal Campbell
Dan Webster	Henry, Ia	Sam S Cannaday
Pekin	Washington, Ia	Geo Waltz
Coghill	McMinn, Tenn	Jas C Carlock
Trent's Chapel	Hancock, Tenn	Ambrose Brewer
Smithfield	Henry, Ky	Fleet H Goodridge
Portage des Sioux	St Charles, Mo	Henry Lesirur
Tuality Plains	Washington, Oregon	Alvin T Smith
North Yam Hill	Yam Hill, Oregon	Benj E Stewart
Yoncalla	Benton, Oregon	Jas B Riggs
Lafayette	Yam Hill, Oregon	Hardin D Martin
Lackemute	Polk, Oregon	Harrison Linnville
Harris' Ferry	Washington, Oregon	Philip Harris
Santiam	Linn, Oregon	Russell T Hill
Williamette	Yam Hill, Oregon	John M Forest
Chehalem	Yam Hill, Oregon	Danl D Bailey

Names Changed: Dry Valley, Union Co, Pa, changed to Winfield.
Lenn's Creek, Kanawha Co, Va, changed to Winfield.
Greenwood, Union Co, Ga, changed to Mount Eolia.
Perry, Jefferson Co, Fla, changed to Beaseley.
Baker's Springs, Polk Co, Ark, changed to Stewart's Springs.
Bath, Franklin Co, Indiana, changed to Misersville.
McLeansville, Jackson Co, Tenn, changed to Clementsville.

Orphans Court of Wash Co, D C. Letters of administration on the personal estate of Robt T Brown, late of Wash Co, deceased. –Philip B Brown, adm

Died: on Feb 24 last, at the residence of his son, in the vicinity of N Y, Mrs Ann W Evans, for many years a resident of Wash City, but originally of Portsmouth, N H, the widow of the Hon Richd Evans, of the latter place, deceased in 1816. She has left, besides her children, many relations & friends, who will cherish her memory with affection.

Valuable real estate at auction in Gtwn, on Mar 25: belongs to the estate of the late Allen Scott, deceased, viz: part of lots 32, 35, & 36, fronting 122 feet 2 inches on the north side of Water st, & extending partially back to the Chesapeake & Ohio canal, with 2 large 3 story brick warehouses, & a 3 story brick dwlg, with back bldg. Also, all of lots 43 & 44, & part of lot 45, fronting 76 feet 3 inches on the south side of Water st, extending to the channel of Potomac river: with a small 2 story brick tenement thereon. Also, part of lot 65, in old Gtwn, fronting 24 feet on the east side of Congress st, with a 2 story brick dwlg house. Terms at sale. –E S Wright, auct

The Terre Haute [Ia] Express says that on Sunday week 4 persons were drowned in the Wabash river. It seems that Mr Hatfield & 2 grown sisters, with Mrs Clark, but recently married, were out on the river in a skiff, when the skiff capsized, & all these persons were drowned. One man & Miss Ireland, who were on board, were rescued.

Criminal Court-Wash-Tue. 1-Thos Wilson was found guilty of an assault upon Mr John L Wirt, a police ofcr at the Capitol. 2-Richd Martin, free negro, found guilty of petit larcency, and sentenced to 4 months in jail. 3-John Rady, found guilty of assault with intent to kill, was sentenced to 6 years in the penitentiary.

Methodist Conference held lately at Winchester, Va, adjourned last Sat. Appointments made for the Potomac District, during the ensuing year.
Potomac Dist: Norval Wilson, Presiding Elder
Alexandria: S Asbury Roszel, Saml Rodgers, Job Guest, sup.
Washington: Foundry & Asbury: L F Morgan, J W Bull. Wesley Chapel: Wm B Edwards, Saml Kepler, sup. McKendree Chapel: Wm Hamilton, John A Collins, sup. Ebenezer, Thos Myers, M A Turner, sup. Ryland Chapel: J S Gorsuch, Jas M Hanson, sup. Union Chapel: Chas McElfresh.
Gtwn: John Lanahan, A J Myers.
Fairfax: J M Grandin, John H Ryland
Stafford: J M Green, J N Hank
Fredericksburg: B N Brown
St Mary's: T Cornelius, J Bunting, Wm Evans, sup.
Charles: Robt Smith, one to be supplied.
Bladensburg: John Smith, John C Dice.
Rockville: Wm Prettyman, M D Conway, B Barry, sup.

Orphans Court of Wash Co, D C. Letters of administration on the personal estate of Henry Howison, late of Wash Co, deceased. –Juliet V Howison, admx

THU MAR 20, 1851
Nashville, Tenn, Mar 11. Mail robbers arrested on Tue. Several letters containing money failed to come to hand, & Dr J J Burnett, U S Mail Agent for this district, succeeded in arresting at Sequatchee Post Ofc, Marion Co, the Messrs M O & John Thurman, [the latter postmaster at that place,] who have been engaged in extensive mail robberies. The prisoners will be conveyed to Knoxville for trial. –Whig

New Orleans papers mention the death of Cornelius Paulding, a wealthy citizen, who has left $5,000 to the Orphan Boys' Asylum at Lafayette, $5,000 to the Public School Lyceum. The greater portion of his estate is probably to be divided amongst his relations at the North-a brother & 2 or 3 sisters.

Mrd: on Mar 8, at St Louis, Mo, by the Very Rev A O'Regan, Lt Jas A Hardie, 3rd Regt U S Artl, to Mgt Hunter, niece of the late Gen R B Mason, U S Army.

Died: on Mar 19, at the ***Highlands***, Maj Chas J Nourse, late of the U S Army. His funeral will take place at Rock Creek Church, this afternoon, at 4 o'clock.

Died: on Mar 13, at his residence in Harper's Ferry, Va, Henry Stipes, in his 55th year. He was one of the oldest citizens of that place, & died a true Christian.

Chestnut Hill School, 3 miles from Balt, Md, will open on May 1.
-Fred'k Gibson, Principal

Commission on Claims against Mexico: 1-Memorial of Henry Wright, administrator of Wm Bunce, claiming for supplies furnished to the Mexican navy in 1827: claim is not valid against the Republic of Mexico: not allowed. 2-Memorials taken up for consideration: that of Elisha Riggs; of Jose Maria Caballero; & of Theophilus Labucere. 3-Memorial taken up for consideration: that of John F Bullock, adm of Edw Hill, deceased, claiming for expulsion from Matamoros, seizure of corn there, & imprisonment at Monterey. 4-Memorials taken up for consideration: that of Franklin Cooper, assignee of Wm Barton; of Geo Y Wethered; & of Jonah Rogers, adm of Augustus Rogers, deceased, claiming for the seizure of the schnr **Nolson** & imprisonment at Laguna in 1833. 5-Memorial of Paul Raukert, claiming for goods destroyed at Matamoros previous to the war of 1846: claim is not valid against the Republic of Mexico: not allowed. 6-Memorial in behalf of Mrs Mary Santangelo, widow & sole legatee of Orazio Santangelo, submitted by Mr Chas Callaghn, as her rep, claiming for the banishment of the said Orazio from Mexico in 1826: claim is not valid against the Republic of Mexico: not allowed.

Died: at the Washington Infirmary, Peter Hausenpflute, aged 50 years, a native of Germany, & for some years past a resident of Harrisburg, Pa. [No death date given-current item.]

Household & kitchen furniture at auction: on Mar 23, at the residence of Hon Geo B Badger, on Missouri ave, between 3rd & 4½ sts. -Dyer & McGuire, aucts

Criminal Court-Wash: 1-John W Hamilton, charged with refusing to aid Isaac Stoddard, a county constable, in the discharge of his duty, was tried & found guilty.

FRI MAR 21, 1851
Yesterday the surgical amputation of the thigh of a female 22 year old patient was performed at the Gtwn Almshouse by J M Snyder, M D, assisted by Drs Magruder, Matthews, Semmes, Davidson, & Riley, jr. The patient was put under the influence of chloric ether, & in 25 seconds the amputation was effected. The patient has been for many months prostrate in consequence of a scrofulous degeneration of all the tissues of the leg.

Telegraphic dispatch received from New Orleans at the War Dept yesterday announcing the death of Brevet Maj Gen Geo M Brooke, which took place at San Antonio, Texas, on Mar 9. Gen Brooke entered the army, from Va, May 3, 1808, as 1st Lt in the infty: promoted to rank of Capt May 1, 1810; to Major the 4th Infty in 1814; to Lt Col of same regt Mar 1, 1819; & in Jul, ___ to the rank of Col in the 5th Infty. His brevet was that of Lt Col, Aug 15, 1814, for gallant conduct in the defence of **Fort Erie**; his second was that of Col Sep 17, 1814, for distinguished & meritorious services in the sortie from **Fort Erie**. He was made a Brevet Brig Gen Sept, 1824, for 10 years' faithful service as Col, & he was brevetted a Maj Gen May, 1848, for meritorious conduct, particularly in his performance of this duties in the prosecution of the war with Mexico. Fort Brooke, at Tampa Bay, was established by & received his name in 1824, where he was for a number of years. At the time of his death he was in command of the military dept, Texas, & engaged in planning an expedition against the Indians.

Hon Thos H Benton, with his daughter, Mrs Jones, family & servants, are at the Astor House, N Y, where Mr Benton is to superintend his daughter's emarkation to visit her husband in Calif.

Died: yesterday, at her residence in Wash City, after a brief illness, Madame Carvallo, the excellent & universally respected consort of Don Manuel Carvallo, the esteemed Minister of the Republic of China.

Died: on Mar 20, of consumption, Mr Allen A Thompson, Printer, in his 51st year. His funeral is tomorrow, 10 o'clock, from his late residence on F st, between 13th & 14th sts.

Died: on Mar 20, at Gtwn, after protracted illness, Jane Anna Guy, in her 24th year. Her funeral will take place from the residence of her brother-in-law, Levi Davis, on Market st, this afternoon, at 3: 30 o'clock.

Died: on Mar 18, at **The Hive**, near Hagerstown, Md, of bilious pleurisy, Wm H Fitzhugh, eldest son of the late Col Wm Fitzhugh, of Livingston Co, N Y.

Coroner's Inquest: the dead body of a man, named Geo Vermillion, was found last Tuesday in the Wash canal near 6th st. Verdict: he came to his death, having fallen into the canal while he was under the influence of intemperance.

Valuable manufacturing property for sale in Lynchburg, Va: will be sold on Apr 10 next: the Factory Lot, Bldgs, Machinery, & Fixtures, belonging to the Lynchburg Manufacturing Co; also, the Mill-house now used as a Distillery. Property is in Lynchburg, on the Blackwater creek. –Richd G Morriss, Pres, Lynchburg Mfgr Co.

To Arba K Maynard. You are hereby notified that I hereby revoke, & annul, & declare void the Power of Atty, or instrument which you procured from me, & for which you have paid no consideration whatever, purporting to give you power to make a contract with the quartermaster of the marine corps, & others, for the manufacture of my patent firearms, under my patent dated Sep 12, 1848, which Power of Atty was dated Oct 4, 1850, & which I have been informed you have caused to be recorded in the Patent Ofc. I hereby forbid you from making any contracts in my name for the manufacture of firearms. —Christian Sharp, in the presence of Francis King & Geo Mackay, Fred 20, 1851.

Trustee's sale of dwlg house, by 2 deeds of trust, one dated Feb 21, 1844, & the other dated Sep 16, 1848: for sale on Apr 22, lot 19 in square 28 in Wash City, D C, with the 2 story brick dwlg-house thereon, recently occupied by Mr S E Scott. The lot fronts on the south side of north K st. —Jno Marbury, Trustee

Christian Sharps. In presence of Francis King & Geo Mackay, recorded in Liber H 2, page 325, of transfers of Patent Rights. —Thos Ewbank, Com'r of Patents

SAT MAR 22, 1851
Commission on Claims against Mexico-taken up for consideration: 1-Memorial of John Chas Beales, claiming for destruction of his property, in 1836, by the invading Mexican army. 2-Memorial of Cassius C Young & others, heirs at law of Guilford D Young, & of Eliz, his wife, the original memorialist, claiming for the service of the said Guildford, who fell in the war for Mexican independence. Claims severally are not valid against the Republic of Mexico, & were accordingly not allowed.

On Tue 4 men belonging to the U S steamer **Susquehanna** were shot on the wood wharf in Portsmouth, Va, by the keeper of a groggery named John Cooper, who was immediately arrested. The men had previous difficulty with Cooper for not paying for liquor. He discharged his gun at 3 of the sailors, John Walsh, Robt McGee, & Saml Reed, who were mortally wounded, & Saml Shannon was severely wounded. McGee had his elbow shattered to pieces & his arm was amputated the same evening, but he is not expected to recover.

A Sad Accident-Death of a Good Man: Balt, Mar 21. Mr John S Skinner, Editor & Proprietor of the Plough, the Loom, & Anvil, met with a fatal accident here this afternoon, about 3 o'clock. While in the post ofc bldg, he accidentally fell through the cellar door, his head striking a granite sill, & fracturing his skull. He never spoke afterwards, but died about 7 o'clock in the post ofc bldg. Mr Skinner was probably 70 years of age. His afflicted wife was present soon after the accident occurred, as were also ex-Mayor Davies & other relatives.

Died: yesterday, in Wash City, Mrs Catharine Adams, consort of Mr Leonard Adams, in her 69th year. Her funeral is on Sunday, at 12 o'clock, from the residence of her husband, on N Y ave, between 12th & 13th sts.

On Thursday, after Mr Jesse S Butts, living on G, between 12th & 13th sts, an employee of the Post Ofc Dept, had left left home to attend to his business, his wife departed, [it is said in search of a servant,] intending to return in a short time. The eldest child, Clara, aged 6 or 7 years, by some means had her clothes took fire and when the mother returned, the girl was found lying on her face, life extinct. 3 other small children were in the room. -Republic

Died: on Mar 20, Mrs Eliz D Thompson, in her 73rd year. Her funeral is on Sunday, at 3 o'clock, at the residence of her son, Henry Thompson.

MON MAR 24, 1951
Senate: 1-Bill for the relief of H J McClintock & Mansfield Carter. 2-Bill for the relief of the administrator of Maj Fred'k D Mills, deceased. 3-Act for the relief of Jos D Ward & Isaac Watts Griffith.

Phil, Mar 22. Geo Alberti was sentenced to 10 years in the penitentiary & fined $1,000; Frisby, his accomplice, was sentenced to 8 years in the penitentiary, & fined $700. Both were connected with the kidnapping of a colored child, taking it to Md, & selling it into slavery. 2-McFadden, the druggist, convicted of manslaughter, by causing the dead of a young woman last summer, by administering morphine through a mistake, was sentenced to 3 months in the penitentiary. 3-John C Deal, Thos Sales, & Geo Elliott, were committed by Mayor Gilpin this morning, to answer for the murder of Chas Blaney, who was killed during an affray yesterday afternoon.

Orphans Court of Wash Co, D C. Letters testamentary on the personal estate of Chas J Nourse, last of Wash Co, D C. –Chas J Nourse, exc

Despatch from Cincinnati: Augustus A Addams, the tragedian, died there on Mar 19.

Sale of the real estate of the late Robt W Bowie, lying in Nottingham district, PG Co, Md, sold at trustee's sale on Tue last. The **Connick Farm** of 390 acres, was purchased by Mr Benj Swann, at $36.25 per acre. The plantation called **Mattaponi** had been divided by com'rs into 5 lots. The first lot, of 136 acres, principally in wood, was purchased by Mr Jas S Morsell, at $26 per acre. The second, 240 acres, by Messrs Robt Rhiselin & Fielder Bowie, at $32 per acre. The third, 350 acres, by Mr Michl B Carroll, at $33 per acre The fourth, 241 acres, mostly in wood, by Mr Robt J Young, at $16 per acre; & the 5th lot, [being the dower,] with the dwlg house & mill, containing 300 acres, was bought by Mr Jas J Bowie, at $10 per acre. The personal property, heretofore sold by the executor, for upwards of $30,000.

Commission on Claims against Mexico: 1-Memorial of Andrew Wylie, jr, administrator of Saml Baldwin, deceased, claiming for seizure of schnr **Montezuma**, imprisonment, & personal outrages & sufferings, being taken up for consideration: same was valid claim against the Republic of Mexico: same was allowed accordingly; the amount to be awarded subject to the future action of the Board. 2-Memorial of Wm L Scott, claiming for seizure of $6,000 in specie at Chihuahua in 1831: claim is not valid against the Republic of Mexico: same was not allowed.

Died: on Sat last, at his lodgings in Wash City, after a lingering illness, of pulmonary consumption, Hon Isaac Hill, of N H, formerly Gov'r of that State, & during 6 years a Senator from it in Congress.

Died: on Mar 23, after a painful illness of several months, John Clayton, in his 77th year. He was a native of Norfolk, England, but for the last 35 years a citizen of Gtwn, D C. His funeral is today at 4 o'clock, from his late residence on Bridge st.

Died: on Mar 22, in Wash City, Mr Wm Ward, aged 75 years. He was a native of Ireland, & for nearly half a century a resident of Wash City. His funeral is today at St Patrick's Church, at 9 o'clock.

Died: on Mar 12, at the residence of Dr Saml Wilson, in Surry Co, Va, Mrs Annie Eliza Hunnicutt, wife of John A Hunnicutt, in her 34th year.

Died: on Mar 22, at an advanced age, Hon Saml Green, formerly Judge of the Superior Court of the State of N H, & for the last 12 years a clerk in the ofc of the Sec of the Treasury.

Criminal Court-Wash-Sat. Chas Bentz alias Chas Brandt, a German, was put upon his trial on the charge of false swearing to enable a certain party to obtain a land warrant from the Gov't. Several witnesses were called to prove that the prisoner could not speak the English language, & is a man of weak intellect. G C Grammer was sworn as interpreter.

Trustee's sale of land: by decree of the Chas Co Court, sitting as a Court of Equity: public sale on Apr 23, at the store of Wm Simmons, called *Partnership*, in Chickamuxen, the following tract of parcel of land, called *Fairfax's Pleasure*, lying in Chas Co, Md, of which Ann L Fairfax, late of Preston Co, Va, died seized & possessed. The above named land was originally called by various names, & consisted of various tracts or parts of tracts. They were called by the above name in a resurvey made by John Fairfax, the husband of Ann L Fairfax, & by the plot & name of said Resurvey they are to be sold, & contain 795 acres, more or less. Mr Walter A Haislip, who lives near the lands, will show them.
-R Sinnett Reeder, Trustee

Hardware Store for sale: wishing to retire from business as early as practical. Apply to E Lindsley, between 9th & 10th sts. Wash.

Shocking tragedy on the Isthmus of Panama, recently: two boatloads of American passengers, consisting of 12 persons, including 4 ladies, while proceeding up the Chargres river were murdered by a gang of Jamaica [negro] & Carthagena boatmen. The bodies of 7 of them were afterwards found & interred: Thos McDermott, 274 Greenwich st, N Y. Jos Brooks, corner of Dey & Broadway, N Y Fidell Pepin, a native of Gap, in the higher Alps. Honore Landry, of Paris. J W Steele, Waterloo, Indiana. Catherine Cameron, residence unknown. A man named Patrick, residence unknown.

Household & kitchen furniture at auction: on Mar 27, at the residence of Mrs O J Preston, on D, between 12th & 13th sts, next door to C P Sengstack. –A Green, auct

TUE MAR 25, 1851
Mrd: on Mar 18, by Rev Mr French, Leopold Neumeyer to Margaret A, eldest daughter of Josiah Eagleson, of Balt.

Died: on Mar 22, Theodore F, aged 5 years, 2 months & 12 days, only son of John M & Adeline Mankins, after a short but painful illness. His funeral is this morning, at 10 o'clock, from the residence of his grandfather, on 19th st.

Public sale on Mar 26, in front of the Mayor's ofc, Alexandria, Va, that well improved farm called **Cavanton**, in said county, containing 65 acres, more or less. **Cavanton** commands a fine view of the Potomac river & adjoining country: comfortable 2 story frame dwlg-house & out-bldgs. –Susan Smythe

Commission on Claims against Mexico: ordered to be received: 1-Memorial of Peter Kerr, claiming for loss of part of cargo of schnr **Hannah Elizabeth**, chased ashore by a Mexican war schnr: taken up for consideration. 2-Memorial of Jesse E Brown, adm of Wm J Russell, claiming for a portion of damage by seizure & confiscation of schnr **Alert**, at Tampico, in 1829: taken up for consideration. 3-Memoiral of Jas W Zacharie, assignee of Asmus C Bredall, claiming for false imprisonment. Memorial of the same, assignee of the same, claiming for the seizure & pillage of the schnr **Lodi**, at Corpus Christi, in 1838. 4-Memorial of Hetty Green, admx of Pardon C Green, claiming for seizure & detention of ship **Transit**, at Campeachy, in 1828. 5-Memorial of Geo & Peter Laffler, claiming for seizure & destruction of a flatboat at Tampico, in 1838, & for consequent damages. Taken up for consideration: 6-Memorial of Wm Murphy, claiming for expulsion from the city of Vera Cruz on May 14, 1846, & for consequent damages. 7-Memorial of John Browner, receiver of the Pelican Ins Co of N Y, claiming to recover insurance paid on cargo of schnr **Caroline**.

The funeral of the late Judge Saml Green will take place from the house of Miss Briscoe, 7th & Pa ave, today, at 3:30 p m.

Launch: at the foot of 7th st, from Geo Page's yard, the beautiful steamer **Champion**, built by Geo Page, & sold to Capt Henry J Straudberg, of Balt, will be launched on Thu at 3 o'clock, tide permitting.

John Jay Bradley, a man of liberal education, a Greek scholar, & formerly an editor of a paper, died in Boston jail on Thu, where he had been confined for a week past for debt. He was in the last stage of consumption when sent to jail, & could scarcely get up the steps for weakness. The creditor peremptorily refused to release him unless the money was paid. His father was applied to, but he refused to interfere. They had a quarrel, but it does not appear that the father knew fully of his son's condition. The debt was $200.

The principal business done in the Police Court of Boston on Wed last, was the fining of divers young men for smoking in the streets, making that practice an expensive luxury.

Elected Police Magistrates for Wash City, yesterday: Saml Drury, John D Clark, John L Smith, Benj K Morsell, Wm Thompson, Jas Crandell, & Craven Ashford. Mayor sent in the following nominations for Police Constables: John Dewdney, Harrison, Craig, Wm A Boss, J F Wollard, E G Handy, R R Burr, John Davis, W A Mulloy, Josiah Adams, John Willett, Isaac Stoddard, & W B Mitchell: confirmed. H W Barnaclo-postponed; John Grinder, postponed.

Wm Turner, M D, of N Y C, has petitioned the Legislature of the State of N Y to make the professional practice of blood-letting a penal offence.

A verdict of $9,975 has been awarded to Lyman Raymond against the city of Lowell, for personal injuries sustained by him, owing to a defect in the streets, in Oct, 1845.

Marshal's sale: by 3 writs of fieri facias: sale on Apr 1 of: lot 3 in square 292, Pa ave, between 12th & 13th sts; lot 22 in square 368, on 9th st, between M & N sts; lots 1 & 10 in square 370, 9th & Mass ave, with improvements; lot 4 in square 371, 10th & K sts; lot 12 in square 559, on N J ave, between K & L sts; lot 27 in square 327, subject to lease; lot 2 in square 865; half of lot 7 in square 654; lot 4 in square 1066; lot 3 in square 1,055: seized & levied upon, & will be sold to satisfy Judicials, [numbers & person not given,] to Mar term, 1851. –Richd Wallach, Marshall, D C

For rent: a fine eligible house on D st, between 9th & 10th sts; lighted with gas. Apply to John Foy, at the Republican House. The property can be bought at private sale if not rented.

Dissolution of the copartnership of Hoffar & Mattingly, Dentist, on Mar 22, by mutual consent. G E Mattingly is retiring from the concern, & recommends Dr Hoffar, who has long experience in dental surgery, & who will continue the business.
–A M Hoffar, G E Mattingly

WED MAR 26, 1851
Wash Corp: 1-Cmte of Claims: bill for relief of Jas Kenally. Same cmte: bill for relief of Walter Hawkins. Same cmte: bill for relief of John Bower: recommended that it be rejected. 2-Mr C B Cluskey, resigns as Surveyor of Wash City.

Wash City Ordinances. 1-Act for the relief of Wm W Davis: fine imposed for a violation in relation to licensing coal yards, is remitted; provided Davis pay the cost of prosecution. 2-Act for the relief of Wentlin Santer: fine imposed for an alleged violation in reference to licensing wagons, carts, & drays, is remitted: provided Santer pay the cost of prosecution.

Commission on Claims against Mexico: 1-Memorial of John H Mears, claim for losses by expulsion from his mines in San Luis Potosi, in Oct, 1846: taken up for consideration. 2-Memorial of John Bonte, claim for violation of grant of exclusive navigation by steam of river Tobasco, loss of steamboat: taken up for consideration.

In Chancery. Catherine Mackall vs D English et al. The bill states that Henry Foxall, late of Gtwn, devised & bequeathed all his estate, subject to certain charges & legacies, to David English, Walter Smith, Leonard Mackall, & Jacob Hoffman, to hold & manage upon certain trusts, with power to sell & re-invest. that said D English, W Smith, & L Mackall received said estate, & undertook said trusts, & acted therein for a long time; that they were entitled to compensation in the form of a commission on the personal estate received by them, & all sales & collection; & no such compensation was received by any of them except D English. Walter Smith is dead, & Richd Smith is his exec; that Jacob Hoffman is dead, & his distributees disclaim all right to such commissions; that David English is dead, & Robt M English & Richd Henderson are his administrators; that Leonard Mackall is dead, & cmplnt is his excx. In a suit of McKenney et al vs D English et al, the claim of commissions by the trustees aforesaid was considered by this Court & allowed, & the rate of commissions settled; that cmplnt is satisfied with the adjustment then made, & claims the amount therein allowed to Leonard Mackall & 1/3rd of that allowed to Jacob Hoffman. It further shows that David English, as the last surviving trustee of Mr Foxall's will, constituted David English, jr, P T Berry, & Wm McK Osborne, trustees jointly with himself, & the estate has now survived to them. It asks a decree requiring the trustees to pay to cmplnt the amount due according to the adjustment aforesaid, & states that the dfndnts Robt M English & Richd Henderson, reside out of D C. Same to appear on or before the 3rd Mon of Oct next, in this Court, to show cause, if any they have, why a decree should not pass as prayed.
–John A Smith, clk

The funeral of Madame Carvallo, the wife of the Minister of the Republic of Chili, took place on Mon. The ceremonies at St Patrick's Church, F st, were attended by an immense crowd of persons. The high mass was sung by the Rev Mr Slattery, assisted by Rev Messrs Lyne, Lanegan, Flanagan, & Lynch. The funeral sermon was pronounced by Rev Mr Moriarty, of Balt. A long train of private & public carriages proceeded to the Congressional Cemetery, where the remains were deposited in the family vault of J H Causten, the father of the deceased. -Republic

Major Noah died on Sat last, nearly 66 years of age, having been born in Phil on Jul 19, 1785, & was connected with the press for over 40 years.

Criminal Court-Wash-Tue. Henry Buete, charged with fraud & perjury, found guilty. It was painful to see the wife & 3 children of the prisoner seated on the same bench with him, waiting eagerly the result of the trial.

Died: on Mar 23, Jas Taylor, a native of England, in his 41st year.

THU MAR 27, 1851
John Goodman, a venerable esteemed citizen of Phil, died at his residence in that city on Sunday last, in his 88th year. He was born at Germantown, Phil Co, in 1763; engaged in the revolutionary struggle, & was present with the army at the battle of Trenton.

A portion of the Military Asylum Board, [including Gens Scott, Wool, Jones, & Lawson, & Col Larned,] paid an official visit to the Heights of Gtwn on Tue last. They examined the place known as *Woodley*, which contains 100 acres, & is reputed to be one of the handsomest places in the District; formerly the residence of Philip Barton Key, but now the property of Col Lorenzo Thomas, U S A. The Board also visited *Linnean Hill*, the property of Mr Pearce.

Postmaster Gen est'd the following new Post Ofcs for week ending Mar 22, 1851.

Ofc	County, State	Postmaster
Harwich Post	Barnstable, Mass	Ephraim Doane
East Gainesville	Wyoming, N Y	Ezra Warriner
Dykeman's	Putnam, N Y	Junia Dykeman
East Marion	Suffolk, N Y	Benj C Tuthill
Arsenal	Alleghany, Pa	Wm Smith
Fillmore	Centre, Pa	Wm J Furst
Arnim Creek	McKean, Pa	John P Evans
Manatawny	Berks, Pa	Isaac Youder
Grosse Isle	Wayne, Mich	Chas Fox
East Berlin	St Clair, Mich	Wm H Baker
Lawton	Van Buren, Mich	Andrew Longstreet
Bone Creek	Ritchie, Va	Geo Collins

Brixton	Alexandria, Va	Wm Jenks
White Oak	Ritchie, Va	John F Lawson
Big Meadow	Grayson, Va	Calvin Green
Lumber Bridge	Robeson, N C	Stephen Cobb
Five Mile	Pickens D, S C	Chas Thompson
Chick's Springs	Greenville D, S C	Alfred Taylor
Cedar Spring	Benton, Ala	Robt M Draper
Hadens	Madison, Ala	John T Haden
Hermitage	Point Coupee P, La	Wm G Bozeman
Salmagundi	Washita P, La	Wm McDanald
Arcadia	Bienville P, La	S P Sutton
Bendy's Landing	Tyler, Texas	H W Bendy
Double Spring	Benton, Ark	David Chandler
New Goshen	Vigo, Ia	Jeremiah Clark
Will's Point	Benton, Ark	David Chandler
Redfoot	Obion, Tenn	John L Moultrie
Doudsville	Pendleton, Ky	G B Sharp
Clarion	Grundy, Ill	John M Clover
Fitzhenry	Igle, Ill	L O Brien
Hyde Park	Grundy, Ill	John Calrus
News	Calhoun, Ill	Jas B Gilman
Cross Roads	Johnson, Ill	Wesley Reynolds
Whitefield	Marshall, Ill	Lewis M Yokum
Uniontown	Indian Territory, Mo	Robt Rabitaille
Stoughton	Dane, Wis	Forrest Henry
Collins	Manetoowac, Wis	Wm N Adams
Nevada	Green, Wis	Jeremiah Lovelace
Brock's Crossing	St Croix, Wis	Elias Brock
Harrisville	Marquette, Wis	Jas Harris
Hopewell	Mahaska, Iowa	Isaac Mills
Decorah	Winneshich, Iowa	C Day
Grand River	Wayne, Iowa	Harvey B Duncan

Names Changed:
Huntington, Morthampton Co, Va, changed to Cherry Store.
Grind Stone, Daviess Co, Mo, changed to Victoria.
Ulso, Wash Co, Wis, changed to Mitchell.
Linn, Monroe Co, Iowa, changed to Lagrange.

Millard Fillmore, Pres of the U S A, recognizes Jose Maria Gaitan, who has been appointed Consul Gen of the Republic of New Granada, for the U S A. Mar 21, 1851. Also, J de Fremery, who has been appointed Consul of Mecklenburg-Schwerin, for San Francisco, in Calif. Mar 24, 1851.

Valuable bldg lot, with a large stone foundation, near the residence of W W Corcoran, at auction, on Apr 5: square 165, in Davidson's subdivision, on H st & Conn ave, adjoining the spacious bldg of Com Shubrick. There is erected on it a new bluestone foundation for a house 36 X 58 feet, with petition walls all laid in hydraulic cement. -A Green, auct

Geo F Dyer, [late of the firm of Dyer & Brother,] Real Estate & Stock Broker, offers his services in the purchase of real estate & stocks: ofc 10th & Pa ave.

Circuit Court of Wash Co, D C-in Chancery. Thos Blagden, vs the heirs at law of Jas Hoban, deceased. John F Ennis, trustee, reports the sale of lot 16 in square 80, for $438 42-100, & the undivided half of square n w of square 695, for the $70, to John F Callan, & the purchaser has complied with the terms of the sale.
–John A Smith, clk

Senate: 1-Cmte on Naval Affairs: asked to be discharged from the further consideration of the memorial of A G Benson: which was agreed to. 2-Cmte of Claims: bill for the relief of Danl Winslow. 3-Ordered that Fontaine J Davenport, Alpheus S F Davenport, John B Eddins, Jacob Hickman, Hannibal Faulk, Morgan O Ross, Eli W Ross, the heirs of Jas L Henderson, C H Morrison, & A P Brittingham, severally have leave to withdraw their petitions & papers.

Criminal Court-Wash-Wed. 1-Chas Weidig, convicted of willful & corrupt perjury in 2 cases, was sentenced, in one case, to be imprisoned 4 years in the penitentiary. In the other a nolle prosequi was entered. The sentence to take effect from & after Mar 31. 2-Chas Brandt, alias Bentz, sentenced to 4 years in the penitentiary: effective Mar 31. 3-Augustus Honschild, convicted of forgery upon the Gov't in 2 cases, was sentenced to 4 years in the penitentiary. 4-Henry Buete, convicted of perjury, was sentenced to 4 years in the penitentiary, to commence 2 days from & after the rising of the Circuit Court, the prisoner's counsel having taken exceptions to the proceedings in the Circuit Court.

The 17 year old son of widow Angell, of Pawtuxet, R I, was shot through the heart on Sat, while on a gunning excursion. One of his companions carried his gun carelessly, & it went off. The poor lad screamed, fell senseless, & died in 10 minutes.

Mrd: on Mar 18, at N Y, by Rev Mr Carder, Lt Henry W Stanton, U S Dragoons, to Miss Sarah Macomb, daughter of the late Maj Gen Macomb, U S Army.

FRI MAR 28, 1851
For sale: the elegant & commodious House now occupied by the Sec of the Navy, on H st. Apply to Dr Frailey, Gen Land Ofc.

The death of Mr Ferdinand Suydam, of the firm of Boyd & Suydam, & formerly of Suydam, Sage & Co, of N Y, occurred at Buffalo on Mar 23, from a stroke of paralysis. He was one of the oldest & most respected merchants, being in business over 40 years.

Notice: All persons indebted to the estate of Robt T Brown, deceased, for groceries, etc, are to settle their accounts, as I desire to close the business as early as possible. Mr J Shaw is duly authorized to settle the same, & will remain at the store in Jackson Hall with Messrs Brashear & Scott for that purpose. –Philip P Brown, adm

Commission on Claims against Mexico: 1-Memorial of Pierre Soule, atty of Ernest Eude, Clement Duhamel, & Jos Dirbis, the firm of Eude & Co, of New Orleans, claiming for the American registered schnr **Fraternitie** & her cargo, captured & destroyed at Nautla, on May 13, 1847: claim not valid against the Republic of Mexico: not received. 2-Memorial of Jas W Zacharie, assignee of Francis Cheti, claiming for the value of the schnr **Constitution** & her cargo, condemned at Alvarado, in 1824, by a prize court: claim is valid against the Republic of Mexico for the value of the vessel only, & the same was allowed accordingly: amount to be awarded subject to the future action of the Board. 3-Memorial of Andrew J Brame, filed on Mar 25, for losses sustained by the capture of the schnr **Julius Caesar** in 1837: ordered to be received: claim was valid against the Republic of Mexico, & same was allowed: amount to be awarded subject to the future action of the Board. 4-Memorial of Jos Bosque, claiming for seizure of cargo of brig **Harriet**, driven on shore near Tampico, in Mar, 1824: claim was valid against the Republic of Mexico, & same was allowed: amount to be awarded subject to the future action of the Board.

Mr Walter Edelin, a highly respectable citizen of PG Co, Md, was accidentally shot on Tue. His son had been out hunting, & on his return placed his gun against the front door of his father's dwlg. Mr Edelin opened the door to go out, the gun fell & went off, the contents lodging in his leg, just below the knee. Dr Bayne was soon in attendance, & found it necessary to amputate the leg, but it availed not. Mr Edelin lingered until night, when death put an end to his sufferings. –Alex Gaz

Patrick Waters, a boy employed in Scarlett, Dodd & Co's Suspender Factory, at the Hedenberg Works, Newark, N J, came to a shocking death on Tue. He was caught by the arm in a belt attached to the machinery, & was revolved around the shaft for nearly 2 minutes, before he could be extricated. He was taken up dead.

Died: in the city of Richmond, Va, after a few hours illness, Rev John Schermerhorn, in his 65th year. He was an ofcr under Gen Jackson's administration as Indian agent in the Western States, & was at the time of his death attending to some lands he had recently gained by a suit in Richmond. This notice is given that his family & friends may learn of his death, & that he had every attention paid him in his last hours. [No death date given-current item.]

Circuit Court of Wash Co, D C-in Equity. Tweedy, Mozier & Co, vs A Coquillard & Geo W Ewing. The dfndnt, Alexis Coquillard, was indebted to the cmplnts, in 1841, in the sums of $4,212.31, $4,359.74, & $300, for which he gave his notes, which they still hold, & which are unpaid; that, as collateral securities for those debts, he assigned to them the notes & mortages of 3rd parties, which they have endeavored to collect, & of the proceeds of which they render an account, showing a balance still due to them of not less than $6,800; that Coquillard, in 1841, as further collateral security for said debt, assigned to the the proceed of certain claims, of which a list is filed with the bill, which had been allowed by Com'r W B Mitchell in favor of certain citizens of the U S against the Indians, under the treaty with the Ottowas, Chippewas, & Potawattamies, which said claims had been purchased by Coquillard, & he had procured powers of atty, to be executed by the claimants to Suydam & Kevan of N Y; that the said assignment by Coquillard to the claimants embraced so much of said claims as should be left after said Suydam & Kevan had been satisfied of a debt due by Coquillard to them; that Suydan & Kevan assigned the whole of said claims to cmplnts; that by an act of Congress, of Sep 30, 1850, the said claims were ordered to be paid by the Treasury Dept; that Coquillard, confederating with said Geo W Ewing, & intending thereby to defeat & defraud cmplnts, subsequently procured from the said persons, to whom the said sum had been adjudicated by said Com'r Mitchell, powers of atty, in the name of said Ewing, & revoking the said powers previously given to said Suydam & Kevan, & the said Ewing is now claiming the said sums of money. The bill prays for an account of the amounts due by Coquillard to cmplnts, & a decree for its payment, & an injunction to restrain Coquillard, Ewing, or any one else, from receiving the said sums of money until the further order of the court. Coquillard & Ewing both reside out of the jurisdiction of this court. They are to appear on or before the 3rd Mon of Oct next. By order of the Court: John A Smith, clerk

Hon Thos Burnside died on Tue last, at the residence of his son-in-law, W E Morris, of Germantown. He was one of the State of Pa's Reps in Congress 30 odd years ago. He was in his 68th year at the time of his decease.

SAT MAR 29, 1851
Commission on Claims against Mexico: 1-Memorial of Mary S Wetmore, admx of her husband, Alphonso Wetmore, deceased, claiming for duties illegally levied at Chihuahua, in 1828: suspended on Mar 17: memorial does not set forth a valid claim against the Republic of Mexico: ordered not to be received. 2-Memorial of Wm B Hatch: claiming for overcharge of tonnage duties at Vera Cruz in 1843: valid claim against the Republic of Mexico: allowed accordingly: amount to be awarded subject to the future action of the Board. 3-Memorial of Abner Woodworth, claiming for expulsion from Parras, on Dec 24, 1846, & for consequent losses: not valid claim against the Republic of Mexico: not allowed.

Senate: 1-Ordered: Leave to withdraw the documents of H J McClintock, Harrison Gill, & Mansfield Carter, for compensation for services rendered at the Great Namshaw, sub-agency of the Sac & Fox Indians. 2-Ordered: that Fred'k Vincent, adm of Mezchase & Malett, have leave to withdraw the documents relating to said claim.

Died: on Mar 12, in New Orleans, Jas W Doughty, a highly respectable & esteemed merchant of St Louis, Mo, aged 35 years.

Foreign Items: 1-Chas Stanhope, Earl F Harrington, Viscount Petersham, & Baron Harrington is dead. In his early days he was an intimate companion of George IV, then Prince Regent. His wife was Miss Maria Foote, the celebrated actress, by whom he leaves an only daughter, Lady Jane St Maur Blanche Stanhope. [No death date given-current item.] 2-Napoleon Junot, Duke of Abrantes, elder of the 2 sons who survived the Marshal, has just died, in his 44th year, in a lunatic asylum near Paris. [No death date given-current item.]

Died: on Mar 25, at his residence, in PG Co, Md, Clement Baden, in his 69th year. During the late war with England, he held a commission in the service of his native State, & was frequently called into active service. In later life he filled for many years the ofc of magistrate, with credit to himself & usefulness to the public. He has left a numerous & highly respectable family to mourn his loss.

MON MAR 31, 1851
On Sat last, the dead body of Benj Young, an old resident of Wash City, who had been missing by his family for several days, was discovered in the Potomac, near the Long Bridge. The Coroner, with the jury, returned a verdict in conformity to the facts as they appeared in evidence.

John H Cooke elected Cashier of the Farmers' Bank of Va, in place of John G Blair, deceased.

Wash City Ordinance: 1-Act for the relief of John Brown: $20 to be paid him for a reimbursement of money paid by him for a stable license, the property used by him as such destroyed by fire.

Dr Jas M Alden, one of the Associate Physicians at the Marine Hospital, Staten Island, died on Wed of typhus fever.

The Harrisburg American says that Mr Callender, of York, died suddenly in the cars on his way home on Thu. He had just effected an insurance upon his life in the sum of $5,000 in the Keystone Mutual Ins Co a few hours before, & left Harrisburg in apparent health.

The Portsmouth [Va] Whig of Wed: murder was committed at Deep Creek, in this county, last night, by Uriah Cherry by shooting. The murdered man was his brother, Solomon Cherry. [Apr 3rd newspaper: Uriah Cherry was arrested on Thursday, not far from his own dwlg. The prisoner's own daughter was the only witness to the bloody deed.]

Dissolution of copartnership existing under the firm of Lusby & Duvall, by mutual consent. The business will be conducted by W T Duvall. –Jos Lusby, W T Duvall

Explosion of fire-damp in the Wash Co coal mines, at **Fort Griffith**, Pa, on Mar 21, which resulted in the death of two of the number, Messrs Nesbit.

Commission on Claims against Mexico: 1-Memorial of Francis Meyer, claiming for advances & services in the expedition of Gen Mina, in 1816, [suspended on Jun 17, 1850,] was again examined: claim not valid against the Republic of Mexico: same was not received. 2-Memorial of Mgt Ward, admx of Elliot Ward, deceased, master of the schnr **St Croix**, claiming for losses by the seizure of said schnr, & imprisonment of person, at Aransas bay, in 1834: claim was valid and allowed: amount to be awarded subject to the future action of the Board.

Died: in Wash, Jas Causten, infant son of Manuel & Mary de Carvallo, of Chili: born on the 16th & died on the 30th of Mar, 1851-10 days after his mother.

Died: on Mar 30, Mrs Elenor Harbaugh, consort of Jos Harbaugh, in her 69th year. Her funeral is on Tue at 10 o'clock.

Died: on Mar 29, Sally Bogan Ott, in her 12th year, 3rd daughter of John D & Mary Ann Ott, of Wash City. Her funeral is from the residence of her father, on Vt ave, between H & I sts, at 3 p m, this day.

TUE APR 1, 1851
Monument Hill Ice Depot: subscriber is able to supply the public with a choice article of ice during the ensuing season. –Jno Pettibone

Valuable lots for sale in the business part of Wash City: lot 3 & half of lot 5 in square 382, Louisiana ave. Lot 3 in square 260, on the Canal, between 13th & 14th sts. Lot 5, in square 260. Lot 3 in square 229, on Ohio ave. Lot 8 in square 324, on C st, near 14th sts. Apply to Edmund Law Rogers, 12 South Fred'k st, Balt, Md.

Wanted: a good cook, one who thoroughly understands her business, & can bring good recommendations, may hear of a situation by applying at the residence of Rev S Pyne, corner of H st & Vt ave.

Mr Abiel Chandler died on the 22nd ultimo, at Walpole, N J, & has left by will $50,000 to Dartmouth College, to establish a school of instruction in the practical & useful arts of life. He has also given $1,600 to the N H Asylum for the Insane, & made many bequests to his relatives & friends. The N H Asylum for the insane is made residuary legatee.

Household & kitchen furniture at auction: on Apr 4, at the residence of the late Dr J B Waugh, on F st, between 13th & 14th sts: also a family horse, carriage & harness. –Dyer & McGuire, aucts

Trustee's sale of valuable house & lot: Chancery-Circuit Court of Wash Co, D C. Wiltberger et al vs Cain et al. Undersigned will sell at auction: the whole of lot 8 in square 728, Wash City, & part of lot 7 in said square, adjoining said lot 8, fronting on East Capitol st, together with a 3 story brick house & back bldg, & stabling. Sale on the premises on Apr 23. The property has been occupied as a boarding-house for a number of years. –Chas H Wiltberger, trustee -Amon Green, auct

For sale: highly improved Farm of 300 acres, whereon the subscriber resides, in Fairfax Co, Va. Also, another well improved farm of about 130 acres, adjoining the above. I also have the agency for selling another small Farm, of about 100 acres, with good improvements on it, adjoining both of the above tracts. Apply in person or by letter to the subscriber; if by post, direct to **Prospect Hill**, Va.
–Thos Ap C Jones, U S Navy, near Prospect Hill, Va.

Sale of **Clifton Farm**: having determined to move to the West, I will sell this farm on which I live, called **Clifton**, in Fauquier Co, Va, 4 miles west of Warrenton, containing between 700 & 800 acres. The improvements consist of a large frame dwlg-house, a large stone barn, & grist-mill; stabling for 20 horses. –A M Payne References: R E Scott, Fauquier; Duff Green, Falmouth; B Day, Warrenton; Gen Jno R Wallace, Alexandria.

Yesterday, John Heard, an active & ingenious rigger, fell from a scaffold near the top of the wall of the east wing of the Patent Ofc to the 3rd floor of that bldg, being a distance of about 30 feet. He had both legs broken & was seriously injured in the head. He was taken to the Wash Infirmary, where prompt attention was paid to him. He is in a very painful & dangerous situation. [Apr 2nd newspaper: the unfortunate rigger Hurse, who was so dreadfully injured by falling from the scaffold in the interior of the Patent Ofc on Mon, died of his injuries yesterday.] [Note: Heard/Hurse.]

Died: on Mar 31, Thos Dixon, son of John & Mary Ann Hands, aged 8 years. His funeral will take place from his father's residence on 4½ st, at 4 o'clock this afternoon.

Wholesale larceny of the Ericsson Boats, a transportation line between Phil & Balt, was detected. Geo Bennett, Wm Cole, & H T Lowry were arrested in Phil on Mon last. These were employed on the steamer **Union**, & many articles were recovered from the house of one of them. They were all committed for further examination. On Thu, Thos R Scott, the agent of the company in Phil, came down to this place & caused warrants to be issued for John Price, Francis Devalenger, John Iler, & Richd Wingate, all residents of Chesapeake City, & employed by the company. Their premises revealed a large quantity of goods of various descriptions. The Elkton Whig says that it is confidently asserted by some that Wingate & Devalenger were not aware the goods were stolen.

Orphans Court of Wash Co, D C. In the case of Saml S Williams, administrator de bonis non of Edw Worthington, deceased, the adm & Court have appointed Apr 22 next, for the settlement & distribution of the estate of said deceased, of the assets in hand, so far as the same have been collected & turned into money.
–Ed N Roach, Reg/o wills

WED APR 2, 1851
Orphans Court of Wash Co, D C: sale on Apr 7, 1851, of the goods & chattels, 3 chairs, 1 table, shaving horse, 3 spades, & bucket, the property of the late Adam Sweitzer, of said county, on the premises lately occupied by the said deceased, near the Catholic burying ground, or Mr Gilman's residence, on the boundary line.
–A E L Keese, adm

Millard Fillmore, Pres of the U S A, recognizes Geo Aikin, who has been appointed Consul of Her Britannic Majesty, for the State of Calif, to reside at San Francisco.
-Mar 29, 1851

Alleged Legislative corruption: an investigation is going on in the N Y Senate relating to charges made against the Sgt-at-Arms of that body, Mr Geo W Bull, to the effect that he, seconded his certain members, has been attempting to levy black mail on the proprietors of gambling houses in N Y, by promising to suppress a bill pending in the Legislature for the more effectual suppression of gambling.

The Hon Wm Clark died at his residence in Dauphin Co, Pa, on Fri last. As State Treasurer, Member of Congress, & Treasurer of the U S, Judge Clark became extensively & favorably known, not only throughout Pa, but the Union.
–Harrisburg Telegraph

Col Spencer, a citizen of Lebanon, Ky, was accidentally killed by his own son on Wed. They had gone out together to the barn to shoot rats, when the unfortunate shot was fired. The father died almost instantly. The son is an estimable young man of 21 years, & suffers indescribably.

Mount Hope Boarding School for Boys, Loudoun Co, Va, will commence on Apr 4. Scholars sent to the Point of Rocks will be conveyed to the school free of charge by giving timely notice. Address Eli P Hirst, **Mount Hope**, near Snickersville, Loudoun Co, Va.

Valuable lot at Public sale: J W Osborn & wife vs Chas S Matthews & others, heirs at law of Wm P Matthews, deceased. Sale on Apr 25, of lot 2 in square 488, fronting on E st, near the Judiciary Square, now divided into 2 good bldg lots. –H Naylor, Chas Pettit, Lewis Johnson, J F Callan, & W Redin, Com'rs. -A Green, auctioneer

Orphans Court of Wash Co, D C. Letters testamentary on the personal estate of Wm Ward, late of said county, deceased. –Wm H Ward, exc

Died: on Apr 1, Laura Virginia, infant daughter of Wm A & Wilmina E Richardson.

THU APR 3, 1851
Mrd: on Apr 2, at St John's Church, Balt, by Rev Mr Webster, Mr Geo R P Britt to Miss Georgianna H Mitchell, both of Balt, Md.

Gentlemen invited to attend the examination of the Cadets in Jun next at the Military Academy at West Point:
1-Robt H Gardiner, Maine
2-Wm Dwight, Mass
3-Prof A W Smith, Conn
4-Hon Francis Granger, N Y
5-Gen Jas L Gaither, Md
7-Prof Jas Phillips, N C
8-Col Wm P Bowen, Ga
9-Anthony H Dunlevy, Ohio
10-Henry W Huntington, La
11-Dr Saml Breck, Ala
12-Hon Thos Randall, Fla
13-Rev John H Lathrop, L L D, Wisc
14-Gen Jesse B Browne, Iowa
15-Hon Jefferson Davis, Miss

Fire in North Woodstock, Ct: several days since. The house burnt is the gate-house on the turnpike, between the villages of North & South Woodstock. Mr Phillips, the tenant of the house, led himself & his wife, & rushed into the street. He went back to get the children who were asleep in the second story, but alas, too late. Three of the children died in the flames, & the 4th died soon after. Mr Phillips was injured so much as to lose his sight. He is an Englishman, & 3 of his children died by starvation & sickness in the Atlantic voyage, while the other four were reserved for an even more horrible death.

Postmaster Gen est'd the following new Post Ofcs for week ending Mar 29, 1851.

Ofc	County, State	Postmaster
Sprout Brook	Montgomery, N Y	Benj Wendell
Abbottsford	Westchester, N Y	Stephen Crosby
Willing	Alleghany, N Y	Hiram York
Dresserville	Cayuga, N Y	Arnold Swift

South Erin	Chemung, N Y	John Mitchell
Wyncoop's Creek	Chemung, N Y	Thos Sweet
May Flower	Otsego, N Y	Loring Dow
North Branch	Sullivan, N Y	Isaac R Clements
Alsion	Burlington, N J	W W Fleming
Mooreheadville	Erie, Pa	Jos T Morehead
Fostoria	Blair, Pa	Jacob Easterline
Benezette	Elk, Pa	David B Winslow
Smith's Cross Roads	Morgan, Va	John W Engle
Sun Rise	Bath, Va	John P Erwin
Osanippa	Chambers, Ala	Wm Hughes
Fair Play	Panola, Texas	Joshua F Gill
White Oak	Jefferson, Ark	Edw Bell
Ridge Post	Davidson, Tenn	Jonathan B Green
Hope	Stewart, Tenn	Wm C Jones
Fillmore	Bledsoe, Tenn	J R Wheeler
Long Hall	Caldwell, Ky	Alfred C Brown
Ophir	La Salle, Ill	C P Eastman
Aripe	Bureau, Ill	David Brown
Cheney's Grove	McLean, Ill	John Prother
Jamestown	Clinton, Ill	Wm H Uzzell
Plum Hill	Washington, Ill	Christian Ninelist
Leepertown	Bureau, Ill	Jas Nickerson
Moravis	Appanoose, Iowa	Edw Rich
Nottingham	Davis, Iowa	Benj Adams
Divide	Marion, Iowa	John A Scott
Poy Sippi	Marquette, Wis	Geo Hawley
Centre Creek	Iron, U Ter	Geo A Smith
Utah Lake	Utah, U Ter	Isaac Higbee
Miller's Creek	Davis, U Ter	John S Fullmer
Lecompte Valley	U Terr	Isaac Morley
Brownville	Ogden, U Ter	Isaac Clark

Names Changed:
1-Gilbertsville, Otsego Co, N Y, changed to Butternutts.
2-Sandy Creek, Mercer Co, Pa, changed to New Vernon.
3-Matthewsville, Pocahontas Co, Va, changed to Dunmore.
4-Beddington, Berkeley Co, Va, changed to Hainesville.
5-Buffalo Hill, Orange Co, N C, changed to Dial's Creek.
6-Moreauville, Avoyelles parish, La, changed to Borodino.
7-Lowryville, Madison Co, Ill, changed to Alhambra.
8-East Arena, Iowa Co, Wisc, changed to Dover.

Commission on Claims against Mexico: 1-Memorial of Terry & Angus, claiming detention of property at the siege at Puebla: valid & allowed accordingly. 2-Memorial of John Beider, claiming for damages by the seizure & condemnation of merchandise, at Cacatecas, in 1841: valid & allowed accordingly. 3-Memorial of Geo Lafler, Peter Lafler, & Tomaso Paroles de Walley, admx of Saml Walley, claiming for expulsion from Tampico on Jun 12, 1846, & for consequents stoppage of business & loss of property: valid and allowed accordingly. 4-Memorial of Hetty Green, admx of Pardon C Green, claiming for the seizure & detention of the ship **Transit**, of which he was master & owner, at Campeachy, in 1828: not valid claim against the Republic of Mexico: not allowed. 5-Memorial of Ashael P Brittingham, claiming for damages by seizure of the brig **Ophir**: examined. 6-Memorial of Gen Don Jose Maria Jarrero, claiming, as a Mexican citizen the amount of certain drafts originally made by Gen Herrera to cover advances by Bernard Bowdoin, a citizen of the U S, in aid of the early cause of Mexican independence, which drafts had, before the treaty of Guadalupe Hidalgo, been assigned to Gen Jarrero by Wm S Parrott, an American citizen, in payment of a debt: the Board said the former claim was definitely settled by the mixed commission under the convention of 1839, & that the memorial, consequently, be not received; that the late claim, however rightful against the Mexican Gov't, cannot be allowed, because, as not the property of an American citizen at the date of the treaty of Guadalupe Hidalgo, it was not meant to be protected by that treaty. 7-Memorial of Rufus K M Baynum & others, heirs at law of Jas P Baynum, deceased, claiming for injuries sustained by him in 1835 & 1836, while mate on the brig **Ophir**: ordered not to be received. 8-Memorial of Edwin Seagur, for himself & the other heirs of Lewis Seagur, claiming compensation for his services as an ofcr in the Mexican army: ordered not to be received. 9-Memorial of Geo W Van Stavoren, for seizure of tobacco at Vera Cruz in 1839, which was, on Feb 13 last, ordered to be reconsidered: nothing in the testimony proves the claim to be valid: not to be received. 10-Memorial of Jas W Zacharie, assignee of Asmus C Bredall, claiming for the assignor's false imprisonment & expulsion in 1845; he also is claiming for seizure & pillage of the schnr **Lodi** at Corpus Christi in 1838: first claim is valid & ordered to be received. The 2nd claim is not valid against the Republic of Mexico, & not allowed.

FRI APR 4, 1851

The Court House of Wellborn, Coffee Co, Ala, was burnt a few days ago, with all the county & circuit books, papers, & records of all descriptions. It is supposed to be the work of an incendiary.

The Pres of the U S has appointed the following Cadets "at large" to the Military Academy: Sons of ofcrs who were killed or died in service: Francis L Vinton, W H Penrose, J H Hill, Wm B Nowland, & Chas B Watson. Sons of ofcrs now in service: R B Screven, F L Childs, & A S Cunningham. From civil life: Jas O Whistler & N L Powers. Dist of Columbia: Edw W Williams.

We learn from the Phil papers that preparations are making for a large issue of <u>three cent pieces</u> from the U S Mint at an early day. By authority from the Treasury Dept, a great part of the silver bullion fund will be converted into these pieces.

We are informed that Rev David Caldwell, of Va, has accepted a call to become the Pastor of Christ Church, Gtwn. He was formerly located in Norfolk, whence he was appointed Chaplain to the Univ of Va, which compliment he concluded to decline, for the purpose of coming to Gtwn.

Terrible scenes at Socorro, New Mexico: 1-Capt Dobbins, formerly of the 3rd infty, who was a follower of the expedition as a hunter, killed a Mr Wakeman on the way up to El Paso, & afterwards committed suicide in San Elezario, at the quarters of Col McClellan. 2-On Feb 29 the robber band, seeking a man named Clarke, [E C Clarke, said to be son of J H Clarke, U S Senator from R I,] went to a fandango or dancing party where he was, & maltreated the whole party of men & females. The leader, Alex'r Young, assisted by John Wade, Marcus Butler, & Wm Craig, fell upon Clarke & gave him 9 or 10 mortal wounds. Chas Gates was badly shot. Wade, Butler, & Craig were searched for & seized by a large party of Americans & Mexicans. Young, the ringleader, escaped. A reward of $400 was offered for the arrest of Young. He was arrested on the 10th, brought to Socorro on the 11th, found guilty, condemned, & executed on the same tree where his companions had been hung. Maj Bartlett repeats that since these dreadful examples Socorro has been perfectly quiet & orderly.

Died: Mar 27, at Keokuk, Iowa, Geo Piercy, son of the late Capt John McKnight, of Alexandria, Va.

Harrisonburg Republican of Sat: Jas Henton, a young man, with several others, went to the house of Mr John Clatterbuck for the purpose of lynching him for some offence alleged against him; in attempting to break into the house of Clatterbuck, a son of Clatterbuck, 14 or 15 years of age, shot Henton, from the effects of which he died. Young Clatterbuck immediately gave himself up, but was promptly discharged.

Commission on Claims against Mexico: 1-Board re-examined the claim of John Powell, assignee of Thos Powell, in the case of the schnr **Escambria**: claim to be adjudged valid & allowed accordingly: the amount to be awarded subject to the future action of the Board. 2-Memorial of John C Gary, adm of Louis P Cook, claiming for losses sustained by the capture of the schnr **Susannah** in 1845: same be now received, & allowed accordingly: the amount to be awarded subject to the future action of the Board.

Sale by order of the Orphans Court of Wash Co, D C: on Apr 7, at the residence of the late Nicholas Travers, on Pa ave, between 12th & 13th sts: furniture, household effects, silver, & kitchen furniture & utensils. –Dyer & McGuire

Died: on Apr 3, after a painful illness, Capt Chas Bradford, of Duxbury, Mass, in his 85th year, long a respected citizen of Alexandria, & for some years past of Washington. His funeral is from the residence of his son-in-law, S Masi, on E st, between 9th & 10th sts, at half-past 3 o'clock this afternoon.

SAT APR 5, 1851

Southern paper announces the death of the late Gen Brooke, who will be remembered with what occurred on the Canada frontier during the war of 1812: One who served with him in the war of 1812, & knew him intimately, has often spoken in terms of the highest enthusiasm of his gallantry & generosity. At an early age he entered the army as Lt. The war of 1812 found him a Capt in the U S Infty. On the Canada frontier he was greatly distinguished, having been twice brevetted for brave & gallant conduct in action. When Gen Brown had fallen back from the Falls of Niagara, after the battle of Lundy's Lane, followed by a much superior force, he threw himself into **Fort Erie**, where he was besieged without other hope than that afforded by the gallantry of his small command, until reinforced by troops ordered from Plattsburg, a distance of 100 miles. The besiegers made gradual approaches every night, by throwing up embankments & digging entrenchments, secured by the darkness of the night. One night it was discovered, by the sound of labor & other circumstances, that they had approached so near that, unless they could be driven off before completing their work, their fire would be exceedingly disastrous to our troops within the fort. Gen Brown ordered battery & battery to open upon them without effect; owing to the darkness of the night no proper direction could be given to the shot. In this dilemma the gallant Brooke volunteered to convey to the works of the enemy a dark lantern, with which he climbed a tree, hanging it some distance above the enemy's works, leaving open a small aperture facing the fort, enabling the guns to be put in proper range to fire with precision on the working party. A few discharges only were requisite to drive them off with a loss, & save the fort. The siege was afterwards forcibly raised by a sortie, in which this gallant soldier bore a conspicuous part.

Richd R Sheckell, of Gtwn, has sued the old trustees of the Commonwealth [abolition] newspaper, at Boston, for libel, for having asserted that he had induced a colored man, Wm Ringold, to leave Mass & visit his friends in D C, where, it is alleged, Ringold was arrested & sold as a fugitive from bondage Damages are laid at $5,000, the writ returnable to the Supreme Judicial Court, to be holden at Springfield on the last Tue of the present month.

Mr Ashbel Mix, respectable farmer of Bristol, died Mar 26 from effects of a dose of corrosive sublimate, taken by mistake. It was prepared as a bed-bug poison. He was about 50 years of age.

The little Canal Steamer, launched last Mon at Easby's ship yard, has been viewed by many persons since her being moored in the Wash canal, in the rear of the Eagle Iron Works. Mr McKinstry says she, the steamer **Roselia of Washington**; measures 58 feet in length, & is 9½ feet in breadth. She was built for Messrs John Pettibone & Co of Wash City.

Wash Corp: 1-Ptn from Danl Rowland, for the remission of a fine: referred to the Cmte of Claims. 2-Bill for the relief of Jas H Shreeves & Harrison Taylor: passed. 3-Bill for the relief of Timothy O'Neale: referred to the Cmte in Improvements: passed. 4-Cmte of Claims: bill for the relief of J B Lokey: passed.

Boston Journal says that on Thu week a gentleman of that city invited all his surviving brothers & sisters, with their wives & husbands, to dine with him. They all responded to the call but one brother & the husband of one sister. Their ages were as followed:
Wm, 81/his wife-74   Seth, 66/his wife-58
David, 79   Sybil, 64/her husband-75
Abraham, 77   Marshall, 62/his wife-58
Polly, deceased/her husband-76   Darius, 57/his wife-42
Alice, 69/her husband-74   Almira, 56
Betsy, 68
The two absent were Chas, aged 71, & Almira's husband, whose age is not known. Two members of the family have died-one brother & one sister. [There is no surname given.]

Died: on Mar 30, at his residence, **Locust Grove**, PG Co, Md, in his 49th year, Benj M Duckett, after a brief but violent attack of inflammatory fever. He was extensively known & universally respected. He was devoted to the wants of his family in the various relations of husband, father, & master. He left a devoted wife & 5 children, with many relatives, friends, & acquaintances, to mourn his loss.

Wash City Ordinances. 1-Act for the relief of Berry & Mohun: sum of $92.23 be paid to them for repairing the roof of the City Hall. 2-Act for the relief of Jas Kanalay: fine imposed on a charge of forestalling the market, is remitted: provided Kanalay pay the costs of prosecution. 3-Act for the relief of Walter Hawkins: fine imposed for violation of law in relation to free negroes, is remitted. 4-Act for the relief of J B Lakey: to be paid $43.25, for work done in Ward 7. 5-Act for the relief of Wm B Wilson: to be paid $48.65, balance due him for laying certain flag footways in the 3rd Ward. 6-Act for the relief of Timothy O'Neale: pay him $22.16, the sum due him for materials furnished for laying flag footways.

Mrs J E Dow has taken the house recently occupied by Mr Cochran, on F st, between 13th & 14th sts, where she has 2 or 3 large airy rooms unoccupied. She can also accommodate a few day boarders.

In Chancery, Apr 1, 1851. Thos C Worthington et al vs Thos H Kent et al. The object of the petition of Jas Kent, adm of Jos Kent, filed in the above cause, is to have the distributive share of Jos Kent, jr, of the proceeds of sale of Sarah Salter's real estate, applied to the payment of a claim against said Jos Kent, jr, & Thos P W Neale, on their joint & several single bill to the said petitioner for $1,117, with interest from Feb 11, 1840. The petition states the execution of said single bill; that the same with interest is wholly due; that the said Kent & Neale have no property in this State out of which payment of the said debt can be enforced, & that the same will be lost to the petitioner unless the said share be applied to the payment thereof. It also states that the said Kent & Neale reside beyond this State, to wit, in the State of Arkansas. Kent & Neale are to appear in this Court on or before Sep 20 next.
–Louis Gassaway, Reg Cur Can/Wash

MON APR 7, 1851
On Sat, as a laborer, Michl Burns, was employed in pulling down the walls of the bldg east of Browns' hotel, when the chimney in falling struck his head & inflicted a fatal injury. He died yesterday morning. He was a native of Ireland, aged about 33 years, & a single man. His body was interred yesterday evening.

Lewis Sinsheimer & Co, have opened this day, Apr 1, a new store, with a new & choice stock of Spring Clothing, called the Union Clothing Store, near the corner of 3rd st.

Navy Dept: Gen Order: Apr 7, 1851. The Navy Dept announces to the Ofcrs of the Navy & Marine Corps the demise of Cmdor Alex'r S Wadsworth, who died at his residence, in Wash City, on Apr 5. –Will A Graham, Sec of the Navy

The Balt Patriot of Sat announces the death of Col Jacob Small, formerly Mayor of Balt, & for many years one of its most exemplary & popular citizens.

The ship **Ivanhoe** lost: from N Y for Liverpool, was seen ashore on the Round Shoal of Nantucket Feb 24, with all sail set, by the ship **Joseph Walker**, arrived here from N Y: wind S S E, moderate. Pieces of her wreckage were picked up off Nantucket. All must have perished, unless rescued by outward bound vessels. She was in command of Capt Magee, with a crew of 28 persons. The passengers were: Achison Moore, North of Ireland; John Irwin, Peter Kelley, ___ Condon, Jas Clark, Thos Carter, Jos Rushworth & wife, Thos Metcalfe, John Crosby, Thos Smith, John Kearns, Wm White, Thos Brennan, Michl Shograsby, & Christy Conner, German.

Shocking death occurred on the Hudson river railroad on Thu last. Mr Christopher Jaycox, aged about 60 years, was struck by a train as he walked on the track. The deceased was an industrious & temperate man, the owner of quite a large landed estate, & the head of a respectable family. —Poughkeepsie American

Naval: Cmdor Geisinger is appointed Govn'r of the U S Naval Asylum in Phil, to take command on the 1st of May. —North American

Orphans Court of Wash Co, D C. Letters of administration on the personal estate of Thos H Gilliss, late of Wash Co, deceased. —W B Todd, adm

Died: on Apr 5, Cmdor Alex'r S Wadsworth, of the U S Navy, in his 61st year. His funeral will take place from his late residence, **Franklin Row**, at 12 o'clock on Tue.

Died: on Apr 5, after a painful & protracted illness, Mrs Harriet Knobloch, in her 43rd year. Her funeral is today at 3 o'clock, from her late residence on 19th at H st.

Commission on Claims against Mexico: 1-Memorial of Aaron Leggett, claiming for damages by the production of forged documents to the defeat of his claim before the Mixed Commission: allowed. 2-Consideration of the several memorials of Mich Dougherty, Ferdinand Clark, & Danl E Smith, claiming for losses sustained by the seizure & confiscation of the schnr **Louisiana** in 1824: allowed. 3-Memorial of Edw M Robinson, exc of Jos Fleming, who was surviving partner of the firm of Fleming & Marshall, claiming for duties illegally exacted at Tampico in 1839 & 1840: allowed. 4-Memorial of Walter L Cox, adm of Jas G A McKenney, claiming for the destruction of his property at Chiapas, in May, 1841: claim is not valid against the Republic of Mexico: not allowed.

N Y, Apr 4, 1851. Sudden death in N Y C yesterday, of Philo Rust, for many years the keeper of the best hotel in Syracuse. He was boarding at the Astor House at the time, with his wife. It appears that he got into a carriage & went up to 9th st to consult his physician in regard to the gout, with which he was at times afflicted. Arriving at the place, & opening the coach door, the driver found Mr Rust in a fit. He conveyed him into the physician's, where he expired before the driver had time to return with his wife.

TUE APR 8, 1851
The Hon Ransom Halloway, late a member of the 31st Congress from the State of N Y, died at Mount Pleasant, PG Co, Md, on Apr 6, of typhoid fever & inflammation of the bowels, after an illness of about 2 weeks. He was on a visit to his wife's relations prior to his return home. His remains will be taken to N Y for interment.

Teacher wanted: a young gentleman, qualified to teach the classics & the higher English branches. Address the undersigned at Upperville, Fauquier Co, Va.
–Henry T Dixon

Howard Gaz: a daughter of Mr Larkin Murphy, aged 5 years, & a daughter of Mr Seth W Warfield, aged 4 years, were burnt to death at Cooksville, a few days ago, by their clothes taking fire.

Notice to residuary legates of Nelson Reed, deceased. By decree of Balt Co Court, as Court of Equity, dated Mar 22, 1851, & passed in a cause therein pending between Jas Dudley, for himself & other legatees of Nelson Reed, deceased, & Wm Baker & Wm Geo Baker, trustees under the will of said Nelson Reed, the Auditor of Balt Co Court, in order to a distribution of the funds in the hands of said trustees, is required & directed to ascertain & report to said court, upon the information & proofs that may be produced, who were the children, of Mary Barton, Rebecca Myers, Eliz Eichelberger, [who were sisters of testator's wife, Nancy Reed,] Jos Burneston, [who was a brother of testator's wife,] Jas Reed, Isaac Reed, [who were brothers of the testator,] Eliz Maril, Rebecca Lloyd, & Jane Bewley, [who were sisters of the testator,] living at the death of Nancy Reed, the testator's widow, who died Sep 29, 1849, or having died before said Nancy Reed, left issue living at the death of Nancy Reed, & what were the names & relationship of such issue then living of such children deceased prior to the death of said Nancy Reed, &, also, to ascertain & report whether Saunders Alex'r Reed, Robt S Reed, [brothers of the testator,] & Anna Toreyson, [sister of the testator,] or either, & which of them were dead at the time of the death of said Nancy Reed, & if either of them were so dead, who were the children of such decedent living at the death of said Nancy Reed, or having died before said Nancy Reed, left issue living at the death of said Nancy Reed, & what were the names & degrees of relationship of such issue so living at the death of said Nancy Reed; & also to ascertain & report who were the children of Dinah Dudley, living at the death of said Nancy, or having died before the said Nancy Reed, left issue living at her death, & the names & degree of relationship of such issue; & also to report, if any of the parties entitled & living at Nancy Reed's death, have since died, who are now the personal reps of such decedents, & upon the expiration of the time limited in this notice to report to the said Court the persons who may have established their title to participate in said fund. Now, in pursuance of said decree, all persons entitled under the will of said Nelson Reed, deceased, are notified to appear & produce the proofs of their title before the said court, on or before Sep 1, 1851, & that in default of such appearance & proof, the parties so failing to appear will be excluded from any participation in said funds, & that the same will be distributed among the parties so appearing & proving their title.
–Wm Baker, Wm Geo Baker, trustees, Balt

Hon Geo P Marsh, U S Minister at Constantinople, is with his family making the tour of Egypt & Palestine. At the last letter received by their friends, they were in Cairo.

From Calif: a gambler named Wroe had been condemned & hung under the Lynch code at Sacramento city. His offence was the shooting of Mr Myers for interfering in a quarrel, & he was executed in 5 hours afterwards.

Mrd: on Mar 31, at Columbia, Fluvanna Co, Va, by Rev Mr Clover, Jas M Estes, of Palmyra, to Susan R, daughter of Jos Hodgson.

Marshal's sale: by writ of fieri facias, under the lien law: public sale on May 5, of one 2 story frame dwlg-house erected upon lot 3 in square 282, in Wash City, seized & levied upon as the property of John McRoddy, & will be sold to satisfy Judicials 63, to Mar, 1851, in favor of Mary A Harvey & Michl Coombs, adms of Henry Harvey. -Richd Wallach, Marshal D C

Commission on Claims against Mexico: 1-Memorial of Danl N Pope, claiming for costs illegally exacted at Tabasco in 1833, & for losses arising from destruction of property in 1834: claim not valid against the Republic of Mexico: not allowed. 2-Memorial of John M Togno, which was rejected on Feb 3 last: same is valid & allowed. 3-Memorial of Jas Mac Gregor, adm of Wally & Donaldson, claiming for violation of charter & stopping of cotton mill at Tampico in 1836: not valid against the Republic of Mexico: not allowed.

WED APR 9, 1851
Postmaster Gen has est'd the following new Post Ofcs for week ending Apr 5, 1851.

Ofc	County, State	Postmaster
Hazardville	Hartford, Conn	D B Dorman
Pendleton Centre	Niagara, N Y	Henry Pickard
Allensville	Allegany, N Y	Saml Southard
Mixtown	Tioga, Pa	Jas Pritchard
Columbia Centre	Licking, Ohio	Jacob Cornell
Ramer	Montgomery, Ala	Wm C Gunter
Huddleston	Pike, Ark	Nathl Gray
Cane Bottom	Lauderdale, Tenn	Wm H Cowan
Mil Institute	Franklin, Ky	J T Dickinson
	Crawford, Ill	S G Swearingen
	Atchinson, Mo	R D Russell
Plainfield	Bates, Mo	Robt S Carpenter
Burbois	Franklin, Mo	John Seaton
Leland's Mills	Sauk, Wis	L B Needham
Moundville	Marquette, Wis	R B Brown
Marion	Konosha, Wis	Saml T Rice

Elk Hart	Sheboygan, Wis	Fred D Spalding
Eau Pleipe	Portage, Wis	John B Dube
Florence	Fremont, Iowa	Jas H Clarke
Osage	Fremont, Iowa	Harlow C Kingston
Nicot	Linn, Iowa	Geo C Perkins
Glenn's	Clark, Iowa	Alonzo Williams

Names Changed:
1-McArthurstown, Athens Co, Ohio, changed to McArthurs.
2-Maple Bottom, Iredell Co, N C, changed to Rocky Creek.
3-Knob Creek, Barren Co, Ky, changed to Antioch.
4-Mortimer, Lake Co, Ill, changed to Newport.

Jas Nolan, a waiter on board the steamship **Arctic**, was arrested at N Y on Fri for taking up a letter at the post ofc belonging to Wm Leery, containing drafts for $2,000, which Nolan got cashed. The prisoner has been identified by the post ofc clerk, but the money has not been found.

Important from the Plains. 1-Lt Myers, 5th Infty, just in from ***Fort Arbuckle***, says that the traders from the Prairies bring the report of the death of Wild Cat & two of his companions, Chickasaws. It is reported that they were killed by the Comanches. 2-The Wichetaws, Kechies, & Osages have banded together for the purpose of exterminating the Tonkaways, who are cannibals, & very much dreaded by all the other tribes.

Appointments by the Pres: 1-Wm H C Mills, of Ga, to be U S Marshal for the district of Ga, in place of W M Brown, resigned. 2-Chas W Davis, to be Sec of the Board of Com'rs on Claims against Mexico, in place of Edw W Johnston, resigned. 3-Jos N Fearson & Pierce Shoemaker, to be Justices of the Peace for Wash Co, D C.

Hon Wm Case, Whig, was re-elected Mayor of the city of Cleveland, Ohio, on Apr 7, by 350 majority. A majority of the Council Whig. Cleveland, is in Mr Senator Wade's Congressional District.

Wash Corp: 1-Ptn from J R McCorkle for the remission of a fine: referred to the Cmte of Claims. 2-Ptn from Jas Handley & others, in reference to depositing gas tar in square 454: referred to the Cmte on Police. 4-Act making an appropriation to pay a balance due to Caleb Buckingham: passed. 5-Act for the relief of John A Sauer: passed. 6-Ptn of Wm Cammack & others, for grading & gravelling 14th st west, from K to Boundary st: referred to the Cmte on Improvements. 7-Ptn of C Edmonston & others for improvement of N Y ave: referred to the Cmte on Improvements. 8-Ptn of Benj Bean, praying indemnity for the loss of a horse killed by falling into the canal at the bridge on L st; & also the ptn of sundry citizens on the same subject: referred to the Cmte of Claims.

Parasols for sale: a large stock, at very low prices. –W M Shuster & Co, 8th & Pa ave.

In Chancery: Circuit Court of Wash Co, D C: Edw Owen vs John Ennis & al. The Trustee in the above cause reports the sale, on Nov 13, 1850, of lots 5 & 6, in subdivision of part of lot 5, in square 518, in Wash City, to Edw Owen for $570, & the purchaser has since complied with the terms of sale. –Jno A Smith, clerk

Edmanuel Fisher, charged with stealing sundry articles, property of John Dalton, was arrested yesterday afternoon at the railroad depot by ofcrs Busher & Westerfield.

Telegraphic Report: Balt, Apr 8. Lt Jas Ridgely, who met with a severe fall from the Exchange Hotel some time ago, is now dangerously ill, & not expected to survive many hours. [Apr 10th newspaper: Lt Ridgely died on Apr 8. He was a young man of excellent heart & undaunted courage, & his death will be mourned by many warm friends.]

The remains of the late Cmdor Wadsworth were interred yesterday in the Congressional Cemetery with the honors due to his rank in the U S Navy. A company of Marines preceded by the Marine Bank, playing a solemn dirge, formed an escort to the funeral cavalcade, which consisted of naval ofcrs, friends of the deceased, & strangers.

For rent: well furnished house, nearly new. Apply to D A Gardner, N Y ave & 15th.

THU APR 10, 1851
From New Mexico: a short time before the party left Santa Fe, a body of Indians made a descent on Dr Conelly's ranch, & drove away between 7,000 & 9,000 sheep. The Dr had been particularly unfortunate in the frequency of such losses. Much danger is apprehended from them during this spring. The Utahs have leagued with the Apaches for the purpose of infesting the Santa Fe train near its termination in the Territory. The two tribes will be joined by the Pueblos. Some alarm is felt for the mail carriers, no less than for the traders & emigrants. Mr Merritt finished taking the census of New Mexico only a few days before starting for the Senate. The Territory contains a population of 61,574, of which 650 are Americans. Among the Mexicans over 20 years of age there is one in every 103 who has learned to read.

C W Roback, astrologer, was arrested in his rooms in Phil on Mon, charged with swindling a colored man out of a sum of money by gammoning him into the belief that he could cure his wife of some ailment by the power of conjuration. The conjurer was taken through the streets in his cap of crescent & stars. He was ordered to find bail in $1,000 to answer.

Died: on Apr 8, in Gtwn, of consumption, Miss Mary Miller, daughter of Wm Parsons. Her funeral is this afternoon, at 3 o'clock, from the residence of her father, on High st.

Official: Dept of State: Wash, Apr 8, 1851. Information received from Amos B Corwin, U S Consul at Panama, that the following citizens of the U S, places of residence not known, have died in the American hospital at that place, & that no effects belonging to any of them were left in his possession, viz: Thos Jones, John M Devor, & Jas Bird, from the American schnr **Juliet**.

Trustee's sale: by order of Montg Co Court, at a Court of Equity, in the case of Adam Robb & others vs Henry Harding, adm of Thos F W Vinson & others: public sale on May 28, at Spates' Hotel, in Poolesville, all those tracts or parts of tracts in said county, called ***The Resurvey on Cor's Basket***, & ***The Revsurvey on Plantire***, containing 324¾ acres of land, 265 acres which are assigned as the widow's dower, & will be sold subject to her interest therein. –Robt W Carter, Trustee

Commission on Claims against Mexico: 1-Several memorials of Louis S Hargous were taken up, the first claiming for losses from his expulsion from Vera Cruz in Jun, 1846; the second for indemnity for imprisonment & detention after his expulsion; the third for indemnity for the use of his steamboats by the Mexican authorities in 1845: each claim is valid against the Republic of Mexico & allowed: the amounts to be awarded subject to the future action of the Board. 2-Memorial of Isaac D Marks, claiming damages for expulsion from Matamoros in 1845: claim is valid and allowed: the amount to be awarded subject to the future action of the Board. 3-Memoiral of Elisha H Saulnier, claiming for his expulsion from the city of Vera Cruz, & losses thereon: claim is not valid & not allowed.

FRI APR 11, 1851

Commission on Claims against Mexico: 1-Memorial of Mathew G Warner representing himself to be the brother & agent of Jonathan J Warner, claiming indemnity for personal injuries sustained by said Jonathan: could not be received: rejected. 2-Memorial of Andrew Mayer et al, filed on Apr 8: claim is valid & allowed accordingly: the amount to be awarded subject to the future action of the Board. 3-Memorial of Isaac Graham, filed on Apr 8: claim is valid & allowed: the amount to be awarded subject to the future action of the Board. 4-Memorial of Jos W Henry, filed on Apr 7: claim is valid, & allowed: the amount to be awarded subject to the future action of the Board. 5-The Board then proceeded to the consideration of a motion filed on Apr 7, for a reversal of the order of the Board adopted on Feb 28, 1850, rejecting the memorial of Fred'k Freeman: it appearing that Freeman has not returned to the U S, & has been unable to subscribe the said memorial, & for other reasons set forth in the opinion of the Board thereon, ordered that the said memorial be received: same was allowed accordingly: the amount to be awarded subject to the future action of the Board.

Mr Richd H Weightman, a native of Wash City, appointed by the Pres of the U S one of the agents for the Indians in Mexico, left here on Wed for that Territory, taking with him his family.

Returned from Calif: among those arrived at N Y from Calif are Col Collier, Mr Bartol, & Mr John Wethered. Mr Collier may become a permanent resident of our State, with his family. Bartol and Wethered may also bring their families with them on their return.

Hon Orville Hungerford, formerly a Rep in Congress from the State of N Y, died at his residence in Watertown on Sun last, in his 61st year.

Orphans Court of Wash Co, D C. Letters testamentary on the personal estate of Chas J Nourse, late of Wash Co, deceased. –Chas J Nourse, exc Claims to be presented to Chas Abert, atty-at-law, F st, near Treasury Dept.

From the Calif newspaper: 1-Feb 22 & 23 witnessed a tremendous excitement in San Francisco, which for several hours was expected to result in the execution, by the populace, of 2 men, Stuart & Wildred, noted scoundrels, who nearly murdered Mr Jansen, a highly respectable merchant of the city, & robbed him of $2,000.
2-English gambler, Fred'k J Rowe, was less fortunate at Sacramento city. He shot Mr Chas A Myers, an industrious resident of that place, through the head. Rowe was convicted of murder & in 5 hours hung in the presence of an assemblage of several thousand persons. Mr Myers, the man who was shot, came from the vicinity of Columbus, Ohio, & has left a wife & several children. Fred J Rowe, the man who was hung, was about 22 years of age. 3-Judge Sallus has been murdered at Naps, in an affray with a man named McCauly. The difficulty arose from a legal decision made by the Judge. 4-J C Holmes, a lawyer of some eminence, committed suicide a few days since. Pecuniary embarrassments, it is said, prompted the act. He belonged to N Y.

Household & kitchen furniture at auction: on Apr 16, at the residence of Mrs Macdaniel, on 9th st between D & E sts-superior household furniture.
–C W Boteler, auct

Mrd: on Apr 1, at **Solona**, Fairfax Co, Va, by Rev F N Whaley, Jas T Close, of Saratoga Co, N Y, to Miss A Eliza Sherman.

Died: on Apr 10, at his residence, in Bladensburg, the Rev John Smith, of the Methodist Episcopal Church. His funeral is tomorrow at 10 o'clock.

Notice: All persons having claims against a balance due from the U S to Henry Grosh, late a seaman in the naval service, deceased, are notified to present them at the ofc of the 4th Auditor of the Treasury within 2 months from the date thereof.

Camden, S C, Apr 4. Court commenced on Mon last, Judge Wethers presiding. On Tue last, Saml J Love was arraigned for the murder of Robt J Lester. Jury returned a verdict of guilty, accompanied by a recommendation to mercy. On Thu, Saml Wilson Love, the father of Saml J Love, who was indicted for aiding & abetting his son in the murder of Mr Lester, was tried by the same jury. He was acquitted upon this verdict: We find the dfndnt Saml W Love guilty of excusable homicide.

SAT APR 12, 1851

Telegraphic dispatch from Detroit: Brig Gen Hugh Brady, of the U S Army, was accidentally killed in that city on Thu, by falling from his carriage. He was upwards of 80 years of age, & universally beloved. He originally entered the Army in Mar, 1792, from the State of Pa. He was a short time out of service, but re-entered it as a Col of Infty in Jul, 1812, & has continued in the Army from that time till the day of his death.

Circuit Court of Wash Co, D C-in Chancery, #734. Wm A Bradley & Sydney A Bradley, his wife, vs Levin M Powell, Jeannette C Powell, his wife, Chas M Thruston, Sarah Thruston, Wm T Thruston & others.. This suit is to procure a decree for a sale of certain tracts. lots, part of lots, & parcels of land in Wash City & County, in D C, the property of one Buckner Thruston, late of said city, now deceased. The bill states that some time during the year 1845, Buckner Thruston, of Wash City, died seized of a certain property, & intestate, leaving as his heirs at law Sydney A, intermarried with Wm A Bradley, Jeannette C, intermarried with Levin M Powell, his daughters, Thos L Thruston, Alfred Thruston, & Chas M Thruston, his sons, Horatio Gates Thruston, Eliza Thruston, Jeannette Thruston, & Dickerson Philips Thruston, his grand children, being children of Robt Thruston, his son, who departed this life leaving the said intestate; that since the death of said Buckner Thruston, his son, the said Alfred & Thos L Thruston, have departed this life intestate, leaving their widows & children as follows: that is to say, Sarah, widow of said Thos L & Chas M, Helen K, & Thos W, his children & heirs at law; & Fannie C, widow of the said Alfred & Jeannette B, Alfred B, & Sydney, his children, & heirs at law; that the aforesaid Horatio Gates, Eliza, Jeannette, Dickerson Philips, Chas M, Helen K, Thos W, Jeannette B, Alfred B, & Sydney Thruston are infants, under the age of 21 years; that the said Buckner Thruston, during his lifetime, executed a certain instrument in writing, whereby he charged the whole of his estate with the payment of an annuity of $600 per annum; that by reason of said charge, so as aforesaid made in said instrument of writing, & by reason of the infancy of the aforesaid infants, the aforesaid property being indivisible, a sale is prayed; & it is further prayed that out of the proceeds of said sale a sufficient amount may be placed at interest to pay the said annuity of $600; & the bill further states that the said Sarah Thruston & Chas M Thruston, reside out of D C. Absent dfndnts to appear in this Court on or before Oct 20 next. –John A Smith, clerk

Commission on Claims against Mexico: 1-Memorial of David Douglas, claiming damages sustained by his expulsion from Chihuahua in 1846, [filed on Mar 11, 1851:] claim is valid against the Republic of Mexico: claim is allowed: the amount to be awarded subject to the future order of the Board.

Died: on Apr 10, Mrs Eleanora Falconer, widow of the late Elisha Falconer, of Fred'k Co, Md, in her 64th year of her age. Her funeral will take place from the residence of her son, Mr R J Falconer, on Sat at 3½ o'clock, on 7th st.

Dept of State, Wash, Apr 11, 1851. Information received from the U S Consul at Lima of the death of both Mr Edw J Storer [late Purser U S Navy] & his wife, on board the British steamer **Bolivia**, while on their passage from Panama to Callan. The Consul has forwarded to this Dept a copy of the inventory which was taken of the effects left by the deceased.

Mrd: on Apr10, by Rev Mr Morgan, Mr Thos W Snape, of England, to Miss Mary A Pierce, of Wash City.

Mrd: on Feb 11, by Rev Mr Tillinghast, Mr Chas Allen to Mrs Mary E Baggett, both of Gtwn.

Died: on Apr 11, John Wingerd, 2nd son of John P & Ann Wingerd. His funeral will be from the residence of his parents on Green st, near Gay, Gtwn, this afternoon at 3 o'clock.

Died: on Fri last, Mr Jas Carbery, aged about 59 years. His funeral will take place from his late residence on Sat at 3 o'clock.

Came to the subscriber, at **Oak Grove**, near Wash, on Apr 10, a drove of hogs, 16 in number, which the owner or owners can have by coming forward, proving property, paying charges, & taking them away. –Benj I Fenwick

MONDAY APR 14, 1851
The steamship **Georgia** sailed from N Y on Fri with 225 passengers for Charges. Among them were the Rev Jas P Miller & another missionary for Oregon, where they are going under the care of the Assoc Presbyterian Synod of North America.

Register's Ofc, Wash, Apr 4, 1851. List of the persons who have taken out licenses during the months of Jan thru Mar, 1851.

Auctioneer license: Boteler, Chas W; Green, A; Marshall
Ballard Entertainment license: Dempster, W R
Billard Table license: Porter, Wm T

Cart license:
Ager, Uriah-2
Baltimore, Thos
Brooks, jr, Edm'd
Bowie, Jas
Brown, Rachael
Casteel, E O
Dwyer, Edw

Duvall, Jesse-2
Fitzgerald, John
O'Leary, Arthur
Page, Geo-2
Payne, Robt
Page, L S
Ritter, W

Rice, E
Sheriff, G L
Seaman, Richd
Simms, John
Tunion, W
Unisck, John

Circus license: Welsh, Rufus
Concert license: Potter, J S

Dog license:
Aylmer, R R
Alexander, Francis
Ailer & Thyson-3
Atkins, David-3
Abert, J J-2
Alexander, C
Arth, P
Anderson, Garret-2
Adams, Caleb
Allen, G F
Abbot, Jos
Acton, E
Ashdown, Wm
Black, Jane
Brown, John
Brent, Elton
Boak, G W
Brunner, W
Byrne, Theresa
Bowen, A
Bell, Eliz
Briel, Michl
Browning, P W
Bruce, Chas
Biggs, Levi
Bache, A D
Brady, Peter
Byrne, C R
Bead, Thos
Brown, Jas
Brown, H

Bates & Bro-3
Buckley, Jas S
Boyle, C
Beckley, Enos E
Bogan, B L
Barber, Geo
Brown, Wm
Brashears, Wm B
Brooks, B
Brown, A
Bully, A F
Brown, Geo
Bowey, Jno
Bohlayer, Jno-2
Black, Moses
Brown, Jas
Brown, J F
Brodbeck, J
Boak, Michl
Bell, Wm
Barber, Jos
Burr, H A
Bennett, Alex
Barrett, Thos, jr-2
Beckett, W
Briscoe, W
Brereton, J-2
Brown, Wm
Brent, J C-2
Beasley, Jos
Brooks, H

Brown, Marshall
Brown, T P
Baldwin, G L
Boarman, S B
Barsochlin, Jno
Birch, Mgt
Butler, M
Benner, Henry
Bradley, A T-2
Brannegan, Jno
Burns, Geo
Cash, Leonard
Clark, H A
Curson, Saml
Clokey, R B
Calalane, A
Chew, John
Crippe, Wm McL
Castell, Jno
Claveloux, M
Coke, Wm
Clark, Wm
Cross, Thos B
Crutchett, J-2
Casparis, Jas
Caden, J
Combs, R M
Calvert, Betsey
Coyle, J F
Chiseltine, E
Cassell, J T

Cornish, H	Downs, Sol'n	Fisher, Philip
Clark, J W	Derrick, A H-2	Ford, Jno W
Chubb, J M-2	Dooley, M	Fink, Casper
Cross, J C	Detter, Thos	Fox, Grace Ann
Clements, R H	Dodson, J B	Guttridge, W
Chavis, G G	Douglass, Jno	Gladmon, A
Castell, Edw	Delaney, Caleb	Green, Muntsay
Copp, Moses	Dorsey, Isaac	Goolrick, J C
Clements, J N	David, Jas	Gray, Thos K
Caton, John	Davis, Abel G	Goodall, Thos
Coltman, C C	Evans, H	Grantt, Jas T
Cross, Jos	Everett, T T	Griffith, W A
Clark, Cornelius	Evans, French	Gayer, B-2
Coyle, Fitzhugh	Espey, J	Goddard, Thos
Caldwell, J F	Edelin, Sarah	Gildermeister, H
Conlan, Peter	Elliot, W P	Galt, M W
Cox, Clem	Edelin, Jas-2	Glick, J H
Croggon, Isaac	Emert, H	Gibson, Jno
Connor, Jno	Eickorn, R	Garrett, M
Cowling, Edw	Earle, Robt	Gordon, Jas
Cammack, Wm	Evans, J D	Graham, H
Conner, John	Ehrmontrout, J	Greason, Wm
Clements, Jno T	Evans, T	Grimes, M H
Carter, Luke	Ergood, Jesse	Givney, B
Corrington, Bernard	Ennis, Philip	Gunn, Geo
Dodson, J	Ennis, J F	Garrett, G W
Douglass, Wm	Fletcher, Jno	Grimes, Jno F-2
Drumell, Saml	Ford, Jas	Green, J W
Donovan, Wm	Ferguson, Wm	Glorious, Geo
Davis, Wm-2	Francis, Richd	Harris, A
Dunnington, C W	Fretz, J	Handay, S
Davis, J Y	Filton, Wm H	Hess, Jacob
Dankworth, F	Fairfax, W M C-2	Hanly, Jane
Donohoo, W J-2	Foster, E	Huger, C
De Vaugn, S	Forrest, S	Herold, A G -2
Dyson, Chas	Fraeler, Chas	Haliday, Henry
Diggs, Thos	Ford, Wm	Hickman, Anthony
Dent, B	Fleming, J	Hobbie, S R
Dermott, Ann R	Fearson, J C	Howard, Jos-2
Dawes, F	Fitzgerald, J	Howie, P G
Dulin, W	Fields, Geo	Hill, H
Doe, M	Fugitt, F J	Hitz, Ann
Douglass, H	Fister, John	Hiss, John-2
De Saules, P A-1	Feeney, W	Heitmiller, A-2

Hanson, Saml
Hawkins, M
Hicks, Chas
Hall, John
Horning, J R
Hancock, Andrew
Horsthamp, H
Hollidge, J
Harkness, T F
Harbaugh, V
Hume, F
Hoffman, H
Hickman, J L
Hanson, G D
Handy, S W
Hepburn, jr, P
Howard, J
Henning, Stephen
Hall, Edw
Hutton, H
Howard, Geo T
Hammersley, Ed
Huntt, Geo G
Ingle, Jno P
Idemanar, J
Jenkins, E E
Jefferson, F
Jones, Jas
Jones, Alfred-3
Jones, Raphael
Jordon, Harriet
Jacob, G
Jones, J B
Johnson, Richd
Jamieson, J M
Jackson & Bro, B L
Johnson, Richmond-2
Johnson, Townley
Johnson, Isaiah
Jamieson, E
Johnson, Lewis
Jourdan, J A
Johnson, Wm P
Jones, Noah

Jackson, Susan
Jackson, A
Killian, John
Kingman, E
Killian, L
Kidwell, A C
Krafft, J M-2
Klomann, Chas-2
Kuhl, H
Kidwell, Jos
Klopper, F A
Kroeber, W
King, Thos
Kauffman, Geo
Kealey, D E
Knott, Geo A
Keyworth & Lewis
Klientienst, J P
Kibby & Co, J B
Kepler, Henry
Kelleher, Jas
Laub, J Y
Lloyd, J T
Lauman, Chas
Lewis, J E
Lauxman, M
Little, Peter
London, W H
Lusby, Saml
Lee, Josias
Law, Jno Geo-2
Leddy, O
Lederer, C
Linkins, Danl
Lawson, Thos
Lindsley, H
Lord, Wm
Lewis, Saml
Leypoldt, A
Lavender, J
Lowe, Jos
Landrick, J
Lee, Wm
Lehmann, A

Lee, Jos
Little, Peter
Lambell, R H
Middleton, C
Muse, L
Magruder, B
Marr, J H
Mason, Jos
Mille, Andrew
Munch, C H
Mustin, Thos
Miller, R A
Marks, S A H
Miller, Chas-2
Marshall, Wm
McClery, J
McClery, E J
McCoy, B M
Mankins, Jas
Mecklin, J R P
Marshall, Thos
Mitchell, J
Middleton & Beall
Mansfield, John
McPherson, J
Magruder, F
Minor, Richd
Murphy, John
Mullen, B-2
McQuay, Benj
Miller, Jos
Mills, R T
Myers, Mary
McHaughten, Geo-2
Murray & Semmes
Martin, Wm
Milburn, T
McElfresh, J W
Moore, Helen
Martin, J W
Marsi, G J
McLean, Jas P
Milburn, T
McKim, J F

Mattingly, Geo	Page, B P	Saur, L
Madison, Jno	Plant, G H	Sengstack, S P
McGreevy, Pat	Paine, Mgt	Springman, J M
Mills, Clark -2	Pumphrey, J	Scott, S
Moore, Jas h	Phillips, G W	Scifferle, J
McDermott, M-2	Parker, Geo	Smoot, J H
Myers, Chas	Poletti, J	Sanders, Richd
Nokes, Jas	Payne, L S-2	Sessford, Thos
Nardin, Jos	Plumsell, Thos	Smith, John C
Naylor, F Y	Pettibone, Jno	Stepper, A
Neale, L	Padownowsky, F	Simpson, J T
Noerr, A	Roux, A	Sioussa, F
Noble, M-2	Riordan, J	Siouss, J
Nicholls, J M	Rhodes, Jas	Simpson, Tobias
Nugent, E E	Redfern, Saml	Slight, J P
Newton, Isaac	Rawlings, D	Shed, J J
Nepp, Danl	Roberts, J M	Scott, Leonidas
Nelson, Jno	Rutter, Amelia-2	Sandford, L-2
Newton, Benj	Roth, Ambrose	Shreve, S
Nugent, Eli	Rappetti, Jos	Schad, B-2
Ormand, E	Randall, N K	Sweeny, H B
O'Neale, H G	Robinson, J	Spignall, M
Orem, J B	Richardson, L	Stewart, J C
O'Donoghue, P	Raily, B J L	Stonestreet, Wm
Owens, Benj	Ray, A	Steiger, W F
Olenstein, C	Rupp, W	Shultz, Geo
Owner, Jas	Riggs, E	Stoddard, Isaac
Otterback, Philip-2	Ruff, J A	Semmes & Co, J H
Parke, Wm	Rochat, H	Stock, Geo
Palmer, H	Rappetti, G	Stewart, Geo
Polizzi, V	Ready, W	Smith, Thos
Page, Y P	Riley, T W-2	Schlab, W
Perkins, T G	Raub, Jno P	Scott, W B
Pullin, J	Robinson, Jno	Smallwood, Dennis-2
Peel, Rosin	Reed, E	Speake, Letitia
Parton, F B	Rogers, C L	Stone, W
Page, Ann	Reed, B W	Spicer, Fred'k
Pleasonton, S	Schwartze, A J	Shuts, John
Peck, Jos-2	Shields, Thos	Stepper, A-2
Pursell, Thos	Sweater, Adam-2	Shultz, D
Pettit, Chas	Smith, Jos	Scott, Geo B
Pumphrey, L	Stutze, G F	Stettinius, Saml
Piper, J R	Speiden, Wm	Shultz, Jos
Peters, Thos	Sewell, Richd	Simms, Wm

Tastett, N	Tanner, Saml	Weber, C
Tanner, Lettie	Tompkins, R	Winchester, Robt
Tucker, J T	Visser, J	Warrington, M K
Tarlton, L A	Vidal, Richd	Wilson, W
Tibball, Eliz	Vonderlick, I	Watterson, Geo
Tabler, Wm J	Van Reswick, J	Willett, V-2
Turtohn, Jno B	Wade, Hiram	Wilkinson, E
Todschnider, F	Watson, W H	Wheeler, E-2
Thomas, Saml	Wilson, J D	Wallis, Wm
Thomas, Chas	Webster, Chas	Werner, J H T
Talbot, Geo	Wilcox, C G	Westerfield, D
Thomas, Geo	Wever, Jos	West, John-2
Talbot, W	Walker, D	Wright, W S
Tilghman, H H	Waite, M H	Webb, Wm B-2
Thomas, Chas-1	Wagner, Nich's	Wallace, Lydia
Travers, Elias-2	Wilson, J M	Wheat, Wm-2
Toping, Geo-2	Williams, T J	Wirt, J L
Thomas, Jos	Washington Semr'y	Wadsworth, A
Tunion, Sarah	Watson, E A	Winter, W H
Tenney, Ponpey	Warner, Chas	Wright, Jas
Taylor, R A	Warner, Henry	Whitwell, Jno C
Turpin, J S	Wilson, Jas	Wagaman
Trott, Thos P	White, Wm	Wurner, Chas
Thompson, J R	Weeden & Ryther	Walker, Dorcas

Dwarf license: Strange, W E

Hack license:
Beckett. W,	Flemming, Jas	Mullen, Wm S
Bowen, Jas A	Kierman, Chas	Wormley, A
Cumming, M A B	Miller, Edw	Wright, Jas

Hats, caps, etc, license:
Barr, J R	Follar, John	Marshall, Wm
Crandall, Jas	Howe, Walter	McLain & Harry
Ewell & Co, J	Lane, C H	Ring & Lieblick

Hog license: Clarke, A L

Huckster license:
Angus, J	Burns & Thomas	Bayliss, C
Atkins, D	Brown, Chas	Baxton, John
Bowie, Jas	Brown, R	Bradley
Bereton & Bro	Ball, T A	Bickelle, Jno

Biggs, H D	Jas Wallace	Poole, Wilson A
Crozgon & Son, J	Hill, John S	Richardson, C F E
Caldwell, J H	Hughes, Thos	Sherwood, S
Crump, J T	Hawkins, Philip	Shreve, John
Cunningham, R	Hawkins, E	Shreve & Co, S
Caldwell, M	Hough, W W	Spignall, M
Crown, J P	Haynes, Wash'n	Stewart, J C
Cole, John	Howel, W P	Sis, John
Cruit, Jas	Jones, Alfred	Selt, W
Campbell, W W	Johnson, W T	Sherwood, Thos
Donaldson, T G	Jenkins, D	Shreve, C H
Dulany, A	Johnson, W C	Tucker, Jas
Dulany, C	Jones, Nash	Thompson, W H
Davis, Jas	Mullikin, J W	Triplett, T J
Donaldson, Thos G	Murray, W A	Weed, Isaac C
Dyson, C	Moore, H W	Wallace, Jas
Eickorn, Geo	McQuay, Benj	Wagner, Nich's
Eickorn, R	Mankins, G W	Williams, W T
Franklin, Jacob	Newmyer & Co	Wilson & Co, J
Fearson, J C	O'Neale, Hillary	Wallingsford, W
Fowler, W R	Oyster, G M	Wallace, Jas
Garret, M	Paul, Isaac	Yeatman, J H
Gates, Chas L	Payne, C H	Yeatman, T J
Transferred to-	Peddicord, J	

Ins Agency license:
McKean, S M
Radcliff, J T

Weed, Edwin C
Webb, Pollard-2

Livery Stable license:
Brown, John
Pumphrey, Levi-3

Shrieve, Jas H
Walker & Kimmell

Merchandise license:

Adams, Mgt	Hugunan, A C	Stevens & Co
Brown, J D	Lanphier, E	Scrivener, Thos
Brown, Marsellus	McDevitt & Robinson	Sherry, Dominick
Boulanger, J	Marshall, Wm	Sheweetzer, Peter
Buckingham, C W	Martin, A W	Venable, Wm J
Cock & Martin	McLain & Harry	Wright, W S
Clark, Lemuel	Prebram, S M	Whaley, Henry H
Funk, N	Riggles, Thos	
Garder, Mary E	Swaggert, Jos	

Omnibus license: Weiden, H A-2

Retail license:
Costigan, John
Collins, Dennis
Crump, D O
Duvall, Jas
David, Philip C
Fugett, Thos M
Howling, Patrick
Hagerman, Henry
Jones, W H
Mangnus, Fred'k
Malone, Lawrence
Posey, Middleton
Peerce, J M
Rowle, Jas
Regan, Jas
Sullivan, John T
Tolson, John F
Wimsett, Jos

Stable license: Cowling, Edw

Tavern license:
Allen, Russel
Dorsey, Prisley W
Kelley, John
Moore, J L
Shaeffer, Casper
Upperman, Wm H
Wingenroth, F

Theatrical license:
Adelphi Theatre-2
Davenport, T D
Potter, J S
Willell, M

Shop license:
Barrow, Danl
Coombs, R M
Dalton, John
Deckman, Henry
Juneman, Geo &
Barber, Casper
Porter, W T
Snyder, Chr

Slut license:
Benter, W F
Gunton, Thos
Krafft, P
McKean, S M
Mills, Clark
Peters, Mary
Pumphrey, L
Peters, Thos
Wallace, Lydia

Ventriloquism license: Kerby, G W

Wagon license:
Newton, B
Polk, S C
Wright, W S
Waters, Thos
Walbridge, H D

Persons fined during the months from Jan thru Mar, 1851:
Bush, Wm: hack
Benter, Wm F: keeping dog
Berry, Ferdinand: selling liquor
Brown, Bazel: keeping dog
Blagden, Thos: keeping dog
Brown, Michl: keeping do

Dunond, Sol: keeping dog
Dickman, Henry: selling liquor
Easby, Wm: keeping dog
Evans, Travers: keeping dog
Greenfield, H C: selling liquor
Goldin, Jno A: selling liquor
Gensler, Henry: keeping open contrary to law
Hoover, Andrew: keeping dog
Hazel, Z: keeping dog
Herbert, Henry: keeping dog
King, Patrick H: keeping dog
Lomex, Elias: keeping dog
Mills, Clark: 2-keeping dogs
McCanplin, Jos: keeping dog
Omeara, Wm C: keeping dog
Ore, Sarah J: selling liquor
Otterback, Henry: keeping slut
Phillips, Mary: selling liquor
Pumphrey, Levi: livery stable-3
Powell, Abm: keeping dog
Plumsill, Thos: keeping dog
Pudorowsky, T: keeping dog
Rice, Edw: keeping dog
Smallwood, Dennis: 2-keeping dogs
Speaks, Leticia: keeping dog
Stettinius, Saml: keeping dog
Upperman, Wm H: keeping open bar on Sunday
Welsh, Rufus: circus-6 fines
Waters, Thos: wagon
Wilson, Jos: keeping dog
Waller, Jas D: keeping dog

Frightful murder of a child. Fri last, at Balt, John Rumpf, son of Jacob C Rumpf, 6 years of age, left his home at 2 P M on Thu to go to school, which he never reached, & could not be found until 4 P M the next day, when his body was discovered in an old slaughter house, dreadfully cut & bruised. Two boys, one 16 & the other 19 years old, have been arrested, & warrants are out for 3 others. These boys were seen beating a child & dragging him along on the day above mentioned. [Apr 17th newspaper: Henry Long, a negro boy of between 12 & 13 years of age, who lived with Mr Bankard, committed the murder of John Rumpf.]

Small farm-23 acres, near the country seat of J H King, & adjoining the college grounds, for sale. Improvements: comfortable small cottage. Will be sold at the auction rooms of E S Wright, Gtwn. –B Forrest -Edw S Wright, auct

Commission on Claims against Mexico: 1-Memorial of Louis S Hargous: claim is valid against the Republic of Mexico: allowed: the amount to be awarded subject to the future action of the Board. 2-Memorial of Geo & Peter Lafler claim is valid against the Republic of Mexico: allowed: the amount to be awarded subject to the future action of the Board. 3-Memorial of Saml Toby, surviving partner of the firm of Thos Toby & Brother, of New Orleans, claiming for the value of a part of the cargo of the Mexican schnr **Columbia**, confiscated by the Mexican authorities in 1825: claim is not valid against the Republic of Mexico: not allowed.

TUE APR 15, 1851
Household & kitchen furniture at auction: on Apr 25, at the farm of John F Clarke, on old Bladensburg road, adjoining the farm of Col Dundas. Also, all his farming utensils, stock, family carriage, wagons, carts, & farm of 200 acres. Also, a comfortable House, new Stabling, & other improvements. -Dyer & McGuire, aucts

U S Patent Ofc, Apr 12, 1851. Ptn of Danl E Stilwell, of N Y, N Y, praying for the extension of a patent granted to him on Jul 17, 1837, for an improvement in the manufacture of soap, for 7 years from the expiration of which takes place on Jul 17, 1851. -Thos Ewbank, Com'r of Patents

Commission on Claims against Mexico: 1-Memorial of A P Brittingham: Board of the opinion that it is not to be received. 2-Memorial of Wm S Parrott, claiming indemnity for losses resulting from forced loan & illegal proceedings of Mexican tribunals, & also for the amount for a bill of exchange drawn by Gen Herrera on Gen Victoria for supplies furnished to the Mexican patriots in 1816: first 2 items are valid, the 3rd item is not valid: the amount to be awarded subject to the future action of the Board. 3-Motion for rehearing the case of Rhoda MacRae, filed Dec 10, 1850, asking to be allowed interest on the sum to be awarded to her under the decision of Dec 13, 1849: interest should be allowed: claim is valid and allowed accordingly.

Suicide at New Orleans-New Orleans Delta of Apr 3. A few days ago, Chas Roussel, a poor French tailor, on St Chas st, decided with his wife that they both would commit suicide by drinking arsenic. After he had taken the fatal potion, she changed her mind and decided she had better bear the ills we have, than fly to others that we know not of.

WED APR 16, 1851
The Hon David Daggett, late Chief Justice of Conn, son of Thos Daggett, of Attleborough, Mass, was born in that town on the last day of the year in 1764. He entered Yale at age 14, where he graduated with distinction in 1783. For 65 years his life has been identified with the history & prosperity of New Haven & Conn. He was long a Professor of Yale College. Judge Daggett died on Apr 12 at the advanced age of 86 years.

The steamboat **Yanke**, of Galena, was ready on Sep 22, 1850, for the St Paul exploring party. Her ofcrs are as follows: Capt M K Harris; Clerk, G W Girdon; Pilot, J S Armstrong; 1st Engineer, G W Scott; 2nd Engineer, G L Sergeant. Touching Mendota, they took on board the Jos Laframboise & family, bound up the Minnesota river to his trading post at Little Rock. At *Fort Snelling* we were joined by a part of the 6th Regt band. Homeward bound, Mr Armstrong, the pilot, was assisted at the wheel by Mr Brissette. Music was provided by Messrs Foster, Morgan, & Kirk, of the 6th Regt band, aided by Mr Eldridge with his violin.

For rent: 3 story brick dwlg, with back bldgs, over Bastianelli & Co's fancy store, west of & next to Campbell & Coyle's hardware store, on Pa ave. Apply to G C Grammer.

The sloop-of-war **Germantown**, has received orders to join the African squadron. She will be the flag ship of Cmdor Lavalette, & will relieve the ship **Portsmouth**, Cmdor Gregory, now out about 19 months. Ofcrs of the **Germantown**: Cmder, Jas D Knight; Lts, Edw R Thompson, Jas H North, Geo Colvocoressis, Geo W Rogers; Purser, Wm A Christian; Assist Surgeon, A Nelson Bell; Acting Master, Julius S Bohrer; Marine Ofcr, 1st Lt John D Simms; Midshipmen, John Taylor Wood, Wm H Ward, Dominick H Lynch, Edw P McCrea, Wm H Toon, John K Lagow, Wm H Maffitt; Boatswain, John Burrows; Gunner, Wm W Fisher; Carpenter, Ebenezer Thompson; Sailmaker, Theodore G Herbert.

Wash Corp: 1-Ptn from S A Pugh for the improvement of certain streets in the 4th Ward: referred to the Cmte on Improvements. 2-Ptn of M Talty for compensation for a sewer destroyed by the Corp: referred to the Cmte of Claims. 3-Ptn of Wm Fletcher, praying indemnity for a horse lost by falling over an embankment in the First Ward: referred to the Cmte of Claims. 4-Ptn of Jas E Bowen & others, for grading & gravelling K st north: referred to the Cmte on Improvements. 5-Ptn of Wm Easby, praying the abatement of a nuisance on square 925, in the 6th Ward: ordered to lie on the table. 6-Ptn of Jas Killeher, praying indemnity for loss sustained by an obstruction in one of the streets in Wash City: referred to the Cmte of Claims. 7-Act for the relief of P H King: passed.

Household & kitchen furniture at auction: on Apr 23, at the residence of David H Burr, 9th & E sts. -Dyer & McGuire, aucts

By deed of trust dated Mar 1, 1849, recorded in Liber J A S #4, folios 266 thru 269, of the land records of Wash Co, D C: public auction, on May 17, of 1 square acre of ground, with improvements, fronting on the eastern line of 7th st, bounded on the north by W D Beall's lot, & on the south by that of A M Gattrell.
-Dyer & McGuire, aucts

Household & kitchen furniture at auction: on Apr 23, at the residence of David H Burr, 9th & E sts. -Dyer & McGuire, aucts

On Monday a number of journeymen blacksmiths & wheelwrights formed a procession at the Navy Yard, & marched to Capitol Hill, down Pa ave, with martial music. The object was a strike in favor of the 10 hour system. They entered the workshop of an industrious blacksmith, Casper Offenstein, who resides on Capitol Hill, & because he refused to join their ranks, the strikers struck him several hard blows in his dwlg house, hurting, at the same time, Mrs Offenstein, by striking her also in the dwlg. Ofcr Mulloy was sent for, & Ofcrs Handy, Wollard, Cox, Westerfield, Busher, Williams, & Keese aided in the arrest. Persons who were held to bail: Thos Kelly, Michl Boyland, Philip Custace, John Ruckingham, Jas Drudge, & Andrew Boyland. John Lyons escaped from the ofcrs, but was arrested in the evening by Ofcr Davis. Another belligerent, John Eagleson, was arrested on Mon in Benter's Refectory, after another affray.

Postmaster Gen est'd the following new Post Ofcs for week ending Apr 12, 1851.

Ofc	County, State	Postmaster
Pleasant Valley	Chittenden, Vt	Martin Richardson
Narrows	Jefferson, N Y	Thos W Collins
S Harrisburgh	Lewis, N Y	Sewall Hill
Schooley's Mountain	Morris, N J	Jacob Cole
Red Oak Grove	Burlington N J	Wm Greig
Buena Vista	PG Co, Md	Wm T Duvall
New Grenada	Fulton, Pa	C W H Moore
Harmarville	Alleghany, Pa	John Miller
Lamartine	Clarion, Pa	David Eshelman
Forwardstown	Somerset, Pa	Saml Hollison
Bemis Creek	Somerset, Pa	Wm Graham
Bradensville	Westmoreland, Pa	Wm S Braden
Sipesville	Somerset, Pa	Levi Hoffman
Waynesfield	Auglaize, Ohio	Eran G Atkinson
Aurelis	Washington, Ohio	G G Grubb
East Richland	Belmont, Ohio	John A Haines
Mohawk Valley	Coshocton, Ohio	Jas Moore, jr
Buckeye Furnace	Jackson, Ohio	Almond Soule
Conine	Licking, Ohio	Thos J Hahan
New Somerset	Jefferson, Ohio	Geo C Saltsman
East Westville	Mahoning, Ohio	DAnl P Pettit
Beachland	Chattooga, Ga	Francis J Grogan
Hutton's Fork	Wilkes, Ga	Wm Lunceford
Rauleson's Ferry	Columbia, Ala	Wm A Sheffield
Ridge Grove	Macon, Ala	Jas Charlton

Manack	Lowndes, Ala	P T Graves
Douphin	Blount, Ala	Josiah Truss
Carthage	Tuscaloosa, Ala	David B Gladney
Landersville	Lawrence, Ala	Saml D Houston
Webster	Winston, Miss	John W Darby
Cotton Grove	Pontotoc, Miss	C L Herbert
Beaverdam	Clark, Miss	Thos J Williford
Manchac House	Travis, Texas	Wm Pelham
Monterey	Red River, Texas	Marcus W Caudle
Justus' Mills	Hempstead, Ark	John Justus
Cedar	Allen, Ia	Hugh Thomas
New Prospect	Orange, Ia	C F Teachemacher
South Nashville	Davidson, Tenn	Wm W Parks
Campbell's Rest	Sullivan, Tenn	S R N Patton
War Gap	Hawkins, Tenn	John W Phillips
Chaplaintown	Barren, Ky	John F F Jewell
Orion	Richland, Wis	Chas R Traxlar

Name Changed: Schooley's Mountain, Morris Co, N J, changed to Springtown.

Mrd: on Apr 7, in Gtwn, by Rev F G Binney, Adonis L Yerby, of Wash, to Mary S, daughter of Jos Radcliffe, of Gtwn.

Died: at the residence of his nephew on C st, between 12th & 13th sts, Mr Jos Knox Boyd, a resident of Wash City for the last 19 years. His funeral will take place on Apr 17, at 3 o'clock. [No death date given-current item.] [Apr 18th newspaper: Obit of the late Jos Knox Boyd: one action in his life sufficient to give honor to the longest life. The daring exploit of the burning of the frig **Philadelphia** in the harbor of Tripoli, to prevent the Turks from availing themselves of their prize, at night, within musket shot of their batteries, must be fresh in the minds of his country men. It was only to be accomplished by volunteers. 70 brave men instantly offered their services, the deceased was among the first. The sequel is known, it is recorded upon the brightest page of history. One by one these gallant men have descended to their graves. A few days since but 2 remained; & now the gallant Cmdor Morris is the sole survivor of that patriotic seventy.]

Died: on Sun, at N Y, Maria Graham, wife of Cmder John S Chauncey, U S Navy, & eldest daughter of the late David Graham.

THU APR 17, 1851
Fire at Bladensburg. The dwlg of John Bowie, [a new bldg lately erected,] was entirely consumed last Mon night. The furniture on the lower floor only was saved. The property was partially insured.

Incident of the War of 1812. This narrative was written in a hurry by Gen Brooke, at my request, when I was at Detroit in Jun, 1842, when Gen Brooke commanded at that place. -T W P. In 1814 the American army was besieged in **Fort Erie** by the British army, commanded by Gen Drummond. A redoubt was under construction by the British, some 200 yards from **Fort Erie**; which, if completed, would have commanded perfectly the American works. Gen Gaines, commanding the American troops, thought it necessary to attempt the destruction of this redoubt, & Lt Col Brooke volunteered to place a light in the line of the redoubt, by means of which the artillery might direct their fire to that point during the night. Col Brooke, assisted by 2 boys from Lt Col Harris' dragoons, bearing a lantern, placed it within the British sentinels, very near the redoubt; & by daylight the work was destroyed. The first fire of our artillery, commanded by Major [now Col] Fourney, killed & wounded 15 of the enemy's working party. Col Brooke ascended a tree in the direction of the work, covered the lantern with a coat, which was attached by a cord some 20 or 30 yards long. When he descended, he pulled the coat from the lantern by the use of the cord, & displayed the light to the besieged.

Alexandria, Apr 15, 1851. Affray last Sat: Capt Jas F Crawley, of the schnr **David Carter**, from N C, with his mate, refusing to go into one of the booths for the purpose of gambling, were violently assailed by a party, & driven from the wharf with stones. The captain turned upon his assailers with a dirk, & Mr Alex'r Turley, a workman recently employed at the Foundry, was stabbed in the abdomen, & died yesterday. The capt & mate, for want of evidence charging them with guilt, were discharged. Inquest was held yesterday by C Neale, & a verdict rendered that the deceased came to his death by a wound from a dirk knife, inflicted by Capt J F Crawley, in self-defence. –Gazette [Apr 18th newspaper: the verdict "in self defence," was not in the verdict rendered. An ofcr has been dispatched to Norfolk to arrest Capt Crawley, & to being him back to this city. Alexandria Gaz.]

Public Schools: Special meeting of the Board of Trustees was held yesterday at the City Hall. Present the Mayor, [Pres of the Board,] Messrs Farnham, Abbot, Haliday, Harbaugh, Bacon, Donoho, McKim, Walsh, Randolph, & Pearson. Mr John Fill, teacher of the Male Primary School in the 2nd School District, was elected to supply the vacancy occasioned by the resignation of Mr H McCormick in the 3rd District. Mr De Maine, assist teacher in the 2nd Distrist School, was elected to supply the vacancy. Mr T M Wilson was elected assist teacher in place of Mr De Maine.

Cooper Female Academy, in Dayton, Ohio, is seeking some competent person to succeed Mr E E Barney, who has been employed for several years as the Principal, & is retiring at the end of the school year. Address the Trustees: Saml Forrer, Pres; Robt C Schenck, J D Phillips, E W Davis, Robt W Steele, Richd Green: Board of Trustees.

Valuable real estate in Gtwn & Wash at auction. As the surviving excecutor of the will of my father, & with the consent of the heirs, I will expose to sale at auction all his real estate in Gtwn & Wash: lot 1, in Beatty & Hawkins' Addition, on High st, with a brick store & dwlg house, & a 2 story brick house & back bldg, both fronting on High st & having an entrance on Gay st. Also, the west half of lot 1 of the slip fronting on Gay st, with the frame house theron. Lot 6, with the Plough Factory thereon, fronting on High st & 135 feet on Dumbarton st, now occupied by Mr Libbey. Also, lots 8 & 9 of the slip fronting on the north side of West st, near High st, & 256 feet on Valley st, with the frame house fronting on the latter street. Also, lot 3 in square 168, in Wash City, on G st, & 59 shares of the Stock of the Farmers & Mechanics Bank of Gtwn. –Francis A Lutz, Exc, & for himself & the other heirs. –Edw S Wright, auct

Household & kitchen furniture at auction: on Apr 21, at the residence of Mr Jas Fullalove, on Bridge st. The House, which is very commodious, is for rent. Apply to Mr Fullalove on the premises, or to the auctioneer, E W Wright.

Mrd: on Apr 12, at Rochester, N Y, at St Luke's Church, by Rev H W Lee, Maj E S Sibley, U S Army, to Miss Charlotte H, youngest daughter of the late Seth Saxton, of that city.

FRI APR 18, 1851
John Clines was hung at Freehold, N J, on Fri last, for the murder of Jas Shields.

Commission on Claims against Mexico: 1-Amounts to be awarded to the several claimants, with a rate of 5% per annum to be computed on all claims which have been allowed for property lost, or contracts unfilled, unless a different rate of interest was stipulated in such contracts from the origin of the claim to Apr 16, 1851, when the commission will expire: & thereupon the Board awarded to:
John Wilkins, exc of Saml Lowder: $15,937.50
Saml Thruston, adm of Henry Ryder: $5,703.66
Geo B Fisk: $5,447.92
Wm D McCarty, assignee of John Woolsey: $2,657.81
John A Bradstreet: $42,697.47
Nathl M Whitmore, adm of Simon Bradstreet: $2,697.47
Jos Adams, assignee of Wm B Grant: $4,046.21
Jas R Byram, assignee of Wm B Grant: $1,378.74
John N Swazey: $1,421.92
John Curtis, adm of Abner Curtis: $1,421.93
Wm Lewis: $1,421.93
Jonathan Farnham: $1,421.93
Abner Lane: $1,421.93
Mgt Meade, admx of Richd W Meade: $5,791.66
Jas Johnston, adm of J P Wallace: $5,811.87

Benj Holbrook: $887.50
John Belden: $5,342.87
Jas O'Flaherty: $8,221.25
Wm W Corcoran, assignee of B B Williams & Jos H Lord: $15,051.00
Dorcas Ann Plumer, admx of Robt Plumer: $5,217.26
Patrick Hayes: $6.192.56
Wm Homan: $187.75
Wm H Freeman, adm of Edw B Freeman: $921.40
Chauncey Child & Hezekiah Child: $8,986.66
John Smith: $1,400.00
John Baldwin: $71,400.00
Asa Fish: $1,062.50
Chas Mallory: $1,062.50
Stephen Morgan: $1,062.50
Geo Wolf: $1,062.50
Simeon Fish: $1,062.50
Henry Ashley: $1,062.50
Lymas Dudley: $265.62
Sanford Stark, exc of Jesse Craig: $531.25
Simeon Fish, exc of Simeon Gallup: $1,062.50
Ambrose H Burrows, exc of Geo Haley: $265.63
Norman Sherwood: $1,000.00
Hiram Conch: $660.00
Robt C Patterson: $650.00
Nathan Barkley: $800.00
Jas C Duval, adm of Z M P Duval: $800.00
Stewart Foster, adm of Chas Foster: $840.00
Saml Collins: $660.00
Nathan Barkley, adm of Moses Nolan: $425.00
Harrison C Allensworth: $650.00
Jas M Gatewood: $600.00
Silas M Knight: $750.00
David Hull: $500.00
Hezekiah D Maulsbey, adm of Geo G Alfred: $1,000.00
Desha Bunton: $4,543.54
John W Bunton: $2,869.72
Jas J Kendall: $2,110.03
Danl Slack & Geo W Hathaway: $4,329.21
Augustus Leftwich, assignee of Chas R Kennedy: $3,174.64
Henry P Bates, adm of Johnson H Alford: $1,470.90
Roderic T Higginbotham: $4,405.00
Jas Reed, assignee of Andrew Moore: $11,487.18
Malcom Sandeman & Co: $1,415.46
Jas Reed: $11,262.50

Jas Reed, assignee of Frederic A Sawyer: $621.15
Jas Reed, assignee of Bennet & Sharpe: $16,006.57
Jas Reed, assignee of Brandon, McKeune & Wright: $6,459.22
Wm H Rogers: $1,456.86
Richmond Sherwood, adm of Oran Sherwood: $10,971.15
Jas Love, adm of Pallas Love: $650.00
Pierre Choteau, jr, adm de bonis non: $81.772.00
John W Simonton & John A Heath: $3,080.49
Philo B Johnson: $750.00
Jas Cochrane: $750.00
Mercantile Ins Co of N Y: $25,936.70
Richd Harding: $243.00
John Hartshorn: $1,458.30
John Galbraith, assignee of Francis B Webster: $480.00
Cornelius P Van Ness & Jas A Dickens: $120.00
Mary Hughes, admx of Geo Hughes: $20,000.00
Henry Cheatham: $660.00
DAnl Davis: $500.00
Thos B Cottrell: $340.00
Henry May, adm of Ann P Bouldin: $41,223.62
New Orleans Canal & Banking Co: $4,370.70
Jas Kelly: $2,000.00
John P Schatzell: $6,250.00
Henry Gisner: $625.00
Geo S Miller: $1,250.00
Henry Breeze: $1,250.00
Joachim Fox: $625.00
Pierre Suzeneau, adm of Emile Suzeneau: $625.00
Adolphe Suzeneau: $625.00
French Strother: $1,250.00
Elihu D Smith: $3,125.00
Geo East: $6,000.00
Archibald Stevenson: $17,400.00
Simeon Remer: $1,250.00
Sanford Kidder: $1,875.00
Jas H Clay: $2,816.66
Atlantic Ins Co of Phil: $4,020.12
Edw Hoffman: $1,031.25
John A Robinson: $16,179.84
Volney Ostrander: $660.00
Chas Stillman: $4,562.50
Geo W Van Stavoren: $2,040.00
Wm Richardson: $2,804.00
Rufus K Furnage: $2,468.00

Wm S Underhill: $805.00
Lewis H Polock: $4,603.50
Ann T Kelly, admx of Wm H Lee: $3,676.50
Wm S Misservy: $6,000.00
Fred'k Bunge & Albert Southmayd: $3,569.97
John C Jones: $4,961.97
Alpheus B Thompson: $8,060.37
Thos O Larkin: 16,474.23
Thos O Larkin & Talbot H Green: $4,608.52
Jos B Eaton: $3,033.22
Benj T Reed: $8,038.54
Mgt P Hallet, admx of John Hallet: $4,103.50
Henry Stevens: $1,250.00
Chas Danforth, surviving partner of Godwin, Clarke & Co: $24,702.35
Hannah Ulrick: $1,181.03
Lucius H Armstrong & Jas Jackson: $5,402.88
Geo W Van Stavoren: $9,045.24
Jas S Thayer, adm of Jas Treat: $1,025.50
Fred'k E Radcliff, adm of Augustus Radcliff: $1,025.50
Saml Jobson: $5,568.76
Geo N Downs & Geo S Owen: $941.60
Jas L Rudolph: $1,250.00
Sanforth Kidder: $160.25
Francis del Hoyo, adm of Francis Arenas: $19,000.00
Jesse E Brown: $2,100.00
Jos Andrews: $1,720.00
Jonas P Levy: $3,675.00
John Claiborne, adm of Thos Hassard: $3,500.00
Elisha Riggs: $13,320.00
Jose Maria Cabellero: $3,069.00
Theophilus Labruere: $3,797.49
John F Bullock, adm of Edw Hill: $37,026.56
Jonah Roers/Rogers, adm of Augustus Rogers: $6,650.00
Geo T Wethered: $3,125.00
Chas H Cooper: $2,472.00
Jesse E Brown, adm of Wm J Russell: $2,100.00
John Brouwer, receiver of Pelican Ins Co of N Y: $1,933.82
Peter Kerr: $6,294.85
Wm Murphy: $12,500.00
Benj Burn: $2,978.50
Andrew Wylie, jr, adm of Saml Baldwin: $75,000.00
John H Means: $152,125.00
Jas W Zacharie, assignee of Francis Cheti: $6,975.00
Andrew J Brame: $1,042.44

Jos Bosque: $11,750.00
Wm B Hatch: $317.55
Mgt Ward, admx of Elliot Ward: $1,850.00
John Boute: $7,175.00
Jeremiah C Terry & Jas W Angus: $9,166.00
Jas W Zacharie, assignee of A C Bredall: $10,000.00
John Belden: $106,431.00
John Powell, assignee of Thos Powell: $12,922.90
Michl Dougherty: $10,125.00
John Christian: $1,374.50
Jos Bolles: $2,821.25
Andrew Meyer & Jos Meyer, excs of Andrew Meyer: $2,144.50
Rhoda McRae: $11,380.50
Isaac Graham: $38,125.00
Jos W Henry: $1,800.00
Frederic Freeman: $750.00
John Parrott: $63,541.00
Geo Laffler & Peter Laffler, surviving partners of the firm of Wally & Laffler: $31,125.00
Ann B Cox, excx of Nathl Cox: $110,355.25
Calvin J Keath, adm of Saml Elkins: $129,282.97
Louis S Hargous: $530,682.29
Wm S Parrot: $26,750.00
Ferdinand Clark: $86,786.29
Franklin Chase: $33,573.00
John E Gary, adm of Louis P Cook: $2,846.66
Danl E Smith: $3,375.00
Edw M Robinson, exc of Jos Fleming: $1,633.93
Geo A Gardiner: $321,560.00
Isaac D Marks: $3,750.00
Louis S Hargous: $72,000.00
John M Togno: $4,112.50
Aaron Leggett: $109,296.00
Christian Alby: $3,397.70
Franklin Cooper, assignee of Wm Barton: $1,357.25
Geo Douglass & Edgar S Van Windle, assignees of Wm S Parrott: $88,000.00
W W Corcoran, assignee of Geo A Gardiner: $107,187.50
Nathan C Folger, assignee of Chas Guenet: $2,0155.60
Franklin C Gray: $3,736.45   Dexter Watson: $750.00
Lewis M Dreyer: $845.18   David Douglass: $2,450.00
Danl Collins: $6,434.37   Sidney Udall: $2,500.00

The Hon Wm Beatty, a prominent Democratic candidate for Canal Com'r, died at his residence in Butler Co, Pa, on Friday last.

The birth place of Washington: from the Alexandria Gaz. ***Arlington House***, Apr 14, 1851. Account of Jun, 1815: I sailed in my own vessel **Lady of the Lake**, a fine schnr of 90 tons, with Messrs Lewis & Grymes, bound to ***Pope's Creek***, Westmoreland, carrying with us a slab of freestone, having the following inscription: "HERE, The 11th of Feb, 1732, [old style,] Washington was born. We anchored some distance from the land, &, taking to our boats, we soon reached the mouth of Pope's or Brydge's Creek, & fell in with McKenzie Beverly, & several gentlemen on a fishing party, & also with the overseer of the property that formed the object of our visit. We enveloped the stone in the Star-Spangled Banner of our country, & it was borne to its resting place in the arms of the descendants of 4 Revolutionary patriots & soldiers, Saml Lewis, son of Geo Lewis, a Capt in Baylor's regt of horse, & nephew of Washington; Wm Grymes, the son of Benj Grymes, a gallant & distinguished ofcr of the Life Guard. the Capt of the vessel, the son of a brave soldier wounded in the battle of Guilford; & Geo W P Custis, the son of John Parke Custis, aid-de-camp to the Cmder in Chief before Cambridge & Yorktown. Health & respect, my dear sir. –Geo W P Custis

Mrd: on Apr 15, by Rev Mr Gorsuch, Mr Edw S Allen to Miss Martha Cammack, daughter of Mr Wm Cammack, all of Wash City.

Died: on Apr 16, in Wash City, Geo Strickland. His funeral is this day, at 9 o'clock, at the dwlg of Mrs James, F st, between 12th & 13th sts.

Died: on Apr 16, Ernest, son of Z D & H P Gilman, in his 3rd year.

Wash City Ordinances: 1-Act for the relief of Jas H Shreves & Harrison Taylor: the fines imposed for alleged violations of an ordinance in reference to pavements, is remitted: provided they pay the costs of prosecution.

Very valuable improved property at auction: on May 1, in front of the premises, Favier's, on 19th st, near Pa ave: lots 1, 2, & 13, in square 119, fronting 98 feet on 19th st & 129 feet on H st, with a 2 story frame & a 1 story brick bldg.
-Dyer & McGuire, aucts

SAT APR 19, 1851
Household & kitchen furniture at auction: on Apr 30, at the residence of the Hon David A Bokee, in the house formerly occupied by the late Doct May, on N J ave.
-Dyer & McGuire, aucts

For rent: a warehouse, suitable for a Grocery & Food Store, on 7th st.
–Wm B Kibbey

Orphans Court of Wash Co, D C. Letters of administration on the personal estate of Magdalin Dembirh, late of Wash Co, deceased. –J B Bragdon, adm, Balt, Md.

New Counties in Va: the Bedford [Va] Sentinel says: a new county, to be called Craig, has been formed out of parts of the counties of Botetourt, Giles, Monroe, & Roanoke. A county to be called Upshur has been formed of of parts of the counties of Randolph, Barbour, & Lewis. Another, to be called Pleasants, in honor of Jas Pleasants, formerly Govn'r of Va, has been formed out of parts of the counties of Wood, Tyler, & Ritchie.

Macon [Ala] Republican of Apr 3. Difficulty between Lewis P Breedlove & Jacob Segrest on Mar 29, resulted in Mrs Breedlove being severely shot. Mrs Breedlove got between Segrest & her husband, & received the load of the rifle in her fore-arm, which it dreadfully lacerated. The ball buried itself between her shoulder & neck. Mrs Breedlove is the sister of Segrest, & the parties have for some time been at law about the property of Segrest's father, who died some time last year.

Female Teacher wanted: H P Powell, Middleburg, Loudoun Co, Va.

Delaware College: summer session will commence on Apr 30. –W S F Graham, Pres; Jas L Miles, Sec of the Board of Trustees.

For sale, lots in Gtwn, near the Canal Basin: the subscriber, as surviving Exc of Thos S Lee, late of Fred'k Co, Md, deceased, will offer at public sale, on May 15, four lots of ground in Deakins, Lee & Casanave's addition to Gtwn, being lots 24 & 25, on Montgomery st, & lots 32 & 33 on Greene st. –J Lee, exc of Thos S Lee

Died: on Apr 18, Mary, consort of Stephen Pleasonton, Fifth Auditor of the Treasury, in her 67th year. Her funeral is on Tue, at 12 o'clock.

Died: on Apr 18, Maj Erastus T Collins, of the Pension Ofc, in his 58th year. His funeral is on Sunday, at 3 o'clock, from the residence of Mr Tingle, 12th & F sts.

Died: a few days ago, at White Sulphur Springs, Greenbrier Co, Va, Jas Calwell, after a few hours' illness, in his 78th year. He was a native of Md, & for any years a merchant in Balt, but since 1818, he was the popular proprietor of the White Sulphur Springs, where he died generally respected & highly esteemed.

Died: on Apr 14, in Fred'k Co, Md, after a severe illness, Thos C Farquhar, aged 31 years & 10 months.

The subscriber, formerly of Brown's Restaurant, has taken & fitted up King's Hotel, near Jackson Hall, & is prepared to receive transient & permanent boarders.
–R W Allen

MON APR 21, 1851
Copartnership: the subscribers have associated with them Mr Robt A Hooe, in the business of Drygoods Dealers: to be conducted under the name of Hooe, Brother & Co. –P H Hooe & Co

Sale at auction of square 937: by deed of trust from Dennis Vermillion & wife, dated Nov 15, 1847, recorded in the land records of Wash Co, D C, in Liber W B 138, folios 239 to 241: with a 2 story brick dwlg, with outbldgs: the square fronts on Md ave, D st, & 9th & 10th sts. –C W Boteler, auct

Fire on Friday destroyed 2 dwlgs, occupied by Mr Ennis & Mr Baltzell. The property was insured.

The Kent Co massacre. Havre de Grace, Apr 18. An ofcr from Chestertown arrested Nicholas Murphy, on the charge of being one of the murders of the Cosden family at the Gtwn Cross Roads, in Kent Co. Murphy testified that he & Thos Drummond were out together on the night of the murder hunting muskrats. Drummond confessed, declaring that Murphy, Sheltonk Ford, Sills, & Taylor are parties who committed the bloody outrage.

From Calif: two men, who gave their names as Jas Baxter, of Maine, & Chas Simmons, of Mass, suffered death on Mar 7, under the Lynch code, at Consumnes. They were accused of being horse thieves. The people denied them even the forms of a trial, & hung them up a few moments after arresting them.

The large & beautiful hotel, the *Oceanic House*, at Coney Island, N Y, kept by C M Rogers, was entirely destroyed by fire, together with most of the furniture, on Thursday. The fire is supposed to have been caused by some defect in the chimney.

Chas Wickliffe, died on Apr 8, at his residence, Bardstown, Ky, of lockjaw, caused by injuries received by falling from his horse.

Died: yesterday, in Wash City, Mrs Amelia Dunn, in her 81st year. Her funeral is this afternoon, at 3 o'clock, from her late residence over the Bank of Washington.

TUE APR 22, 1851
New Books: The House of <u>Seven Gables</u>, a roman, by Nathl Hawthorne, Boston. Ticknor, Reed & Fields. [Fresh from the magic pen of Hawthorne & the dainty press of Ticknor & Co.]

From New Orleans: we learn by Telegraph of the death of Judge Bullard, of Lousiana & a Rep from that State in the last Congress. He had been in ill health for some time previous to his decease. [No death date-current item.]

The Savannah Republican announces the death, in that city, on Thursday last, of Geo Schley, in his 60th year. He was a native of Md, but has spent the greater part of his life in Georgia. In 1825 he was appointed Postmaster of Savannah by Pres Adams, & remained in that ofc continuously up to the time of his death, having seen in these 26 years 7 Presidents past out of ofc.

Paintings & furniture at auction: on Apr 28, by order of the Orphans Court of Wash Co, D C, at the late residence of the late Rev J Vanhorsigh, next door to St Peter's Church, on Capitol Hill. -A Green, auctioneer

Confectionary, glass jars, household & kitchen furniture at auction: on Apr 28, by order of Reuben Collins, in the house occupied by Mrs Campbell, on Pa ave, between 2nd & 3rd sts. -A Green, auctioneer

Household & kitchen furniture at auction: on Apr 24, at the residence of Mr Hamersly, on 9th st, between E & F sts. -Dyer & McGuire, aucts

Household & kitchen furniture at auction: on Apr 25, at the residence of Mr Abern, at 19th & F sts. -A Green, auctioneer

Wash City Ordinance: 1-Act for the relief of John A Sauer: the late surveyor, C B Cluskey, has made an error in the survey of a lot belonging to Sauer, & the error not having been ascertained until the said Sauer had nearly completed a frame tenement thereon: the Mayor is to directed to pay Saur $175, to defray the expenses for damages sustained by Sauer in erecting a frame house on lot 10 in square 535.

Sale of valuable real estate & iron works in Monongalia Co, Va: by decree of the Circuit Superior Court of Law & Chancery for said county, rendered in the cause wherein John Tassey & others were plntfs, & Evan T Ellicott & others were dfndnts. Sale at Morgantown, in said county, on the 4th Mon in Jun next: all that property lying along & near Cheat River, know as the Monongalia Iron Works, the same that was conveyed by said John Tassey & others to said Evan T Ellicott & others, containing 15,000 acres of land, whereon are a Rolling Mill, Forge, Foundry, Nail Factory, Grist & Saw Mill, all driven by water power, together with 3 Blast Furnaces. –Edgar C Wilson, W T Willey, Com'rs

Reward for return of lost dog, Zac. Zac is quite honest, good looking, & very amiable.

J A Ruff, Boot & Shoe Store, Pa ave, near 4½ st.

Millard Fillmore, Pres of the U S A, recognizes E C Angelrodt, who has been appointed Vice Consul of Baden, for the State of Missouri, to reside in St Louis. Apr 18, 1851

Detroit Daily Advertiser of Apr 16: announces the death of Gen Hugh Brady, Brevet Major Gen of the U S Army. He died yesterday, at his residence on Jefferson ave. His death was the result of an accident, occasioned by the fright & running away of his horse, which he was himself driving, which took place on Apr 10. Gen Brady was born in Jul, 1768, & was nearly 83 years of age.

Mrd: on Apr 16, in Trinity Church, Wash City, by Rev Dr C M Butler, Mr Jas C Walker, of Tenn, to Miss Caroline C Christian, of Va.

Fire at Palmer Depot on Wed, laid almost its entire business part in ruins. The fire broke out in the wooden bldg owned by Elisha Converse, & occupied by M C Munger as a general dry goods & grocery store. –Springfield [Mass] Republican

WED APR 23, 1851
Household & kitchen furniture at auction on Apr 24, at the residence of the late Jas Carbery, deceased, corner of E st south & 6th st west. -Dyer & McGuire, aucts

Boarding: Mrs Worthington's, F st, near 13th, Wash City.

Trustee's sale of valuable real estate: pursuant to a decree of the Court of Chancery of Md: public sale on May 13, all that part of land now in the possession of Mrs Norah Digges, being part of Chillum Castle Manor, in PG Co, Md, containing about 230 acres. Apply to D C Digges, Atty at Law, Upper Marlborough; to Geo A Digges, residing near the premises, or to the subscriber in Balt. –R S Steuart

For rent: comfortable 2 story brick dwlg on 8th st, between E & F sts. Possession given in a few days. –John F Boone, 12th st, between F & G sts.

Postmaster Gen est'd the following new Post Ofcs for week ending Apr 19, 1851.

Ofc	County, State	Postmaster
Bucksport Centre	Hancock, Maine	Nehemiah Cole
Mianus	Fairfield, Conn	Shadrach M Brush
Mashapany	Tolland, Conn	Jared D Sessions
Crittenden	Erie, N Y	Seymour Putnam
Grand Island	Erie, N Y	Danl Morgan
La Salle	Niagara, N Y	Henry Clarke
North Parma	Monroe, N Y	Jas A McFarland
Hasting's Centre	Oswego, N Y	Jonathan D Parkhurst
Southampton	Somerset, Pa	Thos J Kennedy
Perote	Ashland, Ohio	Abraham Fast
Pleasant Plain	Clermont, Ohio	I B Young
Hale	Hardin, Ohio	Michl Printz
Durand	Henry, Ohio	Geo Stebbins

Sylvania	Licking, Ohio	Sidney Whipple
Philo	Muskingum, Ohio	Cornelius Fearns
Howland	Trumbull, Ohio	John Crooks
Deardoff's Mills	Tuscarawas, Ohio	Wm M Shreeves
West Salem	Waye, Ohio	John Deck
Pioneer	Williams, Ohio	W Norris
Wilson's Creek	Knox, Ia	Thos W Williams
Ridgeville	Randolph, Ia	Arthur McKnew
Yankeetown	Huntington, Ia	Solomon Smith
Celestine	Dubois, Ia	Jos Stregle
Peach Orchard	Lawrence, Ky	Allen Borders
Clover Hill	Green, Ky	Jos Perry
Magnolio	La Rue, Ky	D J Harris
Pageville	Barren, Ky	John E Holman
Ralphton	Fulton, Ky	R S McFadden
Creve Coeur	St Louis, Mo	Washington, Ross
Central	St Louis, Mo	Jos Valdejo
Bellmonte	St Louis, Mo	John C Gunning
Bonhommes	St Charles, Mo	Thos Boyer
Hamburg	St Charles, Mo	Wm King
Centreville	Montgomery, Ark	Enoch S Haynes
Julia Dane	Davidson, Tenn	Jas H Jones
Black Jack	Scott, Ark	Chas C Burton
Barrcksville	Marion, Ala	Edw Connaway
Coloma	Cherokee, Ala	Wm H Edwards
Timber Creek	Hunt, Texas	Stephen Marshall
Shiloh	Union, La	W A Milner
San Elizario	Soccorro, N Mex	Wm Smith
Albuquerque	Bemalillo, N Mex	John Webber
Frontero	Soccorro, N Mex	Thos White
Soccorro	Soccorro, N Mex	Vincente St Vraine

Names Changed: [Post ofc.] Springfield, Yell Co, Ark, changed to Parkersburg.
Mitchell, Washington Co, Wis, changed to Ulao.
Olio, Sheboygan Co, Wis, changed to Mitchell.
Meadway, Burke Co, Ga, changed to Joy's Mills.
Redding Mills, Berrien Co, Mich, changed to Dayton.
McDowall, Crawford Co, Pa, changed to Sterlington.

Great bargain in watches & jewelry: Canfield, Brother & Co, 227 Balt st, & Chas st, Balt, Md.

Wash Corp: 1-Ptn of Ann Washburn, praying that certain taxes assessed to her may be remitted: referred to the Cmte of Claims. 2-Ptn of J T Clements & others, for the laying of certain flag footways in the 4th Ward: referred to the Cmte on Improvements. 3-Cmte of Claims: bill for the relief of D J Bishop: recommended the rejection of the bill. 4-Cmte on Police: bill for the relief of F H Poston: reported the same without amendment. 5-Bill for the relief of David Westerfield was taken up: referred to the Cmte on Police.

Household & kitchen furniture at auction: on Apr 24, at the residence of Mr Lawrence, on 14th st, between H & I sts, in *McDuell's Row*. -A Green, auctioneer

Mrd: on Mon, by Rev John C Smith, Mr Jas Ford to Miss Sarah Dove, all of Wash City.

Mrd: on Apr 21, in the Church of the Ascension, by Rev L J Gilliss, the Rev Henry J Windsor, Rector of East New Market Parish, Dorchester Co, Md, to Miss Susan Harriet, daughter of the late Cephas W Benson, of PG Co, Md.

THU APR 24, 1851
We learn from the Norfolk papers that Cmdor Jas Barron, of the U S Navy, died at his residence in that city on Mon last, in his 83rd year. He was the senior ofcr in the Navy, which [having been previously an ofcr in the marine service of the State of Va during the Revolutionary war,] he entered as a Lt on Mar 9, 1798, & received his present commission of Capt on May 22, 1799. His whole term of service in the U S Navy exceeded 53 years. He had not, however, been on duty at sea since 1807, in which year he commanded the American frig **Chesapeake** at the time of her unfortunate encounter with the British frig **Leopard**, which came near involving the U S in war with England. Until his last illness, the weight of years had but slightly bowed his tall, majestic person, or dimmed the luster of his bright & intellectual eye, or paled the florid glow of health on his manly cheek. He departed in full possession of the faculties of his mind, serene, resigned, & without pain. [Apr 25th newspaper: We were in error in stating that the late Cmdor Barron had served in the marine service of Va in the Revolutionary war. It was his father who served Va during that war.] [Apr 26th newspaper: The late Cmdor Barron: since the publication of our last paper we have received from an authentic source the following particulars: Capt Jas Barron, the father of the late Cmdor Jas Barron, was Cmder-in-Chief of the Naval Forces of the State of Va during the Revolutionary war; & his son Jas, [the late Cmdor,] was a midshipman in the service of Va, & an aid to his father to the close of the war.] [Apr 29th newspaper: As a matter of interest to the survivors of the family, it is proper to correct an error in a late statement in this paper. Cmdor Walter Brooke was cmder-in-chief of the State naval forces of Va during a part of the Revolutionary war. He having resigned, Cmdor Jas Barron succeeded him as cmder-in-chief, & served to the end of the war.]

For rent, furnished Parlors & Chambers. Inquire of Mrs Fleury, *Vaunum's Row*, Pa ave, at 9th & 10th sts.

On Tuesday will be sold the wreck of the schnr **Lewellyn**, with several cords of green Oak Wood. Sale upon the shores, between Lambell's & Page's wharves. –Henry D Gunnell, Com'r 7th Ward

Archbishop Eccleston's funeral will be this morning at the Convent, in Gtwn, at 7 o'clock, to walk from that place to the railroad depot in Wash. The Pastors of the different Churches are requested to cause the bells to be tolled from 7½ to 9 o'clock. [Apr 25th newspaper: The body of Archbishop Eccleston will lie in state in the Cathedral in Balt until Sat, & then be placed in the vault below the altar of the church, by the side of the remains of Archbishops John Carroll, Amrose Mareschal, & Jas Whitfield.]

Mrd: on Apr 22, by Rev Jas B Donelan, Chas Edw Thomas, of Norfolk, Va, to Miss Jane Eliz, daughter of Ephraim French, of New Milford, Conn.

Mrd: on Apr 22, in Balt, by Rev Mr Berry, Dr Louis Marshall, jr, to Mgt W McVean, all of Gtwn, D C. [Apr 25th newspaper: Mrd: on Apr 22, in Balt, by Rev Mr Berry, Dr Louis Mackall, jr, to Miss Mgt W McVean, all of Gtwn, D C.]

Died: on Apr 22, in Gtwn, D C, of pulmonary consumption, Miss Maria Bootes, eldest daughter of the late Saml Bootes. Her funeral is on Thu at 5 o'clock, from her late residence on Bridge st.

Died: on Apr 23, Rose Frances Trenholm, aged 9 months. Her funeral is this afternoon at 3½ o'clock, from the residence of her parents, on E st near 10th.

FRI APR 25, 1851
Geo Parcell, bar-keeper in the Franklin House, at Columbus, Ohio, was shot dead on Sunday night last by Thos Spencer, of Adelphi, Ross Co. No explanation is given of the motive for the murder. Spencer was committed to jail.

Verdict against the railroad engineer: at the Coroner's inquest held at Geneva, on the body of Mr Riley, killed by a collision on the railroad at that place a few days since, the jury returned a verdict that the accident was caused by the gross carelessness of Robt Dixon, engineer of the accommodation train, & recommending that the coroner cause him to be arrested.

Died: on Apr 22, Chas Eugene Vanvallenburg, aged 1 year & 3 months. His funeral is today at 3 o'clock, from the residence of his parents, on 12th st, between G & H.

The following notice will convey sad intelligence to numerous relatives & friends in Balt & Alexandria. Mrs Lawrason was previous to her marriage Miss Carson. The writer of this has known her for 50 years, & a more lovely girl was not in the town she lived in, or a more affectionate devoted wife, kind mother, or generous friend. From the New Orleans Commercial Bulletin of Apr 14.
+
Died: on Apr 11, after a short illness, at the residence of her son, in this city, in her 60th year, Mrs Eliz Lawrason, wife of the late Thos Lawrason, of Alexandria, Va.

At Richmond, on Mon, the jury in the cause of H B Allison agreed upon a verdict of guilty, & assessed his term in the penitentiary at 5 years. Allison was arrested in Wash City, as a confederate of 2 pickpockets, who robbed several gentlemen in the African Church in Richmond, at a public exhibition, the past winter.

Mrd: on Apr 22, at St Matthew's Church, by Rev Jas B Donelan, Mr Jas C Eslin, of Wash Co, D C, to Miss Harriet E Lanham, of P G Co, Md.

Mr John Masterson, of Lancaster City, met with an accident on Fri last, while returning from his contract on the Columbia railroad, which has since resulted in his death. He was riding a fractious horse, & was thrown from the animal.

SAT APR 26, 1851
The Indiana Argus states that an entire family of 12 persons, viz: John Hanagan, his wife, & 6 children, Mrs O'Donnel, Patrick Slave, 1 adult person, [name unknown,] & one child of John O'Donnel, were burnt to death in their house last week, at Elizabeth, Harrison Co. When the neighbors reached the burning dwlg all its inmates were dead.

Trustees of the Upper Marlborough Academy wish to engage a suitable person to take charge of the institution as Principal. By order of the Board: Jno B Brooke, Pres

Explosion on Mon last of the British steamer **Comet** as she was preparing to leave Oswego, N Y. Royal David & Jas Carroll, engineers of the boat; John O'Connor & Jas Church, waiters; & Thos Quiggin, foreman, were killed.

Ladies with letters in the Wash Post Ofc, Apr 26, 1851- Wm A Bradley, P M

Adams, Miss A D	Burgwin, Mrs M A
Anderson, Mrs S A	Benham, Mrs M L
Bowen, Mrs Alv'a	Bowen, Miss Sa J
Barrow, Miss Cath	Blount, Mrs Eliz
Burman, Mrs El'h	Burnet, Mrs Virgi'a
Brent, Mrs Jane W	Curtis, Mrs L
Brown, Mrs My A	Christ, Pauline
Bennett, Mrs Mary	Cobb, Mrs U E

Dabney, Mrs Chr'a	Michon, Ida
Dunscomb, Mrs J E	Miner, Mrs Marg't
Doyle, Mrs Louisa	Murphy, Maria
Dixon, Mrs Mary	McDowell, Mrs S
Divan, Mrs	Osborne, Miss M
Donoho, Mrs Mary	O'Donoghue, Miss M
Demar, Miss Prisc'a	Pollard, Mrs
Ebbett, Miss El'h	Peck, Mrs S
Erter, Mrs Cath	Robinson, Mrs A W-2
Ford, Eliza	Reynolds, Mrs E
Fitzhugh, Mrs Jane	Remond, Mrs E-2
Fisher, Mrs M C	Rushton, Mrs Maria
France, Mrs Mary A	Riggs, Mrs
Gibson, Mrs Ann	Smith, Miss Sally
Gale, Miss Anne M	Stetinius, Miss B
Gordon, Mrs Fras	Stinger, Miss D H
Gamble, Miss Sarah	Smith Mrs M A
Hall, Miss Anna M	Springer, Mrs R R
Hume, Miss Va	Stewart, Mrs Sarah
Harman, Mrs El'h	Thompson, Miss E
Harrison, Mrs	Tansill, Mrs Fanny
Halehran, Rachael	Watson, Miss A
Jacobs, Mrs Jane A	Walker, Mrs Cath
Jamaison, Mrs M E	Williams, Hillery S
Jones, Mrs Judith F	Wilkinson, Eliz
Jacobs, Mrs Sarah A	Wood, Miss M C
King, Mrs Jane	Wilson, Miss M E
Lewis, Mrs Ann S	Watkins, Susannah
Landsdale, Miss Cor	Wade, Mrs S
Lowe, Charity	Worthinton, Mrs Wm
Matthias, Mrs Ann	

Letter from Cmder Chas T Platt, commanding U S ship **Albany**, dated Tampico, Apr 1, 1851, communicating to the Navy Dept information of the death of 1st Lt Edw Lloyd West, of the Marine Corps. Lt Edw Lloyd West, of the marine corps, died at sea on the 30th ultimo. We sincerely sympathize with his afflicted widow & her children in this sudden & distressing calamity. [To A K Hughes, Acting master, Sec.]

Mrd: on Apr 24, by Rev C M Butler, Mr John Wiley, formerly of Phil, to Miss Emily F Brown, of Wash.

Mrd: on Apr 24, at St Mary's Church, by Rev Mr Alig, John Bohn to Eliz Martell.

Mrd: on Apr 23, Mr Michl Brick to Margaret Cray.

Mrd: on Apr 10, Jeremiah Nolen to Martha Gorden.

Mrd: on Mar 8, Timothy Hourly to Juliana Hourly, all of Wash City.

Died: on Apr 24, at his residence in Wash City, Dr Chas Beale Hamilton, in his 60th year. Dr Hamilton entered the navy in 1811 as surgeon's mate, & served under Cmdor Warrington during the whole of the last war with Great Britain, with distinguished usefulness & ability. After the war he continued in the naval service for several years as surgeon, & finally resigned his commission to practice his profession, as a surgeon & physician. Preferring agriculture to the profession of medicine, he abandoned the practice except within a very limited circle, & purchased a farm a few miles from Washington. His funeral will take place at 12 o'clock today, from his late residence on south B st, Capitol Hill.

Died: on Apr 24, Saml Thos Pettit, son of Chas Pettit, in his 26th year. His funeral is tomorrow at 3 o'clock, from the residence of his father, on E st, between 5th & 6th sts.

Died: on Thu, at Phil, Brevet Maj Thos B Linnard, of the Corps of Topographical Engineers, U S Army, in his 41st year.

Died: on Apr 25, at the St Charles Hotel, Jeanet St Clair, infant daughter of Geo A D & Mary V Clarke.

Fire broke out yesterday in the wooden bldg occupied as a Ten-pin Alley by Mr John M Farrar, at Missouri ave & 6th st, & was entirely destroyed. Also destroyed was the carpenter's shop occupied by Mr Morsell; a frame bldg occupied by Mr Bowen, hack driver; & a newly finished frame bldg belonging to Mr F Magruder, wood merchant, & which he intended to enter upon yesterday.

Household & kitchen furniture at auction: on Apr 30, at the residence of the late Wm Ward, deceased, on H st, near 6th st. –A Green, auctioneer

The subscriber is authorized to sell at private sale square 747, with the improvements thereon, known as *Cazonova*, near *Pearson's Mill*: located between M & N sts north, & Dela ave & 3rd st east. Improvements consist of a commodious frame dwlg, stables, & other out houses. –Chas S Wallach

By virtue of a supplemental decree of the Circuit Court of Wash Co, D C, sitting in Chancery, passed in a cause wherein Thos Blagden is cmplnt & John F Callan [adm] & others are dfndnts: I shall sell on May 9, the following: part of lot 2 in square 147, & part of lot 2 in square 148: both lots on B st, between 18th & 19th sts.
–John F Ennis, Trustee -A Green, auctioneer

MON APR 28, 1851
Edw Colston, of Berkeley Co, Va, a gentleman wel known throughout the Commonwealth for all the qualities which a adorn a man & Christian, died suddenly on Wednesday night at his residence.

In the Municipal Court at Boston, last week, Dr Timothy H Smith, charged with having killed 2 children by malpractice, was tried on a charge of manslaughter. The Jury did not agree on a verdict. They acquitted him of the charge on one child, & in the case of the other stood 5 for conviction & 7 for acquittal.

The creditors of the late Simon Fraser, deceased, are to call at my ofc, 6th & Canal sts, on May 22, to get their dividend of the assets of the personal estate of said Fraser, deceased. -Wm Bird

The U S sloop-of-war **John Adams**, Cmder Barron, bound to Madeira & Coast of Africa, salled from Hampton Roads on Thu. List of her ofcrs: Cmder, Saml Barron; Lts, Henry French, George T Sinclair, J A Doyle, Johnson B Carter, Isaac G Strain; Surgeon, Wm B Sinclair; Master, Jas Higgins; Assist Surgeon, Jas F Hustus; Midshipmen, John Irwin, C F Thomas, B Boyd, jr, Marshall C Campbell, Chas A Babcock, Geo F B Barber; Capt's Clerk, Saml Barron, jr; Boatswain, Wm Black; Gunner, John Owens; Carpenter, Wm Hyde, Sailmaker, Wm Mahoney.

Mrd: on Apr 23, at Trinity Church, by Rev Mr Pyne, Albert Ray to Amanda J, daughter of Capt R E Clary, U S Army.

Mrd: on Thu last, at the Theological Episcopal Seminary, Alexandria Co, Va, by Rev Mr Lockwood, Felix Richards to Miss Ann Amelia H Macrae, all of said county.

Mrd: on Apr 10, in St Peter's Church, Balt, by Rev Mr Williams, Richd H Hagner to Annie M, daughter of the late Dr Hungerford, all of Calvert Co, Md.

TUE APR 29, 1851
The Govn'r of the State of Tenn has appointed the Hon A O Nicholson Chancellor for the Middle District of Tenn, vice Hon Terry H Cahal, deceased.

The late Archbishop Saml Eccleston was the last of five who have filled the principal see of the Catholic Church in the U S. The first was the Most Rev John Carroll, born in Md in 1735, consecrated on Aug 15, 1790, & died on Dec 3, 1815; the second was the most Rev Leonard Neale, born in Md in 1746, succeeded Archbishop Carroll, & died on Jun 18, 1818; the third the Most Rev Ambrose Marechal, born in France in 1768, succeeded Archbishop Neale, & died on Jan 29, 1828; the fourth the Most Rev Jas Whitfield, born in England in 1779, succeeded to Archbishop Marechal, & died on Oct 19, 1834; the fifth & last, who died last week, was born in Md in 1801, succeeded Archbishop Whitfield, & died on Apr 22, 1851. –Balt American

Rose Farm for sale: I will sell for the owners the above named estate: 4 miles from the Fauquier Sulphur Springs, Va, containing nearly 1,000 acres: improvements consist of a substantial dwlg & necessary out-houses. Apply to Rice W Payne, Atty for E G Rose & Brothers, Warrington, Va.

For sale at public auction on May 7: in front of the Courthouse in Warrenton, Va, my Farm, known as the ***Mountain View Farm***, containing 186 acres, more or less: improvements are a dwlg house, large barn, & many necessary out bldgs.
–Hugh T Douglas, Fauquier Co, Va

Pretty villa for sale, near ***Linnean Hill***, [Joshua Peirce's] about 2¼ miles from the Centre Market: house is a very neat ornate Cottage, new & well built, situated on the wooded hill overhanging Rock Creek: a little domain of 20 acres. The proprietor sells only because he has gone to reside in Richmond. Apply to Mr Franck Taylor, bookseller, Jas M Carlisle, atty at law, Randolph Coyle, civil engineer, or Geo W Riggs. -Edw Wm Johnston

Obit-from the Phil Inquirer of Apr 23. Died: on Friday last, at Washington, Mrs Mary Pleasonton, wife of Stephen Hopkins, & daughter of the late John Hopkins, of Lancaster Co, Pa. To the partner of her bosom & her surviving children, she has left a rich legacy of virtues to be cherished.

Died: on Apr 23, at the Infirmary, Geo Homewood, a native of England, but for the last 18 or 20 years a resident of Washington.

Died: on Apr 26, at ***Hopeton***, of scarlet fever, Benj Ernest, aged 2 years, 1 month & 2 days, son of Jos C & Mary K Lewis.

Danville, Pa, Apr 28. The Methodist Church in this place ws struck by lightning yesterday while the congregation was at prayer. The electric fluid passed down the steeple into the centre of the church, instantly killing Mr Geo Peusye, & seriously injuring 8 others in different parts of the church.

Household & kitchen furniture at auction: on May 5, at the residence of Wm Darby, on N J ave, near B st, Capitol Hill, all his furniture. -Dyer & McGuire, aucts

Furnished house for rent: 2 story house on 19th st, between F & G sts, at present occupied by me, together with the furniture. –John M Barclay

WED APR 30, 1851
Orphans Court of Wash Co, D C. Letters of administration, with the will annexed, on the personal estate of John Butler, late of said county, deceased.
–Walter Butler, adm w a

Wash Corp: 1-Ptn from T Burk for permission to occupy a stable as a livery stable: referred to the Cmte on Police: passed. 2-Cmte of Claims: asked to be discharged from the further consideration of the ptn of M Talty, & that it be referred to the Cmte on Improvements. 3-Cmte of Claims: act for the relief of R McCorkle, & an act for the relief of Wm Pegg.

Postmaster Gen est'd the following new Post Ofcs for week ending Apr 26, 1851.

Ofc	County, State	Postmaster
Ashleyville	Hampden, Mass	Edw Kneeland
Berlin Falls	Coos, N H	John C Merrill
Centre Canistro	Steuben, N Y	Phineas O Stephens
Stockholm Depot	St Lawrence, N Y	Dason W Stearns
Olivet	Armstrong, Pa	John McGreary
Tippecanoe	Fayette, Pa	John B Patterson
Crownsville	Anne Arundel, Md	M Diffenderfer
Peach Grove	Fairfax, Va	Eliphalet R Merry
Antaugaville	Antauga, Ala	Wm P King
Rural	Jasper, Mo	Harrison B Jackson
Turkey Foot	Scott, Ky	Thos L Moore
Rough Creek	Grayson, Ky	John H McDaniel
Merriville	Montgomery, Tenn	W D Meriwether
Bee Branch	Pettis, Mo	Benj Prigmore
Unionopolis	Anglaize, Ohio	Rob C Layton
Snooksville	Defiance, Ohio	Peter Snook
Cokesburg	Licking, Ohio	Wm S Gleason
Bird's Run	Muskingum, Ohio	Wm M Miskimins
Paulding	Paulding, Ohio	Alex S Latty
Van Buren	Clinton, Ill	Jeremiah Mulford
Unity	Alexander, Ill	Hugh P Craig
Fair Weather	Adams, Ill	Abraham High
Clyde	Whitesides, Ohio	Thos Milner
Forestville	Delaware, Iowa	Wm Turner
Mount Parthenon	Newton, Ark	Thos K May
Lamartine	Washita, Ark	Chas Fittz
Walnut	Jefferson, Iowa	Forrest W Heard
Pleasant Grove	Desmoines, Iowa	Jas E Shellady

Names Changed: Bare's, Monroe Co, Ohio, changed to Baresville.
Burton, Chautauque Co, N Y, changed to Allegany.
Abington Centre, Luzerne Co, Pa, changed to Waverley.
Greenock, Crittenden Co, Ark, changed to Aldham.
Kaukaulin, Brown Co, Wisc, changed to Kaukauna.
Rogersville, Anderson Co, S C, changed to Evergreen.

Mrd: on Apr 28, by Rev Dr Pyne, of St John's Church, Washington, His Excellency Alphonse De Borboulon, Minister from France to China, to Katharine, youngest daughter of Alex'r Norman Macleod, formerly of Isle Harris, Scotland.

Clerk wanted: a young Man, between 17 & 21 years of age, who writes a fair hand, & wishes to learn the Grocery business. Apply to Jos Wimsatt, Dealer in Groceries, corner of Pa ave & 13th st.

John R Griffith, a boy 16 year old, accidentally hung himself in Delaware Co, Pa, on Apr 17. It is supposed he slipped & fell from the plank, as when discovered, his neck was dislocated, & his feet were resting on the ground.

On Fri last, while the friends of Mr Sumner, in Reading, were celebrating his election by a discharge of cannon, a premature discharge took place, by which Mr Eben Buxton had both arms blown off, making it necessary to amputate them above the elbow. His recovery is doubtful. Mr Lewis Gleason had his right arm & 2 fingers of his left hand blown off.

THU MAY 1, 1851
The Martinsburg Gazette of Apr 22, announce that Col Edw Colston, of this county, is no more. He was suddenly stricken, on Apr 23, at **Honeywood**, his late residence, when he had just closed a conversation with a member of his family. He fell from his chair & instantly expired. His excellent lady & 2 elder children were absent from home at the time of their sudden bereavement.

The Hon Robt McLane, late chairman of the Cmte of Commerce in the House of Reps, & Philip Hamilton, son of Alex'r Hamilton, & late Counsellor of N Y C, have formed a co-partnership & will practice law hereafter in San Francisco. N Y Courier & Enquirer

For sale: the stock & good-will of an old & well established Boot & Shoe Store, on Pa ave, & now doing a fine business. The subscriber is desirous to sell on account of an engagement in other business. Apply to John H D Richards, at P A Brenner's, Pa ave.

By virtue of an order of distrain for house rent due to Ambrose Lynch by Jas Osborn, I will expose at public sale, on May 8, in front of the Centre Market house, 3 wheat fans, 1 cutting machine, 1 dairy cooler, 2 milk pans, 1 boiler, 1 can, & a lot of lumber. H R Maryman, Constable

By virtue of 2 writs of fieri facias, at the suit of Michl Thompson, against the goods & chattels of Thos Llewellyn, I have seized for public sale, on May 8, 1 sideboard, 1 table, 1 clock, 1 stand, 1 bucket, 1 horse, 1 cart, & a lot of cart gear: in front of the Centre Market house, for cash. –H R Maryman, Constable

Sudden & melancholy death. We learn that Mr John C Mullay, of Pa, a clerk in the Indian Bureau, was on Tuesday taken with an apoplectic or epileptic attack, & died within a few hours. His wife was promptly summoned, & was by his side when he expired. Mr Mullay was in his 38th year, & greatly respected for his general intelligence & high qualifications for his official trust. His funeral is this afternoon at 4 o'clock, from his late residence on H st, near 18th st.

Died: on Apr 30, in Wash, at the residence of her daughter, Mrs Louisa Delany, on Missouri ave, Mrs Mary Ann Villard, widow of the late Mr R H L Villard, of Gtwn, D C, in her 53rd year. Her funeral will take place this morning at 11 o'clock, from Trinity Church, [corner of 3rd & C sts.]

Obit: died-on Mar 16, 1851, at Jackson Court-house, Va, Mrs Jane H, consort of Fleet Smith, [late of Wash, D C,] in her 66th year. She had been for the greater portion of her life a communicant in the Presbyterian Church, & cherished in her old age, when bowed down by continued infirmity & disease, the hopes of a blessed immortality.

FRI MAY 2, 1851
In Nuremburgh, in Bavaria, is the terrestrial globe constructed by Martin Behaim, [or Boehm,] the friend & associate of Columbus, & which it has been asserted by those who never saw it give the priority of discovery to Behaim. This globe was begun in 1491, & completed Aug, 1492. It is in the mansion adjoining the Lindauer gallery, & said to be the earliest in existence.

Great Bargains in Furniture & other Housekeeping Goods, on 7th st, nearly opposite the Exchange Bank. –N M McGregor

A slander suit of Asahel Fairbanks & wife vs Saml R Burroughs, all of Warren, was concluded before the Supreme Court at Worcester, Mass, last Fri, by a verdict of $1,000 damages in favor of the plntf. The Worcester papers pronounce the verdict a most righteous one.

Ordained to the ofc of Deacon by the New England Conference on Sunday last, was the Rev Robt J Lawrenson, a native of Balt. This young clergyman was brought up in Wash & was for some time employed as a mechanic in the navy yard.

Mrd: on Apr 30, by Rev Mr Morgan, Mr Henry F B Pardon, of England, to Miss Virginia C M Barron, of Wash City.

Mrd: on Apr 29, at Haddock's Hills, near Wash, by Rev Danl Lynch, of Gtwn College, John F Boone, of Wash, to Henrietta H Dyer, of the same place, daughter of the late Capt Jos Tarbel, U S Navy.

Died: on Apr 29, John Blackston Riley, aged 23 years, 3rd son of the late Thos R Riley, of Wash City. His funeral is on May 2, at 4 o'clock, from the late residence of his father, corner of 9th & H sts, Island.

N H paper: Benj C Cadun, of Cornish, a few days ago, excited by liquor, was abusing a favorite horse; his son, about 18 years of age interfered, when the father made an assault upon him with a pitchfork. The young man seized it by the prongs, held it firmly, when the old man let go, fell backwards, & died.

Mr John Cousins, of Belfast, Maine, who recently returned from Calif, had purchased a farm in Monroe, & went with ofcrs to take possession of it on Apr 26, when the occupants, an old man named Jewell & his son, resisted, & Mr Cousins was shot dead from a window of the house. Gen Cunningham, the deputy sheriff, procured a larger party, & they surrendered. The Jewells are said to be very bad men. Mr Cousins had been married but a few days. The farm formerly belonged to Wm Sullivan, of Boston. -Boston Post

For rent: desirable residence at the corner of F & 11th sts. Rent very low. Inquire of E J McClery, corner of 14th & E sts.

Information wanted of Abel M Griggs, a native of Flemington, N J, but a resident of Wash for near 30 years, having left that place Feb 20, 1848; since which time nothing has been heard from him. Any information respecting him, addressed to Mary Griggs, Wash, will be thankful received by a distressed family.

SAT MAY 3, 1851

In the case of the State of Md against Geo W Burnham, indicted for larceny of a portion of the money stolen from Messrs Adams & Co's Express, the jury, on Thu, returned a verdict of not guilty, & he was accordingly discharged from custody.

On Wed, Andrew Rutledge & Alex'r Carkaden, employed in the distillery of N C Ely & Co, Wmbsburgh, N Y, lost their lives by inhaling carbonic acid gas, evolved by the fermentation of molasses. Rutledge accidentally fell into a cistern in which molasses was working, & Carkaden, in his efforts to rescue him, shared the same fate.

Extensive stock of groceries, liquor, & store fixtures at auction, on May 7, at the Grocery Store of S P Tench, on Garrison st, Navy Yard. -A Green, auctioneer

For rent: large dwlg house on I st, between 20th & 21st st, recently occupied by M Bols le Comte, the French Minister. To examine the premises, the key may be found at the grocery store of Saml Stott, Pa ave & 20th st. For terms apply to Mr Stott, or to the owner, Francis Markoe.

Dwlg house for rent: 2 story brick house on First st. Apply to W B Tenney, Gtwn.

By writ of fieri facias, at the suit of Mary A Laskey, guardian & next friend of John M Laskey, an infant, against the goods & chattels of Wm Davis, & to me directed, I have seized sundry articles, property of Wm Davis, for public auction, on May 10, in front of the Centre Market-house, Wash, D C. –H R Maryman, Constable

N Y, May 2. Michl Mulrey entered the eating saloon of Geo Ricketts, in Chatham st, this morning, drew a pistol & shot the attendant dead. The attendant knew Mulrey did not have the means to pay for what he ordered, & refused his demands.

Mrd: on May 1, in Phil, by Rev J Y Ward, Mr John B Ward, of Wash City, to Miss Louisa P, daughter of E W Davis, Counsellor at Law, of Phil.

Mrs B Sprigg, on C st, between 3rd & 4½ sts, has several very pleasant rooms for the accommodation of Boarders.

Mrs M A Hills will open on Sat a beautiful assortment of Summer Millinery, on Pa ave, opposite Harper's.

MON MAY 5, 1851
Circuit Court of Wash Co, D C-in Chancery. Henry Dangerfield vs Mary Mudd et al. Bill in this case states that the cmplnt recovered a judgment against Ignatius Mudd in the Circuit Court of Wash Co, D C, Mar term, 1841, for $674.99, with interest, on $279 from Aug 1, 1840, on $195 from Aug 15, 1840, & on $195 from Aug 28, 1840, & costs; which judgment remains yet unsatisfied. It further states that Ignatius Mudd is dead, & Mary Mudd has been appointed by the Orphans Court of Wash Co, D C his admx; that the personal estate of Ignatius Mudd is insufficient to pay his debts, & it is necessary to sell his real estate; that he was heretofore seized of lot 13 & part of lot 14 in square 299, & conveyed the same to Clement Cox in trust to secure certain debts; that Walter S Cox was constituted trustee under said conveyance by decree of the Circuit Court after the death of Clememt Cox, & has recently sold a portion of lot 13 to pay a debt secured by said conveyance, but that the residue of said property is subject to the general debts of said Mudd, & it prays to have it sold to pay them. It further states that Ignatius Mudd left 2 children, Emily B Mudd & John H C Mudd, & John H C Mudd is not a resident of D C. Same to appear in this Court on or before the 3rd Mon of Oct next. –Jno A Smith, clk

Mrd: on Apr 29, at Balt, by Rev Geo W Burnap, Henry Rolando, U S N, to Ann Eliz, daughter of Dr Jno Buckler.

Died: on May 2, John George, son of J G & Lydia Weaver, aged 2 years, 4 months & 9 days.

Household & kitchen furniture at auction: on May 15, at the residence of J W Jones, corner of 4½ & N st. On the same day & place, will be sold the dwlg house & storehouse of Mr Jones. The lots are 40 thru 42, in square 503, forming the corner, 90 feet on N st & 135 feet on 4½ st. -A Green, auct

Obit: the late Maj Linnard, whose decease in the full meridian of manhood has just occurred in Phil, was a native of that city. He graduated at the Military Academy, & was commissioned a Lt in the 2nd Regt of Artl in 1830. Whilst serving with his regt in Fla, during the Seminole war, he was selected by Maj Gen Jesup, then commanding the Army of the South, as a member of his staff, & served as aid-de-camp to that Gen in the active campaigns of 1836 thru 1838. In 1838 he was transferred to the Topographical Engineers, & promoted to captaincy in 1842. In 1846 he joined the headquarters of Gen Taylor, in Mexico. Exposure & privation in the work of which he had the charge-the erection of an iron lighthouse on the southern extremity of Cape Florida-induced the disease which terminated his life. He came home, at last, only in time to die in the midst of his weeping family, & surrounded by those whom most he loved.

Wash City Ordinances: 1-Act for the relief of P H King: to pay him $30 for the unexpired term of his tavern license 2-Act for the relief of Traves Evans: fine imposed for violation in keeping a dog without license, is remitted: provided Evans pay the cost of prosecution. 3-Act for the relief of Thos Burk: he is hereby permitted to use & occupy as a livery stable the private stable & premises now occupied by him on lot 6 in square 257.

Judge Edmonds pronounced sentence of death in the Court of Oyer & Terminer in N Y last Fri, on Aaron B Stukey, for the murder of Zeddy Moore, & on Jas Wall for the murder of Michl Casey. Their executions will take place on Jun 28.

TUE MAY 6, 1851
Valuable Farm Houses, cows, hogs, farming utensils, & furniture at auction: on May 16, at the farm known as **Melrose**, about 1 mile above Bladensburg, adjoining the farm of Messrs Lounds & Cross. The farm contains about 200 acres. Upon it is a beautiful modern-built two & a half story cottage house, nearly new; & many out-bldgs. -A Green, auct

We learn from Harrisburg that Gov'n'r Johnston has nominated the Hon Geo Chambers, of Franklin Co, to fill the vacancy on the Bench of the Supreme Court of Pa caused by the recent death of the Hon Thos Burnside.

Gen Elijah J Roberts, late a State Senator from the Lake Superior District in Michigan, died in Detroit on Wed last. He was a practical printer, & was formerly associated with Maj Noah in the N Y Inquirer. He died in the 64th year of his age.

Levy Court of Wash, on Mon last, the Pres designated the following Justices of the Peace to be members of the Levy Court for Wash Co, D C, for the term of 1 year, viz: Henry Naylor, Chas H Wiltberger, Chas R Belt, Joshua Peirce, Lewis Carbery, Wm R Woodward, Robt White, Saml Drury, Benj K Morsell, John F Cox, & Jas Crandell.

Obit: The late Mrs Mary Ann Villard was a native of Phil, but had been a resident of D C for the last 35 years. She passed into the rest that remaineth for the people of God, after protracted & dreadful sufferings. –C M B

Obit: died-on May 1, at Woodsfield, Ohio, after a short but severe illness, Mr Enos M Morris, in his 24th year, son of the Hon Jos Morris. During the administration of Pres Polk the deceased was a resident of Wash. –F

Died: on May 3, of dropsy in the chest, Benjamin Franklin, son of Martha Jane & the late Benj Franklin Coston, aged 5 years & 4 months.

Household & kitchen furniture at auction: on May 7, at the residence of Wm Darby, on N J ave, near B st, Capitol Hill. -Dyer & McGuire, aucts

For rent: desirable 2 story brick dwlg, 2nd door east of the Union Hotel. Apply to E S Wright, or to Jas Fullalove, Gtwn.

Mount Pleasant Retreat. John Foy has removed from his old establishment, the Republican House, on D st, to the large & commodious mansion, nearly opposite the north gate of the Capitol. Plentiful supply of the usual luxuries.

WED MAY 7, 1851
The St Louis Republican notices the arrival of Col Sumner, of the 1st U S Infty, en route from Santa Fe, to take command of the Military force in that dept.

Albany Knickerbocker: the sloop **Meridian**, of Castleton, was upset when near Barrytown, in the squall of Thu last. Mrs Aaron Goodwin, Miss Vosbrugh, & one of the crew, Rufus Feathersby, were drowned.

In the Supreme Court of R I, on Wed, the jury in the suit of John A Perkins vs Frances Horsey, for a breach of promise of marriage, rendered a verdict of $3,000 for the plntf.

U S Patent Ofc, May 6, 1851: ptn of Chas H Titcomb, of Lowell, Mass, adm of Edgar M Titcomb, deceased, formerly of Andover, Mass, praying the extension of a patent granted to said Edgar M Titcomb for an improvement in a machine for spinning woolen roving, for 7 years from the expiration of the patent, which takes place on Jul 29, 1851. Thoe Ewbank, Com'r of Patents

Lamentable accident in Churchville, N Y, on Thu last, when a young man named Potter accidentally shot Miss Lyon. She is not expected to live. Potter became frantic with grief, ran from his home, & has not been heard of since.

Postmaster Gen has est'd the following new Post Ofcs for week ending May 3, 1851.

Ofc	County, State	Postmaster
Friends	Chautauque, N Y	Nehemiah I Finn
Angola	Sussex, Del	Peter R Benton
East Troy	Bradford, Pa	N Smith, 2nd
W Franklin	Bradford, Pa	Mordecai Chilicote
Prospect Mills	Lycoming, Pa	Jas Striker
Edge Hill	Montgomery, Pa	Danl Stout
Stewartsville	Westmoreland, Pa	Thos J Chalfant
Monticello	Jasper, Ga	Henry A Dickinson
Ellington	Outogamie, Wis	Rodney Mason
Moselle Furnace	Franklin, Mo	Geo L Nuckolls

Mrd: on May 6, in the Church of the Ascension, by Rev L J Gilliss, Elijah W Day, of Port Tobacco, Md, to Miss Mary Latimer, of Wash City.

Notice: the subscriber has left the papers connected with his former Land & Gen Agency in charge of Wm Jas Stone, jr, Counsellor at Law, F & 14th sts.
–Sam D King

For rent: 3 story brick house on 6th st, at present occupied by Purser Stockton, will be for rent from Sep 1st next. Apply to Mr Francis Mohun, east wing of the Patent Ofc.

Summer Millinery: Miss E Dashiell will open on May 8: south side of Bridge st, 1 door west of Jefferson st, Gtwn, D C.

On Sat last Mr Valentine Bartle, his wife Catharine, & a little child only 12 months old, residing on a small farm on the Ridge road, about 9 miles from Phil, were found cut & mangled in a most frightful manner, & completely dead. The remainder of the family, 3 children, were found secreted in a barn, to which they had fled for safety. It was evident they were killed with an axe. A young Italian or German, who had formerly worked on the farm, is supposed to have committed the fiendish deed, & a reward of $200 is offered for his apprehension.

Accident on the Mississippi river, near Carrollton, on Apr 28, in the upsetting of a skiff, which contained Mr Geo Logan, his 3 sons, & 5 negroes, all of whom drowned except Mr Logan & one of his sons.

Wash Co, D C: I hereby certify that Wm Barnes, of said county, brought before me, as a stray trespassing on his enclosures, a dark gray gelding. —B K Morsell, J P [Owner is to come forward, prove property, pay charges, & take him away. —Wm Barnes]

Orphans Court of Wash Co, D C. Letters of administration on the personal estate of John C Mullay, late of said county, deceased. —Cath D Mullay, admx

Wash Corp: 1-Ptn from John C McKelden, John C Rives, & others: act authorizing the construction of a reservoir in the alley in reservation 10, for the extinguishment of fires: passed. 2-Ptn from Geo W Stewart, for refunding half the original cost of a well & pump at the corner of H & 12th sts: referred to the Cmte of Claims. 3-Resolution submitted appointing Saml Drury, A G Ridgely, & Jas W Sheahan com'rs to hold an election in the First Ward, on Jun 2, for one member of the Board to fill the vacancy caused by the resignation of Saml Drury, adopted. 4-Cmte on Improvements: bill for the relief of Mary Ann & Abigail McMinn: passed. 5-Cmte on Finance: bill for the relief of Fanny Buchanan: passed. 6-Ptn of Jas Martin, praying indemnity for injuries done to his long boat caused by an obstruction in the Wash canal: referred to the Cmte of Claims. 7-Cmte on Police: bill for the relief of John M Farrar: passed.

$100 reward for runaway mulatto woman named Judy, who left on Nov 4, 1850. —Wm Major, 9 miles south of Culpeper Court-house.

THU MAY 8, 1851
The Hon Saml R Thurston, late Delegate in Congress from the Territory of Oregon, died on Apr 9, while on his way from Panama to San Francisco, on board the steamer **California**. His disease was dysentery. Senator Gwin, a passenger in the same steamer, had been seriously though not alarmingly ill, & was better on Apr 9.

Almira Beasly, a girl of 16, has been arrested at Providence on a charge of poisoning her brother, only 15 months old, by giving him arsenic. One witness said she told her that she gave arsenic to both her brother & her other sister. She was fully committed for trial for murder.

The Camanches, in their marauding excursions on the Southwestern frontier, frequently carry off white children. In the **Fort Smith** Herald of Apr 18, a poor man named Hart, of Refugio Co, Texas, had his oldest boy, age 12, stolen by the Comanches on the 11th. The father offers $200 reward for his recovery.

Miss Sarah A Chapell, from Lynn, was killed at Marblehead on Sunday. She was in a carriage, near the fort, when the horse became startled, & backed over a descent of about 20 feet, falling upon & crushing her so that she died instantly.

The chancery suit brought by Clarissa, a mulatto woman held as a slave, to assert her freedom, against B E Ferry & wife, who claimed to be her owners, was decided in the Franklin Circuit Court, in favor of Clarissa, & a decree establishing her freedom rendered by Judge McHenry. She had been detained in Pa by a former owner, for 7 months, & as personal attendants, only 6 months is allowed. –Frankfort [Ky] Commonwealth, Apr 29

Calif: Wildred & Stuart, indicted for the murderous attack upon & robbery of Mr Janson, have been tried & found guilty of assault with intent to kill & robbery. Stuart was sentenced to 14 years in the penitentiary, the most the Jury could give him. He has since been taken to Yuba Co, to be tried for murder. Wildred was sentenced to 10 years in the penitentiary.

The Cincinnati Commercial of Wed last notices the death of 2 persons of Asiatic cholera. One was a man named Dominick Gallary, who had recently arrived from New Orleans, & the other was a woman named Naughton, who had been taken from the steamboat. Her son was ill with the same disease, & not expected to recover.

Mrd: on Apr 29, at St Mary's Church, by Rev Mathias Alig, John Freeman to Miss Carolina Walter, both of Washington City.

Mrd: on May 4, by Rev Mathias Alig, Thos Donoho to Miss Jane Murter, of Washington City.

Mrd: on May 6, by Rev Mr French, John F Mullowny, late U S Consul at Tangiers, to Miss Amanda L Turpin, of Wash City.

Died: on Apr 18, in Jackson City, Miss, in her 44th year, Mrs Ann Eliza Johnson, consort of the Rev W P C Johnson, of St Andrew's Church of that city, leaving several children & numerous friends to mourn her loss. Mrs Johnson was a native of Fairfax Co, Va, & a niece of the late Judge Bushrod Washington, under whose hospitable roof at **Mount Vernon** she spent much of her youth.

Died: on Mar 15, on board the sloop-of-war **Warren**, off San Francisco, Lt Wm H Thompson, of the U S Navy.

Montg Co land for sale: 155 acres, within 4 miles of Rockville, [the county town,] & adjoining the farm of Roger Brocke, jr. Improvements are not of much value, there being only a small log house, surrounded by fruit trees. If not disposed of before May 22, it will on that day be offered at public auction, at the tavern kept by Mr Thos L F Higgins. Address Thos McCormick, Alexandria, Va. N B: Improved property in Washington would be taken in exchange, if desired.

Orphans Court of Wash Co, D C. Letters of administration on the personal estate of Saml Baldwin, deceased, late a resident in the Republic of Mexico.
—Andrew Wylie, jr, adm

The copartnership existing under the firm of McLaughlin & Duff is this day dissolved by mutual consent. All persons having claims against the said firm will present the same to Geo McLaughlin for settlement; & all persons indebted to the same will make payment to him. —Geo McLaughlin, Andrew Duff

In the matter of Chas S Matthews, the heirs of Wm P Matthews, Jas W Osborn & Eliza Ann his wife, Richd S Matthews, Ann Matthews, Benj H Dorsey & Henrietta his wife, Andrew S Matthews, & Alex'r McD Matthews, heirs at law of Wm P Matthews. The Com'rs on Apr 25, 1851, made sale at auction of the easternmost half of lot 2 in square 488, to Jas W Osborn, for $1,044.44; & of the westernmost half of the same lot to Andrew Rothwell, for $1,331.61; & the purchasers have complied with the terms of the sale. —Jno A Smith, clerk

By deed of trust from John G Gary, recorded in Liber W B 122, folios 211 thru 213, I will sell at public sale, at the auction rooms of Messrs Dyer & McGuire, in Wash City, on Jun 10 next: lots 5 thru 14 in square 152: said lots contain 120,217 square feet. J B H Smith, trustee -Dyer & McGuire, aucts

For rent, to a private family, a House, with back bldg, near Pa ave. Inquire at the store of Messrs Jas Galligan & Son, 7th & Pa ave.

FRI MAY 9, 1851

A young man, Chas Roberts, of Brodentown, N J, was run over by the train from N Y, which passed over him, killing him instantly.

A pear tree in N Y, bearing yearly noble & delicious fruit, still remains undisturbed in the yard attached to the old domicile of the late Peter Bonnett, in Frankfort st, near William, having been planted by his progenitors in the 17th century.

The Nat'l Monument, a weekly journal, is to be published in Wash, under the sanction of the Wash Nat'l Monument Society, Jas C Pickett, Editor & Publisher.

Laying the corner stone of Brown's Hotel: this corner stone for the rebuilding of Brown's Hotel was laid on May 8, 1851. Tillotson P Brown & Marshall Brown, proprietors & owners, under the supervision & architecture of John Haviland, of Phil; J Sniffin & Gilbert Cameron, [contractors of the Smithsonian Instutite,] contractors & builders; Thos Lewis, Bricklayer; Lawrie & Stewart, Stone Masons; Schneider & Martin, Iron Works; Brown & Sioussa, Plasterers; Foster & Evans, Plumbers; W H Harroer, Tinner; Parker & Spalding, Painters; Jas B Lokey, Excavator.

Mrd: on Thu, at Wesley Chapel, by Rev Mr Kenny, Thos W Grayson, Editor of Wash [Pa] Examiner, to Miss May Eliz, daughter of Mr A Green, of Wash City.

Millard Fillmore, Pres of the U S A, recognizes Armory Edwards, who has been appointed Consul General of the Republic of Nicaragua, to reside at N Y. May 5, 1851

Valuable bldg lot at auction: on May 18, in front of the premises, lot 5 in square 168, in Davidson's subdivision: located on F st, immediately in the rear of the residence of Com Warrington. –Francis A Lutz, Surviving Executor

For rent: 3 story brick bldg adjoining the residence of Mrs Wm Brent, on Delaware ave, Capitol Hill, now occupied by Mr Fred'k Skinner, & to be vacated on or about May 15. Apply to John Carroll Brent, at his ofc, C & 4½ sts, or his residence on Delaware ave.

SAT MAY 10, 1851
Dr Wm B Wilson, of Phil. died suddenly on Wed, at the Washington Hotel, in that city. He was seized with a violent hemorrhage & expired instantly. He had not been in good health for some time previously.

Nat'l Medical Convention: the following gentlemen were elected ofcrs for the ensuing year, 1851, on the recommendation of the nominating cmte:

Dr Jas Moultrie, of S C, Pres   Dr J B Flint, of Ky, Sec
Dr Geo Heyward, of Mass, V P   Dr Isaac Hays, Sec
Dr R D Arnold, of Ga, V P   Dr P C Gooch, Treasurer
Dr D R Wellford, of Va, V P

Explosion at Patterson, N J, yesterday, at the establishment of Messrs Rogers, Ketchum, & Grosvenor, in the testing of a new locomotive. The bodies of 4 killed were taken from the ruins-Amos Whitehead, superintendent; Thos Bustard, mechanic; John McNamara, apprentice; & Patrick Dougherty, laborer. Wm Warren, foreman of one of the depts., was severely bruised & scalded, & lower jaw broken; he is not expected to recover. 24 others were wounded, some of them severely. The want of sufficient water in the boiler was the cause of the explosion.

Mr Saml Stettinius, of Wash City, was arrested on Wed on the charge of forging the assignment of a land warrant, to the prejudice of Henry C Carter, a U S marine, now residing in the State of Delaware. Justice Donn decided to hold the accused to bail in the sum of $1,000 to await further proceedings. Mr Stettinius was released from custody.

Situation wanted as a Teacher: a young gentleman, a recent graduate of a Northern college, desires a situation at the South as private tutor or principal. Address S A Barrett, Cambridge, Mass.

Highly improved Farm at public sale: on May 27, known as the **Laurel Farm**, in PG Co: contains 610 acres: with 6 tenements on different parts of the farm, some of them in cottage form. Title indisputable. –Cannon, Bennett & Co, aucts

Orphans Court of Wash Co, D C. Letters testamentary on the personal estate of Thos Collins, late of said county, deceased. –David P Kurtz, exc

Balt, May 9. Judge Nicholas Brice, of the Balt City Court, died at his residence on North Chas st, in this city last night, after a lingering illness of some 2 years. He had been very infirm from age, being 80 years old, & has not occupied his seat on the bench for more than 18 months. He was appointed to the judgeship in 1817.

Died: yesterday, in Wash City, in her 72nd year, Mrs Catharine Goldsborough, relict of the late C W Goldsborough. Her funeral is tomorrow, at 3 o'clock, from her late residence at Mrs Ford's, corner of F & 19th sts.

Died: May 9, Mary A Holland, daughter of John E & Susannah Holland, in her 10th year. Her funeral is Sunday at 2 o'clock, from the residence of her father, on H, between 6th & 7th sts.

MON MAY 12, 1851
Mr Michl P Smith, an estimable citizen of Clearspring, Wash Co, Md, left his home on Easter Monday for Balt & Wash, & was to return in 4 or 5 days. He has not been heard of since he got out of the cars at the Relay House. He had in his possession from $10,000 to $15,000, & it is feared he may have been murdered. The Hagerstown papers state that his family are in the greatest distress concerning his safety, & request any one who may know anything concerning him to communicate with his brothers, Jas & John Smith, at Clearspring. –Balt American

The brig **Commerce**, from Bathurst, arrived at Boston on Tue, & the capt reports that on Fri he fell in with a boat & 11 men, who proved to be the surviving members of the crew of the ship **Minerva**, which was reported as capsized & all on board lost. Johnson, the cook, who is from Nantucket, died shortly after being taken on board the **Commerce**. Of the survivors, Capt Marchant & Mr Gorham, a baker, were taken into Holmes' Hole.

Mr Danl Wilcox, of Portsmouth, was choked to death whilst at his dinner on Thu, at the Pelham House, Newport, in endeavoring to swallow a piece of beef.

A day of two since, while Coroner Abel Kelley, of Kennebunk, Me, was holding an inquest upon the body of Wm Tenan, of the same, who had committed suicide, Kelly suddenly fell from a chair & died shortly afterwards.

Elijah Pease, an old farmer of 75 years, residing in Potsdam, St Lawrence Co, N Y, wanted to buy a farm, & went into Canada with a Mrs Smith, who professed to have one to sell, [left by her first husband, a Mr France,] under feigned circumstances. Here Pease & Mrs Smith traveled as man & wife, & while stopping at Kingston, Pease sickened & died, from what was found to be poison administered by Mrs Smith. She took possession of his money, $600, & sold his horse & wagon, but was soon arrested & her guilt exposed. Mrs Smith has a husband living, & Pease leaves a wife & grown-up children. It was then remembered that her first husband died quite suddenly. –Springfield Repub

The largest individual tax paid in N Y is by Wm B Astor. Last year he paid into the city treasury the sum of $23,891 for taxes. The assessed value of his property in that city is $2,600,300.

Two brothers residing in Guildball, Vt, by the name of Pelom, last week, got into a dispute, which resulted in the death of one. One attacked the other with a stake, & he in self defence struck him on the head with his fist, the blow fracturing his skull. The injured man lived about 6 hours.

Terrible affray last week in Daviess Co, Ky, resulted in death. The dispute was between the Payne & Turnbull families, about a fence or boundary between their respective estates, which were adjoining each other. One of the Paynes was killed outright, & others, in each family, were desperately wounded.

Nathan Taylor, Dr Luce, Benj Aylworth, Jas McDaniel, sen, Jas McDaniel, jr, & G H Brown, were arrested last week at Lanesborough, Pa, on a charge of counterfeiting.

Capt Morris Stanley, aged 86, a native of Wales, who came to this country with the late John Jacob Astor, & was engaged in several battles on board American vessels of war during the Revolution, died at his residence in Phil last week.

Three Cent Coin. Supplies of this new & desirable coin have been put into circulation, & prove very convenient The country will demand an abundant supply of them.

The jewelry shop of John Klein, South 3rd st, Phil, was on Wed robbed of property valued at $3,000-being nearly the entire stock. Albert & Jos Klein & Abraham Landis, sons & nephew of the proprietor of the store, have been arrested, charged with the robbery. The property was found on the premises of Abraham Landis, the nephew.

Household furniture & personal effects, at auction: on May 22, at the residence of the late Maj John C Mullay, deceased. -Dyer & McGuire, aucts

Mrd: on May 7, in Brooklyn, N Y, by Rev Dr Bethune, at the residence of her father, Miss Caroline Eliz, youngest daughter of Robt Speir, to Leonard Cassell McPhail, M D, late Surgeon U S Army.

Died: on Mar 28, at Memphis, Tenn, Wm Lanphier, in his 78th year. He was born in Fairfax Co, Va, & was a descendant of the Hugenots. His grandfather & father emigrated from Ireland to this country in 1732, & settled at Port Tobacco, in Md. Since 1784 he had been a resident of Alexandria, Va, until he moved to Memphis in 1845.

Died: on Apr 14 last, at the residence of her son-in-law, P D G Hedgman, in Stafford Co, Va, Mrs Hannah B Hedgman, relict of John G Hedgman, for many years delegate from that county, in her 72nd year.

Died: yesterday, after an illness of 9 weeks, Wm W Billing, the only son of the late Wm W Billing, aged 12 years & 5 months. His funeral is this evening, at 4 o'clock, from the residence of his mother, on H st north, near 6th st.

Died: on May 10, after a few hours' illness, Emma Elberta, aged 2 years, 10 months & 2 days, youngest daughter of Greenberry & Thomazine M Rowzee.

Farms & lots for sale, on the Brookvile road: 38 acres, with suitable bldgs. Refer to Chas Bunting, Cottage Post Ofc, Montg Co, Md.

All persons having claims against the personal estate of the late Mrs Dorcas Galvin will please present their accounts without delay. -J P Pepper, J W Hicks, excs

Orphans Court of Wash Co, D C. Letters testamentary on the personal estate of Chas B Hamilton, late of said county, deceased. -E Hamilton, excx

TUE MAY 13, 1851
Wash City Ordinances: 1-Act for the relief of Chas Stewart, jr: to pay him $150 for balance due for paving flag footways in Ward 2. 2-Act for the relief of Mary Ann & Abigail McMinn: the sum of $22.77, erroneously assessed against them for certain improvements in square 377, be remitted.

Orphans Court of Wash Co, D C. Letters of administration on the personal estate of Anna Whitmore, late of said county, deceased. -Geo Mockebee, adm

Last night a man named John Day, a bricklayer of Wash City, fired a revolver at his wife, Catharine Day, which caused her death in about half an hour. Mrs Day had been separated from her husband, & was living with her father in D st, between 13th & 14th sts. She was walking with her sister, &, seeing her husband coming near then, she hastened away. Day fired his revolver twice. Day was arrested by ofcr Boss, & committed to jail. [May 14th newspaper: The jury find that the said Catharine V Day was standing at her father's door on May 12, 1851, in company with her brother, sister Mary, her cousin, & Catharine B Keener, when John Day, her husband, came up to the party, & some words passed between the deceased & her husband, & he said, "I'll shoot you," & then pulling a pistol from his pocket, the deceased ran to get into the house, pursued by Day, & when entering the kitchen door, she was shot by said Day.]

On the life of the late Cmdor Jacob Jones: he wanted to be buried in his native State, Delaware, & on Oct 26, 1850, the last sad ceremony was performed with military honors. He was born near the town of Smyrna, Kent Co, Delaware, in Mar, 1768; at the time of his death, Aug 3 last, he was in his 83rd year. His father was an independent farmer & his mother was of a family greatly respected. She died while he was an infant; his father soon followed her to the grave, & at 4 years he was an orphan. He studied medicine under Dr Jas Sykes, of Dover. He married the sister of the distinguished gentleman under whose directions he commenced the study of his profession, & continued his residence in Kent until the death of that lady. At age 31 he entered the U S Navy. On Feb 22, 1801 he rose to the rank of Lt; on Apr 20, 1810, he was made a master commandant; & on Mar 3, 1813, he was promoted & rated as post capt in the U S Navy.

WED MAY 14, 1851
Postmaster Gen est'd the following new Post Ofcs for week ending May 10, 1851.

Ofc	County, State	Postmaster
North Collins	Erie, N Y	Paul H White
Mill Brook	Warren, N Y	John A Russell
Bristolville	Barry, Mich	Solomon P Hess
Rix	Ionia, Mich	Jos W Sprague
West neck	Kalamazoo, Mich	Friend C Bird
Attica	Lenawee, Mich	Chas Perry
Mill Point	Ottawa, Mich	L M S Smith
Wales	St Clair, Mich	Benson Bartlett
Antrim	Shiswassee, Mich	John Near
South Aeworth	Sullivan, N H	Jas M Holden
Pontiac	Erie, N Y	Isaac N Candee
Schraslenburgh	Bergen, N J	J C Quackinbush
Black Horse	Middlesex, N J	A V P Davison
Pedricktown	Salem, N J	Hudson A Springer
West Windham	Bradford, Pa	Jos B Webster

Cherry Hill	Erie, Pa	Ira Harrington
Coal Port	Indiana, Pa	John Fulton
Drehersville	Schuylkill, Pa	Jacob Dreher
Clark's Corner	Ashtabula, Ohio	Ashael K Warren
Waller	Rose, Ohio	Beroth Eggleston
Oak	Williams, Ohio	John Stubbs
Riceville	Pittsylvania, Va	L W Clements
Farmington	Ritchie, Va	S S Austin
Paddy Mills	Shenandoah, Va	Thos Edwards
North Fork	Washington, Va	Abraham Linder
Midway	Giles, Va	Jos Kyle
Hayter's Gap	Washington, Va	Ota H Ward
Tunnel	Augusta, Va	John R Hopkins
Elevation	Johnston, N C	D H Holland
Creachville	Johnston, N C	S P Horton
Canoe Creek	Burke, N C	Wm Alexander
Clay	Yancy, N C	J D Woodward
Branch Island	Pickens, S C	Jos Yenny
Sugar Hill	Hall, Ga	Jas A Thomas
Indian Creek	Jackson, Ga	Russel D Park
Fancy Bluff	Glynn, Ga	Francis D Scarlett
Ocklockney	Thomas, Ga	Wm McLeod
Gum Pond	Baker, Ga	Wm B Crawford
Everett's Spring	Floyd, Ga	Thompson Everett
Leo	Habersham, Ga	Champion Ferguson
Halawaka	Chambers, Ala	W H H Griffin
Dover	Yazoo, Miss	D M Lewis
Albemarle	Carrol, Miss	Thos Hubbard
Percy's Creek	Wilkinson, Miss	W C Walker
Tunica	West Feliciana, La	Oliver P Robinson
Union	Jasper, Texas	Jno Henderson
Olivet	Russel, Ala	Jas B Hall
Jinny Lind	Sebastian, Ark	Thos Yadon
Hale	Ogle, Ill	A Wilban
Illinois City	Rock Island, Ill	E Beardsley
Wythe	Hancock, Ill	Lyman L Calkins
Boon's Lick	Howard, Mo	N M Bonham
Mount Prospect	Whiteside, Ill	Jas Haukey
Pilot Hill	Mason, Ill	Jas More
Bell Plain	Marshall, Ill	Nathan Patton
Moultonville	Madison, Ill	Orris G Moulton
Romeo	McHenry, Ill	Jas Cross
Wellington	Lake, Ill	Peter Loron

Prairie	Lewis, Mo	M L Williams
Stony Point	Jackson, Mo	Jacob Gregg
Oakley	Lewis, Mo	Bayly R Glascock
Dairy	Scotland, Mo	Levi Myers
Heath's Creek	Pettis, Mo	Aaron Jenkins
Hallsville	Boone, Mo	John W Hall
Looney's Creek	Marion, Tenn	Jos B Kelley
Foster's Mills	Johnson, Ia	Philip G Robison
Little Eckhart	Elkhart, Ia	David Eldridge
New Bethel	Marion, Ia	Rich O'Neal
Zion	Grant, Ia	Henry Egbert
Hurt's Mills	Harrison, Ia	Jacob Greiner
Olive	Marion, Ia	Peyton Bristow
Grayson Springs	Grayson, Ky	Theo Munford
Luda	Washita, Ark	John Carr

Names Changed: Greene, Kennebeck Co, Maine, changed to Greene Corner.
Greene Depot, Kennebeck Co, Maine, changed to Greene.
Gary's Ferry, Duvall Co, Fla, changed to Middlebury.
Eden, Harris Co, Texas, changed to Hamblin.
Cheat River Depot, Preston Co, Va, changed to Section.
Howes, Concordia Parish, La, changed to Tooley's.
Cave Spring, Scott Co, Ky, changed to Springdale.
Bluff, Mercer Co, Ill, changed to Pope's Mills.
Loretto, Sauk Co, Wisc, changed to Dellton.
Oak Ridge, Green Co, Ind, changed to Owensburg.

Adm Sir Edw Codrington, one of the oldest flag ofcrs in the British navy, died in London on Apr 27, in his 82nd year. He was Lt of the Queen Charlotte, in Howe's memorable victory of Jun 1, 1794. At the battle of Trafalar he was Capt of the Orion. He was also Capt of the Fleet, in the Chesapeake & at New Orleans, in 1814.

On May 8, while crossing the Ohio river in a ferry boat, below New Albany, Ind, with a buggy & horse, W H Parker, of Tenn, was drowned. His horse took fright & jumped into the river. Mr Parker endeavored to extricate the horse from the buggy, & both were drowned.

At Alexandria, on Sun, Mr Wm Page, Deputy Grand Master of the Masonic Fraternity, whilst delivering a lecture in the Wash Lodge room, suddenly fell & instantly expired. He leaves a large family, & was generally esteemed.

Mrd: on May 13, in Trinity Church, Wash, by Rev Dr Butler, Mathew Harrison, of Va, to Harriette L, daughter of Gen Walter Jones.

Mrd: on May 8, in Balt Co, Md, by Rev Mr Hamner, Saml B Beyer, of Wash, D C, to Miss Sarah A, daughter of Jas Reeside, of Balt Co.

Died: on Apr 29, in Cincinnati, Ohio, of typhoid fever, Chas H Goldsborough, 2nd son of the late Chas W Goldsborough, of Wash City.

The funeral of Mrs Catharine V Day will take place this afternoon, at 2 o'clock, from the residence of her father, Geo W Freedley, on D st north, between 13 & 13½ sts.

Marshal's sale: by 2 writs of venditioni exponas: public sale on Jun 9, of a certain Flour Mill in Gtwn, D C, on Water st, being parts of lots 34, 35, & 38, on which is a 3 story brick house used by Robinson & Anderson as a grocery store, in virtue of a certain account of the said plnts, filed in the Clerk's ofc of Wash Co, against the said dfndnt, as trustee of Francis H P Robinson: seized & levied upon, & will be sold to satisfy judicials #5, to Oct, 1851, Wm T Duvall vs Robt Ould, & #6, to Oct, 1851, Mayndier Mason vs Robt Ould, trustee of Francis H P Robinson.
–Richd Wallach, Marshal of D C

THU MAY 15, 1851
Wash Corp: 1-Ptn from Jos Ingle, exc of Catharine Coyle & Jas Casparis, for relaying the curb stone, pavement, & gutter from the alley on the south side of square 688 to N J ave: referred to the Cmte on Improvements. 2-Cmte of Claims: asked to be discharged from the further consideration of the ptn of Clark Mills: ordered to lie on the table. 3-Cmte of Claims: bill for the relief of Wm O Jones: ordered to lie on the table. 4-Ptn from L H Berryman & others, for the improvement of Va ave: referred to the Cmte on Improvements. 5-Ptn from Saml Butt, for payment for medicine furnished the out-door poor: referred to the Cmte on the Asylum. 6-Ptn from J F Wollard, asking a settlement of his accounts as police constable of the 3rd Ward: referred to the Cmte on Police. 7-Ptn from Wm Cox, asking compensation for the arrest of Frank Camper, on a warrant charging him with the murder of Martin Ragan. 8-Ptn from A E L Keese & Wm Cox, asking compensation for arresting Sandy Sprig, who assaulted, with intent to rob & kill John Hutchinson, both of which were referred to the Cmte on Police. 9-Bill for the relief of David Westerfield: passed. 10-Ptn of Saml Adams, praying remission of a fine: referred to the Cmte of Claims. 11-Com'rs appointed to hold elections in the several Wards on the first Monday of June:

Saml Drury	W A Kennedy	Saml Hanson
A G Ridgely	E C Dyer	John R Queen
Jas W Sheahan	Peter F Bacon	Saml S Briggs
Elexius Simms	Geo S Gideon	Thos Kelly
Michl P Callan	F A Klopfer	Saml Byington
John D James	Chas Munroe	B S Kinnsey
Geo Crandell	J T Van Reswick	John E Foulkes

Miss Saunders, in Louisiana, has recovered $12,000 damaged from Wm L Shaw for defamation of character. What the slander consisted of is not stated.

Fine Durham Bull Calf at Auction: on May 17, in front of my Auction Room, a Calf belonging to Mr Chas B Calvert. Terms cash. –A Green, auctioneer

At Cincinnati on Fri last a carpenter named Ezra O'Hara was shot dead by a man named Warwick, from Lexington, Ky. On the same day, Mrs Mason, widow of the late Dr Mason, entered the law ofc of John M Wilson, & deliberately fired a double barreled pistol twice at him. The balls fortunately missed him. She fainted immediately afterwards, & was taken away insensible.

Mrd: on May 14, in Wesley Chapel, Wash, by Rev G W Israel, Jas Williams, of Montg Co, Md, to Martha A Israel, of the former place.

Died: on Tue last, at Balt, after a short illness, in his 62nd year, Gen Wm H Marriott, long a respected resident of that city, & formerly the Collector of the port of Balt.

For sale, a valuable Farm in Alexandria Co, Va, containing 110 acres. Apply at the Law Ofc of the subscriber, on 5th st. –Edw Swann

FRI MAY 16, 1851
Household & kitchen furniture at auction: on May 19, at the residence of the late Thos Collins, deceased, on 8th st, between G & H sts. –P Kurtz, adm
–A Green, auctioneer

Household & kitchen furniture at auction: on May 21, at the residence of Capt Aulick, on 13th st, between E & F sts. –A Green, auctioneer

Valuable bldg lots at auction: by decree of Orphans Court of Wash Co, D C, sitting in Chancery: public auction on May 20, of lot 32 in square 87, fronting on 7th st, between F & F sts. At the same time: lot 6 in square 1,078, at the corner of 15th st east & K st south. By order of Sarah Ann Mount, Guardian.
–Dyer & McGuire, aucts

On Wed afternoon, while two of the hands [Lewis Payne] Dennis Dacy] at **Oak Hill Cemetery** were engaged in blasting rock; a premature explosion of the powder took place, seriously injuring them both. Mr Payne had one of his hands so much shattered that it is thought amputation will be necessary, & Mr Dacy had his face & eyes badly injured.

Wanted: a competent female servant to do the house work of a small family. Also, a girl of 12 to 15, to nurse. Inquire for Wadsworth, at the recent residence of Capt H B Sawyer, 1st Ward, nearly opposite the Six Bldgs, Wash. –D Wadsworth

Dr A J Schwartze has resumed the practice of medicine: ofc on Pa ave, near 3rd st. The Apothecary & Drug business will in the future be conducted by his son, John Schwartze.

SAT MAY 17, 1851

Having found it expedient to visit Calif, to return on or about the last of Aug next, I have entrusted all my business matters to the care & attention of Maj Wm B Scott, of Wash City, to whom all persons having business relations with me are respectfully referred. -Beverly Tucker

For sale: that valuable 2 story brick dwlg & bakery, on East Capitol st, being the next lot to the corner fronting on the Capitol square, & being part of lot 10 in square 728. The house is now occupied by Mr Langley as a bakery, at the annual rent of $150. -Thos Jarboe

The oldest woman in the world is supposed to be one Mary Benton, now residing at Elton, in Durham Co, England. She was born on Feb 12, 1731, & is of course in her 121st year. She is in possession of all her faculties, perfect memory, hearing & eyesight. She cooks, washes, & irons in the usual family avocations, threads her needle, & sews without spectacles.

Cornell S Franklin has been appointed Naval Ofcr, ad interim, of the Port of N Y, in place of the late Philip Hone, deceased.

Steam boiler explosion on May 14 at the foundry of J P Morris, at Richmond, near Phil, killing Mr Hugh Sweeny, who had his head blown off, & so seriously injuring Messrs J B Reynolds & Wm M Sheppard, they are not expected to live. Two other men are missing.

Wash City: a man, David Rowles, well known to our Criminal Court, was arrested yesterday by ofcr Mulloy, on suspicion of robbing the dwlg of Mrs Nisbet, on C st, between 3rd & 4½ sts, on Thu. The prisoner was fully committed for trial.

For rent: commodious 3 story brick house at the corner of Md ave & 10th st. Rent moderate to a good tenant. Apply on the premises, or to the subscriber, at his yard, Railroad Depot. –M G Emery

Circuit Court of Wash Co, D C, in Chancery. Blagden vs Callan, adm, & heirs at law of Jas Hoban, deceased. John F Ennis, the trustee in the above cause, reported the sale of part of lot 2 in square 147, to Chas H Van Patten for $168, & part of lot 2 in square 148 to John F Callan for $25; & the purchasers have complied with the terms of the sale. -Jno A Smith, clerk

Lincoln W Pettibone, a young man of talent & great promise, a lawyer by profession, retired to a room below his ofc, at Delaware, on May 12, & shot himself through the head with a rifle, producing instant death. The cause of this rash act was not ascertained.

Rev Chas Hill committed suicide on May 9, at Leominster, Mass, aged 65 years. He had the preceding Sabbath officiated in the pulpit. No cause given for the unhappy deed.

Mrd: Thu, by Rev John C Smith, Bushrod Jolly to Miss Lucinda J Brewer, both of Upperville, Va.

Died: Thu, Adelaide Carothers, daughter of John T & Emily S Given, aged 4 years & 9 months.

Musical Instruction: formerly Prof of Music in St Mary's College, Balt, & more recently in St Timothy's Hall, Catonsville, Md, announced that he will give lessons on the Piano Forte, Organ, Flute, & other instruments. Apply at the residence of Rev J R Donelan, St Matthew's Church, or at the Piano Store of Mr Richd Davis, Pa ave. –J Theo McKenna, Organist St Matthew's Church

The public are warned not to trust any one on my account, except my daughters, without a written order, in each case, from one of them or from me. –Th S Jesup

MON MAY 19, 1851
Rev Erskine Mason, D D, Pastor of Bleecker st Presbyterian Church, N Y, died on Wed after an illness of several months. His age was 47.

On May 3 several Cadets of the Western Military Institute at Drennon Springs, Ky were preparing their guns for a hunting expedition, when young Mr Harlitt, a Cadet, pointed it at his personal friend, young Mr Forestall, & pulled the trigger. The discharge so severely wounded Forstall that he died a few days afterwards.

In the Circuit Court of the U S for the District of Georgia, on May 13, his honor Judge Nicoll presiding, Theodore Orville Brown, of Augusta, [age about 17 years,] was convicted of embezzling from the U S mail on 2 indictments, & sentenced to 10 years hard labor in the State's prison for each offence.

By virtue of 3 writs of venditioni exponas, I shall expose at public auction, on Jun 20, lots 19 thru 22 in square 117, with improvements thereon, situated on M st, Wash City, the property of John T S McConchie, seized & taken in execution at the suits of John F May. –H R Maryman, Constable

Local: yesterday a violent storm passed over out city, during which the large barn of Wm J Stone was struck by lightning, & the barn & contents were destroyed, including 3 valuable horses. The lightning also struck the house occupied by Mr H H McPherson, apothecary, 7th & H sts, where slight damage was done. Mr J Connolly's cabinet maker's shop, was also struck, but escaped with slight injury.

Millard Fillmore, Pres of the U S A, recognizes Johannes Jacob Ludwig Herrlich, who has been appointed Vice Consul of Sweden & Norway, for San Francisco, Calif. May 17, 1851

Mrd: on May 15, by Rev Mr Massey, J T Radcliff, of Wash, to Louisa Harrison, daughter of the late Jos Harrison, of Talbot Co, Md.

Mrd: on May 15, by Rev Mr Hodges, Mr Stark B Taylor to Miss Mary Ellen Norris, all of Wash.

Mrd: on Wed last, by Rev C A Davis, Thos Shackelford to Frances Davis, both of Prince William Co, Va.

Mrd: on Thu, by Rev C A Davis, Herry Yeatman to Susan Amelia Thompson, all of Wash City.

Clermont, an elegant country seat, near Alexandria, formerly the property of Gen Mason, but more recently owned by Levin Powell, was on Sat purchased by Capt Frances Forrest, of Wash City, at $10,020. It contains 312 acres of land, besides the costly dwlg & other houses.

Coroner's Inquest: on Sat last, before Thos Woodward, it appeared that the death of John Merinder, a sailor, was caused by receiving a blow from Capt John Powell, of the schnr **Patrick Henry**, on May 8, while the schnr was off White Point, on the Potomac, near the Va shore.

Orphans Court of Wash Co, D C. Letters of administration, with the will annexed, on the personal estate of Julian Montandon, late of said county, deceased.
-Elias Travers, adm w a

TUE MAY 20, 1851
Wanted immediately: a first rate Servant-Woman, who can come well recommended. Also, a Chambermaid, slaves preferred. Best wages will be given. Apply to Mrs C Woodward, on H st, between 9th & 10th sts.

Household & kitchen furniture at auction: on May 23, at the residence of Mr Geo Deffner, on Pa ave, between 21st & 22nd sts. -Dyer & McGuire, aucts

St Mary's Female Seminary, St Mary's Co, Md. The Board desires to procure a Principal & 2 Assist Teachers for the ensuing scholastic year, commencing on Sep 1 next. The ofc of Principal has heretofore been held by a member of the Protestant Episcopal Church, & it is desired by the Trustees to fill the place with one of that denomination. It is also desirable that one of the Assist Teachers should be a member of the Roman Catholic Church. Principal salary-$350; Assist Teachers-$300. Apply to the undersigned, at Leonardtown, St Mary's Co, Md: H G S Key, Wm I Edelen, & Jas T Blakistone.

Wash Corp Ordinances. 1-Act for the relief of D J Bishop: fine imposed for a law in relation to licenses, is remitted: provided Bishop pays the costs of prosecution. 2-Act for the relief of David Westerfield: $10.95 to be paid him for the balance due him for services rendered while acting as police ofcr of the 7th Ward.

Circuit Court of Wash Co, D C-in Chancery. Wm H Irwin, vs Alex'r H Lawrence, adm, & Priscilla Dines, heirs at law of Hanson Dines, deceased. The Trustee reports he sold lot 12 in square 798, in Wash City, to John B Magill, for $70, & the purchaser has paid the purchase money. The Trustee also made a report, stating that Jas Pullen, the original purchaser of lot G in square 797, Wash City, having made a transfer of his said purchase of said lot to Almericus Zappone, has complied with the terms of said sale. Ratify same. -Jno A Smith, clerk

For rent: a brick Coach House & Stable in the rear of **Gadsby's Row**. Also, the Barber Shop attached to the Row. Apply to J H McBlair.

WED MAY 21, 1851
On Tue last, a youth in the town of Fredericksburg, named Gideon Hazlup, was burnt to death by the explosion of a barrel of whiskey, the contents of which ignited from a candle in his hand.

At New Orleans, on May 10, while Mrs Ramos, wife of the Alderman of that name, was seated in the sleeping apartment of her children, a camphine lamp exploded, setting fire to the bed curtains & burning the children most horribly. One died shortly afterwards, & the other sister was not expected to survive. The 3rd child was also much injured.

Sad accident on May 6: Mr C Bulwinkle, of Walhalla, S C, together with Mrs Bulwinkle & child, were thrown from a vehicle in which they were driving, by the horse taking fright. They were so badly injured that Mr Bulwinkle & his child died in a few hours; Mrs Bulwinkle, though seriously hurt, is said to be recovering. Mr Bulwinkle was an intelligent & enterprising German, one of the chief of the German settlement, & his loss will be severely felt & sorely lamented by his countrymen. –Pickens Courier

Sir Richd Parkenham, formerly Envoy to the U S, & who has been on the retired list since his leaving Wash, is appointed her Majesty's Minister at Lisbon.

Sarah H Hurst, daughter of one of the Swiss Bell Ringers, was drowned on May 1 in the Contocook river at Fisherville, N H. She was 10 years of age, & lost her hold when crossing Sawyer's bridge, & fell into the swift stream.

Postmaster Gen est'd the following new Post Ofcs for week ending May 17, 1851.

Ofc	County, State	Postmaster
Prairieville	Barry, Mich	A T Allen
Spring Creek	Berrien, Mich	Geo Drake
Pine Plain	Montcalm, Mich	Timothy S Coates
Ora	St Clair, Mich	Ira Marks
Pumpkin	Southampton, Va	Jas M Grizzard
Griffithsville	Cabell, Va	Alex'r Griffith
Bunger's Mill	Greenbrier, Va	Wallace Robinson
Durbamville	Orange, N C	Jasiah T Moore
Pleasnat Oaks	Mecklenburgh, N C	S H Elliott
Green Hill	Rutherford, N C	Wm B McEntire
Edisto Mills	Edgefield, S C	Patrick J Coleman
Sugar Creek	Telfair, Ga	Murdock H McRae
Heronia	Telfair, Ga	Hiram Swain
Farriorville	Pike, Ala	Jos W Hubbard
Milbridge	Giles, Tenn	Saml H Stout
Westview	Hamilton, Tenn	Saml T Igon
Rally Hill	Maury, Tenn	Duncan McRae
Waldo	Wright, Mo	Elias W Walls
Russell's Store	Boone, Ill	Jas M Russels
Pioneer	Greene, Ill	Jordan W Calvin
Night's Prairie	Hamilton, Ill	John B Lockwood
St Joseph's	Champaign, Ill	Jos S Kelly
St Jacob	Madison, Il	Jacob Schroth
Cypress Creek	Johnson, Ill	Jacob Keisler
Ney	De Kalb, Ill	Curtis Goodsil
Oneonta	Sauk, Wis	Joel Hunter
Bear Creek	Sauk, Wis	John Bear
Roslin	Marquette, Wis	P C Gray
Rocky Run	Columbia, Wis	Jesse F Hand
Mount Pleasant	Greene, Wis	L W P Morton
St Mary's	Lafayette, Wis	Richd Morrill
Pin Hook	Grant, Wis	J M Robinson

Name Changed: Stoneham, Oxford, Maine, changed to North Lovell.

Mr Jas McAllister was killed by lightning during the storm of Tue, at Chesapeake City, Cecil Co, Md. He was going to his house, & his wife was at the door to meet him, when he was suddenly struck down. His hat & boots were torn to atoms, & his death instant.

Mr Wm Piggford, a native of this county, died a few days ago, aged 87 years, after living with his wife 65 years, whom he has left a widow to mourn her loss. He is one of 6 brothers & sisters, whose average age is 80. He has left an only daughter, now 63 years old; & not one of them ever took a dose of medicine from a physician, were ever bled or blistered, until they attained the age of 60; but have lived temperately & used but little animal food. Within 10 miles of Sill's Creek, on which this family was raised, there has never occurred a case of pulmonary disease or consumption. –Wilmington, [N C] Come

Geo W Slocum, a resident of Genoa township, Delaware Co, Ohio, deliberately murdered his wife on May 15, & then attempted to cut his own throat, but failed, & is now in jail. He is about 45 years of age, & is said to have been intemperate.

At a large gathering at Cannelton, Ind, some days ago, an explosion took place, breaking the arm of Mr Jas Cavender, & killing the 14 year old son of Mr Leming.

Mrd: on May 17, by Rev O B Brown, Chas G Griffith, of Balt, to Miss Frances, daughter of Hazard Knowles, of Wash.

Died: on May 18, of scarlet fever, Clarence S M, aged 4 years, 6 months & 15 days, son of J G & Lydia Weaver.

Died: on May 11, at Buffalo, Ebenezer F Norton, aged 77 years. Mr Norton, some 25 years ago, represented his district in Congress.

Died: on May 13, at Poughkeepsie, N Y, Mary Eliz Cunningham, eldest daughter of Gen Walter Cunningham, of that city.

Desirable land for sale: 200 acres on the Eastern Branch, within one mile of Wash City. Apply at the Potomac Savings' Bank, opposite the Post Ofc, to T M Hanson.

THU MAY 22, 1851
The house of Robt Sherwell, in Columbia st, near Pierrepont, Brooklyn, N Y, has been rented for Jenny Lind, who intends making that city her residence for the ensuing 3 months. It is understood that her cousin, together with Benedetti, Salvi, & Belletti, will reside with her.

Household & kitchen furniture at auction: on May 26, at the residence of Mrs M H Turpin, on 10th st, between D & E sts. -A Green, auctioneer

Pianos & Music: in stock are 2 magnificent Louis XIV Pianos, & a number of 7, 6¼ & 6½ centual Pianos from the renowned factory of Chickering, Boston.
-Richd Davis, Pa ave

Wash Corp: 1-Ptn from Daman Foller & others, for a foot-bridge over the run at the intersection of N Y ave & North Capitol st: referred to the Cmte on Improvements. 2-Cmte on Police: bill for the relief of J F Wollard, police ofcr of the 3rd Ward: passed. 3-Bill for the relief of Wm Pegg: passed. 4-Cmte of Claims: asked to be discharged from the further consideration of the ptn of Danl Rowland: which was agreed to.

Mr John Wilson, of Charlotte Co, Va, was murdered on his plantation on May 13. He was found in a branch, his body perforated by a rifle ball. Life was not extinct when he was first found, but he had passed the power of speech, & survived but a few hours. He was unmarried, aged about 30, & generally esteemed in his neighborhood.

Henry Wellman was killed, at Cincinnati, on Thu week, by being run over by a fire-engine.

Steamboat disaster near Phil on Mon, off Greenwich Point: the steamer **Ohio**, of the Union line, [the regular packet between Phil & Newcastle,] was so much damaged that she sunk in 20 minutes after the collision. The Gloucester steamer **Commodore Stockton** ran into the Ohio. The body of a young man, named Taylor, a clerk in a hat store at Charleston, [S S,] has been removed; Mr John Finlay, of Balt is missing; Dr Wood, Gen Taylor's son-in-law, lost all his baggage & many valuable papers; Lt Wise, lost his baggage & $1,000; Mrs Toothaker, [so spelt in our dispatch,] of Wash, lost her baggage & money, but saved her child; John Wills, of Balt, who swam ashore, recovered his baggage.

Administrator's sale of the extensive & valuable private stock of wines of the late Mr Hussey, former Proprietor of the Eutaw House, Balt. The undersigned, Administrator of Asabel Hussey, deceased, will sell at public auction on May 20, at the warehouse 365 Balt st, the very valuable stock. –Isaac Dillon, Adm
-Gibson & Co, aucts

Died: on Tue, after a painful illness, Thos Greeves, in his 68th year. Truly, his end was peace! His funeral is this evening, at 4 o'clock, from his late residence on 5th st, between M & N sts.

FRI MAY 23, 1851
Furnished house or parlors to rent: located near the President's Grounds. Inquire of D A Gardner, on N Y ave, next to 15th st.

Valuable Gtwn Property at Public Auction: on Jun 11, the north part of lot 23 in Beall's addition to Gtwn, fronting on the west side of Washington st 25 feet, improved by a 2 story brick dwlg & back bldg. For particulars inquire of Mr John Myers, Gtwn, or address Saml Hunt, Agent for the heirs, 167 Balt st, Balt, Md.

First Ward Ice Cream Saloon has re-opened 2 fine rooms, between 17th & 18th sts, on Pa ave, for the accommodation of ladies & gentlemen, for the best of Ice Cream, Cakes, & all kinds of Confectionaries. –Jacob Brodbeck

$5 reward: left Balt yesterday, & came to Wash City in the cars of last evening, 2 boys, about 13 years old, Wm Cary & Geo Fox. The reward will be paid for information of the whereabouts of Wm Cary by his distressed mother, on application to Timothy Shannon, porter of the Nat'l Hotel.

County Court of Balt, before Judge Legrand, in the case of Miss Caroline Seeger vs John F Bartholdt, an action of damages for breach of promise of marriage & seduction, a verdict in favor of the pntf rendered for $3,000 damages, the largest amount of damages in a case of this kind which has ever been rendered in this Court.

Wash City: the two towers on Trinity Church at 3rd & C sts, will be erected by Mr John Cameron, who superintends the operations of the workmen who are employed to build these towers, that they will be of an octagonal shape, each tower terminating in a spire.

Mrd: on May 20, in Gtwn, by Rev Dr Ryder, Wm G Hardy, M D, to Mrs Matilda Hill, both of the District.

Mrd: on May 22, at the Foundry M E Church, by Rev L F Morgan, Rev Robt Kellen, of Concord Biblical Institute, to Miss Euphemia Jane, eldest daughter of Abner Young, of Wash City.

Died: on May 18, at Smithtown, Long Island, N Y, by Rev J C Edwards, J Crutchett to Miss Marcia Augusta Smith, daughter of the late Richd Smith, of Smithtown.

Died: on May 22, after a long & painful illness, Mrs Eleanor Maria McIntosh, [daughter of the late Thos Foote, of London,] wife of J M McIntosh, formerly of Va, but for the last 12 years a resident of Wash City. Her funeral is today at 10 A M, from the residence of her husband, on the corner of 10th & L sts.

SAT MAY 24, 1851
The Marquise de Livry died on May 1 at the Chateau de Lasson, [Calvados.] She belonged to one of the oldest families in France. Her father, who was a captain in the service of Louis XVI, was guillotined, & she was detained in the prison of St Lazare, & only avoided a similar fate by making her escape in disguise.

Appointment by the Pres: Harlow Case, Collector of the Customs at Sandusky, Ohio, vice John Youngs.

$5 reward for strayed or stolen small red & white Cow. I will give the above reward upon her delivery at my residence, 9th st, near H st. —Charlotte D Sandy

Reuben Weed, arrested in Bethany, Conn, on Apr 8, for breaking into & entering the house of Mrs Lucy L Beecher, in the day time, & threatening the lives of Mrs Beecher & her children, was found guilty, & sentenced to 30 days in the county jail. He was committed the same day. On Sun he was found dead, hung by the neck from the door of his cell.

P G Co Court, as a Court of Equity. John H Clagett & Catharine J his wife, & Harriet E Beans, vs Jas Edelen. The suit is to procure a decree for the sale of certain lands & real estate in said county, of which Henry A Edelen died seized & possessed; & also to obtain a decree for rents & property received from said land against Jas Edelen, who has been in possession of the premises for 12 years. The bill states that Henry A Edelen died about 1835 intestate, & without ever having been married; that he died seized & possessed of **Locust Hill**, & **Fort Adams**, in said county; that he left the following persons, his brother & sisters & heirs at law, to wit: Horace Edelen, Jas Edelen, Wm M Edelen, Aloysius Edelen, Jos Edelen, who died intestate & without ever having been married, Emily Edelen who intermarried with Benedict J Semmes, Mary Olive Edelen, who married Thos F Semmes, Catharine Edelen, who married John H Beans, the parent of the said cmplnts, Catharine & Harriet E Beans, & both of whom left the said cmplnts their only children & heirs at law; Matilda Edelen, who married ___ Bowen, of Calvert Co, Md; Celeste Edelen, who married Saml C McPherson; that the said cmplnts are entitled to one undivided eleventh part between them of the said lands & real estate, & to the one undivided tenth part of the interest & share of the said Jos Edelen in said lands & real estate; that the said Jas Edelen has purchased the interest of all the heirs at law & persons entitled to said premiums, except the interests of these female cmplnts, & has been in possession of the said premises for 12 years, receiving the rents, issues, & profits; that the said cmplnts have derived no benefit or advantage from the said lands, nor have they received any thing from the said Jas Edelen on account of the rents & profits; that the said lands are not susceptible of an advantageous partition among these entitled to them, & that it would be for the benefit & advantage of all interested to have the land sold for the purpose of division; & also prays for a decree against the said Jas A Edelen for rents & profits, & that the said Jas Edelen resides out of the State of Md. He is warned to appear in this Court on or before Nov 1 next.
–Edmund Key   -John B Brooke, Clerk of PG Co, Court.

Household & kitchen furniture at auction: on May 26, at the residence of Mr John Knoblock, on 19th st. -Dyer & McGuire, aucts

Circuit Court at Milwaukee, Wis: May 16, Jas Holliday, one of the most esteemed members of the bar of that city, while pleading a case was suddenly taken ill, & before he could be removed from the Court expired. His death was caused by rheumatism of the heart.

Wash Corp: 1-Ptn from Geo Parker & others, asking an appropriation for a display of fireworks on Jul 4: referred to a select cmte. 2-Ptn from P W Browning & others, remonstrating against the erection of gas works on square C, on Maine st: referred to the Cmte on Police. 3-Bill for the relief of Joshua Peirce: ordered to lie on the table.

Mrd: on Apr 30, at *Elmwood*, near Princess Anne, by Rev John Crosdale, Mr Geo S Atkinson to Miss Eliz Jackson, 2nd daughter of the late Col Arnold E Jones, of Somerset Co, Md.

Died: May 23, in Wash City, Letitia McCreery Walker, daughter of the late Saml Purviance Walker. Her funeral is today at 4 o'clock, from the residence of her mother, on 6th st.

Died: yesterday, Wm Thomas, son of Edw & Mary A Gallant, aged 5 years. His funeral is tomorrow, at 5 o'clock, from the residence of his father, on 6 st west, between O & P sts.

MON MAY 26, 1851
Rev Wm Tracy, lady, & 5 children, Missionary from Madura, South India, has returned to N Y after an absence in India of 15 years.

Boston Post records the death of Saml Cushman, aged 68, of Portsmouth, N H. He was for several years a Rep in Congress, & had held the ofc of navy agent at Portsmouth, & other public trusts.

Alleghany Co Court at Cumberland, Md: 1-On Thu the Court sentenced Michl Milan, for 6 years, for an assault with intent to kill, during a riot on the Balt & Ohio Railroad line; Wm Conly, 5 years; Timothy Flarity, 6 years; John Cain, 5 years; John Kelly, jr, 5 years; John Kelly, [Humpback,] 6 years: all for the same riot. 2-R W Clarke was convicted of killing his wife on Apr 29. He stranguled her: sentence of imprisonment for 18 years, for murder in the 2nd degree. Clarke is about 30 years old, & a shoemaker by trade.

Accident on May 16: the iron bridge across Benson, upon the Lousiville & Frankfort Railroad, near Frankfort, broke down while the large car in which the hands boarded & slept was crossing it: Mr Edmund Bacon, of Frankfort, a worthy mechanic, was thrown into the water & drowned. Others were injured, some seriously.
-Commonwealth

The trial of Henry B Kimbrough, a young man from Columbus, Ga, charged with robbing the post ofc of a package of money containing $6,000, took place in Savannah on May 17. Jury could not agree. A new trial will come on in August.

Patrick Kennedy was killed by lightning & 15 others prostrated on the plank road between Evansville & New Albany, Indiana, on Sat last.

Miss Jacobs & her infant brother were drowned at Cleveland, Ohio, by their carriage being backed into the canal, the horses having taken fright at a drunken man.

Valuable improved property at auction: by decree of the Orphans Court of Wash Co, D C, confirmed by the Circuit Court of Wash Co, D C, sitting in Chancery. Public auction on Jun 23, of lot 6 in square 73, with 2 story frame house & back bldg, on north K st, between 21st & 22nd sts. –Julia A Parris, Guardian
-Dyer & McGuire, aucts

Hon Levi Sweetland, of Coventry, Conn, for many years Judge of Probate for that district, committed suicide by hanging. [No death date given-current item.]

House for sale: frame cottage. Inquire at Howell's Grocery Store, 9th & L sts.

Household & kitchen furniture at auction: on May 30, at the residence of Mr Daniels, on Pa ave, near 3rd st. -Dyer & McGuire, aucts

For rent: comfortable & commodious well finished dwlg house, with out-bldgs, with cistern & pump of excellent water in the yard, with a bathing-room. Possession on or before Jul 1 next. –F Forrest [No address was given.]

Died: on Fri last, James, infant son of J W & Sidney J Moorhead, of Wash City.

TUE MAY 27, 1851
Nat'l Eating House: <u>Green Turtle soup</u> ready at 11 o'clock. Families served as usual. -Walker & Shadd

Handsome bldg lots at auction, on May 30th: I shall sell by order of the Dean of the N M Faculty, lot 7 in square 389, on G st, located between 9th & 10th sts. Also, lot 1 in square 552, on P st & 1st st. –Dr J F May, Dean -A Green, auctioneer

Valuable bldg lots at auction, on Jun 1: By deed of trust from Nicholas Barry to Asa Gladman, dated May 21, 1850, recorded in Liber J A S 13, folios 497, of the land records of Wash Co, D C: sale of part of lot 6 in square 494: fronts on E st, between 4½ & 6th sts. –Asa Gladman, Trustee -A Green, auctioneer

Seneca Quarries for rent: apply to C H Nourse, Seneca Mills, Montg Co, Md.

A young daughter of Mr Hastings, of Jamaica, Vt, while on a visit to the house of a friend in Londonderry, was shot by a boy who playfully pointed a gun at her, & snapped it.

Obit-died: on May 14, at Staunton, Va, Mrs Fanny Peyton Brown, widow of the late Gen John Brown, first Chancellor of the Staunton district, aged 88 years. She was the daughter of Henry Peyton & Mgt Sallarue, & was born at Milford, Prince Wm Co, in the Colony of Va, in 1762. She lost 3 brothers in the conflicts of the Revolution. Her mind & memory were unimpaired by her great age. [May 29th newspaper: Permit me to correct an error in the obituary notice of Mrs Brown. Col Harry Peyton married Mgt Gallahue, not Sallarue. Valentine Peyton, a captain in the army of Gen Lincoln, at Charleston, in 1780, was killed in a redoubt while defending it against a charge of the enemy when that city fell into the hands of the British. He was the son referred to, & I have often heard my Father mention the circumstance. –C]

From Europe. Queen Isabella, of Spain, has the misfortune to break her leg in descending from her carriage at Aranjuez.

Died: on May 26, Mrs Mgt Kelly, in her 17th year, after a painful & most distressing sickness of 4 weeks. Her funeral will be from the residence of her father, Mr Edw McCubbin, on 8th st, near Pa ave, this day, at 2 o'clock.

Died: on May 26, at College Hill, D C, after a very short illness of congestion of the brain, Lemuel P Bacon, son of Rev Joel S Bacon, D D, President of Columbia College, aged 12 years. His funeral is this day, in the College Chapel, at 4 o'clock.

Died: on May 18, at Warrenton, Va, [where she had gone but a few days previous,] Mrs Catharine Powell, widow of the late Maj Burr Powell, deceased, of Middleburg, Va.

$5 reward for strayed Grey Horse. –Isaiah King, East Capitol st, between 4th & 5th.

Jas E Kerr, a young man, in the lower part of Iredell Co, N C, on Sat week, in fixing the lock of a loaded gun, the gun accidently went off, sending the contents through the crack between the logs of a house, hitting a woman by the name of Peggy Duncan, who was sitting up in bed in the room, & killed her instantly.
–Lincoln Courier

WED MAY 28, 1851
The venerable Judge Simeon Baldwin, of New Haven, [father of Hon Roger S Baldwin, late U S Senator,] died at his residence in that city on Monday, in his 90th year. His life had been one of eminent usefulness, in various public stations.

Wash Corp: 1-Ptn of Henry Kuhl: for improvement on L st: passed. 2-Act for the relief of E G Handy: passed. 3-Act for the relief of Chas Dyson: passed. 4-Act in favor of Philip Boteler: passed. 5-Ptn from Mrs Susan M Burche, in relation to the hauling of gravel from N J ave & 2nd st: referred to the Mayor. 6-Cmte of Claims: bill for the relief of Chas Rison: passed.

Whiting Sheldon, of Belchertown, was killed by the freight train on the Western railroad on Thu afternoon, about 6 miles east of Springfield, Mass. He was struck when racing his wagon with another man, & paid no attention to the coming train. The horse escaped.

On Wed, Christopher Hickman, about 17 years of age, while oiling the machinery in Welt's rolling mill, in Newport, Ky, was caught between 2 heavy iron rollers, & passed through them with the rapidity of lightning. The body was completely ground to powder. Cincinnati Gaz

The Cosden Murders: from Chestertown: a man named Shaw was arrested in Newcastle Co, Dela, & brought to Chesterday on Sat last. He made a full confession, acknowledging that he was one of the party at Cosden's house on the night of the murder; that Abe Taylor shot Mr Cosden, & also Mrs Cosden, when she came into the yard; that Shelton murdered Miss Cosden, & went upstairs & killed Miss Webster; that, although Murphy & himself were present, they had nothing to do with the murder. Drummond was not one of the party engaged in the murder.
–Balt American of yesterday

Mr Reynolds Carpenter, of Pownal, Vt, lost $4,000 while traveling West to purchase wool. A few days since $3,439 came back to Vt in a package by express, the conscience stricken sender sent an anonymous letter.

Postmaster Gen est'd the following new Post Ofcs for week ending May 24, 1851.

Ofc	County, State	Postmaster
North Fayette	Kennebeck, Me	Saml S Walton
Stump Bridge	Madison, Miss	Wm Law
Grimesville	Grimes, Texas	Rufus Grimes
Maple Springs	Red River, Texas	Wm G Miller
Star	Walker, Texas	Joshua D Robinson
Millwood	Collins, Texas	Jas Smith
Chepultepeck	Benton, Tenn	Hiram Peirce
Olympus	Overton, Tenn	Abram Grimsley
Chesher's Store	Anderson, Ky	W G Chesher
Port Perry	Perry, Mo	Jos T Clark

Name Changed: Livonia, Wayne Co, Mich, changed to Plank Road.

Mrd: on May 27, by Rev Wm B Edwards, Ammon Green to Miss Ann Maria Lazenby, all of Wash City.

Died: on May 19, suddenly, at Louisville, Ky, Mrs Adela Culver, consort of Dr F B Culver, & 2nd daughter of Hon Amos Kendall.

$5 reward for strayed from the residence of the subscriber, **Green's Row**, Capitol Hill, a large size red & white Cow. –Thos Rynd

The subscriber informs that he will be absent from Wash City for a short period, & his business will be conducted by his son, J C Green. -A Green, auctioneer

The partnership existing between Thos Hunter, of Gtwn, D C, & Jos Dowling, of Sandy Hook, Wash Co, Md, is this day dissolved by mutual consent; the papers relative to the said firm are in the hands of Mr Geo Waters, of Gtwn. –Jos Dowling, Sandy Point, Md.

THU MAY 29, 1851
Longevity-returns of the 7^h Census: 1-Sucky Wright, colored, 120 years of age; 19th Ward, Balt City, Md. A note on the return by the Assist Marshal: this old woman is undoubtedly the age here put down. Jacob Ennals, who is 66, married her granddaughter, &, at the time of the Revolutionary war, in 1775, she had a child 25 years old. Her documents attest the fact of her being as represented. 2-Mary A Beacham, white, 104 years. This old lady lives in Tremont st, at the corner of Mulberry st, 19th Ward, Balt City, & the day the Assist Marshal called she was actively engaged in the yard washing clothes. 3-Mary Cross, white, 102 years. South Caroline, Anderson, district. A note of the Marshal says: I found Mrs Cross carding, & was informed that she carded rolls enough in a day to spin 6 cutts.

Railroad accident on Mon, when the Springfield train of cars reaching the crossing on the north side of Hartford the switch turned the wrong way, the passenger train ran into a gravel train on the branch road, instantly killing 2 Irishmen, John Murphy & Malachi Carey. The third, Anthony Manion, was fatally injured.

Fatal accident from looking at the ascension of Madame Delon in her ballon. Yesterday, a young man, Edw Snyder, employed as a clerk in the store of Messrs Wm L Laws & Co, in Phil, fell from the top of the bldg into an area on Merchant st, & instantly broke his neck & legs. He was 19 years of age, & highly esteemed by his employers.

Household & kitchen furniture at auction: on May 31, by order of the Orphans Court of Wash Co, D C: at the residence of the late Anna Whitmore, at N & 6th st, on **Greenleaf's Point**. –Geo Mockebee, adm -A Green, auctioneer

Mrd: on Tue last, by Rev O B Brown, Mr John Keithley to Miss Mary Rigsby, all of Wash City.

Died: on May 28, Lucinda Alberter, youngest daughter of J C & Cecilia Maria Cook, aged 6 years, 4 months & 2 days. Her funeral is this morning at 9 o'clock, at her father's residence, Md ave, corner of 7th st.

$200 REWARD. The undersigned, sons of John Yokely, deceased, having come to believe that Howard P May is the murderer of their father, & the said May having fled the country, will pay the above reward to any person apprehending & confining the said May so that they can bring him to trial for the aforesaid murder. May is about 5 feet 10 inches high, light hair, grey eyes, sharp prominent features, & has his names engraven with India ink upon one of his arms, on the inside of the arm, between the wrist & the elbow. He is about 25 years old, & weighs from 145 to 160 pounds. -Solomon Yokely, David Yokely, jr, Lexington, Davidson Co, N C.

FRI MAY 30, 1851
Mrd: on Thu, in the Fourth Presbyterian Church, by Rev John C Smith, Mr John H Walker, of Balt, to Miss Roanna E Phillips, of Wash City.

Mrd: May 28, in Balt, by Rev Mr Ross, Erickson H Taneyhill to Mary E Taneyhill, both of Calvert Co, Md.

Liberal reward for return of gold watch lost, below the Foundry, on the Canal towpath. Return to Mr Bryan, collector of tolls for the Chesapeake & Ohio Canal Co. -Jacob Snively

New Haven Palladium of May 26. The Hon Simeon Baldwin expired at his residence in Church st, this morning, in his 90th year. The infirmities of age have been for some time nearing him down to his grave, & this morning the pulse of life stood still. He was the father of the Hon Roger S Baldwin, late Senator in Congress from this State. Judge Baldwin, was born at Norwich, on Dec 14, 1761; graduated at Yale College in 1781; in 1783 was appointed Tutor in the College-until 1786, when he was admitted to the bar in this city. In 1803 he was elected a Rep in the 8th Congress of the U S.

Orphans Court of Wash Co, D C. Letters of administration on the personal estate of David Ruppert, late of Wash Co, deceased. –Joanna Ruppert, admx

Portland, May 28. Mrs Preble, widow of Com Edw Preble, died in this city last evening, aged 81 years. Few women have done so much in unostentatious benevolence as she did, & her memory will be held in respect by those who knew her best. She has left quite a large amount of property.

SAT MAY 31, 1851
Ex-Govn'r Hugh McVay, of Alabama, died at his residence in Lauderdale Co on May 9, in his 85th year. He was for 30 years identified with the legislation of Alabama, commencing at the time of the establishment of the Territorial Gov't.

Died: on May 30, Abraham De Camp, of N Y C, from congestion of the brain, aged 52 years. His funeral is tomorrow at 2 o'clock, from the residence of his brother, on D, between 9th & 10th sts.

Died: May 27, at Balt, Ida Leslie, only child of A Ross & Eliza J Ray, aged 19 months & 17 days.

Jno T Ryon requests all persons indebted to him to call & settle their accounts, as he is desirous of closing up his business at speedily as possible, & will be at the counting room of his late place of business for that purpose.

Obit-died: on May 20, at Eastern Hill, D C, after a brief existence of a few hours, the infant daughter of Dr W A & R C Manning. And also, at the same place, on May 26, Mrs Rosette Caroline Manning, wife of Dr W Wilfred A Manning, & daughter of Maj Ignatius Manning, after a short period of great suffering, aged 33 years, 9 months & 10 days. This devoted wife & fond parent has thus early been summoned to the angelic choir, already adorned by 3 most interesting infants, co-heirs of heaven, leaving a most disconsolate husband & heart-stricken relatives & friends to mourn their irreparable loss.

Trustee's sale of property: by deed of trust from Jas Duff to the subscriber, dated May 23, 1849, recorded in Liber J A S, folios 55 thru 57, of the land records of Wash Ci, D C: sale on Jul 1, of lot 6 in square 87, in Wash City; & the east portion of lot 8 in square 87; at the intersection of N Y & Va aves, between 10th & 21st sts. –J L Smith, Trustee -Chas W Boteler, auct

Plantation for sale: in Campbell Co, Va, formerly owned by Maj Branch, & afterwards by Col Spencer, containing about 939 acres: improvements are good, & its situation very healthy. Apply to Mr Mathew B Nowlin, residing near the land, or the undersigned in Richmond. –Lewis Webb, Wadsworth, Turner & Co, Hubbard, Gardner & Carlton, Van Lew & Smith.

MON JUN 2, 1851
Knowing the loss of time & inconvenience of sending servants, the subscriber has attached to his Family Grocery, Tea & Variety Store an Express-wagon, for the early delivery of all articles that may be ordered from him. –Z M P King, I & 15th sts

Two new houses for rent: one on 6th st, between D & E sts, in which I reside; the other on C, between 4½ & 6th st. –L Hunter

Household & kitchen furniture at auction: Jun 9, at the residence of the late Wm H Dietz, F st, between 12th & 13th sts, by deed of trust, dated May 3, 1849, from Wm H Dietz to Jas Walters, recorded in Liber J A S 2, folios 415 to 418.
–Dyer & McGuire, aucts

On Fri Saml Shoemaker, a laborer at Easby's quarry, whilst blasting rock, met with an accident which it is feared will cost him his life. He was ramming a charge, when the power ignited from a spark which fell from the steel rammer. Little hopes are entertained for his recovery. –Gtwn Reporter

The Eastward train of cars from Syracuse on Wed ran into a horse & buggy at a road crossing near the Vernona station. The horse was instantly killed, & the man driving it, Mr Jacob Near, residing in the vicinity, was fatally injured. He died in about an hour of the accident. Mr Near was about 65 years of age.

Arrest of Strang, the Mormon King of Beaver Island. The Detroit Daily Advertiser of May 27: on May 26 the U S iron steamer **Michigan** arrived at our dock, having on board the U S Marshal Knox & his posse, U S DA, Hon Geo C Bates, & Adjt Gen Schwarz, having returned from Beaver Island, whence they went last week in pursuit of Jas J Strang, & three of his dutiful subjects, Jos Ketchum, Finely Page, & Wm Townsend. They were arrested, being charged with obstructing the U S mail, & assaulting with arms the mail carrier, counterfeiting U S coin, & depredations upon Gov't lands. Strang was formerly from Chautauque Co, N Y.

Lemuel Woodward, a farmer of Plainfield, Conn, & worth half a million dollars, came to his end on Sun last, when he was killed by a 2 year old heifer. His son-in-law, Mr Gallup, found him. It is difficult to imagine what could have caused the attack on the part of the heifer.

Orphans Court of Wash Co, D C. In the case of Jas C McGuire, administrator, with the will annexed, of Dolly P Madison, deceased. The Court & administrator have appointed Jun 24 next for the settlement of the said estate, with the assets in his hands, so far as the same has been collected & turned into money.
–Ed N Roach, Reg/o wills

Obit-died: on Thu, at Queenston, near Princeton, Robt E Hornor, Doorkeeper of the U S House of Reps. His disease was consumption, & for the last 6 weeks he has been confined to his room & bed. He disclosed on his death-bed the fact that he had discovered 2 years ago the insidious but sure approach of the disease. He was in his 51st year. –Trenton [N J] Gaz

Died: on May 27, after an illness of only 5 hours, of effusion on the brain, Mary, infant daughter of Eustace E & Rebecca O'Brien, aged 1 year, 7 months & 18 days.

Died: on May 12, at Cedar Hill, near Franklin, Ky, Mrs Anna Innis, relict of the Hon Henry Innis, & mother of Mrs J J Crittenden. This lady was one of the pioneers of Ky, & has been the pride of her State. Her early days were spent in the wilderness, & in the society of such men as Clarke, St Clair, Wayne, Shelby, Scott, [of the battle of Monmouth,] Wilkinson, [who bore the news of Burgoyne's surrender,] Boone, Henderson, Logan, Hart, Nicholas, Murray, Allen, & Breckridge. She saw Washington as he led his broken army through the Jerseys, & as he returned in triumph from Yorktown. Her tenacious memory retained all that she had seen. Providence had been kind to her in all his dealings with her. He had blest her in her children.

Mr Jas Brisbane, one of the oldest & most respectable citizens in Western N Y, died at Batavia, on May 29. He has for many years occupied a distinguished position in the financial world. He leaves a large estate to his 2 sons, Albert & George. The former gentleman is the well known Fourierite philosopher.

Mr Warden Cresson, of Phil, while in Jerusalem, embraced the Jewish religion. On his return, at the instigation of his family, was indicted before a jury of 6 persons, who returned a verdict that he was insane, & ordered his property to be placed in the hands of commissioners appointed for that purpose. Mr Cresson, aggrieved at this decision, carried his case before the Court of Common Pleas. The jury returned a verdict that the said Warden Cresson was perfectly sane & fully capable of managing his own affairs.

TUE JUN 3, 1851
Millard Fillmore, Pres of the U S A, recognizes E C Angelbody, who has been appointed Consul of the Kingdom of Saxony, for the port of St Louis. May 31, 1851

Wash City election of yesterday, resulted in the choice of Wm J McCormick as Register; Robt J Roche as Collector; & Henry W Ball as City Surveyor.

The public is informed that the house advertised by G B Armstrong, as a summer residence, is the property of Thos Lumpkin, & is rented for one year by the subscriber. Possession cannot be obtained until May 1, 1852. –P M McGill, 12th st, between M & N

At the recent session of the U S Circuit Court for the District of Vt, the Hon Saml Prentiss presiding, the case of the U S vs Jacob Slingerland was disposed of, by the dfndnt's being found guilty, & sentenced to the penitentiary for 5 years. He was a lawyer from N Y, aged 58 years, who was indicted for forging & altering papers for procuring pensions, & transmitting the same to the Pension Ofc in this city, & fraudently procuring pensions thereon.

John Thompson, son of Mr John Thompson, 10th st, near E st, aged 9 years, was accidentally drowned in the canal of Wash City. He went down to the water to wash his shoes, when he lost his balance & fell in. He was carried to the adjacent dwlg of Mr Davidson, where every means of restoration were fruitlessly resorted to by Drs Butt & Garnett, & Mr W C Choat, the latter applying a strong galvanic battery. -Telegraph

Fatal rencontre at Lexington, Ky, on Sunday week, between Jacob Cassell & Wm Carpenter, young men & respectable mechanics. A fight between them terminated in Carpenter's being shot dead on the spot. The other was arrested & committed to prison.

The N H Gazette, published in Portsmouth, N H, is the oldest paper in New England, & is now in its 97th year. The Lancaster Democrat says that the first number was worked off, upon a sheet of coarse cap paper, by Danl Fowle & his negro man Primus, containing 4 pages, each 10½ inches long by a little less than 10 inches broad.

Mrd: on May 22, at **Evermay**, Claiborne Co, Miss, by Rev Wm Baxter, Alex'r C Bullitt, one of the editors & proprietors of the New Orleans Picayune, & late editor of the Republic, to Miss Fanny Smith, daughter of the late Benj Smith, of Ky.

Died: on May 2, in Duxbury, Mass, Capt Joshua Brewster, of that place, aged 88 years. He was a descendant of Elder Wm Brewster, one of the Pilgrims who came over in the ship **Mayflower**, & landed at Plymouth in 1620.

WED JUN 4, 1851
David G Bright, father of Senator Bright, of Indiana, died at Madison on May 29, aged 77 years. He was a gentleman of great moral worth.

It is Ex-Pres Herrera, of Mexico, & not Paredes, whose death is reported by the latest arrival from Vera Cruz.

Edw F Dougals, Jas Clements, & Thos Benson, convicted of the murder of Asa A Havens, 2nd mate of the barque **Glen**, were sentenced to death at N Y on Monday last, & are to be executed on the last Friday in Jul.

Mrd: on May 28, at Scranton, Pa, the residence of Dr Throop, by Rev Mr Mitchell, S W Thompson to Sarah Hale, 2nd daughter of J V N Throop, of Wash City.

Mrd: on Jun 3, by Rev Mr Hodges, John C Metcalf to Julietta M Massoletti, all of Wash.

Died: on May 30, in Phil, Henry Turk, infant son of Thos H & Ellen Lane, of Wash City.

Wash City Ordinances: 1-Act for the relief of Chas Stewart, jr: the sum of $6.86 is appropriated to him for making a culvert on I & 13th sts. Act for the same: sum of $12.99, for balance due him for flag footways on 15th st. Act for the same: sum of $36.69, a balance due for footways on 18th st. 2-Act for the relief of Wm Pegg: fine imposed for violation of the law in relation to carts, is remitted; provided he pay the cost of prosecution. 3-Act for the relief of Chas Rison: fine imposed for an alleged violation in relation to taking earth from the public streets, is remitted: provided he pay the costs of prosecution. 4-Act for the relief of J R McCorkle: fine imposed in relation to concerts & public exhibitions, is remitted: provided he pay the cost of prosecution. 5-Act for the relief of Chas Dyson: fine imposed for an alleged violation of law relative to the construction of frame bldgs, is remitted: provided he pay the cost of prosecution. 6-Act for the relief of Wm Pettibone: sum of $5 be paid to him for a fine imposed on him for an alleged violation of the law in relation to keeping dogs. 7-Act for the relief of Fanny Buchanan: the sum of $24.13 be paid to her, that amount erroneously paid by her for taxes on part of lot G in square 319. 8-Act for the relief of A E L Keese & Wm Cox, County Constables: to be paid $75 each, as compensation for their energetic, untiring, & successful efforts in discovering & arresting the perpetrator of the murderous assault on & robbery of John Hutchison, in Wash City, on Feb 2 last. 9-Act for the relief of J H T Werner: to pay him $26.75, for furnishing locks & keys for the desks in the chambers of the Board of Alderman & Board of Common Council. 10-Act for the relief of E G Handy, police ofcr of the 3rd Ward: to pay him $65.67, being the balance found due to him on the settlement of his police accounts up to May 23, 1851, as certified by the accounting ofcrs of this Corp. 11-Act for the relief of John M Farrar: to pay him for the unexpired term of his license for keeping a bowling saloon, which was destroyed by fire on Apr 25 last; provided Farrar return his license to the Register. 12-Act for the relief of J F Wollard: the sum of $97.72 be paid him in settlement of his account as police ofcr of the 3rd Ward to May 1, 1851. 13-Act in favor of Philip Boteler: permission is given Boteler to use the bldg now on lot 16, in square 169, as a livery stable, any existing law to the contrary notwithstanding: provided Boteler give to the Mayor written consent to the same of persons interested in the adjoining property. 14-Act making an appropriation to pay Peter Little for work done on G st south: the sum of $278.15 be paid him for said work. 15-Act making appropriation to pay John Fletcher for work done on south G st: the sum of $41.06 be paid him for said work.

Orphans Court of Wash Co, D C. Letters testamentary on the personal estate of Saml Greene, late of said county, deceased. –Hugh W Greene, exc

The Tahlequah Advocate of May 13 says that Danl Vann & Lewis Ross have both declined being candidates for the station of Principal Chief of the Cherokee Nation.

In Chancery. Jno C Jones vs Alfeus B Thompson. The bill states that the cmplnt was engaged as a merchant at the Sandwich Islands, & in 1830 formed a general copartnership with the dfndnt A B Thompson for one year; that after the expiration of the year the said cmplnt employed Thompson as his supercargo, & was often jointly interested with him in individual transactions at the Sandwich Islands & in Calif, & large advances were from time to time made by cmplnt to Thompson, who became indebted to complnt in the amount of $30,000 & upwards; that in 1833 cmplnt dispatched the vessel **Loriot** to Calif with Thompson as supercargo; that the vessel was seized by the Mexican authorites, & Thompson was imprisoned, & suffered sundry injuries; that, in consideration of his indebtedness to cmplnt, said Thompson executed a written assignment to cmplnt of his claim against the Mexican Gov't for satisfaction for said injuries, & a power of atty to cmplnt to prosecute the claims, & said assignment is mislaid or lost; that cmplnt left Calif in 1840, & since his departure, & perhaps in some instances before, Thompson furnished supplies to the Mexican Gov't, from the joint property of himself & cmplnt, to the amount of $2,500; &, as to the claim arising out of said transaction, said Thompson & cmplnt are partners, & cmplnt is entited to the whole claim on account of the general balance due to him. It further shows that the Board of Com'rs upon claims against Mexico, established under the act of Congress of Mar 3, 1849, have awarded to said Thompson, on account of said claims, the sum of $8,060.37; that cmplnt is entitled to said sum of money, & has notified the Sec of the Treasury of his intention to contest the payment thereof to Thompson. It asks that Thompson may be required to answer, & may be enjoined from receiving the amount aforesaid; & further states that Thompson is a resident of the State of Calif. It is ordered that cmplnt appear in Court, in person or by solicitor, on or before the 3rd Mon of Oct Next.
–Jno A Smith, clk

Candidates who have received permission to present themselves at the Naval Academy, Annapolis, Md, on Oct 1 next, for the purpose of being examined as to their qualifications for admission into the Navy as Acting Midshipmen.

Names	States	Cong District
1-Edmund S Allen	Conn	3rd
2-Adolphus G Armington	Indiana	3rd
3-Newton H Gist	Indiana	8th
4-Saml McKee	Ky	6th
5-John Campbell	Ky	10th
6-Christopher H Dabbs	Louisiana	4th
7-Thos O Selfridge, jr	Mass	8th
8-John S Barnes	Mass	6th
9-Edmund O Matthews	Missouri	2nd
10-Geo H Perkins	N H	3rd
11-Saml A Smith	N J	5th
12-Richd W M Graham	New Mexico	

13-Geo H Cooke	N Y	22nd
14-Montgomery Sicard	N Y	20th
15-Carlton W Seely	N Y	27th
16-Henry B Dox	N Y	29th
17-Jason C Erwin	N C	1st
18-Jos McD C Jay	N C	1st
19-Geo J Sloan	N C	4th
20-Beverly Daniel	N C	6th
21-Chas H Crandal	Pa	12th
22-J Marx Etting	Pa	17th
23-David D McLeod	Pa	24th
24-E M Seabrook	S C	7th
25-Edw Lee	Tenn	3rd
26-John H Stevens	Tenn	5th

Postmaster Gen est'd the following new Post Ofcs for week ending May 31, 1841.

Ofc	County, State	Postmaster
South Andover	Oxford, Me	Jas Stevens
Bee Line	Allegran, Mich	Jas M Heath
Rabbit River	Allegran, Mich	Simeon Howe
Welaka	Putnam, Fla	Lewis H Bryant
Munsonville	Putnam, Fla	Asa Munson
Mount Hope	Tyler, Texas	Hamilton W Carter
Kemp	Kaufman, Texas	Levi Noble
Bushby Creek	Williamson, Texas	Thos E Palts
Sun	St Tammany, La	Matthew Richardson
Shady Grove	Washington, La	Abram A Harvy
Chulafiuna	Randolph, Ala	E Prior Reeves
Walldon's Ridge	Marion, Tenn	Edwin Newy
Barclay	Whitesides, Ill	J M Wilson
Mier	Madison, Mo	Eli Duncan
Sylvester	Greene, Wis	Chas F Thompson
Berry	Dane, Wis	Jos Bowman
Hoosier Grove	Greene, Wis	Leroy C Wallace
Coon Prairie	Crawford, Wis	Peter Lamoree
Golden Lake	Waukesha, Wis	Wilhelm Scheuber
Newton Corners	Jefferson, Wis	Jona L Byington
Chequist	Davis, Iowa	Isaac Sweeney
Silverville	Lawrence, Ia	Robt McAfee
Hector	Jay, Ia	John C Brewington
Ditney Hill	Dubois, Ia	Saml Jacobs
Spring Borough	White, Ia	H H Birdsall

Repton	Clark, Ia	John Wroughton
Blackford	Hancock, Ky	Richd C Jett
Otsego	Ray, Mo	Jason N Baker
Torah	Linn, Iowa	Isaac Ford

Names Changed: Point Smith, Franklin Co, Ala, changed to Chickasaw.
Lockranzy, Cherokee Co, Texas, changed to Linwood.
Frog Level, Newberry Co, S C, changed to Prosperity.
Branchtown, Cherokee Co, Texas, changed to **Fort Lacey**.
Brownsville, Johnson Co, Ark, changed to Enterprise.
Grand Prairie, Prairie Co, Ark, changed to Brownsville.
Reagan's Bluff, Monroe Co, Ark, changed to Aberdeen.
Bissell's, Grant Co, Indiana, changed to Trask
Phill's Creek, Jersey Co, Ill, changed to Fidelity.

THU JUN 5, 1851
Appointment by the Pres: Alex'r D Moore, Collector of the Customs, Wilmington, N C, vice Robt G Rankin, resigned.

Stockton Journal of Apr 29: we learn from Mr Scott, of Bonsell & Scott's Ferry, that on Sun last a band of 4 Mexicans, horse & cattle thieves, were arrested on the San Joaquin. They were first seen passing Mr Danl Patterson's ranch with 50 head of cattle, having the brands of R Livermore, Dr Marsh, & Senor Alviso. They were arrested, & a jury of 20 citizens was summoned, & they were found guilty. One of the prisoners was a vaquero of the notorious Jin Beckwith. They gave their names as Ramon Dias, of Hermosillo, Timoteo Sandoval, Luis Gracia, Francisco Galvez, & Jesus Moreno, of Maxatlan, Mexico. They were hung on Mon morning, at 10 o'clock.

Clifton Farm in Culpeper Co, for sale: containing about 640 acres, can be bought at private sale upon terms to suit the purchaser. It has a comfortable houses for overseer & negroes, barn, & other necessary out-bldgs. Mr Wm Glassell & Mr John Glassell, living in the neighborhood, will show the farm. Address me, Josiah Wm Ware, exc of John Glassell, deceased, at Berryville, Clarke Co.

Valuable real estate in Gtwn for sale: Jun 17, the property advertised by Geo Smith, the subscriber, as surviving exc of Thos L Lee, late of Fred'k Co, Md, deceased: sale of lots 24 & 25 on Montgomery st; & lot 32 & 33 on Green st. Title indisputable. –J Lee, surviving exc of Thos L Lee.

Mrd: on Tue, at Balt, by Rev Mr Killen, John T Mason, Surgeon U S Navy, to Mary, daughter of the late Thos R Johnson, of St Mary's Co, Md.

Died: on Jun 3, Wm Harrison Ward, in his 37th year. His funeral is today at 4 o'clock, from the E st Baptist Church.

Died: yesterday, after a painful illness. Mr Wm Linkins, sr, in his 64th year. His funeral is this afternoon, at 4 o'clock, from his late residence on L st, near 18th st.

Died: on Jun 3, Harvey L, aged 1 year & 4 months, son of Wm & Mary A Phillips. His funeral is this afternoon, at 4 o'clock, from the residence of his parents, on 7th st, near the Northern Market.

FRI JUN 6, 1851
Z W Potter, the U S Consul at Valparaiso, & family, returned to N Y in the ship **Empire City** on Tue.

Hon Chas & Mrs Haddock, Mr & Miss McCurdy, Jas Lawrence, C F Stansbury, Capt J R Sands, Col Van Alen, Lts L B Avery, Caldwell, Parrott, G H Preble, J Duer, & Miss Kimball had invitations to Queen Victoria's Ball. —Boston Post

Ex-Pres Pedraza died in the city of Mexico about May 15. He had been suffering with a long & painful illness.

It was 6 years on May 26, since Sir John Franklin sailed from Sheerness on his dangerous expedition, & the chances of his safety at the present time are but slight indeed. Still his hopeful wife is active in her efforts to promote attempts for his discovery.

Wash City Ordinance: 1-Act for the relief of Michl Talty: that the sum of $60.50 be paid to him for the loss sustained by him in the destruction of his sewer across N Y ave, on 12th st, by the Corp. —Silas H Hill, Pres of the Board of Common Council; B B French, Pres of the Board of Aldermen. Approved Jun 3, 1851: Walter Lenox, Mayor

Mrd: Jun 3, by Rev Mr Lenaghan, Mr John Johnston to Mrs Eliz Ann Mulliken, both of Wash City.

Wash Co, D C. This is to certify that Jas Pumphrey brought before me as an estray, a sorrel Horse. —J W Beck, J P [Owner is come forward, prove property, pay charges, & take him away. —Jas Pumphrey]

Trustee's sale of Mules: by deed of trust from Jos Dowling & Thos Hunter: sale on Jun 11, in front of Vanesson's stables, on Congress st, near the canal Gtwn: public auction. -Jos G Waters, trustee

Wanted, a wet nurse, for an infant 2 months old. Apply to Dr Wm P Johnston, 7th st, between E & F sts.

SAT JUN 7, 1851

Circuit Court-Wash: the Kosciusko case: This morning the chancery case was taken up. Maj G Tochman opened it by reading the pleadings of the heirs of Kosciusko. The object is to obtain a decree commanding the present administrator de bonis non of the estate of Gen Kosciusko, [Mr Lewis Johnson,] the administrator of the estate of Geo Bomford, [Mr J B Smith,] & the sureties of Bomford upon his administration bond of the estate of Kosciusko, [Messrs Jacob Gideon, Ulysses Ward, J B H Smith, Jas Carrico, Saml Stott, & Geo C Bomford, the son of the deceased Geo Bomford,] to account before the auditor for the assets of the estate of Gen Kosciusko; & also to obtain an order commanding the sureties of Geo Bomford, deceased, administrator of Kosciusko's estate, to being into Court the sum of $43,504.40, with interest, due from Jan 1, 1847, which Geo Bomford detained in his hands, as is proved by his account, settled with the Orphans' Court, on Jun 7, 1848. This protracted litigation of 30 years duration, is approaching to the close.

$100 reward for runaway negro man John Jourden: age about 32. He has a sister living at Mr Chas Miller's, near the Navy Yard, in Wash. He has also an aunt living in Wash. Any letter addressed to me at Buena Vista Post Ofc, PG Co, Md, will meet with prompt attention. –Basil T Duckett

Millard Fillmore, Pres of the U S A, recognizes Adolphe Eugene Bandelier, who has been appointed Consul of the Swiss Confederation at the port of St Louis, in the State of Missouri. –Jun 4, 1851

Duly elected in Wash City on Jun 2, 1851, for members of the Board of Alderman & Board of Common Council, & for Assessors in the 2nd, 4th, & 6th Wards.

Wm B Magruder	Silas H Hill	John J Mulloy
Wm T Dove	Chas P Wannall	Jas A Gordon
Saml E Douglass	Jos Bryan	Wm Morgan
Horatio N Easby	John W Maury	A W Miller
Jas Kelly	Thos H Havenner	Jas Cull
John Wilson	M P Mohun	Geo Page
Nicholas Callan	John P Pepper	D B Johnson
Joel Downer	John L Wirt	Ephraim Wheeler
John F Ennis	John C Brent	John Van Reswick
Jos Borrows	Thos Hutchingson	

Assessors: Geo H Plant; Danl E Kealley; Washington Lewis

Died: on Jun 5, Nathl Plant, aged 62 years. His funeral is this evening, at 4 o'clock, from his late residence, at the corner of C & 13th sts.

Died: on May 28, at his residence, ***Stony Arbor Farm***, PG Co, Md, Mr Raphael C Edelen. He has left an interesting family to mourn his loss, & a large circle of friends. -F J W

MON JUN 9, 1851

Judge Wm B Turley, of Jackson, Tenn, died on May 27, at Raleigh, Shelby Co, of the effects of an accidental wound received on Fri at the same place, where he had arrived on his way to Memphis. -Eagle

Richmond papers: violent affray in Lynchburg, Va, on Thu, between Mr Saunders, a son of Dr Jas Saunders, a member of the State Convention, & Mr A W C Terry, the Editor of the Lynchburg Virgininian. The difficulty originated in some strictures by the Virginian on the course of Dr Saunders in regard to the basis question. The Dr replied through the Lynchburg Republican, in a card of some length & bitterness. On Thu Saunders met Terry in the street, & Saunders struck Terry with a walking stick. Terry and Saunders drew revolvers & fired, exchanging shots on each side, & each party received 2 wounds, & each of them one shot in the body, which it was feared may prove mortal. [Jun 10th newspaper: Mr Jas Saunders died on Thu, the day on which his combat with Mr Terry, of Va, took place. Mr Terry was then alive & expected to recover.] [Jun 12th newspaper: Letters from Lynchburg announce the painful intelligence that Mr Terry died on Sun last. -Richmond Enquirer]

Mrd: on Jun 5, by Rev John Lanahan, Solomon Stover, of Fred'k Co, Md, to Miss Hester A Travers, daughter of Capt Jabez Travers, of Wash.

Mrd: on Thu last, in Gtwn, by Rev J J Murray, W H Dougal, of Wash, to Miss M Virginia, daughter of Morris Adler, of the former place.

Mrd: on Jun 4, at *Goodwood*, PG Co, Md, by Rev Mr Mackenheimer, Francis M Hall to Rosalie Eugenia, eldest daughter of Chas H Carter.

Died: on Feb 11, 1850, in the region of Great Salt Lake, Mr Richd J A Culverwell, in his 49th year. The deceased was a native of Balt, Md, but for the last 15 years a resident of Wash City. He leaves a wife & several children to mourn his loss.

In Chancery. Francis B Stockton vs the heirs of Geo Bomford, deceased. The bill in this case states that Susan Decatur, about 1823, conveyed to Geo Bomford lot 22 in square 167, in Wash City, to hold to him & his heirs in trust, first to secure a debt of $640, which was afterwards paid; &, secondly, for the use of Mrs Eliz Ewell & her heirs forever. That the said Geo Bomford hath died, leaving heirs, viz: Laura, the wife of Richd C Derby; Ruth, the wife of John S Paine; Geo C Bomford, Erwin E Bomford, & Jas S Bomford, upon whom the said trust hath devolved. That the said Eliz Ewell, by her deed with covenants of warranty, hath conveyed, for a full & valuable consideration, all her interest in the said lot to the cmplrt; & the object of the bill is to obtain from the said heirs of Bomford a conveyance of the legal estate so vested in them. And it appearing that the said named heirs of Geo Bomford are not residents of D C: same to appear on or before the 3rd Mon of Oct next.
–John A Smith, clerk

The oldest Sovereign of Europe is Ernest, King of Hanover. On Jun 5 he completed his 80th year. He is the only surviving son of Geo the Third, & was formerly known as the Duke of Cumberland. He, instead of Victoria, acceded to the throne of Hanover on the death of his brother, Wm the Fourth, in Jun, 1837, on which day the thrones of England & Hanover were separated-the prevalence of the salic law preventing the accession of females.

Appointment by the Pres: Lewis Sutton, of Balt, Md, Appraiser at large, vice Hugh W Evans, declined.

Through the commendable exertions of Mr John P Hilton, a watchman in the Treasury bldg, the dwlg of Jas H Causten, on F st, the roof of which took fire in the night some weeks ago, was saved from destruction. In extinguishing the fire Mr Hilton's clothing were very much damaged; on hearing which Mr Causten made Mr Hilton an equivalent donation, at the same time returning him thanks for his kind act.

TUE JUN 10, 1851
The Norfolk Beacon states that the U S war-steamer **Susquehanna**, Capt Wm Inman, was to sail from that port on Sat for the East Indies. She bears the pennant of Cmdor J H Aulick, of the East India squadron, & will call at Rio Janeiro to land the following passengers: M Macedo, Brazilian Minister to the U S; D Gondin, his Sec of Legation; Hon Robt C Schenck, Minister to Brazil, & Franklin Clark, Sec of Legation; Hon John S Pendleton, Charge d'Affaires to the Argentine Republic. The following is a complete list of the ofcrs of the **Susquehanna**: Com John H Aulick; Capt Wm Inman; Lts, S W Godon, Thos T Hunter, J B Randolph, Foxhall A Parker, Geo H Cooper; Passed Assist Surgeon, Chas Eversfield; Assist Surgeon, Chas T Fahs; Purser, Garret R Barry; Chaplain, Edmund C Bittinger; Master, John Matthews; Cmdor's Sec, Ferdinand Coxe; Capt's Clerk, W T Inman; Purser's Clerk, John H Hartzell; Purser's Steward, F C Hampton; Surgeon's Steward, Edw Meade; Chief Engineer, Saml Archibald; 1st Assists, Geo F Hebard, Henry H Stewart; 2nd Assists, Edw Fithian, Eli Crosby, J C E Lawrence; 3rd Assists, Thos A Shook, Alex Henderson, Stephen D Hibbert; Capt Marines, Wm B Slack; Passed Midshipmen, John Kell, John W Bennett; Midshipmen, Robt L May, F A Boardman, Wm H Cheever, Chas E Hawley, E C Stockton; Boatswain, Richd Follins; Gunner, Chas B Oliver; Carpenter, John Green; Sailmaker, Wm Ryan.

Academy of Richmond Co annual election to be held on Jul 5. For particulars apply to Robert Walton, Pres pro tem: Augusta, Ga, May 31, 1851.

Family bread & home made biscuit, domestic pies, & superior crackers: send orders to the 3rd door north of Odd Fellows Hall, 7th st: J C McKelden.

The Cincinnati Gazette states that Hiram Powers' statue of the Greek Slave has been forwarded thence to its fortunate owner in Wash City, Wm W Corcoran, to be placed in his private gallery.

Benj F Brown, a few years since a reputable ofcr in one of the public depts of the U S Gov't, & afterwards a candidate before the House of Reps for the ofc of Doorkeeper, has been arrested & brought to Wash City, where he is now in jail, in default, we believe, of $20,000 bail, charged with a fraud committed upon the Gen Land Ofc by means of forgery. —Telegraph [Jun 11th newspaper-corr: W S Brown was brought from N Y to this city under the charge of forging land warrants, not Benj F Brown, who is his brother.]

Circuit Court of Wash Co, D C: in the matter of the ptn of Bradley Dickson for the partition of the real estate of which the late Thos Dickson died seized; the com'rs appointed by the Circuit Court of Wash Co, D C to divide the said real estate having made their return to the Court, & reported that the said property would not admit of division without loss & injury to the parties interested, & having returned the real value thereof in current mony; it is therefore by the Court, May 15, 1851, ordered that unless the heirs-at-law of the said Thos Dixon, & all others who may have a right to elect to take the said real estate at the valuation returned by the said com'rs, do, on or before the 3rd Mon in Oct, 1851, so elect to take, the said real estate will be sold by the said com'rs. John A Smith, clerk [Note 2 spellings of Dickson/Dixon. The correct spelling is Dixon. Bradley is the son of Thos Dixon.]

Stock of Millinery, dry goods, by order of the Orphans Court of Wash Co, D C, at our auction rooms on Jun 16, the entire stock of the late Mrs Magdalene Dumberth, of Gtwn, D C, deceased. -Dyer & McGuire, aucts

Millard Fillmore, Pres of the U S A, recognizes Theodore W Riley, who has been appointed Consul of the Republic of Chili, for the city & State of N Y. Jun 9, 1851

Mrd: on Jun 5, by Rev Mr Callahan, Allen J Dorsey to Miss Mgt R Shreeve, all of Wash City.

Mrd: on Jun 3, by Rev Smith Pyne, Chas Vinson, of the Treasury Dept, to Mrs H R F, widow of the late Capt E A Capron, 1st Artl, U S A.

Died: yesterday, Agnes Cushing, infant daughter of Jas & Mary F Goldborough, aged 5 months.

WED JUN 11, 1851
Mrs Gore Langdon, lately deceased in London, has left her maid the interest for life of L10,000.

Postmaster Gen has est'd the following new Post Ofcs for week ending Jun 7, 1851.

Ofc	County, State	Postmaster
Huntsville	Litchfield, Conn	Chas Hunt
Belsano	Cambria, Pa	Jas Kane
Carter Camp	Potter, Pa	T B Abbott
Hopewell Centre	York, Pa	Wm Wallace
Dibertsville	Somerset, Pa	Solomon G Miller
Madisonburgh	Wayne, Ohio	Chas E Graeter
Park's Mills	Franklin, Ohio	Jeremiah Leasure
Nova	Ashland, Ohio	Jas Young
Good Hope	Fayette, Ohio	Hugh Campbell
Whigville	Noble, Ohio	Henry Taylor
Lauraville	Baltimore, Md	John Gambrill
Shoal Creek	Benton, Ala	Geo R Cole
Sapp's Cross Roads	Blount, Ala	Vestal Beeson
Chananhatchy	Tallapoesa, Ala	John R Brooks
Keas Bridge	Chickasaw, Miss	Thos T Enochs
Chance Prairie	Burleston, Texas	J J Kidd
Vine Grove	Washington, Texas	Jas H Holt
Hale's Point	Lauderdale, Tenn	Rush Byrne
Mount Val Springs	Blount, Tenn	Wm McTeer
Oddville	Harrison, Ky	Hez'h M Whitaker
Eminence	Washington, Oregon	Chas E Fox
Lebanon	Marion, Oregon	John S Hunt
Cincinnati	Polk, Oregon	Joshua Shaw
Dayton	Yam Hill, Oregon	Chris Taylor

Names Changed: Shannon, Yala Busha Co, Miss, changed to Pine Valley.
Nuzums' Mills, Marion Co, Va, changed to Valley Falls.
Steubenville, Steuben Co, Ind, changed to Pleasant Lake.
Blair's Ferry, Roane Co, Tenn, changed to Blairsport.
Hoadley, Racine Co, Wis, site & name changed to Cypress, Kenosha Co.
Randolph, Columbia Co, Wis, changed to Randolph Centre.

Desertion in the army: the loss annually to Gov't is enormous-every man who deserts robs the Gov't of $50 directly, & indirectly much more. One-eighth of the whole army deserted last year, & last month 16 out of 56 men of Capt Hatch's company, at Rochester, deserted. Congress can & will remedy this difficulty. –N Y Express

The undersigned have formed a copartnership, for the purpose of conducting a Plumbing, Copper, Tin, & Sheet-iron establishment. Having many years experience in the above branches. Establishment corner of 6th st & Pa ave.
–McLaughlin & Townley

Providence Journal: the oldest soldier on record: the celebrated soldier Polowaski, who was 127 years old, & resided at the Hotel de Invalides, died at Paris on May 6, by an attack of pleurisy. The funeral of this man of 4 monarchies & 2 republics was attended by a vast number of people. The above paragraph going the rounds of the papers recently, is doubtless substantially correct, except as to the age & name of the party. It probably refers to Golembiowski, or, as it is spelled in his certificate of the Legion of Honor, Kolembeski. When we saw him 4 years ago he resided at the guard-house in the garden of the Luxenbourg Palace. He did not look to be over 80 years of age, had a good appetite, conversed freely, retained all his senses, & his hair, though showing the silver livery of advised age, was far from being white. In person he was short & well-built. He was born in Poland Mar 1, 1731, & had been 70 years in active military service, having at age 14 entered as one of the body guards of Stanislaus. He has been in 39 general battles, & was 5 times wounded. Since 1814 he has resided in Paris. He was 120 years & 2 months at the time of his death.

At Providence, on Thu, a jury assessed $1,800 damages upon Thos Wood for trifling with the affections of Mary Curran, in refusing to marry her after he had promised so to do.

Millard Fillmore, Pres of the U S A, recognizes Jas Dempsey, who has been appointed Vice Consul of Sweden & Norway, at Alexandria, in the State of Va. -Jun 10, 1851

Balt, Jun 10. The Mayor yesterday sent in a message to the Councils stating that a defalcation of about $6,000 had been discovered in the accounts of Col H S Sanderson, late City Collector under the administration of Col Stansbury, & from a hasty survey of the books other deficiencies were apparent to a large amount. The defalcation occurred in the books of Mr P A Egerton, deputy collector under Col Sanderson. Mr Egerton is denying having made any false entries

Mrd: on Jun 2, at Gtwn, by Rev Mr Lanahan, Mr Geo N Beale to Miss Eliz B, daughter of Col J H Wheeler, of N C.

Superior wines & old brandy in bottles at auction, on Jun 17: the private stock of the late J L M Smith, of Balt. -Dyer & McGuire, aucts

THU JUN 12, 1851
Valuable real estate for sale in Clarke Co, Va: by decree of the Circuit Court of Clarke, rendered May 13, 1851, in the case of Holmes, etc, vs Holmes' heirs: public sale on Jul 24 of tract containing about 360 acres; 1½ miles southeast of Berryville, the county seat of Clarke. It is one of the most desirable farms in the Valley of Va. Premises will be shown by called upon the subscriber, or Province McCormick, Berryville, Clarke Co, Va. -Geo W Bradfield, Com'r

Citizens Retreat: the subscriber, having lately taken the large Hotel, at the foot of Long Bridge, in Wash, invites the patronage of the public in general. -Geo Sinclair

$50 reward for a man calling himself Chas Lee, who came to my stable & hired a Horse & Buggy, on May 10th, & who I have not heard from since. –Levi Pumphrey

By 2 writs of fieri facias, at the suits of Darius Clagett & Jas B Dodson, trading under the firm of Clagett & Dodson, & against Jas W Plant, against the good & chattels of W A Powell, I will offer for public sale, on Jun 19, in front of the Centre Market house, in Wash City, sundry articles of Powell's, including bowls, chairs, oilcloth, curtain, shovel window shades, & 2 trussels, etc. –H R Maryman, Cnstbl

Jos Seigfried, who has contracted to paint the spire of the Presbyterian Church on Main st, in Chilicothe, Ohio, ascended on Thu, to within some 6 feet of the top, by ingeniously attaching a block-&-tackle to a hook, & fastening the lower end to a large basket. While in a perilous position he felt himself growing faint & he immediately slipped down into his basket, where he lay, some 10 minutes. If he had fallen he never would have known what hurt him. –Chilicothe Gazette

U S Patent Ofc: 1-Ptn of Richd Imlay, of Phil, Pa, praying for extension of a patent granted to him Sep 21, 1837, for an improvement in the mode of supporting bodies of railroad cars. 2-Ptn of John & Chas Hanson, of England, praying for the extension of a patent granted to Benj Tatham, jr, & H R Tatham, as assignees of the said Hansons, on Mar 29, 1841, for an improvement in making pipes or tubes of lead. 3-Ptn of Reuben Daniels, of Woodstock, Vt, praying for the extension of a patent granted to him Oct 7, 1837, for an improvement in shearing machines. 4-Ptn of John Thomas, of Plainfield, N J, praying for the extension of a patent granted to him on Dec 20, 1837, for an improvement in drydocks.
–Thos Ewbank, Com'r of Patents

For rent, on Jul 1, the upper part of a 3 story brick house, with a good kitchen & dining room under the 1st floor. Inquire of Mr Moore, in the corner row, Mrs Wise, **Duff Green's Row**, or -Jas Williams, 7th st.

Jas Jasper Orcutt, one of the incendiaries arrested at Utica, N Y, some time ago, has been found guilty of arson in the 1st degree, & sentenced to death. Aug 1 is the day appointed for his execution.

Valuable 4 story brick house on 4½ st at auction: on Jun 16, sale of the house & lot, on 4½ st, near Pa ave & C st, adjoining Dr Boyle's residence. -A Green, auctioneer

Square 936 at auction: on Jun 18, fronting on Md ave & F, between 9th & 10th sts. The above square is immediately opposite the Brick Cottage owned by the late Mr Vermillion. -Dyer & McGuire, aucts

Public sale of Real Estate: by deed of trust from Andrew Johnson to the undersigned trustee, dated May 17, 1850, recorded in Liber J A S 13, folios 418 thru 421, of the land records for Wash Co, D C: sale of part of square 416, along T st north to 8th st. –John H Goddard, jr, Trustee -A Green, auctioneer

Sale on Jun 18, of the entire stock of Andrew Coyle & Son, at their store, on Pa ave, near 7th st. We deem it unnecessary to enter into particulars, but respectfully refer to the printed catalogue. -Dyer & McGuire, aucts

Balt, Jun 11. We announce the death of Mr O C Tiffany, one among our most opulent merchants & respected citizens. He died suddenly this morning at his residence in Franklin st, of heart disease. He was about 60 years of age.

The public are notified that on Sun, Jun 15, at 10 o'clock, the ceremony of Dedication will take place at the new Trinity [Catholic] Church, in Gtwn, D C. The Right Rev Dr Carbonell, Bishop of Toronto, will officiate on the occasion. Tickets of admission 50 cents each.

Died: on Jun 7, Marion Eckford, the wife of Lt F Stanly, U S Navy, & daughter of F R Tillou.

Died: on Jun 3, Wm C McClasky, son of Wm T McClasky, aged 7 months.

Died: yesterday, Mr Geo Bean, in his 54th year. His funeral is today at 2 o'clock.

FRI JUN 13, 1851
Circuit Court of Wash Co, D C-in Chancery. A H Lawrence, cmplnt, vs Aaron Leggett. The cmplnt, by his bill filed in pursuance of the 8th section of the act of Congress, approved Mar 3, 1849, entitled, an Act to carry into effect certain stipulations of the treaty between the U S A & the Republic of Mexico, of Feb 2, 1848, claims $5,464.80 out of an award made by the Board of Com'rs under the said act of Congress in favor of said Aaron Leggett for $109,296.00. The bill alleges that the dfndnt had promised to said cmplnt a liberal compensation & per centage out of any award that might be made to him by said Board, for services to be rendered by said cmplnt in the prosecution of said dfndnt's claim; that cmplnt did perform the services required, & spent much time & labor in the preparation of said claim for intelligible action; that an award was made, & that 5% of said award is a reasonable allowance for said services. Said dfndnt not having appeared nor answered, & it appearing to the satisfaction of this Court that the dfndnt is absent from D C, he residing in the State of N Y, it is now ordered that the 3rd Mon of Oct next be assigned for the appearance & answer of said dfndnt to the bill. Jas Dunlop
-Jno A Smith, Clerk -A H Lawrence, for cmplnt

N Y, Jun 12. Jos Brewster, a halter, fell into the hold of the ship **Challenge** this morning, & was instantly killed.

The Hon M A Martin died on Jun 3, at his residence near Clarksville, age 51 years. It is remarkable that 3 citizens of Tenn so distinguished as jurists & men of intellect as Judges Turley, Cahal, & Martin should have died so suddenly & in so short a time of each other. –Nashville Banner

Official: War Dept, Adj Gen Ofc, Wash, Jun 10, 1851. Gen Orders #29.
A Gen Court Martial, to consist of 13 members, will assemble in Wash City on Jun 23, for the trial of Brevet Brig Gen Geo Talcott, Col of Ordnance.
Detail for the Court:
1-Bvt Maj Gen D E Twiggs
2-Bvt Maj Gen J E Wool
3-Bvt Maj Gen P F Smith, Col Mounted Riflemen
4-Bvt Maj Gen B Riley, Col 1st Infty
5-Bvt Maj Gen G Gibson, Commissary Gen
6-Bvt Brig Gen J B Walbach, Col 4th Artl
7-Bvt Brig Gen S Churchill, Inspector Gen
8-Bvt Brig Gen J G Totten, Col Corps of Engineers
9-Bvt Brig Gen N S Clarke, Col 6th Infty
10-Bvt Brig Gen T Childs, Major 1st Artl
11-Col J J Abert, Corps of Topographical Engineers
12-Col J B Crane, 1st Artl
13-Bvt Col J Plympton, Lt Col 7th Infty
Bvt Maj J F Lee, Judge Advocate
By order of the President. –R Jones, Adj Gen

Govn'r Hunt, of N Y, has issued a proclamation, offering a reward of $600 for the apprehension of Thos Root, Wm Malumpy, Danl Ryan, & Thos McMahon, fugitives from Wash Co, where they are indicted for the murder of Patrick McCarty.

The schnr **S Marvin**, of Racine, was capsized on Lake Michigan in the gale of May 22, & all on board drowned. The persons lost were Capt W P Denton, Alex Atwood, mate; Harvey Sawson, Jas Underhill, Philip Kinsley, & a Welchman, name unknown, hands on the vessel. The passengers were Robt Myers, of Delaware Co, N Y, & Wm Bunch, a mulatto from Manistee.

Mrd: on Jun 10, by Rev Mr Nelson, John Marbury, jr, of Gtwn, D C, to Juliet, daughter of the late A B Murray, formerly of Balt.

Mrd: on Jun 10, at Martinsburg, Va, by Rev D Francis Sprigg, Geo F Harrison, of Elkora, Cumberland Co, Va, to Miss Rebecca Holmes Conrad, 2nd daughter of David Holmes Conrad.

Naval: Passed Midshipman Pollock, sailing-master of the ship **St Louis**, had been court-martialed for cutting down with a cutlass a seaman on board the ship, & was sentenced to be discharged from the squadron. The crews belonging to the vessels of the squadron were in good health.

John Moffett was arrested on Wed at Gtwn, charged, in the warrant first issued by Justice P Gorsuch, of Balt, with an assault & battery with intent to kill Barbara Tretler, of that city; also, with robbing the said female of $200 in gold & silver. The prisoner was identified & committed to jail to await the requisition of Gov Lowe.

Died: on Jun 12, in Wash City, in her 29th year, Louisa Pemberton, wife of Chas W Forrest, & daughter of the late Chas J Nourse. Her funeral is today, at 4 P M.

Died: on May 26, in Wash City, Miriam Phillips, daughter of Thos & Emily S Blagden, aged 7 months & 10 days.

SAT JUN 14, 1851
Died: on Jun 12, after a long & painful illness, Mrs Catharine Minitree, in her 65th year. Her funeral is today at 10 o'clock, from the residence of her son, on Md ave, between 4½ & 6th sts.

Died: on Jun 12, Mgt Mariah Edwards, daughter of the Rev Wm B & Eliz A Edwards, of Wash City, in her 9th year. Her funeral will take place from the Wesley Chapel on Sun, at 3 o'clock.

Died: Jun 11, in Wash City, Emma, only daughter of Wm & Cordelia Mitchell, aged 22 months.

Mormon violence on Beaver Island. Cincinnati, Jun 13. A man named Thos Bennett, & his brother, Saml, have been shot on Beaver Island by a party of 50 Mormons.

Public sale of valuable real estate on the Potomac River: by decree of Montg Co Court, as court of Equity, in the case of French Forrest & others vs Moreau Forrest, the subscriber, as Trustee: public sale on Jul 19, at the City Hall in Wash: all the lands in Montg Co of which the late Jos Forrest was seized & possessed at the time of his death, either in his own right, or in the right of his wife, except lot 3, heretofore sold to Wm H Offutt. The land contain 565 acres, more or less. The improvements consist of a dwlg house & other out-houses. –R J Bowie, Trustee

Michl McNamara, who was at work on the scaffold very insecurely fastened in the rear of the Nat'l Hotel, Wash City, fell therefrom yesterday into the street. He is not expected to recover.

Shamrock Hill for sale: situated about 2¼ miles of the Capitol, & adjoining the lands of Washington Berry & Jas Moore: with a fine dwlg house on the premises containing 14 apartments, with barn, smoke-house, & milk-house. Apply to Junius J Boyle, U S N.

Rooms for rent: Mrs Stetson, on Pa ave, between 3rd & 4½ sts.

For sale: a large 3 story brick bldg on 8th st, between G & H sts. Apply to Mrs A S Young, 4½ st, near the City Hall.

MON JUN 16, 1851
Mrd: on Jun 11, Mr Jas Lewis to Miss Ellen Eliz Dubant, all of Wash City.

Died: on Fri, Maria S, only child of Mrs H Ulerich. Her funeral is today at 4½ o'clock, at the residence of her mother, 15th st.

Mr Wm H Cox, of St Louis, who committed suicide at Congress Hall, Albany, on Mon last, by cutting his throat, had arrived the day before from N Y C, where he had been led into a series of excesses.

TUE JUN 17, 1851
Appointments by the Pres: 1-Thos W G Allen, Surveyor of the Customs, Suffolk, Va, vice Benj Reddick, resigned. 2-Nicholas J Keefe, of N J, to be Consul of the U S for the port of Laguyra, in the Republic of Venezuela, in place of Louis Baker, removed. 3-Timothy Darling, to be Consul of the U S for the port of Nassau, New Providence, in place of Julius C Kretschmar, removed.

For sale: lot 26 in square 252, on 13th st, between G & H sts, Wash. Apply to Miss Eliz Clark, Greenmount, Hookstown road, Balt.

Dewaw's Fireworks factory, at Jersey City, was blown up last Sat, & killing Mr Dewaw instantly, who was alone in the bldg at the time.

Valuable 20 acre lots at auction: sale on Jun 21, on the premises, two valuable farms of 20 acres each, know as a part of the Worthington estate, situated between the 7th st Turnpike & the Piney Branch road. -Dyer & McGuire, aucts

Valuable bldg lots at auction: by decree of the Circuit Court of Wash Co, D C, in Chancery, made in a cause wherein Thos E Brannan & others are cmplnts, & Wm F Brannan & others are dfndnts: sale on Jul 17, of lot 5 in square 374, on which is a small bldg. On Jul 18, I shall sell lots 7 thru 11, in square 213; lot 5 in square 374 on H st, between 9th & 10th sts; & the other lots front on 15th & M sts, & Mass ave. –Jas W Sheahan, Trustee -A Green, auctioneer

Valuable farm in Anne Arundel Co for sale: containing 1,114 acres with a convenient brick dwlg, & all necessary out-houses. Mr Geo Hamilton, living on the premises, will show the same. Address the subscriber, John Hamilton, living near Port Tobacco, Chas Co, Md.

Trustee's sale of real estate: on Jun 27, by deed of trust recorded in Liber W B 113, folios 134 thru 136, a land record for Wash Co: a 2 story frame house & lot; situated in square 367, lot 52, [subdivided,] on 9th st between N & O sts, fronting on 9th st. Belonging to the estate of the late Sarah Brown, deceased. -A Green, auctioneer

Circuit Court of Wash Co, D C, sitting as a Court of Chancery, Oct term, 1850. Thos Wilson, cmplnt, vs Geo C Bomford, Jas V Bomford, Irvin Bomford, Richd C Derby & Louisa Derby his wife; Jas S Payne & Ruth Payne his wife; & John D Kurtz, administrator & only heir at law of John Kurtz, deceased, & others, dfndnts. The bill states that Geo Bomford, deceased, & Clara his wife, by their deed, dated May 6, 1845, conveyed to Wm W Corcoran, his heirs & assigns, part of lot 79, in the original limits of Gtwn, in D C, & the cotton factor bldg thereon, & part of the machinery attached, in trust to secure the payment of $10,000, a debt due from said Bomford to Thos Corcoran, & with a condition therein that on the payment of said debt by the said Bomford, his heirs, or assigns, the said Trustee should release & convey said premises to the said Bomford, his heirs, or assigns; that afterwards the said Geo Bomford & Geo C Bomford, being indebted to the Trustees of the Farmers' & Mechanics' Bank of Gtwn, in D C, in the sum of $12,000, on sundry notes drawn by the said Geo Bomford, & endorsed by said Geo C Bomford, by their deed dated Jan 3, 1848, conveyed a portion of the same part of the said lot 79, so as aforesaid conveyed to W W Corcoran, & the cotton mill bldg thereon, & the machinery, to John Kurtz & Clement Cox, & their heirs, to secure the payment of the last mentioned debt, with power to sell the said premises at public auction, if said notes were not paid at maturity. The bill further states that the said Geo Bomford died insolvent; that letters of administration on his estate were granted by the Orphans Court of Wash Co, D C to Jonathan B H Smith; that the said notes fell due & remain unpaid, & in arrears; that the said Clement Cox died in the lifetime of the said Geo Bomford, having never interfered in the matter of the said trust, leaving John Kurtz, on the demand of the said Trustees of the Farmers' & Mechanics' Bank, they being the holders of the said part of the said lot 79 conveyed as aforesaid to W W Corcoran, which was conveyed to him the said John Kurtz & the said Clement Cox by the said deed of Jan 3, 1848, & the cotton mill bldgs thereon, & the machinery, for sale at public auction on Oct 17, 1848, to pay said debt, in conformity with the requirements of the said deed, & on that day sold the same, free from all incumbrance, to the highest bidder; that the cmplnt was the highest bidder, & the purchaser of the said premises, for the sum of $30,000, a full, fair, & adequate price therefore. The bill further states that the said cmplnt complied with the terms of sale, having paid to the said John Kurtz the sum of $10,000 in hand, & passed to him his bond for the residue of the purchase money, payable in 3 annual instalments of

$6,666.66 2/3 each: that the instalment of 1849 fell due in the lifetime of said John Kurtz, & has been paid; that the proceeds of said sale have been applied, as required by the terms of sale, & as far as necessary, to pay the debt due to the said Thos Corcoran, & charged on the said lot & bldg, & the said debt has been fully satisfied; that the said John Kurtz has departed this life intestate, leaving John D Kurtz his only child & heir, who declines to meddle with the trust devolved on him in the premises by the death of his father; that cmplnt will be prepared to pay the remaining instalments of his purchase money when they fall due; that there is no person competent to receive the same, or to release & convey to him the said premises when paid for. The object of the bill is to have a Trustee appointed by this Court, in the stead of the said John Kurtz, deceased, to complete the unfinished trusts of the said deed of Jan 3, 1848; that on the final payment of the said purchase money, such new trustee, & the said Wm W Corcoran, the trustee named in the deed of May 6, 1845, made to secure the said debt to Thos Corcoran, may, by deeds to be made & executed by them, convey & release the premises in the deed of Jan 3, 1848, mentioned to the cmplnt, his heirs, & assigns. The persons named as dfndnts in the said cause, do not reside within the D C, & cannot be found therein, it is by the Court, Mar 3, 1851, ordered that the said named absent dfndnts appear in this Court on or before the 4th Mon in Oct next. –Jno A Smith, clerk

Mrd: on May 27, in Rockville, Md, by Rev Basil Barry, Maj Matthew Markland, of Wash City, [formerly of Ky,] to Miss Caroline S Hall, daughter of the late Dr E J Hall, of Balt Co.

Died: on Jun 9, at Madison, Conn, Emily Joanna Hand, youngest daughter of the late Jos W Hand, of Wash City, aged 11 years.

Died: on Jun 15, in Wash City, at her father's residence, on G st, Frances Eliz Henry McDowell, 3rd daughter of Gov Jas McDowell, Rep in Congress from Va.

Died: on Jun 16, in his 8th year, William, an interesting son of Wm & Catharine Begman. His funeral is today at 10 A M, at his father's house on 13th & E sts.

Died: on Jun 16, Jesse William, infant son of Elias & Rachel Yulee, aged 9 months. His funeral is today, at 5 o'clock, from Mrs Rice's boarding-house, on Capitol Hill.

WED JUN 18, 1851
The *Tiber* originally passed across what is now Pa ave, about 50 paces west of the brick arch. At this point the only bridge then was the trunk of a tree, & higher up, near the late railroad depot, was a ford, over which, by means of several large stones, foot passengers were enabled to cross. It was over this rustic bridge that the procession headed by Gen Washington, passed to lay the corner-stone of the *Capitol* in 1793.

Kosciusko's trial: the case came up upon the bill filed by the heirs of Gen Kosciusko, on Sep 26, 1848, against Lewis Johnson, the actual administrator de bonis non of Kosciusko's estate; Jonathan B H Smith, administrator of the estate of Geo Bomford, the former administrator of Kosciusko's estate; & Jas Carrico, Sam Stott, Geo C Bomford, Jacob Gideon, Ulysses Ward, & Jonathan B H Smith, sureties upon the administration bonds of Geo Bomford. The object of the suit is to compel the dfndnts, by decree, to account for the assets of the estate before the auditor; & to obtain an order commanding the sureties of Geo Bomford to bring into Court $43,504.40, with interest since Jan 1, 1847, which their principal, Mr Bomford, admitted, in his last account settled with the Orphans' Court, to be due from him as administrator of the estate of Kosciusko. The case was opened by Maj G Tochman, who argued it for 2 days, with great ability. The facts are these: Gen Kosciusko, in 1798, left in the hands of Mr Thos Jefferson $17,099.99. He simultaneously left with Mr Jefferson a will dated May 5, 1798, authorizing Mr Jefferson to employ this fund upon his death for the purpose of purchasing & educating such negroes as he may choose. Kosciusko then executed another will, in 1806, in France, by which he bequeathed, out of the same fund, $3,704 to Mr Armstrong, of N Y; of course, pro tanto, he revoked his first bequest. [This legacy, by accumulation of interest, swelled to the sum of about $17,000. It is this will of 1806, which, a few days ago, the jury by their verdict declared not to be the last will of Kosciusko.] At the time when Kosciusko executed those two wills [of 1798 & 1806] he was also possessed of about 215,000 fra-in France, England, & Switzerland, which he then left undisposed of. It was contended by the counsel of the heirs that his original intention was to leave that fund to his next of kin, to be taken by them under the statute of distribution. But he subsequently made acquaintances & formed an intimate friendship with Mr Zeltner & his family, with whom he resided in France during 20 years, & made up his mind to give to that family a considerable portion of his property. This he did by the subsequent wills, dated Jun 4, 1816, & Oct 10, 1817, which he executed at Soleure, in Switzerland, during his temporary sojourn there. By the will of 1816 he bequeathed to sundry members of Mr Zeltner's family about 100,000 francs, & directed that hey be paid out of his general property which he should possess at the time of his death; directing further to employ for that purpose, in the first place, the funds which he had in the hands of Mr Hottinger, his banker, in Paris; he them peremptorily revoked all former wills & codicile, & declared the will of 1816 to be his last will. By the will of 1817 he only bequeathed [specified therein] property to other sundry members of Mr Zeltner's relatives, & let the will of 1816 in every other respect unchanged & in full force. The first administrator of the estate was Benj L Lear. He settled with the Orphans' Court 4 accounts; by the last, filed on Feb 5, 1831, he admitted that on that day he had in his hands in various stocks $27,991.08 of Kosciusko's assets. Upon Lear's death in 1832 Geo Bomford, who was executor & administrator cum testaments annexe of Lear's estate, obtained letter of administration de bonis non of the estate of Kosciusko, & settled his first account as such administrator with the Orphans' Court on Mar 15, 1839. By this account Bomford admitted that upon Lear's death came into his hands as administrator de bonis non of the estate of Kosciusko $31,785.27½, in various stocks purchased & left as Kosciusko's assets by his predecessor. Bomford settled 9 accounts with the Orphans' Court. By the last, filed on Jun 7, 1827, he admitted that on that day was due from him as administrator of the estate $43,504.04, with interest since Jan 1, 1847. The estate of Kosciusko appears to have swelled to the sum of $64,000 or $65,000. In 1845 the heirs instituted legal proceedings against Bomford, to compel him to either to bring the moneys of the estate into Court or to give a new security. They succeeded in obtaining 2 new administration bonds in the penalty of $60,000, to which the dfndnts named above became sureties of Bomford. The dfndnts pleaded that they are not liable for the assets which Bomford collected & wasted before they entered into security for him. The case is now under advisement of the Court.

Col John H Sherburne, the U S Agent, has been unable to find the grave of Paul Jones, at Paris, while an English shipmaster deposes that he has seen his grave-stone at Cronstadt. Paul Jones was a rear admiral in the Russian service, & a monument might be placed to his memory at Cronstadt. But he died in Paris Jul 18, 1792, & was buried there on the 20th. The Nat'l Assembly sent a deputation to attend his funeral; & a funeral discourse was pronounced over his remains by Mons Marron, a Portestant clergyman of Paris. Still it cannot be discovered now where his grave was made. –Boston Courier

San Francisco: the leading item of news is the occurrence of another terrible conflagration at San Francisco, which is reported to have laid in ashes property to the amount of $15,000,000.   dan

Plan of addition to the Capitol has at last been adopted. Reminiscences of Washington.

Postmaster Gen has est'd the following new Post Ofcs for week ending Jun 14, 1851.

Ofc	County, State	Postmaster
Big Creek	Steuben, N Y	Carius Bennel
Scalp Level	Cambria, Pa	Geo Englebach
Arden	Berkley, Va	John Dunn
Savannah	Macon, N C	Isaac Ashe
Bay River	Craven, N C	Jas Miller
South Creek	Beaufort, N C	Josephus Reed
Black Jack Valley	Spartansburg dist, S C	Elias Bearder
Clayton's Mills	Pickens dist, S C	Carter Clayton
Sandy Flat	Greenville dist, S C	John M Crotwell
Union Line	Spartansburg dist, S C	R L Duncan
Fair Forest	Union dist, S C	W P Gee
Bethany	York dist, S C	Wm McGill
New Centre	York dist, S C	Myles Smith

Millville	Cherokee, Ga	Ira R Foster
Skitt's Mountain	Hall, Ga	Ashford Quinn
Bruceville	Pike, Ala	Joel Rainer
High School	Jackson, Miss	P A Kent
Homochitto	Franklin, Miss	Nathan Bunckley
Estis	Tallahatchie, Miss	Jas Moore
Red Hill	Wayne, Miss	Wm Chapman
Zion Hill	Amite, Miss	Isaiah Cain
Downsville	Union Parish, La	Philemon Wilhite
Sandifer's Store	Carroll, Ky	Jas S Sandifer
Sagon	Dupage, Ill	Smith D Pierce
Jacobs	Pike, Mo	Benj F Jacobs
Boon's Grove	Washington, Ark	B F Reagor
Niona	Pulaski, Ark	J C M Hicks
Irish Creek	De Wit, Texas	Arthur Burns

Names Changed: 1-East Cutchogue, Suffolk Co, N Y, changed to West Southold. 2-Buncombe, Walton Co, Ga, changed to Logansville.

Died: on the [paper folded,] instant, at the residence of Dr Garnett, of Wash City, Spencer Sergeant Wise, infant son of the Hon Henry Wise, of Va.

Quincy [Ill] Whig of Jun 3rd announces the death, in that city, of Mrs Eliz Odell, wife of A C Odell, on Jun 1. On the Fri before, her son, Alfred, & on Sat, her 2 daughters, Ellen & Eliza, died of the same disease. Thus were 4 members of the family consigned to the grave.

Valuable residence on the Heights of Gtwn at public sale: by decree of the Circuit Court of Wash Co, D C, as a court of Chancery, in the cause of the ptn of John Cox, trustee, #109 Chancery: sale of the residence know as the *Cedars*, on Fayette st, & 7th. The dwlg house is a commodious 3 story bldg. Lots 209 & 211 in Threlkeld's Addition to Gtwn, at Fayette & 8th sts, each fronting on Fayette st. Part of lot 28, of Old Gtwn, fronting on Bridge st, with a frame dwlg house.
–Walter S Cox, trustee -Edw S Wright, auct

Criminal Court-Wash: Grand Jury:
Wm Gunton
Thos F Simms
Thos Young
J F Haliday
Beniah Willett
B F Middleton
Wm H Edes
Esau Pickrell
Wm Selden

Andrew Hoover
Thos Havenner
Henry Haw
B O Tayloe
Geo Thomas
Geo W Young
Alex'r Ray
Ephraim Wheeler
Robt Clarke

Geo Parker
Geo Waters
Geo Poe
Petit Jury:
Edw Bradford
Otho R Vermillion
Norley L Adams
Henry Parker
Jas K Plant
Jas Barnard
Gabriel Barnhill
Humphrey O Whitmore
Bertrand E Hays
Wm Cammack
Edw Birckhead
Thos P Tench
Saml Hanson
Geo A Bohrer
Rezin Beck

P M Pearson
Saml Kirby
Thos Blagden

Wm Kurtz
Chas Mann
Wm Tucker
Archibald R Quantirl
Landon W Worthington
Henry E Marcellus
John R Scrivener
Jas Clephane
John McDermott
Alex'r Talbot
Eugene Laporte
Saml Drury
Saml Wardell
John R Ruff
Wm S Macpherson

The Criminal Court-Wash- 1-Sentenced Mediperis, a Mexican, convicted at a former term of an assault on Miss Parkhurst, to pay a fine of $5 & costs.
2-Ezekiel Young, jr, charged with refusing to aid ofcr Stoddart in the discharge of his duty was found not guilty.

Mrd: on Jun 10, in Vt, by Rev Bishop Hopkins, Jas G Rumsey, of Detroit, Mich, to Augusta J, eldest daughter of Gen John A Arthur, of Burlington.

Orphans Court of Wash Co, D C. Letters of administration on the personal estate of Nathl Plant, late of Wash Co, D C. –Eliz Plant, admx

THU JUN 19, 1847
The partnership under the firm of A Hatch, jr, & Co is dissolved by mutual consent. The business will hereafter be conducted by A Hatch, jr, at the old stand on Pa ave, between 6th & 7th sts. –A Hatch, jr, S B Webb

A W Scowell, a printer 80 years of age, the oldest in the U S, commenced his apprenticeship of 7 years in the King's printing ofc, London, in 1784, 68 years ago. The Boston Mail says he was a soldier under Sir John Moore, at Corunna, in 1809, where he received a ball in his right arm. He was present at the burial of Sir John, & remembers the minutest particulars of the scene. He was with the Duke of Wellington through his whole campaign, & lost an ankle bone by a grape shot in the battle of Waterloo. This verteran typo is one of the swiftest & best compositors in Boston.

Circuit Court of Wash Co, D C-in Chancery. Mgt Ashton, by her next friend Thos P Hereford, vs Wm M Stewart & others, heirs at law of Ann Stewart, deceased. The object is to procure a decree for a conveyance of certain lots of ground in Wash City, D C. The bill states that Hugh M Stewart, who had 8 daughters, several of whom intermarried, during his lifetime made to each of them before their intermarriage, except his daughter Sally, who died an infant, a certain advancement in personal property; to the cmplnt, one of his daughters, he gave a certain negro woman & her future increase, which said negro woman afterwards had 5 children, all of whom were owned & possessed by the cmplnt until they were grown & had become very valuable; that the the said negroes were sold by Ann Stewart, the mother of the cmplnt, & with her consent, upon the express condition that the proceeds arising from the sale should be invested in certain real estate for the use, benefit, & behoof of the cmplnt; that lots 14 & 15, in square 224, Wash City, with improvements, were so purchased for the benefit of the cmplnt; that Ann Stewart, to whom the said lots were originally conveyed, repeatedly admitted that said lots were bought with the proceeds of sale & hire of said negroes, & always promised, & frequently expressed her intention to convey or devise to the said cmplnt the said lots of ground; that said cmplnt continued from the time of the purchase of said lots down to the time of the filing of her said bill in the action possession thereof, claiming them as her property; that said lots were neither conveyed nor devised to cmplnt; that Ann Stewart died on Aug 13, 1849, leaving the following persons her heirs at law, to wit: Susan C, the wife of Jeremiah Williams, Adam Duncan Stewart, Wm M Stewart, Hebe, wife of Thos R Gedney, Arabella, wife of John McKee, Ann C, wife of Chas L Carter, the said Ann & her husband died before said Ann Stewart, leaving the following children, all of whom are of age, to wit: Duncan S Carter, Judith Carter, Hebe, wife of Wm Ashbey, Judith, wife of Edwin Carter, Ellen, the wife of Wm B Boggs, Marion, wife of Wm Rhodes; the said Marion having died before the said Ann Stewart, leaving the following infant children, to wit: Mary Nancy, Catharine, & Wm. The bill prays that the said heirs at law may be made dfndnts to said bill, & that they be required to convey said lots of ground to said cmplnt, & that a guardian ad litem be appointed for such of the heirs at law as are infants. The said bill further states that Adam D Stewart, Arabella & her husband John McKee, Duncan S Carter, Judith Carter, Hebe & her husband Wm Ashby, & Wm H Rhodes, & the aforesaid infant children, reside of the the District of Columbia. Same to appear in this Court on or before the 3rd Mon of Oct, 1851. –Jas S Morsell, Assist Judge Circuit Court of D C. -Jno A Smith, clerk

Criminal Court: During a visit paid to this city some time ago by the N Y firemen a riot occurred in front of the Franklin Engine House, when Mr E Rodburn, standing at the door of Willard's Hotel, was shot by some unknown person & severely wounded. Yesterday Washington Rollins & Wm Baker, charged with rioting on the occasion above alluded to, were put upon their trials. The jury acquitted Baker, & found Rollins guilty.

Berkeley Springs, Va: the Hotel is ready for the reception of company, with accommodations increased & greatly improved. Stages now run daily between this & Sir John's, on Balt & Ohio Railroad, distant 2½ miles only. –John Strother

Smithsonian Institute: ofcrs appointed to serve during the ensuing 6 months:
Prof Jos H Henry, Pres
O C Wight, Rec Sec
Dr L D Johnson, V A
E Given Caruthers, Reader
Z C Richards, Cor Sec
J E Thompson, Librarian
Z C Richards, W T Eva, & O C Wight, Exec Cmte

Died: on Jun 17, Furman Black, jr, aged 7 years & 5 months, only son of Furman & Sarah A Black. His funeral is today at 4 o'clock, at the Nat'l Hotel.

Died: on Jun 6, at Terre Haute, Ind, John M Wheat, in his 49th year, son of the late John Wheat, of Greenleaf's Point, Wash.

J A Simpson, Artist, is prepared to execute Portraits in a superior style. He can be found at the room of the Cmte on Pensions, basement, from 10 to half past 3 o'clock daily.

St Louis: 1-On Jun 16-Mrs Larrier, of Messrs Ludlow & Smith's theatrical company, died of cholera, at the same theatre. Mrs Blanche, another member of the company, was instantly killed while on the stage, by the falling of a weight behind the scenes. 2-The will of Judge Mullanphy was opened on Jun 17, & he bequeaths one-third of his estate, $200,000, to the city in trust, for the relief of emigrants, & the remaining $400,000 goes to his heirs.

FRI JUN 20, 1851
Six men were burnt to death at one bldg in the recent fire on May 3 at San Francisco, to wit: Capt Welch, Lewis Richland, Edw McCahill, Leon Greenbann, Reuben Baker, Nesbaum, & Rosenthal. Gen Jas Wilson was seriously injured.

Criminal Court-Wash-Thu. 1-Nelson Sims found guilty of an aggravated assault & battery. 2-Francis Cole, tried for an assault & battery, acquitted. 3-Jas T Bartley, tried on a charge of larceny, not guilty. 4-Mary Lee, charged with larceny, was under trial when the court adjourned.

Springfield [Mass] Republican of Tue. Govn'r McDowell, of Va, has been compelled by domestic affliction to decline the invitation given him by a union of parties in Springfield to deliver an Oration here on Jul 4. "Your letters have found him watching beside the sick bed of a beloved child, whose health, which has been a source of the deepest anxiety with him for many months past, has recently & rapidly so completely sunken under the power of pulmonary disease as to justify his worst fears in regard to her." –Sally C P McDowell

Appropriations made during the 2nd session of the 31st Congress.

1-Act for the relief of the legal reps of Robt S Burrough & of Stephen Hopkins: for fees alleged to have been withheld from them by the U S, & which had accrued between Jun 1, 1799, & Jun 30, 1805: $709.82

2-Act for the relief of the widow of the late Col Wm Gray, of Ark: the difference of pay & allowances between a lt col of cavalry & a lt col of infty: indefinite.

3-Act for the relief of the administrator of Maj Fred'k D Mills, deceased: the value of the horse & equipage of the deceased lost at the battle of Churubusco, in Mexico: $200.

4-Act for relief of Wm Hardin: for expenses incurred & moneys paid by him in defending a suit to recover money he had procured for the use of the Gov't: $600.

5-Act for relief of J H McClintock, Harrison Gill, & Mansfield Carter: To H J McClintock, for his services as farmer for the Sac & Fox Indians at the Great Nemahaw sub-agency, in 1846, & for the hire of 2 hands employed & paid by him: $142.20
To Harrison Gill, for his services as assist farmer for said Indians at the same place & time: $58.66 To Mansfield Carter, for his services as assist blacksmith for said Indians, at the same place & time: $89.33

6-Resolution providing for an adjustment of the accounts of John D Colmemeil, Pres of the Ohio & Miss Mail Line Co: for transporting the mails of the U S between Nov 15, 1832, & Jul 15, 1833: indefinite.

7-Resolution in relation to the accounts of John De Neufeille & Son: any balance which may be found to be due to said firm, to the party or parties legally entitled to receive the same: indefinite.

8-Act for the relief of Charlotte Lynch: only surviving child of Lt Col Ebenezer Gray, of the 6th Regt of the Conn line, who served in the army of the Revolution from the beginning of the war to its close, as an equivalent for the loss sustained by him by the substitution of the commutation certificates, issued in 1783, for the half-pay for life, to which he was entitled: indefinite.

9-Act for the relief of Dunning R McNair: the amount of fines improperly imposed on him, while he was mail contractor on route from Bedford to Washington, in Pa: $425.

10-Act for the relief of the legal reps of the late Gen Walker K Armistead, U S Army: money which he paid out for & on account of the U S Army, whilst in command at **Fort Monroe**, in 1834, & which was not adjusted with the Gov't during his life: $687.40

11-Act for the relief of Saules J Bowen: for his services as clerk in the ofc of the 2nd Auditor of the Treas Dept, from May 1, 1846 to Jul 1, 1847: $533 33

12-To A W Babbitt, as delegate from the Territory of Utah, for mileage & compensation: $2,460.

13-To W S Messervey, as delegate from New Mexico, for mileage & compensation: $2,460.

14-For compensation to John Ryan, a deputy surveyor general of Wisconsin & Iowa, under his contract of Jun 22, 1850: $567.73

Mrd: on Wed, at Balt, by Rev Mr Foley, at the residence of H B Majesty's Consul, Lt D Ammen, U S Navy, to Maria Catharine Jackson.

Died: on May 8, at San Francisco, Calif, Mr Thos McCalla, son of John M McCalla, late 2nd Auditor of the Treasury Dept.

Died: on Jun 19, Henry Stanford, infant son of Wm H & Sarah E Stanford. His funeral is today, this morning, from his father's residence, Capitol Hill, North Capitol st.

Died: on Jun 17, Augustus, son of Caroline & L A Fleury, late of the Quartermaster Genrl's Ofc, aged 15 months.

Died: on Jun 19, George W, infant son of Jas & Mgt Selden, aged 4 months & 13 days.

Died: on Jun 8, in Alexandria, Va, of scarlet fever, George Dashiel, aged 18 months; & on Jun 15, Cardlyn Dennis, in his 7th year, only sons of Geo D & Sarah Ellen Fowler.

Situation wanted, by a respectable woman, as assist housekeeper, & to do chamber work, or to take charge of an infant, in some respectable family; would have no objection to travel with a family. Apply to John C Keating, on C st, between 9th & 10th sts.

Foreign Item: the death of the Earl of Shaftsbury & the Right Hon Richd Lalor Sheil is announced. The latter gentleman died at Florence on May 25.

Circuit Court of Wash Co, D C. Wm H Martin, cmplnt, vs Thos Powell, John Powell, Peter Laidlaw, the New Orleans Canal & Banking Co, & John D Fink, dfndnts in chancery. The undersigned, Wm H Martin, by his bill, filed in pursuance of the 8th section of the act of Congress of the U S A, approved Mar 3, 1849, entitled an act to carry into effect certain stipulations of the treaty between the U S A & the Republic of Mexico of Feb 1, 1848, claims the whole amount of the 2 several awards made by the Board of Com'rs, the one in favor of John Powell, assignee of Thos Powell, for the sum of $12,922.90, as indemnity for the schnr **Escambia**, the other in favor of the New Orleans Canal & Banking Co, for the sum of $4,370.70, as indemnity for the schnr **Louisiana**. The bill of Wm H Martin alleges that as security in a bond executed by Thos Powell in the sum of $47,500 to the judge of the Court of Probates for the city & parish of New Orleans, La, conditioned for the faithful performance by said Thos Powell of his duties as dative executor of the estate of one Sarah Baume, of New Orleans, deceased, he was compelled by judgments & executions & did pay as security for said Thos Powell to the dfndnt, John D Fink, as dative executor of the said estate of Sarah Baume, deceased, appointed after the removal by the Court of the said Thos Powell, the sum of $20,000; that said Fink executed to said Wm H Martin, an instrument bearing date Feb 16, 1837, acknowledging the receipt of said sum of money, & subrogating him, said Martin, in all the rights of him, the said Fink, as dative executor as aforesaid. Moreover, the bill alleges that by the laws of La your orator, Wm H Martin, was subrogated to all the rights of the rep of said estate of Sarah Baume, deceased, & had an equitable mortage on the claims of said Thos Powell on the Republic of Mexico for the vessels **Escambia** & **Louisiana**. The bill charges the claim set up by John D Fink to the said awards to be illegal & invalid. The bill further charges that the assignments respectively made by Thos Powell to Peter Laidlaw, & by him to the New Orleans Canal & Banking Co, & by said Thos Powell to John Powell, by means whereof the Com'rs were induced to make the awards for indemnity to said John Powell, as assignee of Thos Powell, for the schnr **Escambia**, & to the said New Orleans Canal & Banking Co, as assignee of Peter Laidlaw, who was assignee of Thos Powell, were fraudulent, not bona fide, not made upon valuable consideration, but were assignments made mala fide, to hinder, delay, & defraud the creditors of said Thos Powell, & to evade the obligation of said Thos Powell for $47,500, with sureties for the faithful discharge of the duties of his ofc as dative executor as aforesaid. The bill charges that Thos Powell became insolvent; that the cosecurities of the said Martin in the bond of $47,500 became insolvent, so that said Martin has been compelled to pay the said sum of $20,000 in consequence of his being bound in said bond as security for said Thos Powell, & can have no satisfaction therefore, except by setting aside the fraudulent assignments made by said Thos Powell of his claims to indemnity for the schnr **Louisiana** & **Escambia**; the object of the bill is to set aside the assignments as fraudulent & invalid, & to have the amount of said awards for the schnrs **Escambia** & **Louisiana** applied to the satisfaction of the moneys paid by the cmplnt as security for Thos Powell, & the bill prays for general relief. The dfndnts are all absent from D C, & the said dfndnt, John Powell, resides in the State of Va. Same to appear on or before that 3rc Mon of Oct next. –Jas S Morsel, Assoc Judge Circuit Court D C -John A Smith, clerk -John Carroll Brent, Alex'r H Lawrence, Geo M Bibb for cmplnt

SAT JUN 21, 1851
The Alta California of May 15 reports the total loss of the ship **Commodore Preble**, Capt Ballard, on the North Reef, Humboldt Bay, on May 6. Capt Ticknor, of the steamer **Sea Gull**, carried the passengers & crew to San Francisco. The **Commodor Preble**'s cargo was saved. She had on board about 100 passengers.

Public sale: by decree of Chas Co Court, as Court of Equity: sale on Jul 23, at the Courthouse door in Port Tobacco, Chas Co, Md, the whole of the real estate of which Johannes D Starke died seized & possessed, known as ***Clifton***, containing about 1,000 acres, more or less. It has upon it a new & splendid dwlg house, & every outhouse in perfect repair. Geo Dent, whose farm lies adjoining, will show the premises. -Fred'k Stone, Trustee

Thos U Walter, of Phil, architect for the extension of the Capitol, arrived in Wash City on Thursday. The work, it is presumed, will commence without further delay.

Circuit Court of Wash Co, D C, in Chancery. Saml Redfern vs Barbara A Parker et al. John F Ennis, the trustee, reports that on Nov 2, 1849, he sold part of lot 4 in square 141, Wash City, to Allison Nailor, for $660, & that he has complied with the terms of the sale; that on Mar 31, 1849, he sold part of lot 3 in square 56, Wash City, to W J Mosely, for $295, & he has complied with the terms of the sale.
–Jno A Smith, clerk

Mrd: on Jun 19, by Rev Mr Morgan, Mr A F Hines to Miss Sarah A Fickett, all of Wash City.

Mrd: Jun 19, by Rev Mr Gilliss, Mr Edw A Smith to Miss Eliz Davis, all of Wash City.

Died: on Jun 2, of cholera, on the plains, about 90 miles from **Fort Leavenworth**, Dr Alfred W Kennedy, Surgeon in the U S Army. Also, of the same disease, & about the same time, his son, Worsley, in his 4th year. Dr Kennedy, accompanied by his wife & children, was on the line of march to New Mexico, with a detachment of U S troops that had been concentrated from different military posts at **Fort Leavenworth**. The cholera first broke out among the troops at the Fort on May 29 & 30, & before leaving that post 11 of the soldiers had died. Dr Kennedy had just arrived from **Fort Scott**. In 1840 he was commissioned Assist Surgeon in the U S army, & received the first honor among a large number of applicants examined at the same time. He had been almost constantly in active service.

A Good Farm Wanted: the advertiser has just arrived from England, & wishes to fix his location in the neighborhood of Wash, if he can meet with a farm to suit his mind, a piece of from two to five hundred acres of good land. Apply in person to John Keyworth, at the residence of Robt Keyworth, between 9th & 10th sts, Penn ave.

Died: on Jun 19, Miss Susan Wright, daughter of Mrs Sarah Wright, of Wash City.

Died: yesterday, at Balt, Rev Danl McIlton, long an active Clergyman of the Methodist Church, in his 70th year.

Died: on Jun 20, in Wash City, Mrs Mary M Telfair, formerly of Rhode Island.

MON JUN 23, 1851
The N Y papers announce the decease of the widow of the late Chancerllor Kent. She died on Thu, at Orange, N J, at age 83 years.

Abraham Taylor, another of the persons charged with the massacre of the Cosden family, whose trial was removed from Kent to Elkton, in Cecil Co, was found guilty of murder in the 1st degree.

Orphans Court of Wash Co, D C. Letters of administration on the personal estate of Geo Bean, late of said county, deceased. –Ann Bean, admx

From Oregon: Wm Kendall, convicted of murder, was executed at Salem, on Apr 18, amid a large concourse of spectators.

The Albany Argus notices the recent death of Jas B Weed, the only son of Thurlow Weed. His sudden demise in the flower of manhood was unexpected & universally deplored.

Fire in North Groton, Mass, on Jun 13, Mrs Annable & 2 daughters were burnt to death, leaving Mr Annable, a cabinetmaker, & one little son, who survived the catastrophe.

The <u>Mounted Rifles</u>. This regt of the U S troops arrived at San Francisco, from Oregon, on the Gov't propeller Massachusetts, on May 6. They are ordered home, by way of the Isthmus, & in a few days we may look for them to arrive heres. List of Ofcrs: Brev Col W W Loring; Maj G B Crittenden; Assist Surgeon L H Holden; Assist Surgeon C H Smith; J N Palmer, Lt & Adj; Brev Maj J S Simonson, C F Ruff; Brev Lt Col A Porter; Capts L Jones, N Newton; 1st Lt A J Lindsey; Brev Capts T Claiborne, R M Norris; 1st Lts J May, F S K Russell; 2nd Lts G H Gordon, W B Lane, W E Jones; Lt W G Howland; Lt W Hawkins. –Panama Star

Criminal Court-Wash-Sat: 1-Mary Lee, charged with larceny, found guilty, but recommended to mercy: sentenced to be imprisoned 6 hours in the county jail & fined $1. 2-John Meyer alias Jacob Meyer, found guilty of forgery: sentenced to 4 years in the penitentiary.

Died: on Jun 21, T Egerton Browne, of the Post Ofc Dept in his 59th year.

Died: in Upperville, Va, on Jun 19, Mary Eliz, daughter of Rev Henry W Dodge, aged 2 years & 6 months.

TUE JUN 24, 1851
The Jacksonville [Fla] Republican of Jun 12, records the death of Dolly, a negress, aged 116 years. She was the slave of H D Holmead, of that place. She was remarkable for her tenacious memory of events connected with the American Revolution, having acted as cook & servant to several ofcrs of the Southern army during the war.

Nicholus Murphy, another of the murderers of the Cosden family in Kent Co, Md, has been convicted of murder in the 1st degree. This is the 3rd of the gang who has been found guilty.

Quebec, Jun 16. Mr Patterson, who owned the **Montmorenci Falls**, & all the land on both sides of the river for 20 miles up & down, died the day before we were there. He was a Scotchman by birth, & came to Canada a poor boy; but worked his way up, until he died one of the richest men of the province.

3,000 acres of land for sale: my estate known as **Brothwick**, in Dinwiddie Co, with a commodious dwlg. I desire to sell because of the remoteness of my residence from this plantation, & my inability to give it my attention. Mr Jones, who resides on the premises, will show the lands. –Richd Jones, Blacks & Whyte's, Nottoway Co, Va.

The dwlg house of Col Warthen, of Washington Co, Ga, was burnt to the ground last week, & his only son, aged about 15, & another lad, were burnt to death.

The U S Military Academy: the first instructor appointed to West Point was W A Barron, captain of engineers, appointed Apr 1, 1802. The 2nd was Jared Mansfield, captain of engineers, appointed May 3, 1802. Mr Barron was acting Professor of Mathematics, & Mr Mansfield acting Prof of Natural & Experimental Philosophy. These 2 gentlemen were the only teachers at West Point for the next 2 or 3 years. In that time Gen Jos G Swift, of the engineers, Gen Armistead, of the engineers, Col Bomford, of the ordnance, & Col McRee, of the engineers, were cadets. The Academy remained in this form till 1812, when, in preparation for the war with Great Britain, it was re-organized. The first Professors appointed were: Jared Mansfield, Alden Partridge, Christian E Zoeller, Fiorimond de Masson. Mansfield remained 16 years; Partridge remained 5 years; Zoeller 7 years; & Mr Mason, 3 years. In 1817, Col Sylvanus Thayer, now stationed in Boston, was appointed Superintendent, remaining 15 years. There are now, including the Military Staff, 40 Professors, Teachers, & Assistants.

Judge Bryan Mullanphy died suddenly at St Louis on Jun 14. He was the only son of the late John Mullanphy, of this city, from whom he inherited a very large estate, valued now at half million of dollars. He died unmarried & in the prime of his manhood.

Criminal Court-Wash-Mon. The U S vs W H Stevens: the dfndnt was indicted for an assault with intent to kill David Moor, by striking him severely with a brick on the head. The jury found him guilty of an aggravated assault, & sentenced him to be fined $1 & be imprisoned 3 months in the county jail.

Mrd: on Jun 17, at Sing Sing, N Y, by Rev Dr J McVickan, Peter Berry, of Gtwn, D C, to Priscilla, daughter of the late Roderick McLeod.

Circuit Court of Wash Co, D C-in Chancery. Danl B Brown vs Jonas P Levy, & Hon Thos Corwin, Sec of the Treasury. The bill states that on or about Jan 5, 1847, one Jas S Carpentier obtained a judgment in the Superior Court of the State of N Y against the said Jonas P Levy for $215.85, which judgment belonged in equity to Edw R Carpentier, of the State of N Y, & was duly assigned to him. That execution was issued on said judgment to recover the amount thereof, but without effect. That thereupon, on application to the proper Court, the said cmplnt, Danl B Brown, was appointed receiver of the estate & effects of the said Jonas P Levy, & vested with the entire power & control over the same, & that the said estate was under the order of the Court, & by the proper deed & indenture of the said J P Levy, assigned to the said cmplnt; that as a part of the estate so assigned was a claim of the said Jonas P Levy upon the Gov't of Mexico, upon which an award in favor of the said Levy had been made by the Board of Com'rs under the law & the treaty with Mexico, allowing him the sum of $3,675, which remained in the U S Treasury. Cmplnt claims to be entitled to receive & distribute the said amount, under & by virtue of the said order of the Court & the assignment of the party among his creditors, agreeably to the intent & effect of the said assignment. The said dfndnt, Jonas P Levy, is not an inhabitant of D C. Same to appear in this Court on or before the 3rd Mon of Oct next. –Jno A Smith, clerk -D A Hall, solicitor

John Tilghman, who was convicted at the Fall term of Craven Co [N C] Superior Court of the murder of Jos J Tilghman, was executed on Jun 14, about half a mile from the county jail. A large concourse of people, between 4,000 & 5,000, were there.

Caution: my son, John C Siebel, a minor, having left my family & control without my consent, this is to forewarn all persons not to trust him on my account, as I shall not hold myself responsible for any debts, obligations, or dealing of his whatsoever. -Geo C Seibel

Died: on Jun 13, in St Louis, Mo, of pulmonary consumption, Jas Brooks, aged 28 years. The deceased was a native, & for a considerable period a resident of Wash City, where he leaves a number of relatives & friends to lament his early death.

Died: on Jun 20, at his residence, in PG Co, Mr Anthony C W Page, in his 36th year.

Died: on Apr 6, on board the steamer **Fremont**, at sea, when 8 days out from Rio de Janeiro, on her way to Calif, Mrs Maria C McLane, wife of Allan McLane, U S Navy, & daughter of the late Richd Bache, of Phil. Her death was calm & peaceful. She was buried at Valparaiso, in the Foreign Burial Ground.

WED JUN 25, 1851
Orphans Court of Wash Co, D C. Letters of administration on the personal estate of Thos Egerton Browne, late of said county, deceased. –Thos Browne, adm

The high Military Court convened by a General Order for the trial of Col Talcott, on charges preferred against him by the Sec of War, was opened yesterday with a full Court, Maj Gen Twiggs presiding. The charges, consisting of alleged insubordination & disrespect to the Head of the War Dept, in regard to certain contracts for ordnance supplies, were read: & the trial was begun by the examination of Hon Chas M Conrad, Sec of War, in support of the charges.

Harvey Dayton, late cashier of the State Bank at Morris, N J, was convicted on Sat last of perjury. The bank failed about 2 years since, under circumstances exciting strong suspicions of fraud.

Miss Mary Spencer fell through a hatchway in the store of Mr L Chapman, N Y, on Sat, & was almost instantly killed. She was employed on the premises in the manufacture of pocket-books, & was on the trap door conversing, when the door tilted, & she fell the whole distance from the 5th story to the 1st floor. She was a native of Nottingham, England, about 30 years of age.

Wash Corp: 1-Ptn from David Atkinson, for the remission of a fine: referred to the Cmte of Claims. 2-Ptn from John M Jameson & others, for the grading & gravelling of 2nd st: referred to the Cmte on Improvements. 3-Ptn of Christopher Cammack & others, for grading & paving the alley on square 224: referred to the Cmte on Improvements. 4-Ptn of Wm J Tabler & others, for setting the curbstone on squares 529 thru 532: referred to the Cmte on improvements.

Died: on Sunday, at Phil, Chas N Buck, in his 76th year, a native of Hamburg, but for 55 years a resident of that city, & Consul-Gen from the Gov't of the city of Hamburg.

Died: on Jun 19, suddenly, at West Point, N Y, Mrs Eliza Gaither, of Montg Co, Md, relict of the late Henry C Gaither, & mother of Gen Wm Lingan Gaither, Pres of the Senate of Md. She had accompanied her son to West Point, where he, as a member of the Board of Visiters, was in attendance on the annual examination at the Military Academy. The trip was looked to as calculated to improve her health, which had been for some time seriously impaired.

Died: on Jun 20, at the residence of its grandfather, Thos Mustin, in Wash City, Mary Sophia, infant daughter of the Rev Thos & Annie S Jones, of Newville, Va.

Died: on Jun 23, at **Maple Hill**, near Wash City, Robt S P, son of Geo & Harriet McCeney, in his 2nd year. His funeral is today at 10 o'clock, from the residence of his parents.

Household & kitchen furniture at auction: on Jun 27, at the residence of Hazard Knowles, on 12th st, near Pa ave. –C W Boteler, auct

Postmaster Gen has est'd the following new Post Ofcs for week ending Jun 21, 1851.

Ofc	County, State	Postmaster
Mittineague	Hampden, Mass	Wm Barrows
Dickersonville	Niagara, N Y	Wm Pool
Cattaraugue	Cattaraugue, N Y	Salmon L Johnson
Morris Cross Roads	Fayette, Pa	Benj F Hellen
Harmony	Clark, Ohio	Jos Wise
Milo	Defiance, Ohio	David Wattenbe
Fairfax	Highland, Ohio	Benj F Pulliam
New Metamora	Washington, Ohio	R G Laughlin
Hurrican Bridge	Putnam, Va	Albert J Beckett
Monteithville	Stafford, Va	Jas Monteith
Whiteday Glades	Monongalia, Va	Wm Carrothers
Shirley	Tyler, Va	Wm P Jones
Millard	Jackson, Va	Reuben Harrison
Box Creek	Cherokee, Texas	John A Box
Constitution	Franklin, Ark	D L Bowland
Rome	Clarke, Ark	Joshua D Stewart
Oak Hill	De Kalb, Indiana	Thos Fosdeck
Cuba	Owen, Indiana	Wm L Hart
Bloomingsburgh	Fulton, Indiana	Jos Brelsford
Stephen's Chapel	Bledsoe, Tenn	Jos Hixson
Cotton Wood Grove	Bond, *	Davis S McCord
Sutton's Point	Clay, *	Wm Fennimore
Utica	La Salle, *	Jas Clark
Saline Mines	Gallatin, *	Wm Warford
Washburn	Marshall, *	Chas L Maxwell
Sacton	Clark, *	Jesse Draper
Lambs Point	Madison, *	Wm J Rosberry
Huntley Grove	McHenry, *	Stewart Comins
Warm Fork	Oregon, Mo	Wm C Cathey
Lisbon	Linn, Iowa	Danl Runkel
Nautrille	Bremer, Iowa	John H Messinger
Fulton	Jackson, Iowa	Wm Marden
Webster	Alamskee, Iowa	Adna C Perry
Chatham	Buchanan, Iowa	Chas Melrose
White Breast	Clark, Iowa	Bernard Arnold
Morning Sun	Louisa, Iowa	Wm P Brown
Adario	Waukesha, Wis	Danl Root

Names Changed: Kossuth, Jackson Co, Tenn, changed to New Columbus. Staffordsburg, Kenton Co, Ky, changed to Beauford. [*lil]

Administrator's sale by order of the Orphans Court of Wash Co, D C. Sale on Jun 26 at the store lately occupied by Julian Montandon, deceased, on Pa ave, between 12th & 13th sts, all his personal effects. –E Travers, adm -Dyer & McGuire, aucts

Household & kitchen furniture at auction: on Jun 27, at the residence of Hazard Knowles, on 12th st, near Pa ave. –C W Boteler, auct

Mrd: on Mon, by Rev John C Smith, Mr Calvin T Hartman to Miss Ann H Walker, all of Wash City.

Mrd: on Jun 19, by Rev Mr Cushman, Jno Ober to Miss Frances L Clarke, youngest daughter of the late Robt Clarke, all of Wash.

For rent: 2 story frame house on N Y ave, between 12th & 13th sts. Inquire of H Leddy, corner of 11th & I sts.

$5 reward for return of 2 milch cows that were stolen or strayed. –Ellen Sinclair, 21st st west, north of K st.

THU JUN 26, 1851
By way of New Orleans we have a report of the death of Brevet Brig Gen Matthew Arbuckle, of the U S Army, who died on Jun 11, at **Fort Smith**, on the Arkansas river. He entered the Army from the State of Va 52 years ago. At the time the cholera was raging with great fatality amongst the newly arrived troops, of whom some 30 have died.

Rockville [Md] Journal: a large body of land lying near the Potomac river, known as the Winn property, has just been sold to a gentleman from the State of N Y for $5 per acre. The tract contains some 700 or 800 acres.

New Britain, Conn Jan 29, 1851. Henry Meigs, sen: Dear Sir: I have a series of the Nat'l Intell, tri-weekly, beginning with the first year of Gen Jackson's administration, bound up, in full size of the paper, to the end of this [last] year. I offer the Board of Directors this series. I am now on the verge of my 88th year. –G W Murray [We regret to state that this was one of the last epistles of G W Murray. He was seized with severe illness, & has died. -Chas Turrell]

Criminal Court-Wash-Wed. 1-John Lyons, indicted for an assault upon Wm A Mulloy, constable, while acting in the discharge of his duty, was found not guilty. The dfndnt was then tried for an assault upon Caspar Offenstein, & found guilty. The Court sentenced Lyons to pay a fine of $5. 2-Thos Kelly pleaded guilty to a indictment for an assault on Caspar Offenstein: he was fine $5. 3-Richd H Adamson, John Ellis, & John Eggleston, tried for a riot, were found not guilty.

Alfred Brest was arrested yesterday by P B Belt, a constable, charged with stealing $200 from Marshall's auction store about 6 weeks ago. He was fully committed for trial.

U S Patent Ofc, Wash, Jun 25, 1851. Ptn of Nathl Adams, of Cornwall, N Y, praying for the extension of a patent granted to him for an improvement in a machine for moulding & pressing brick, for 7 years from the expiration of said patent, which takes place on Sep 8, 1851. –R C Weightman, Acting Com'r of Patents

Farm for sale: the subscriber offers his Farm in PG Co, Md: contains 178½ acres. City property would be taken in part payment. Inquire at Buell & Blanchard's Printing Ofc, 6th st, south of Pa ave.

Died: on Jun 24, in Wash City, Geo Taylor, in his 91st year. His funeral will take place at 10 o'clock this morning, from Mrs Clare's boarding-house, corner of Louisiana ave & C st. [On the first page of the newspaper: Geo Taylor and his costume of a by-gone time, which he always adhered to, will be missed by those he greeted on his walks. He has left several children, among them 3 gallant sons, who have seen service in the ranks of the defenders of their country-the elder, a Col in the army; the 2nd, an ofcr of the Navy; & the 3rd, a Lt in the Marine Corps.]

Died: on Jun 24, George, son of the late Florence S & Wenefred McCarthy, aged 18 years. His funeral is today at 4 o'clock, from his late residence, on F st, between 6th & 7th sts.

Wash City: Mayor's Ofc, Jun 25, 1851. Selected members of the Auxiliary Guard:

John H Goddard, Capt	T Cross	John L Fowler
Jos Goodyear	John E Little	Jas Simms
Abraham Dixon	Jas Bean	Henry Horskamp
John Frere	Israel Wasson	Thos Gooden
Isaac Ross	Wm M Mockbee	Mason Piggott
Wm Hickerson	Washington Lewis	Solomon Hubbard
Jos Williamson	Geo H Grant	Thos W Jones
Henry Thomas	Francis W Colclazier	J W Smith
Henry P Queen	Thos A Clements	Wm Cox
Thos E Williams	Edw Thomas	Walter Lenox, Mayor
John Simonds	Jos W King	

FRI JUN 27, 1851

The owners of the house on square 728, called the **Brick Capitol**, [now occupied by Mrs H V Hill,] are to meet there on Jun 27, & as the subject of selling the property will then be considered, & a full attendance of the owners is required.
–John P Ingle, trustee

Mrd: on Jun 24, by Rev Jas B Donelan, Mr Augustus Voss to Miss Lucy Amanda Frances Mann, all of Wash City.

Mrd: on Jun 17, by Rev Mr Tillinghast, Dr Wm Eustace, of Richmond, Va, to Miss Martha Virginia Laub, of Wash.

Mrd: last evening, by Rev Mr Davis, Mr J W Jordon to Miss Mary Eliz Westerfield, all of Wash City.

Died: on Jun 26, after a sudden illness, Porter Gillet, infant son of the Rev R R & E M Gurley. His funeral is this day, at 3:30 o'clock, from the residence of his parents, on 12th st.

This day published the Life & Character of John Paul Jones, a Capt in the U S Navy during the Revolutionary war, by John Henry Sherburne, with an appendix containing an official list of ofcrs of the navy, ships of war & regulations, from 1776 to 1851. Price: $2. –Adriance, Sherman & Co, #2, Astor House. For sale by Wm Adam & F Taylor.

The estate of Judge Mullanphy, who lately died at St Louis, is valued at $600,000. By his will he bequeathed a third part of it to the city of St Louis, in trust, to constitute a fund to furnish relief to all poor emigrants & travelers coming to St Louis on their way bona fide to settle in the West.

The U S steam-frig **Saranac** arrived at Pensacola on Jun 9, from Havana. Since her arrival a serious illness has broken out on board, by which upwards of 80 ofcrs & men are on the sick list. No deaths yet reported. Cmder J G Pendergrast has assumed the command of the **Saranac**.

SAT JUN 28, 1851
For rent: a 3 story frame house on H st, between 4½ & 5th sts. Inquire of Mr Edmonson, next door.

Household & kitchen furniture at auction: on Jun 30, at the residence of Mr Ball, on E st, between 9th & 10th sts. -Dyer & McGuire, aucts

The death of the Hon Spencer Jarnagin, formerly a U S Senator from the State of Tenn, is announced in a telegraphic dispatch from Memphis. He is reported to have died of cholera, Jun 24.

The three men recently convicted of the murder of the Cosden family, Wm Shelton, Abraham Taylor, & Nicholas Murphy, were sentenced to death by Judge Chambers, at Chestertown, on Thu. [Jul 4th newspaper: Gov Lowe, of Md, has fixed the first Fri in Aug as the day of execution, at Chestertown, of Taylor, Shelton, & Murphy.]

All those in any way indebted to the subscriber are earnestly requested to call & close their bills to Jul 1, by cash or short notes. —Z D Gilman

Trustee's sale of valuable property: by decree of the Circuit Court of Wash Co, D C: sale on Tue, of the north half of lot 8 in square 348, fronting on 11th st west, near Pa ave; & lot 21 in square 253, fronting on north G st, between 13th & 14th sts; belonging to the estate of the late Col Wm Brent, deceased. —John Carroll Brent, trustee -A Green, auct

Died: yesterday, at his residence on **Rock Creek**, Abner C Pierce. His funeral will take place tomorrow at 3½ o'clock.

Charlottesville Female Academy will be resumed on Sep 1. In consequence of the resignation of Mr Albert Holladay, arising from the ill health of his family, the Trustees desire to obtain an experienced & competent Teacher as Principal. Apply to Egbert R Watsson, Sec of the Board of Trustees, Charlottesville. Va. Trustees:
V W Southall   J H Timberlake   A P Magruder
R K Meade   John R Jones
E R Watson   Wm A Bibb

Obit-died: Miss Mary L K Strider, only daughter of Saml Strider, of Jefferson Co, Va, is no more. She took cold during the Christmas holydays; it fell upon her bust & lungs, slightly at first, but afterwards the inflammation attacked the brain with a fierceness that baffled the skill of the best physicians & attentive nurses. She died on Jan 22, 1851, in her 17th year, at the Wesleyan Female College, at Wilmington, Delaware. —Qui Noscet

Died: on Jun 21, at Fayetteville, N C, Dr Thos Nash Cameron, a native of Va, but who had resided in Fayetteville for 55 years. He had been often chosen to the highest municipal ofc of the town, & had more than once represented the county in the Legislature of the State.

Died: on Jun 20, at Nashville, Tenn, Mrs Jane Ellen Cheatham, consort of Col E S Cheatham, of Springfield, Tenn, & eldest daughter of Hon E H Foster, aged 29 years.

Died: on Jun 24, at Kent Island, Queen Ann's Co, Md, in her 23rd year, Miss Maria Louisa Gibson, after an illness of only a few days, which she bore with Christian fortitude & perfect resignation.

Died: on Jun 27, in Wash City, Hannah, in her 27th year, consort of the late Dennis Buckley, of Balt, a native of Cork, Ireland. Her funeral takes place on Sunday morning, at 5½ o'clock, from her late residence on 11th st, near Md ave.

MON JUN 30, 1851
Mr Chas L Brace, of Hartford, who has been engaged the last year in a pedestrian tour through Europe, was imprisoned on May 27, in Gros Werdein, Hungary, under the false accusation of being one of the Democratic Revolutionary Cmte & an agent of Ujhazy. Mr McCurdy, our Minister at Austria, is making efforts for his release. –Hartford Cour [Jul 17th newspaper: Trieste, Jun 26, 1851. Mr Brace has been released from imprisonment. Secret combinations are planning against the Gov't, & the recently discovered actors hung.]

The Shadwell Cotton & Woollen Factory, in Fluvanna Co, near Charlottesville, Va, was destroyed by fire on Jun 21. It was the property of Mr John Timberlake.

U S ship **Germantown**, Port Praya, Cape Verde, May 20, 1851. This ship arrived here on May 14, bearing the broad pennant of Com E A F Lavallette, to relieve the ship **Portsmouth**, Com Gregory, which ship sails for the U S tomorrow or next day. List of the ofcrs of the U S ship **Germantown**: Cmdor, E A F Lavallette; Cmder, Jas D Knight; Lts, E R Thomson, J M North, G M Colvocoressis, G W Rodgers; Surgeon of Fleet, Wm F Patton; Acting Purser, Wm Cushman; Assist Surgeon, A N Bell; Marine Ofcr, J D Simms; Acting Master, R M McArann; Midshipmen, J T Wood, Shepherd, Ward, Toon, Taylor. The brig **Porpoise** is also here, & sails tomorrow for Madeira & Windward Islands. List of the Ofcrs of the brig **Porpoise**: Lt Commanding, Jas L Lardner; 1st Lt, J Sheppard Bohrer; Acting Master, C W Wooley; Midshipmen, J Heileman, Wm Gwin; Purser, J C Eldridge; Passed Assist Surgeon, Jas I Brownlee.

Accidental death of a hero of the war of 1812: at the Brooklyn navy yard, on Tue last, John Deacon, one of the ship-carpenters employed upon the U S steamer **Fulton**, fell from the staging, a distance of 20 feet, striking his side & head upon the floor beneath as to cause his death within an hour. He was upwards of 70, & for many years employed at the yard. He was employed as a carpenter on board of the ship **Enterprise** during her engagement with the ship **Boxer,** in the last war with England, & at a most critical moment rendered signal service. The **Enterprise** had received a shot in her bow, & the water poured in so rapidly as to threaten speedy destruction. Deacon, at his own request, was slung over the bows, & succeeded in nailing a side of sole leather over the opening, which effectually stopped the progress of the water. He was so injured by the rolling & pitching of the ship, & by the intense cold, that he never entirely recovered. Cmdor Kearney, [who commanded the **Enterpirse** at that time] has often referred with pride & gratitude to the gallant daring of John Deacon.

Jas Burnham, son of Mr Andrew Burnham, of Mount Vernon, N H, was drowned on Sun week, in a mill-pond in that town, while bathing.

For rent: well finished 2 story dwlg house, with basement, on I between 18th & 19th sts. Apply to Jas Eveleth, on 19th st, between G & H sts.

Another child was killed at N Y last week on account of a mistake by the clerk of a druggist in putting up a prescription. His name is Austin Secor. He was arrested & held to bail to answer for the fault.

Mr Chafin, brakeman on a freight train of the Vt Central Rairoad, was instantly killed on Tue, when passing under a bridge, his head came in contact with the timbers of the bridge, shockingly mutilating it, & scattering his brains in all directions.

Fatal accident in the Pyrotechnic Works in Jersey city, a few days ago, killing the proprietor Mr Dawes. Since that accident they have been superintended by a young man named Wm Duffy, who was killed in another explosion there on Tue.

Dreadful murder in the village of Wmsburgh, opposite N Y, on Sat, when Laurence Reilly, residing at 110 north Fourth st, murdered his wife, Ann, aged about 20 years, & his wife's mother, Mary, wife of Patrick Golden, who was about 50 years of age. A girl, Eliz Conroy, about 19 years old, who resided in the bldg, received a dangerous stab under the left breast. Jealousy is said to have instigated Reilly to these foul deeds. He was immediately committed to jail.

Valuable improved property at auction: by decree of the Circuit Court of Wash Co, D C, sitting in Chancery: public auction on Jul 5, on the premises, at the corner of C & 1st sts, east of Capitol: lots 17 & 18 in square 725, with a 2 story frame house thereon. -Eliz Elliot, Guardian -A Green, auct

Mrs Clark has been arrested near Stilesville, Ind, for poisoning Mr Richd Treat & his 6 children, 3 of whom he had by Mrs Clark's daughter, Mr Treat's first wife, & 3 by his second wife. It was the second marriage that caused wicked old Mrs Clark to have arsenic put in the bread. 30 persons partook of it, & some were not expected to recover.

Orphans Court of Wash Co, D C. Letters of administration on the personal estate of Rutha Owen, late of said county, deceased. –Michl R Berry, adm

Criminal Court-Wash-Sat. 1-Frank Bell found guilty of theft-2 offences: sentenced to 3 months in the county jail for the first offence; & for the second offence 1 year in the penitentiary. 2-C Calvert, guilty of petit larceny: sentenced to 4 months in jail. 3-W Better, convicted of petit larceny: sentenced to 6 months in jail. 4-Buck Lacy, convicted of assault & battery: sentenced to 3 months in jail.

Mrd: on Thu, in the Fourth Presbyterian Church, by Rev John C Smith, Mr Jas A Johnson to Miss Cassandra Virginia Bangs, all of Wash City.

Mrd: on Jun 26, by the Rev Mr Edwards, Edward Hall to Susan Lowndes, daughter of Wm B Jackson, all of Wash City.

Mrd: on Jun 18, at St Louis, Lt John W Davidson, Adj First Dragoons U S Army, to Miss Clara B, daughter of Geo K McGunnegle, of St Louis.

Mrd: on Jun 24, by Rev Jas Todd, Mr Geo B Laird to Miss Virginia F, daughter of the Hon Henry J Miller, of Rockingham Co, Va.

Died: on Jun 8, Sabbath morning, at Dwight Mission, Cherokee Nation, Rev Danl S Butrick, for more than 30 years a faithful & useful missionary of the American Board of Foreign Missions among the Cherokee people.

TUE JUL 1, 1851
Country Boarding: the Cottage 8 miles north of the Post Ofc, 7th st, is now ready for summer boarders. Ref to Mr J F Callan, corner of E & 7th sts.

$5 reward for a Lady's Gold Watch, lost at or after leaving the Rev John C Smith's Church, 9th st, on Sunday last. Leave at this ofc, of with me at the Senate Post Ofc. –John M Jameson

Farm for sale: intending to remove to the West, I offer the farm on which I now reside, about 2 miles from Bladensburg, PG Co, Md: contains about 300 acres: the dwlg house is large & in good repair. Inquire of the subscriber, John Cooper, on the premises.

In Chancery, Jun 27, 1851. Ordered that the sale made & reported by Thos Marshall, trustee for the sale of Harriet R Marshall's real estate, be ratified: amount of sale reported to be $5,404.10. –Louis Gassaway, Reg Cur Can

We learn from a gentleman who was a passenger on the boat **Ben West** from the Missouri river, that Maj Luke Lea was accidentally killed by being thrown from his horse a few days since, about 4 miles from Westport. He was found in a sitting position in the corner of a fence, dead. Maj Lea was an agent for the Pottawatomie, Kikapoo, & other tribes of Indiana, at the *Fort Leavenworth* Agency. –St Louis Republican [Jul 17th newspaper: Letters were received at the Indian Bureau the day before yesterday from Mr Com'r Lea, from St Paul's, Minn, which report him well, & busily employed upon the business which took him to the West.]

For rent: several desirable rooms, at the house formerly occupied by Walter Jones, on the corner of 6th & D sts. –J P Crutchett

Naval: 1-The U S storeship **Lexington**, for the Pacific, is fitting out at Brooklyn. Lt Jas Rowan has been ordered to take command of her. 2-The frig **Macedonian** is to be razeed into a corvette. She was captured from the English in 1812.

The Minnesota Democrat of Jun 10 notices the departure from *Fort Snelling* of the 6 Sioux Indians arrested on the charge of the murder of Andrew Swartz. They were handcuffed & placed in a wagon, guarded by 25 dragoons, to be taken to Sauk Rapids, Benton Co, for trial. They were in charge of H L Tilden, Marshal of the Territory, & went on singing their death song. The Indians made an escape and 5 of them were shot & killed by the Dragoons. One of the Indians killed was the man who murdered Andrew Schwartz. The remaining Indian proceeded at once to Little Crow's Village, 6 miles below St Paul. No attempt was made to arrest him.

Valuable private dwlg at auction: by the power vested in me as truste: public auction on Jul 15, of part of lot 5 in square 288, fronting on G st, between 11th & 12th sts: with a 2 story brick dwlg, & brick back bldg. --S S Williams, trustee
-A Green, auctioneer

The Pres of the U S, through the Marshl of D C, yesterday extended a cordial invitation to the Masonic Fraternity to be present & assist in the laying of the corner stone at the Capitol, on Jul 4. B B French, Grand Master, accepted the invitation.

Yesterday a laboring man, of athletic frame, visited St Patrick's Church on some business with the Pastor. He was violently attacked with an apoplectic fit & died in a short time. We learn that his name was Holden, & that his brother was a resident of the 7th Ward.

The following Justices of the Peace were yesterday elected Police Magistrates of Wash City for the ensuing year commencing Jul 1, 1851.

Saml Drury	B K Morsell	Jas Crandell
John D Clark	W Thompson	Craven Ashford

Died: on Jun 27, Eleanor Jane Bedingfeld, only daughter of O Bedingfeld Queen [now in Calif] & Sarah Queen, aged 18 months & 10 days.

Died: on Jun 29, of congestion of the brain, Mary Lincoln, eldest & only daughter of J James & Mary F Greenough.

WED JUL 2, 1851
Mr Fred'k Lutz has been appointed agent for Wash City to obtain subscriptions to the Nat'l Monument Journal.

Property for sale: 4 dwlg houses & a corner store, on N J ave. Inquire of J B Iardella, Druggist, Capitol Hill.

Postmaster Gen has est'd the following new Post Ofcs for week ending Jun 28, 1851.

Ofc	County, State	Postmaster
E Wallingford	Rutland, Vt	Joel Constantine
Big Lick	Hancock, Ohio	Andrew Moore
Bingham	Clinton, Mich	Geo W Estis
Fogo	Allegan, Mich	Jas Redpath
Adaline	Marshall, Va	Thos T Parriott
Crab Orchard	Wythe, Va	John C Shannon
Rocky Ridge	Anderson dist, S C	Asa P Vandiver
Coonsboro	Orangeburg dist, S C	Jos W Leary
Jalappa	Dooly, Ga	Stephen T Burgess
Union Centre	Miami, Indiana	Oliver Caulk
Pond Creek Mills	Knox, Indiana	Jacob Small
Howard's Mills	Montgomery, Ky	John Furley
Wexford	Alamackee, Iowa	Edw Stafford
Strawberry Hill	Muscatine, Iowa	Wm N Towndraw
Welton	Clinton, Iowa	Thos Wright
Mount Hope	Delaware, Indiana	Jas A Ginger
Clermont	Fayette, Iowa	Chas Sawyer
Vega	Henry, Iowa	Jos M France

Names Changed: Mansville, Hancock Co, Maine, changed to Tilden.
Matildaville, St Lawrence Co, N Y, changed to Colton.
Evansville, Jefferson Co, N Y, changed to Evans' Mills.
Gold Hill, Chambers Co, Ala, changed to Waverley.
Oakville, Union Co, Ark, changed to Three Creek.

In a few days I shall offer for sale or rent the brick house in which I reside, surrounded by a beautiful large rural garden, full of flowers, fruits, & vegetables: adjoins the residence of the Minister from Spain, on the most elevated part of Capitol Hill. I also have a brick house & stable near the above. –Stephen Scott, B st

$5 reward to whoever returns to me a horned Milch Cow. –Julius A Peters, Wine store, Pa ave, near 10th st.

Desirable private residence at auction: on Jul 9, the lot & improvements in square 690, known as the residence of the late Dr May, on Capitol Hill. It fronts on N J ave: has a 3 story brick dwlg, back bldg, & stable. -Dyer & McGuire, aucts

Orphans Court of Wash Co, D C. Letters of administration on the personal estate of Wm H Ward, late of said county, deceased. –Sarah Ward, admx

The death of Gen Arbuckle, of the U S Army, at **Fort Smith**, on Jun 11, is confirmed by the Arkansas papers. He was about 75 years of age, & at the time of his death, he was in command of the 7th Military Dept of the Army.

Died: on Jul 1, at Balt, after a few days illness, Mrs Anna Jane Meiere, wife of Prof J Meiere, & daughter of the late Rev Christopher MacAllister, D D T C D.

Died: on Jul 1, of congestive intermittent, Wm Marion, son of Wm Q & Eliz A Force, aged 6 months. His funeral is this day, at 10 o'clock.

THU JUL 3, 1851

Wash Corp: 1-Ptn of C L Coltman, for the remission of a fine: referred to the Cmte of Claims. 2-Ptn of Jas Robertson, for the remission of a fine: referred to the Cmte of Claims. 3-Act for the relief of Darl Linkins: referred to the Cmte of Claims: passed. 4-Cmte of Claims: asked to be discharged from the further consideration of the ptn of John M Jameson: which was agreed to. 5-Ptn of Johnson Simonds, praying to be indemnified for certain damages incurred by him in consequence of the change in the grade of N J ave: referred to the Cmte of Claims.

The Detroit papers announce the death, by accidental drowning, of Capt Jas S Thompson, formerly of the U S Army, & son-in-law of the late Gen Hugh Brady.

An investigation was had yesterday before Justice Smith into the death of Chas Lucas, a man who has resided in Wash City for the last 3 or 4 years, died suddenly on Tue in a stable attached to the tavern of H Horschamp, near 7th st, between L & M sts. On Jun 22, the deceased, had some quarrel with Henry Davis, residing on O st at 7th, & was very severely beaten & bruised by Davis, whose wife Eliz Davis, joined her husband in the assault upon the deceased. They were both arrested.

During a performance at the St Louis theatre on Jun 16, a large flat-iron, suspending a lamp from the ceiling, slipped, striking Mrs Shea on the top of the head. In a moment she fell dead upon the stage, which was soon covered with her blood. Mrs Shea came to this country as Miss Kemble, & is the grand-daughter of Stephen Kemble, & grandniece of the famous Mrs Siddons. Her husband is at present in New Orleans.

Dr Josiah K Skeen, a highly valued citizen of Jacksonville, Ill, retired to bed in good health last Tue week, & started suddenly from his sleep, exclaiming that he had cholera. He drank a large tumbler of brandy & some essence of peppermint, which occasioned his death in a few hours. He did not have cholera.

Mrd: on Jul 1, at the Church of the Epiphany, by Rev Mr French, D R Goodloe, of N C, to Miss Mary E Waring, of Gtwn, D C.

Mrd: on Jun 25, in Pitt Co, N C, by Rev Mr Croghan, Wm Grimes to Miss Eliz, daughter of Thos Hannahan.

Died: on Jun 23, at the residence of her father, in Waterford, Saratoga Co, N Y, Florilla, daughter of the Hon Hugh White, M C, in her 21st year.

Died: on Jun 30, Lawrence Smith, infant son of John & Mary C Dhalgren, aged 7 months & 16 days.

FRI JUL 4, 1851
Graduates at West Point:the following statement gives the names of the Cadets of the first class who have graduated at West point at the recent annual examination, the order of general merit, & the particular corps & regts for which its members are recommended by the Academic Board:

Recommended for the Corps of Engineers:
1-Geo L Andrews, Mass
2-Jas St C Morton, Pa

Topographical Enginners:
3-Geo T Belch, Ohio
4-W G Welcher, Tenn

Artl, or Ordnance, Infty, Mounted Riflemen:
5-A Piper, Pa
6-Jas Thompson, N Y
7-Caleb House, Mass
8-Kenner Garrard, Ohio
9-B Hardin Helm, Ky
10-Ed H Day, Tenn
11-Alvan C Gillen, Tenn
12-Dewitt N Root, N Y
13-A J Perry, Conn
14-Isaiah N Moore, Pa
15-J Edwards, jr, Maine
16-A J S Molinard, N Y
17-H E Maynadier, D C
18-David Bell, Indiana
19-R Williams, Va
20-J Medleshall, Indiana
21-M Parks, jr, N C
22-Hyatt C Ransom, N y
23-A McRae, N C
24-Chas E Norris, Indiana

Infty, Dragoons, or Mounted Riflemen:
25-Gordon Chapin, Va
26-J C Kelton, Pa
27-W H Morris, N Y
28-Jas Curtis, Ill
29-R E Patterson, Pa
30-T J C Amory, Mass
31-N D Whipple, N Y
32-H C Hodges, Vt
33-Jas Daniel, N C
34-Roger Jones, jr, D C
35-Adolphus F Boad, Ohio
36-M Smith, Ala
37-E A Palfrey, La
38-Jno T Shaff, D C
39-H F Witter, Pa
40-J G Tilford, Ky
41-J B Green, N Y
42-L J Baker, N C

They will, after a month's leave of absence, be transferred, as brevet 2nd Lts, to the several corps & regts for which they have been recommended.

Valuable farm for sale in PG Co, Md: the farm on which the subscriber now resides: containing 211 acres, with a good dwlg house & all necessary out houses. Terms accommodating. –Alex'r H Tolson

Laying of the corner-stone of the extension of the Capitol: L J Middleton, Marshal of the First Division; Dr Wm B Magruder, Marshal-2nd Division; G A Schwarzman, Marshal-3rd Division; Jos Libbey, Marshal-4th Division; M Thompson, Marshal-5th Division. J Madison Cutts, Marshal, at the ceremonies at the Capitol. Aids: Geo S Gideon, Wm H Winter. Assist Marshals:

Isaac Hall
J D Hoover
V Marion Burche
Dr H P Howard
J T Mitchell
J R Ashby
Richd H Laskey
P H Hooe
F Little
G W Yerby
John Potts

Thos F Morgan
Isaac R Wilson
Peter Wilson
Wm R Woodward
Geo McNier
H H Heath
B O Payne
R E Doyle
W O Niles
John Macauley
Peter M Pearson

Leonidas Knowles
A T Harrington
John D Clark
R C Ray Campbell
J R Harbaugh
Jos Lyons
John C Winn
R A Morsell
Robt W Keyworth

The following gentlemen have been selected from the States & Territories, & will report to Jas M Cutts, for duty as Marshals, at the Capitol:

Saml B Paris, of Maine
Geo J Abbott, of N H
J H Adams, of Mass
Wm Hunter, of R I
A R Wadsworth, of Conn
Henry E Robinson, of Vt
Archibald Campbell, of N Y
A VanWick, of N J
Robt Morris, of Pa
Geo P Fisher, of Dela
Abram Barnes, of Md
Robt Chew, of Va
Wm W Morrison, of N C
Henry J Kershaw, of S C
L McIntosh, of Ga
Chas K Sherman, of Ala
-Richd Wallach, Marshal of D C

Lewis L Taylor, of Miss
Stephen Duncan, of La
Geo W Thompson, of Ohio
Richd Henry Lee, of Ky
Moreau Brewer, of Tenn
Robt G Hedrick, of Ind
Nichols Vedder, of Ill
Edw M Clark, of Mo
E B Culver, of Ark
S Yorke AtLee, of Mich
Robt A Lacey, of Fla
Jos F Lewis, of Texas
Henry Clay Henderson, of Iowa
O Alexander, of Wisc
G S Oldfield, jr, of Calif
A M Mitchell, of Minn

Mrd: on Wed, by Rev John C Smith, Mr Henry Fisher to Miss Ellen Ann Barrett, all of Wash City.

Mrd: on Jul 3, by Rev Mr Marks, Mr Jos Fowler, of Anne Arundel Co, Md, to Miss Mary Ann Virginia Brown.

Mrd: on Jul 3, by Rev Mr Marks, Mr Julius Henry Piles to Miss Harriet Sansbury.

Mrd: on Jun 26, 1851, at Fredericksburg, Va, by Rev G W McPhail, H M Hieskell, U S Navy, to Miss Emily L H Badger, of that place.

Stock of Grocery & furniture at auction: on Jul 9, in the house occupied by Mr Henry Rochat. -Dyer & McGuire, aucts

MON JUL 7, 1851
Hon Cave Johnson, late Postmaster Gen, has been appointed by the Govn'r of Tenn to the ofc of Judge, made vacant by the death of Judge Martin.

Wash Co, D C: Nicholas Kuhland, of said county, brought before me, an an estray, trespassing upon his enclosures, a bay horse. –Saml Drury, J P [Owner is to prove property, pay charges, & take him away. –N Kuhland]

The Powell Estate on the Schuylkill, belonging to Col John Hare Powell, has recently been sold for $350,000. The dividing up of this splendid property will greatly stimulate improvements in the suburbs of Phil.

Stephen Walsh, claimed at N Y as a fugitive from justice, under the Ashburton treaty, was discharged by the Com'r on Wed. He was a deserter from the British army, &, for the purpose of bringing him under the effect of the treaty, he was charged with stealing the keys with which he unlocked the guardroom in which he was confined. The magistrate held that he did not take them with an intent to steal, & therefore the taking was not a felony.

Bloody tragedy near Lynchburg, Amherst Co: Dr Lorenzo D Williams, of Amherst, son of Jno M Williams, had eloped on Sunday, with the eldest daughter of Capt Richd G Morris, age 19, with the purpose of marrying her. The couple, with one of Williams brothers, & Mr Edmund Hill, took the Charlotesville route for Wash City. The family of the young lady getting wind of the elopement, Capt Morris & his son Richd G Morris prepared pursuit. They overhauled them in Charlottesville. When Williams party & young Richd Morris were at the supper table in Lovingston, Nelson Co, where they accidentally put up at the same hotel, young Morris threw his plate into the face of Williams. Williams, Morris, & Hill then commenced shooting, which resulted in the death of young Morris & of Hill, & mortally wounded Dr Williams. Young Morris was shot by Williams' brother Robt. Hill was shot by Morris, & Williams was shot by him in the side or back. The father & daughter made their escape in their room up stairs. Revolvers were used by all parties. [Information from the Jul 8th newspaper is included in the above: supplied the given names of the men.] [Jul 21st newspaper: Williams is entirely out of danger; Hill is improving, with a fair prospect of recovery.]

Millard Fillmore, Pres of the U S A, recognizes Royal Phelps, who has been appointed Consul Gen of the Republic of Costa Rica, for the U S. Jun 30, 1851

Cornelius Regan, aged 31 years, died in the House of Correction at Springfield, Mass on Jul 1, having starved himself to death by a fast of 6 days. He was incarcerated for 30 days, or till he could pay a fine of $5 & costs. Attempts to persuade & even to force him to eat were in vain.

Mrd: on Sat, by Rev John C Smith, Mr Thos Mullone to Mrs Ann O'Meara, all of Wash City.

Mrd: on Jul 3, by Rev Jas B Donelan, Mr John S Everett to Miss Ann Rebecca Freeman, all of Wash City.

Died: on Jul 4, in Wash City, aged 45 years, Mrs Dorothy Mattingly, after long & painful sufferings, which she bore with meek submission.

Died: on Jul 3, in Richmond, Va, after a protracted illness, Henningham H Lyons, consort of Jas Lyons, in her 52nd year.

Died: Jun 25, at Poplar Run, Orange Co, Va, Garland Ballard, about 55 years of age.

Died: on Jun 30, at the residence of her son, in Waynesburg, Va, Mrs Rachael Hines, of Wash City, in her 58th year, after a short illness of 8 days. Her funeral is on Tuesday at 5 o'clock, at the Foundry Church.

Died: on Jun 29, at the residence of his grandfather, Wm G Yerby, of Upperville, Va, Oscar, infant son of A Oscar & Bettie Yerby, of Essex Co, Va, aged 14 months.

Administrator's Notice: the undersigned, appointed by the County Court of Alexandria Co, Va, adm, with the will annexed, of Gen John R Wallace, late Marshal of D C, deceased, requests all persons indebted to said estate to make payment to Lucien Peyton. -Christopher Neale, adm w a

TUE JUL 8, 1851
Congressional candidates for Congress in Indiana:

Whig:
Lemuel Q De Bruler	Saml W Parker	Schuyler Colfax
Roger Martin	Eli P Farmer	Saml Brenton
Johnson Watts	Edw W McGaughey	

Democrat:
Jas Lockhart	Wm Daily	Ezra Read
Cyrus L Dunham	Thos A Hendricks	Graham N Fitch
John L Robinson	Willis A Gorman	Jas W Borden

Freesoil: Geo W Julian
Independent Democrat: Geo N Carr

Candidates for Congress in Alabama: election on the first Monday in Aug.

Union Whig:
C C Langdon, of Mobile
Jas Abercrombie, of Russell
Wm S Mudd, of Jefferson
Alex'r White, of Talladega

Southern Rights Democrat:
John Bragg
John Cochran, of Barbour
Sampson W Harris, of Coosa
David Hubbard, of Lawrence
W H Garrett, of Cherokee
R G Earl, of Benton,
J L M Curry, of Talladega
Geo Reese. of Chambers
T A Walker, of Benton

Anti Compromise Dem:
John Erwin, of Greene
John A Winston, of Sumter
Wm S Inge, of Sumter

Union Democrat:
Gideon Freierson, of Tuscaloosa
Wm R Smith, of Fayette
Francis H Jones, of Lauderdale
W R W Cobb, of Jackson
Robt Murphy, of DeKalb
Jefferson Faulkner, of Tallapoosa

Appointments by the Pres: 1-David A Bokee, Naval Ofcr for the Port of N Y, vice Philip Hone, deceased. 2-Egbert Benson, Appraiser at large, vice Mathias B Edgar, declined.

Teacher wanted in the Warrenton Male Academy. —R A Ezzell, Principal

Accident at Brown's new hotel yesterday, when bricks on the 4th floor sunk under the weight. Jas *Hanrahan died last night. Michl Hanrahan & Archie Brown [colored] were supposed to be fatally injured. & taken to the Infirmary. [Jul 9th newspaper: Jas *Hinnahan who died, was married on Jun 6 last. The other sufferers are improving.] *2 splgs

Orphans Court of Wash Co, D C. Letters of administration on the personal estate of Erastus T Collins, late of said county, deceased. —Ellen D Collins, admx

Criminal Court-Wash-yesterday. 1-Jas Riggles was found guilty of keeping a house of ill fame: sentenced to 3 months in the county jail. 2-Thos & Ann Creighton, found guilty of selling liquor without a license: fined $16. 3-Martha Plant, found guilty of an assault: fined $1 & 10 days in jail.

Farmers' & Mechanics' Bank, Gtwn: Jul 3, 1851. The Trustees have declared a dividend of 2½%, payable to Stockholders or their legal reps on demand.
—Wm T Lang, cashier

WED JUL 9, 1851
A boy named Patrick Connell, 11 years old, was killed in Wmsburgh on Jul 4, by the accidental discharge of a pistol in the hands of Patrick Sherry.

Postmaster Gen has est'd the following new Post Ofcs for week ending Jul 5, 1851.

Ofc	County, State	Postmaster
South Carthage	Franklin, Maine	Wyman V Tainter
West Wash'n	Lincoln, Maine	Henry D Doe
Crawford House	Coos, N H	Jos L Gibb
Glendale	Berkshire, Mass	John H Strong
Hill Side	Oneida, N Y	Alfred Rogers
Lime Hill	Bradford, Pa	J F Chamberlain
Hick's Run	Elk, Pa	John L Dale
Sporting Hill	Lancaster, Pa	Jacob Summy
Seltzerville	Lebanon, Pa	John Seltzer
Klingerstown	Schuylkill, Pa	John Wrist
Catoctin Fur'ce	Fred'k, Md	Peregrine Fitzhugh
Lewistown	Fred'k, Md	Jesse Landis
Holly Mills	Oakland, Mich	Marcus L Young
West Townsend	Sandusky, Ohio	Wm H McIntyre
Riley Centre	Sandusky, Ohio	Jas Parks
Fetterman	Taylor, Va	David C Narris
Mountain Falls	Fred'k, Va	Jas A Russell
North Creek	Beaufort, N C	Wm Satchwell
Rural Hill	Conecuk, Ala	Peter L Johnson
New Providence	Pike, Ala	Bryan S Brooks
Siden	Carroll, Miss	C R Wright
North Point	Pulaski, Ark	Henry Buchman
Bayou Pierre	De Soto Parish, La	Robt G Hayden
Baker's Gap	Johnson, Tenn	Henry J Mony
Massack	McCracken, Ky	Thos B Haynes
Clifty	Todd, Ky	Jno C McGehee
Willow Hill	Jasper, Ill	Saml B Todd
*Castlenn	Jefferson, Ill	John W Treese
Windsor	Henry, Mo	Thos J Means
Louisville	Fayette, Iowa	Josiah Goddard
Amity	Scott, Iowa	Philip Baker
Gardiner City	Oregon	Geo L Snelling
Mouth of Willamette	Clark, Oregon	Ellis Walker
Rickreal	Polk, Oregon	N Ford
Rome	Marion, Oregon	Christ'r C Cooley
Myrtle City	Oregon	Levi Scott

*Paper was folded---possible name.

Names Changed: Bienbeim, Schoharie Co, N Y, changed to South Gilboa.
Camp Mills, Floyd Co, Va, changed to Laurel Creek.
McBride Mills, Heard Co, Ga, changed to Union Mills.
Parry's, Panola Co, Texas, changed to Davis.
Oak Grove, Montgomery Co, Indiana, changed to Linden.
Popano, Whitley Co, Indiana, changed to Etna.
Delaware, Jersey Co, Ill, changed to Rhoad's Point.

Wash Corp: 1-Act for the relief of John Fletcher: passed. 2-Act for the relief of J T Barnes: passed. 3-Nomination of Geo T McGlue as scavenger of the 1st Ward: referred to the Cmte on Police. 4-Cmte of Claims: asked to be discharged from the further consideration of the ptn of Jas Robertson: agreed to. 5-Bill for the relief of Jas Keleher: referred to the Cmte of Claims. 6-Cmte of Claims: asked to be discharged from the further consideration of the ptn of Johnson Simonds: agreed to. 7-Cmte on Improvements: ptn of Wm J Tabler & others for footways: passed.

Mr Alfred Crawford, the well known agent of the Phil Railroad & Citizens' Union Line of steamboats, died suddenly at his residence on Sunday. –Balt Patriot

Mrd: on Jun 22, by Rev Jas P Donelan, of St Matthew's Church, John C Seibel to Miss Sarah R Ross, both of Wash.

Mrd: Jul 6, by Rev Dr Morgan, Martin L B Josetti, of Wash, to Miss Anna Berry, of PG Co, Md.

Died: on Jul 4, Wm L Ogden, in his 66th year.

Died: on Jul 2, at Annapolis, Mary T, 2nd daughter of the Hon John Johnson, in her 17th year, of a severe attack of bilious fever.

Wanted 2 or 3 spirited & sound working Cabinet Makers. Inquire of Wm A Griffith, Marble Worker.

Valuable property for sale: the Grist Mill on Four-mile Run, between Alexandria, Va, & Wash, D C. Attached to the Mill are a brick dwlg house & 35 acres of land. Machinery is in complete order. Will be sold at auction, in front of the Mayor's ofc, in Alexandria, Va, on Jul 17. –Chas E Lippett, Alexandria

Wash City Ordinance: 1-Act for the relief of Danl Linkins: to pay him $17, the balance due him for trimming & gravelling N Y ave, between 9th & 10th sts west.

Valuable farm at auction: on Jul 26, **Oak Grove**, containing 122 acres, with a block house & log stable; 2½ miles from Gtwn. Title indisputable.
-Dyer & McGuire, aucts

Criminal Court-Wash: 1-Albert Beach, convicted of taking money under false pretences, was sentenced to 18 months in the penitentiary.

Catharine Colfer & John Colfer, arrested on Jul 4 on being concerned in the robbery of Honora Roche, an elderly Irishwoman, of gold & silver, of the value of $400, were committed for trial.

On Monday Messrs Dyer & McGuire, auctioneers, sold the following real estate:
Washington.

Square	Lot	Cents	Purchaser
228	4	13 ¾	Wm McKinstry
228	5	9 ½	Wm B Todd
228	6	9 ¾	Wm B Todd
228	7	10 ¼	Wm B Todd
228	8	10 ¾	S P Franklin
228	10	15	Lloyd N Rogers
637	3	3	Andrew Rothwell
637	7	2 ¼	Hugh McCormick
637	8	2 7/8	L N Rogers
637	9	2 ¼	Andrew Rothwell
685	6	20 ¾	L N Rogers
685	14	15 ¼	L N Rogers
689	16	11	Wm B Todd
690	10	1 ¼	C B Cluskey
692	4	4 ½	Wm B Todd
692	10	½	Dr C H Van Patten
692	11	1	David A Hall
692	12	1 ½	L N Rogers
693	4	2 ½	L N Rogers
693	6	2	H McCormick
693	9	1 7/8	H McCormick
693	10	2 ½	R M Coomb
693	24	1	L N Rogers
693	26	7/8	R Wallach
693	27	7/8	Wm Marshall
694	4	2 ½	Wm Marshall
694	8	1 ¼	Wm Marshall
694	9	1 1.4	Wm Marshall
732	20	2 ¼	Dr C H Van Patten
732	21	1 ¾	Dr C H Van Patten
732	31	3	Geo Watterston
732	35	1 4/10	H McCormick
732	36	1 6/10	Dr C H Van Patten

732	37	1 5/8	J P Ingle
743	Part of 1	2 ¾	M Kelly
743	2	1 ½	Capt J H Goddard
743	3	1	H McCormick
743	15	5/8	L N Rogers
743	16	3/8	L N Rogers
743	18	3/8	L N Rogers
743	10	6/10	Capt J H Goddard
743	12	1	Capt J H Goddard
743	11	1	H McCormick
744	Part of 1	2 ¼	K H Lambell
744	2	2 ¼	K H Lambell
766	Part of 1	2 3/8	C Greenwell
766	5	½	S P Franklin
766	Part of 6	2 ½	S P Franklin
766	7	2 1/8	S P Franklin
766	8	2 3/8	S P Franklin
766	9	3	M Kelly

For rent: 2 story brick house on C st, between 2nd & 3rd sts, opposite Trinity Church. Apply to F Nailor, or to Jno C Burche, Indiana ave.

THU JUL 10, 1851
Dr Eyre Read, the Democratic nominee for Congress in Indiana, in opposition to the gallant McGaughey, has withdrawn from the contest.

Mrs Hannah Roach, a native of Ireland, died on Sunday, at her residence in Albany, in her 106th year.

Mrd: on Tue, by Rev John C Smith, Mr Wm Carey to Miss Eliz Kerr, all of Wash City.

Mrd: on Jul 8, at Balt, by Rev Dr Wyatt, Dr Wm Boteler, of Fred'k Co, Md, to Maria Sidney, daughter of the late Geo A Hughes.

Mrd: on Jul 8, at Balt, by Rev Dr Wyatt, Anthony Kennedy, of Martinsburg, Va, to Mgt Smith, daughter of the late Hon Christopher Hughes.

On the banks of the Anacostia river, about a mile from **Giesboro**, our enterprising fellow-citizen, Thos Blagden, is cultivating a farm in a very superior manner, making it one of the most beautiful retreats in this vicinity.

Official: War Dept: Adj Gen Ofc, Wash, Jul 7, 1851. General Orders #35. Promotions & Appointments in the U S Army, made by the Pres since the publication of Gen Orders #15, of Mar 13, 1851.

I-Promotions

Medical Dept
Assist Surgeon Chas M Hitchcock, to Surgeon, Feb 13, 1851, vice Hammond, deceased.

Corps of Topographical Engineers:
1st Lt Wm H Emory, to be Capt, Apr 24, 1851, vice Linnard, deceased.
2nd Lt Amiel W Whipple, to be 1st Lt, Apr 24, 1851, vice Emory, promoted.
Brevet 2nd Lt Francis T Bryan, to be 2nd Lt, Apr 24, 1851, vice Whipple, promoted.

2nd Regt of Dragoons:
1st Lt Oscar F Winship, to be Capt, Jun 30, 1851, vice Saunders, resigned. [Co H]
2nd Lt Thos J Wood, [Adj of the Regt,] to be 1st Lt, Jun 30, 1851.
2nd Lt Jas Oakes, to be 1st Lt, Jun 30, 1851, vice Winship, promoted. [Co D]
Brevet 2nd Lt Chas W Field, to be 2nd Lt, Jun 30, 1851, vice Oakes, promoted. [Co G]

Regt of Mounted Riflemen:
1st Lt Andrew J Lindsay, to be Capt, Jun 30, 1851, vice Backenstos, resigned. [Co H]
1st Lt John G Walker, to be Capt, Jun 30, 1851, vice Tucker, resigned. [Co K]
2nd Lt Geo W Hawkins, to be 1st Lt, Jun 30, 1851, vice Lindsay, promoted. [Co D]
2nd Lt John P Hatch, to be 1st Lt, Jun 30, 1851, vice Walker, promoted. [Co L]
Brevet 2nd Lt Geo W Howland, to be 2nd Lt, Jun 30, 1851, vice Hawkins, promoted. [Co C]
Brevet 2nd Lt Eugene A Carr, to be 2nd Lt, Jun 30, 1851, vice Hatch, promoted. [Co K]

1st Regt of Artl:
Brevet 2nd Lt Jas P Flewellen, of the 2nd Artl, to be 2nd Lt, Feb 22, 1851, vice Tillinghast, promoted, to stand on the Army Register below Lt Amos Beckwith. [Co K]

2nd Regt of Artl:
2nd Lt John McL Taylor, to be 1st Lt, Jun 30, 1851, vice Lansing, resigned. [Co F]
2nd Lt Lloyd Beall, to be 1st Lt, Jun 30, 1851, vice Edwards, resigned. [Co D]
Brevet 2nd Lt John A Mebane, to be 2nd Lt, Jun 30, 1851, vice Taylor, promoted. [Co L]
Brevet 2nd Lt Armistead L Long, of the 3rd Artl, to be 2nd Lt, Jun 30, 1851, vice Beall, promoted. [Co B]

3rd Regt of Artl:
2nd Lt Horatio G Gibson, to be 1st Lt, May 26, 1851, vice Hammond, resigned. [Co I]
Brevet 2nd Lt Richd Arnold, to be 2nd Lt, May 26, 1851, vice Gibson, promoted. [Co M]

1st Regt of Infty:
Henry Bainbridge, of the 5th Infty, to be Lt Col, Jun 11, 1851, vice Wilson, promoted to the 7th Infty.
2nd Regt of Infty:
Lt Col Ethan A Hitchcock, of the 3rd Infty, to be Col, Apr 15, 1851, vice Brady, deceased.
1st Lt Nathl Lyon, to be Capt, Jun 11, 1851, vice Smith, promoted to the 5th Infty, & Canby, Assist Adj Gen, who vacates his regimental commission. [Co B]
2nd Lt Tredwell Moore, to be 1st Lt, Jun 11, 1851, vice Canby, Assist Adj Gen, who vacates his regimental commission. [Co G]
2nd Lt Thos W Sweeny, to be 1st Lt, Jun 11, 1851, vice Lyon, promoted. [Co D]
Brevet 2nd Lt Austin N Colcord, to be 2nd Lt, Jun 11, 1851, vice Moore, promoted. [Co K]
Brevet 2nd Lt Jos T Haile, to be 2nd Lt, Jun 11, 1851, vice Sweeny, promoted. [Co D]
3rd Regt of Infty:
Maj Dixon S Miles, of the 5th Infty, to be Lt Col, Apr 15, 1851, vice Lee, promoted to the 6th Infty.
5th Regt of Infty:
Lt Col Gustavus Loomis, of the 6th Infty, to be Col, Mar 9, 1851, vice Brooke, deceased.
Capt Wm Hoffman, of the 6th Infty, to be Major, Apr 15, 1851, vice Miles, promoted to the 3rd Infty.
6th Regt of Infty:
Major Francis Lee, of the 4th Infty, to be Lt Col, Mar 9, 1851, vice Loomis promoted to the 5th Infty.
1st Lt Edw Johnson, to be Capt, Apr 15, 1851, vice Hoffman, promoted to the 5th Infty, & Easton, Assist Quartermaster, who vacates his regimental commission. [Co D]
2nd Lt Geo W Lay, to be 1st Lt, Apr 15, 1851, vice Easton, Assist Quartermaster, who vacates his regimental commission. [Co B]
2nd Lt Chas T Baker, to be 1st Lt, Apr 15, 1851, vice Johnson, promoted. [Co D.]
Brevet 2nd Lt Wm P Carlin, to be 2nd Lt, Apr 15, 1851, vice Lay, promoted. [Co A]
Brevet 2nd Lt Alden Sargent, to be 2nd Lt, Apr 15, 1851, vice Baker, promoted. [Co B]
Brevet 2nd Lt Jas L Corley, to be 2nd Lt, May 6, 1851, vice Tubbs, resigned. [Co E]
Brevet 2nd Lt Elisha G Marshall, of the 5th Infty, to be 2nd Lt, May 15, 1851, vice Davis, dismissed. [Co I]
7th Regt of Infty:
Lt Col Henry Wilson, of the 1st Infty, to be Colonel, Jun 11, 1851, vice Arbuckle, deceased.
Capt Jos R Smith, of the 2nd Infty, to be Major, Jun 11, 1851, vice Bainbridge, promoted to the 1st Infty.
1st Lt Robt S Garnett, to be Capt, Mar 9, 1851, vice Rains, promoted to the 4th Infty. [Co A]

2nd Lt Wm L Cabell, to be 2nd Lt, Mar 9, 1851, vice E K Smith, promoted. [Co E]
8th Regt of Infty:
1st Lt Chas L Jordan, to be Capt, May 15, 1851, vice Screven, deceased. [Co D]
2nd Lt Edw Blake, to be 1st Lt, May 15, 1851, vice Jordan, promoted. [Co H]
Brevet 2nd Lt Jas McIntosh, to be 2nd Lt, May 15, 1851, vice Blake, promoted. [Co K]
II-Appointmentss
Medical Dept
Wm H Tingley, of Pa, to be Assist Surgeon, Mar 24, 1851, vice Hitchcock, promoted.
John J Milhau, of N Y, to be Assist Surgeon, Apr 30, 1851, vice Hewit, resigned.
Aquila T Ridgely, of Md, to be Assist Surgeon, Jun 30, 1851, vice Kennedy, deceased.
Corps of Engineers: rank: all Jul 1, 1851: to be 2nd Lt:
1-Cadet Geo L Andrews
2-Cadet Jas St C Morton
Ordnance Dept
3-Cadet Geo T Balch
4-Cadet Wm T Welcker
1st Regt of Dragoons:
14-Cadet Isaiah N Moore [Co A]
19-Cadet Robt Williams [Co C]
20-Cadet John Mendenhall [Co H]
2nd Regt of Dragoons:
9-Cadet Ben Hardin Helm [Co G]
18-Cadet David Bell [Co A]
24-Cadet Chas E Norris [Co E]
Regt of Mounted Riflemen:
22-Cadet Hyatt C Ransom [Co D]
23-Cadet Alex McRae [Co A]
34-Cadet Roger Jones, jr [Co H]
40-Cadet Jos G Tilford [Co B]
42-Cadet Laurence S Baker [Co G]
1st Regt of Artl:
7-Cadet Caleb Huse [Co A]
11-Cadet Alvan C Gillem [Co H]
17-Cadet Henry E Maynadier [Co C]
2nd Regt of Artl:
6-Cadet Jas Thompson [Co D]
10-Cadet Edw H Day [Co F]
13-Cadet Alex'r J Perry [Co H]
3rd Regt of Artl:
5-Cadet Alex'r Piper [Co B]
12-Cadet De Witt N Root [Co F]

15-Cadet John Edwards, jr [Co G]
4th Regt of Artl
8-Cadet Kenner Gerrard [Co D]
16-Cadet Albert J S Molinard [Co E]
1st Regt of Infty:
41-Cadet Jas B Greene [Co D]
2nd Regt of Infty:
27-Cadet Wm H Morris [Co E]
28-Cadet Jas Curtis, jr [Co H]
35-Cadet Adolphus F Bond [Co K]
3rd Regt of Infty
21-Cadet Martin P Parks, jr [Co D]
31-Cadet Wm D Whipple [Co G]
33-Cadet Junius Daniel [Co K]
4th Regt of Infty:
32-Cadet Henry C Hodges [Co E]
5th Regt of Infty:
39-Cadet Henry F Witter [Co K]
6th Regt of Infty:
26-Cadet John C Kelton [Co K]
29-Cadet Robt E Patterson [Co H]
38-Cadet John T Shaeff/Sharff [Co G]
7th Regt of Infty:
25-Cadet Gurden Chapin [Co H]
30-Cadet Thos J C Amory [Co A]
37-Cadet Edw A Palfrey [Co D]
8th Regt of Infty:
36-Cadet Melancthon Smith [Co B]
+
John S Evans, of Ky, to be Military Storekeeper in the Ordnance Dept, May 7, 1851, vice Simmons, resigned.

III-Casualties
Resignations:
Brevet Lt Col Jacob B Backenstos, Capt Mountained Rifleman, Jun 30, 1851.
Brevet Maj Stephen S Tucker, Capt Mounted Riflemen, Jun 30, 1851.
Brevet Maj Richd P Hammond, 1st Lt 3rd Artl, May 26, 1851.
Capt Wm H Saunders, 2nd Dragoons, Jun 30, 1851.
1st Lt Arthur B Lansing, 2nd Artl, Jun 30, 1851.
1st Lt Geo Edwards, 2nd Artl, Jun 30, 1851.
2nd Lt Caleb E Irvine, Mounted Riflemen, Jun 30, 1851.
2nd Lt John L Tubbs, 6th Infty, May 6, 1851.
Brevet 2nd Lt Wm R Calhoun, 1st Dragoons, Apr 26, 1851.
Assist Surgeon Henry S Hewett, Apr 30, 1851.
Military Storekeeper, Jas W Simmons, Ordnance Dept, Apr 30, 1851.

Commissions vacated under the provisions of the 7th Section of Act of Jun 18, 1846.
1st Lt Langdon C Easton *6th Infty, Apr 15, 1851, Assist Quartermaster.
1st Lt Edw R S Canby, *2nd Infty, Jun 11, 1851, Assist Adj Gen.

Declined:
Chas Duvall, of Louisiana, the appointment of Military Storekeeper in the Ordnance Dept.

Deaths:
Brevet Maj Gen Hugh Brady, Col 2rc Infty, at Detroit, Mich, Apr 15, 1851.
Brevet Maj Gen Geo M Brooke, Col 5th Infty, at San Antonio, Texas, Mar 9, 1851.
Brevet Lt Col Richd B Screven, Capt 8th Infty, at New Orleans, Louisiana, May 15, 1851.
Brevet Maj Thos B Linnard, Capt Topographical Engineers, at Phil, Pa, Apr 24, 1851.
Surgeon Wm Hammond, at Benicia, Cal, Feb 13, 1851.
Assist Surgeon Alred W Kennedy, near Council Grove, on Santa fe route, Jun 3, 1851.
*Regimental commission [only] vacated.
By order, R Jones, Aadj Gen

$5 reward for return of strayed Mare. Mr A Holmead, west of Centre Market

FRI JUL 11, 1851
Public sale on Jul 22, on Irwin's wharf, the steamboat **Joseph Johnson**, now in running order. Her engine was built by Watchman & Bratt, of Balt, & is now in good order. -S J McCormick, auct, Alexandria

Gen Jas Miller, who served with distinction in the last war, with Great Britian, died at Temple, N H, on Mon. After the war he was appointed Govn'r of Arkansas Territory, & for a long series of years held the post of Collector of the port of Salem, resigning it in 1849. Since that time he has been a resident of his native State, N H. The immediate cause of death was apoplexy.

The life of Major Lemuel Purnell Montgomery, of the 39th Regt U S army, who fell at the battle of the Horsehoe, on Mar 27, 1814, will shortly be published by Baker & Scribner, N Y. The work will be written by Rev T H Headley. The life of Col Henry Clay, jr, & other ofcrs of the Mexican war, will also be added. The brother of this brave ofcr, [Mr C P Montgomery] is the general agent for the work. Major Montgomery's pistols have recently been presented to the Nat'l Institute by his brother, the holsters & silver butts of which were originally presentd by Gen Jackson to Col Hugh Montgomery, the father of Maj L P & Mr C P Montgomery. Mr Varden, Curator at the Nat'l Institution, will act as special agent for the work in this city. -Telegraph

Portland, Jul 10-three brothers named Clough, a Mr Ranlett, of Monmouth, & Chas Clark, of Newport, were drowned in Cucknowanging Pond

Millard Fillmore, Pres of the U S A, recognizes Friedrich H Steil, who has been appointed Consul at Nassau, for the State of Texas, to reside at Galveston. —Jul 9, 1851

Our fellow citizen, Dr D B Clarke, is contributing a full share to the improvements on the part of the Island between 10th & 12th sts. His spacious & beautiful hall is a great acquisition; the Odd Fellows' Hall, in the centre of the same ward, is also commenced under most favorable auspices.

Congressional Cemetery. The ground recently added to the former site is nearly all taken, & is already improved by the erection of many beautiful monuments & other memorials. The Methodists are emulating the example of their Protestant Episcopal neighbors, by enclosing a large portion of their ground, which, up to the present time, has remained unoccupied.

At auction, Dyer & McGuire, aucts, disposed of 2 two-story brick houses on Marble alley, for $2,150. Purchaser, Mr Henry Oelricks.

To landholders: wanted a tract of land eligible for settling 50 or 100 families in farming & other industrial pusuits. Location, description, price, & terms required. Address, post paid, H N Gilbert, Land agent, Wash.

Sister M de Sales, Superior of St Vincent's Female Orphan Asylum, in 10th st, takes this method of thanking Dr Wm Gunton for the gratuitous use of the steamer **Columbia**, on Wed last, in conveying the orphans from this city to Alexandria, & Mr Parker, Pres of the boat **Thomas Collyer**, for returning them from Alexandria to Washington, also without charge. The inmates of St Vincent's had a day of recreation of which they will ever be mindful & ever grateful.

Yesterday G C Grammer was unanimously re-elected Pres of the Patriotic Bank of Wash.

Mrd: on Jul 10, in Alexandria, Va, by Rev C B Dana, Dr Wm Kleipstein to Miss Mary A, daughter of Rebecca Taylor, all of that place.

Died: on Jul 10, Mrs Maria H Waller, wife of J D Waller. Her funeral is this evening, at 3 o'clock.

Died: on Jul 10, Geo Washington, infant son of Maria P & Wm E Spalding, aged 4 months & 18 days. His funeral is today, at 5 o'clock, from their residence, on H st, between 21st & 22nd sts.

SAT JUL 12, 1851

Highly improved estates & valuable timbered land on the lower James River for sale. The undersigned, requiring his undivided attention elsewhere, from residing on his estate, will sell on the premises, publicly, on Sep 23, *Sandy Point*: 33 miles from Petersburg; more than 4,000 acres. The subdivisions will be nearly as follows, of which surveys & maps will be exhibited. 1-*Upper Quarter*, 841 acres, with frame dwlg, kitchen, & necessary out-houses. 2-*Upper Teddington*, the family residence, 797 acres, with a commodious wooden dwlg & many out-houses. 3-*Lower Teddington*, 716 acres, with a new framed dwlg & out-houses. 4-*Neek*, 707 acres, with a small new frame dwlg & some out-bldgs. 5-1,200 acres of timbered land. Also, for sale, all my stock. Mr Nicol, residing at *Sandy Point* is prepared to show the property in my absence. -Robt B Bolling, Petersburg

The death of Gen Jas Miller is announced as occurring in Temple, N H, on Jul 7. The immediate occasion of his death was a stroke of paralysis, which he received on Jul 4. Gen Miller was 76 years of age. He was born in Petersboro', N H, & was bred to the profession of the law. In 1810 he entered the U S army, & served with distinction throughout the last war with Great Britain. He rose rapidly from rank of capt to that of major general. He was present at Tippecanoe, under Gen Harrison, but was prevented by sickness from taking part in the battle. He rendered eminent services in the battles of Chippeway, Bridgewater, & Lundy's Lane. He was late appointed Govn'r of Arkansas; held the post of collector of the port of Salem, which he resigned in 1849. He has since been a resident of his native State of N H. —Salem Freeman

Chas Co Court, sitting as a Court of Equity, Feb, 1851. Eliz Lloyd & others, vs Thos H Buckner. This suit is to procure a deed of conveyance for certain tracts of land in said county, which were in 1835 sold by the dfndnt, Thos H Buckner, to one Menchin Lloyd, deceased, of whom the cmplnts are the heirs at law. The bill states that in 1835 Thos H Buckner sold real estate, which is particularly described therein, unto Menchin Lloyd in his lifetime, for $8,500, according to the provisions of said Lloyd's bond for the same, therewith filed; that the possession of the said real estate was delivered to the said Menchin Lloyd, & was held by him until his death, & has ever since been & is now held by his heirs at law, the cmplnts in this case; that the whole amount of the said bond for the purchase money for the said real estate has been full paid & satisfied to said Thos H Buckner; that the said Menchin Lloyd died in 1841, leaving the said Eliz Lloyd, his widow, & a certain Eugene Lloyd, Mary Emily, who has since intermarried with Thos Lloyd, Eliz T who has since intermarried with Chas C Perry, Francis Eliza, & Josephine, his children & heirs at law; & that the said Thos Buckner resides out of the State of Md. The cmplnts are to appear in this court on or before the 4th Mon of Oct next. —Peter W Crain. —R H Mitchell, Clerk Chas Co Court

Died: on Jul 11, Helen Parris Gilman, wife of Z D Gilman. Her funeral will be on Sunday at 4 o'clock, from the residence of her husband, corner of C & 3rd sts.

Geo Long, the negro boy, about 12 years old, who some weeks ago murdered a child, John Rumpf, at Balt, has been found guilty of murder in the first degree. The Jury recommended the Govn'r to commute the punishment of the prisoner to imprisonment in the Penitentiary for life.

Col G W Hockley died at the residence of Col Kinney, at Corpus Christi, on Jun 9. He was one of the most distinguished soldiers in the Revolutionary army of Texas, & served with great credit in the battle of San Jacinto. He was the Sec of War during the administration of Gen Houston. His death will be deplored throughout the State. –Texas paper

O'Ferrall's Boarding-house, at Bath, Berkeley Springs, Va. John O'Ferrall, having moved back to Bath & resumed business at his old stand, in connexion with his son, were ready to receive company on Jul 1. –John O'Ferrall & Son

For sale: the Gloucester Iron Works, at Gloucester, N J. Apply at the works, or 133 Market st, Phil, C M & J C Siter.

MON JUL 14, 1851
The venerable Dr Nott, now in his 97th year, was present at the celebration at Hartford, Conn, on Jul 4, & closed the services in the Church by pronouncing the benediction. Henry Gibson, a survivor of Gen Washington's Life-Guard attended the celebration at Newburgh, N Y. This aged veteran completed his 100th year on Feb 18 last, but still retains his strength & recollection in a remarkable degree-the reward of a temperate & well-spent life. He was in the battle of Princeton, Trenton, & Yorktown, & was with Washington during his encampment at Newburgh.

Mr T D Davenport, the father of Miss Davenport, who, 2 or 3 months ago, became favorable known in Wash City as an actress at the Nat'l Theatre, died at Cincinnati, Jul 6.

Mr Hugh Sisson, of Balt, is just finishing a block of marble prepared to the order of the Md Grand Lodge of Odd Fellows, & designed as a contribution to the Washington Nat'l Monument. The front bears a beautifully sculptured American eagle, of life-like proportions, & bearing aloft the national crest, surrounded by the insignia of the Order of Odd Fellowship. The Grand Band of the Independent Order of United Brothers have also authorized Messrs Baughman to prepare for them an elegant stone, designed as their contribution to the Washington Monument.

Medical Society of D C meeting Jul 14-at the Wash Infirmary. –T B J Frye, M D, rec sec

Millard Fillmore, Pres of the U S A, recognizes Heinrich Ferdinand von Lengerke, who has been appointed Consul of Oldenburg, for the State of Calif, to reside at San Francisco. Also, Carl Fr Adae, who has been appointed Consul at Oldenburg, for the State of Ohio, to reside at Cincinnati. –Jul 11, 1851

The telegraph brings intelligence that Jas J Strang, the self-styled King of the Earth, & the rest of the Beaver Island Mormons, who were indicted with him for obstructing the U S mail & other offences, have been promptly acquitted. The jury gave no credence to the witnesses for the prosecution, who were chiefly Mormon seceders, & personal enemies of the accused. –N Y Com Advertiser

The result of the Court-Martial lately held in Wash City, which has, in the opinion of that Court & in that of the Pres of the U S, required the dismission of Gen Talcott from the Army. Finding & sentencing of the Court. After mature deliberation on all the evidence adduced, the Court finds the accused, Brevet Brig Gen Geo Talcott, Col of the Ordnance Dept, as follows:
Charge I: specification, guilty & guilty of the charge.
Charge II-specification, guilty & guilty of the charge.
Charge III-1st specification, guilty, except the words therein, & had previously reported to the Sec of War.
2nd specification, not guilty
3rd thru 7th specifications, guilty
and guilty of the charge.
Sentence.
The Court does sentence him, Brevet Brig Gen Geo Talcott, Col of the Ordnance Dept, to be dismissed the service. Executive Mansion, Jul 8, 1851. I hereby confirm the same. -Millard Fillmore
III-Brevet Brig Gen Geo Talcott accordingly ceases to be an ofcr of the army from this date. The confidence naturally reposed by him in the head of his corps furnishes undoubtedly some apology for his course, but cannot justify it.
IV-The Gen Court Martial, of which Brevet Maj Gen Twiggs is President, is dissolved. By command of the Pres: R Jones, Adj Gen

Mr T D Davenport, the father of Miss Davenport, who, 2 or 3 months ago, became favorable known in Wash City as an actress at the Nat'l Theatre, died at Cincinnati, Jul 6.

Died: on Jul 13, Mrs Mary Attridge, in her 79th year. Her funeral is today at 4 o'clock, from the residence of her son-in-law, Mr Abraham Butler, on 13th st.

Died: on Jul 10, at the residence of his grandfather, Agricola Favier, of hydrocephalus, Agricola Armand, aged 7 months & 11 days, son of Armand & Honorine Jardin.

Died: on Jul 3, at Phil, in her 19th month, Annie, only daughter of Jas R Smith, & grand-daughter of Wm G W White, of Wash City.

Real estate sales: 1-By A Green-in square 725, lots 17 & 18, corner of C & First sts, east of the Capitol, improved by a 2 story frame house: sold to Mrs Mitchel for $1,270. 2-Lot 11 in square 763, fronting on C st south, between 2nd & 3rd sts east, to Mr Jas McGrann, at 2½ cents per foot. 3-In square 453, lot 9, 4½ st, between C & D sts south, sold at 10¼ cents to Mr O'Brien.

New Centre Market-House. The rapid growth of Wash City, has awakened considerable interest in a new market-house, to take the place of the present bldg on Pa ave, between 7th & 8th sts. Robt Mills, Architect, having been requested to furnish a plan, accompanied with a drawing of such market-house, has submitted a plan to the Mayor. The bldg to extend from 7th to 9th sts, 560 feet in length by a wide not less than 60 feet; 76 butcher's stalls, 10 x 18 feet; 28 vegetable stands, 10 x 7 feet; 28 poultry stalls, 10 x 18 feet; 2 stores, 50 x 20 feet, on 7th st; 4 stores on Pa ave, 30 x 20; besides several small rooms for market masters on each side of the grand central entrance from Pa ave & the rotundo under the clock-tower. The revenue table states that such a bldg can be erected [except the steeple] for $100,000.

Criminal Court-Wash-Sat. Henry Davis, convicted of an assault upon Chas Lucas, a short time previous to the death of the latter, was sentenced to 4 months in jail.

Desirable ready furnished house for rent in First Ward: at the corner of F & 21st sts, at present occupied by Mrs McLaughlin, is now for rent, either in whole or in part. Apply to Rd Smith.

TUE JUL 15, 1851
Aaron Burr in 1795 was the owner of nearly one-fourth block fronting Nassau, Cedar, & Liberty sts, & Broadway. He was an eminent lawyer with an extensive practice. At one period his practice was worth $10,000 a year. In 1800 Col Burr was elected to the ofc of Vice-Pres of the U S. On Jul 11, 1804, he retired from political life. The fatal termination of the duel with Hamilton, & the verdict of wiful murder, rendered by the coroner's jury, caused him to absent himself from this past of the country. He fled to England, where his papers were seized, & himself thrown into prison, & returned to N Y in 1812 & resumed the practice of law at 15 Nassau st. The effort was unsuccessful, & he soon fell into decay in mind, body, & estate. Mathew L Davis, his last solitary friend, stuck to him closer than a brother, & had him lodged in a solitary hut, with a lonely window, on a desert sand-bank in the wilds of Staten Island. Here, through the bounty of Mr Davis, he lived for 18 months; & here on Sep 14, 1836, died Aaron Burr, in his 81st year, with not a friend to close his eyes, or wipe the dew-drops of death from his brow. Burr was buried at Trenton, N J. –Laurie Todd, in the House Journal.

Wm Britton, a young man residing with his mother in West Phil, was on Wed shot accidentally by an elder brother, recently returned from the South. They were examining a pair of pistols, in the room of the young man, one of which was loaded.

Brevet Col H K Craig [lately Lt Col of the Ordnance] succeeds by seniority & appointment to the rank of Col of that Dept. Col C is an old & experienced ofcr, having entered the Army as 2nd Lt of Artl on Mar 17, 1812.

Distressing casualty at West Elkton, in this county, on last Sat week, when Mr Wheeler & his lady were looking through the new steam mill, when Mrs Wheeler's clothes were caught, & herself drawn through between the wheels, cutting both her legs off near the knee, & one arm near the body. She died after 3 hours agony. Mrs Wheeler was cut off in the prime of life, leaving a young family & a devoted husband to mourn their irreparable loss. –Eaton [Ohio] Register of Jul 3

Death of Col Luke Lea, Indian Agent of the *Fort Leavenworth* Agency. From the Kansas Ledger. He died on Jun 17, whilst on his way from Westport, Mo, 1½ miles out, to his residence at the old Agency. He was thrown from his horse and died in a very short time. Mr Justice, a citizen, & some black people got to him before he expired, but too late to relieve him. Col Lea was from the State of Tenn-one of her favorite sons. He served gallantly in Fla, under Gen Jackson, in the Indian wars; was a member of Congress for 4 years from East Tenn; & for 30 years was Cashier of the State Bank & Register of the State Land Ofc of Tenn, with great applause. He received the appointment to the ofc of Indian Agent of the *Fort Leavenworth* Agency, in 1849, from Pres Taylor; he was highly respected by the Indians under his charge & the citizens of Western Missouri.

Died: on Jul 13, Rittenhouse, aged 11 months, infant son of Levi D & Jennis Slamm. His funeral is this morning, at 10 o'clock, from the residence of his grandfather, B K Morsell, Pa ave.

Died: on Jul 12, in Gtwn, of a short illness, at the residence of his father, in his 28th year, John H, son of Henry C Matthews.

A very important arrest was made in Balt, on Sat, of a man known by the name of Wm Stetler, who, it is alleged, has long been engaged in counterfeiting the gold & silver coin of the U S. The prisoner was delivered into the custody of Marshal Roberts, to be taken to Phil, where the crime of forgery had been committed. –Balt Patriot

Police ofcr Gillespie, of N Y, was killed there Thu, during an affray amongst some sailors, which he was endeavoring to suppress. Thos Brown, 2nd mate, & John Brown, sailor, of the ship **Columbia**, arrested on charge of striking the fatal blow.

On Tue last when a rain storm passed over the city, Mr Andrew J Trimble, seeing his wooden boat break from it fastenings, jumped aboard a skiff to overtake it, when he was struck by lightning and instantly killed. Mr Free, who sat near him, was prostrated by the concussion, & remained apparently inanimate for a long time. –Louisiana [Mo] Banner

From Europe: the Earl of Derby died on Jun 30, & Earl Stanley succeeds to his title.

Cleveland, Ohio, Jul 10. This morning, the hack belonging to the Farmers' Hotel was driven down to the landing, for a man named Barry, his wife, & 2 children, who came in on a propeller. While the driver was absent the horse & hack went into the river, & the wife & 2 children were drowned. -Herald

Child Lost: wandered from the residence of his uncle, on Sat last, a little boy named Rody Connor, aged 5 years. He was seen on 13th st, near N Y ave, on Sat. Any information that will lead to his restoration will be thankfully received by his distressed parents. –John Connor, living on 5th st, above I st.

Real Estate: 1-Mr A Green, auct, sold last evening a lot containing about 20,000 feet of ground on 7th st extended, between the boundary line & T st, at .03 cents per square foot, to Mr P W Dorsey. 2-Mr C W Boteler sold a 3 story house & lots on 11th st, next door to Pa ave, & part of the estate of the late Jos K Boyd, for $5,000, to G A M Randall.

WED JUL 16, 1851
Peter Harmony, for many years one of the most prominent merchants of N Y C, died at his residence there on Sat. He was at his ofc [Peter Harmony's Nephews & Co] 3 or 4 days ago in usual health. He was far advanced in years.

Mr Thomas, of Algiers, died from the explosion of a camphine lamp.
–New Orleans Bltn

Benj W Richards died on Sunday. He had for several years been in declining health. -Phil American

Wash Corp: 1-The nomination of Henry Martin as Inspector of Tobacco: confirmed. 2-Bill for the relief of Johnson Simonds: passed. 3-Act for the relief of Thos C Wilson: passed.

Valuable property for sale: by decree of the Circuit Court of Wash Co, D C: the trustee of the real estate of the late Col Wm Brent, deceased, will offer at public auction on Jul 22: lot 21 in square 253, fronting on north G st, between 13th & 14th sts. –John Carroll Brent, trustee -A Green, auctioneer

Postmaster Gen has est'd the following new Post Ofcs for week ending Jul 12, 1851.

Ofc	County, State	Postmaster
Craneville	Essex, N J	Silas S Thompson
Heverlyville	Bradford, Pa	Edw McGovern
Rough & Ready	Schuylkill, Pa	Gabriel Herb
New Moscow	Coshocton, Ohio	John Bown
Gap Creek	Ashe, N C	Wm H Gentry
Amity Hill	Iredell, N C	Ebenezer McNeily
Avoca	Lawrence, Ala	Thos Masterson
Hamilton	Butte, Cal	Lyman Bristol
Double Springs	Calevaras, Cal	David Shall
Bidwills' Bar	Butte, Cal	Edmund Shepherd
Shasta	Shasta, Cal	Robt W Crenshaw
Mckolumne Hill	Calevaras, Cal	Jas B McKinney
Centreville	Nevada, Cal	C D Cleveland
Jackson	Calevaras, Cal	Henry R Mann
Point Magre	Avoyelles Par, La	Lewis White
Charity	Lincoln, Tenn	Robt M Whitman
Irvinesville	Nicholas, Ky	John B Taylor
Bluff Dale	Desmoines, Iowa	Eber M Bradley
Champoag	Marion, Oregon	Robt Newall

Name Changed: Cobaltville, Middlesex Co, Conn, changed to Cobalt.

New Orleans Jul 12. 1-A duel was fought today between *Dr Thos Hunt & John W Frost, of the New Orleans Crescent, in which Frost was killed, having received a ball through the heart. Writs have been issued against Dr Hunter & his seconds on the charge of murder & of being accessory thereto. 2-The Trinity Catholic Church, which was seized by the Sheriff in consequence of some difficulties between the Bishop & Pastor, has just been destroyed by fire. It was possibly the work of an incendiary, a party to the quarrel. Loss $25,000. The difficulty alluded to respecting the Catholic Church was between Bishop Blanc & the Rev Mr Guidziorowesky as to the right of possession. While the latter gentleman was officiating there, the Bishop appointed another priest to supersede him, & Mr G refused to relinquish the church, in which proceeding he was sustained by many of the congregation. The Bishop appealed to the law, & the judgment of the Court placed him in possession of the property. [Jul 19th newspaper: *Dr Thos Hunt was the brother of Col T G Hunt.]

Household & kitchen furniture at auction, & the personal effects of Geo Bean, deceased: sale on Jul 25, on the corner of 3rd & N sts, Navy Yard. –Ann Bean, excx -A Green, auct

Millard Fillmore, Pres of the U S A, recognizes Saml John Gower, who was appointed Consul of Austria, for the port of San Francisco, Calif. Jul 14, 1851

Railroad accident: the morning train of cars on the Susquehanna Railroad from York, due here at 8 o'clock, did not arrive till half past 12. The through burden trains ran off the track near Burns' in Balt, Co, and Mr Clark, fireman, was killed; Mr Meredith, an old & faithful conductor of the Messrs Smalls, of York, was seriously injured, & not expected to live. –Balt Patriot

The Annual Commencement of the Washington Seminary, under charge of Rev John E Blox, Pres, took place yesterday at the Nat'l Hall. The following pupils, all in uniform, participated, viz:

John Keyworth	Adolph Kieckhoefer	H McCormick
Chas N Carvallo	Chas F Williams	Geo T Cox
Wm D Porter	Willard Fitzgerald	Geo Dubant
John G Dooley	Henry Hempler	Saml Savage
Wm H Sweeny	R Mohun	Wm Kirby
Fred'k D Stuart	Thos B Dyer	Geo King
Chas W Sioussa	Henry H Morton	Walter H Ratcliffe
Richd C Bronaugh	Geo P Houston	Jas R Dobbyn
Walter H Ratcliffe	Malcolm Wallingsford	Henry Ridgely
Lawrence R Thomas	Marcellus W Stoops	Wm C Reynolds
Walter C Briscoe	Eugene Fitzgerald	John Howlett
Jas N Callan	Walter Drury	Press B Sands
Timothy Cronin	Richd Washington	J Hoban Sands
Jas W Orme	Jas C Reynolds	Jos B Towers
Chas B Masi	Edw Kirby	

Mrd: on Jul 15, by Rev Jas Rider, Pres of Gtwn College, Edw G Dyer to Bettie Elton Belt, both of Wash City.

Mrd: on Jul 10, by Rev Wm Edwards, Mr Geo M Head to Miss Barbara Tilley, both of Wash City.

Died: on Jul 12, at Kent Island, of bilious dysentery, in his 6th year, Wm G W, eldest son of Jas L White, of Wash City.

Died: on Jul 10, at **Poplar Hill**, Montg Co, Md, [the residence of Thos Connelly,] Sallie Ellis, only daughter of Saml C & Lydia A Espey, of Wash City, aged 9 months.

Died: on Jul 15, Christopher Columbus, son of Christopher & Fred'k Hager, aged 1 year, 3 months & 21 days. His funeral is today at 4 o'clock.

Died: on Jul 15, Mary Alice, youngest daughter of John A & Catharine P Kirkpatrick, aged 18 months. Her funeral is today at 4 o'clock, from the residence of her father, on D, near 13½ sts.

THU JUL 17, 1851

New Book: The Campaigns of the Rio Grande & of Mexico, with notices of the recent work of Maj Ripley: by Brvt Maj Isaac I Stevens, U S Army: N Y, published by D Appleton & Co, pp. 108: Washington, Taylor & Maury.

The death of Mr Frost, at New Orleans, in a duel a few days ago, grew out of a discussion which ought to have had no personality about it, being a simple question amongst political friends as to who woul made the most eligible candidate of their party, & their district for a seat in Congress. The gentleman who was killed was the Editor of the New Orleans Crescent, & his antagonist was Dr Thos Hunt, brother of Col Theod G Hunt, a member of the Bar, who had been named by his friends to run for Congress, & was warmly opposed by the deceased, as well in his newspaper as in a public meeting.

Peter B Hoge, the son of the Postmaster at Scottsville, was arrested on Fri last, on a charge of robbing the mail, & is now in jail in Charlottesville. He is only 16 years of age, though he has had the management of the ofc there for 3 years past, his father being engaged in teaching school. —Petersburg [Va] Intelligencer

John Slater died at N Y during the past week, the victim of hydrophobia. The 3 year old son of Mr Weeks, died at N Y this week from a bite he received some 4 weeks ago.

Fatal accident on Monday, at the bookbindery of Jacob Bumstead, 22 Ann st, N Y, when two girls employed there fell through a trap door & fell from the 4th to the 1st floor. Mary C Dyke died on the way to the hospital, & Catharine Brady was severely bruised, but is expected to recover.

Obit-died: on Jul 11, in his 44th year, Dr Jno H Sellman, of Anne Arundel Co, Md. He leaves a wife & children to mourn their loss. As a master he was kind & indulgent; his social qualities were unsurpassed, & no one could be where John Henry Sellman was & not feel its influence. —Davidson, Jul 14, 1851.

U S Circuit Court at Balt, on Tues: Judge Taney delivered the opinion of the Court in the case of Baring, Brothers, & others vs the executors of Robt Oliver, a bill filed on the chancery side of the Court, involving a claim to upwards of $50,000. The case was as to whether the answers made by Mr Oliver more than 20 years ago, to an attachment then obtained to affect funds alledged to be in his hands as trustee of Lyde Goodwin, were made in good faith, or were false & fraudulent, as alleged by the cmplnts. In the judgment of the Court, there is nothing to justify so grave a charge as that of perjury & fraud against a man who had been dead for 17 years. The bill was dismissed. John Nelson, Benj C Howard, & H W Davis, for cmplnts; Reverdy Johnson & J M Campbell, for respondents. -American

The person who, in my absence from home, took away my carryall on Sat last, worth $75, is requested to return it, or publish the cause in the Nat'l Intell.
—Timothy Buckley

From the Cape of Good Hope: At Tambookies, Capt Tylden had a battle with the rebels, in which 216 of them were killed.

Mr John E Gowen, of Boston, contractor for removing the last U S steamer **Missouri** from the harbor of Gibraltar, sailed from Balt on Sun, in the clipper brig **Chatsworth**, for his destination.

Annual Commencement of Columbian College, D C, was held yesterday, in the large Baptist Church on E st, & was attended by the Pres of the U S, the Mayor of the City, & a very large audience. Rev Dr Bacon, Pres of the Institution, addressed the Throne of Divine Grace. Individual orations were delivered by: Geo S Bacon, Cayuga Co, N Y; John Browne Budwell, Jas City Co, Va; Wm E Duncan, Amherst Co, Va; T Brooke Edwards, Wash City; Wm C Gunnell, Wash City, [Mr Gunnell was excused;] Joshua P Klingle, Wash Co; Reuben R Owens, King Geo Co, Va; Wm Y Titcomb, Boston, Mass; Geo G Whitfield, Hinds Co, Miss; Ulysses S Willey, Marion Co, Va. The First Degree in the Arts & Sciences was conferred on Peyton K Randolph, & the Second Degree was conferred upon W J H Carleton, of Ga; Jonathan Tilson, of Vt; Richd H Woodward, of Va; & David J Yerkees, of Pa, alumni of the institution. The Second Degree was also conferred on Saml G Kerr, of Md; Rev Alfred Holmead, of Wash City, & Franklin Haven, of Mass.

For sale: farm containing nearly 200 acres, 1¼ miles from Beltsville, PG Co, Md: with a frame house & out-houses. Willing to exchange it for city property.
—Chas Miller, Centre Market

Valuable farm for sale in Albemarle: ***Blair-Park***, containing about 1,600 acres: by decree of the Circuit Court of Albemarle, in the case of Watson, guardians, etc, vs Henderson & others, pronounced on May 28 last, to make sale of this estate: all necessary farm bldgs exist on this estate; but the improvements likely to be needed for a family, are wanting. Mr Brown, the manager will show the property.
—Alex Rives, E R Watson, Com'rs, ofc in Charlottesville.

Gtwn Free School held its annual exhibition yesterday in the late Methodist Episcopal Church, occupied by the school. As an incentive to the youth of his native town, W W Corcoran, has committed to the Trustees of the School $100, to be distributed to the 4 boys of the school most distinguished for scholastic proficiency & good conduct. The further munificent sum of $75 has been appropriated by the Corp for premiums. The 4 fortunate youths were: Wm Jackson, Jas H Burns, Philip Craig, & Hamilton Moreland. 165 boys are under the charge of Principal Wm H Craig & Assist Jas A Burns. 50 girls are under the care of Mrs Guy.

In the war of the Revolution, Henry Peyton, of Va, lost 3 sons.

For rent: 2 story brick house on Pa ave, next door to Dr Magruder. Apply to Saml Stott, Pa ave & 20th st

Died: yesterday, in Wash City, Mr Marcellus Simpson, in his 52nd year. His funeral will take place from the residence of Louis Marceron, on Pa ave, near the Navy Yard, this evening, at 4 o'clock.

Died: on Jun 14, at Galveston, Texas, Jos Ellis Whitall, late of Iberville Parish, La, eldest son of Saml Whitall, of Gtwn, D C.

Died: on Jun 10, at Cairo, in Egypt, on his return from China, David W C Olyphant, of N Y, in his 63rd year.

Died: on Jul 16, in Wash City, after an illness of only 3 days, Jas Lawrence, son of Jas L White, aged 6 months & 16 days. His funeral is this morning at 10 o'clock.

Valuable bldg lots for sale in Wash City. Apply to the proprietor, J Crutchett, Capitol Hill, Wash.

FRI JUL 18, 1851
Wash: we understand that the Grand Jury of Wash Co yesterday made Presentments against Geo A Gardiner & John C Gardiner, for perjury; & against Mears for presenting false papers.

Cornelius McCaullay, of Phil, has been appointed Consul to Belfast, Ireland. He is a native of Ireland, long known as a highly respected merchant in Phil.

Jonathan Fountain, son of Mr Fountain, merchant, 306 Broadway N Y, drowned in Saratoga lake on Sun, when bathing in deep water, he called for help.

Elected Dirs of the Bank of the Old Dominion, on Tue last; located in Alexandria: Wm Fowle, Lewis McKenzie, Danl F Hooe, Wm G Cazenove, John J Wheat, Robt H Miller, Stephen Shinn, Wm N McVeigh; Wm F Phillips, Warrenton.

Official: Headquarters of the Army, Adj Gen's Ofc, Wash, Jul 12, 1851. Announcement of the death of a veteran soldier, Bvt Brig Gen Matthew Arbuckle, Col of the 7th Infty, who died on Jun 11, after a short illness, at his post, *Fort Smith*, Ark. He entered the Army, as Ensign of Infty, Mar 3, 1799; & had a long & continuous service.

We learn from Boston that on Sat, while Benj Howard, merchant on Central wharf, was riding in his carriage, with his wife, sister, & niece, the horses ran away, & the party were all thrown out. Mr Howard's sister died from the injuries she sustained.

Killed by Lightning. 1-The wife of Eben G Bartholomew, of Harlem, Winnebago Co, Ill, was killed, by lightning while asleep in bed with her husband & child. Mr B received a slight shock. The child was severely burnt. 2-The New Haven Palladium states that Mr Danl Beach, of Terryville, Plymouth, was killed by lightning on Thu last, as he lay in bed, with his wife along side of him, had one of her limbs below the knee paralyzed. She, however, walked a ¼ mile to a neighbor's to procure assistance, & was recovering.

Mr Wm Webb, daughter of the late Benj Webb, of Wilmington, Dela, was found dead in the bathing tub at her residence near Wilmington, on Jul 10. It is supposed that the coldness of the water caused a sudden rush of blood to the head.

Obit-died: The mournful sympathies of many friends make it fit that some slight public tribute be given to the memory of Helen Parris Gilman, wife of Z Douglas Gilman, & daughter of Govn'r Parris, formerly of Maine. Removing in her youth with her parents to this city, she has through the years performed her domestic, social, & religious duties that the affections of many gathered around her, & many a heart was smitten with deep sorrow to hear of her unexpected death. [Jul 12th newspaper: Helen P Gilman died on Jul 11.]

Mr Geo Gelation, a well-known sportsman at **Fort Hamilton**, caught a shark in the Narrows on Tue, measuring between 7 & 8 feet long. --N Y Mirror

Died: on Thu last, in Wash City, Mrs Amelia Poston, aged 70 years. She was for many years a resident of Alexandria.

Died: on Jul 9, at St Louis, Mo, Richd H Simms, of Wash City, in his 23rd year.

Died: on Jul 14, at Phil, Cmder Thos J Leib, U S Navy, in his 49th year.

Died: on Jul 12, at the Naval Asylum, Phil, Thos Johnson, seaman, aged above 100 years. This old tar is believed to have been the last survivor of the gallant crew who so well sustained Paul Jones in his desperate conflict with the ship **Serapis** in 1779.

Died: on Jul 14, at Sandy Spring, Md, Caleb Bentley, in his 90th year. He passed an active & varied life, & mantained throughout an unblemished reputation, & the respect & love of an extended circle of relatives & friends.

Railroad accident on Wed on the New Haven railroad, near New Rochelle, dangerously wounded Mrs Adams, of Cleveland, & Mr E Foster, his wife & daughter, of Indiana.

Valuable estate at auction: by deed of trust from Wm B Scott & wife, to the undersigned, dated Jun 12, 1849, recorded in the land records of Loudoun Co, Va: public auction, on Aug 4, at the Auction house of Dyer & McGuire, Wash City, a tract of land containing 1,206¾ acres, more or less, with improvements, in Loudoun Co, Va, bounded by the Potomac river, the land of Col John M McCarty, the land of the heirs of John Dulen, & the tract called the **Woolington tract**. –Wm D Nutt, A McLean, Robt W Latham, trustees

The delightful Cottage on the corner of I & 17th sts west, is on the point of completion. Mr Matthias Duffy, of Gtwn, is its proprietor, as he has been its sole architect. It has the general form of the letter T, contains 9 lovely rooms, 3 on each floor. The house was built for sale, & surely must soon find an appreciating purchaser.

Sale of Real Estate, made a day or 2 since in Gtwn. The mansion of the late Col Cox, situated on the Heights, & now occupied by Mr Scott, was sold for $6,700, being $3,200 above its assessment. Mr Scott was the purchaser.

Sale of Real Estate. Dyer & McGuire sold at public auction on Wed, a large number of lots, among them lot 9 in square 14, [4,087 sq ft] on Pa ave, near Gtwn, to C B Clusky, at one cent per foot. Square 411, lot 9, on the Island, [2,259 sq ft] to Jas Magee, at .06 per foot. Lot 2, in square 628, .03¾ per foot, to B H Cheever.

SAT JUL 19, 1851
For sale or rent: a large commodious brick dwlg house on G, between 10th & 11th sts; nearly new; was occupied by the Hon Cave Johnson for 5 years, & last by Ex-Govn'r McDowell. –C Woodward, Pa ave, between 10th 11th sts.

Died: Jul 13, at the residence of her son, Thos Henderson, in Fauquier Co, Va, Mrs Orra M Henderson, relict of the late Richd H Henderson, of Leesburg, Va, in her 66th year.

Died: on Jul 19, Miss Mgt Dayly, aged 14 years. Her funeral is today, at 10 o'clock, from 10th st, between E & F sts.

Anderson Dana died at Wilkesbarre on Jun 24, aged 85 years. He was a boy at the time of the ever memorable Wyoming massacre. His father & brother-in-law were killed there, when he fled with his mother, her family, & others to Connecticut.

Howard University conferred on Wed at the commencement exercises at Cambridge, Mass: the honorary degree of Dr of Divinity on Rev Alonzo Hill, of Worcester; Rev John Adams Albro, of Cambridge; Ref Rufus Phineas Stebbins, of Meadville, Pa; & Rev Stephen Higginson Tyng, of N Y. The honorary degree of Dr of Laws was conferred on: Geo Sewall Boutwell, Govn'r of Mass; John J Crittenden, Atty Gen of the U S; Benj Faneuil Dunkin, Chancellor of S C; Sylvanus Thayer, Col Engineers in the U S Army; Alex'r Dallas Bache, Superintendent of the U S Coast Survey; Jos Henry, Sec of the Smithsonian Institution; & John Amory Lowell, of Boston. The degree of Master of Arts was conferred on: Rev Nathl Hall, of Dorchester; Ormsby McKnight Mitchell, Dir of the Astronomical Observatory, Cincinnati; Simeon Borden, of Fall River; Wm Raymond Lee, of Roxbury; Jonathan Kimball, of Lowell; Jas Rhoades, of Phil; & John Danl Runkle, of Cambridge.

Accident on the New Haven Railroad on Wed resulted in injuries to: Mrs Andrews, of Cleveland, Ohio; Miss Andrews, of Cleveland, Ohio; Mrs Seymour, of Stanford; Mr & Mrs Wiggins & 2 children, of N Y; Mr E S Foster, wife, & daughter, of Indiana; Miss Clark, of Hartford; Mr Dyer, of Ireland; Leroy Taylor, of Newtown, Conn; H L Plumb, of Stockbridge, Mass; Aaron Curtis, of Bristol; Chas Cooke, of Winsted; Chas Booth, of Stanford; Capt Bassett, of Bridgeport; Smith Booth, of Bridgeport; a son of Isaac Berry, of Phil; Wm Bristling, of Gardiner, Me; D H Lockwood, a brakeman; Mrs & Miss Funnel, Misses Nason, Gregg, Powell, Moore, & Cogel, all of Goucester, N J. Miss Miller, of Mass, is reported to be dead.

On Wed last John S Wormley, of Chesterfield Co, Va, deliberately shot down his son-in-law, Anthony S Robiou, of the same county, at a house in the neighborhood of the Black Heth Pits. Both parties had been at variance some time previous. Wormley was a lawyer by profession, & Robiou was formery Deputy Sheriff of the county, a man of wealth. -Richmond Times

Late from Calif: 1-Jas F Grahan, a nephew of the Sec of the Navy, & 4 others, were drowned at San Puebla Bay on May 28.

Mr Alfred White, of West Baton Rouge, met a sudden & shocking death on Jul 4. He was washing the legs of his horse, when the animal suddenly sprang off, dragging the unfortunate man with him, throwing him against the fence & trees, crushing his head. -New Orleans Bulletin

MON JUL 21, 1851
The funeral of Mrs Ann Sands, one of the oldest inhabitants of Brooklyn, N Y, took place on Fri. She was 90 years of age, & was the mother of Capt Joshua Sands, now in Europe, in command of the U S ship **St Lawrence**. She was greatly esteemed by a wide circle of acquaintances.

San Francisco, Calif-execution of a robber. John Jenkins, alias Simpton, came to his death on Jun 11, by strangulation, caused by being supended by the neck with a rope attached to the adobe bldg on the plaza, at the hands of, & in pursuance of, a preconcerted action on the part of an association of citizens styling themselves a cmte of vigilance, of whom the following members are implicated by direct testimony, to wit: Capt Edgar Wakeman, Wm H Jones, Jas C Ward, Edw A King, T K Battelle, Benj Raynolds, J S Eagan, J C Derby, & Saml Brannan. This was signed by T M Leavenworth, foreman, A M Comstock, J C Griswold, E Kingsbury, W J Shaw, E Blair, Wm M Eddy, John D Gott, & Frank Turk, jurors of inquest. The Cmte of Vigilance issued a circular setting forth the objects of their association, & is unwilling that a few of their associates should be selected by the coroner's jury, avowing the responsibility of the outrage for the following named persons:

S E Woodworth
S Brannan
E Borham
F A Woodworth
Geo J Oakes
Frank S Mahoney
Francis E Webster
R D W Davis
Jas C Ward
Wm N Thompson
Wm H Jones
R S Watson
Clinton Winter
Edw A King
Geo Mellus
Jas B Huie
W A Howard
J D Stevenson
B Frank Hilliard
Henry Dreschfelt
Chas R Bond
S W Haight
Jas Ryan
B B Arrowsmith
Geo H Howard
Wm Browne
S E Teschmaker
Caleb Hyatt
Robt Wells
C H Brinley
Saml R Curwen
H D Evans

J W Salmon
Jas F Curtis
John Y Bryant
Benj Reynolds
L Hulseman
E Kirtus
A W Macpherson
A G Randall
Jno S Eagan
Thos Deblois
J C L Wadsworth
N T Thompson
Stephen Payran
Wm Hart
N Reynolds Davis
C Spring
Geo M Garwood
Gabriel Winter
A Wheelwright
R S Lemot
Jas Shindler
B J Fourgeaud
Jesse Southam
J W Ryckman
A Jackson McDuffie
Z H Robinson
W S Bromley
R D Headly
Geo D Ward
A Ottenheimer
S B Marshall
C L Wilson

B H Davis
Hazen Hazeltine
W H Taber
P Frothingham
W Iken
Isaac Bluxome, jr
Z E Schenck
Geo D Lambert
Lothrop S Bullock
Geo Austin Worn
John P Haff
John W Ryder
E Bothcher
Jos F Haman
Thos W Walker
Theodore Kulnman
Saml Mark
J Seligman
Jos E Dall
DAnl J Thomas, jr
J F Von Lengerk
Julius D Shultz
J E Farwell
J E Derby
J Pratt Stevens
Jacob P Leese
F J West
Thos McCahill
Edgar Wakeman
W T Coleman
W Peake
A Wardwell
J S Clark
Jonas Minturn
Saml A Sloan
E H Clark
Lloyd Minturn
W B Lucas
H R Haste
F O Wakeman
J F Teschemacher
J Thompson
Huie J W Jackson
Wm L Hobson

Wm Meyer
Jos R Curtis
W H Tillinghast
John G McKaraher
Wm H Graham
J F Hutton
Jno Raynes
J H Fisher
Horace Morrison
John H Watson
Joshua Hilton
F L Dana
John Quincy Cole
Jas Pratt
O P Sutton
Geo W Douglass
Wm G Badger
A J Ellis
Chas H Vail
S J Stabler
Henry M Naglee
W Forst
Wm J Sherwood
Otis F Sawyer
A L Tubbs
E W Travers
W N Hortin
N D Hill
Wm Langerman
Eugene Hart
B E Babcock
T K Batelle
J C Treadwell
Hartford Joy
Aug Belknap
Wm Burling
J F Osgood
Horatio P Gates
Thos N Casneau
E Kemp
Jer Spalding
Wm C Graham
J Mead Huxley
Jno M Coughlin

Chas Minturn
Saml Moss, jr
Geo Clifford
Howard Cunningham
C O Brewster
Chas Soule, jr
Chas L Case
Chas L Wood
Robt P Belden
Chas Moore
Wm Fell
N Smith
Jas R Duff
Jas Dows
John O Earle
E M Earle

E W Crowel
R M Cooley
J L Van Bockkelin
A H Gildermiester
Chas N Hill
Geo N Blake
Saml S Phillips
J Neale, jr
Dewitt Brown
Chas Del vechio
F A Atkinson
E F Baker
Jos Post
Chas Miller
F Argenti
Jas King, of Wm

Calif casualties: 1-Dr Reuben Knox, of St Louis, John Allen, of Burlington, Vt, Jas F Graham, of N C, [nephew of Hon Wm C Graham, Sec of the Navy,] Mr Davis, of Maine, & an Indian boy were drowned in the bay of San Francisco on May 28, by the swamping of a boat in which they had embarked for San Pablo. Mr C Wheeler, of New Bedford, who was the only person saved, clung to the oars of the boat, & succeeded in getting on shore in an exhausted condition. 2-On May 30, at Park's Bar, on the Yuba river, about 20 persons attempted to cross the river in a boat too heavily laden, which upset by striking against a rope, & the following persons were drowned: Danl Baney, Wayne Co, Ohio; B Moodisbang, do; Stephen Lewis, jr, Richmond Co, Ohio; John Stull, do; Saml Miller, do; Chas Cox, do; Henry Van Tilbauth, do; Henry A Hodge, Otsego Co, N Y; F Jouguo, Bordeaux, France; Fargandie, do; Vincent Mathieu, do; & one man unknown. 3-W G Brown, recently from N Y, was killed in an affray with Dr Redding, at Webberville, early in June. 4-Michl Fallon, of Roxbury, Mass, was drowned in the North Fork of the American river on Jun 6. 5-Maj Francis Fountain, a Frenchman, was killed at Smith's Bar, North Fork Feather river, recently, by the fall of a bucket, while he was engaged in digging a hole. He was in the Mexican war, where he held the ofc of Sergeant Major under Col Harney. 6-Martin Schmidt, a German, formerly of N Y, was killed at San Francisco, on Jun 11, by jumping or falling into a well 40 feet deep, while suffering under an attack of delirium tremens. 7-Capt Jas Everson, of N Y, was recently drowned at Red Mountain bar, Toulumne river, by the sinking of a boat. He was 39 years old. 8-Passed Midshipman Wm De Koven, of Conn, aged about 24 years, died very suddenly on board the surveying schnr **Ewing**, at San Francisco. He died probably from apoplexy. 8-Capt Snow, of Thomaston, Maine, was murdered by 2 Mexicans on Jun 10, who stabbed him as he was weighing some gold dust in his tent in Dragoon Gulch, neat Sonora.

An ancient mourning ring was ploughed up a few weeks since at the country-seat formerly occupied by the illustrios Fulton, near Oak Hill, Columbia Co, N Y. It is of gold, very thick & heavy, & on its outer circle bears an inscription in gold letters on a black ground, as follows: "Peter Schuyler, O B J shp, 1753, aet 30 6." Whether the gentleman whose death is recorded by this memento was the father of brother of Gen Schuyler, a patriot of the Revolution, must be determined by those who are better acquainted with the history of the family. In a book of genealogies the Schuylers intermarried with the Van Rensselaers & Livingstons, & it is possible that they were also related to the Fulton family. –N Y Com Advertiser

For sale: desirable farm in Fauquier Co, Va, adjoining the Somerville Post Ofc, at present occupied by Dr S T Taylor: contains about 600 acres, with a 2 story frame house, & all necessary out bldgs & houses. Apply to John T Cochrane, at Mrs Manning's, 13th st, just below F. If not sold privately, it will be sold at public auction, on Aug 26, by -Dyer & McGuire, aucts.

Valuable improved property for sale on Aug 5, on the premises, one 2 story brick dwlg house, on the south side of H st, between 17th & 18th sts, & recently occupied by the late Maj J C Mullay. -Dyer & McGuire, aucts

On Fri last Mrs Durham, wife of Mr Jas H Durham, who keeps a boarding-house in **Green's Row**, Capitol Hill was shockingly burnt by the sudden explosion of a passage lamp filled with camphine or ethereal fluid. She was lighting the lamp when it burst.

Mr Crutchett's new House, with an observatory surmounted, is making quite a show on the brow of the Capitol Hill. The tower-top is 90 feet from the ground.

Orphans Court of Wash Co, D C. Letters testamentary on the personal estate of Abner C Peirce, late of said county, deceased. –Tho Carbery, exc

Mrd: on Jul 2, at Balt, J W Nicholls, of Nashville, Tenn, to Miss Mary A, daughter of the late Dr Morgan P Pitts, of Norfolk Co, Va.

Died: at the residence of her son-in-law, W D Porter, U S Navy, Mrs E A Beale, the widow of the late Geo Bealle, sr. Her funeral is today at 11 o'clock, on F, near 6th st. [No death date given.]

Died: on Jul 19, in Wash City, in her 35th year, Mrs Mary Ann Worthen, wife of Chas Worthen, leaving him & 5 children to mourn her loss. Her funeral is today at 4 o'clock, from the family residence on 10th st, between L & M sts.

Died: yesterday, of a lingering illness, in his 49th year, Mr Henry Howard. His funeral is today at 3 o'clock, from his late residence on 5th st west, between Mass & K st north.

TUE JUL 22, 1851
In the absence of their parents 2 little girls, 5 or 6 years old, one a daughter of Mr John A Root, the other of Mr Hathaway, both of Haydenville, Mass, undertook to sport upon a raft above Hayden's button factory. In the act of getting on the raft they pushed it from shore, & were carried over the dam, a fall of 12 or 15 feet. As the raft rose, a little hand was seen clinging to it, & a man plunged into the river, seized the hand, drew out the girl, & found the other clinging to one of her feet. Neither sustained any injury.

Criminal Court-Wash-Mon. Trial of John Day for the murder of his wife: Hon Judge Crawford presided. For the prosecution, Philip R Fendall, U S D A, assisted by Wm R Woodward. Messrs Jos H Bradley & Edwin C Morgan appeared for the defence. The Jury was composed of Notley L Adams, Edmund Bradford, Saml Wardell, John D Scrivener, Chas Mann, John A Ruff, Eugene Laporte, Chas Turner, Thos J Williams, Chas F Lowrey, Elijah R Taylor, & Lewis Wright. The first witness called was Miss Catherine B Creamer, who since Nov last had been an inmate of the family of Mr Fridley, [the late Mrs Day's father.] Court adjourned. [Jul 23rd newspaper: Mr & Mrs Fridley, the father & mother of the deceased, Capt Goddard, Dr Stone, & ofcr Boss, who arrested Day soon after the fatal deed, were severally examined. The Court adjourned.]

Mscl: In 1819 Geo Clymer, of Phil, invented the Columbian Press, which was patented in this county & England, & came extensively into use here at least. In 1819 or 1820 the firm of Mr Hoe commenced bldg power presses, with but indifferent success.

Wheeling Gaz: John Loudon, who was arrested a few days since for counterfeiting, while on his way to Va under charge of ofcrs succeeded, while at the Goddard House, at Marysville, in taking something that caused his death. He died on Jul 11.

Mrd: on Jun 25, in Raleigh, N C, by Rev Dr Mason, Bradley T Johnson, of Fred'k, Md, to Jeannie C, daughter of Hon R M Saunders.

Died: on Jul 16, at Gtwn, D C, Chas B Lucas, in his 31st year, son of Wm & Eliza Lucas.

Died: on Jun 21, at **Fort Leavenworth**, Mo, Thos F, infant son of Mary T & Dr Jos K Barnes, U S Army.

Valuable bldg lots at auction: by decree of the Circuit Court of Wash Co, D C, sitting in Chancery, made in a cause wherein Thos F Brannan & others are cmplnts, & Wm F Brannan & others are dfndnts: sale on Jul 24, of lots 7 thru 11 in square 213, on 15th & M sts & Mass ave. And on the corner of 15th & M sts is a large frame bldg, with basement fitted up for storeroom. —Jas W Sheahan, Trustee
-A Green, auctioneer

Boarding & Day School: on I st, between 9th & 10th sts. Mrs C & Miss M A Cox will resume their duties, as teachers, in this Seminary on the first Mon in Sep next.
References:
Wm Jones, M C, Wash
Jas F Haliday, do
A F Cunningham, do
Gen R C Weightman, do
Rev Mr Prettyman, Female Institute, Wilmington, Del
R C Bowie, Balt
Saml M Janney, Springdale Boarding School, Loudon Co, Va
Rev F Jacobs, Charleston, S C

Wm Noel & Geo K Boyd, jr, Venetian Blind-Makers & Upholsterers, Pa ave, between 9th & 10th sts: old blinds repaired; & fancy split blinds, of all sizes.

Ripe grapes & grape vines of the best varieties at auction: on Jul 23, vines cultivated in pots by Mr John Howlett, & so mature as to be fitted for fruiting at the next season. -Dyer & McGuire, aucts

WED JUL 23, 1851
Mr Jonathan Olcott, the oldest inhabitant of Hartford, Conn, died in that city on Jul 16, at age 93. He had enjoyed unusual health for one of his age, & on the day before his death he was able to walk about the house. On Jul 4 he rode in the procession with the soldiers of the Revolution.

Postmaster Gen has est'd the following new Post Ofcs for week ending Jul 19, 1851.

Ofc	County, State	Postmaster
Township	Albany, N Y	Cornelius Way
East De Kalb	St Lawrence, N Y	John H Bartlett
Manor Hill	Schoharie, N Y	Orson Phelps
Groff's Store	Lancaster, Pa	Saml G Groff
Buena Vista	Alleghany, Pa	Robt Hamilton
Forks of Potomac	Hampshire, Va	N B Guthrie
Organ Church	Rowan, N C	Moses Barringer
Olinda	Fayette, Ala	Dale C Barmore
Butler Spring	Butler, Ala	Jas Reynolds
Mechanicsville	Russell, Ala	Jas Sharman

Waccoochee	Russell, Ala	Wm A Treadwell
Retreat	Grimes, Texas	Josiah W Ogden
Woodlawn	Jasper, Texas	R A Richardson
Allum Creek	Bastrop, Texas	Thos Alford
Meadows	Van Buren, Ark	A H Smith
Grand Glaze	Jackson, Ark	E B Califf
Paint Rock	Cocke, Tenn	Jas Weaver
Mount Pelis	Weakley, Tenn	Robt K Waddy
Grundy	Pulaski, Ky	Fountain C Graves
Paris	Linn, Iowa	Robt C Powell
New Castle	Jackson, Iowa	John Shurlock

Names Changed: 1-North Collins, Erie Co, N Y, changed to Shirley.
2-Blythe, Schuylkill Co, Pa, changed to Tuscarora.
3-Ouachita City, Union parish, La, changed to Hamilton.
4-Good Springs, Mead Co, Ky, changed to Meadville.
5-Bear Creek, Jay Co, Ind. changed to West Liberty.

Post ofcs in Calif:

Post Ofc	County	Postmaster
Benecia	Solano	Rufus Brackett
Bidwell's Bar	Butte	Edmund Shepherd
Centreville	Nevada	C D Cleaveland
Culloms	El Dorado	S S Brooks
Double Springs	Calaveras	Danl F Shall
Empire	Tuolumne	Edw Conway
Fremont	Yolo	H A Weeks
Graysonville	Tuolumne	J W VanBenchoten
Green Springs	[blank]	J C Parks
Horr's Ranch	Tuolumne	B D Horr
Hamilton	Butte	Lyman Bristol
Jackson	Calaveras	Henry R Mann
Junction	Contra Costa	Robt Livermore
Knight's Ferry	San Joaquin	Kewis Dent
Livermore's Ranch	Contra Costa	Robt Livermore
Los Angeles	LosAngeles	Henry Eno
Louisville	El Dorado	Geo G Blodgett
Mariposa	Mariposa	H B Edwards
Martinez	Contra Costa	Oliver C Coffin
Marysville	Yuba	Jas Cushing
Mokelumne Hill	Calaveras	Jas B McKinney
Monterey	Monterey	A Randall
Mountain Inn	Tuolumne	Josiah Williams
Napa	Napa	M H N Kendig
Nevada	Nevada	A M Blanton

Nicolaus	Sutter	F H Russell
Oak Spring	Tuolumne	Drury Shoemake
Placerville	El Dorado	Thos C Nugent
Rough & Ready	Nevada	Marcus Nutting
Sacramento	Sacramento	R A Edes
San Francisco	San Francisco	Jacob B Moore
San Joaquin	San Joaquin	Rich M Harmer
San Jose	Santa Clara	J D Happe
San Jose Mission	Santa Clara	J J Vallejo
San Juan	Monterey	Edw Smith
San Diego	San Diego	Richd Rust
San Luis Rey	Los Angeles	[blank]
San Luis Obispo	San Luis Obispo	Sam A Pollard
Santa Clara	Santa Clara	Fletcher Cooper
Santa Cruz	Branciforte	Alex McLean
Santa Barbara	Santa Barbara	Henry Carnes
Stockton	San Joaquin	Jona Tittle
Sonora	Tuolumne	Rich F Sullivan
Sonoma	Sonoma	L W Boggs
Shasta	Shasta	Robt W Crenshaw
Tuolumne City	Tuolumne	Paxson McDowell
Trinidad	Trinity	L B Gilkey
Vallejo	Sonoma	Lyman Leslie
Vernon	Sutter	Grand C Addison
Wood's Diggings	Ruolumne	Robt Turner
Yuba	Yuba	H Fairchild

Death of a White Mountain patriarch: on Tue, Abel Crawford, departed this life. He died after a lingering & painful illness, at the advanced age of 86 years. He was one of the earliest settlers in those wild & secluded regions, having resided for about 60 years on the spot where the **Mount Crawford House** now stands, about 6 miles below the Notch valley. –Boston Journal

New Orleans Courier of Jul 10. This morning at 94 Hospital st, the residence of Dr Vigne, lay the bodies of his wife, his son Jules, aged 9, Louis, aged 7, & another still younger, all shrouded in the habiliments of death. Yesterday they were in perfect health; today they are all dead, victims of cholera. Only last week a similar visitation fell upon the family of Mr Valeton, auctioneer, who went with his family to Pass Christian, carrying with them the seeds of disease. In two days he & his children, his uncle Mr Cucullu, & a servant girl all perished of cholera. P S: A post mortem examination of the bodies of Mrs Vigne & her 4 children by an eminent physician traces their untimely death to poisoning, from a copper pot used for cooking.

The Paper Mill belonging to Mr Peter B Hoffman, in Balt Co, was consumed by fire on Sat, & one of the operatives, Jas Smeaton, was burnt to death in the flames.

Next Fri is appointed for the execution of Chas F Douglass, Edw Benson, & Fred'k Clements, the 3 sailors convicted of the murder of the 2nd mate of the bark **Glen** in Sep last. They are said to be resigned to death. –N Y Commercial Advertiser

Wash Corp: 1-Ptn from Jas Crutchett against the changing the course of <u>Tiber Creek</u> in square 630: referred to the Cmte on Improvements. 2-Cmte of Claims: act for the relief of David Atkins: passed. 3-Ptn of Thos B Griffin & others, for grading K st: referred to the Cmte on Improvements. 4-Ptn from Thos A Walters & others, for opening M st, between 21st & 22nd sts: referred to the Cmte on Improvements. 5-Bill for the relief of Robt Beale: referred to the Cmte on Improvements. 6-Cmte on Police: nomination of Geo Y Bowen as Sweep of the Second Ward: ordered to lie on the table. 7-Ptn from W G Ridgely, asking that certain taxes paid by him be refunded to him: referred to the Cmte of Claims. 8-Ptn from Geo Cover & others, to grade N Y ave: referred to a select cmte. 9-Ptn of John M Martin, for remission of a fine: referred to the Cmte of Claims. 10-Ptn of Thos Williamson, praying remission of a fine: referred to the Cmte of Claims. 11-Ptn of Selby Parker & others, & of John E DeVaughan & others, praying certain modification of the laws for licensing the sale of liquors: referred to the Cmte on Police. 12-Ptn of Alfred Shucking, praying permission to retain the enclosure of a certain st: referred to the Cmte on Police. 13-Ptn of Jas Casparis, asking permission to increase the size of the area in front of his premises on A st south: referred to the Cmte on Improvements. 14-Cmte of Ways & Means: asked to be discharged from the further consideration of the ptn of Ann Washburn: which was agreed to. 15-Ptn of Wm Greenwell & others, praying modification of the laws licensing the sale of liquors: referred to the Cmte on Police.

Mr Meredith, the conductor of the freight train on the Balt & Susquehanna railroad, who was dreadfully injured by an accident near Parkston on Tue, died at York that evening.

Telegraphic dispatch received on Mon, announced the sudden decease of Mr David Weaver, at Louisville, Ky. Mr W was one of our most extensive butchers. A few weeks ago, in company with his father-in-law, in his usual health, left on a visit to his brother in Missouri. Before he reached the home of the brother, he was arrested by a disease which, in a few hours, proved fatal.

Died: on Jul 14, at Concord, N H, of consumption, Charlotte Packard, youngest daughter of Capt John Manahan, for many years a resident of Wash City, aged 16 years & 1 month. The numerous friends of the bereaved father in this city sincerely sympathize with him in his affliction.

Mrd: on Jul 21, by Rev John W French, S Powhatan Carter, U S Navy, to Caroline C, daughter of Saml J Potts.

Died: on Jun 21, in the city of Raleigh, N C, in his 80th year, Mr Wm Peck, a merchant of 50 years' standing. Mr Peck was born in the borough of Norfolk, Va, on Apr 1, 1772; soon after removed to Petersburg, where he resided until Feb 8, 1798, at which time he came to N C, & located as a merchant in our city. For many years he was the confidential friend of Mr Jos Gales, the grandfather of the present editor of the Register, &, like him, will stand out prominently in the memory of his fellow citizens, a bright example of unaffected simplicity, modesty, & goodness.
-Raleigh Reg

Extensive sale of groceries, liquors, & cigars: on Jul 29, at the store occupied by Mr J H Knott, corner of N Y ave, H & 13th sts. -Dyer & McGuire, aucts

THU JUL 24, 1851
Lynch law in Calif in regard to the execution of Jenkins: J P Noyce, a police ofcr, sworn, refused to answer any questions. He had been a citizen of San Francisco for 2 years, & feared not for himself but for his family. Wm Devier, of Balt, endeavored to prevent 2 men from tolling the engine-house bell as a signal for the execution, & also David C Broderick, who swore to seeing Capt Wakeman acting conspicuously, & others he named, in the hanging. Ira Cole testified; heard Capt Wakeman call for a belaying pin to make fast the rope.

The will of Wm Rayland, of Caroline Co, Va, providing for the freedom of all his slaves, 90 in number, & if contrary to the law of Va for them to remain therein, then for their removal to, & establishment at his expense, in some free State, has been sustained against the suit of the heirs by the Supreme Court of Va. The slaves are to be transported shortly to one of the free States of the Union, or to Liberia.

The U S sloop of war **Vincennes**, Cmder W L Hudson, was at Acapulco Jun 16, to sail next day for San Francisco. She had 31 on her sick list, with Panama fever, but no serious cases. The fever was of a mild type.

Some 80 years since, the frig **Hussar**, in passing through Hurl Gate, laden with supplies for the troops of his most obstinate Majesty George III, struck some dangerous rock known as the Pot, springing so bad a leak as to make it necessary to run her ashore. It was supposed that a large sum in gold was in her hold, besides arms. We learn by the Wetchester Gazette that Messrs Howe & Pratt, who have engaged some time in clearing away the rubbish by which the wreck is incumbered, are now in a fair way to realize the reward of their labors. They are now in close proximity to the gold.

Fatal accidents in N Y on Sat: Richd McDougald, while driving a coal cart, fell under the wheel & died instantly. Edw Balier, hod carrier, fell from a scaffolding on St Marks st & was killed. Wesley Dallou, foreman of the carpenters at 49 Maiden Lane, slipped while upon the roof & fell to the lower floor, & was taken up lifeless. John Daley, age 6 years, fell from a pile of wood in West st, & fractured his skull & died.

A son of Mr D P Williams, about 5 years old, was stung in the hollow of his foot by a bee near Vincent town, N J, on Jul 18. His leg soon became stiff and swollen, & the pain extended throughout his whole body. On Jul 15, the surface of his body in the region of the heart became black, & he died in great agony.

Wm & Mary College, Wmsburg, Va: will re-open on Oct 8. Faculty:
Rt Rev John Johns, D D, Pres & Prof of Moral Philosophy & the Evidence of Christianity.
Judge Beverly Tucker, Prof of Municipal & Constitutional Law.
Benj S Ewell, Prof of Math & Natural Science.
Morgan J Smead, Ph D, Prof of Languages.
Henry A Washington, Prof of History & Political Economy.
Rev Silas Totten, D D, Prof of Intellectual Philosophy, Belles Lettres, & Rhetoric.
Robt Gatewood, adj Prof of Math.
M J Smead, Sec of the Faculty

Criminal Court-Wash-Wed. The following named witnesses testified:

Jas A King	John H Sessford
Richd M Downer	Dr W P Butt
Henry Hoffman	Wm H Scott
Jas H Summers	Geo T Fridley, brother o/late Mrs Day
Wallace Grant	Mary M Fridley, sister of the deceased

[See Jul 22nd newspaper-more on the trial of John Day for the murder of his wife.]

Official: War Dept, Adj Gen's Ofc, Washington, Jul 19, 1851: Gen Orders #39. Promotions in the U S Army made by the Pres since the publication of Gen Orders #35, of Jul 7, 1851.
I-Promotions
Ordnance Dept
Lt Col Henry K Craig, to be Col, Jul 10, 1851, vice Talcott, dismissed.
Maj Rufus L Baker, to be Lt Col, Jul 10, 1851, vice Craig, promoted.
Capt Edw Harding, to be Major, Jul 10, 1851, vice Baker, promoted.
1st Lt Peter V Hagner, to be Capt, Jul 10, 1851, vice Harding, promoted.
2nd Lt Geo Deshon, to be 1st Lt, Jul 10, 1851, vice Hagner, promoted.
Bvt 2nd Lt Stephen V Benet, to be 2nd Lt, Jul 10, 1851, vice Deshon, promoted.
3rd Regt of Artl:
Bvt 2nd Lt Chas S Winder, to be 2nd Lt, Jul 21, 1851, vice Patten, resigned. [Co H]

H-The Sec of War directs the assignment of ofcrs of Ordnance to duties & stations as follows:
Lt Col Baker, to be Inspector of Arsenals & Armories, in place of Lt Col Craig, promoted.
Maj Symington, to Watervliet Arsenal, N Y.
Maj Bell, to Allegheny Arsenal, Pa.
Maj Harding, to Watertown Arsenal, Mass.
Capt Huger, to Harper's Ferry Armory, Va.
Capt Bradford, to Charlestown Arsenal, S C.
Capt Ramsay, to **Fort Monroe** Arsenal, Va.
Capt Thornton, to N Y Arsenal, N Y.
Capt Whitely, to St Louis Arsenal, Mo.
Capt Talcott, to Augusta Arsenal, Ga.
Capt Hagner, to Frankford Arsenal, Pa.
1st Lt Wainwright, to Detroit Arsenal, Mich.
1st Lt Callender, to Kennebec Arsenal, maine.
1st Lt Kingsbury, to Little Rock Arsenal, Ark.
The Col of Ordnance will give the necessary preliminary instructions for carrying out the foregoing assignments.
Resignation: 2nd Lt Geo Patten, 3rd Artl, Jul 21, 1851.
By order, R Jones, Adj Gen

FRI JUL 25, 1851
Homicide in Miss: Mr A S Strawhun was shot by Dr W P Hebard, at Aberdeen, Miss, on Jul 8. Dr Hebard was admitted to bail in a bond of $5,000.

Orphans Court of Wash Co, D C. Letters of administration on the personal estate of Eliz A Beale, late of said county, deceased. –Allen P Bowie, adm

Wash Corp Ordinances. 1-Act for the relief of Jas T Barnes: to be paid $452.07, being the balance due him for grading I st. 2-Act for the relief of Johnson Simonds: $50 to be paid to indemnify Simonds for injuries done to his premises in consequence of the alteration of the grade of N J ave, between A & C sts. 3-Act for the relief of John Fletcher: to be paid $22.40 for laying a gutter across I st. 4-Joint resolution to allow Saml Byington to grade So Capt st.

Gtwn College Annual Commencement yesterday. The following order of exercises was observed:

John E Plater	John C Hamilton
F Mathews Lancaster-	Robt W Harper
Valedictory	Thos King
Jas M Cutts	Henry W Brent
Julius A Choppin	Dominic O'Byrne
Eugene C Longuemare	Jas R Randall

Wilfrid B Fetterman
Wm X Wills
Degree of A M was conferred on:
John W Archer, of Va
John C Riley, M D, D C
John C Longstreeth, Pa
The degree of A B was conferred on
John C C Hamilton, D C
Wm X Wills, Md
Edwin F King, D C
The same degree of A B was conferred on the following students of the College of the Holy Cross, near Worcester, Mass:
Jas A Durwin, Mass
John Power, Mass
Wm M Smith
John W Archer

John Reid, M D, Md
Rev Jas A Healey, Ga
John A Brownson, Miss

Lafayette J Carrill, La
F Mathews Lancaster, Md
Dominic A O'Byrne, Ga

Edw D Boone, D C
Ludger Lastrapes, La

Fred'k Female Seminary will resume on Sep 1. –H Winchester, Pres

Criminal Court-Wash-Thu. The trial of John Day: witnesses for the defence have since been examined: C P Sengstack, jr, Jas A Conner, Wm H Thomas, Jas Bowen, Lemuel Herbert, Dr F Howard, Mrs Beron, Solomon Beach, Wm Maxwell, Peter M Dubant, & Lemuel Williams.

Versailles, Ky, Jul 18-St Clair J Buford, of this county, in a rencontre with Geo W Carter, former sheriff, was killed, & Carter was so injured that he is not expected to survive. Carter drew a pistol & shot Buford dead on the spot. Carter had been beaten with a stick.

Hardward & cutlery at auction: on Jul 30, at the store occupied by N M Iardella & Brother. Also the store fixtures. -A Green, auctioneer

Wash City improvements. 1-John Rice, of Phil, has obtained from W W Corcoran, a contract for bldg 4 of the 8 first class dwlgs, intended by that gentleman to be erected in the First Ward, & Downing & Brother, of Wash City, have a contract for 2 of them. Mr Corcoran has commenced adding another wing to his residence. This gentleman recently purchased from Matthew St Clair Clarke, the well known house on K st north, near St John's Church. Mr E Swann's elegant 4 story mansion is on Louisiana ave, near Judiciary Square: builder was Mr Walker. On H st we observe a row of houses in course of erection: row belongs to Mr J F Brown, & is being built by Ager & McLain.

Mrd: on Jul 22, by Rev Mr Slattery, Mr Washington F Darnes to Miss Ann Columbia May, all of Wash City.

Mrd: on Jul 22, at St Mary's Church, by Rev Mr Alig, Mr Wm Cord to Miss Mary Theresa Schlatmann, both of Wash City.

Mrd: on Jul 14, by Rev Mr Alig, Michl Ulrick, of Pa, to Miss Mary Ellen McKelyutth, of Wash City.

Mrd: on Jun 12, by Rev Mr Alig, Mr Wm Sullivan to Miss Emma Fitzpatrick, both of Wash City.

Died: on Jul 20, suddenly, at the *Grove*, Prince Wm Co, Va, Mr Saml Latimer, in his 46th year, leaving an affectionate wife & a large family of children. Mr Latimer fell a victim thus early in life to a cancer, which, less than a year ago, appeared to be entirely removed by the knife.

Died: on Jul 21, at Louisville, Ky, Peter Hume, aged about 40 years, a resident of Phil, but known & valued here as elsewhere.

Sale of Wash City property, on Wed at public auction. Lot 14 in square 455, was sold to John Throckmorton for .21¾ cents a sq ft; 2 story brick house & lot, on G st, sold to E Roe for $970; lot 2 in square 552 sold to J F Wollard for 4½ mills; lot 1 in square 858, sold to Capt John Goddard, for 4 mills; lot 5 in square 389, sold to Capt Jones, for 5¼ cents; lot 8 in square 389, sold to T B Goddard, for 4½ cents; lots 21 & 22 in square 390, to E A C Goddard, for 3 cents a foot. Nearly all these lots are on the boundary of the city.

SAT JUL 26, 1851
For rent: the dwlg part of the house on the corner of 10th & I sts. Apply to Jos A Deeble, south side of I, between 9th & 10th sts.

House wanted: to purchase a good brick dwlg, suitable for a family residence, for which a fair price will be paid in cash. Apply to H M Morfit, 4½ st, Wash.

Board of Commissioners on Claims against Mexico: 1-The claim of Geo A Gardiner, for loss of property consequent on his expulsion from the State of San Luis Potosi, in Mexico, in Oct, 1846. He was sole proprietor of certain silver mines from 1814 up to his expulsion on Oct 24, 1846. The cause alleged for such order or expulsion was the near approach to the State of San Luis of the invading army of the U S, & that citizens of the U S, suffered to remain in the State, would give intellignce to the army of their country. The Mexican troops set fire to & destroyed his bldgs, stripping him of all his property. Board decides the claim is a valid claim against Mexico, & the same is allowed; the amount to be awarded subject to the further action of the Board. –Geo Evans, Caleb B Smith, Robt T Paine, Com'rs

The U S sloop of war **Preble**, which has been fitted out at the Navy Yard, Brooklyn, for a School-ship for the institution at Annapolis, is now ready to receive her crew.

Capt Henry A Nagle was arrested in Phil on Tue, upon a warrant issued by the Criminal Court in this city, based upon an indictment by the Grand Jury. The Phil Ledger says: Capt Nagle is charged with presenting a claim to Philip Clayton, 2nd Auditor of the Treasury Dept at Wash, for expenses incurred by Capt Quail, of the 2nd Regt of Pa volunteers, which, it is alleged, contained fraudulent charges.

Chas F Douglass & Edw Benson, 2 of the sailors lately convicted of mutiny & murder of the mate of the barque **Glenn**, were hung yesterday at N Y. Jas Clements, who was convicted of the same offence, was respited by the Pres until Aug 22, for the reason that Benson, who admits his own agency in the murder & mutiny, & charges Douglass with being the actual murderer, strongly asserts the innocence of Clements, who also declares he is not guilty. On the scaffold both men exculpated Clements.

Mr Wm H Taylor, a young lawyer, formerly of Savannah, was killed in Nassau Co, Fla, on Wed of last week, in a shocting affray with Mr E W Clark.

Puritan Courtship: a short time after the death of Mrs Standish, the bereaved capt found his heart filled with tender interest to Miss Priscilla Mullins, daughter of Mr Wm Mullins. He made his wishes known to the father, through Mr John Alden, his messenger. Priscilla was called into the room, heard his every word, & then said: Prither, John, who do you not speak for yourself. Henceforward he visited for himself, & ere their nuptials were solemnized in due form, & Miss Priscilla Mullins became Mrs John Alden.

Criminal Court-Wash-Fri. Witnesses in the trial of John Day, for the murder of his wife:

John Brower	Mrs Eliz Bright	Mrs Ann Wood,
Jos B Tate	Saml Wroe	[Day's mother]
Geo W Sears	Mrs Susannah Boteler	
Wm H Fanning	J O Whitney	

Mrd: on Jul 24, at Wash, by Rev Wm Hodge, Mr Thos A Mitchell, of Annapolis, Md, to Miss Isabella C Mayo, of Richmond, Va.

Died: on Jul 25, Annie Booth, aged 22 months & 19 days, youngest daughter of John B & Sarah A Turton. Her funeral is today at 4 o'clock, from their residence on H st, between 21st & 22nd sts.

Farm hand wanted: Henry Douglass, Florist.

Forest School, ***Owings' Mills***, Balt Co, Md, 11 miles on the Riestertown Road, accessible by turnpike & York railroad. For particulars address Rev Jos Nicholson, Owings' Mills, Balt Co, Md.

Public Notice: all persons indebted to the estate of the late Gen R Wallace, deceased, residing in Wash & Gtwn, D C, are to make payment to Lucien Peyton, or to myself, & to no other person. –Christopher Neale, Adm of Gen J R Wallace

MON JUL 28, 1851
A child of Capt Woodhouse, about 2 years old, was burnt to death at Fair Haven, Ct, on Tue, when its clothes took fire from some matches with which he was playing.

Glimpses of men, things & places: Quincy, Mass, Jul 22, 1851. I am writing from ***Old Braintree***. I visited Quincy and saw the old mansion house of the Adamses: I was shown the principal parlor where the Hon Chas F Adams, son of the late Pres John Quincy Adams, soon appeared & received us. He owns a fine dwlg of modern construction on a hill near by, called ***Mount Wollaston***, but he prefers the old mansion where Pres John Adams lived & died; where Pres John Quincy Adams was born; the east room had the same furniture & pictures that were very much as his grandfather left them. There are portraits of his grandfather & grandmother, & a portrait of their only daughter, & that of her husband, Col Smith, of N Y. Also a portrait of Jefferson, & one of Gen Warren. On wandering through the burying ground close by the road side, I found several inscriptions of historic interest. "John Quincy, jr, born 23rd of Feb, 1711; died 26th of April, 1775. And Abigail Quincy, his wife, born [blank]. To their united & beloved memory this monument is erected by their only surviving child. [This surviving child, I suppose, is the present aged Josiah Quincy, the first Mayor of Boston, & late Pres of Harvard University, who now resides in Quincy, near the village.] Another marble slab read as follows: In memory of Jos Adams, son of Jos, senior, & grandson of Henry & of Hannah, his wife, whose maiden name was Bass, a daughter of Thos Bass & Ruth Alden, parents of John Adams, & grand-parents of lawyer John Adams. [The lawyer John Adams, I suppose, was the eldest Pres Adams.] Another inscription read as follows: Rev John Hancock, 5th minister of the first congregational church of this town, & father of John Hancock, the patriot. Died May 7, 1744, in his 42nd year. Another record of the Adamses, probably erected by the elder Pres Adams, read as follows: In memory of Henry Adams, who took his flight from the Dragon persecution in Devonshire, in England, & alighted with 8 sons near ***Mount Wollaston***. One of his sons returned to England; &, after taking time to explore the country, four removed to Medfield & the neighboring towns; two to Chelmsford; one only, Joseph, who lies here at his left hand, remained here, who was an orginal proprietor in the town of Braintree, incorporated in the year 1639. This stone & several others have been placed in this year by a great-great-grandson. –Birds-Eye

On Thu the wife of Michl Kilroy, charged in Boston for beating his wife, refused to testify against him, saying it was her own fault. She refused to give him money to buy more liquor, when he was already intoxicated. She said he was a good husband, & the father of her 5 children. The Court was obliged to order her to give bonds in $100 to appear as witness, &, if not given, the ofcrs were instructed to commit her.

Household & kitchen furniture at auction: on Jul 30, at the residence of J S Butts, on G st, near 12th st. -Dyer & McGuire, aucts

Academy of the Visitation, Gtwn, D C: Annual Distribution of Premiums took place on Jul 23. Premiums to: [All names are preceded by Miss.]

Imogen Penn, Lynchburg, Va
Virginia Foote, Jackson, Miss
Marion Ramsay, Wash, D C
Rosa Ford, Wash
Mary Ann Borremans, Wash, D C
Amanda Clare, Wash, D C
Ellen Roche, Wash, D C
Cath. Tilghman, Eastern Shore, Md
Eliz O'Donnoghue, Wash, D C
Carrie Kiger Gwin, San Fran, Calif
Harriet Thayer, Petersburg, Va
Cora Lallande, of New Orleans, La
Maria Yerby, Richmond, Va
Jan Neale, Chas Co, Md
Helen Williams, Lynchburg, Va
Virginia English, Gtwn, D C
Florence Rielly, Gtwn, D C
Mary Ledlie, Pittsburgh, Pa
Mary White, Charleston, S C
Eliz Poe, Gtwn, D C
Anne O'Donnoghue, Gtwn, D C
Jane Carroll, Gtwn, D C
Frances Fetterman, Pittsburgh, Pa
Ann Foote, Jackson, Miss
Josephine Clements, Gtwn, D C
Amelia Stoops, Gtwn, D C
Caroline Rielly, Augusta, Ga
Geraldine Bellinger, Charleston, S C
Sarah Jones, Lynchburg, Va
Mary Spalding, Wash, D C
Caroline Noland, Montg Co, Md
Ann Eliza Ashe, Wilmington, N C
Florence Greenhow, Wash, D C
Eliz Fulmer, Wash, D C
M J Smoot, Gtwn
Josephine Smith, Newburyport, Mass
Ernestine Blache, New Orleans, La
Caroline Brent, Montg Co, Md
M A Murray, Gtwn, D C
Frances Offutt, Gtwn, D C
Nina Fremont, San Francisco, Calif
Rosa Selden, Lynchburg, Va
Bettie Watson, Richmond, Va
Gertrude Greenhow, Wash, D C
Julia Laub, Gtwn, D C
Mary Prizzini, Richmond, Va
M A Bell, Petersburg, Va
S Howell, Princeton, N J
Josephine Laub, Wash, D C
Sallie Ellicott, Balt, Md
Bessie Boyce, Gtwn, D C
Emma Woolard, Gtwn, D C
E McAtee, Gtwn, D C
Adle Welsh, Gtwn, D C
Mary Drill, Gtwn, D C
Frances Turner, King Geo Co, Va
Lilla Bonner, Wash, D C
E May, Gtwn, D C
M A Ellis, Gtwn, D C
Ellen White, Charleston, S C
Mary Gwin, San Francisco, Calif
Virginia Cooledge, Gtwn, D C
Clara Wildman, Columbus, Ga
Mgt Walker, Milwaukee, Wisc
Virginia Springer, Cincinnati, Ohio
Frances Turner, Balt

Cecilia Lyon, Balt
Virginia Laub, Wash, D C
F Walker, Milwaukee, Wis
Eliza Carvallo, Santiago, Chili
Eleanor Bellinger, Barnwell, S C
Mgt Duer, Cincinnati, Ohio
Pauline Blache, New Orleans, La
Alice Semmes, PG Co, Md
C Williams, New Orleans, La
Caroline Brent, Wash, D C
Eliza Howle, Wash, D C
Mary Burke, Eastport, Maine
Ellen O'Donnoghue, Gtwn, D C
Ada Semmes, Gtwn, D C
Alice Edelin, PG Co, Md
Ellen Waring, Montg Co, Md
Ernestine de Vaudricourt, Wash, D C

Victoria Brent, Chas Co, Md
Mary Watkins, Newbern, N C
Eliza Palmer, Montg Co, Md
Cassie Selden, Lynchburg, Va
C Wilson, PG Co, Md
A Branch, Petersburg, Va
Lucy Gwin, San Francisco, Calif
L Mignot, Charleston, S C
A Goszler, Gtwn
J Meem, Gtwn
Mary Gore, Balt
Eliz White, Charleston, S C
Josephine Jones, Lynchburg, Va
Celestia Neale, Chas Co, Md
Geraldine Bellinger, Charleston, S C
Mary Cecilia Gore, Carroll Co, Md
Caroline Brent, Montg Co, Md

Mr Caleb S McClennen, sailmaker, of Boston, was drowned in the harbor near that city on Fri last, in endeavoring to save the life of a lad who fell from a yacht, & drowned.

Jos B Marks, a notary public of New Orleans, committed suicide a few days ago, while on his way from La to New Orleans, by jumping from the steamboat into the river. He was a native of S C, but had been a resident of New Orleans for many years. -Bee

Danl Hennessey, of Charlestown, & Miles McFarland, of Boston, got into a quarrel on Fri, on board a vessel belonging to the former, in the Charles river. They scuffled & finally went overboard & sunk. Both drowned.

Died: on Jul 24, at N Y, in his 34th year, *Chales Henry Oakley, M D, U S Navy. [*Copied as written.]

Died: on Jul 16, at the residence of Bernard Jones, jr, Collinsville, Ill, David W Foutz, of Va. His effects are in the possession of Mr Jones, who desires to hear from his family.

Rev Fr Barber will succeed Rev J E Blox, as Pres of the Wash Seminary, as the latter gentleman is about to change his residence to Fred'k City, Md.

TUE JUL 29, 1851
Loss of lives by the upsetting of a boat on Mill Pond on the Chateaugay river last Monday night: Jas Ayres, Garret Persey, jr, Sophronia Persey, Mary Crippen, & Eamed Daley. Their ages were from 17 to 20 years old.

Mr Cabet, the Chief of the Communist colony at Nauvoo, Ill, has returned to Paris to stand his trial for swindling. He is now 70 years old. He once held the high post of Procureur General. This was in the early part of the reign of Louis Philippe. As soon as he reached Paris, he surrendered himself to the police & was sent to prison.

Chancery sale of valuable property: by decree of the Circuit Court of Wash Co, D C, dated Jul 21, 18_1, in a cause wherein Edw McGuire is cmplnt & Richd G Briscoe is respondent: sale on Sep 1, on the premises, all the estate, interest, & term of years yet to come & unexpired, under a certain indenture of lease from Fred'k May to Michl McCarty, dated Aug 17, 1835, recorded in Liber W B 39, folios 391, in part of lot 29 in square B, with improvements. The lease is for the term of 99 years from Aug 1, 1835, renewable forever, & at the yearly rent of $114.90, payable quarterly, & contains a privilege of purchasing the fee on payment of $1,915. On the premises is a 2 story brick house, used as a store & dwlg, & other improvements.
–Walter D Davidge, Trustee -Dyer & McGuire, aucts

Mr Danl Benjamin, residing in Mansfield township, N Y, is now upwards of 90 years of age; served as a private during the Revolutionary war; has ever been temperate & industrious in his habits, & is an excellent citizen.

Mrs Durham, wife of Mr Jas H Durham, who a few evening since was severely burnt by the explosion of a camphine lamp, died yesterday morning. Mrs Durham was an excellent lady, & her family has the sympathies of a large circle of acquaintances.
+
Died: on Jul 28, in Wash City, in her 51st year, Mrs Nancy W Durham, wife of Mr Jas H Durham. Her funeral is this morning, at 10 o'clock, from the residence of her husband, on Capitol Hill.

Mr Bodisco, the Russian Minister, & his lady, & a party of ladies & gentlemen, went up to Norfolk on Fri last from Old Point in the steamer **Star**. The visited the navy yard & the U S ship **Pennsylvania**, Cmder Saunders, where they were received with the usual honors & salutes.

WED JUL 30, 1851
On Sat the sloop **Rebecca Ford** was struck by a violent squall & capsized in the North river, on her way from Kingston to N Y. Mrs Mary E Cragin & Miss Eliza Allen were drowned.

Fire & loss of lives on Sat at Browntown, Bradford Co, Pa, in a frame shanty used by the contractors of the North Branch Canal extension, when it was consumed by fire, & Abraham Fisher, Henry Fisher, contractors, & Hannigan, superintendent, & Goldsmith, the cook, perished in the flames. [Jul 31st newspaper: the men were first murdered and house burnt to conceal the act. One contractor, it is presumed, had $3,000 in his possession to pay off his workmen.]

Postmaster Gen has est'd the following new Post Ofcs for week ending Jul 26, 1851.

Ofc	County, State	Postmaster
Merritt	Barry, Mich	David W Smith
Fillmore	Macomb, Mich	Wm F Myers
New Way	Licking, Ohio	E D Stratton
Pickereltown	Logan, Ohio	Lewis Cowgill
Patmos	Mahoning, Ohio	Levi A Leyman
Moore's Ordinary	Prince Edward, Va	Chas Waddell
New Castle	Hampshire, Va	Jos Workman
Cedar Hill	Augusta, Va	Wm H Ott
MdElroy	Doddridge, Va	Israel Allen
Smith's Bridge	Robeson, N C	John Smith
Union	Washington, N C	Wilson W Mizel
Flat Creek	Buncombe, N C	Jefferson Garrison
Jewell Hill	Madison, N C	David Farnsworth
Dallas	Abbeville, S C	Nimrod W Stewart
Lynchburgh	Sumter, S C	Elisha Spencer
Beaver Dam	Middleburgh, S C	Wm L Leggett
Big Wanhoo	Hall, Ga	John F Rives
Cedar Ridge	Murray, Ga	F W McCurdy
Fort Buffington	Cherokee, Ga	John K Moore
Marthasville	Macon, Ga	John R Cook
Buck Head	Pike, Ala	Danl W Jefcoart
Sandifer's Mills	Copiah, Miss	S D Ramsey
Sookalena	Lauderdale, Miss	Wm G Calhoun
Yarborough	Bossier Parish, La	Arthur Yarborough
Seven Leagues	Smith, Texas	Geo W Patterson
White Sulphur	Green, Tenn	Cain Broyle
Eclipse	Macon, Tenn	Jas H Eubank
Fern Creek	Jefferson, Ky	Squire Hardman
Flat Woods	Izard, Ark	Levi Long
Cromwell	Noble, Ind	Abel Mullin
Sylvan Dale	Hancock, Ill	Benj J Wright
Richfield	Adams, Ill	Thos R Jones
Allen's Grove	Lee, Ill	Horatio G Howlett
Paradise	Coles, Ill	John Cunningham

Creesville	Jefferson, Iowa	David Langhery
Illyria	Fayette, Iowa	Oliver P Gallagher
Wah-ta-Wah	Adair, Iowa	Wm Alcom
Tippo	Davis, Iowa	John Allen
Greene	Wapello, Iowa	Jos H Glover
Clayton	Clayton, Iowa	John R Dunkin
Lycurgus	Alamakee, Iowa	John A Wakefield
Jamestown	Winneheik, Iowa	Jas Cutler
Union Prairie	Alamakee, Iowa	Darwin Patterson
Black Creek	Marquette, Wis	Berj Haigue
Chaunceyville	Manitoowoc, Wis	C H Eaton
Braunf Is	Manitoowoc, Wis	A McNulty
Long Lake	Marquette, Wis	Josiah B Crooker
Beechwood	Sheboygan, Wis	R C Brazleton

Names Changed: 1-Burnett's Corner, Dodge Co, Wisc, changed to Noyesville. 2-Paradise, Coles Co, Ill, changed to Wabach Point.

Mr C H Ehler, an apothecary, was burnt to death by the upsetting of a camphine lamp, which he was trimming, at Louisville, on Wed.

Mrd: on Jul 28, in Christ Church, Wash, by Rev Mr Hodges, Canratt Scotoozsler to Miss Louisa Lapolt, all of Wash City.

Mrd: on Jul 28, in Ryland Chapel, by Rev J S Gorsuch, Mr Washington O Berry to Miss Amy Hart.

Mrd: on Jul 29, at St Mary's Church, by Rev Mr Alig, Mr Philip Miller to Miss Louisa Gramlich, all of Wash City.

Mrd: on Jul 28, in Wash City, by Rev Jas Laurie, D D, Wm B Hale, of Winchester, N H, to Harriet Amelia, daughter of Mr Weight Porter, of Hartford, Vt.

Mrd: on Jul 22, by Rev Mr Edwards, John Wm Earp to Miss Matilda Gardnier, both of Wash City.

Died: on Jul 18, in Mobile, Ala, in his 31st year, Mr Geo W Wallace, formerly of Wash City.

Died: on Jul 29, Chas Vernon, aged 14 months & 8 days, only child of S J & Hannah Ober. His funeral is from Messrs Adams', at 10 o'clock, this day.

Farm at private sale: part of **Chillum Castle Manor**, in PG Co, Md, adjoining the lands of Messrs Duvall & Matthews, & the farm recently sold by J M Donn, to Mrs Heildman: contains 132 acres. –S C Crawford

Rev Elisha Ballentine, who for a few years past has been the efficient & beloved Pastor of the Four-and-a-half street Presbyterian Church, is about to resign, with a view to improve his health.

THU JUL 31, 1851
Mr R R Nelson, a passenger on board the steamboat **Penobscot**, Capt Clark, from N Y, bound to Phil, accidentally fell overboard on Sat last, & was drowned.

U S Dist Court at Springfiled, Ill: 2 young men, Hiram Purcell & Elias Warfield, indicted for robbing the mail, pleaded guilty: both being 18 years of age, were sentenced to 3 months' in the penitentiary. [This leniency is more like encouragement than punishment of a crime for the commission of which there can be no excuse.]

Roxbury, Mass, Jul 30. Gen Dearborn, Mayor of Roxbury, formerly Collector of the Port of Boston, died at Portland, Me, yesterday.

The Charlestown [Va] Spirit of Jefferson announces the deaths of Buchanan C Washington & John Yates, two of the wealthiest citizens of that county. Mr Washington died on Sunday, in his 61st year; Mr Yates on Jul 6, at age 75, in Cumberland, Eng, his native place, where he was on a visit.

Mary M Fridley, younger sister, & Geo W Fridley, brother to the late Mrs Day, who had previously given in their evidence in chief, were again called to the stand.

Criminal Court-Wash-Wed: the case of John Day: witnesses examined for the rebutting testimony:

Geo Clark	Mrs Ann Little
Hiram Clark	Geo Payne
Chas Fraley, jr	Leonard O Cook
Augustus Roux	Walter Lenox, Mayor of Wash
Albert W Martin	H O Whetmore
Caleb Buckingham	Mrs Sarah Whetmore

The Grand Jury for this Dist on Tue: among their final acts was the finding of a true bill against John Carlos Gardiner for false swearing; & a true bill against J Hamilton Mears for fraud on the Govn't. Gardiner was arrested on Jul 17 for perjury, but not until Tue was the indictment found.

Teacher wanted at Leesburg Academy, Leesburg, Va. Address to the subscriber, Pres of the Board of Trustees, Wm H Gray.

Died: on Jul 29, after a lingering illness, Mrs Mary F Owen, wife of Edw Owen, of Wash City. Her funeral is today at 5 o'clock, from her residence, on south B st, opposite the Smithsonian Institution

Died: on Tue last, in Wash City, Mrs Louis Adellvig. The deceased was a native of Germany, but for several years a resident of Wash City, in her 82nd year. Her funeral is this afternoon, at 4 o'clock, from the residence of her son-in-law, Wm Grupe, on Pa ave, between 4½ & 3rd sts.

Murder in Loudoun Co, Va, on Thu last: quarrel took place between Mr Lee Thompson & a Mr Clarke, a school teacher, in the neighborhood of Leesburg, which resulted in the death of Thompson. It was brought about by Clarke's having punished Thompson's children while under his charge & in his school. Clarke was arrested, & is now in the jail at Leesburg. Thompson leaves a wife & 6 children. –Alex Gaz

FRI AUG 1, 1851
Boston, Jul 30. We learn from *Holmes' Hole*, that the dwlg house of Mr Morris was struck by lightning, & Mr Morris was killed instantly. Mr Francis Nye, painter, was also killed while at work in his shop, & several others in the bldg were stunned.

In Chancery: Dillon vs Garretson. By decree passed: auction, on Aug 18, lot 1 in square 324, Wash City. –D A Hall, trustee -C W Boteler, auct

Situation wanted as nurse or chambermaid, or as assist housekeeper, by a respectable woman. For particulars inquire of Mr John Caton, on C st, between 9th & 10th sts.

Sale of valuable land, the real estate of the late Abner C Pierce, as may be necessary to pay his debts & the legacies now due of his late father. That portion of his land upon the Piney Branch Road, from the land of Mr Bodisco to the Wash & Rockville Turnpike, about 360 acres, offered for sale, in lots from 5 to 50 acres. –Tho Carbery, exc

Contributions to the Washington Monument:

Chas Loring	Assist Marshal	Maine	$40.80
John H McGee	Do	Va	$8.50
W P McCorcle	Do	Va	$6.00
C D Cobb	Do	Missouri	$113.60
Felix H Hull	Do	Va	$2.00
John M Becton	Do	Texas	$45.05
H K Bell	Do	Do	$10.20
Saml A Moore	Do	Do	$33.15
A S Baker	Do	Do	$18.70
Chas Bennett	Do	Pa	$34.20

Abm Morrison		Johnston, Pa	$11.00
Maria M Espy		Ohio	$10.00
W W Corcoran	Annual contribution	Wash, D C	$50.00
B B French		Do	$3.65
John McGough		Pa	$10.00
Saml N Purse		Missouri	$2.00
H F Tallmadge	U S Marshal	N Y	$1000.00
L H Colton	Do	Wisc	$190.98 3rd py't
A A Pettingell	Do	Conn	$234.00 5th py't

Orphans Court of Wash Co, D C sale of cow & calf at auction: on Aug 2, the property of Mrs Whitmore, deceased. Terms cash. –Geo Mackabee, adm –John Robinson, auct

The U S storeship **Lexington** sailed from N Y on Mon last bound to the Pacific, with stores for the use of our squadron cruising in that ocean. Her ofcrs are:
Lt Commanding, Wm Radford   Geo S King, Passed Midshipman
John Stuart, Acting Master   John C Hunter, Purser
Edw C Stout, Passed Midshipman   Jas Suddards, Surgeon
T Scott Fillebrown, do   E St Clair Clarke, Capt's Clerk

Proposals will be received for extending the culvert that crosses 10th st west, between G & H sts north. –Francis B Lord, Com'r of the 3rd & 4th Wards, Wash.

Portland, Me, Jul 30. Jos S Atkins, of *Mount Vernon*, was struck by lightning & instantly killed, on Sat last, while mowing in a field. His son, standing near him, was knocked down senseless, but resuscitated.

Mrd: on Jul 29, by Rev Jos S Collins, Mr Orford Boucher to Miss Margaretta Skidmore, both of Gtwn, D C.

Died: on Jul 31, Mary O'Leary, wife of John O'Leary, of consumption, in her 27th year. Her funeral will be from the residence of her husband, 4½ st, near Md ave, Sat, at 3 o'clock.

Died: on Jul 29, in her 30th year, Frances, beloved wife of John G Deeble, a native of Ireland, but for the last 2 years a resident of Wash City. Her disease was consumption, which she bore with Christian fortitude.

Died: on Jul 30, in Balt, of paralysis, after an illness of 2 weeks, Peter Foy, in his 71st year.

Died: on Jul 31, Henrietta, infant daughter of Jas C & Henrietta Greer, aged 2 years & 4 months. Her funeral will take place today, at 2 o'clock, from the residence of Wm Green, 10th st.

SAT AUG 2, 1851

The death of Gen Henry A S Dearborn, of Roxbury, Mass, occurred at the residence of his son-on-law, Hon A H W Clapp, at Portland, Maine, on Tuesday, after a painful illness of 10 days. He was the son of Maj Gen Henry Dearborn, Sec of War during the whole of the 2 terms of the Jefferson Administration, & during the war of 1812 filled the post of Cmder-in-Chief of the Army. The deceased Gen [the son] derived his title from the ofc of Adj Gen of the State of Mass, which he held for several years; an ofc which in his State is not a title merely & a sinecure, but one of reponsibile duties & labors. Graduate of <u>Wm & Mary College</u>, Va, in 1803.

U S Patent Ofc. Ptn of Sewall Short, of New London, Conn, praying for extension of a patent granted to him Oct 6, 1837, for an improvement in railway ovens, for 7 years from expiration of the patent, which takes place Oct 6, 1851. –Thos Ewbank, Com'r of Patents

The Hagerstown "Torch Light," which for the last 30 years has been ably conducted by the late Wm Bell & his sons, ceased to exist with the number of Thursday. Messrs Mittag & Sneary, the proprietors of the Herald of Freedom, having purchased the establishment, will unit the 2 papers & conduct them jointly under the name of "Torch Ligth & Herald of Freedom."

Late storm on Sat last was destructive in the western part of Md: the barns of Messrs Danl Stoner & Wm Merring, in Carroll Co, were destroyed by lightning. The barn of Mr John F Simmons, of Fred'k Co, was destroyed. The orchards on the premises of Abraham Augustine were entirely prostrated. –Balt Patriot

Geo W Sickner & his 3 brothers, & 2 or 3 of their associates, have been arrested & committed to jail at Elmira, N Y, on a charge of counterfeiting. Their dies, paper, & rollers, fell into the hands of the police.

The Bangor Courier of Mon contains the particulars of the accident of the steamer **Governor**, by striking on White Head Ledge on Sat, during a thick fog, with about 200 passengers on board. The passengers & their belongings were transferred to the steamer **Boston**. Rev Joshua N Danforth, of this District, was on board.

Ladies with letters in the Post Ofc, Wash, Aug 2, 1851.

Alexander, Mrs A-2	Allen, Miss Jane
Ambrose, Mrs Fanny	Adams, Miss Julia
Aborn, Mrs Mary T	Brown, Miss C J
Anderson, Miss M R	Browne, Mrs E E

Berry, Miss Ellen'a
Beale, Miss Eliza A
Barthels, Miss Hen
Biss, Mrs Lethe
Beall, Miss M A
Barry, Miss Sarah J
Banton, Miss Sarah
Butler, Miss M A
Carman, Miss A-2
Carr, Miss Eliza
Collins, Mrs Anne'a
Collins, Mrs Corn'a
Coleman, Miss M A
Chandler, Miss M
Coye, Mrs Mary A
Chew, Mrs Tabitha
Davis, Miss Car'e A
Davis, Miss Eliz J
Dick, Mrs Eliz
Duvall, Miss E R
Dickson, Harriet A
Dupuy, Miss Lizzie-2
Donahoe, Miss M
Dea, Mary
Ferrie, Mrs Anna
Fowke, Miss Lucy
Fletcher, Mrs L
Farmer, Mrs L-2
Fedray, Mrs M A
Fairchild, Mrs Jane
Hall, Mrs Caroline
Hoge, Miss Eliz
Heeler, Jean
Huddleson, Miss M A
Hamilton, Miss M V
Hoban, Miss Susan
Hutchison, Mrs S W
Lynch, Mrs M A
Lounda, Miss Sarah
Landie, Eliz
Lockwood, Mrs J A
Moss, Mrs Eliz
-Wm A Bradley, P M

Moore, Miss L A
Mead, Mrs Mary A
Maddison, Mrs M
Miller, Ann Virg'a
McMagee, Mrs M W
McKan, Miss Mary
McCauley, Mrs M
McHarvey, Mrs A or
J W McHarvey
McGermy, Bridget
McDonald, Mrs J
Neal, Mrs Amelia
Offutt, Miss Anna E
Parker, Miss Ella
Pumphreys, Miss R A B
Quinn, Miss Cath'e
Queen, Miss Charl
Richstein, Miss B C
Reed, Miss Emma
Rozier, Mrs H A
Reese, Mrs
Radcliff, Miss M A
Roby, Mary E
Smoot, Mrs B M
Saul, Mrs John
Stewart, Miss Luc'a
Stinger, Mrs Rev'a
Turner, Mrs B C
Tyler, Miss Corn'a
Thompson, Mrs H
Tolson, Miss M E-2
Taylor, Mrs Sarah
Waters, Miss A C
Warner, Ann M
Winter, Mrs Eliz
Wilson, Mrs Eliz
Williams, Mrs G C
Washington, Hen'a
White, Miss Luc'a
Wallace, Mrs N A
Wood, Mrs A
Yerby, Miss Lucr'a

Died: on Jul 30, at Leesburg, Va, aged 1 year & 10 days, Howard S, 2nd son of Alpheus L Edwards, of Wash City, late of Chattanooga, Tenn.

MON AUG 4, 1851
Letter from Paris: Bache McEvers, Pres of the N Y Ins Co, died suddenly of a stroke of apoplexy. He was walking in the street, with Mr Dudley Selden, when attacked. Mr McEvers was 52 years old, & succeeded his father, Chas McEvers, as Pres of the Company in 1838, & held the ofcr for 13 continuous years. [No death date given- current item.]

On board the ship **Devonshire**, Capt Hovey, which sailed from Portsmouth for N Y on Jul 2, the small-pox made its appearance on the first day out. One person was attacked and the patient was placed in the sternboat, hanging at the davits, entirely clear from the ship; a small house was built over it with tarpauline & stakes, in which he was comfortably sheltered, & here he was nursed, & attended until he was entirely cured. The ship arrived at N Y on Sat; the passenger, who is now perfectly well, having never left the boat in the whole course of the voyage. None of the other passengers were attacked by the small-pox, the precaution taken by the captain having proved perfectly successful.

Cyrus F Ballard was lately shot by Conrad Decker, in Ellery, Chautauque Co, N Y, & dangerously wounded. Decker had sold his wife to Ballard for 2 shillings, &, becoming dissatisfied with the bargain, undertook to kill him.

On Sat last, the house of Esquire Stalford, of Wyalusing, Bradford Co, was destroyed by fire, & 4 men, residents of this vicinity, were consumed. They were Mr Henry Fisher, about 50, & Abraham Fisher, his son, aged about 23, residents of South Wilkesbarre; Thos Flanaghan, aged 25, a resident of Plymouth, & a man named Goldsmith, whose home, we believe, was in this borough. Mr Fisher was a contractor on the North Branch Canal, & occupied as an ofc a room in Mr Stalford's house. Mr Coolbaugh alone escaped. Mr Stalford & family were asleep in other parts of the house & escaped the flames. Mr Fisher is supposed to have had several hundred dollars in the office.

Fatal accident at Millstone Point, Waterford, Ct, on Jul 28, which resulted in the death of Mr Wm Frazer, of the firm of Butts & Frazer. He was standing some 200 feet from a blast, when a fragment of the rock, weighing some 50 pounds, struck & killed him.

$200 reward for runaway negro man James Marshall, who ran away from the subscriber, living near Upper Marlboro, PG Co, Md, on Jul 26. He is about 22 or 23 years of age. -Chas Hill

Mr Saxton Bently, a teacher in a public school at Manhasset, Long Island, was drowned on Mon in Success Pond while bathing with a companion. He was a young man of rare promise, esteemed & loved by all who knew him. His parents reside in Lebanon, Conn.

Public sale: by decree of Chas Co Court-Court of Equity: sale on Sep 2 next, of the real estate of which the late Saml I Briscoe died possessed, called **Hill Serene**, & containing about 600 acres. The farm lies on the Wicomico river, & has a good dwlg house & all necessary out-houses, in first rate repair. The estate cannot be sold for less than $6,500. -John W Mitchell, Fred'k Stone

Mobile Tribune: the large Wm Jennings estate, which lies in England, seems to have claimants in all parts of the country. He was an old miser, who took great pleasure in accumulating. He was born about 1700 & died in 1798, leaving no issue & intestate. The whole value of this property in 1848, according to English authority, exceeded L8,000,000, or more than $40,000,000, a sum which would made its possessor, we imagine, the richest man in the world. Who are the heirs? The impression among eminent legal men is that the true heirs are the descendants of the family of Mr S S Jennings of this city. Instructions were sent twice to this country for the descendants of Chas Jennings, who came hither from England in 1681.

The Hydropathic Co which purchased Barnum's residence at Iranistan, Conn, have been unable to pay for it; so that it has gone back again into his possession, &, it is said, will be occupied by his family.

Died: on Jul 16, at the village of Stoke Newington, near London, Eng, in her 66th year, Jane, wife of Pishey Thompson, formerly & for many years a resident in Wash City. None knew her but to love her, None nam'd her but to praise.

TUE AUG 5, 1851
Foreign Gleanings: Lady Noel Byron has set to work on her estate 200 unemployed frame-work knitters. She has offered them a bonus of 10% on all moneys which they will place in her hands during the first 12 months.

Teacher wanted: the Trustees of Union Academy, Snowhill, Md, wish to engage a teacher to take charge of the Academy: salary will be $500 per annum.
–Wm U Purnell, sec

Storm on the Missouri River-fire-& loss of life. The ofcrs of the steamer **Duroc** bring news of sad character: on the 18th instant at Oregon, Mo, the hotel of Mr F N Pollock was struck by lightning & consumed by fire; Mr Pollock was killed. Mr Jabe was burnt to death; Mr Jas D Fortune escaped, but died a few hours after; Mr Hades died. Mr Jas Thorp, violently bruised, is not expected to survive. Mr Sypes is expected to recover. -St Louis Republican

Rappannock Academy & Military Institute, Caroline Co, Va. Geo G Butler, A M, Principal: Rev Alex Shiras, A M, Assoc Principal; John R Jones, Dept of Tactic & Math. Next session will commence on the 1st Monday of Oct ensuing, & close on the 4th Wednesday in Jul, 1852. Terms: $160, payable half upon entrance, & remainder at Mar 1.

University of Md will begin on Oct 15 & close on Mar 1, 1852.
Nathan R Smith, M D, Surgery
Saml Chew, M D
Jos Roby, M D
Wm Power, M D
Richd H Thomas, M D
Geo W Miltenberger, M
Wm E A Aiken, M D, Dean
Balt, Md. -Jul 1, 1851

For rent: nearly new 3 story brick dwlg house on Pa ave, near the Capitol square. Apply to J P Fugitt, Blagden's Wharf.

Jos T Kessler, Teacher of Music, has removed his place of residence south side of Pa ave, between 9th & 10th sts, nearly opposite Mr Davis' music store.

For rent: 2½ story brick house on 11th st, near G st. Apply on the premises to Mr Nicholas Callan. –Jas Maguire

For sale: valuable lot fronting 26 feet on F st, between 9th & 10th sts, with a small 2 story brick house on the alley. Apply to Mrs Sarah Moore, adjoining the lot.

Store on 11th st for rent: now occupied by N M McGregor. Possession on Sep 10 next. Apply to Geo Lowry, Gtwn.

For sale: the entire stock of a Music store on Pa ave. Mr D O Hare, on the premises, will show the same & make known the terms.

Died: on Aug 3, after a lingering illness, Harriet, aged 54 years, wife of Jacob A Bender. Her funeral is today at 4 o'clock, from her late residence on F st, near 7th.

Died: on Jul 29, at his residence, near Fairfax Court-house, Hiram Fuller, Editor of the Fairfax "News." He was born in South Salem, N Y, but in the spring of 1844 he purchased a farm in Fairfax Co, & removed there with his family. In Aug, 1819, he became the editor & proprietor of the "News.

Died: on Jul 12, at his residence, near **Fort Smith**, Ark, after a few hours' illness of cholera, Col Wm Duvall, in his 69th year. Col Duvall was a native of Fred'k Co, Md, & was the oldest surviving member of a noble Huguenot family. He removed with his family to **Fort Smith** [to fill an important ofc under Gov't] about 22 years since. His remains were interred in his family vault beside his excellent wife, near the residence of his son-in-law, Maj Rector.

Died: on Jul 19, at *Fort Hamilton*, N Y harbor, Bettie Blaney, daughter of Lt Col J H Eaton, U S Army, aged 10 months.

WED AUG 6, 1851
Wash Corp: 1-Ptn from Jos Ingle, exc of Catharine Coyle & others, regarding the relaying a pavement on the south side of square 688: referred to the Cmte on Improvements. 2-Cmte of Claims: act for the relief of Francis Dacy: passed. 3-Ptn from Geo Sinclair, for remission of a fine: referred to the Cmte of Claims. 4-Cmte of Claims: bill for the relief of T P & M Brown for expenses incurred in entertaining the members of the Pennsylvania Legislature: passed. 5-Ptn of John E Bailey, praying the remission of a fine: referred. 6-Ptn of W H Clampett & others, for changing the grade of K st: referred to the Cmte on Improvements. 7-Ptn of Jos Shillington & others, for a flag footway across Pa ave: referred to the Cmte on Improvements. 8-Act to pay the balance due Danl Linkins. 9-Ptn of Geo Cover & others: for examining the grade of N Y ave: read & adopted.

Thos Gewin & Jas McCollum were both killed a few days ago in a re-encounter, near De Kalb, Miss. They were near neighbors, & a feud had existed between their families for some time. Armed with guns, they both fired, & both were killed.

Aaron Milhado, Pres of the Va Bank in Norfolk, died on Fri week, at the Bath Alum Springs. His health for some time had been very infirm.

Died: on May 6 last, at Santa Fe, New Mexico, of erysipelas, in his 19th year, Alex'r Gordon Beall, son of Col Benj L Beall, U S Army, & grandson of the late venerable Geo Taylor, of Wash City.

Died: on Jul 29, in PG Co, Md, of dysentery, Lucy Fairfax, only daughter of Lt A B Fairfax, & the late Sarah C Fairfax, his wife, aged 1 year & 5 months.

Foreign Item. 1-Dr Lingard, the celebrated historian of England, died at his residence, Hornby, on Jul 17, aged about 81 years. For some time his health has been failing. 2-The well-known picture by Benj West, of Penn's Treaty with the Indians, was sold about 3 weeks ago at Christie & Mason's, in London, for L441. At the same sale [that of Mr Penn of Stoke Pogeis] a large family picture by Sir Joshua Reynolds, with some of his infantine beauties in many parts, was sold for L367 10s. 3-The mortal remains of Madame Letitia, [mother of the Emperor Napoleon,] & of Cardinal Fesch, have been removed from Rome to Ajaccio, in Corsico, the native place of the Bonaparte family. The Corsican papers of Jul 8 contain accounts of the ceremonies. None of the members of the Bonaparte family appear to have been present.

Episcopal Institute for Young Ladies, n w corner of 9th & E sts, will resume on Sep 1. -Wm J Clarke, Principal

Criminal Court-Wash-Tue: The Jury asked to be discharged because they could not agree upon a verdict. Judge Crawford sent word to them that the Court had no power to discharge them. The Jury returned about 5 o'clock: Mr Middleton, the clerk, called their names; the clerk called for their verdict; Mr Saml Wardell, their foreman, in a firm tone, but evidently under the influence of deep feeling, replied, handing a paper to the Clerk. "Guilty as indicted, with this recommendation." The paper disclosed the fact that John Day had been guilty of the murder of his wife, & was accompanied with a recommendation to the Executive for a commutation of his punishment. The Court: The Executive has no such power. Mr Bradley: the penalty is death. The D A asked to have the verdict recorded. The Clerk proceeded to call the names, & Notley L Adams, Edmund Bradford, Saml Wardell, & John B Scrivener each rose & audibly responded "Guilty." Chas Mann replied "Not Guilty." Whereupon the Jury were ordered to return to their chamber. Another message was sent to ascertain whether or not they could change their recommendation to Executive clemency, instead of commutation of punishment; which was replied to in the affirmative. [Aug 8th newspaper: correction: the error consisted in our having stated that the Court replied in the affirmative to a message from the Jury, inquiring whether they could change their recommendation to Executive clemency instead of a commutation of punishment, when the fact was that the Court declined to answer the question.] [Aug 11th newspaper: Mr Mann was not the only member who prevented an earlier agreement, there having been one other juryman who took the same view of the case as Mr Mann.]

Dwlg for rent: on G st, near the State Dept, now occupied by the undersigned, will be for rent on Oct 1. Apply at the 3rd Auditor's Ofc: John S Gallaher.

On Sunday, the Rev Mr Blox, of the Roman Catholic denomination, delivered his farewell discourse in St Patrick's Church, to a crowded & deeply affected auditory.

On Monday, Mr Johnson, whose stable was destroyed by fire on Sunday, secured & brought before Justice John L Smith, a negro fellow named Henry Douglass, alias Brooks, charged with setting fire to his premises. Another negro, Geo Simms, appeared as the principal witness, & in the examination the fact leaked out that the informer had accompanied Douglass to the vicinity of Mr Johnson's grounds. They both were committed to await the action of the Criminal Court. A colored woman, Mary Lewis, was also sent to jail for false swearing on the examination.

The bldg of the New Gas Establishment: east of 4½ st, between Md ave & the city canal: main bldgs are 8 in number; the great excavation for the gasometer is a perfect circle of 90 feet in diameter, & 20 feet in depth; the walls will be 3½ feet thickness, & will contain 400,000 bricks. The brickwork is under the charge of Mr Peter Havener, who works subject to the contractors for the bldg, Messrs Jones & Co, of N Y C.

Criminal Court-Wash-Tue: 1-Noah Lawrence was convicted for larceny. 2-Henry Plummer, free negro, was sentenced to 1 year imprisonment & fined $1 for an assault on a small child, daughter of Mr Uniacke.

THU AUG 7, 1851
Storm in Fayette Co, Pa: on Jul 26 a tornado struck: the chimney of Geo Wetsell's large log bldg, that the family occupied, came down & crushed Mrs Wetsell. A child in a cradle was unhurt. The barn & dwlg of Mr Arrison was destroyed, & Mr & Mrs Arrison were badly hurt. The residence of Rev Mr Rose was left with but a small angle of the first story. The hat of one of the boys was found on the farm of Col Bute, 3 miles distant. Mr Jas Stewart took his wife & a child to the basement, & the house was gone. He found his 2 other children stunned but not hurt. The residence of Mr Strong withstood the blast, but his barn lost part of its roof. Col Bute's main dwlg house escaped injury. A grand child, a small child of Mrs Archibald, had its skull fractured; another was slightly injured. The storm came down upon the premises of Zachariah Ball. The bldgs belonging to Gen H W Beeson were left with their foundations. The house occupied by Mr Kinsil was unroofed. A large log barn belonging to Levi Downer, was blown down. Mr Sebastian Rush, on the Nat'l Road, had the roof of his new barn, just finished, partly unroofed.

Entire stock of groceries at auction, on Aug 9, on the west of the market, on the canal, occupied by J W Boucher. –Barnard & Buckey, Gtwn

Postmaster Gen has est'd the following new Post Ofcs for week ending Aug 2, 1851.

Ofc	County, State	Postmaster
Montgomery Centre	Franklin, Vt	Columbus Green
Ringville	Hampshire, Mass	Ethan C Ring
West Batavia	Genesee, N Y	Elisha W Croff
Hawkinsville	Oneida, N Y	Sterry Hawkins
Massena Centre	St Lawrence, N Y	Augustus Wheeler
Hickory Run	Carbon, Pa	Saml Saylor
Irishtown	Mercer, Pa	Jas Miller
Fort Wilkins	Houghton, Mich	Danl D Brockway
Bridgeport Centre	Saganaw, Mich	Saml C Munson
Prospect Lake	Van Buren, Mich	Huram Jacobs
Nobleville	Noble, Ohio	Jas Hellyer
Williamstown	Montgomery, Ohio	Cornelius R Wilson
Rochester Depot	Loraine, Ohio	Giles Gilmore
Greersville	Knox, Ohio	Robt Greer
Industry	Hamilton, Ohio	John Kennedy
Home City	Hamilton, Ohio	Aaron Lyon
New Harmony	Brown, Ohio	Deloss Laughlin
Ford	Geauga, Ohio	Franklin Dickinson
Havana	Huron, Ohio	Loomis E Ransom

Moody's Mill	Morgan, Ohio	Robt McMichael
Renosa	Laurens Dist, S C	T Wier
Mollihorn	Newberry Dist, S C	John N McCrackin
Aspen Grove	Calhoun, Fla	Jas H Parker
Salsada	Butler, Ala	A C Fuller
Monthalia	Pancla, Miss	B W Morris
City Point	Itawambee, Miss	Chas H Laws
Halifax	Panclo, Miss	John Bishop
Yuba	Yuba, Calif	H Fairchild
Louisville	El Dorado, Calif	Geo G Blodgett
Empire	Tuolumne, Calif	Edw Conway
Martinez	Contra Costa, Calif	Oliver C Coffin
Santa Clara	Santa Clara, Calif	Fletcher Cooper
Knight's Ferry	San Joaquin, Calif	Lewis Dent
Mariposa	Mariposa, Calif	H B Edwards
Trinidad	Trinity, Calif	L B Gilkey
Horr's Branch	Tuolumne, Calif	B D Horr
San Joaquin	San Joaquin, Calif	Rich M Harmer
Livermore Ranch	Contra Costa, Calif	Robt Livermore
Vallejo	Sonoma, Calif	Lyman Leslie
Tuolumne City	Tuolumne, Calif	Paxson McDowell
Rough & Ready	Nevada, Calif	Marcus Nutting
Green Springs	Calif	Josiah C Parks
Obispo	San Luis Obispo, Calif	Sam A Pollard
Nicolans	Sutter, Calif	F H Russell
Oak Springs	Tuolumne, Calif	Drury Shoemaker
San Juan	Monterey, Calif	Edw Smith
Sonora	Tuolumne, Calif	Rich F Sullivan
Wood's Diggings	Tuolumne, Calif	Robt Turner
Grasonville	[blank,] Calif	J W Van Benschoten
Mountain Inn	Tuolumne, Calif	Isaiah Williams
Marysville	Yuba, Calif	Jas Cushing
Colerain	Jackson, Ark	Saml McCall
Cherry Grove	Saline, Ark	Thos H Crawson
Trouble Hill	Scott, Ark	Isaac D Williams
Reform	Union, Ark	John M Hicks
Loran	Whitley, Ind	Wm A Clark
Bergersville	Johnson, Ind	Geo B McCann
Ludlow	Dubois, Ind	John H Damewoor
New Elizabethtown	Hendrick's, Ind	Thos C Parker
Coatesville	Hendrick's, Ind	Wm H Shield
Blue Spring	Stewart, Tenn	A A Boyell
Hindmare's Hill	Coffee, Tenn	Pleasant H Price

Hale's Point	Andrew, Mo	Miles Hale
Jenkin's Creek	Jasper, Mo	Wm Dunn
Norway	Miller, Mo	T C Degraffenried
Cook's Store	La Fayette, Mo	Mordecai M Cook
Stringtown	Cole, Mo	Luke E Ray
Hazledell	Cumberland, Ill	John Devall
Green Garden	Will, Ill	Jas Hudson
Farmer's Farm	Iroquois, Ill	Geo G White
Iron Hills	Jackson, Iowa	Robt Templeton
Waicpista	Fon du Lac, Wis	Anson C Stowe
Luzerne	Fon du Lac, Wis	Giles A Titus
Lagoda	Fon du Lac, Wis	Marcus Brown

Names Changed: 1-Portersville, New London Co, Conn, changed to Mystic River. 2-Poplar Grove, Newberry District, S C, changed to Beth Eden.

The death of M Daguerre, the Inventor of the Daguerreotype, & a distinguished chemist, is announced. Scarcely a dozen years ago when the first pictures taken in this country by means of the daguerreotype were exhibited. The price of admission to this novel show, of 25 or 30 pictures, was .50 cents. –Boston Journal
[No death date given-current item.]

On Thu night last a tavern in Oregon, Holton Co, kept by F A Pollock, was struck by lightning & consumed. The following are the sufferers as afar as we have learned their names: F A Pollock, the landlord, & Jas Fortune, of Holt Co; ___ Bush, Wm Tharp, & Wm Sypes. Two were burnt to death & others have since died.
–St Jos Gaz, 23rd

At Newark, N J, on Mon, Edwin Drum, an Irishman, aged about 25 years, was assassinated by Mgt Garraty, a young servant girl to whom he had been paying attention for some time previously, but whom he had deserted & was married to another on the Sunday preceding his death. He was stabbed with a carving knife by Mgt while he was walking in the street with his wife, & died almost immediately. Mgt has not been seen or heard from since.

Criminal Court-Wash-Wed. 1-Noah Lawrence, guilty of stealing spoons & forks from Dr J F May, was sentenced to 3 years in the penitentiary. His young wife accompanied him during his trial, & also on his return to jail.

Died: on Aug 6, Mary Elizabeth, daughter of John & Caroline Granenger, aged 3 years, 9 months & 10 days. Her funeral will be from the residence of her uncle, Chas E Rison, K st, near 13th st, this afternoon, at 2 o'clock.

Assist Teacher wanted in a Classical school. –B F Stem, Fredericksburg, Va.

Analostan, or Mason's Island, in the Potomac, opposite Gtwn, D C, is offered for sale. For terms inquire of John Marbury, Atty at Law, Gtwn.

Limestone land for sale: the undersigned, wishing to give more attention to his profession, offers for sale the Farm on which he resides, in Warren Co, Va: contains about 260 acres: bldgs are very neat & comfortable dwlg, prettily situated. Address the undersigned at Nineveh, Warren Co, Va: David Funsten.

FRI AUG 8, 1851
Fire in San Francisco, Calif, on Jun 22, Sabbath morning: W G Badger who had just rebuilt from the fire in May, suffered a loss of about $20,000; Rev Mr Williams Presbyterian Church was consumed; Gambling House, called Polka; Dr Stout's large boarding house; & brick store owned by Markwald & Casper, Jackson st: all consumed.

From South America. Saml Eckel, newly-appointed U S Consul for Taleahuano, arrived in the last steamer with his lady.

Household & kitchen furniture at auction: on Aug 9, at the residence of Col J H Eaton, on I st, between 10th & 11th sts. -Dyer & McGuire, aucts

San Francisco, Calif: 1-A marauding party of 12 men, commanded by a Capt Irving, were all killed by the Indians of the Cohuilla tribe, near Los Angeles. They deserved their fate. 2-A party of 9 men, under Capt Fitzpatrick, have been cut off by the Indians, &, as is supposed, all murdered, at Rogus river.

Died: on Aug 6, of dropsy, Richd H Hardington, in his 48th year. His funeral will be from his late residence, Garrison st, near the Navy Yard, today at 3 o'clock.

Died: on Wed, Mary Frances, only daughter of B Birch, in her 18th year. Her funeral is from the residence of her father, 4th st, between F & G sts, this evening, at 4½ o'clock.

SAT AUG 9, 1851
The first jury trial which ever was held in Panama occurred there on Jul 16. It was composed of 90 persons. The case left to them was that of Rafael Quintana, the last of the Chagres murderers, whom they found guilty.

The Stockholm journals state that Mlle Jenny Lind has just purchased one of the largest estates in Sweden, that of *Beckarshoerg*, in the Province of Nykoping.

Died: on Aug 8, Meury White, eldest daughter of M H & Susan B Stevens, aged 3 years, 9 months & 10 days. Her funeral will be from the residence of Mrs Adams, on Pa ave, this morning at 10 o'clock.

Jul 25th, our village was the scene of a painful tragedy, that resulted in the death of Mr Anderson Baldwin, one of the most respectable citizens in the county. Mr Baldwin & Maj Holland became engaged in a political controversy. Holland struck Baldwin with his fist, who returned the blow. They were on the point of being separated, when Orlando Holland, the son of Maj Holland, drew a knife & struck Baldwin. He expired in about half an hour. –Crawford Alabamian, Jul 31.

Rumford Academy, King Wm Co, Va, will be in session from Sep 1 to Jul 1 following. Mr Geo W Upshaw has been engaged as Assistant. Mr John H Pitts, Principal, graduated at this institution, with the highest honors of his class, in Jul, 1844, & since that period has been discharging the duties of a Teacher in Fleetwood Academy. For particulars address: Jno H Pitts, Aylett's Post Ofc, King Wm Co, Va.

MON AUG 11, 1851
Eight persons drowned during a squall on Thu when a small boat capsized opposite the Sailors' Snug Harbor, on Staten Island, N Y: the party consisted of Mrs Green, belonging to N Y, her 4 children & nurse, & 2 sailors living at the Snug Harbor. Mrs Green kept an Eye Infirmary. The party were going on a picnic excursion.

Mrd: on Jul 19, at Mobile, Ala, R Carrese Brent, of Md, to Miss Janet Miller, of Mobile, Ala.

Died: on Aug 5, in Balt, Mrs B Cottringer, relict of Garrett Cottringer, formerly of Phil, & confidential friend of the last Robt Morris, Sec of Finance of the U S, & ex-Sec of the North American Land Co, Phil. She & her daughter were well & favorably known & their merits appreciated in Wash City, during some years' residence, & in conducting a Female Academy.

Four executions in Md on Fri last: Amos Green, negro, was hung at Ellicott's Mills, & Abraham Taylor, Nicholas Murphy, & Wm Shelton were hung at Chestertown, the latter for the murdering the Cosden family. Except Shelton, they all died protesting their innocence of the crimes for which they suffered. When the trap of the gallows fell, from some disarrangement of the rope the noose around Murphy's neck slipped, & he fell to the ground. Murphy again mounted the scaffold & endured the penalty of the law.

Died: on Jul 21, at ***Prospect Hill***, Montg Co, Md, James Mason, son of Ebenezer Peyton & Mary E Piggott, aged 22 months.

John M Smith & Mr R O Lyman were killed on Jul 24, while engaged in surveying the Indian lands on Wolf river, Iowa. A tornado came up, during which a large tree was blown directly across the tent, striking Mr Smith & Mr Lyman on the head & killing them instantly, & seriously wounding Davis Howard. The remaining men were to return to Dubuque, to be reorganized by the U S Surveyor General.

Orphans Court of Wash Co, D C. Letters of administration on the personal estate of Jas Goddard, late of Wash Co, deceased. –A Goddard, adm

On Fri, as 2 little boys, sons of Thos C Donn, were playing with a fire-arms, the eldest boy, 10 or 12 years of age, received a charge of shot in his right leg; the younger son was slightly injured. Dr Edelin attended the boys, & they are doing well.

TUE AUG 12, 1851

The dead body of a woman, supposed to be that of the wife of John Cookson, of Pawtucket, Mass, was found last week mysteriously buried at Seekonk, R I. Cookson, about the time the body was discovered, took passage in the schnr **Oregon**, bound from Providence to some part of Va, but the vessel was forced by bad weather to put into N Y. He has been arrested & sent back. He denies the murder & says he has no doubt his wife is still living in Seekonk.

Mr Robt Limehouse, a resident of Charleston, died on Aug 6, in his 91st year, being the oldest inhabitant of that city.

Terre Haute, Ind, Aug 4, 1851. R W Thompson states that there is a mistake associating his name, as atty, regarding the claim of Dr Gardiner against Mexico.

Norborne Hall School, Boarding & Day School for Young Ladies, at Norborne, Martinsburg, Va, will be re-opened on Sep 15. –Mrs Jane R Codwise, Principal

Desirable improved Island lots for sale: property of the late Mrs Mary T Walsh, deceased: sale on square 501, Aug 16, of lots 13 thru 16, part of lot 17, & lots 20 thru 25. John Carroll Brent, John Marbury, Trustees -A Green, auctioneer

Mrd: on Jul 28, by Rev Dr Bunting, Mr Remigius Burch, of Wash, to Miss Ann Bernard, of Little Hackney, St Mary's Co, Md, daughter of the late Bernard Blackiston.

Died: at Chicago, Ill, after a few hours' illness, of cholera, Walter Butler, brother of Benj F & Chas Butler, of N Y C. Mr Butler was the oldest member of the family, & removed from the State of N Y to Chicago after the monetary embarrassments of 1842. His oldest [& 3rd] daughter, accompanied by his eldest son, were absent on their bridal tour, having been married 3 weeks previous. His 2^{nc} daughter [also married] was ill, & unable to reach her father's bedside to receive his blessing. Thus died, in the full vigor of manhood, one eminently qualified with every virtue to command the administration of men & the approval of God. [No death date given- recent communication.]

Died: Aug 1, after a protracted illness of severe suffering, George, youngest son of Gold S Silliman, of Brooklyn, L I.

Died: on Aug 4, at the residence of the Hon Andrew Stewart, Uniontown, Pa, Eliz Stewart, daughter of Chas E & Mary E Swearingen, of Wash, D C, aged 1 year & 11 months.

Sale on Aug 18, of a lot of ground on 15th & M sts, containing 5,475 square feet, more or less; with a 2 story frame house. Title indisputable. –Eliza Bates -Asa Farr, Agent

New & valuable dwlg for sale: subscriber wishes to dispose of his fine House, which is just completed, on the corner of 3rd & C sts: the house is 44 x 43 feet. Mr A Baldwin will show the bldg, or myself. –Z D Gilman

Army movements: Companies A & H, of the 4th Artl, now stationed on Govnr's Island, have been ordered to some point at present unknown. The ofcrs are Capt J B McCown, Bvt Capt G W Getty, Bvt Cap R O Drune, Quartermaster; Lt David N Couch, Lt Jas C Booth. –N Y Com Advertiser

WED AUG 13, 1851
Postmaster Gen has est'd the following new Post Ofcs for week ending Aug 9, 1851.

Ofc	County, State	Postmaster
Mackerel Corner	Carroll, N H	John L Leavitt
North Uxbridge	Worcester, Mass	Wm H Dudley
Tuna	Cattaraugus, N Y	Henry Heath
Salmon Creek	Monroe, N Y	Wm C Slayton
Millburne	Columbia, N Y	Philip Groat
Wassaic	Dutchess, N Y	Orville Gridley
North Winfield	Herkimer, N Y	Josiah W Warner
Ketchumville	Tioga, N Y	Henry Ketchum
East Ashford	Cattaraugus, N Y	Alonzo White
Pontico	Cayuga, N Y	Osman Rhoades
Bangall	Dutchess, N Y	Alonzo Buel
Palmyra	Burlington, N J	Isaiah Foy
Macopin	Passaic, N J	Abram W Pulis
Penn	Lancaster, Pa	Isaac Staufer
Fountain Mills	Chester, Pa	Danl Stubbs
Barre Forge	Huntingdon, Pa	S M Green
North Industry	Lawrence, Pa	Wm Law
New Florence	Westmoreland, Pa	Geo C Osburn
Bedminster	Bucks, Pa	Elias Ott
Franklinville	Montour, Pa	Lloyd Thomas
Shoustown	Alleghany, Pa	John Hamilton

Forest Oak	Montgomery, Md	Jos Thompson
St Dennis	Baltimore, Md	W M Townsend
Shelemiah	Cecil, Md	Elihu B Hull
Ashley	Delaware, Ohio	Horatio S Miller
Berryville	Highland, Ohio	Braden Smith
Rock Mills	Rappannock, Va	Wm S Yates
Spring Hill	Hernando, Fla	Peter W Law
Lloydsville	Brenton, Ala	Wiley Vise
Beaver Creek	Dale, Ala	Richd C Floyd
Big Creek	Dale, Ala	Green B Johnson
Friendship	Bath, Ala	Danl McCormick
Cooper's Well	Hinds, Miss	Inman Williams
Bearden	Lavaca, Texas	Kinchew Mayo
Mormon Island	Sacramento, Calif	John W Shaw
Two Bayou	Washita, Ark	Robt F Green
Cannon's Store	Sevier, Tenn	Wm H Cannon
Sweet Water	Menard, Ill	Geo M Saunders
El Dorado	Fayette, Iowa	Eli Elrod
Wayne	Henry, Iowa	Sylvester Smith
Scotch Grove	Jones, Iowa	John E Lovejoy
Niles	Appanoose, Iowa	F N Sales
Centre Hill	Washington, Iowa	Geo A Ellsworth
Kentuck Grove	Risley, Iowa	Jas T Cooke
Catalamet	Lewis, Oregon	Jas Birnie

Names Changed: 1-Leistville, Pickaway Co, Ohio, changed to Camp Charlotte. 2-Laporte, Warren Co, Pa, changed to Freehold.

Mr Jos Taylor Janney, of Newtown. Bucks Co, Pa, drowned at Square Beach on Sunday. He was a good swimmer, but ventured too far. The current carried him off.

Education of Young Ladies: 121 Marshall st, Phil, Pa: will commence on Sep 1 next.
References:
Hon Walter Lowrie, N Y   Rev Albert Barnes, Phil
Rev J McDowell, D D, Phil   Mr Jos Ingle, Wash, D C
Col S D Patterson, Phil   Rev H Malcolm, D D, Phil
For further information apply to Gilbert Combs, Principal, 124 Marshall st, Phil.

Election for Judicial Ofcrs in the State of Missouri, last week, as follows: Hamilton R Gamble, Wm B Nafton, & John F Ryland are elected by the State at large as Judges of the Supreme Court.

Mr S W Jewett, of Vt, has imported at a cost of $30,000, an improved breed of French marino sheep, pure descendants from the Gov't merino sheep of Spain.

A boat containing Mr Rufus Reed, of Providence, his 2 daughters, 2 Misses Porter, of Providence Island, & 2 other persons, names not ascertained, was upset in a gale near Bristol on Sunday. The 4 young women were drowned. Mr Reed sustained himself by swimming, the other 2 by clinging to a portion of the mast in the water, until rescued.

Lot for sale: deed of trust to me directed, dated Sep 25, 1849, recorded in the land records of Wash Co, Liber J A S 7, folios 435 thru 438: sale of lot 9 in square 582, fronting on 2nd st, between Va ave & D st. –P M Pearson, trustee
-Dyer & McGuire, aucts

Bldgs lots at auction, Aug 30: deed of trust from John Allmand & wife, dated Aug 27, 1742, recorded in the land records of Wash Co, D C, in book W B 94, folios 481 to 484: will be sold at Public Auction, all of lot 13 in square 218, on K st; also, all of lot 18 in square 453, except 5 feet front, on G st. By order of the trustee.
-A Green, auctioneer

On Monday the extensive bldgs formerly occupied by the Globe printing ofc, & more recently by the Union newspaper, were sold at auction for $11,700. Mr Wm H Winder was the purchaser.

Valuable house & lot at auction: by deed of trust from Gardner Green & wife, dated May 4, 1851, recorded in the land records of Wash Co, D C, in book W B 13, folios 506 to 509: auction on Sep 16, of lot 5 in subdivision of square 283, fronts on L st & Mass ave, improved by a 2 story brick dwlg. By order of the trustee.
-A Green, auctioneer

Mr Geo Scott, an elderly & much respected citizen residing near the Navy Yard, was found dead in his bed on Monday last. He had retired to bed on Sunday night, apparently in good health. Death by the visitation of God was the verdict.
-Telegraph

The District Tent of the Order of Rechabites held its meeting at the Navy Yard on Mon, when the following were elected ofcrs for the ensuing term:
Levin Jones, of Gtwn, Past District Chief Ruler
Jas Young, of Balt, District Chief Ruler
Wm D Serrin, of Wash, District Deputy Ruler
A H Jones, of Cambridge, Md, D Recording Scribe
John Garrett, of Gtwn, D Financial Scribe
John Mills, of Wash, District Treasurer
J Carter, of Wash, D L
J E Alford, of Balt, D Chaplain
Lewis Slicer, of Balt, D G

Col Ogilvie, Judge Advocate Gen, died at Poouah on Jun 17, of paralysis succeeded by gangrene. He was 64 years old, & had been 45 years in India

Mrd: on Aug 9, in the Catholic Church at Harper's Ferry, by Rev Mr Plumnkitt, Miss Apollonia Jagiello, of Lithuania, Poland, & Maj Gaspar Tochman, formerly of Warsaw, Poland.

Mrd: on Aug 11, by Rev Mr Donelan, John E Herrell to Henrietta Q Mahorney.

Died: on Aug 11, in Wash City, Margaret Beatley, wife of C Beatley, in her 42nd year. Her funeral will be from her late residence on 22nd st, between B & C sts, today at 4 o'clock.

Died: on Aug 3, in Norfolk, Va, Mrs Chloe Ann, wife of the Rev Wm McKenney, Chaplain U S Navy.

Died: on Sat last, in Wash City, Portia, daughter of Robt A & Anne Sommerville, aged 2 years, 1 month & 19 days.

Died: at Appleby, Harford Co, Md, Catharine Scott, wife of Wm Murray Maynadier, in her 68th year. [No death date given-current item.]

THU AUG 14, 1851
Relic of the Revolution: Jordan L Mott, of Mott Haven, recently sent to the Smithsonian Institution a blunderbuss, taken out of the wreck of the British frig **Hussar**, which was sunk in the East River above Hurlgate in Nov 1780. The piece has lain in the salt water for 70 years. The barrel, lock, & screws, all the iron work of the gun, are entirely destroyed, yet the brass work is in a most perfect state of preservation. Prof Henry observes that it is interesting on account of the historical associations connected with it, but also as exhibiting the unequal action of salt water on 2 metals simultaneously exposed to corrosion. –N Y Courier

On Sunday last 2 young girls, Jeannette Merrick & Sarah Hanlon, were drowned in the East River, near N Y, by the capsizing of a rowboat. There were 9 in the boat & it was upset by the steamboat **Rough & Ready** as they passed. Assistance was rendered, but in vain. The bodies of the girls were recovered the next morning.

A young boy named Wilhelm, about 14, living at 197 Hester st, N Y, attempted to commit suicide on Mon by shooting himself through the heart with a pistol. He had just returned from his work to his dinner, when he went into a room & discharged a pistol at his breast. His recovery is doubtful.

Robt Whitlock, of Albany, committed suicide on Fri by hanging himself in his room. He was only 17 years of age.

Ralph Whitehead, an Englishman, was found drowned in French river, near Webster, Mass, a few days since. He had previously offered a man $200 to kill him. The deceased was of intemperate habits, which led to insanity.

The Norwalk Gaz states that a little girl 8 years old, Harriet Sherwood, on Jul 28, was killed when she tried to enter the school house through a window, when she was caught by the neck by the window coming down upon her, & when found life was extinct.

Mrd: on Aug 13, by Rev U Ward, John S Hopkins, of Gtwn, to Miss Hester E Dashiell, of Gtwn.

Died: Jun 28, at **Burnside**, his residence, in Granville Co, N C, Patrick Hamilton, in his 63rd year.

Hon Caleb B Smith will remove to Cincinnati about Sep 1, where he will devote himself to the practice of the Law, having formed a partnership with the eminent legal firm of Spencer & Corwine. The people of Indiana will regret to lose Mr Smith as a citizen. Ohio & the Queen City may be proud to claim him as a citizen. –Newcastle [Ind] Cour

Wash Corp: 1-Act for the relief of O J Prather: passed. 2-Ptn from Danl Rowland: referred to the Cmte of Claims. 3-Ptn from Jane L Graham & others, for setting curbstones & paving the footway in front of squares 168, 141, & 120: referred to the Cmte on Improvements. 4-Ptn from Collin P Bayliss for remission of a fine: referred to the Cmte of Claims. 5-Bill for the relief of Edw Cowling: referred to the Cmte on Police. 6-Act for the relief of Geo Sinclair: passed. 7-Cmte of Claims: asked to be discharged from the further consideration of the ptn of C L Coltman: agreed to. 8-Ptn from W Jos Smith & others, for curb stone & footway: referred to the Cmte on Improvements. 9-Ptn of John Ousley & others, asking damages for injuries done to their property in square 250, by the late rains: referred to the Cmte on Improvements. 10-Ptn of Geo Parker & others, in relation to drainage: referred to the Cmte on Improvements. 11-Ptn of Capt Jos Smoot & others, in relation to the pavement in front of **Franklin Row**: referred to the Cmte on Improvements. 12-Bill for the relief of Jas B Greenwell: passed.

The Journal des Debats of Jul 27 says that the judgment against M Cabet, the leader of the Icarian colony of communists at Nauvoo, has been reversed by the appellate court, & that he is discharged.

Liberal reward for return of runaway, Thos Lambert, an indented apprentice to the Tin & Sheet-iron business; age is 19 years old. –F Y Naylor, Pa ave

T Drury, wishing to engage in another business, offers his stock of Boots & Shoes at private sale. Call at the old established store, Pa ave, between 19th & 20th sts.

Potomac Fire Ins Co: John Marbury has been chosen the Pres of this Company.

Landon Female Seminary for sale: the subscriber having renewed his connexion with the Va Institute, at Staunton, will sell his Seminary, know as Landon: located in Fred'k Co, Md, on the great mail route to the West, 33 miles from Wash. Address Rev R H Phillips, Staunton, Va.

Lots 21 & 22, in square 127, fronting the residence of Col Abert, containing 13,557 square feet, were sold on Tuesday by Mr Green, auctioneer, to Mr A H Mechlin, at .25 per square foot.

The messenger sent to Maine to ascertain of Mrs Cookson, the supposed murdered woman, was still alive, has sent a dispatch to the magistrate at Pawtucket stating that she is. Her husband was accordingly released, & the question is revived as to the identity of the murdered woman.

Land for sale: the subscriber offers several tracts in PG Co, Md, on the road leading from Wash to Nottingham, from Upper Marlboro to Piscataway, or from Alexandria to Upper Marlboro. The tract vary in size. Apply to Chas B Calvert, Nat'l Hotel, Wash.

Suitable reward will be paid at Mrs Ann Hill's, on H st, between 14th & 15th sts, for the detection of the thief who, on Tuesday, broke into her stable & took a buffalo skin, the coachman's clothes, & other articles.

Important sale of valuable property: on Aug 20, on the premises, the ***Farmers' Hotel***, on the corner of D & 8th st, together with the large brick stable & frame carriage house adjoining: located on lots 1, 2, & part of 3, in square 407, fronting 134½ feet on D st. -Dyer & McGuire, aucts

FRI AUG 15, 1851
Died: on Jul 27, at 27 Paterson st, Kingston, Glasgow, in Scotland, Mary Katherine, daughter of David Munroe, of Wash. D C.

From Calif: 1-A Spanish woman was hung in Downieville, in the Sacramento Valley, for murdering a man named Cannon, on Aug 7. 2-David Hill, from Cortlandt Co, N Y, has been executed at Sonora. On the stand he said that he had robbed & stolen, & done many acts of crime, but had never shed blood, & he threw himself upon the mercy of the people. [No date given-current item.]

Storm at Springfield, Mass on Sat: the house of Mr E Coombes was struck by lightning, & a Frenchman, Louis Lord, employed in Mr Coombes' backyard, was instantly killed. Miss Emmeline Bliss, in the room below, had her shoes ripped off. When off Bristol a boat with 8 persons in it capsized, & 4 drowned: 2 daughters of Mr Rufus Read, ages 16 & 10, of this city; & 2 daughters of Mr Potter, who reside on the island of Prudence, & with whom the family of Mr Read was boarding during the heat of the summer months.

Died: on Jun 30th last, at Sacramento City, Calif, Alfred Howell Tidball, in his 24th year, youngest son of the late Alex'r S Tidball, of Winchester, Va.

The wife of Geo Rives, 449 Commercial st, Boston, died on Thu last from an overdose of laudanum, while suffering from tic doloreux.

The Case of Cookson: the most singular incident connected with the affair is, that the sister of Mrs Cookson, on viewing the deceased body found, was confident it was that of her sister, whose remains she supposed that she recognized not only by her teeth & hair, but by a scar & other marks upon the breast & body. The husband does not appear to have been annoyed at his arrest & detention.

Business stand for rent in Wash, D C: 3 new stores at the corner of 7th st west & Market Space: will be completed & ready for possession on Oct 1. Also for rent, a very large warehouse next to the corner store. Apply to the subscriber, at Miss Briscoe's, south side of Pa ave, between 4½ & 6th sts. –Anne R Dermott

On Fri last, Mr Geo P Riker, merchant, of Montplier, Vt, while on a fishing excursion, slipped from a high rock & fell about 12 feet, striking his head. He died soon after.

U S vs John Day: the reasons for a new trial. First: That N L Adams, one of the jurors in said case, did, before he was sworn as such, form & expressed an opinion; he having said, with an oath, to Richd Brooke, that "a man who would shoot his wife, or had shot his wife, as John Day had done, should be hung without judge or jury," or words to that effect. Second: That the wife & daughter of Mr Wardell, one of the jurors in said case, did visit him, the said Wardell, in private, after the jury had retired to make up their verdict; & did talk with him about the trial. Third: That the said Wardell did communicate a part or the whole of these conversations to Mr Mann, one of the jurors in said case, telling him that the people had said to his [Wardell's] wife & daughter that he [Mann] had perjured himself on this case, & urged this on the said Mann as a reason why he should convict the dfndnt. Fourth: That newspapers containing remarks about the case were obtained by the jury. Fifth: The the knowledge that there was hereditary weakness of mind, or insanity, in said Day's ancestors has come to the knowledge of the dfndnt's counsel since the trial.

Boston, Aug 14. John Stevens, a broker, committed suicide this morning by cutting the main artery of his right leg. He died in his chair.

Very valuable improved property at auction, on Aug 25: 2 lots in square 74, with 3 story brick bldg, & the brick bldg attached to the same, on Pa ave, known by the name of Six Bldg, now in the occupancy of Lts Balch & Porter.
-Dyer & McGuire, aucts

SAT AUG 16, 1851

Jesse Lott, & his brother-in-law, Saml McKinnon, were struck by lightning on Sat last, while in the woods, which caused their instantaneous death. Lott was 28, & young McKinnon 16. –Mobile Herald & Tribune, Aug 7

Negroes killed by lightning: on Jul 23, Mr John Reeves, residing near Bolivar, with 7 negroes, repaired under a large tree when a clap of thunder was heard & lightning struck the tree. Mr Reeves had just been with them, & before the tragedy, went to recover his horse, and then went to the house. At the usual time for returning home, none of the hands made their appearance. They were all found dead by the tree.
-Bolivar [Tenn] Herald

Gen John M Duffield, a well-known citizen of Mississippi, died at New Orleans on Aug 6. He had but the day before returned from Texas.

Com'rs Ofc, Alexandria, Va, Aug 13, 1851. Notice: Richd C Mason, Wm Dodge & Sarah his wife, Mary K Mason, & Lucilla Mason, plntfs, vs Geo T Mason, Wm Brent's Administrator, Geo McGill, the Farmers' & Mechanics' Bank of Gtwn, R C Washington, John Carter, J G Smoot, Benj Hallowell, & Wm Morgan, dfndnts. By a decree of the Circuit Court of Alexandria Co, pronounced on Jun 12, 1851, one of the masters of said Court was directed to inquire & report to the Court the names of the creditors of Richd B Mason, entitled to participate in the assets conveyed by the deed of trust in the proceedings mentioned from said Richd B Mason to the said Richd C Mason, & the nature & amount of their respective claims, & the evidence thereof, together with what interest may be due thereon, respectively. Also whether any & which of them are entitled to any preference in the distributaion of the proceeds of the property conveyed, when the same shall be sold, & the grounds whereon such preference is claimed & allowed. And that said master do cause publication to be made in one or more newspapers, requiring all the creditors of said Richd B Mason, entitled to participate in the proceed of said trust-fund, to appear before him, & prove their respective claims by a certain day by him to be limited, & that in default thereof they will be excluded from all participation in the assets distributable under said deed. On Sep 15, 1851, in the Market-house bldg, Alexandria, Va, the Com'rs will receive the claims of the creditors of Richd B Mason. -Wm C Yeaton, Com'r

Cincinnati, Aug 14. The steamer **Dacotah** exploded at Peoria, Ill, on Sat. She was bound for Minnesota, for the accommodation of a number of settlers who were on board. Killed were Mr Haywood & 2 children; Wm Baker, wife, & child; H Foster, C Van Sykle, 3 children of B Woodworth, H Barnes, & Mr Moffatt.

Mrd: on Thu, by Rev John C Smith, Mr Jos A Blau to Miss Laura V Freeman, all of Wash City.

Mrd: on Aug 12, at the Mansion House, Alexandria, Va, by Rev Elias Harrison, Maj Thos A Harris, of the U S Army, to Miss Imogen Porter, daughter of the late Com Porter, U S Navy.

Died: on Aug 4, at *Stony Harbor*, her late residence, near Piscataway, Md, after a painful illness of 7 months, Mrs Sarah Ann Edelen, consort of the late Raphael C Edelen, in her 53rd year.

Died: on Aug 14, in Bladensburg, Md, Philip F Brown. His funeral is from the residence of his father, at 10 o'clock, today.

Mrs Choate has removed to 4½ st, & Pa ave, where she has Millinery Goods & Ladies Dress Caps constantly on hand.

MON AUG 18, 1851

Since the death of Marshal Sebastiani there now only remain 5 marshals in France. Soult, nominated in 1817; Gerard, in 1830; Reille, in 1849; Jerome Bonaparte, in 1814; & Excelmans, in 1815. Jerome Bonaparte was nominated by the Emperor in 1814, but his appointment was not ratified until after the Revolution, by the Pres of the Republic.

Sad accident in Plympton, Mass, on Sunday last, by which Deacon Lewis Bradford, of the Congregational Church, lost his life. His wagon upset & he was thrown to the ground. He gasped several times & died. It appeared his neck had been broken by the fall. He was 84 years of age, & was Town Clerk at the time of his death, which ofc he had filled for 39 years.

Peter Sky, one of the warrior chiefs of the Onondagas, died at the Castle on Monday last at the advanced age of 96 years. He was a true friend to the U S, & in the war of 1812, when Gen Porter called for volunteers to protect the Niagara frontier, the Onondaga chiefs & warriors were among the first to answer the call. They sustained the whole brunt of the battle of Chippews, under their gallant but unfortunate chief, La Fort, who was killed in the action; while the subject of this notice received a severe & dangerous wound, for which he has since drawn a pension from Gov't. –Syracuse [N Y] Standard, Aug 13.

Rev Dr Stephen Olin, Pres of the Westleyan Univ, at Middletown, Conn, died at that place on Sat, after a long & painful illness. He was one of the most eminent ministers of the Methodist Episcopal Church.

Capt Brower, of the brig **Lowder**, arrived at N Y from the African coast, states that in Apr last the brig **Englishman**, Capt Harris, of Bristol, England, was capsized in a tornado off Fernando Po. There were about 30 persons on board, & only one of whom, a native of Africa, was saved. He was picked up, floating on a spar, on the 3rd day after the disaster by an English ship from Caenarvon bound for Fernando Po. Among those on board the **Englishman**, were Rev G W Simpson & lady, of the Presbyterian Board of Missions of N Y, & Mrs Harris, wife of the captain.

At Boston, on Aug 14, Edw Everett, of this city, was thrown from his carriage, his horses having become unmanageable through fright. He was dragged a short distance & received a wound on the back of the head. He was removed to the house of his relative, Mr Jas Boyle, 18 Harvard st, with whom he was residing for the present. His situation is a critical one.

The decision of Judge Warden, in the application of Fanny Wright D'Arusmont against her husband for alimony, was delivered on Monday last. She was divorced from her husband by a decree obtained in Tenn courts, & filed a bill to recover back the entire or a large proportion of the property deeded by her to her husband as her trustee, & in the opinion delivered Judge Warden allows her alimony in a sum equal to the amount which she would be entitled to under the trust deed, $1,000 per annum. The Court did not express any opinion as to the force of the trust deed, & made the allowance, not as a provision under the trust deed, but as alimony pendente life.

The Whigs of Anne Arundel Co, Md, met in Convention at Annapolis on Tue, & made the following nominations of candidates.
For the House of Delegates: Thos R Kent, Gabriel H Duvall, & Robt Lemmon, jr.
Clerk of the Circuit Court: Jos H Nicholson; Register of Wills: Benj E Gantt
Judges of the Orphans' Court: Dr S Gambrill, Dr Geo A Barber, & Noble Stockett.
State's Atty: B T B Worthington; Surveyor: John Duvall
County Com'rs: Danl T Hyde, Gassaway Winterson, P W Wainwright, Wm Williams, Eli Gaither, & John Sellman.

The diplomas conferred as rewards of merit upon the youth of the public schools was printed from an engraved plate designed & executed by Mr John H Arnold, a young artist of Wash City. The principal figure in the vignette embellishment is Geo Washington in early manhood, equipped as a surveyor, with compass & Jacob staff. In the distance, in shadow, is seen a new rising Washington Monument, surrounded by a halo.

Rittenhouse Academy, corner of 3rd & Indiana ave. O C Wright, Principal; Assistants: A G Carothers, & D L Shorey. Prof D E Groux, Teacher of Modern Languages. Prof R Gibson, Teacher of Drawing. Apply to the Principal, or to Mr Carothers, or at the Bookstore of W M Morrison.

Mrd: on Aug 14, at Balt, by Rev Mr Tarring, E Dorsey Etchison, of that city, to Miss Rachel A Stephens, of Wash.

Died: on Aug 15, of typhoid fever, Edmund B Darnall, in his 20th year, youngest son of Francis I & Mary Darnall, PG Co, Md.

Died: on Aug 12, at **Powhatan Hill**, the residence of Col Edw T Taylor, in King Geo Co, Va, after a protracted illness, in her 23rd year, Mrs Louisa R T Jenifer, the wife of Jas L Jenifer, & daughter of Wm H Taylor, of **Mount Airy**.

Wholesale Watch & Jewelry Store: H Miller & Co, Importers, & Manufacturers, have leased the old stand formerly occupied by Messrs Canfield, Brother & Co, at Chas & Balt sts, #227, to be opened about Jul 20. –L H Miller & Co

Ran away from the subscriber on Aug 11, John Wilson, an indented apprentice to the Tin & Sheet-iron business. Age 17 years. A liberal reward will be paid to any person returning him to F Y Naylor, Pa ave.

TUE AUG 19, 1851
The following gentlemen have been appointed by the South Carolina Institute as Delegates to the World's Fair in London, viz:

Hon Wm Aiken	Joshua Lazarus	John W Rice
Chas D Carr	Wm Lebby	E M Seabrook
Dr Peter C Gaillard	W M Porcher	Richd Stone
Wm Gregg	F Richards	Chas Warley

Tennessee election: the Congressional Delegation will stand as follows, being a Whig gain of 1 member, as compared with the last Congress:

Andrew Johnson, Democrat, re-elected	Wm Cullum, Whig, gain
Albert G Watkins, Whig, re-elected	Isham G Harris, Democrat, re-elected
Josiah M Anderson, Whig, re-elected	Fred'k P Stanton, Democrat, re-elected
Geo W Jones, Democrat, re-elected	Christopher H Williams, Whig, re-elected
Jas H Thomas, Democrat, re-elected	
Meredith P Gentry, Whig, re-elected	

$5 reward for lost or stolen dog, a large dog of mixed Newfoundland & St Bernard's breed. -Geo Watterston

Indiana election: the Delegation to the next Congress:
Andrew Lockhart, Dem
Cyrus L Dunham, Dem
John L Robinson, Dem
Saml W Parker, Whig
Thos A Hendricks, Dem
Willis A Gorman, Dem
John G Davis, Dem
Danl Mace, Dem
Graham N Fitch, Dem
Saml Brenton, Whig

The <u>Patapsco Female Institute</u>, near Ellicott's Mills, Md, Mrs Lincoln Phelps, Principal: will re-open Sep 25.

Died: on Jul 11, 1851, at **Shepherd's Hill**, Caroline Co, Va, John Woolfolk, after an illness of 15 days, in his 47th year.

The Providence Post says that Martin Van Buren is as buoyant & elastic now as he was 20 years ago; & adds that one reason perhaps is, that he had not drank intoxicating liquors in the last 30 years, & is remarkably regular in every thing save his politics.

WED AUG 20, 1851
Ranaway on Aug 16, from my residence, **Missouri Mills**, 4½ miles from Dumfries, Pr Wm Co, Va, my negro man Geo Posey. He was purchased of Mr Wm Beaty, near Front Royal, Warren Co, Va. Mr Beaty was the executor of Thos John, of the same county. I will give a reward of $50 if taken in the State of Va, or $75 if taken in any other State. -Thos Golding

The Peoria Republican give the particulars of a late disaster: explosion of the steamer **Dakotah**, on Aug 9, bound for Minnesota Territory. Henry Barns, part owner, dangerously injured; Benj Woolworth, Capt, dangerously injured, recovery doubtful; Alpheus Chapman, Engineer; John Selby, M Thompson, David Robbins, Miss Amanda Cutler, Reuben McKee, Edgar Chase, & Milton Howe, dangerously injured; Mrs Barnes & child, Mrs Chapman & child, Mrs Selby, Mr Moffit & wife, Mrs Hayward & 2 children, Mrs Thompson & 3 children, Jas Lathrie, Mr Emmons, Edw Roe, John Palmer, Abner Kenwick, Amos Hopkins, Pitts Hopkins, slightly injured; a child of Benj Woolworth, child of Henry Barnes, 7 years old, child of Mr Moffit, 9 years old, dead; Mr Haywood & 2 children, Mr Baker, wife, & child, Miss Harriet Foster, Chas Van Winkle, not found. The **Dakotah** was owned by Messrs Franklin Warson & Henry Barnes.

Cumberland Civilian: on Sun last, as the canal boat was passing through the Four Locks, below the Tunnel, a fight sprung up on board, between a white man named Snyder, attached to one of the boats, & George, a negro, belonging to the estate of Henry Bevans, deceased. In a short time they found themselves in the lock, & both drowned. Their bodies were afterwards found in the lock.

Mr Edw Everett, of Wash City, who was thrown from a carriage in Boston on Wed, is recovering from the effects of the accident.

Chestertown jail, Aug 6. Letter from a convict to his mother. My Dear Mother: I have seen you for the last time in this world; on the day after tomorrow I shall close my life on the gallows. I acknowledge on many occasions I sinned against you, & set at defiance your words of reproof & advice; & often have you cautioned me against the paths I was pursuing, & predicted that they would terminate in a disgraceful death. I can say nothing to comfort or console you, except to protest my innocence. I enclose you a lock of my hair, which I hope you will keep in memory of your unfortunate & miserable son. –Wm Shelton

Orphans Court of Wash Co, D C. Letters of administration de bonis non on the personal estate of Robt T Brown, late of Wash Co, deceased. –Adam C Brown, adm de bonis non

Wash Corp: 1-Ptn from E F Queen, for the erection of a patent balance hay-scales, at or near the Northern Market: referred to the Cmte on Police. 2-Ptn from J F Wolland & others, for improvement of N st: referred to the Cmte on Improvements. 3-Act for the relief of Geo W Steward: passed. 4-Nomination of Geo T McGlue, as scavenger of the First Ward: rejected. 5-Ptn of Mrs M C Davis, asking remuneration for damage done to her property by the late heavy rains, by the grading of I st: referred to the Cmte of Claims. 6-Cmte of Claims: asked to be discharged from the further consideration of the ptn of A Addison: agreed to.

Valuable farm for sale: on Sep 15, the Farm on which Saml M Beall formerly resided, on the road leading from Seneca to Gtwn: farm divided into 2 tracts, one of 165 acres, the other 60 acres. Improvments are a comfortable frame dwlg, stables, barn, & other out-bldgs. Letters address to Rockville Post Ofc, will be attended to. –Oratio Clagett

Postmaster Gen est'd the following new Post Ofcs for week ending Aug 16, 1851.

Ofc	County, State	Postmaster
Rawson	Cattaraugus, N Y	Josiah O Perry
New Boston	Lewis, N Y	Thos Taylor
West Salem	Mercer, Pa	Jas W Mossman
Pocahontas	Somerset, Pa	Philip Boyts
New Upton	Gloucester, Va	Edw Sears
Ashton	Carroll Parish, La	A Karppe
Tomahawk	Searcy, Ark	Esaias Baker
Millard	Jefferson, Ind	John T Hamilton

Name Changed: Farmington, Ritchie Co, Va, changed to Oxford.

Copartnership: G W Yerby has associated with him in the Dry Goods business E P Miller, of Jefferson Co, Va: business will be the firm of Yerby & Miller.

John Armstrong, a well-known citizen of Maysville, Ky, died at his residence in that city on Tue last. He was a resident of Maysville for nearly half a century, & by his energy & intelligent industry had amassed a very large estate.

U S Surveying steamer **Jefferson**, Sea-Bear Bay, Patagonia, May 31, 1851. Steamer wrecked on her way to Calif. Left Montevideo, May 19; gale on May 25; ship knocked on her beam ends. We reached the nearest island on May 28, completely worn out, & our poor little ship a perfect wreck. No inhabitants here, other then a few men digging guano on Penguin Island, about 7 miles distant. We have been ordered upon a survey of the ship, & were unanimous in condemning her. We will come in a ship the captain has chartered, & expect to sail for the States in about 6 weeks. -Cor Phil Evening Bulletin

On Aug 22, I sell at at the Parsonage near Rock Creek Church, the household effects of the Rev Henry W Woods, late rector. Also, a first rate carriage & family horse. -A Green, auctioneer

THU AUG 21, 1851

The extensive establishment of Elisha W Thompson, at Keyport, N J, known as the Keyport Pavilion, was destroyed by fire on Aug 10. It was a favorite resort during the bathing season. Mr Thompson's loss is about $11,000.

Rev Mr Bissey was struck by lightning in the Methodist Church at New London, Chester Co, on Sunday last, when he had just concluded his sermon. He died instantly. Mr Bissey was esteemed by the Church, in which he has for many years been a faithful laborer. –Phil Penn

Mr Jacob Quackenbush, on Sat week, was at Keyport, with his wife & friends, for the purpose of bathing. While bathing he was suddenly discovered drowning, & before those present could reach him life was extinct. –Monmouth [N J] Enquirer

Mrd: on Aug 19, by Rev W T Eva, Colville Terrett, U S Navy, & Miss M Anna F Mathews, eldest daughter of the late Capt Wm P Mathews, of Balt, Md.

Mrd: on Jul 14, at *Oakwood*, near Fayette, Missouri, by Rev Mr Dunn, Horace Everett, of Gainesville, Ala, to Mary, eldest daughter of A Leonard, of the former place.

Mrd: on Aug 13, at the seat of Capt O H Berryman, Fauquier, Va, by Rev A Compton, Fenton Mercer Ewell to Miss Alberta Otwayanna Reynolds.

Died: on Jul 15, suddenly, at Gtwn, D C, to the inexpressible regret of his family & a large circle of friends & associates, Dr Wm Sothroron, in his 65th year.

Died: on Aug 5, at **Fort Snelling**, Minnesota Territory, Sarah D Hendrickson, wife of Capt T Hendrickson, U S Army.

Died: on Aug 19, Sarah Ellen, infant daughter of Wm Henry & Mgt Kelly, & grandchild of Edw & Susan McCubbin, of Wash City.

Utica, Aug 18. Jeremiah Blake, a clerk in the store of E Classen, of this city, was drowned at the foot of the first flight of stairs, at the Falls, this afternoon. He was there on a visit, with his wife, who was ascending the stairs a little before him, & upon turning around to speak to him she discovered him struggling in the water, from which it was impossible to rescue him.

The copartnership existing under the firm of J W Baden & Brother is this day dissolved by mutual consent. Persons indebted to the late firm are to make payment to J W Baden, at the old stand, Pa ave, near 6th st. –J W Baden, T E Baden
[J W Baden has purchased the entire stock of the firm, & will continue the Hardware Business at the old stand.]
+
A Card-I have this day sold my stock of Hardware to Lindsley & Baden, who will continue the business at the old stand. I am retiring from the business.
-R E Lindsley
+
Howard Lindsley & Thos E Baden will conduct business at the old stand, on Pa ave, between 9th & 10th sts.

On Aug 8, Wm Stafford accidentally shot Mr David Rea, in Shelby township, Ia. Both men went wild turkey hunting when Rea shot Stafford. Mr Rea has left a wife & a large family of children to lament his untimely end.

<u>Washington Seminary</u>, D C: will recommence on Sep 1. –Saml Barber, Pres

FRI AUG 22, 1851
Fire Ins: Potomac Ins Co, Gtwn, D C. Directors: Gtwn:

John Marbury	Joshua Riley	Wm G Ridgely
Robt Read	Stephen Cassin	Wm Clabaugh
Richd Cruikshank	Wm Emmert	
Jeremiah Orme	Wm H Edes	
<u>Washington:</u>		
Wm B Todd	Wm P Johnston	John Purdy

John Marbury, Pres; Henry King, Sec

W O Berry & Wm E Beach have formed a copartnership under the firm of Berry & Beach, in the Tinning & Sheet-iron business in all its branches.

The Misses Quincy will resume their duties of teaching on Sep 1. A few children can be accommodated with board from Mon to Sat, or permanently if desired. Apply at their residence, **Franklin Row**.

SAT AUG 23, 1851

The steamer **Habanero**, while cruising off Bahia Honda, 40 miles west of Havana, captured a part of 50 patriots, who were unarmed in 4 boats, steering for New Orleans. They were carried to Havana, & on the 16th instant, were placed on board another Spanish frig lying in port, & were executed the next morning, by being shot on the public road in Havana, in the presence of 20,000 spectators. List of the executed:

Col W S Clendennen
Capt F S Server/Sewer
Capt Victor Kerr
Capt T B Veacy
Lt Jas Brandt
Lt J O Brice/Bruce
Privates:
W H Howes
Saml Mills
Edw Rulman
Geo A Arnold
B J Wregy
Wm Wiseman/Niseman
Anselmo Torres Hernandez
Patrick Dillon
Thos Hearsey
Saml Reed
H T Finne/Vinne
M Phillips
Jas L Manville
G M Green
J Salmon
Napoleon Collins
N H Fisher
Wm Chilling
G A Cook

Lt Thos C James
Dr John Fisher
Dr K A Touquignet/Tourniquet
Sergeant J Whitesides
Sgt A M Catchett/Cochett
Adj R C Stamford/Stanford

S O Jones
M H Hall/Ball
Jas Buxet
Robt Caldwell
C C Wm Smith
A Ross
B B Ronke/Brourke
John Christoles/Christdes
Wm B Little
Robt Cantley
John G Sanks
Jas Stanton
Thos Harnot
Alex'r McIleer/McIlcer
John Stubbs
John Ellis
Wm Hogan
Chas A Robinson

*The names following / are the spelling of the same name found in the Aug 25th newspaper.

The creditors of Chas Wilson, miller, Gtwn, D C, are to produce to the subscriber by the first Monday of Nov next their respective claims, showing the amount due, & proved by affidavit. –John Marbury, trustee

Foreign Item: Harriet Lee, the author of the Canterbury Tales, once so famous, died lately at the advanced age of 95. It was from these tales that Byron took the plot & characters of his Werner, reproducing the work with the most servile fidelity to the incidents & personages.

Notice: the creditors of Wm Crawford, jr, deceased, late of Gtwn, D C, are to produce to the subscriber by the first Monday in Nov next their claims against his estate, showing the amount due, & proved by affidavit. –John Marbury, trustee

Dwlg house & lots for sale: on north side of Prospect st, Gtwn, opposite the residence of Geo Poe, jr. –John Marbury

Mrd: on Aug 21, by Rev Wm B Edwards, Wm H Jones to Mary F, 2nd daughter of Chas L Coltman, all of Wash City.

Died: on Aug 22, Dorothy H, widow of Jno Storer, in her 81st year. Her funeral will take place from the residence of her son-in-law, J K Hanson, today at 4 o'clock.

Died: in Aug 19, at the residence of Rev C M Callaway, Jefferson Co, Va, Sarah Virginia, youngest daughter of Saml D & Matilda S King, aged 3 years & 27 days.

MON AUG 25, 1851
Isaac R Harrington, Postmaster for the City of Buffalo, died at that place on Aug 20.

From Oregon: the Oregon Spectator confirms the death of Capt Stewart, in an action with the Indians, on Jun 17, at Table Rock, on Rogue River, 12 or 15 miles from the traveled road. The Indians were lying in ambush, & fired on the riflemen as they passed. A conflict ensued, in which about 20 Indians were killed, & many were wounded. Capt Stewart was wounded with an arrow, & survived till the next day. Lt Peck was also severely wounded.

The man who went over Niagara Falls, several days since, was Jeremiah McMurray, a gardener, from Grand Island. He had been to Chippewa to sell vegetables, &, being intoxicated there, fell asleep in his canoe, & was not aroused until the boat reached the first rapids, when it was too late.

Died: on Aug 23, by accidental drowning, Chas S West, aged 29 years. His funeral is today at 3 o'clock, from the residence of his father, Mr John West, on 7th st.

TUE AUG 26, 1851
Col Ross, of the 7th Infty, died at Boston on Sunday at the Revere House. He was formerly of Md.

Andrew McCorrie, aged 22 years, of Fall River, was washed off the rocks at Seaconnet Point, while fishing on Wed last, & drowned. Mr Treat, who was with him, made an unsuccessful attempt to save him. Gen Combs was also washed from the rocks yesterday, & came near being lost.

Sale of mountain lands: by authority of the last will & testament of Corbin Griffin, deceased: sale on Sep 21, before the Courthouse door of Hardy Co, a tract containing 4,225 acres, lying on New-Creek Mountain, in Hardy Co, Va. Apply to Wm Seymour, Moorefield, or to the subscriber at Wmsburg, Va. –Robt P Waller, exc of Corbin Griffin, deceased.

Valuable farm at auction: on Aug 28, on the premises, *Conjurer's Defeat*, on Oxen Run, Wash Co, now occupied by Mr Sears & the widow Evans, containing 180 acres. -Dyer & McGuire, aucts

Mrd: on Aug 24, by Rev L F Morgan, Mr A H Markland, of Ky, to Miss M L Simms, daughter of Mr Sampson Simms, of Wash City.

Died: at the residence of P F Bacon, Washington F Murray, of Louisville, Ky, aged 28 years. His funeral is today at 4 o'clock. [No death date given.]

WED AUG 27, 1851
Stolen from my room over Mr Lloyd's Confectionary Store, yesterday, a Gold Hunting Watch, made by Tobias, #1905. It can easily be told by a small dark spot on the face. A liberal reward will be given for its recovery. –E Downing

Orphans Court of Wash Co, D C. Letters of administration on the personal estate of David Weaver, late of said county, deceased. –Henry Weaver

Notice: all papers relative to the estate of the late Jesse E Dow, have been left in my hands, & persons having business with the administrator, or wishing to settle claims due to the estate, will please call on me. –B B French, Atty at Law

The undersigned, having relinquished his interest in the Gtwn Dyeing Establishment, informs that he has purchased the Dyeing Establishment lately occupied by L J Denham, on Pa ave, between, 9th & 10th sts. –John T Berkley

Wanted to hire, 2 respectable women, either colored or white, one for a cook & the other for house work. Apply to Misses Rooker's Seminary, 6th & F sts.

Postmaster Gen est'd the following new Post Ofcs for week ending Aug 23, 1851.

Ofc	County, State	Postmaster
Smith's Ridge	Farifield, Ct	Chas Baraclough
Feura Bush	Albany, N Y	Robt Coughtry
Indian Fields	Albany, N Y	Judson Lamereux
Somers Centre	West Chester, N Y	Wm E Teed
Constantia	Delaware, Ohio	L R Ryant
Bonyer's Knob	Fayette, Va	Ruth Hughart
Clay's Point	Lewis, Va	Adam H Varner
Sugar Hill	Marion District, S C	Neal Carmichael
Winchester	Macon, Ga	Jas A Stubbs
Troublesome	Clinch, Ga	Jesse P Prescott
Gum Swamp	Pulaski, Ga	Chas Love
Etna	Paulding, Ga	L P Garrison
Sharp Top	Cherokee, Ga	Ladson Worley
Bulluetah	Leake, Miss	Lewis J Sparkman
Pearl River	Copish, Miss	L Kennedy
Palentine	Benton. Ala	Geo H Borden
Cypress Top	Harris, Texas	David Cole
Point Monterey	Cass, Texas	Norphet Gripton
Milo	Bradley, Ark	John Varnel
Santa Fe	Poinsett, Ark	A D Puckett
Taylorville	Andrew, Mo	Isaiah Bennett
Breckville	Madison, Ky	Absalom B Stivers
Pecolota	San Miguel, N Mex	Wm H Moore
San Miguel	San Miguel, N Mex	Peak Senical

Names Changed: 1-Rosevelt, Oswego Co, N Y, changed to Pennellville.
2-Putnamville, Putnam Co, Missouri, changed to Hartford.
3-Bucklin, Winnebago, Ill, changed to Burritt.

On Aug 19, in Brighton, 5 miles from Cleveland, Ohio, the two story wood house of Mr Onacker caught fire from coals used for cooking. Their five boys ages 2, 11, 12, 14, & 16 perished. Mr & Mrs Onacker had only time to snatch up their sixth child, & last born, a mere infant, who slept with them. –Cleveland Plaindealer

Louisville Journal: a few days since, in Davis Co, in that State, Mr Howard T Taylor & Dr Wilmot were on a hunting excursion, when the gun in the hands of Mr Wilmot accidentally went off, & lodged in the right breast of Taylor. Taylor soon recovered from his fainting fit, but has since been wholly out of his right mind.

For rent: 2 rooms, suitable for ofcs, next door to Adams' Express Ofc. Inquire of J P Pepper, on the premises.

Rev H J Durbin, of the Methodist Episcopal Church, & agent of the American Bible Society for Southern Indians, died a few days ago. He had started from Greensberg, Ind, after preaching, for Vernon, when a storm came up while he was riding through the woods. A tree fell on him, breaking his thigh, & otherwise injuring him. He managed to reach a house, but he died in 4 or 5 days afterwards.

Wash Corp: 1-Ptn of C McCarthy, praying remission of a fine: referred to the Cmte of Claims. 2-Ptn of Lewis Johnson & others, for setting curb & footways on G st: referred to the Cmte on Improvements. 3-Ptn of Jas Flaherty & others, remonstrating against the enclosure of certain streets: referred to the Cmte on Improvements. 4-Cmte of Claims: act for the relief of Benj Blair: read twice. 5-Act to pay a balance due Danl Leakins: passed. 6-Cmte on Improvements: ptn of H Forstkamp & others, for curb stones & footway paved in front of square 423: passed.

Boston Traveller: Mr Wm W Wilson, agent of the U S for the detection of counterfeiters, has arrested in Palmyra, Me, True F Young & Jas French, on charge of counterfeiting. French is said to be a person of some wealth; Young was pardoned out of the State prison a year or more since in order to testify at N Y in the case of Ashley, charged with passing counterfeit money.

Improvements on 7th st: at the n w corner of 7th & Pa ave is the handsome range of bldgs, 5 stories in height, building for Miss Ann Dermott, & are in a state of rapid progress. The adjoining property had been purchased by Mr Saml Fowler, who will erect 2 elegant stores. Mr Coyle's enlarge & improved warehouse will have a new iron front. The firm of Messrs Selden, Withers, Lathan & Co, have purchased the banking house property next to the Patriotic Bank, & are now extending it to 4 stories in height. Opposite these improvements we notice that Mr Wm G Deale has enlarged the store he recently purchased. Mr John C McKelden has rendered the adjoining store handsome by a renovated front, with a large bow window. Large gas-pipes are now being deposited along 7th st, preparatory to a permanent & abundant supply for that section of Wash City.

For rent: 3 story brick house on C st, between 4½ & 6th sts. –Louisa Hunter

Mrd: Sunday, by Rev Mr Marks, Mr Chas W Smith to Miss Eliz Brightwell, both of PG Co, Md.

Mrd: on Aug 14, at St Louis, Lt A Read, U S N, to Miss Constance, daughter of Maj E Steen, U S A.

Mrd: on Aug 23, by Rev Mr Alig, Timothy Murphy to Mgt Donohue.

Died: on Aug 25, Priscilla Fraser, in her 63rd year. She has been a resident of Wash for 45 years. Her funeral is today at 2 o'clock, from her late residence on Half st west, near the Eastern Branch.

Died: on Aug 14, at Louisille, Ky, after 9 hours' illness of cholera, Wm Thompson, aged nearly 13, eldest son of Martha P & Saml Campbell, formerly of Middleburg, Va.

Died: on Aug 14, in the Navy Yard at Pensacola, after a long illness, Geo Lyndall, formerly of Wash City. A large circle of friends mourn his loss, & deeply sympathize with his afflicted widow & children.

Died: on Aug 23, Effie Kate, youngest child of Robt T & Susan Bassett, aged 1 year.

Timothy Divison #1 Sons of Temperance: meeting this evening at 8 o'clock.
-H H Helfer, R S

Mrs H McCormick & sister will resume their school on Sep 1. Terms made known at their residence on 4½ st, south of the avenue, 4th house in the row belonging to Mr Ward.

THU AUG 28, 1851
Mrd in Ashe, N C, on Aug 13, Mr Wm Walters [a dwarf, about 23 years old, & not more than 30 inches tall, & weighs 35 pounds] to Miss Eliz Sawyers, [a full grown woman,] daughter of Martin Sawyers, all of Wythe Co. –Wytherville Republican

A gentleman who resides in Choctaw Co, tells of a difficulty that occurred at Nicholson's store, on Aug 9, between Col John James, the Union candidate at the recent election for the Legislature in Wash Co, & Mr Wm Nicholson; a fight ensued, in which the latter discharged both barrels of a double-barrelled gun at Mr James, killing him instantly. The matter grew out of the election, in which Mr James was defeated. –Mobile Register

Bedford [Va] Sentinel: a boy named Luster, in attempting the other day to carve his name on the Natural Bridge higher than any other, lost his footing & fell 150 feet to his death. [Sep 4th newspaper: the boy fell 25 feet, was not a boy at all, but a young man, & was alive & well 10 days afterwards.]

A girl employed in Mr Dallery's jewelry factor at Wmsburg, N Y, was filling a lighted lamp with camphine, when it exploded. Jane Hanna was severely burnt & died in 3 hours. Jane Thomas was seriously burnt.

Hon Jas McDowell, a Rep in Congress for several years past from the State of Va, & formerly for some years Govn'r of that State, died at his residence near Lexington, Va, on Sunday last, at about the age of 56 years.

U S Patent Ofc: ptn of Chas Porter, of Lynn, Mass, administrator of the estate of E S Curtis, late of Boston, Mass, deceased, praying for the extension of a patent granted to said E S Curtis for the improvement in gristmills, for 7 years from the expiration of said patent, which takes place on Nov 23, 1851. –Thos Ewbank, Com'r of Patents

By order of distrain, & to me directed, from Frances Webb, against the goods & chattels of John Cullum, to satisfy rent due & in arrears, I have this day, Aug 23, 1851, seized sundry articles, to be sold at public sale for cash, on Aug 30. –J A Ratcliffe, Bailiff

Died: on Aug 21, at Fredericksburg, Va, Jas D Harrow, in his 60th year, editor of the Va Herald, one of the oldest papers in the country, with which he became connected early in the present century. For many years he was a member of the Presbyterian Church, & lived a Christian life.

Orphans Court of Wash Co, D C. Letters of administration on the personal estate of Geo B Scott, late of said county, deceased. –Rachel Scott, admx

Miss Heaney's Academy, for the instruction of Young Ladies in the English & French languages, will be reopened on Oct 1. The School, in or near C st, will be soon made known. Address Miss Heaney or Mr Saml Carusi through the City Post Ofc.

New Orleans, Aug 23. Letters received here from Capt Kerr, Maj Stanford, & others who were shot, blame Lopez for abandoning Col Crittenden's company, of whose capture you have already been advised.

FRI AUG 29, 1851
Gtwn Classical & Scientific Academy will resume on Sep 1, at the residence of the undersigned, on West st, near High. –T W Simpson, A M, Principal

Lt Col R H Ross, of the 7th Infty U S Army, died at the Revere House, in Boston, on Sunday, of chronic diarrhea, & his remains were deposited in *Forest Hill Cemetery*, on Monday, to await the final disposition fo his friends. The burial service was performed at the tomb by Rev Mr Lambert, of the Navy. The deceased was a native of Md, & about 45 years of age. He distinguished himself in Mexico, & was brevetted for his gallant conduct at Matamoros, Monterey, & the taking of the city of Mexico, under Gen Scott. His funeral was attended by Col Mansfield, Majors Johnson & Wyse, Capt Brown, Lts Blount & Patten, Dr Murray, & others.
–Boston Pat

Orphans Court of Wash Co, D C. Letters of administration on the personal estate of Geo B Scott, late of said county, deceased. –Rachel Scott, admx

Norfolk, Aug 26. Com Parker, cmder-in-chief of the Home Squadron, yesterday received dispatches from Washington to proceed without delay to the coast of Cuba; & the U S steam frig **Saranac**, Capt Pendegrast, with Com Parker on board, accordingly sailed today for Havana. Orders were also received to dispatch the U S sloop-of-war **Plymouth** to the same destination, but unfortunately the vessel had been at sea some hours [bound to the East Indies] before the order was received. The U S frig **Columbia**, now in ordinary at the Gosport navy yard, is to be fitted for sea with all possible dispatch.

Chief Justice Shaw, at Boston, disposed of a novel case in that city last week. Mr Eben Poole, of Bangor, after permitting his child by a former wife to remain in the care & custody of her grandparents for 10 years, without providing in any manner or degree for her support, attempted to gain possession of her by habeas corpus. The Judge was of the opinion that the interests of the child would be best promoted by allowing her to remain with the grandparents, & that the petitioner had waived his parental right to her custody by having abandoned her so long a time.

By the death of the Duchess of Leuchtenberg, who was a Bavarian Princess, & wife of Eugene Beauharnois, the son of the Empress Josephine, the jewels presented to Josephine by the Emperor Napoleon, & which had since belonged to the Duchess of Leuchtemberg, now become the property of her son the Duke of Leuchtenburg, whose wife is a Russian Imperial Princess, so that poor Josephine's diamonds will in future sparkle on the person of a daughter of the Russian Czar. –German paper

The undersigned [recently Professor of vocal & instrumental music in St Timothy's Hall, Catonsville, Md] informs that he will give lessons on the Piano, Organ, & other instruments. Apply at his residence at Mrs Clair's, over Bank of Wash, or at the Music store of Mrs Anderson, Pa ave. –J Theo McKenna, Organist, St Matthews Church.

Household & kitchen furniture at auction: on Sep 3, in the 2 houses occupied by Mrs Selden on 13th st, between E & F sts. –N Callan, trustee -Dyer & McGuire, aucts

Mrd: Aug 26, by Rev J G Butler, Wm F G Tableman to Miss Sophia L Smith, both of Wash City.

Mrd: Aug 28, by Rev J K Eckard, Geo Wm Yerby to Mary E Phillips, of Harrisburg, Pa.

Orphans Court of Wash Co, D C. Letters testamentary on the personal estate of Dorathy Hanson Storer, late of said county, deceased. –R C Weightman, exc

SAT AUG 30, 1851

The Classical & English School at St Matthew's Church will be opened on Sep 4, & conducted by a Graduate of Gtwn College. Inquire of Rev Jas B Donelan, Rector.

Cincinnati, Sunday last. Barnard Houseman, in a partial state of intoxication, stabbed his son Lewis, mortally wounding him. Barnard was soon arrested. Lewis, a watchman, asked his father not to make so much noise, & this enraged his father.

New Orleans, Aug 22. The schnr **Fairy** arrived today from Havana, having on board the bodies of Col Crittenden, Capt Victor Kerr, & Lt Jas Brandt, who were executed at Havana on Aug 16.

New Orleans, Aug 26. The city is now quiet. A thousand Liberators are waiting for conveyance to Cuba. Gen Felix Huston commands them.

Hon Luke Woodbury, lately nominated as the Democratic candidate for Govn'r of N H, committed suicide by hanging himself to a tree at Antrim, N H, on Aug 27. No cause is assigned for the act. [Sep 2nd newspaper: Mr Woodbury returned from a ride in company with a little son of B B Mussey, of Boston; went to the barn, unharnessed & put up his horse; returned to the house, inquired of his wife & informed she was in the garden. He went to the barn, & remained so long that his wife went to the barn & found it locked. She sent to his brother's store for a clerk, who, upon search, found the body of Mr Woodbury suspended from a timber by a splice rein. Life was extinct. Mr W was about 50 years of age, was a graduate of Dartmouth College, & has been Judge of Probate of this county for several years. He had property of some $25,000, a splendid residence in Antrim. He leaves an estimable wife, but no children. Three of his brothers reside in Antrim, & likewise his mother. It is said the Judge wished to be free from the cares of ofc, & remain a private citizen.]

Died: on Aug 29, at his residence, near Rock Creek Church, Maj Geo A Walker, Paymaster U S Marine Corps, in his 51st year. His funeral is on Sunday, at 10 o'clock.

Died: on Aug 22, at Fayetteville, N C, Capt Wm H Bayne, for 11 years past the Editor of the North Carolinian. The deceased was a native of Wash, D C, but has been a resident of Fayetteville since Jul 4, 1840, at which time he took charge of the "Carolinian." He left a wife & 5 small children to mourn the loss of a kind protector & friend.

School for Young Ladies, 13th near C st, will resume on Sep 15. –Susan Russell

Household & kitchen furniture at auction: on Sep 5, at the residence of A K Parris, on F st, between 13th & 14th sts. -A Green, auctioneer

Geo Pharaoh was executed at West Chester, Pa, on Fri, for the murder of Rachel Sharpless, committed on Sep 28 last. He shot her dead with a gun, while she was unlocking the school house door at West Goshen, Chester Co, she being a teacher there. The wadding used on the occasion matched a torn copy of the Sat Evening Post, which was found in his possession when arrested. His sole motive was to obtain a gold watch belonging to the deceased. The mother of Pharaoh was sister of Jabez Boyd, who was hung at Westchester on Nov 21, 1845, for the murder of Wesley Patton, a lad. Pharaoh was hung on the same gallow, with the same rope.

C W Schuermann, Prof of Music, who for 4 years was an instructor of music in Wash City, has during a stay of some months in Germany, with a view to improving himself in his art, determined to return to Wash, & will resume his instructions by Sep.

TUE SEP 2, 1851
Gtwn College: classes & Lectures resume on Aug 15. –Chas H Stonestreet, Pres.

The Buffalo papers resport that Dr A F Fitch & Wm Gunn, two of the conspirators on trial for injuries to the Michigan Central Railroad Co, died in the hospital of the Sisters of Charity at Detroit on Mon last. Geo W Gay, the person alleged to have fired the depot, died some time ago. –N Y Commercial Advertiser

Mrd: on Sep 1, in Wash City, by Rev J W French, Lt Col Benj F Larned, Deputy Paymaster Gen U S Army, to Eliz R Larned, of Wash City.

Elihu Cresswell, lately deceased, by the terms of his will left his estate to his mother, but liberated his slaves, 51 in number, enjoining upon his executors, Messrs John E Caldwell & L E Simons, of New Orleans, the duty of transporting said slaves to one of the free States. Mr Caldwell has written the Govn'r of N Y, making inquiries relative to removing them. The Govn'r published papers that philanthropic citizens may have a chance to render practical assistance to the much talked of cause of emancipation by receiving the slaves when liberated, & making interest or provsion for their employment or maintenance. All gentlemen so disposed will confer a benefit by communicating with Mr Caldwell.

Jeremiah Speer, of Paterson, N J, advertises his wife Rachael, as having left his bed & board, & cautions people not to harbor or trust her on his account. Rachel speers him back again, in the following, which shows her spunk, at least: NOTICE: I, his wife, say he never had any bed or board for me, but he boarded with my father, & I paid his board. A few months ago he was taken sick, when his mother came with a hired man & wagon & took him away, without my knowledge or my father's consent, & I paid a 3 weeks' doctor's bill for him. When he came back I told him he must go to his mother & stay till he got weaned, before I would live with him. -Rachael Speer.

Six cents reward will be paid for the arrest & delivery to the subscriber of his 2 runaway apprentices, Jas Conlons & August Carl. –J H S Werner

Pittsburgh, Aug 29–accident near Turtle Creek, at any early hour, after a party had assembled at Mr Perchment's tavern, dancing & amusing themselves. On their return home they passed over a precipice known as the *Falls,* when in the dark they got off of the road & fell to the bottom of the crag. Mr McElroy was dead, his body crushed. The young lady with him had her back & legs broken. No hopes of her recovery. –Gaz

Mrd: on Sep 1, in Wash City, by Rev J W French, Lt Col Benj F Larned, Deputy Paymaster Gen U S Army, to Eliz R Larned, of Wash City.

Six cents reward will be paid for the arrest & delivery to the subscriber of his 2 runaway apprentices, Jas Conlons & August Carl. –J H S Werner

WED SEP 3, 1851
Wm S Crittenden: in the midst of the lamentations of fathers & mothers, brothers & sisters, for the death of their dearly beloved, by the Havana butchery, we knew him first in the Mexican war. He was educated at West Point & graduated with honor. His father emigrated to Arkansas when that State was in its infancy, & died in early life. Will, as he was named by his friends, was a noble specimen of the Ky gentleman; an accomplished soldier. At the close of the Mexican war he resigned his military ofc & became a citizen of New Orleans, where he resided until he embarked with Lopez. If ever a man fell victim to atrocious deception, it was he.
–New Orleans True Delta

Benj L Bowen has recently been appointed Superintendent of Chimney-sweepers of the 2nd Ward, Wash. Those requiring his services to leave their names & residence at Mr Reed's Grocery Store, 14th & F sts, & at his residence, on M st, between 13th & 14th sts.

Household & kitchen furniture at auction: on Sep 8, by order of the Orphan's Court, at the residence of the late Richd H Harrington, deceased, on Garrison st.
-Dyer & McGuire, aucts

Central Academy, 2nd story of the old Medical College, E & 10th sts, will be resumed on Sep 1. –Jas Nourse, Jos Harvey Nourse

Postmaster Gen est'd the following new Post Ofcs for week ending Aug 30, 1851.

Ofc	County, State	Postmaster
Sprout Brook	Montgomery, N Y	Benj Wendell
Pepokating	Sussex, N J	R V Armstrong
Farmersville	Crawford, Pa	Anthony Hollister

Sewicklyville	Alleghany, Pa	John Way
Cravesville	Paulding, Ohio	H N Curtis
Livingston	Crawford, Ohio	Renas Livingston
Pattonville	Hocking, Ohio	John F Roberts
Greenwich Station	Huron, Ohio	Hiram Townsend
Adamsville	Harrison, Va	Peter W Night
Shenandoah Springs	Shenandoah, Va	Noah J Burner
Big Cole	Boone, Va	Augustus Pack
Hamlin	Cabell, Va	Jas C Black
Rocky Hill	Fayette, Va	Saml Flishman
Elk Hill	Amelia, Va	Wm A Milestone
Buckland	Gates, N C	Saml E Smith
Klutt's Tan Yard	Cabarras, N C	Levi Klutts
Soapstone Mo't	Randolph, N C	Mar Hayworth
Harrison Creek	Cumberland, N C	Arthur Melvin
Sweet Water	Watanga, N C	Thos Farthing
Camp Ground	Pickens Dist, S C	Jas Hughes
Crow Creek	Pickens Dist, S C	Robt Stewart
Polk	Clinch, Ga	Simon W Nicolls
Fort Taylor	Benton, Fla	Robt D Bradley
Mountain Home	Lawrence, Ala	D G Ligon
Burk Hill	Yala Busha, Miss	C McCullar
Prairie Lea	Caldwell, Texas	Jas H Callahan
Almond Grove	Red River, Texas	Geo W Parker
Elm	Ballard, Ky	John W Peebles
Walnut Bottom	Henderson, Ky	Benj Faulkner
Bowling Green	Stewart, Tenn	N P Allmon
New Boston	Henry, Tenn	B A Howard
Whitaker's Bluff	Wayne, Tenn	Richd H Whitaker
Calico Rock	Izard, Ark	Jas Jeffrey
Green Grove	Conway, Ark	Benj Murphy
Bloomer	Sebastian, Ark	A J Brooks
Ark	Lafayette, Ark	A J Vanmeter
Grassy Creek	Livingston, Mo	Sol R Hocker
Perkin's Creek	Bellinger, Mo	Jason H Hunter
Fryrear's Mills	Miller, Mo	A Fryrear
Mount Meridian	Pulaski, Mo	Jacob Love
Blakesville	Harrison, Ind	Anderson Brown
Mount Hope	DeKalb, Ind	Jas R Caspar
Fitchburg	Jasper, Ind	Aaron H Larkins

Names Changed: 1-Lincoln, Winnebago Co, Ill, changed to Howard.
2-Green Plains, Hancock Co, Ill, changed to Rocky Run.

Contributions to the Washington Monument:
Assist U S Marshal, G A Smith, Fla: $20.08
Wm Paine, U S Marshal Dist of Maine: $588.86
C H Knox, U S Marshal Dist of Mich: $278.00
E E Buckner, Assist Marshal, Mo: $37.70
J G Walker, Assist Marshal, Va: $26.35
Hugh Kyger, Assist Marshal, Va: $22.00
John T Myrick, U S marshal, Fla, [3rd payment:] $15.30
T S Martin, Assist Marshal, Ga: $21.25
Jennings Maupin, Assist Marshal, Va: $57.20
H B Shepherd, Assist Marshal, Ind: $28.05
John R Hutchison, Oakland College, Miss: $1.00
P F Keavy, H R Davis B F Sibley, H E Wall, P Smith, Board of police of Wilkinson Co, Miss: $50.00
W G Ewing, **Fort Wayne**, Ind: $5.00
J F Bell, contributed by citizens of Bayle Co, Ky: $10.00
Mrs Ogden, primary school #4, 2nd Dist, Washington: $4.00
H Anunally, Yazoo City, Miss: $8.00
W A Read, Parish of Plaquimine, La, [annual contributed] $5.00
E J Meany, Romney Classical Institute, Va: $6.00
Elias Hibbard, Upper Alton, Ill: $2.00
Received from special agents: $608.34

Orphans Court of Wash Co, D C. Letters of administration on the personal estate of Richd H Harrington, late of Wash Co, deceased. –M A W Harrington, admx

For sale: Glass Case, a pair of new & handsome counters. Apply to Chas H Lane, Hat, Cap, & Gentlemen's Furnishing Store, near 4½ st & Pa ave.

THU SEP 4, 1851
Store & dwlg for rent: 13th & H sts. Apply on the premises to Mrs Nott.

Teacher wanted in Easton Academy, Talbot Co, Md. Apply to Sam Hambleton, jr, Pres of the Board of Trustees.

Fox River Courier: Gen Geo McClure died at Elgin Ill, on the 15th ult. He was born in Londonderry, Ireland, in 1771. His parents had been driven by persecution from Scotland. When 20 years old he landed in Balt, where he worked a few months, & then went to Chambersburg, Pa, remaining a few months, & then passing to Bath, Steuben Co, where he resided from 1791 till 1835. In the war of 1812 he commanded a brig on the Niagara frontier. He was at different periods, Judge, Surrogate, & Sheriff. Many years ago he removed to Illinois, where he resided & took an active part.

Teacher wanted in Easton Academy, Talbot Co, Md. Apply to Sam Hambleton, jr, Pres of the Board of Trustees.

Wash Corp: 1-Cmte on Police: bill for the relief of Edw Cowling. Same cmte: asked to be discharged from the further consideration of the ptns of Alfred Shucking & of Jas Flaherty. 2-Bill for the relief of Philip Mackey, praying permission to erect a temporary shed near a brick bldg: referred to the Cmte on Police. 3-Bill for the relief of John E Bailey: rejected.

Mrd: on Sep 2, in Wash City, by Rev Dr Ducachey, of Phil, Somerville Nicholson, of the U S Navy, to Hannah Maria, daughter of Dr Wm Jones.

Mrd: on Sep 1, at the E st Baptist Church, by Rev Mr Kempton, Mr Benj S Myers to Miss Emma Brown, formerly of N Y.

Marshal's sale: on Sep 30, at O & 5th sts, one small frame dwlg house, on lot 8 in square 480; seized & levied upon as the property of Wm Posey, to satisfy Judicials 41 to Mar 1851, in favor of Harkness & Purdy against Posey.
–Richd Wallach, Marshal D C

FRI SEP 5, 1851
There seems to be no doubt that the Spanish Gen Enna was wounded in a battle with Lopez at Carambola. He may have since died. The Havana Faro Industrial publishes, by authority, the following document, giving an account of the forces of Lopez, which was found amongst the papers taken:
Gen in Chief: Narciso Lopez
2nd in Command & Chief of the Staff: John Pragay
Ofcrs of the Staff: Capt Emmrich Radrich, Lts Jos Lewohl & Sigis Rekendorf.
Corps of Adjs: Col Eugen Blummenthal, Capt Ludivig Schlezinger, Lt Ludivig Muller, Sur Henry A Tournique, Commissary G A Cook.
Staff of the Regt of Infty: Col R L Dowman, Lt Col W Scott Haynes, Adj Geo A Graham, Commissary Jos Bell, adj of the regt Geo Parr.
Co A: Capt Robt Ellisi, lt E H McDonald; sub-lt J L Lahuzan; lt R H Brelenbridge.
Co B: Capt John Johnson; 1st lt Jas Dunn; 2nd lt J S Williams; 3rd lt Jas O Reilly.
Co C: Capt J C Brigham; 1st lt Richd Howder; 2nd lt G A Gray; 3rd lt J D Baker.
Co D: Capt Philip N Golday; 1st lt David L Rousseau; 2nd lt John H Landingham; 3rd lt Jas H Howain.
Co E: Capt Henry Jackson; 1st lt Wm Hubbi; 2nd do T A Simpson; 3rd lt Jas Crangle.
Co F: Capt Wm Stewart; 1st lt Jas G Ownes; 2nd lt John G Bush; 3rd lt Thos Hudnall.
Regt of Artl: Ofcrs of the Staff: Chief Wm S Crittenden; Adj R L Stanford; 2nd master of commissary Felix Husten; surgeon Ludovig Hanki.
Co A: Capt J A Kelly; 1st lt F C James; 2nd lt Jas A Stevens; 3rd lt J O Bryce.
Co B: Capt Jas Sanders; 1st lt Philipp S Van Vechten; 2nd lt Brewerly E Hunter, 3rd lt Wm H Craft.

Co C: Capt Victor Kerr; 1st lt Jas Brandt; 2nd lt H T Vienne.
Regt of Cuban Patriots: Cao A: Capt Ildefonso Oberto; 1st lt Diego Hernandez; 2nd lt Miguel Lopez; 3rd lt, Joce A Pianos; 4th lt Pedro Lopez.
Regt of Hungarians: Maj Geo Bontila; Capt Ladislaus Palank; lts Jos Csermelyi, Johan Peteri, Adalbert Kerskes, Conrad Eichler.
German Regt: Capt Hugo Schlicht. Lt Paul Michsel Biro; Cambias: Capt Pietro Muller, Lt Giovani Placosio.

For rent: with or without the furniture, on 15th st, near L st, a frame house, nearly new, in good order, a pump of good water in the yard. Inquire of Alex'r Borland on the premises.

Mrd: on Sep 2, at the Univ of Va, by Rev R K Meade, the Rev Wm McGuffey, Prof of Moral Philosophy in the Univ, to Laura P, daughter of Prof Henry Howard.

Mrd: on Sep 2, at Needwood, Fred'k Co, Md, by Rev Mr Bague. Saml L Gouverneur, of Oak Hill, Loudoun Co, Va, to Mary Digges Lee, eldest daughter of the late Wm Lee, of the former place.

Died: on Sat last, at his residence near Nottingham, Md, very suddenly, of apoplexy, Michl B Carroll, aged about 54. He was a gentleman of wealth & influence, in the prime & vigor of manhood, with a hand & heart open to all around him. His funeral was on Mon; the procession to the grave was more than ½ a mile in length. His negroes [about 100] exhibited deep grief. They were all well & neatly clad, & each one wore a badge of mourning. Mr Carroll has left a widow, but no children.

Wash City Ordinances: 1-Act for the relief of Philip Gormley: that $229.47 be paid to him for balance due for grading K st. 2-Act for the relief of T P & M Brown: to be paid $150, for payment of a claim of theirs against the corp.

Headquarters of the Marine Corps: Adj & Inspector's Ofc, Wash, Sep 3, 1851. Announcement of the death of Maj Geo W Walker, Paymaster of the Corps, who died at his residence in D C on the 29th ult. –P G Howle, Adj & Inspec

SAT SEP 6, 1851
On Mon, at Andover, on the Erie Railroad, Henry Fitzsimmons & lady were instantly killed when crossing the track in front of the locomotive. The gentlemen in charge of the train are blameless. The horse stopped on the track.

Telegraphic dispatch yesterday announced the demise of Hon Levy Woodbury, an Associate Justice of the Supreme Court of the U S, at his residence at Portsmouth, N H. His health had been declining for some months past. [No death date given- current item.]

Southern Press of yesterday announces the death of Beverly Tucker, one of the Faculty of Wm & Mary College. He was about 67 years of age. [No death date given-current item.] [Sep 8th newspaper: error: age should have been 60 years.]

Wm Lovatt was bit by a rattlesnake, which he kept in his house, & died on Tuesday. He endured the most horrible tortures from the time he was bit until his death. –Phil paper

$20 reward for return of strayed pair of Gray Horses, last seen near Mrs Loughborough's, on the River road to Seneca of Poolesville. Deliver to me, or Mr Harry, at Tenallytown, D C. –Thos Marshall, near Gtwn, D C.

Farm for sale: subscriber offers his Farm, in PG Co, containing 178½ acres. Inquire at Buell & Blanchard's Printing Ofc, 6th st, south of Pa ave. –M Buell

Nominations of the two parties of State ofcrs for California, to take place yesterday:

Ofc	Democratic	Whig
Govn'r	John Bigler	P B Reading
Lt Govn'r	Saml Pardy	Drury P Baldwin
Justice Sup Court	Sol'n Heydenfeldt	Tod Robinson
State Treasurer	Richd Roman	J M Burt
State Comptroller	W S Pierce	Alex G Abell
Atty Gen	S C Hastings	Wm D Fair
Surveyor Gen	Wm M Eddy	Walter Herron
Congress	Jos W McCorkle	E J C Kewen
Congress	Edw C Marshall	B F Moore

Calif: Hon E Heydenfeldt has resigned as Judge of the Seventh Judicial Distrist.

Trustee's sale of valuable real estate: by deed of trust from Walter H Finnall: public auction on Oct 7, of the tract of land & winter & spring fishery called The ***Tump***, lying on the waters of Aquia Creek & Potomac River, in Stafford Co, Va. The land contains 738¼ acres. –W P Conway, trustee [On the same day will be sold on the said ***Tump Farm***: the schnr **Wm C Beale**; sloop **Wm J J Murray**; 4 batteaux; 26 capstans; 2 ducking guns, & stock. –Chas Henderson, trustee -Geo W Conway, receiver]

Accident at San Francisco harbor on Jul 27: Capt Gellaly, of the British ship **William**; Mr W H McComb, agent for the owners of that vessel; Capt P Crowell, of the storeship **Charlotte**; Capt J P Ward, formerly in the employ of D Gibb, as master of the vessel; the capt of the British brig **Desire**, & 4 seamen went on a excursion to Contra Costa in a long boat, & in returning a violent wind struck her sails, capsizing the boat, & drowning all except Capt Crowell. Capt Ward belonged to N Y. The seamen were John McGowen, Wm Hunter, Robt Tayor, & Dugald McKenna.

C H Parker, engineer of the steamboat **Penobscot**, from N Y to Phil, fell overboard on the Jersey coast, on Sat, & was lost. He leaves a wife & 4 children in Brooklyn.

New Orleans, Sep 5. Lopez has been executed, & all the Americans who were captured with him have been condemned to the mines.

University of Georgia, Athens: will proceed to elect a Professor of Natural Science: salary $1,700 per annum. Apply at the Institution or to Asbury Hull, sec.

Hagerstown Academy, Instructor wanted. —Jacob Hollingsworth, Pres: Board of Trustees

MON SEP 8, 1851
The Providence Journal announces the death of Dr Levi Wheaton, one of the oldest & most distinguished citizens of Rhode Island. His eventful life covered nearly a century. [No death date given-current item.]

It has been frequently stated that Col Clendenin was among the persons executed at Havana on the 16th. This was the first report, but it was afterwards ascertained that it was Col W S Crittenden, & not Col Clendenin, who was the sufferer. He has not been to Cuba at all. A gentleman, who knows him well, met him at Cario 2 or 3 days since, on his way to New Orleans.

$20 reward for return of strayed or stolen bay Horse. —Thos C Magruder, E st at 6th.

Very desirable private residence at auction: on Sep 17, the lot & improvements in square 690, known as the residence of the late Dr May, on Capitol Hill, fronting on N J ave. The house is a 3 story brick dwlg, with back bldg, & stable.
-A Green, auctioneer

Mrd: on Sep 2, in Gtwn, by Rev Chas McElfresh, Mr Benj R Mayfield to Miss Charlotte L Brown, both of Gtwn.

Mrd: on Thursday, at N Y, at Calvary Church, by Rev Francis L Hawks, Lt Edw Higgins, U S Navy, to Anna Maria, daughter of John C Zimmerman, of that city.

Died: on Aug 28, near Taneytown, Carroll Co, Md, Mrs Mgt Galt, wife of Sterling Galt, in her 53rd year.

Died: on Aug 3, near **Fort Washita**, Lt P A Farrelly, 5th Infty U S Army. On Thursday before his death Lt Farrelly was thrown from a horse, his head striking a stump, which affected the skull & brain, & which is supposed to have caused his death.

Died: on Sep 4, in Germantown, Pa, Mrs Mgt Provest, widow of the late Alex'r Provest, in her 74th year. She was a devoted mother & a firm & consistent Christian.

Died: on Aug 29, 1851, Ann Eliza, daughter of Jas & Jane Keck, aged 11 years & 9 months.

On Aug 31, the little son of Chas H Burgess, residing on B st, near 11th, aged 1 year & 7 months, strayed from the door to the culvert & fell in, & would have drowned had not a gentleman passing at the time saved the little child. The parents feel much gratitude.

TUE SEP 9, 1851
For sale or lease: *Forrest Hall*, a new house on High st, Gtwn, D C. For particulars apply to B Forrest, Gtwn, D C.

Casanovia at auction: on Sep 13: within the Corporation limits, square 747, on north Boundary st: with a very large dwlg, 2 stables & carriage house, servant's house, icehouse, smoke house, & a pump of fine water. -Dyer & McGuire, aucts

Lord Brougham has the honor of being related to Patrick Henry, the great Orator of Va. Patrick Henry's mother was Sarah Winston. His father was John Henry, of Aberdeen, Scotland. John Henry's mother was Jane Robertson, sister of Dr Wm Robertson, the Historian, from whom Brougham is descended.

Died: on Sep 4, at the residence of his father adjoining this city, Jonathan M Seaver, a member of the Religious Society of Friends.

Died: on Sep 8, after a long & painful illness, Mrs Eliz Ruff, in her 61st year. Her funeral is today at 3 P M, from the residence of her son, E st, between 5th & 6th sts.

Died: on Sep 7, Wm Waters, Boatswain in the U S Navy, in his 50th year. His funeral is today at 2 o'clock, at the Navy Yard.

Died: on Sep 8, Capt Saml Killmon, aged 63 years, a native of Dorchester Co, Md, but for the last 30 years a resident of Wash City. His funeral will move from the late residence of the deceased, 13th st, this morning at 10 o'clock.

Obit-died: on Aug 19, 1851, at Jackson Court-house, Va, Fleet Smith, late of Wash City. The deceased was for a long time a resident of Leesburg, Va, & practiced the profession of the law in Loudoun & neighboring counties. He was licensed to practice by Edmund Pendleton, Spencer Roane, & Robt White, Judges of the Gen Court of Va, in 1798. He removed to Wash in 1820; he also resided for a few years in St Mary's Co, Md. His loss to the surviving relatives of his family will long be deplored.

Valuable & handsome property at auction: known as **Fairview**, being part of square 513, lots 3 thru 6, 22 thru 24, 30 thru 32, & 42 thru 45, all adjoining: improved with a frame house 32 x 38 feet: fronts on north M, between 4th & 5th sts. Title indisputable. -A Green, auctioneer

WED SEP 10, 1851
Wash Corp: 1-Ptn from Jos Downing & others for grading the alley in square 400: passed. 2-Nomination by the Mayor of Peter M Pearson as a member of the Board of Health: confirmed. 3-Ptn of Jas Casparis to widen an area in front of his premises in the 5th Ward: passed. 4-Cmte of Claims: act for the relief of Francis Holden: passed. 5-Ptn from J L Elliott & Evan Hughes, for setting the curb-stones & paving the footway in front of square 286: passed. 6-Ptn of Caroline Cox, praying for curbstone at square 342: referred to the Cmte on Improvements. 7-Communication from the Register, enclosing the names of Jenny Cowper & Eliza Rives as the only persons who have complied with the law of Dec 10, 1850, concerning free negroes, mulattoes, etc: referred to the Cmte on Police.

Saml Fowler, Merchant Tailor, will in the future be at the store of P H Browning, under the U S Hotel. Those indebted to him will settle up with him or with P W Browning, as he wishes to close up his old affairs without delay.

Postmaster Gen has est'd the following new Post Ofcs for week ending Sep 6, 1851.

Ofc	County, State	Postmaster
Morrisonville	Clinton, N Y	John T Finn
Pleasant Hall	Franklin, Pa	Chas Wheeler
Dillingersville	Lehigh, Pa	Erwin Burkhalter
Moscow	Luzerne, Pa	Thos Depew
West Nanticoke	Luzerne, Pa	Levi M Smith
Bossardsville	Monroe, Pa	Jos A Bossard
Ogdensburgh	Union, Pa	Theodore Harding
Hall	York, Pa	Michl S Bowers
Flat Creek Mills	Campbell, Va	Edmund J Early
Fowler's Knob	Nicholas, Va	Wm E C Trent
Sugar Run	Wetzel, Va	Robt W Kirby
Chronicle	Lincoln, N C	Obor Munday
Swan Pond	Wilkes, N C	Wm W Hampton
South Saluda	Greenville dist, S C	Wm F Hunt
Ford's Store	Franklin, Ga	Henry Ford
Reynolds	Houston, Ga	Thos Lewis
Sterling	Montgomery, Ga	Wm A McLeod
Toombs	Richmond, Ga	Jas Palmer

The prisoners at Havana: the following are the names, so far as officially published, of the members of the expedition against Cuba who have been captured by the authorities of that Island, & are now held as captives. This list, it will be seen, does not include the whole of 155 men who are said to be prisoners.

N Y: Elias Otis, Michl O'Keennen, John Danton, Lt P S Van Vechten, M L Hefren.
Washington: Capt Robt Ellis, Thos Hilton.
Mobile: Lt E H McDonald, D D Waif, H D Thomason, Chas A Donues, Eman'l R Wier.
New Orleans: Lt Jas G Dwen, Lt J G Bush, W Wilson, W Miller, P Lacoste, M Lieger, P Mileman, Henry Smith, John Cline, Geo Forster, C Knoll, Nicholas Port, John Martan, Patrick McGrath, Chas S Daily, Jas Fiddes, S H Prenell, Conrad Taylor, Thos Denton, C A McMurray, J Patan, Conrad Arghlir, Jose Chiceri, G Richardson, John B Brown, Thos S Lee, Capt Jas Aquelli, Harvey Williams, Franklin Boyd.
Phil: Thos Little, Commissary J A Simpson, Geo Wilson.
Ky: Lt D D Rousseau, Lt Robt McGrier, J D Hughes, Wm H Vangale, Francis B Holmes, Malbone H Scott.
Memphis: Lt W H Craft.
Alabama: J D Prenit, W L Wilkinson, C Cook.
Charleston: Jas Chapman.
Galena, Ill: Jas Brady.
Petersburg: Henry B Hart.
St Louis: Jacob Fonts, Preston Faces.
Va: Wm Cameron.
Mississippi: Thos Mourou, Wilson E Rieves.
Ohio: Isaac Freeborn.
U S: Cornelius Derby, Peter Falbos, Benj Harrer.
England: Wm Caussans, John Nowes.
Ireland: Henry B Metcalfe, Geo Metcalfe, Jas Porter, Thos McDellans.
Cuba: Bernardo Allem, Julio Chasagne, Francisco Curbia y Garcia, Ramon J Arno, Jose Dovren, Manuel Martinez, Antonio Hernandez, Martin Melesimo.
Germany: Johannes Sucit, Edw Wisse, Wilhelm Losner, Robt Seelust, Ciriac Senepli.
Hungary: Georg Bautista
New Grenada: Andrew Gonzalez.
Alquizar: Francisco A Leve.
Bayomo: Manuel Diaz
Navarre: Antonio Romero.
Spain: Francisco J Zamora.
Not stated: Antonio L Alfonso, Manuel Aragon, Jose Bojjantoie y Rabina, Joaquin Casanova, Miguel Guerra, Wm Mackinney, Dandrig Seay, Leonardo Sujliorit, J D Baker, Luis Bander.

The Missouri Republican announces the death of Mr Sylvester M Bartlett, Editor of the Quincy [Ill] Whig, a pure-minded man.

A new paper in Texas: The Rio Grande, a new weekly paper, published at Brownville, Texas, by O F Johnson & F J Parker: price is $5 per annum.

Mrd: Sep 9, by Rev Thos Lockett, Mr Jos Fowler to Miss Alcuzera Barnhouse, all of Wash City.

Died: on Sep 8, after a protracted illness, Mary Ann Hurley, aged 34 years, widow of John Hurley, & eldest daughter of Wm & Susan Dant. Requiescent in pace! Her funeral is today at 4 o'clock, from her father's, on D, between 2nd & 3rd sts.

Orphans Court of Wash Co, D C: the case of Ann Tench & Thos P Tench, adms of Stanislaus Tench, deceased. The administrators & Court have appointed Sep 30th for the final settlement of said estate, as far as the assets collected & turned into money. -Ed N Roach, Reg/o wills

Having taken the house lately occupied by Mrs Whitwell, on 4½ st, I will rent my rooms furnished. −A T Young

Auction of household & kitchen furniture at the Auction Store: on Sep 20, by deed of trust from Seth Lamb to M Thompson, dated Nov 29, 1850, recorded in Liber J A S 18, folios 61, 62, land records of Wash Co, D C. −M Thompson, trustee
-A Green, auct

Private sale: subscriber offers his Farm near the old Fred'k road from Gtwn, containing from 75 to 80 acres; with a comfortable dwlg house & all necessary out bldgs. Reference may be made to Mr Lewis Carbery. −Wm Morris, Montg Co, Md

$5 reward for apprehension of runaway mulatto boy Wm Burk, my indentured apprentice. −M Barker

For sale: property on D st, near 13th, now occupied by Mr Worthington. The house is of brick, covered with slate. Gas pipes have been introduced into the principal apartments. Apply to John Foy, on Capitol Hill, or to C B Cluskey, at his ofc on Pa ave, at 12th.

Private sale: of lot in square 104, corner of F & 20th sts, Wash, fronting 178 feet on F, near the residence of Maj Turnbull. −B Forrest, Gtwn, D C

THU SEP 11, 1851
J Francis Clements, Atty & Counsellor at Law: ofc on Louisiana ave, between 4½ & 6th st.

News by telegraph from Louisville, Ky, of the death of Mrs Crittenden, the excellent consort of Hon J J Crittenden, Atty Gen of the U S. It is said to have taken place at Frankfort, on Monday last. [Sep 15th newspaper: Mrs Crittenden, wife of Hon John J Crittenden, died on Sep 8, after an illness of 9 days. Our strongest sympathies are with her bereaved husband & family.]

Col Crittenden's last letter. The New Orleans Crescent of Sep 2 contains the following letter from Col Crittenden, who lost his life in the Lopez expedition: ship of war **Esperanza**, Aug 16, 1851. Dear Lucien: In half an hour I, with fifty others, am to be shot. We were taken prisoners yesterday. We were in small boats. Gen Lopez separated the balance of the command from me. I had with me about one hundred-was attacked by two battalions of infantry & one company of horse. The odds was too great, and, strange to tell, I was not furnished with a single musket cartridge. Lopez did not get any artillery. I have not the heart to write to any of my family. If the truth ever comes out you will find that I did not duty, and have the perfect confidence of every man with me. We had retired from the field and were going to sea, and were overtaken by the Spanish steamer **Habanero**, and captured. Tell Gen Huston that his nephew got separated from me on the 13th-day of the fight- and that I have not seen him since. He may have straggled off and joined Lopez, who advanced rapidly to the interior. My people, however, were entirely surrounded on every side. We saw that we had been deceived grossly, and were making for the U S when taken. During my short sojourn in the Island I have not met a single patriot. We landed some forty or fifty miles to the westward of this, and I am sure that in that part of the Island Lopez has no friends. When I was attacked Lopez was only three miles off. If he had not been deceiving us as to the state of things. He would have fallen back with his force and made fight, instead of which he marched on immediately to the interior. I am requested to get you to tell Mr Green of the custom-house, that his brother shares my fate. Victor Kerr is also with me, also Stanford. I recollect no others of your acquaintance at present. I will die like a man. My heart has not failed me yet, nor do I believe it will. Communicate with my family. This is an incoherent letter, but the circumstances must excuse it. My hands are swollen to double their thickness, resulting from having them too tightly corded for the last eighteen hours. Write to John, and let him write to my mother. I am afraid that the news will break her heart. My heart beats warmly towards her now. Farewell! My love to all of my friends. I am sorry that I died owing a cent, but it is inevitable. Yours, strong in heart, W L Crittenden. To Dr Lucien Hensley.

The grand picture recently executed by that able artist, Mr Healey, representing Mr Webster in the act of delivering his great speech, in reply to Mr Hayne, in the U S Senate, was exhibited on Sat in Boston to a select number of persons. This work, we believe, took everyone by surprise, the expectation falling far short of the reality, both in the boldness of the attempt & in the success which crowned it. Mr Healey's reputation will be much raised by this performance. -Courier

Good 2 story frame house & lot at auction: being lot 33, in Naylor & Rothwell's subdivision of square 425, fronting on 7th st, between L & M. House rents for $12.50 per month. Title indisputable. -A Green, auctioneer

Obit-died: near Greensboro, Ala, in his 33rd year, Rev Jas Somervell Marbury, eldest son of John Marbury, of Gtwn, & late Rector of St Paul's Church, Greensboro. [No death date given-current item.]

FRI SEP 12, 1851
Register's Ofc Wash, Sep 5, 1851. Persons who have taken out licenses under the laws of the Corp during the months of Apr, May, & Jun, 1851.
Auctioneer license: Dyer & McGuire

Billards license: Flint, C W

Circus license: Robinson & Edred

Cart license:

Ayler & Thyson	Boyle, J F	Dent, Bruce
Addison & Co, A	Chew, Phil	Dyson, Chas
Adams, Cabil	Connell, Dennis	Deevers, 1-2
Adams, Wm	Chapin, H L	Dove, Wm T
Ashton, C H B-s	Collins, John H	Dowell, John
Abbott, Jos	Cazanove, Peter-2	Dowling, Wm-2
Adams, Saml	Cross, Lloyd-2	De Neale, Wm Y-2
Anderson, Caleb	Crowley, Wm	Delany, L
Adams, Saml	Clements, A-3	De Neale, K
Anderson, Wm	Clements, A N-3	Edes, Philip
Buckley, Jas S	Castell, Edw-2	Emery, M G
Bruce, Chas	Cruttenden, Harvey-2	Elkins, J
Bean, Geo-2	Coltman, Chas L	Eslin, J-2
Bowen, Thos	Chew, John	Fitzgerald, Jno
Brent, Elton	Cannon, W P	Ford, Wm-2
Butler, Mathew-2	Cross, Jos	Fisher, Abm
Bolayer, John	Cook, Saml-6	Fletcher, Jno-3
Barr, Wm-2	Clements & Daly-2	Fletcher, Wm-2
Brown, Robt	Conlan, P	Fowler, Jas
Barrett, Thos J-2	Clark, R B	Ferrall, D
Beckett, Wm	Coyle, Fitzhugh	Fraser, Wm
Brown, Hanson-2	Coltman, C L	Flinn, Jno
Burgess, John-2	Clark, Wm	Gates, Julia Ann
Barnes, Elias	Dick, Moses	Gregg, Saml-2
Beall, E	Davis & Garrett	Green, Manroy
Barnes, Jas-2	Deevers, Wm-2	Gildermester, H-2
Bayly, Wm	Downing, Jos	Garner, Jno F

Greer, Theo J	Lane, John	Owens, Jas
Grinder, Adam	Lyvus, Chas-2	O'Neale, J J
Greason, Wm	Lacy, Emanuel	Orrison, A
Green, Patrick	Lambell, K H-2	Oyuster, G M
Gill, John-4	Linkins, Wm	Pulizzi, V
Garner, John R	Loveless, John	Purdy, John
Greer, A A	Linkins, John	Petinon, Henry
Goings, Sarah	Linkins, Danl-2	Perkins, Saml
Graham, Wm	Lucas, Octavius	Payne, Robt
Gormley, P-2	Linkins, Walter-2	Pegg, Wm
Goings, John	Lomax, Elias	Powers, John
Goings, Jas	Lawson, Wm	Prather, H D-2
Hyde, Rich A	Lewis, Thos	Payne, Saml
Hill, Isaac	Mitchell, Rebecca	Prather, L
Haislip, H-2	Myers, Chas F	Prather, O J
Hagerty, Wm-2	Mason, Jos-2	Plant, Nathl-2
Heltmiller, A	McNew, N C-2	Palmer, John
Harvey & Co, J S-4	Middleton, Eliza-2	Pettibone, John
Hall, John	Mohun, Philip	Powers, J
Hicks, Chas	Mudd, J T-2	Page, Geo-3
Hanson, Chas	Moore, Wm	Peters, John
Hopkins & Co, J S-2	Madison, Cath-2	Parker, H
Hoover, Andw-2	Magruder, Fielder-2	Queen, Jno R
Hanson, Geo	Mills, Jno E	Richardson, L
Howard, Thos	Mothershead, Jno-2	Rhodes, Jas
Hodgkins, John	McGlue, Geo T-2	Robb & Green
Hunsberger & Co	Miller, Chas	Raidy, John
Howell, Thos-2	Mister, J	Redfern, Saml
Hensey, W	Miller, John	Rice, E
Hensey, R	Moran, Wm	Robey, John
Hoover, John	Mocaby, J B-3	Riley, Thos W-4
Horsthump, H	Mitchell, H C	Rowles, J H
Howlett, J W	Mills, Jas H	Ragan, Danl-2
Holoran, M-2	Murphy, John	Ragan, Thos
Harshman, J	Moore, J D W-2	Reid, Andw
Haggerty, Wm	Mercer, Jas	Reid, A
Jolly, John	Mockoby, J B	Rigsbey, A
Jones, Alfred	McKenney, Jared	Rison, Chas
Jones, Andw	Marden, J	Richards, W-2
Key, Saml	Neale, Levi	Stewart, Chas W
King, Chas	Nokes, Jr, Jas-2	Sewall, Richd
Kelly, Wm	Noble, Martha	Simms, Alex
King, Z M P	Noerr, Andrew	Somerville, Arnold
King, J R	O'Hare, C S	Selby, Thos

Simms, Jno
Stone, Thos
Seaman, Richd
Smoot, A E-2
Sinon, John
Scott, Leonidas
Stephenson, Jos
Simms, J M
Simmons, Aug-3
Smallwood, r T
Stone, Wm-2
Smoot, Saml
Stone, Thos
Sampson, H
Stewart, G-2
Sibley, C
Stewart, Chas-2
Stott, Saml
Shea, J-3
Scott, Geo B

Scott, Ann
Sullivan, John
Shepherd, P
Tyler, Robt
Talbert, Wm
Thomas, Saml
Travers, M W-2
Tuxton, Stuart
Travers, Sol-2
Tucker, Wm
Teusdale, Susan F
Unisck, John
Van Riswick
Walker & Peck-3
Walker & Jones-2
Winchester, Robt
Whitney, J O-2
Warner, Henry
Welsh, David
Webster, Rezin

Washington, Wm
Waters, Thos
Williams, Z-2
Ward, John
Williamson, Benj
Ward, W H
Wilson, Jno
West, J P-2
Woods, John
Worden, Wm
Williams, Jesse-3
Wise, Jas A-2
White, Geo
Waters, G
Waters, E-2
Warder, Wm-2
Ward, E-3
Wilkins, Geo
Williams, W F-2
Ward, E-2

Commission license: Dyer & McGuire
Concerts license: Cameron Family; Sanford, S J
Deformed man license: Shipley, S N-1 week

Dog license:

Atkinson, G
Adams, Saml
Aylmer, R R
Benix, Saml
Baggott, Jas
Baker, Jno
Butler, Matthew
Bateman, A
Barry, Mary
Bean, Jas
Burdine, Wm
Bush, Cloann
Branson, P
Bryan, Thos
Boyle, John F
Bowen, M
Burch, Thos W
Bittinger, H
Butler, Henry

Bany, J C
Barnes, Jas
Bohn, C
Brown, L H
Carter, W W
Cowan, Hugh
Cook, Alfred
Craven, Henry
Cook, Saml
Cook, J F
Chew, Wm
Choppin, W
Carson, Saml
Cryer, Benj
Clark, Jos
Connor, W W
Contee, John
Cropley, E S
Duvall, Wash

Deagle, M
Dillon, Wm
Duckett, G
Dozier, J
Doniphan, Edw
Dodge, Hannah
Dowell, John
Defalgo, S-2
Ellicott, Jas
Evans, R F-2
Fletcher, C
Faunce, Mary
Ferrill, Dennis
Foster, Robt F
Fugitt, Thos L
French, Jas A
Fisher, David
Follansbee, Jos
Garner, Geo

Gill, C A
Gunnell, Jas S
Gautier, C
Grinder, Adam
Gray, Wm
Gibson, Louisa
Griffith, Richd
Goss, J F
Godfrey, S A
Gantt, Edw
Griffin, Saml
Gannon, E
Green, O
Garrett, Jas
Greeves, Jno
Graham, Susan
Hazard, H H
Hanson, Cecilia
Howard, Jos
Hutchingson, P
Holmead, J B
Hanson, Richd
Holland, Isaac
Hill, Eliz
Hopkins, G W
Harley, Anderson
Hagar, Mrs
Hickman, Jos
Harris, Warner
Huggins, F B
Harry, Geo
Ingram, Wm
Ingram, Wash
Johnson, Wm C
Joyce, Andw
Jesup, Thos J
Jamieson, J M
Kelly, John
Kehl, Jno W
Kirkpatrick, J A
Kaufman, C
Keithly, Saml
Kleindienst, A
Kibble, Alex

King, H
Killian, J G
Laudvaigt, Jno A
Lee, Jas
Lapreux, Lewis
Lee, Richd
Leeswitzet, J
Latham, W
Little, Franklin
Liomim, E
Luxon, Thos
Linkins, J
Laughton, J C
Lovejoy, J N
Lewis, W B
Little, Saml J
Lee, Mary
Lambert, J
Lesberger, H
Lee, Saml
Lomix, Elias
Mason, Enoch
Morgan, Richd
Massi & Co, F
Marceron, Jno L
Morris, Wm
Milstead, Thos
Marks,sr, Jacob
Mudd, Edw
Mansfield, J
Middleton, Rich
Meade, Jas H
McCook, John
Magnus, Fred
Miller, A
Morgan, T P
Maynard, Edw
McMahon, O
Mockobee, J B
McCauley, Jo
Nailor, D
Normon, Jane
Pickrell, J J
Peddicord, Jere'j

Parris, A K
Plant, Jno
Parsons, Jas
Posey, E
Palmer, E
Patterson, Basil
Quigley, Wm
Robb & Green
Rose, Danl
Rose, Jemima
Ross, Rezin
Rhodes Jas
Shadd, Absolom
Suit, K
Simms, Wm
Smith, Thos-2
Snyder, M
Stone, Mrs
Sims, Ann
Shepherd, Peter
Smith, Wm
Sasscer, Wm B
Scott, Wm T
Stewart, C M-2
Schureman, Jane
Simms, A
Spurling, A
Taylor, Geo
Tucker, Stewart
Tilman, Rosa
Talbert, Jas
Thompson, Rich
Tench, Thos P
Thomas, Henry
Thompson, Geo W
Taggart, Jane L
Thomas, E M
Taylor, Chas
Todschnider, R A
Thomas, Geo
Usher, Jno
Ultdorfar, Peter
Vernon, Jno
Viedt, J

Vermillion, W
Wilcox, Chas G
Warner, Nich
West, Jas
Wilkinson, Edw
Weaver, Sandy
Washington, B

Wilson, Jno H
Wallach, Rich
Watts, Saml
Welsh, Davis
Wilson, Chas
Wheatley, Wm J
Wagler, Rich

Warrington, jr, L
White, E E
Williams, S
Wilson, Patrick
Wiley, John
Ward, Francis
Young, M C

Dray License:
Bacon & Co, S
Davidson, Jos
Hall, Edw
Jackson & Bro, B L
Murray & Semmes
Middleton & Beall

Ober, S J
O'Brien, Jas
O'Donnoghue, P&T-2
Pumphrey, Saml
Parker & Co, G & T
Reid, B W

Ryon, R J
Semmes & Bro, B J
Stephenson, Jos
White & Co, E E

Hack license: Harrington, R H; Wormley, Wm

Hats, Caps license: Iddings, Saml; Milstead, Ignatius

Hawking & pedl'g license: Welply, Danl

Huckster license:
Bevans, D H
Brush, T M
Dent, Bruce
Humphreys, M A C

Johnson, D B
Kauffman, C
Roach, Mgt
Sullivan, Jno T

Scott, John
Woody, Edw

Ins Agent license:
Armstrong, G B
De Selding, C-2

Latham, R W
Pairo, Chas W

Menagerie & concert license: Quick & Co, G C

Merchandise license:
Bradwell, T
Carpenter, T
Chase, Wm
Downer, R M
Davis, Geo A
Eckart, T & H
Flood, Geo W
Gates, John N
Hunsberger & Co

Hendley, G & J R
Hilbus, Geo
Holden, Francis
Henry, C F
Ivey, Catherine
Kane, Patrick
Myers & Co, E
Murphy & Co, F J
McDermott, J

Mathiot, Geo
Schwartze, Jno
Walker & Jones
Westerfield, Jas
Worthington, L W
White, M M
Wiley, J

Retail license:

Adams, Saml	Cross, Lloyd	Sullivan, David O
Arnold, S & J	Hamilton, E M	Southorn & Murray
Bray, Geo W	Jackson, Vincent R	Venable, Wm
Cox, John	Milstead, Ignatius	White & Co, E
Clarvoe, J H	Robertson, Danl	Welsh, John

Shop license:

Bailey, John E	Freeman, Jno	Schad, John
Fugitt, F J	Gannon, Edmund	
Flint, C W	Nugent, Thos	

Slut license:

Allen, E W	Heard, Harry	Welsh, David
Clark, Isaac	Simms, Tyer	
Casparis, Jas	Scott, Wm T	

Statuary license: Dexter & Co: 1 week & 1 day
Tavern license: Thomas, Wm
Ten-pins license: Flint, C W

Theatrical license:

Adelphi Theatre	Nat'l Hall	Potter, J S

Wagon license:

Addison & Co, A	Connor, Jas A	Forshee, Moses
Adams & Co-3	Carroll, David	Green, A
Adams, Caleb	Clark, Wm	Gier, B
Baeschlin, Jno	Coyle, Jas	Gildermester, H
Butler, Matthew	Donovan, Wm-2	Green, Edwin
Bolayer, John	Davis & Garrett	Gennaty, Thos
Baden & Bro, J W	Dyer & McGuire	Grimes, J T
Barber, Geo	Desmond, Dennis	Gibson, Joshua
Buckley, T	Dunlap, Henry	Hughes, Geo W
Briscoe, Henry	Davidson, Jos	Howard, John
Brown, Thos	Entwisle, Thos	Hager, C
Beall, D L	Emery, M G	Henke & Maach
Blagden, Thos-2	Emerson, Geo W	Heitmiller, A
Ballinger, Francis-2	Emery, M G	Hager, Mrs
Bully, A H	Favier, A	Horning, G D
Bryan, Jos	Fugitt, Jos	Hall, W
Ballinger, T	Fitzgerald, D	Hamersley, Edw
Craig, Wm	Fister, Jno	Havenner & Br0-2

Hoover, John
Isaac, Hester
Jones, Alfred-2
Jones, Saml W
Jones, Noah
Knott, Geo
Krafft, Jno M-2
Kepler, Henry
Knott, Geo
King, Z M P
Kibbal, E
Lederer, C
Lemnan & Bro
Lancaster, Rich
Mason, Jos
Miller, Michl
McKelden, J C-4
McGregor, N M
Magee, Saml
Miller, Jacob
Miller, Chas
Mills, R T
McGarvey, J
McDevitt, John
Martin, A W
Newton, Benj

Noerr, Andw
Newton, Isaac
Otterback, Philip
Purdy, John-2
Pywell, R R
Pearson & Co, P M
Page & Paytu-2
Payne, Saml-2
Prather, H D
Parker, A
Polk, Saml C
Pettibone John-2
Ritchie, Thos
Rider, geo F
Rhodes, Jas
Roux, A
Riley, Philip
Riley, John
Ramsbury & Ebert
Rawlings, D
Roux, D
Skirving, Jas
Shedd, J J
Stephenson, Jos-2
Simms, J M-2
Swigert, Jos

Straub, Jos
Stewart, G
Sibley & Co, W J
Spicer, Fred
Sibley, Jas
Tenney, Jas
Thomas, Henry-2
Turney, C
Thoms, Geo
Taylor, Robt
Taylor, J H
Thompson, Jas
Tyrill, Michl
Visser, J & J-2
Vonderlick, j-2
Walker & Peck
Waganer, John
Whitfield, L
Wall, C O
Walbridge, H D
Wallace, Saml
Willson, Wm
White, Patrick-2
Weyrick, J
Walker, F
Young, M C

Persons fined during the months of Apr, May & Jun, 1851.

Ackerman, Jacob: merchandise
Acton, Osborn: running 3 carts
Barry, Mary: keeping dog
Baltzer, Mary Ann: selling liquor
Bailey, J C: do
Bayliss, Collin: keeping dog
Butler, David: do
Coburn, John: selling liquor
Carter, Edw: keeping dog
Cole, Jas: do
Cummings, Chas: omnibus
Collins, Dennis: selling liquor
Clark, Stephen: keeping dog
Calvert, Chas B: keeping open bar on Sunday
Corrigan, Bernard: selling on Sunday
Coburn, John: selling liquor

Coyle, Jas: wagon
Contee, Eliz: keeping dog
David, John: do
Duvall, Jas: selling liquor
Downs, John: keeping dogs-2
Davis, Tobias: selling iron
Defalco, Pasqual: keeping dog
Flint, C W: selling liquor
Flint, C W: billiard table
Fugitt, F J: selling liquor
Flint, C W: do-2
Gross, Andw: do
Goddard, Thos B: keeping dog
Gardner, J B: do
Grundy, T B: selling goods
Gere, Mr [alias J Doe: do
Gee, Henry: keeping dog
Gross, Andw: selling liquor on Sunday
Jackson, Edw: keeping a slut
Kerry, John: selling liquor less than a pint
Kelly, Saml: keeping dog
Kelcher, Jas: hacking
Launders, Ann: keeping dog
Lomax, Michl: do
Little, Jas: do
Lee, Moses: do
Lewis, Wm B: billiard table-3
Lee, John: keeping dogs-2
Mead, Edw: keeping dog
Miles, Jas: do
Neale, Horatio: do
Norris, Eliz: selling liquor
O'Leary, John: keeping dog
Phillippis, Mary: selling liquor
Quinn, Danl: do
Reddin, Shadrach: do
Reeside & Vanderwerken: omnibus-4
Ryan, Danl: keeping a slut
Richards, Alfred: selling liquor
Reddin, Shadrach: do
Sullivan, Timothy: do
Seibert, John: do
Scheifner, Edw: do
Thomas, Henry: keeping dog

Tyrell, Mich: wagon
Wormley, Wm: hack
Walker & Shadd: selling liquor
Wood, Jas: keeping dog
Welch, Catharine: opening shop on Sabbath
Weeden, Jas H: selling goods
Wilson, Paul: hacking
Wilson, Thos: hawking goods

Foreign papers announce the death, at Copenhagen, in the Kingdom of Denmark, on Aug 16 last, of Peter Pedersen, formerly for many years Minister from the Gov't of Denmark to that of the U S. He could not have been younger, we think, than 80 years of age.

Saml Bowles, senior, of the Springfield Republican newspaper, died at his residence in Springfield, Mass on Monday. He was 54 years old, & follows to the grave within a few quick weeks a loved & only sister, a grandchild, & his eldest daughter.

Mrd: on Sep 9, at Phil, by Rev H W Ducachet, D D, Robt Le Roy, of N Y, to Amelia, 2nd daughter of Wm D Lewis, of the former city.

Valuable improved property & bldg lot at auction: on Sep 16, immediately after the sale of property by E S Wright, I will offer the property on the corner of 1st & Fred'k sts, improved by a good 2 story brick dwlg. At the same time, a lot at the corner of 1st & Potomac sts. –H N Wadsworth -Barnard & Buckey, aucts

The excessive heat of yesterday made at least one victim of a poor man named Roach, a laborer, as we learn, employed at the foot of the Capitol. He had been in Wash City but a few days, not having long since arrived from his native land. He resided on 6th st, & was a man of about 50 years, & of large frame.

For sale: small 2 story frame house on I st, between 21st & 22nd. Apply on the premises to Jas Read.

Mount Vernon: Geo Washington was blessed with a noble father, who died, however, when he was 10 years old, & with a mother who was the soul of truth & honor. Some one in England recently tried to figure Geo Washington as English born, but in fact he was 3rd in descent from the European stock. His great grandfather emigrated from the north of England to America 118 years before the Declaration of Independence, & grandfather, father & all, were Virginia born. Washington was an Englishman under the Gov't as Colonies; once as a midshipman in British service, a post which he abandoned at the instance of his mother; once & memorably in his youth official expedition to the French commandant on the waters of the Ohio.

SAT SEP 13, 1851

Dr Wm Ingall, sr, well known practitioner in the city of Boston, died at Wrentham on Mon, & was buried Tuesday from Montgomery place. He attained the good old age of 82 years.

On Thursday Mr Geo Earp, of Phil, was seized with a fit of apoplexy, & expired in a few minutes. He was one of the oldest, most respectable, & successful merchants in that city.

Rev Thos H Gallaudet, L L D, died on Wednesday at his residence in Hartford. Mr G was the 1st Principal or presiding ofcr of the Institution for the Deaf & Dumb in Hartford, & was connected with the institution, as a manager, up to the time of his death. –Com Adv

Mrd: on Sep 3, at Westwood, near Nashville, Tenn, by Rev Dr Edgar, Dr Thos R Jennings to Miss Mary Courtney, eldest daughter of Col M Courtney.

For rent: the commodious 2 story double house, [recent residence of Capt H B Sawyer,] situated on Pa ave. Inquire of D Wadsworth, at the house.

Obit-died: at Santa Fe, New Mexico, Capt W H Saunders, a native of Leesburg, Va, & late of the 2nd regt U S Dragoons. He entered the army at an early age, as 2nd lt of dragoons, & served with distinction through the Florida war under Generals Taylor & Worth. He then participated in the brilliant victories upon the Rio Grande & siege of Vera Cruz, which resulted in the complete discomfiture of the Mexican forces, & triumph of the American army. –C [No death date given.]

For rent: the house lately occupied by R H Harrington as a public house, near the Navy Yard gate. Apply to J R Queen.

Wash City Ordinances. 1-Act to pay a balance due to Walter Linkins: the sum of $989.58, for grading K st, from 19th to 21st st. 2-Act for the relief of Jas B Greenwell: To pay him $90, for balance due for constructing a reservoir at 16th & H sts. 3-Act to pay a balance due Danl Linkins: $54.25 to be paid him for work done on the east of 9th st. 4-Act for the relief of Geo W Stewart: to be paid $60, being one half of the expense of erecting a pump at H & 12th sts, in 1836.

Valuable brick house & lot at auction: on Sep 16, by deed of trust from Gardner Green & wife, dated May 4, 1830, recorded in the land records of Wash Co, D C, in book W B #13, folios 506 to 509: all that lot of ground known as lot 5 in square 283: fronts on L st & Mass ave: improved by a 2 story brick dwlg. -A Green, auctioneer

$10 reward for return of stolen small bay Horse, with a saddle & bridle. Bring him to Levi Pumphrey's Livery Stable on C, between 4½ & 6th sts. –Arthur G Pumphrey

For sale: The Virginia Herald, an old established paper in the town of Fredericksburg is offered for sale. –Chas A Harrow, administrator

U S Patent Ofc. Ptn of Nathl J Wyeth, of Cambridge, Mass, praying for the extension of a patent granted to him for the improvement in preparing ice for shipping, for 7 years from the expiration of said patent, which take place on Dec 1, 1851. –Thos Ewbank, Com'r of Patents

Persons having claims against the estate of Richd H Harrington, deceased, will present the same to John R Queen, & all persons owing the said estate will settle the same with the said Queen. –M A W Harrington, administratrix

Cow found: was taken from the canal, a large red horned Cow, which the owner can have by proving the same & paying charges. –Alfred Lomax, Md ave & 4½ st.

Auction of Boots & Shoes, on Sep 15, at the store of T Drury, on Pa ave, between 19th & 20th sts. -Dyer & McGuire, aucts

Real estate at auction: by authority vested in me by the heirs of the late John Simpson: auction on Sep 16 of: property on the corner of High & West sts, formerly the residence of the said Simpson, being part of lot 14, in Beatty & Hawkins' addition to Gtwn, fronting on High st 84½ feet, & on West st 138¾ feet, with improvements. Also, part of lot 7, in the Slip, fronting 71 feet on West st by about 150 deep; very desirable bldg lots. -Saml Hein -E S Wright, auct

MON SEP 15, 1851
Mrd: on Sep 13, by Rev Dr Laurie, Dr Leopold Dovilliers, of St Louis, Mo, to Phillippa, 2nd daughter of Mr Nathl Carusi, of Wash City.

Mrd: on Sep 1, at Gtwn, D C, by Rev Mr Romley, Jos S Duckwall to Virginia M, youngest daughter of John W Bronaugh, deceased, late of Stafford Co, Va.

Balt American of Sat. A party of persons from Balt Co, Mr Edw Gorsuch, his son Dickinson Gorsuch, his nephew Joshua Gorsuch, Dr Thos Peirce, Nathan Nelson, Nicholas Hutchins, & another person whose name we do not know, went into Pa to recover 2 runaway slaves belong to the elder Gorsuch, & who were known to be harboring in Chester Co, at Christiana, between Lancaster & Phil. They secured the aid of a deputy U S Marshal & several police ofcrs from Phil, on Thursday to where the slaves were supposed to be secreted. Near the house they recognized 2 negro men, one of whom was recognized by Mr Gorsuch as his slave. The whites gave chase & the negroes ran into the house. A horn of bugle was sounded by the negroes, & a crowd, mostly blacks, began to collect around the house. As Mr Gorsuch & the party left, a discharge of firearms took place & Mr Edw Gorsuch was instantly shot dead, & his son was wounded in the shoulder. The negroes rushed on the wounded men & beat & multilated them in a shocking manner. The son of Mr Gorsuch was entirely disemboweled by a sweeping blow with a scythe. Mr Josua Gorsuch & Dr Peirce were dangerously wounded. An ofcr from Balt was wounded, though not mortally. The son of Mr Gorsuch, after his father was killed, drew a pistol & shot dead the negro who had fired the fatal shot. He was then set upon & barbarously murdered in the manner we have stated above. In the crowd of some 200, were a number of whites, who not only refused, when called upon by the Deputy Marshal, to assist in the enforcement of the law & the capture of the negroes, but actually encouraged then in their murderous outrages. Mr Gorsuch resided on York road, where he was the owner of a fine farm & valuable mill-seat. His son & others in the party were persons of standing & respectability. Additional Particulars. Since the above was put in type, Dickerson Gorsuch is not yet dead, though his condition is such as to render his recovery extremely doubtful. He was not cut with a scythe, but beaten & clubbed. He is lying at a house in the neighborhood of where the affray took place. Joshua Gorsuch & Dr Peirce, though beaten, were not seriously injured. The former came on yesterday with the body of old Mr Gorsuch, which was buried yesterday. The funeral took place from his late residence on the York road, attended by a large concourse of persons. The negroes in the affray have all left the vicinity. No arrests were made. [Sep 16th newspaper: nine blacks & 2 whites are in custody. The latter are Elijah Castnor & Lewis Hannaway.]

Died: on Sep 14, in Wash City, Philip Ennis, in his 64th year, a native of the county of Wexford, Ireland, & for the last 30 years a resident of Wash City. His funeral will take place from his late residence on 6th st, Sep 16, at 4 o'clock.

Died: on Sat last, Mrs Mary Corcoran, wife of Mr Jos Corcoran. Her remains will be taken from her residence, corner of 7th & H sts, at 3 o'clock this afternoon, to *St Patrick's Burial-Ground*. Friends of the family are invited to attend.

Washington L Underwood, one of the editors of the Helena [Ark] Shield, committed suicide, on Aug 20, by shooting himself through the heart. He had been in delicate health for several months, & was supposed to have been in a fit of insanity.

Dr Sylvester Graham has died at Northampton, Mass. He was the Vegetarian leader & inventor of the Graham Bread.

Household & kitchen furniture at auction: on Sep 17, at the residence of J D Logen, on H, between 17th & 18th sts. -A Green, auctioneer

Very liberal reward for return of strayed dog, of the St Bernard breed.
–John F Coyle

A child named Jenkins, a light mulatto or quadroon, about 6 years of age, fell into the water, near the Long Bridge, on Fri, & drowned.

Fire on Fri in Mr Mattingly's stable, in the rear of his dwlg, on 3rd st east, near the Eastern Branch. Boys had gathered up leaves to make a bonfire, a dangerous act.

For sale: lots 39 & 40, Deaken's Lee's, & Cazenove's addition to Gtwn, fronting on Wash st & canal. Lot 72, on Water st & basin. Also, parts of lots 81, 82, 84, 85, 86, 97, & 98, same additions. Apply to T L Ringgold.

To let, that large & commodious dwlg-house on 13th st, near G st, now occupied by Mr N Carusi. Possession on Oct 1. Apply to A Rothwell, at 7th & I sts.

TUE SEP 16, 1851
Orphans Court of Wash Co, D C. Letters testamentary on the personal estate of Betsey Dowty, late of said county, deceased. –Geo C Ames, exc

Mount Alban Institute: located on the Gtwn Heights; next sesseion will begin Nov 1. For further information address Rev Anthony Ten Broeck, Gtwn, D C.

Boston, Sep 13: Cars on the Eastern Railroad from Portland for Boston, last evening were thrown off the track at Elliott, killed Geo W Palfrey, the engineer, & Clement Pennell, the fireman. Several passengers were badly bruised.

For sale: pew #67, in St John's Church, in the centre aisle, & at a desirable distance from the pulpit. Apply to Dr Richmond Johnson, Winder's Bldg.

Fine enameled coal grates. –W H Harrover, 7th st, opposite the Patriotic Bank.

For sale: 2 lots with dwlg houses on West Market space, & next east of Gadsby

Row, fronting on I st. Terms made known by the subscriber, living 3 doors east of the premises. –Geo Bender

Hungarian emigrants, Wash, Sep 6, 1851. Hungarians who came to the U S from Shumla, Turkey, & who desire to settle in the colony of New Buda, Decatur Co, Iowa. [Letter written to Maj G Tochman & his lady born Jagiello: seeking asylum.]

Ofcrs: Jos Brick	Chas Braun	David Balogh
Martin Koszta	Mathias Snedlak	& his wife
Chas Bukovite	Rudolf Bardy	Etienn Zoka
Chas Lichtenstein	Saml Szabo	Jos Santa
Edouard Scheifele	Chas Szatmaty	Alexandre Laczko
Jos Barcas	Chas Gloss	Francois Polacaek
Jos Nagy	& his wife	Alexandre Feher
Francola Takacs	Etienn Farkas	Francois Incze
& his wife	Jean Horwqath	
Jos Kailing	Pierre Fulop	

Sub-Ofcrs:
Etienn Ajtay
Alexandre Toth
Ignace Fintay
Francois Tegyveressy
Ignace Szabo
Gustav Huszak

Citizen-soldiers
Francois Jakab
Michel Kantner
Geo Tebes
Pierre Kowach
Jean Balla
Etienn Tusa
Etienn Szoboszlay
Jean Gal
Jean Sipess
Etienn Fekees
Georges Bodanek
& his wife
Ladialaus Nemes
Jos Patsy
Michel Lorintz
& his wife
Jos Tomics
Michel Tokes
Jos Fulop
Francois Salamon
Antoin Lorant
Michel Dobezy
Michel Petrenyi
Jos Nyiri
Jean Nagy
Zacharias Lukacs
Jos Brockle

Jean Vargies
& his wife
Luis Grun
Chas Sztacho
Francois Kovach
Jean Bakes
& his wife

Saml Debreczenyi
Francois Szabo
Jos Bilkay
Alexandre Bay
Jean Ban
Ignace Botts
Luis Nemethy
Francois Zrimbo
& his wife
Chas Nemethy
Alexandre Tekete
Jos Hangya
& his wife
Francois Borondy
& his wife
Jean Rozsa
Emericus Vegh
Pierre Homola
Luis Tilip
& his wife
Jean Szekely
Jos Molnar
Alexandre Becser
Jean Vaskovich
& his wife
Saml Gerzso
Etienn Nyircgyjazy
Jean Deme

Etienn Jeney
Jean Bohonyi
Francois Laszlo
& his wife
Alex Kelemen

Alexadnre Kuhn
Jean Krucsanyi
Jean Monly
Pierre Novakovich
Chas Jakab
Etienn Nyilas
Pierre Markus
Jos Vegh
Jos Oszlany
Jos Lajos
Etienn Sulyok
Alexandre Kuhn
Michel Lapadar
Andrew Kovach
Jean Borbely
& his wife
Francois Nyiregyhazy
Antoin Velker
Antoin Sxucs
Antoin Rabathy
Antoin Badalik
& his wife
Francois Sporn
& his wife
Pierre Botta
Jos Schmielt
Laurence Suto

Jos Brick, Notaire du Comte Torontal, chef des émigrés a Shumla; Rep de ses compatriots.
Chas Lichtenstein, Capt
Chas Bukovits, Capt

W H Stanford, Merchant Taylor, north side Pa ave, west of 3rd st, under Gadsby's Hotel. [Ad]

Shannondale Springs, Jefferson Co, Va, for sale. Bushrod C Washington, late Pres of the Board, & John Yates, another stockholder in this delightful Watering Place, having directed by their wills the sale of their stock, the surviving stockholders, in full meeting have directed a sale of the whole stock. Connected with the Springs are 190 acres; bldg in good repair & accommodates 150 boarders. Refer to Dr Ashmead, Dr Mitchell, & Sam F Smith, Phil, Col Seaton & John S Gallaher, Wash, D C, & P Baltzel, Wesley Coles, & editors Sun, Balt. Communications to the undersigned, Pres of the Board, Charlestown, Jefferson City, Va.
–L W Lackland, Pres of the Board of Dirs

Valuable property for sale: by power of atty from Wm Z Beall, offers the *Tavern Stand* at Long Old Fields, PG Co, Md, now occupied by Mr Judson Richardson, with 35 or 40 acres adjoining thereto. Apply to John B Brooke, jr, Atty, Upper Marlborough, Md.

N Y Express: correspondence between Gen Concha, the Capt Gen of Cuba, & Capt Platt, the cmder of the sloop of war **Albany**, resulted in the liberation of Philip Schuyler Van Vechten, one of the party which landed from the Pampero. [Ofcrs Kelly & Haines were also liberated.] Capt Platt recognized Van Vechten, with whose father & mother, resident at Albany, N Y, he had been acquainted.

Mrd: Sunday last, by Rev Mr Alig, Mr John Casey to Miss Mary Ann Flannagan, all of Wash City.

Died: on Sep 6, at Floyd Courthouse, Va, Mr Nathl Henry, about 60 years of age, son of the famous Patrick Henry.

WED SEP 17, 1851
Mrs Sally B Gray, the only remaining daughter of the late Col Richd Taylor, & sister of the late Pres Taylor, died at the residence of F G Edwards, on Sep 6.

Among the passengers in the steamer **Pacific** arrived at N Y from Liverpool, were Prof Silliman, of New Haven; & J C G Kennedy, U S Com'r in regard to the Census.

While Rev John S Gorsuch was preaching in his pulpit at the Ryland Chapel, in this city, on Thu last, the telegraphic dispatch announcing the death of his venerable father by the hands of a negro mob in Lancaster Co, Pa, was placed in his hands. He left the next morning to be at the bedside of his brother, who is dangerously, if not mortally wounded, and to attend the funeral of his father.

Mrd: on Sep 16, at St Peter's Church, Wash City, by Rev Peter Laneghan, Peter T Marceron to Eliz T X Gartland, both of Wash City.

Furnished rooms to let: on 11th st, between G & H sts. –Mrs Hayne

Postmaster Gen est'd the following new Post Ofcs for week ending Sep 13, 1851.

Ofc	County, State	Postmaster
South Brooks	Waldo, Me	John Lane
Globe Village	Worcester, Mass	Wm Monroe
West Littleton	Middlesex, Mass	Peter C Edwards
North Ridge	Niagara, N Y	Orlando B Averill
Greig	Lewis, N Y	John L Williams
Chestnut Hill	Calvert, Md	Rich H Rawlings
Riley	Clinton, Mich	Jonathan Owen
Westphalia	Clinton, Mich	Geo Goder
Mud Creek	Easton, Mich	Joel Baily
Wheatfield	Ingham, Mich	Simon P Hendrick
South Henrietta	Jackson, Mich	Henry Hurd
Alto	Kent, Mich	Danl C McVean
Ridge	Lenawee, Mich	Henry Darling
North Brighton	Livingston, Mich	Guy C Pond
Mercer Salt Works	Mercer, Va	Wm G Heptinstall
Red Level Springs	Alleghany, Va	Sam V Gatewood
Terebinthe	Cumberland, N C	Blackman Culbreth
Belton	Anderson dis, S C	J B Lewis
Kingston	Autauga, Ala	John D Moody
Mount Hilliard	Pike, Ala	H P Wilbanks
Mount Petres	De Witt, Texas	Jas A Crawford
Myatte	Fulton, Ark	Moses T Michaels
Belmont	Sabine Parish, La	Law E Stephens
Lindville	Union Parish, La	Jolie S Bar
New Garden	Ray, Mo	Wm Sample
Wequise	Jasper, Ind	Jas McNeal
Lake James	Steuben, Ind	Clayton Malony
Dongola	Gibson, Ind	Wm C Barrett
Winneshiek	Winneshiek, Iowa	Elias J Topliff
Moneck	Winneshiek, Iowa	Saml D Johnson
Athens	Dodge, Wis	Henry A Ashley
Lincoln	Wansbard, Wis	Wm H Curtis
Stantonville	Calumet, Wis	Lemuel Fields
Power's Mill	Waukesha, Wis	Jos G Rogers
Courtland	Columbia, Wis	Horace Rust
Lynn	Calumet, Wis	Chancey Vaughn
Elk River	Benton, Min Ter	Wm R Marshall

Names Changed: 1-Providence, Wilson Co, Tenn, changed to Felix.
2-Port Gaines, Wahnahta Co, Min Ter, changed to **Fort Ripley**.

Grapes & improved garden plants for sale, at the Garden & Green-house, on 5th st, near N Y ave. —John Howlett

Wash Corp: 1-Act for the relief of Mrs Sarah Butts: referred to the Cmte of Claims. 2-Ptn of H Berrean, praying permission to retain a certain enclosure in front of his property: referred to the Cmte on Police. 3-Ptn of Levi Pumphrey & others, remonstrating against the change asked for by certain memorials in the mode of weighing hay & straw: referred to the Cmte on Police. 4-Ptn of A G Pendleton & others, asking an additional appropriation for the improvement of 2nd st east: referred to the Cmte on Improvements. 5-Ptn of Jas Hollidge, praying permission to retain a certain enclosure in front of squares 510 & 511: referred to the Cmte on Police.

Part of square 545 at auction: by deed of trust from Aaron McAlwe & wife, dated May 2, 1844, recorded in the land records of Wash Co, D C, in Liber W B #10, folios 125 to 129: public auction on Oct 18: fronts on N st, the same comprehending the entire lots 64 & 65, of Jones' subdivision of said square. Improvements consist of a good frame house with 5 rooms, besides a kitchen. -A Green, auct

Administrator's sale of leasehold property, valuable lot of mahogany, cabinet-maker tools, & household & kitchen furniture at auction: on Sep 19: sale of the leasehold of lot __, in square 290, improved by a new brick house, on E st, between 12th & 13th sts. Also the effects of the late Jas E W Thompson, deceased. Lots 14 & 15, in square 534, on 3rd st, between N & O sts, will be sold at the same time. By order of Geo Savage & John D Clark, administrators. -Dyer & McGuire, aucts

Jas Fennimore Cooper died after a lingering illness, at his residence in Cooperstown, N Y. [No death date given-current news item.]

THU SEP 18, 1851
Orphans Court of Wash Co, D C. In the case of John P Pepper & Josiah W Hicks, excs of Dorcas Galvin, deceased: the execs & Court have appointed Oct 7 next for the final settlement of the said estate, with the assets in hand.
—Ed N Roach, Reg/o wills

Col Pragay, the Hungarian, who was killed in Cuba, had happily settled near Galveston, Texas, & was doing well, when duped by the scripholders into the fatal expedition, upon the pretence that the Cubans desired aid & help. He forfeited his life & good prospects in a passionate devotion to liberty, which too late he found he was forcing on the Cubans against their wishes. —Alex Gaz

The Mayor of Buffalo has justly revoked the license of Horace Perkins, the keeper of an emigrant passage ofc in that city, for charging $4 for a steerage ticket to Chicago, when the usual price is $1.50.

John Thos Patterson, age 22 years, went to a fire in Balt on Sat, & got drunk. He then went home, & being sick, went to a window, fell out & broke his neck. —Alexandria Gaz

Mrd: on Sep 16, by Rev J Geo Butler, John McLane Buel to Miss Mary Ellen, daughter of John C Roemmelle, all of Wash City.

Capt Robbins, master of the schnr **Martha Greene**, which arrived at Boston on Tue, reports that on Aug 12, 60 miles from Cape Pine, a boat containing Capt Roallons & 6 men, belonging to the British ship **Hindostan**, bound from Whitby, Eng, to Quebec, which ship foundered at sea, carrying down 8 of the crew. Those saved were landed by Capt Robbins at Shelburne, N S.

Died: on Sep 17, Mrs Lydia Wood, wife of Henry S Wood, in her 51st year. Her funeral will take place from her late residence, Capitol Hill, 4th st, near Pa ave, tomorrow, 2 o'clock.

Died: on Sep 16, in Wash City, after a long illness, Mr Zachariah Hazel, in his 82nd year. His funeral is at his late residence, on Capitol Hill, on Thu, at 2 o'clock.

$10 reward for return of a black horse, stolen from my stable, at Good Hope, on Sep 15. Jos T Mitchell, Proprietor of Good Hope Hotel, D C

Appointment by the Pres: Chas H Ladd, to be Navy Agent for the Navy Yard at Kittery, Maine, & for the Naval Station at Portsmouth, N H, in place of Chas W Cutter, resigned.

Wm McL Cripps, Cabinet-maker, 11th st, near Pa ave, has on hand some very handsome cottage sets of furniture; fancy rush seat chairs; cane seat chairs, & fancy chairs.

$15 reward for return of a horse, stolen on Sep 10. —Richd Griffith, near the Almshouse.

FRI SEP 19, 1851
Gen Dearborn died at Portland on Jul 29, of a malignant disease. Henry Alex'r Scammel Dearborn was born at Exeter, N H, on Mar 3, 1783; was educated at Wm & Mary College, in Va; studied law 3 years in a Southern State, & 1 year in the ofc of the late Justice Story, at Salem. At this time, his father was Sec of War, & Thos Jefferson was the President of the U S. In 1812 he commanded the troops in Boston harbor; in 1831 he was elected to Congress from the 8th district. He held the ofc of Adj Gen of the Commonwealth til 1843; was Mayor of Roxbury, in 1847.

At the last term of the Taylor Criminal Court, in session at Campbellsville, Ky, Taylor Murphy was found guilty of the murder of his wife in May last, & sentenced to be hung on Oct 10. He has since made a full confession of the crime. A brother of Murphy, charged with being an accessory, is now in the Taylor county jail awaiting trial.

Hon G P Marsh, U S Minister at Constantinople, & his wife, arrived at Abeiah, with health greatly improved.

Mr Chancellor S Barber petitioned the Supreme Court of New London Co, Conn, at the Aug term, for divorce from his wife, Phoebe A, on the ground that she is guilty of habitual intemperance & the excessive use of morphine, which, under the Conn statute of 1849, furnish good cause of divoce. Judge Church denied the petition, for the reason that the practices complained of were encouraged by the petitioner himself, & the result of his fault & negligence.

Mrd: on Sep 16, at St Mary's Church, by Rev Mr Alig, Michl Ragan to Mary Agnes Elder, both of Wash City.

Mrd: on Sep 16, at St Mary's Church, by Rev Mr Alig, Martin Yunganz to Mgt Bott, both of Wash City.

Mrd: on Sep 18, by Rev Mr Alig, Mr Wm Hammel to Miss Barbara Vonderlehr, both of Wash City.

Died: the funeral of Saml Mundell, aged 14 years, will take place from the residence of his parents, Marine Barracks, this afternoon, at 4 o'clock. [No death date given-current item.]

Wm L Chaplinn: last autumn the Court of Montg Co, Md, required him to give bail, which he did, for $19,000, on a charge of assault & battery, with intent to kill those who intercepted him while he was driving away from D C 2 slaves, the property, severally, of Hon A H Stephens & Hon Robt Toombs. The venue was changed to Howard Co, Md. At the spring court the bail was declared to be forfeited, he not having made his appearance. The witnesses of this city, Messrs Goddard, Butts Handy, & Smithia, are to be present in court today, when we presume they will be released from their recognizances. Chaplin still being afar from Ellicott's Mills. –Republic

Two boys in West Meriden, Conn, Thos & Wm Daniels, aged 10 & 8, flung powder from a keg they found into a bonfire. They had put powder in their pockets, which took fire and both were badly burnt. Thos died the next morning, & Wm is not expected to recover.

The public are cautioned not to purchase or trade for certain notes signed by me, dated Sep, 1850, payable to L F Harris & Emory Houghton, of Burlington, Vt, as the consideration for which they were given has entirely failed, viz. an alleged patent: improvement on the lime kilns, by which half of the fuel was to have been saved, but which has turned out no saving at all. –Avory E Smoot

Valuable farm & hotel, improved city property, also servant man [24] & woman [60], at auction: on Oct 6, the tract called ***Chichester***, improved by a frame hotel, known as Good Hope, lying on the east side of the Eastern Branch, in Wash Co. Both servants are restricted to the District. Also, lots 4 & 5 in square 1,001, improved by 2 frame dwlgs. -Dyer & McGuire, aucts

On Sep 17, a party of 3 men & 2 boys, all attached to the Marine Garrison, proceeded on a gunning excursion. There were but 3 guns. Wm Wells, a private in the Corps, was extremely desirous to obtain from Saml Mundell, the deceased, his fowling piece, which was repeatedly refused. On their arrival at the grounds of Mr Atchinson, an altercation ensued between Wells & young Mundel, [age 14 years,] during which the latter raised his gun in a menacing position, when Well sprung towards him, seized the piece with one hand, raised it as if he intended to knock the boy down, then fell back a short distance, cocked it, took deliberated aim & fired, lodging the contents of the gun in the left side of young Mundell's neck, killing the boy instantly. Wells was committed to jail. Young Mundell is a son of Orderly Sgt Jos Mundell, universally respected as a most excellent ofcr & citizen. The funeral will take place from the Garrison, today, at 4 o'clock.

Wash City Ordinances. 1-Act for the relief of Joshua Peirce: $145 to be appropriated, to settle his account. 2-Act authorizing Jas Casparis, to widen an area in front of his premises, in the 5th Ward.

We were yesterday presented by Mr Thos Bates, whose charming homestead near Rock Creek Church is so aptly termed ***Pomona***, with a sample of the fruit he has been raising.

Centennial Anniversary of the Founding of Gtwn, D C. By act of Assembly of Md, sitting at Annapolis, May 15, 1771, Com'rs were authorized to survey & lay out a town, to consist of 80 lots, in Fred'k Co, on the Potomac river, above the mouth of Rock Creek. These com'rs were Henry Wright Crabb, John Needham, John Clagett, Saml Magruder, Jas Perry, & David Lynn. The land constituting the site of the projected town was the property partly of Geo Gordon & of Geo Beall. On Sep 18, 1751, the com'rs, Saml Magruder alone absent, met according to law & chose for their clerk Alex'r Beall, who was sworn before John Needham, to register in a well-bound book the certificate of survey of Gtwn, the price of each respective lot, the name of its owner, & time of its being paid for, or of the tender or refusal of the proprietor or proprietors, & the other transactions & proceedings of the com'rs in &

about the town aforesaid. The town was to be called Gtwn, a title variously derived, but believed to be the result of a compromise between the proprietors as individuals & loyal subjects. At one time the name of a possible town there was likely to be **Beallsville**; but that appearing, perhaps, somewhat *two egotistical for those sober & modest times, it was agreed that, as the two proprietors of the site of the intended place gloried in the praenomen George, & as that was also the name of their then sovereign liege the King of Great Britain, the most unexceptionable title should be that which, by act of Assembly & succeeding custom, it has ever borne. Alex'r Beall, the clerk, was also appointed surveyor, & how competent he was for both functions the neat & well kept record & town plots well attest. The area of the town plot was to be 60 acres, comprising 26 acres & eleven-sixteenths of Geo Gordon's land, & the remainder of 33 acres & five-sixteenths of Geo Beall's. It was surveyed & laid out by the appointed surveyor according to the provision of the act of Sep 19, 1751, this day 100 years ago. When application was made to these proprietors to sell their land so surveyed & laid out, they refused to do so on reasonable terms, leaving it incumbent on the com'rs to issue their warrant summoning 17 good & lawful men of Fred'k Co, to be at the Inspection House, to meet on Sep 28, for the purpose of assessing & returning what damages or recompense should be allowed the non-contents for their land. The instrument summoning these 17 was directed to Josiah Beall, coroner of Fred'k Co. On meeting of this Jury, on Feb 27, 1742, the sum of L280 currency [$746.66] was adjudged as a fair & just equivalent for the land, or about $12 7/16ths per acre. By the act of Assembly it was graciously permitted that the two proprietors should have first choice of any two lots apiece they might prefer; &, when the proposition was made to them by the Comr's, Geo Gordon, wisely submitting to what was inevitable, made choice of two lots, as did his more uncompromising neighbor & co-proprietor, but not before making a thorough-going protest in which he notifies the com'rs of his intention to appeal to a higher law. His letter to the com'rs we deem worthy a literal transcription, retaining his own spelling & punctuation: 7th March, 1752. If I must part with my property by force I had better save a little than be totally demolished, rather than have none I accept of them lots, said to be Mr Henderson's and Mr Edmonson's. But I do hereby protest and declare that my acceptance of the said lots, which is by force, shall not debar me from future redress from the com'rs or others. If I can have the right of a British subject I ask no more. God save King George. –George Beall. Witnesses present, Archd Henderson, Nich's Haymond, Clem't Davis, and Thos Lamar. The lots Mr Beall took are among the most valuable now in the town, being situated about where the cotton factories now stand. The purchaser of the first lot was Eliz Beall, who gave L1 10 for it, but paid down on 5s. Sixty-nine lots were sold, coming to L191, of which only L17.5 were actually paid in at the sale. Messrs Beall & Gordon received the purchase moneys, however, & thus acknowledged the validity of the proceedings, thus releasing the Com'rs from all future litigation in respect to the title. As laid out, the street now called High was first entitled Water st, & that part of Bridge st west of Water was called Falls st. The street now called Water, had, in different places the names of the Keys & Wapping. [Oct 1st newspaper: in a brief biography of Danl Boone the honor of the name is claimed by the grandfather of the famous Western pioneer. Shortly after Geo Boone's arrival in this country from England, in 1717, he purchased a large tract of land in Berks Co, Pa, & various other tracts in Md & Va, & among others the land on which Gtwn was laid off, & to which, it is said, he gave his name-a name given to it under the impression that it would afterwards become a town of some magnitude & commercial importance. In some of the old records of Md the fact of the purchase by Boone could be ascertained, &, if ascertained, possibly the fact, from other evidence, of his having given to the town in futuro his own Christian name, as one Pope is said to have given the name of **Tiber** to the creek below the Capitol Hill in Wash, & that of Capitol to the hill itself, which it now bears, from the circumstance of his being named Pope, & his farm near the Capitol Hill, Rome. –W]

SAT SEP 20, 1851
Tremont House, Boston, Mass, having been one of the firm of John L Tucker & Co, the subscriber pledges his best exertions to maintain its reputation.
–Wm H Parker, Boston

Suitable reward for return of strayed or stolen sorrel Horse. –Francis N Brent, residing in Montg Co, Md: Washington & Rockville Turnpike, 8 miles from Wash City.

Died: on Sep 18, Mary Alice Davis, daughter of M A Davis, aged 3 years & 10 months. Her funeral is today at 4 o'clock, on Pa ave, between 4½ & 6th sts.

Grand Railroad Jubilee at Boston. From the Boston Journal of Thu. Yesterday was the first day of the Great Celebration; Col Schouler addressed the Pres: Hon Henry Wilson made an address. Military escort was under Gen Edmands, with the first brigade under Brig Gen Andrews, & 2 regts of selected corps out of the city, & a battalion of riflemen under Maj Saunders. On the extreme right was the 5th regt of artl, under Col Cowdin, comprising the following companies: Bond's Cornet Band. Roxbury Artl, Capt Webber; Wash Artl, Capt W W Bullock; Boston Artl, Capt A H Evans; Columbian Artl, Capt E Thompson.
1st Regt of Light Infty, under command of Col Holbrook, viz: Flagg's Brass Band. New England Guards, Capt Bradlee; Boston Light Guard, Capt Clark; Wash Light Guard, Capt Savory; Boston Light Infty, Capt Ashley; City Guards, Lt Pulsifer; Norfolk Guards, Roxbury, Capt Merrian; Mass Volunteers, Capt Moore; Warren Light Infty, Lt Nichols; Independent Boston Fusileers, Capt Mitchell; Winthrop Light Guard, South Boston, Capt Cassel; Pulaski Guards, South Boston, Capt A J Wright.
A regt of Infty under Col J D Greene, viz: Charlestown Brass Band.
Woburn Mechanic Phalanx, Capt Granner; Lowell Mechanic Phalanx, Capt T G Farmer; Worcester Light Infty, Capt E Lamb; Worcester City Guards, Capt Goodhue; Cambridge City Guards, Capt Geo A Meacham; Davis Guards, Acton,

Capt W E Falkner; Lowell City Guards, Capt Lesure; Charlestown City Guards, Capt Sanger.

A regt of infty under Col Nathan P Colburn, viz: Beverly Light Infty, Beverly; Marblehead Light Infty, Marblehead, Capt Gregory; Salem Light Infty, Capt Endicott; Stoneham Light Infty, Stoneham, Mass, Capt L Dike; Salem Mechanic Light Infty, Capt B R White; Lawrence Light Infty, Capt M Dodge; Winchester Guards, Winchester, Capt Prince.

Battalion of Rifles, under the command of Maj Wm Saunders, consisting of the Mechanic Riflemen of this city, Capt T G Adams; & the Nat'l Rifle Guard of Marlborough, Capt Hope.

Marshals:

Wm H Foster	F Lyman Winship	F W Lincoln, jr
C H Appleton	C F Lougee	Granville Mears
Joel Scott	T W Pierce	J M Wightman
H C Lord	F A Allen	J R Bradford
J B Wheelock	Farnham Plumer	Geo F Train
David S Child	F G Whiston	M F Fowler
J W Bradford	G F Woodman	E F Hall
D E Bates	Geo A Batchelder	E D Cushing

Hon Seth E Sill, one of the Justices of the Supreme Court of N Y, died in Buffalo a few days ago. He had returned from Batavia, where he had been attending a term of the Supreme Court, slightly indisposed, & on the following day was violently seized with the malady which terminated his life.

Rev Levi R Reese, a distinguished minister of the Methodist Protestant Church died, after a short illness, this morning, on the Eastern Shore of Md, whither he had gone on a visit. -Balt Argus

The venerable Jas Montgomery, the Christian poet of England, will be 80 years of age on Nov 5 next, on which day the citizens of his native town of Sheffield intend honoring him by the erection of a statue. [Dec 4th newspaper: Montgomery was educated at the Moravian Establishment at Fulneck, England, & strictly adhered to the tenets of the sect throughout his life. He was employed in boyhood by Mr Gales, father of Jos Gales, of the Nat'l Intell, who was then a bookseller in Sheffield. He was the editor of a radical paper called the Sheffield Iris, was found guilty of sedition, & imprisoned in York Castle, where many of his poems were composed.]

Telegraphic dispatch from Pittsburgh, received yesterday, announced the arrest there of a young man, Haldeman, from Columbia, Pa, who ran away from York, Pa, on Mon with upwards of $3,000 belonging to his father & others, which had been entrusted to him to get exchanged. His arrest was accomplished through the agency of Mayor Gilpin, of Phil, & his special ofcrs. –Phil American

Trustees sale: by decree of the Circuit Court of Wash Co, D C, passed in a cause wherein Martha C Williams & others are cmplnts, & Ephraim Mulliken & others, heirs of John Mulliken, are dfndnts: the subscriber, as trustee, will expose to sale at auction, on Oct 23, lot 11 in square 74, fronting on K st, Wash City, with the dwlg house & other improvements thereon. –W Redin -A Green, auct

Notice: by virtue of an execution, issued by John L Smith, j p for Wash Co, D C, to me directed, at the suit of John Schad against the goods & chattels of W G Williams, I have levied on a lot of lumber, poplar, & pine boards & scantling, as the property of said Williams, which if not redeemed by Sep 23, according to law, they will be sold at public sale, for cash, in the morning. –J A Ratcliffe, Constable

Masonic: the funeral of Brother Henry Morgan, late of St John's Lodge, #11, will take place on Sep 21, at 3 o'clock, from Masonic Hall, 10th & E sts.
-Chas Calvert, Sec

MON SEP 22, 1851

Hon Fred'k Whittelsey died on Fri, at his residence in Rochester, N Y, on Friday, of typhus fever. He was a rep in Congress from the Monroe district from 1831 to 1835.

Hon Jefferson Davis has consented to run as the Secession candidate for Govn'r of Mississippi, in place of Gen Quitman, declined.

Mr D W Ferrall, of Bladensburg, on Monday last shot on one tide, on the flats of the eastern Branch of the Potomac, 96 ortolans, [sora,] 46 reed birds & 2 plover. As the sora can only be shot singly, & the tide serving probably little more than 3 hours, Mr Ferrall's success exceeds any thing we have before heard of in small shot sporting.

On Fri of last week the daughter of Mr C & Mrs Mary Mahony, living in East Granby, Conn, was burnt to death. In the absence of her parents, she got a box of matches, with which she got on a bed & set fire to the bedclothes. She was badly burnt & lived but 2 hours.

Red Republican of Aug 30: fatal affray in Anna Coco settlement, in the parish of Rapides, on Aug 23, two men, Francis Head & Mr Weeks, were killed & others wounded. It grew out of a charge that was made against Head that he had set fire to a house. Mr Hardcastle, the police juryman of the ward, killed Harris, & one of the Sweats, Mr Weeks. Several persons were engaged in the affray, but not arrested.

Mrd: on Sep 18, at Broad Creek House, PG Co, Md, by Rev J Martin, T S Everett, U S Army, to Miss Eliza, daughter of the late Col Thos C Lyles.

Stock of groceries, liquors, & store fixtures, at auction: on Sep 25, at the store occupied by Mr S S Noland, on the corner of 14th & L sts. -Dyer & McGuire, aucts

In Harrison Co, Ind, on Tue, a young man, F McRae, while out squirrel hunting, stood the breech of his gun on the ground, with the muzzle leaving against his breast. The gun went off & killed him almost instantly.

On Sep 5 murder was committed at Port Gibson, Miss, by Geo A Briscoe; his victim was the well known & highly esteemed Jeremiah Chamberlin, Pres of Oakland College. Briscoe went to the college & assaulted Briscoe with the sword from a cane & killed him. The murderer robbed the gallows of its just dues by cutting his throat from ear to ear, & died in a few minutes. It is said that the difficulty originated from political matters. -New Orleans Bulletin

For rent: commodious house in the 1st Ward, now occupied by the Brazilian Minister. For terms apply to Gen Gratiot, Six Bldgs.

TUE SEP 23, 1851
N Y cement for sale in lots to suit purchaser. A constant supply will be kept on hand. Apply to Peter Berry, Water st, Gtwn.

I certify that Judson Walker brought before me a Bay Mare, taken up as an estray trespassing on the farm of John Little. Owner is to come forward, prove property, pay charges, & take her away. Wash Co, D C: J Florentius Cox, J P

The death of Jas Fennimore Cooper took place on Sep 14, at his residence in Cooperstown. For several months past his health had been in a condition which awakened the anxiety of his friends. His works have become permanently incorporated with the best literature of every civilized country. Mr Cooper was born at Burlington, N J, on Sep 15, 1789, & had he lived one day longer, he would have been 62 years of age. His father, the late Judge Cooper, was a large landholder in O s go Co, in this State, residing alternately at Burlington & Cooperstown, & giving his name to the latter township. He entered Yale College in 1802; at 13 he was ill qualified for the attainment of academic distinction; in 1805 he entered the service as a midshipman & remained in the Navy for 6 years. In 1810 he resigned his post in the Navy, & married the lady who survives to mourn his loss, & resided in Westchester, in the vicinity of N Y. After a short time he removed to his patrimonial estate in Cooperstown, & pursued in earnest his career as a writer of fiction: The Spy, The Pioneers, The Pilot, Lionel Lincoln, & The Last of the Mohicans-in 1826. While in Europe for several years, he wrote The Bruro, The Red Rover, & The Prairie. On his return to the U S he wrote The Pathfinder, The destroyer, The Two Admirals, & Wing and Wing.

Orphans Court of Wash Co, D C. Letters testamentary on the personal estate of Zachariah Hazel, late of said county, deceased. –H R Maryman, exc

From the Tarborough Press of Sep 20. Mrd: at Roseneath, in Halifax Co, on Sep 7, by Jas Jones, Mr Richd Williamson, of Missouri, to Mrs Martha L Savage. Mr Williamson was a wealthy old gentleman, living in the extreme western part of Missouri. They met while he was traveling, at the house of his old friend Moses Smith, Mrs Savage, a niece of his wife. When he proposed she told him she was a widow with four responsibilities, which was all she possessed. He said he was rich enough for them all, & finally the marriage came off, & they all started for the far West. May happiness attend them!

Mrd: on Sep 17, at Salisbury, N C, by Rev Prof Morgan, his daughter, Miss Charlotte Eliphel Morgan to E Delafield Smith, Counsellor at Law of N Y.

Bargain: **Pine Grove**, elevated site for a cottage or summer residence, 4 miles from Washington, containing 30 acres. Price only $600 cash. Inquire of Rich B Lloyd.

Postmaster Gen est'd the following new Post Ofcs for week ending Sep 20, 1851.

Ofc	County, State	Postmaster
N Washington	Lincoln, Me	Nelson Calderwood
Lombardville	Cecil, Md	Wm A Long
East Saganaw	Saganaw, Mich	Alfred M Hoyt
Zilwaukie	Saganaw, Mich	Albert C Jones
Purgitsville	Hampshire, Va	Wm S Purgit
Magnolia	Washington, Va	Wm P Milnor
Meadow Dam	Patrick, Va	Jas Reynolds
Crater's Mills	Iredell, N C	John Templeton
Millersville	Barnwell dist, S C	G E Miller
Pleasant Spring	Lexington dist, S C	John Shuler
Juno	Lumpkin, Ga	Wm Burt
Martin's Store	Macon, Ga	A J Easom
Anguilla	Clay, Ia	Allen J Parish
Prairie Ridge	White, Ia	Richd Eastman
Lansing	Porter, Ia	E H Johnson
Hall	Franklin, Ill	Jacob S Clark
Crittenden	Franklin, Ill	Thos E Smith
Boone	Franklin, Mo	Jas B Southworth
Pomona	St Charles, Mo	John Smith
Croked Lake	Marquette, Wis	L G Wood
Chippewa Falls	Chippewa, Wis	Hiram S Allen
Jordan	Greene, Wis	Ora Satterlee
East Hampden	Columbia, Wis	Alfred Topliff
Mouterey	Davis, Iowa	Danl Moyer

Names Changed: East Sand Lake, Rensselaer Co, N Y, changed to East Poestenkill. Marine Settlement, Madson Co, Ill, changed to Marine.

Wanted a female Teacher, in a private family in the country. A Catholic preferred. R B Lloyd, Alexandria, Va

Wash City Ordinance: 1-Act for the relief of Thos McNaney & John Dove: the sum of $559 be appropriated to pay the balance due, for grading Conn ave.

At the risk & expense of Patrick Moran, the former purchaser, I shall expose for sale, at public auction, on Sep 26, a lots of ground on 15th & M sts, with a 2 story house & peach orchard. –Eliza Bates, Z A Farr, Agent -A Green, auctioneer

WED SEP 24, 1851
Havana, Sep 11, 1851. List of prisoners brought to Habana from the late Cuban Expedition under the command of Gen Narciso Lopez, & final disposition of them as far as known. Sent to Spain by steamer **Isael la Catollca:**

Chas A Downer, Mobile
J D Hughes, New Orleans
J St Levy, Quebec
F D Hough, New Albany, Ind
Sent to Spain by ship **Venus:.**
Louis Schlessinger, Hungary
D E De Wolk, Mobild
E H McDonald, Mobile
H J Thomason, Mobile
J Norriss, Mobile
A R Wier, Mobile

Sent to Spain by ship **Primera de Gautemala:**
Joaquin Casanova, New Orleans
Jas Chapman, Charleston
Wm H McKinsey, Bardstown, Ky
C Cook, Ala
Danl Seay, New Orleans
C Noll, Berlin
J D Baker, New Orleans
Henry B Hart, Petersurg, Va
Louis Bauder, Germany
Jacob Faust, St Louis
Benj F Hanna, Balt
Patrick McGrath, New Orleans
J G Dwin, New Orleans
Chas J Daily, New Orleans
D Q Rousseau, New Orleans
S H Furnell, New Orleans
Wm H Craft, Memphis, Tenn
Conrad Tailor, Berlin
J G Bush, New Orleans
Thos Denton, New Orleans
T A Simpson, Phil
C A McMurray, Balt
W W Inslee, New Orleans
Antonio Hernandez, Havana
A T Pruitt, Ala
Elias J Otts, Depotville, N Y
Thos Hilton, Wash, D C
Bernard Allen, St Louis
W L Wilkinson, Mobile
Julio Chassagne, Havana
M Mullen, St Louis
Thos H Lee, New Orleans
P Lacoste, New Orleans
Geo Metcalf, Ireland
Patrick Coleman, New Orleans
H B Metcalf, Ireland
M L Hefron, N Y
Robt M Grider, New Orleans
Jas Brady, Galena, Ill
M K Scott, Ky
Henry Schmidt, New Orleans
Geo R Wilson, Phil
Geo Foster, New Orleans
Wm H Vaughn, Ky

Wm H Cameron, Jefferson Co, Va
Peter McMullen, Ireland
John Denton, N Y
Franklin P Boyd, N Y
Thos R Munroe, Miss
Edw Weiss, Germany
Robt Schutz, Prussia
C Schneck, Baden
Geo Holdship, St Louis
Jas H Hearsey, New Orleans
Luke Scully, New Orleans
Wm Wilson, New Orleans
Thos Daily, New Orleans
Jas M Wilson, New Orleans
Henry Saile, Liverpool
Wm K Hurd, New Orleans
G Bontilla, Hungary
Slezinger, Hungary
Radnitz, Hungary
Curmeli, Hungary
Petrie, Hungary
Kercker, Hungary
Viosg, Hungary
Ngikos, Hungary
Michl Biro, Austria
David Winborn, Miss
Thos Hudnall, New Orleans
H Von Schlicht, Berlin
J B Gunst, New Orleans
Timothy K Henry, Natchez
Howard Purnell
John McKinnis
E Q Bell, New Orleans
John Carter
Bernard McCabe, Ireland
John Murphy, Ireland
Hiram West, Spring Valley, Ohio
Waiting ship at Havana:
C J Duffy, New Orleans
Thos Little, Mobile
Michl Geiger, New Orleans
John D Brown
Geo S Berry, Cincinnati, Ohio

C Sebring
Jas Halpin
Benj Gilman, Cincinnati, Ohio
Edw Crissy
Jas Smith
Hudson Nelson
A R Ludwig, New Orleans
Chas Harrison, New Orleans
Victor Duprat, New Orleans
Henry Stanmyre, New Orleans
Geo Quick, Phil
Henry McHenry, New Orleans
Jas D Donnelly, Pottsville, Pa
Chas Giblin, Cincinnati, Ohio
John Murtigh, Phil
Thos McClelland, Ireland
John McKneiss, Pittsburg
Pedro M Lopez, Venezuela
Pedro Valazco, Cuba, servant of
  Lopez
Manuel Fleury, Cuba
Jacob Harbele, Germany
Louis Hackel, Swiss
Manuel Martinez, Havana
F A Laine, Cuba
F C Mahan, Danville, Ky
John Boswell, Balt
W L Constantine, Canada
Wm Cousans, Lincoln, Eng
H Schmidt, Saxony
Conrad Bechtold, Prussia
Jas Oglevie, New Orleans
Harvey Williams, New Orleans
John Cooper
Jas B Gafin, Ohio

Asher J Phillips, New Orleans
Jacob Jessert
Thos Bryan
John Bachilder, New Orleans
John Brown

In the Hospital, all doing well:
A L Alfonso, Cuba, arm
Manuel Aragon, ____, leg
J B Rurira, Galicia, leg
Preston Essex, St Louis, leg, slight
Robt H Ellis, Wash, D C, left hand
John Cline, New Orleans, thigh, slight
N Port, Prussia, finger, slight
John N Davis, New Orleans, shoulder, slight
Jas Fiddes, Malta, both legs
J G Porter, Dublin, breast & arm, slight
G Richardson, New Orleans, arm, slight
F Curvia, Havana, arm
M J Keenan, Mobile, finger, slight
John Talbot, New Orleans, hand, slight
Jose Douvren, Cuba, side, slight
Wilson A Rieves, Mississippi, leg, slight
Wm Losner, Saxony, finger
Thos McNeil, Lumpkin Co, Ga, sick
L Palanka, Hungary, graze, slight
Wm Miller, Northampton, Eng, finger, slight
J B Weymouth, Nashville, Tenn, hand, slight
John Robinson, England, side, slight
Geo Edgerton, Natchez, sick
+
N Lopez: executed
P S Van Vechten: delivered to Capt Platt
Andrae Gonzalez: in prison
___ Somers, New Orleans: pardoned
Capt Lopez: in prison
Julio Herren: detained here
J A Kelly: liberated
H S Haynes: liberated

Household & kitchen furniture at auction: on Oct 7, at the residence of his Excellency Sergio T de Macedo, on Pa ave, near Gtwn, all his superb furniture, china, glass, family carriages, & horses. -Dyer & McGuire, aucts

Marshall Hall for sale: by deed of trust from the late Wm Page & wife to the subscriber, dated Dec 20, 1850: recorded in the land records of Chas Co, Md: public auction on Oct 4, in front of the Mayor's ofce, Alexandria, Va: contains 377¼ acres: with a large & commodious brick Mansion House, containing 16 rooms, & all requisite out-houses. -Law B Taylor, trustee

Bvt Brig Gen Henry Whiting, Assist Quartermaster Gen in the U S Army, died at St Louis on Sep 16. His death was sudden, & supposed to have been caused by an affection of the heart. He entered the army in 1808. His remains are to be taken to Detroit for interment.

Among the passengers who embarked on the ship **Franklin**, on Sat, for France, was Gen I Watts De Peyster, who visits Europe as well for the benefit of his health as, at the instance & by the direction of Govn'r Hunt, of the State of N Y, to examine into the organization of the French Nat'l Guard, Pressian Landwehr, Swedish Indelta, & other municipal systems of police & defence, in order to submit the result to the Executive.

Edw L Dawson, Barber: 7th st, one door from E st, Wash. [Ad]

Albany, N Y, Sep 22. Accident on the railroad Sat, by which 2 men, Stephen Kiernan, aged 35, & Geo Slack, aged 19, were instantly killed. They were employed on the water-works & were struck by the train as they walked on the tracks on their way home. Kiernan was a widower, & leaves 2 children in Ireland. Slack was unmarried.

Evansville, Ind, Sep 22. Explosion of the steamer **James Jackson**, yesterday, on leaving Shawneetown. List of the killed, wounded, or missing: John Francis, of La, badly wounded & scalded; Philip Rance, of La, do; Capt Simmes, of Natchez, killed; Capt Walker, of Ark, killed; John Grimes, of Vera Cruz, wounded & scalded; Emanuel Brown, of New Orleans, scalded; Sol Warner, negro, of Louisville, killed; Isaac C Green, of Texas, killed; Moses Embray, of Columbus, Ohio, wounded; Austin Johnson, of New Orleans, do; Demsood, of Gtwn, Ky, killed; Mr Fisk & Elised Pitts, of Gtwn, Ky, scalded; Mr Silney, of Ark, do; Jas Craft, of Md, & Chas Alliany, of Louisville, badly scalded; Jas Larkins, of Louisville, do; Wm Warner, late of Providence, do; Isaac McCorckle, of Miss, do; O M Garrott & wife, scalded; Jas McFadden, of Baton Rouge, badly scalded; S C Thomas, of Pa, leg broken; Arnold Lashler, of Ky, & Bend, of Miss, slightly scalded; R H Rishley, of La, slightly scalded; Mary Ehmsel, of Louisville, killed; P K Cochran, of New Orleans, slightly scalded; Danl Marshall, of Ill, slightly scalded; D Hood, of Miss, killed. J J Mitchell, of Maine, badly wounded; Dr A C Kuns, of Louisville, slightly hurt; Judge C Morgan, of La, do; Col V Stewart, of Pa, R E McHallon, of Maine, badly hurt; Allern, of Miss, C C Shackleford, slightly burnt; McEmon, do; Khen, do.

Household & kitchen furniture at auction: on Sep 26, at the residence of Dr Hiram Wadsworth, Dentist, on 1st st. –Barnard & Buckey, aucts, Gtwn.

Proposals will be received until Fri next for excavation to change the course of Tiber creek through square 630, to the culvert now bldg, & also to turn the stream east of the Tiber into it on the south line of Mass ave. –Fra K Lord, Com'r 3rd & 4th Wards.

As 2 locomotives attached to a freight train were coming up from Columbus to Cleveland, the boiler of one exploded, instantly killing S Booth, one of the engineers, & fatally injuring the other. A fireman was also severely scalded.

Chancery Notice: the creditors of Alex'r Shepherd, deceased, are to produce their claims against the estate of said Shepherd, duly vouched, on or before, Oct 3 next. –Walter S Cox, Special Auditor

Mrd: on Sep 20, by Rev Mr Hodges, Edwin Waterman to Maria Amos Lindsay, all of Wash.

Died: on Mon, at N Y, while on his way Eastward, Capt John A Blake, in his 54th year. He has been a resident of Wash City about 20 years, & leaves a family & many friends to mourn his sudden death. His funeral is tomorrow at 10 o'clock, from his late residence, on 11th, near E st.

Died: on Sep 20, Mrs Mgt Ann Young, aged 64 years, consort of Ezekiel Young. The deceased was for many years a resident of Wash City. Her death is lamented by a large family & numerous friends.

Died: on Sep 19, at Harper's Ferry, Va, at the residence of her grandson, the Rev Horace Stringfellow, jr, Mrs Milley Strother, in her 81st year.

Died: on Sep 21, at New Brunswick, N J, Mary H, wife of C L Hardenbergh, & daughter of the late John G Warren, of N Y C.

Harford Co Academy, Bel-Air, Md, E Arnold, L L D, Principal. –Edwin Arnold, formerly of Wash.

THU SEP 25, 1851
Wash Corp: 1-Bill for the relief of Sarah Butts: rejected. 2-Ptn from Benj Bean, asking remuneration for the loss of his horse, which fell from the guard wall into the canal on I st north: referred to the Cmte of Claims. 3-Ptn from Nicholas Hopp & others, regarding curbstones & footway: referred to the Cmte in Improvements. 4-Act restraining the speed of steamboats, with a ptn from Henry W Williams & others on the subject: referred to the Cmte on Police.

For sale: a very handsome dapple gray horse, 5 years old, works finely in harness, sprightly, but perfectly gentle & kind, & the best family horse in Wash. He can be seen for a few days at the Patent Ofc Bldg. Price, $140. –I F Mudd

I certify that Geo McNaughton, of Wash Co, D C, brought before me, as an estray trespassing on his enclosure, a Heifer Calf. –Thos C Donn, J P [Owner is to come forward, prove property, pay charges, & take her away. Geo McNaughton, 6th & G.]

Trustee's sale of improved property: by deed of trust, executed by Chas F McCarthy & Catharine his wife, on Sep 16, 1850, recorded in Liber J A S, 17, folios 135, 136, & 137: public auction of part of lot 17 in square 377, with a 2 story frame house. -Dyer & McGuire, aucts

Died: on Sep 24, at **Mount Hope**, Gtwn, D C, the residence of Wm Robinson, Passed Midshipman Wm H Weaver, U S Navy, in his 25th year. His funeral is on Fri, at 4:30 o'clock, from the above residence.

The funeral of Capt John A Blake is postponed till 3 o'clock this afternoon, in consequence of the remains not having arrived yesterday morning, as was expected. 1-Members of the Grand Lodge to assemble to pay tribute of respect to their late Brother. -R J Roche, G sec 2-Same for the Light Infty. –H Richey, O S 3-Same for Members of the Central Lodge. –Geo W Robinson, Sec 4-Also, the Anacostia & Potomac Steamboat Co: -Geo Page

Information wanted: If Mr John or Thos Burns, sons of Mrs Eliz Burns, are in Washington, [as their mother had been led to suppose,] trying to find her, they are to inquire for her at Dr Green's residence, C st, near 4½ st.

FRI SEP 26, 1851
The late Gen Whiting: the Buffalo Courier pays tribute to the memory of Bvt Gen Whiting, whose recent death at St Louis was announced. Gen Whiting was an old & tried soldier; he has been 43 years in the service, having entered the army in 1808, as cornet of dragoons. He was brevetted to a captaincy in 1814 for meritorious service. He was in the artl for some years, but for about 20 years had been in the staff. He was brother of Maj Whiting, of the 1st artl, & father of Henry M Whiting, 4th artl. He also has a son in the Navy. Gen Whiting was brevetted Brig Gen in 1848 for his services in Mexico & elsewhere. Gen Whiting was a man of fine literary tastes, fond of historical research & by study & application had become an excellent scholar. He paid at one time much attention to the aborigines, their history, or traditions, & we are informed prepared a volume on the subject.

Lambert Norton, late Pres of the State Bank at Morris, N J, & charged with being concerned in defrauding it, was acquitted on Saturday.

For sale: house & land, 2 corners at Chilton's Cross Roads, Westmoreland Co, Va, consisting of 2 dwlg houses, 2 store houses, 2 wells, & excellent water: about 120 acres. Inquire of John Reed, on the premises, or B W Reed, Wash, 14th & F sts.

Household & kitchen furniture at auction: on Oct 2, at the residence of the late F C Labbe, on Pa ave, between 14th & 15th sts. -A Green, auctioneer

The steamer **Pampero**, which has been made to play so conspicuous a part in the late Cuban expedition, was built in Balt some 18 months since for J F Heiss, & Lt Hunter, of the U S Navy. The latter deposed of his interest in her to the former. The **Pampero** in the late movement appeared as the property of L J Sigur, one of the proprietors of the New Orleans Delta. In the paper of Sep 16, the interest of Mr Sigur in the **Delta** had been purchased in Jun last by Mr Heiss, & the presumption is that the **Pampero** was taken in payment. –Balt American

To let: the dwlg portion of a 3 story brick house on Pa ave, in square B. The front room of the lower story is occupied by Mr Staffan as a clothing store. –John P Ingle

Kimberton Farm at auction: on Oct 20: property for a long time was occupied as a Boarding School, in Chester Co, 30 miles from Phil: contains about 117 acres: spacious stone dwlg house; extensive back bldgs. Inquire of Henry Kimber, residing on the premises; or of Isaac Jackson, 70 Marshall st, R V Massey, 205 N 4th st, or of Thos Kimber, 40 N 4th st, Phil. Conditions of the sale will be made known by Abigail Kimber.

Ofcrs of the Navy & other persons who have in their possession Books which belong to the Navy Dept are respectfully requested to return them.
–Jno Etheridge, Chief Clerk

Valuable farm in Alexandria Co, Va, my farm, containing about 120 acres, for sale. It adjoins the farm of Robt Cruett, near the road leading to Ball's Cross Roads.
–Wm Ball

Official: Navy Dept, Sep 25, 1851. Intelligence has reached this Dept that Lt Wilson R McKinney, of the U S Navy, departed this life at Marseilles on Aug 18, 1851. He was attached to the U S razee **Independence**, on the Mediterranean station. His disease having assumed an unfavorable type, the surgeon of the ship deemed it necessary to recommend his removal to the shore as speedily as practicable. This was done, & for some few hours he seemed to revive, but all that skill was of no avail; he expired the 4th day after his removal to the shore. He was interred with all proper ceremonies, the funeral being attended by his brother ofcrs, the American shipmasters in port, & a large number of French ofcrs. [Capt Wm Jameson presiding, Fleet Surgeon Wm Wheelan being appt'd Sec. Lt McKinney was ill on board the ship for one month. He is to be buried at Marseiles. Sympathy to his family. Published by order of Will A Graham, Sec of the Navy.]

The body of the late Capt Blake having been brought on Wed night by railroad from N Y, where he died, was yesterday committed to the tomb. The procession was large & proceeded from the late residence of the deceased to the Congress burial ground, where the corpse was interred.

A letter from Sweet Springs, Va, of Sep 18, mentions the sudden death of Mrs Warner, an interesting lady of Richmond, who after spending the evening of Sep 17th well & cheerful, retired to her chamber, & in the morning was found dead in her bed. Her death was attributed to an affection of the heart.

The barn of Hon N P Tallmadge, at Fond du Lac, Wisc, had been struck by lightning, & all its contents, of grain, consumed.

The notes of the new bank of Bridgeport, Conn, of which Mr P T Barnum is a principal stockholder, have a portrait of himself on one end, & one of Jenny Lind on the other.

To Boarders. Having rented that large & beautiful residence, lately occupied by Mrs Stettinius, on La ave, I am now prepared to take Boarders. –Mary Ann Fowler

Wanted immediately, a good plain cook. Apply to Mrs W C Zantzinger, E st at 8th.

House of the first class for sale: finished for several months: near the corner of G & 10th sts: commodious & lofty. Gas pipes have been laid in the hall, parlor, saloon, & dining room. –Jas Caden

SAT SEP 27, 1851
World's Exhibition, U S Ofc Industrial Exhibition, London, Sep 12, 1851. Dr Playfair seems never to have thought upon the subject of dentistry. Dr Thos Chadbourne, U S, made juror upon this class. Samples of false teeth were sent from the establishments of P E Hawes, of Ambler & Avery, of S Brown, & of J Alcock, in N Y. The specimens of dentistry of O Avery, of Honesdale, Pa, were also superior to any thing of the kind manufactured in Europe. Dr Hitchcock, of Boston, through his friend Mr T Bigelow Lawrence, Attache of the American Legation, exhibited samples of dentists' work. E Barlow, of N Y exhibits a beautiful array of teeth, mounted on 18 carat gold, & soldered with 18 carat gold solder: teeth imitate nature. The enameled teeth of Dr Stockton, of Phil attracted the attention of dentists here, & has caused large orders to be given for their importation. The enameled teeth of Dr Stockton, of Phil, received great favor. J D Chevalier, of N Y, is the only contributor of dentical instruments from our country. -Edw Riddle to J C G Kennedy, Sec Ex Com Nat'l Exhibition.

Wanted: a young man who writes a fair hand, with experience in the dry goods business wants a situation either in a dry goods or grocery store. Address F A Davis, Wash.

Dr John M Bernhissel has been elected Delegate to Congress from the U S Territory of Utah.

Council of N Y Indians on Sep 19, to celebrate the funeral rights of their Grand Sachem, John Blacksmith, deceased, & to elect the Grand Sachem in his place. Ely S Parker [Do ne-ba ga-we] was proclaimed Grand Sachem of the Six Nations. Spencer C Parker, brother of the Grand Sachem, with 8 others, were installed as War-Chiefs, to fill vacancies occasioned by death.

The editor of the Alexandria [Rapides] Democrat is informed by the resident physician on the plantations of Meredith Calhoun that the number of deaths by cholera were 2 whites, Dr Martin & John W Malkey, & 67 slaves.

Jos B Garnier died at St Louis on Sep 11. At the time of his death he was probably the oldest emigrant resident of St Louis, having been there since 1809. He was a native of Marseilles, France, thence he went to Martinique, then to Phil & N Y. In N Y he was a clerk in the house of Peter R Livingston about 1780. In 1800 he removed to St Louis.

On Thu last Mr Wm Ebert, [gunsmith,] at Fred'k City, Md, was accidentally shot while unscrewing a loaded pistol, left at his shop for repairs. The ball entered the abdomen on the right side, & was cut out near the back bone. On Monday mortification supervened, &, we lament to record, terminated fatally.

Madame Dorman will reopen her class for instruction in the French language on Oct 1 at Mrs Ross', n e corner of 9th & E sts.

For rent: commodious brick house at 14th & L sts. Apply to J J Joyce, F & 13th sts.

Died: on Sep 13, at Alexandria, Va, after a long & painful illness, Esther D, wife of Wm Fowle, of that place, in her 62nd year.

Died: on Wed week, suddenly, Mary Brockenbrough, 2nd daughter of Hon Willoughby Newton, of Westmoreland, Va, in her 18th year.

Died: on Sep 17, at White Sulphur Springs, Va, Mrs Columbia Calwell, wife of Wm B Calwel, & daughter of Robt T Gwathmey, of Richmond.

Died: on Sep 16, at **Willow Glen**, the residence of her father-in-law, Hezekiah Brawner, in Chas Co, Md, Mary Jane, wife of Jas T Brawner, in her 23rd year.

MON SEP 29, 1851

N Y Courier of Sep 23. Mr John H Potts, Foreman in one of the largest printing establishments in the U S, the Courier & Enquirer, died yesterday. The Morning Courier was established in May, 1827; the following Dec, we found Mr Potts in the ofc. In a word, he was all that could be required of a Foreman.

Was committed to the jail of Balt City & County, on Sep 18, 1851, by D C H Bordley, a J P of the State of Md, as a runaway, a negro, about 9 years of age; states his name to be John Edw Johnson, that he was born in Balt City, & taken to Phil by a white man about last Christmas. Owner to come forward, prove property, pay charges, & take him away. -Wm H Counselman, Warden of Balt City & County jail.

Hon Lucius Lyon, formerly a Rep & afterwards a Senator in Congress from the State of Michigan, died at Detroit on Fri last.

Michigan railroad conspirators: verdict of guilty rendered on Thu in Detroit. Those found guilty are:

E Champion	Wm Corwin	Erastus Smith
Willard Champion	O D Williams	Ebenezer Farnham
Lyman Champion	A J Freeland	Amny Filly
E J Price	Aaron Mount	E Price

Smith & Farnham were recommended to the mercy of the court. Dr Fitch, charged with being the leader in the conspiracy, died during the trial. [Oct 2nd newspaper: Williams & Filley sentenced to 10 years in the State Penitentiary; Corwin, Mount, E Price, & R Price, Dr Farnham, & Freeland: 8 years each; E Champlin, L Champlin, W Champlin, & Erastus Smith: 5 years each.]

Never have so many persons been convicted of murder in any city of our Union as during the last few months at N Y. On Sat 3 men were sentenced to be executed by hanging in Nov. Their names are Michl Mulvey, Jas Sullivan, & Jos Clark. On the same day Ellen Doyle, convicted of man-slaughter, in killing Catherine Sullivan, was sentenced to 5 years' imprisonment at Sing Sing. She is the mother of 5 children.

The remains of Stephen Girard, the millionaire & benefactor of the city of Phil, are to be removed on Tue next from the Holy Trinity burial ground, where they have been since his death, to Girard College, where a sarcophagus has been prepared for them. This is done by the City Authorities, to restrain whom from carrying their purpose into effect the relatives of the deceased applied for an injunction, which the Court refused to grant.

Examination at Lancaster of the prisoners in the jail, after their arrest, on the charge of participating in the Christiana outrage, was concluded on Thu. Alderman Reigart delivered his decision, fully committing 13 of the accused to the custory of the U S Marshal, to take their trial for high treason against the Gov't. Prisoners committed to answer are Castnor Hannaway & Elijah Lewis, white; Henry Sims, John Morgan, Jacob Moore, Alson Fernsly, Lewis Gale, Lewis Clarkson, Chas Hunter, Geo Wells, Nelson Carter, Jacob Woods, & Geo Williams, colored.

Miss Simons, a young lady, was thrown from a horse a few days ago, in Docgeville, Iowa Co, Wisc. Her foot hung in the stirrup & she was dragged several rods & killed.

Mrd: on Sep 25, by Rev S A H Marks, Mr Jos Johnson to Miss Eliz Chauncey, both of Alexandria, Va.

Mrd: on Sep 25, by Rev Wm B Edwards, Mr Francis J Gibson, of Phil, to Miss Sarah Jane Hall, of Wash City.

Mrd: on Sep 24, at Grace Church, Brooklyn, by Rev Dr Croswell, of New Haven, Rev Edward O Flagg, Rector of Trinity Church, Norwich, Conn. to Eliza W, daughter of Gen Wm Gibbs MacNeill, of N Y.

Died: on Sep 27, in Gtwn, Susan E. 2nd daughter of the late A B Murray, formerly of Balt, Md.

Dissolution of copartnership on Sep 15, by mutual consent. -J T Radcliff, S J Radcliff. J T Radcliff has associated with him Geo T Massey, late of the house of W M Shuster & Co. The firm will be conducted under the style of Radcliff & Co.

Committed to the Balt City & County jail, on Sep 2, 1851, by D C H Bordley, a j p of the State of Md, as a runaway, a negro man, who calls himself Mary Ann Waters, about 28 years of age. He had on when committed a dark figured mousseline de laine dress, blue velvet mantilla, white satin bonnet, & scarf. Says he is free, was born in Elkridge, & has been hiring out in the city of Balt as a woman for the last 3 years. Owner is to come forward, prove property, pay charges, & take said negro away; otherwise he will be discharged according to law. —Wm H Counselman, Warden, Balt City & Co jail

Horses for sale: 13 head of Western Va horses have just arrived at Thos Bakers' Livery Stable. Call & see.

TUE SEP 30, 1851
Postmaster Gen est'd the following new Post Ofcs for week ending Sep 27, 1851.

Ofc	County, State	Postmaster
Hurdtown	Morris N J	Wm B Lefever
Spangsville	C-rks, Pa	Jacob G Spang
Ledersville	Susquehannah, Pa	Wm Eager
Felt's	Ingham, Pa	Alba Blake
Jeffries	Clearfield, Pa	Thos Henderson
Slatington	Lehigh, Pa	Danl D Jones
Mullingar	Warren, Pa	J McMaster
Hellen Furnace	Clarion, Pa	Ham W Longwell

North Pine Grove	Clarion, Pa	Jas Black
Stoch Hill	Clarion, Pa	Geo Alsbourgh
Marionville	Forest, Pa	John D Hunt
Paper Mills	Baltimore, Md	Christian Gore
Bolivar	Frederick, Md	Levi Remsburg
Olney	Montgomery, Md	Jona D Barnsley
Linden	Genesee, Mich	Claud T Thompson
Ashleyville	Macomb, Mich	Alfred Ashley
Frankenmuth	Saganaw, Mich	G A Renzanterger
Vassar	Tuscola, Mich	Wm Johnson
Elden	Clark, Ohio	Ed B Cassilly
Cabell	Carroll, Ohio	Wm Ruledge
Algonquin	Carroll, Ohio	Hiram Topa
Hay's Store	Montgomery, Ohio	Wm Zigler
Sutton's	Williamsburg Dist, S C	Saml S Guild
Lounde's Ferry	Williamsburg Dist, S C	Saml H Lofton
Rough & Ready	Chambers, Ala	Oscar P Jones
Swan Lake	Arkansas, Ark	Quinton D Nicks
Black Hawk	Holt, Mo	Robt Hawkes
Fairmount	Clark, Mo	Jas Owen
Richland Centre	De Kalb, Ia	Geo W Smith
Mount Comfort	Hancock, Ia	Robt M Wallace
Lycurgus	Marshall, Ia	J F Parks
Ivy	Miami, Ia	Robt Cook
Knob Creek	Harrison, Ia	Abm McCawley
Buck Hill	De Kalb, Ia	Cyrus Bowman
Rising Sun	Montgomery, Ill	Wm C Henderson
Clintonville	Kane, Ill	Geo W Woodbury
Webb's Prairie	Franklin, Ill	Elijah Taylor
Bond's Point	Christian, Ill	Thos Simpson
Piney Grove	Hardeman, Tenn	Alfred Riggs
Mouth of Little River	Blount, Tenn	Iredell Wright
Gamble Grove	Fayette, Iowa	Thos Woodle
Poultney	Delaware, Iowa	Hiram Cooper
Dakota	Wasbara, Wis	Chapin M Seley
Brooklyn	Green, Wis	Har P Starkweather
Umatilla	Oregon	A Francis Rogers
Umpqua City	Umpqua, Oregon	Amos E Rogers
Elkton	Umpqua, Oregon	David B Wells

Names Changed: 1-East Hampton Lake, Middlesex Co, Conn, changed to Chatham.
2-Polk, Union Co, Ga, changed to Choestoe.
3-Griffin's Creek, Benton Co, Ala, changed to Cross Plains.
4-Cedar Grove, Wilson Co, Tenn, changed to Cole's Ferry.

5-Warsaw, Portage Co, Wisc, changed to New Haven.
6-Lecompte Valley, San Pete Co, Utah Territory, changed to Manti.
7-Rt Rev W M Green, Bishop of Misissippi had removed his residence from Natchez to Jackson, in that State.

For sale low, a family horse & carriage. Apply to Andrew J Jones, 14th & E sts.

From the first record of the Post Ofc Dept, Benj Franklin, P M G, the following is made: Alexandria, Va, Post Ofc, Josiah Watson. Amount of postage collected from Feb 24, 1776, to Jun 12, 1778, L63 16s 5 d Virginia currency. The books were then kept by Benj Franklin himself, & are still preserved among the archives of the Dept, in his own handwriting, when the whole force of the Dept was Postmaster Gen, at a salary of $1,000 per annum. The present Postmaster Gen is assisted by nearly 200 subordinates in the Dept, & nearly 30,000 throught the country.

Hartford Times: announce the death of Jno J Cleaveland, Clerk of the U S District Court of Conn, & son of the Hon Chauncey F Cleaveland, member re-elect to Congress from that State, , who died in his 28th year. [No death date given-current item.]

Most desirable residence & farm for sale: **Snowden**, the residence of the late Yeamans Smith; in Eastern Va, within a mile of Fredericksburg, with 800 acres in the tract; bldgs are all in complete order, consisting of a large 2 story brick house, with adjoining bldgs. –John L Marye, Wm M Smith, excs of Yeamans Smith.

Wanted, a Nurse for children. Apply to John P Wheeler, at the Post Ofc Dept, or at Mrs Duncan's, D st, between the residences of Hon Danl Webster & Johnson Hellen.

Another survivor of the Cuban expedition has been heard from, Lt Theodore A Stevens, one of Col Crittenden's party. At the time of their capture by the steamer **Haberno**, he jumped overboard & escaped to the shore by swimming. After a month of wandering through the woods & mountains, ragged & shoeless, eating leaves & wild fruit, he surrendered himself to the authorities, & was taken to Havana.

Fairfax farm for sale: about 550 acres, belonging to the widow & heirs of the late John Hunter Terrett, deceased, 8 miles s w of Washington City, where suitable property will be taken in part payment. –John Dowling, Indian Ofc, Wash, D C.

Executor's sale: the personal property of Zachariah Hazel, late of Wash Co, D C, deceased: public auction on the premises, on 2nd st, near Md ave, Wash City, on Oct 2: household & kitchen furniture. –H R Maryman, exc

Extensive sale of groceries & liquor: on Oct 6, at the store occupied by Wm H Upperman, on Pa ave, between 3rd & 4½ st. -A Green, auctioneer

By virtue of 2 writs of venditiona exponas, issued by J D Clark, & one issued by Thos C Don, justices of the peace, Wash Co, D C: at the suits of Nathl Carusi, Wm McCormick, & Jas A Ratcliffe, against the goods & chattels, lands & tenements, rights & credits of Jos Martini, of said county: sale of lot 9 & 10 in square 540, to pay said claims. Sale in front of the premises on Oct 30, 1851. –Wm Coale, Cnstbl

WED OCT 1, 1851
The death of John R Livingston has lately been announced at **Red Hook**, at age 98 years. He was the survivor of a very distinguished family. The most eminent of the family were Chancellor Livingston, of N Y, & the celebrated Edw Livingston, of La. Chancellor Livingston administered the first oath of inauguration to Geo Washington, under that Constitiution, on the spot where the Custom House now is, in Wall st. He afterwards became a patron to Robt Fulton. Edw Livingston, the other eminent brother, was Mayor of the city, Senator in Congress from N Y, Minister Pleni to France, & Senator in Congress from La. Another brother was Peter R Livingston, well know in the political annals of the State, both as a Democrat & a Whig. The sisters of this family were in their alliances remarkable. One of them was Mrs Montgomery, the wife of Maj Gen Montgomery, who fell under the walls of Quebec covered with glory. Another, Maj Gen in the U S Army, appointed by Mr Madison Quartermaster in the army during the Revolution, & present at the surrender of Burgoyne. [Name was omitted.] Another was the wife of John Armstrong, Sec of War under Mr Madison, when Washington was captured by the British, & the reputed author of the Newburgh Letters. The other sisters were Mrs Tillotson, wife of Col Tillotson, writer & politician, & Mrs Garretson, wife of Rev Mr Garretson, of Rhinebeck, a divine of some note. The Livingston family had in their day great estates on the north river. John R Livingston, some 15 yers ago, returned to one of them at **Red Hook**, where he has lived as a country gentleman in a style quite unknown to the 100 acre farmer. He was more than half a century ago one of our principal merchants, & he lived in Broadway [where Mr Plummer's Broadway House now is] in great style & entertained with princely hospitality.

Nelly Moore, an old black woman, who lived near the Brick Meeting House, in Cecil Co, Md, died last week aged about 130 years.

Constantinople, Aug 25, 1851. A young American artist, Mr Walter Gould, of Fredericksburg, Va, lately returned here from Kutaiah, where he spent several weeks with M Kossuth. He had with him full oil portraits of Kossuth, Bathyani, Pertzel, & Wysowski; also that of Saleyman Bey, the Turkish colonel residing there as a com'r in charge of refugees.

Wash Corp: 1-Ptn from Thos Plumsill, asking compensation for services as acting police ofcr of the 6th Ward: referred to the Cmte of Claims. 2-Act for the relief of W B Mitchell: referred to the Cmte of Claims. 3-Ptn of Washington Lewis, for remission of a fine: referred to the Cmte of Claims.

Mrd: on Sep 25, by Rev L F Morgan, Mr Wm Brent Mickum to Miss Sarah Priscilla Ogden, all of Wash City.

Died: on Sat last, in Wash City, Edwin C Weed, in his 57th year, late of Fairfax, Va, & formerly of Greenfield, Saratoga Co, N Y, in which county, as well as in Rensaelaer, he was favorably known as an efficient man of business.

Information wanted of Wm Otterson, a native of Ireland, who left Wash City for Charleston, S C, some 5 years since. Address a letter to his sister, Mrs Matilda Skilling, Wash City.

For rent: new 3 story brick house-3rd & Mass ave. Apply to Saml Wise, 5th & H st.

For rent: 2 story brick house on Md ave, at 13th. Apply to Mrs Cheshire, at Dr Piper's, corner of 9th & sts, near the Patent Ofc.

THU OCT 2, 1851
S J Radcliff, late of the firm of J T Radcliff & Co, has taken the new warehouse #2, 9th st. He will be able to furnish the best Peruvian & other Guanos; & Field & Garden Seed.

Household & kitchen furniture at auction: on Oct 4, in front of our Auction rooms, the effects of the late Govn'r McDowell. -Dyer & McGuire, aucts

Valuable farm for sale: Woodstock, on which Theo Mosher resides, in the neighborhood of the land of Messrs Young, Addison, Blagden, Barry, Jenkins, & others: 370 acres; improvements are new dwgl house & out-bldgs. Possession on Jan 1. -Theo Mosher

The new Govn'r of Ky is Lazarus W Powell. He is a very amusing man, & a very clever one for a Democrat.

Died: on Sep 30, in Gtwn, D C, Mrs Ellen O Farrell, aged 75 years, formerly of Donegaltown Co, Ireland, but for the last 3 years a resident of this town. Her funeral is today at 4 o'clock, from the residence of her son-in-law, Wm Burns, on Bridge st, between Potomac & Market sts.

Hon Harry J Thornton, of Ala, whose appointment as a Com'r of Land Claims in Calif we recently noticed, after being confined to his bed, at Willard's Hotel, in Wash City, for a couple of weeks, from an inflamed hand, proceeding from an accidental injury, was on Monday called upon to submit to the amputation of his left arm, midway between the wrist & elbow. The operation was performed in an admirable manner by Dr Fred'k May, assisted by Drs Miller & Stone. The patient was under the influence of chloric ether, & awoke without having experienced any pain. -Telegraph

Late from Buenos Ayres. Gen D Filipe Ibera, the Govn'r & Capt Gen of St Jago del Estero, is dead.

Teacher wanted: apply to Jas F Gordon, Sec of the Board, Chestertown, Kent Co, Md.

Wash City Ordinances: 1-Act for the relief of Danl Linkins: sum of $522.99, for filling lots in square 40.

Groceries & Liquors at auction: on Oct 2, in the store occupied by Mr Chas Borremans, on Pa ave, near 22nd st. -Dyer & McGuire, aucts

Household & kitchen furniture at auction: on Oct 2, at the residence of the late F C Labbe, on Pa ave, between 14th & 15th sts. -A Green, auct

FRI OCT 3, 1851
Mrs Eliz Prudden Tucker died at St George's, Bermuda, on Sep 8, at the age of 36 years. She was the wife of Hon Tudor Tucker, the Consul of the U S for that port.

On Wed Mr Swartzeman, of the Dead Letter Ofc, destroyed 164 five-bushel bags of dead letters, the accumulation of 3 months. They were all emptied into a ravine near the Wash Nat'l Monument & given to the flames.

Mrs M E Fowler can accommodate 4 or 5 more permanent or transient boarders. Residence on 11th st, near Pa ave, south side. Also, 1 furnished front parlor.

Household & kitchen furniture at auction: on Oct 9, at the house lately occupied by Mrs Whitwell, on 4½ st, between C & Indiana ave. -A Green, auctioneer

For sale: a farm near the turnpike road leading to Balt: contains about 160 acres: improvements consist of 2 frame dwlgs. Apply to Pollard Webb, ofc north side of Pa ave, between 4½ & 6th sts.

$20 reward. Gone again! My negro woman Catharine [alias Kitty Francis] has again absconded. She is about 30 or 35 years of age, dark complexion. –Jno P Hilton

Official: Gen Orders #49: Headquarters of the Army, Adj Gen Ofc, Wash, Sep 27, 1851. Announcement of the death, at St Louis, on Sep 16, of Col & Brevet Gen Henry Whiting, Assist Quartermaster Gen. Gen Whiting was commissioned a Cornet of Dragoons, Oct 20, 1808; served with reputation on the Niagara frontier in the war of 1812 with Great Britain; in the late war with Mexico he filled the high & responsible post of Quartermaster Gen to the Army of Occupation, & shared with it in the glory of the field of Buena Vista. He has left behind a reputation worthy the emulation of his brother ofcrs, & which his children, may well regard as a priceless legacy. –E Jones, Adj Gen

Mrd: on Sep 2, in Gtwn, by Rev Jos S Collins, Edw Waite, formerly of N Y, to Mary A Stetson, late of Alexandria, Va.

Mrd: on Sep 30, by Rev L F Morgan, Mr Jno P Brown to Mary Eliz McBain, all of Wash City.

Mrd: Oct 1, by Rev Mr MacElfresh, Richd Earl to Miss Hannah Davison, all of Wash City.

Died: on Sep 25, at his residence, in Lincoln Co, N C, Hon Jas Graham, in his 57th year. He was the 2nd son of the late Gen Jos Graham, & the last surviving brother of the present Sec of the Navy. He was frequently a member of the Legislature of N C, & a most faithful Rep in Congress for 12 years. [Oct 8th newspaper: the Sec of the Navy left Wash City on Mon on a visit to N C, rendered necessary by the decease of his brother, & may be absent for 2 or 3 weeks.]

Died: on Sep 15, of Asiatic cholera, at Burlington, Vt, Chas S McGuffy, in his 16th year, only son of Rev Wm H McGuffey, Prof of Moral Philosophy in the Univ of Va.

SAT OCT 4, 1851
Ladies with letters remaining in the Post Ofc, Wash, Oct 4, 1851.

Alexander, Miss C
& Alexander, Miss M
Ball, Miss Kate
Baggitt, Miss A
Beall, Mrs Benj B
Ballville, Mixx Cath
Bennett, Eliza
Brown, Mrs S Ann
Bugby, Mrs Mgt
Baker, Miss
Beall, Miss M A
Barry, Mrs Martha
Brashears, Miss M E

Costin, Mrs Amelia
Clark, Mrs Clacy
Cumming, Mrs J G
Dade, Miss Ann M
Dodd, Mrs Anna
Dier, Miss Julia
Forbes, Mrs Eliz
Frazier, Mrs Han'h
Fisher, Mrs Lucy A
Fenwick, Miss E E
Farley, Mrs W
Finch, Mrs Mgt
Gould, Miss Ann M

Guerin, Anna
Green, Mrs Emily
Green, Mrs M A E
Hunt, Mrs Addie C
Hamilton, Miss H
Hill, Mrs J
Hort, Miss Kate
Hayman, Miss arg
Harris, Miss R
Hutton, Miss Sophia
Johnson, Miss C D
Johnson, Mrs Eliz-2
Jefferson, Martha A
Johnson, Mrs J E
Kean, Miss Mgt
Keys, Miss Mary
La Truite, Mrs E
Ludlow, Miss Kate
Lee, Mrs Mgt
Morgan, Miss G
Matthews, Mrs J J
-W A Bradley, P M

Middleton, Mrs L
Moor, Miss Mary R
Mooney, Miss
Malvin, Miss Rebec
McNiell, Miss Mary F-
McCoy, Mrs Martin
McLain, Mrs J C
Noble, Miss T A
Ogden, Miss E W
Pumroy, Mrs Louisa
Rayner, Mrs F L
Stewart, Mrs Chas J
Scroggin, Miss L A
Sage, Miss Louisa
Stone, Mrs Mary F
Tansill, Mrs Ann E
Tyler, Miss Cornelia
Trundle, Mrs Rach'l
Urquhart, Mrs M J
Whitcomb, Mrs M

For rent: 3 story brick house on H & 17th sts, now occupied by Elisha Riggs, jr. Possession on Nov 1 next. Apply to R S Chew, at the State Dept.

Hats & Caps: Fall & Winter Style, 1851. Chas H Lane, Fashionable Hat, Cap, & Gent's Furnishing Estab't.

Orphans Court of Wash Co, D C sale: in the case of the late David Weaver, his administrator, will on Oct 7, sell at auction, at his late residence on the heights, on the Fred'k road, the following property: one good saddle horse, first rate draught horse, market wagon, 9 hogs, & a lot of pigs, 3 hives of bees, grindstones, & furniture. –Henry Weaver, adm -Barnard & Buckey, auct

Miss Mary Legare, sister of the former Atty Gen of the U S, is engaged in the lumber trade at Cedar Rapids, Iowa, & advertises to supply any amount of bldg lumber & boat plank.

Wm R Riley has just opened a large stock of Fall & Winter Dry-goods: corner 8th st, opposite the Market. –Wm R Riley

Died: on Sep 21, in her 21st year, Mrs Mary Frances Marshall, wife of Jaquelin A Marshall, jr, of Fauquier, & eldest daughter of Jos H Sherrard, of Winchester, Va.

Died: on Oct 3, Phebe, wife of J Bartram North. Her funeral is on Sunday at half-past 3 o'clock, from the residence of her husband, on N J ave.

Died: on Sep 28, at her residence near Charlotte Hall, Md, of a short illness, Eliz B Matthews, aged 61 years.

Died: on Sep 20 last, near Memphis, Tenn, on her way home from the North, Mrs Emily Wright, wife of Benj D Wright, U S Navy Agent at Pensacola, Fla.

Died: on Oct 2, in her 6th year, Annie H R, daughter of John & America Willey. Her funeral will take place at the Foundry Church, on Oct 5, at 3 o'clock.

For sale or rent: new 2 story attic brick house, on 9th st, between L & M sts. Rent $175. Inquire of Geo T Langley, within.

MON OCT 6, 1851
The brig **Louisa**, arrived at Salem from Gambia, reports the death of Rev Jas Moore, M D, of the Monrovia Mission, on Aug 26, from an accident on board the **Louisa**.

News had been received of the death of Mr Jas Richardson, the enterprising African traveler, on Mar 4 last. He died at the village of Unqurutus, 6 days distant from Kouka, the capital of Bornou. He had separated from his companions, Drs Barth & Overweg, in Jan last. Mr Richardson was an Englishman.

Advices from Astoria, Oregon, to Aug 27, state that Mrs Gaines, wife of Gov Gaines, died on Aug 13.

Thos Reid & Henry Clements, confined in the Richmond jail under sentence of death for mutiny & murder on board the schnr **John B Lindsay**, in Jan, 1850, made their escape on Tue, by boring through the ceiling or floor over their cell, & thence through the roof of the bldg, from which they descended by tearing their blankets into strips & fastening them together.

Tribute to Col Richd Ross, of Md: graduated at West Point in 1830; served in the Florida war 2 or 3 years with honor; at the first outbreak of the war with Mexico he was placed under the command of the gallant Taylor; during the bombardment of **Fort Brown**, he secured the confidence & respect of all his brother ofcrs; at Monterey he commanded 2 companies of his regt at the time; under Gen Scott, he participated in the siege & capture of Vera Cruz, & was in all the subsequent battles until he was severely wounded at Contreras, just before the capture of the city of Mexico. Though suffering from severe indisposition, he joined his regt in the capture of the first fort & heights of Cerro Gordo, where he laid the foundation of the disease which has terminated his active & useful life. As a son & brother his character was beyond praise. He now lies low in death.

From the Boonsborough Odd Fellow: as Mr Keller, a young man, son of Mr John Keller, residing in Funkstown, aged about 20 years, returning home from Boonsborough, on Sep 30, the horse which he was riding rushed into a buggy, & in falling fell upon Mr K & injured him as to cause his death in a few hours.

Rev Saml Ralston, D D, died at his residence in Carroll township, Wash Co, Pa, on Sep 25, at the advanced age of 96 years, having been in the ministry for 70 years. He retained full possession of his faculties & intellectual vigor up to the hour of his death. He was of the Presbyterian Church.

Mrd: on Sep 15, at Meadville, Pa, by Rev John Barker, D D, Pres of Allegheny College, Lt Geo Hurst, U S Navy, to Miss Clara Van Tassel, formerly of Erie.

Died: on Sep 20, at Mendota, Minn, Henry Hastings, only son of Hon Henry H Sibley, aged 4 years.

The Monticello Watchman of Sep 30th: W R Palmer was found guilty for the murder of his half brother, & sentenced to be hung on Nov 20.

$50,000 worth of property has been bequeathed to the Pittsburgh & Allegheny Orphan Asylum by the late Dr Thos Hartford. He also left property to the poor of Canton, Ohio, worth $10,000.

Store for rent, on Pa ave, 2 doors west of Brown's new hotel. Apply to Wm H Ward.

Orphans Court of Wash Co, D C. Letters of administration on the personal estate of John A Blake, late of said county, deceased. –Mary E Blake, admx

Gtwn improvements: besides the opportunities afforded at **Forrest Hall**, the handsome new establishment of Mr Jas Hicks, at High & Prospect sts, will supply every desired convenience of a public character in the fine rooms above his large & superior store-room. Mr Hicks' neighbor, Mr Michl May, has a bldg containing 2 fine store rooms. On Bridge st, near the market-house, Mr Tenny is replacing an old house with 2 handsome new stores. Mr Wm Hening is putting up a couple of good bldgs near Gtwn College. Mr Muncaster, on east Beall st, opposite the residence of Cmdor Cassin, has recently completed a commodious & handsome dwlg. On Water st, Mr Philip T Berry is making an improvement in his new wharf, on the propery formerly belonging to the estate of the late Thos C Wright. Messrs Wm A Bradley & ___ Thompson, of Wash City, have made large investments this year in Gtwn property. They have become proprietors of **Analostan** or **Mason's Island**, in the Potomac, opposite the town, with a principal view of making it a coal depot. They have also purchased the Water & Bridge st property of the late Gen Mason, below the aqueduct.

Valuable improved property at auction: on Oct 9, a 2 story brick dwlg house, on H st, between 17th & 18th sts, recently occupied by Maj J C Mullay.
–Dyer & McGuire, aucts

New Boot & Shoe Store: on Pa ave, between 4½ & 6th sts. –J M Johnson

$10 reward for strayed or stolen small brown Mare, & a light gray Horse. Paid if delivered to Jas Danford, on the Eastern Branch, Wash Co, D C.

TUE OCT 7, 1851
Oak Hill Cemetery, Gtwn, D C. The managers of this beautiful Cemetery propose to sell the Burial Lots therein at public auction on Friday, the 17th of the present month of October. The lots have been laid out so as to contain each about 300 square feet. Some are of less dimensions. There are also portions of the ground set apart for single graves. A very handsome engraved plan of the grounds, showing the avenues, paths, & lots, by their names & numbers, may be had at 25 cents each at Morrison's and Taylor & Maury's bookstores, Wash; at O M Linthicum's drug store, Gtwn; & of Mr Blunden, the superintendent, at the gate of the Cemetery. The lots have been marked & numbered on the ground to correspond with the map; so that any one with a copy thereof in hand may readily ascertain the number of the lot he may wish to purchase. The price of the lots has been fixed at forty cents per square foot. The privilege to select one of the lots in any part of the Cemetery [except the lots numbered from 1 to 15, inclusive, and lots 50, 124, and 125] will be offered in succession to the highest bidder. The lots will be sold subject to the regulations adopted by the Managers for the good government of the cemetery, which are similar to those in other like institutions. The sale will be held on the premises, and will commence at 11 o'clock A M on the day before mentioned. Terms of sale: One-third of the purchase money, including the premium for choice, will be required on the day of sale, or within five days afterwards; and the residue in six and nine months, with interest from the day of sale. For the deferred payment the purchaser will be required to give his notes, with approved security.
–John Marbury, Pres of the Oak Hill Cemetery Co

Trustee's sale of brick house & lot: at auction, on Nov 6, by deed of trust dated Aug 11, 1848, recorded in Liber W M #145, folios 37 thru 40, of the land records of Wash Co, D C: sale of lot 18 in square 533, fronting on Indiana ave, between 3rd & 4½ sts, with improvements. –Wm H English, trustee -A Green, auctioneer

New line of regular packets. N Y, Alexandria, Gtwn, & Wash Packets. The schnr **Pampero**, Geo Penfield, Master; schnr **Volant**, Merrice Osborn, Master; schnr **Townsend Jones**, S W Dayton, Master; schnr **Mott Bedell**, John Bedell, Master; schnr **Ann**, Benj Bedell, Master; schnr **Le Roy**, Wm Powell, Master Agents: Mott Bedell, & Wm E Jones, 104 Wall st, N Y. Cazanove & Co, Alexandria, Va. Peter Berry, Gtwn

Salona Farm for sale: the former residence of Rev Wm Maffitt, located in Fairfax Co, Va, adjoins the farm of Com Jones, contains 208½ acres; brick mansion, 52 x 32; stone farm house, stone spring house, brick school house, carriage house, cow house, & barn, 62 x 30, with basement. –Elisha Sherman, Langly, Fairfax Co, Va

The people of Grayson Co, Va, met on Sep 23, & offered a reward of $1,000 for the apprehension of Jarvis C Bacon, an Ohio Abolitionist, who recently, under the garb of religion, sowed his vile sentiments broadcast amongst the negroes of that county, stirring them up to revolt.

Superior household & kitchen furniture at auction: on Oct 22, at the residence of his excellency the English Minister, Sir H L Bulwer. -A Green, auct

San Francisco Herald: on Aug 24, the jail was forcibly entered by a division of the Vigilance Cmte, consisting of 36 members, who took 2 prisoners, Saml Whittaker & Robt McKenzie, to the room of the Cmte, on Battery st, where they were hung.

New & valuable dwlg for sale: corner of 3rd & C sts. The bldg will be shown by Mr A Baldwin or myself, Z D Gilman.

Booker Gold Mine for sale: by decree of the Circuit Superior Court of Law & Chancery for Buckingham, pronounced on Sep 15, 1851, in the case of Wm M Moseley & John F Miller, plntf, vs the heirs of Saml Morris, deceased, dfndnts: sale on Dec 4 next, the ***Booker Gold Mine***, in said county, at present in the occupancy of Messrs Wm M Moseley & Co. Correspond with me at Curdsville, Buckingham Co, Va, Alex'r Moseley, Com'r.

U S Patent Ofc, Oct 6, 1851. On the petition of M Sorel, of Paris, France, praying for the extension of a patent granted to him for an improved method of preserving iron & steel from rust or oxidation, for 7 years from the expiration date of Dec 7, 1851. –Thos Ewbank, Com'r of Patents

By 3 writs of fieri facias at the suit of Lewis Paine, Eliz Monroe, & Yerby & Bro, trading under the firm of Albert F Yerby & Adonis L Yerby, against the goods & chattels of Eliza Ricard, in & unto a lot of crockery, one straw bed, one coat, sacking boxes, barrel & contents, rocking chair, matting, carpet, tin ware, & other articles: sale on Nov 11, to satisfy said claims. –J A Ratcliff, constable

Postmaster Gen has est'd the following new Post Ofcs for week ending Oct 4, 1851.

Ofc	County, State	Postmaster
Cobleskill Centre	Schoharie, N Y	Geo Tator
Maspeth	Queens, N Y	David Miller
Boght	Albany, N Y	Wm G Graesbeck
Fisher's	Ontario, N Y	Chas Fisher
Cottage Home	Harford, Md	Levi B Finley

Grassy Creek	Russell, Va	Chas F Bond
Upper Falls of Coal	Kanawha, Va	Richd G Chandler
Harper's Valley	Raleigh, Va	John Shumate
Falls Mill	Cabell, Va	E H Walton
Upland	Mason, Va	Ransom Whitten
Cat Fish	Marion Dist, S C	J W Moody
Philadelphia	Darlington Dist, S C	J G Gatlin
Tanner's Ford	Walker, Ga	Archibald Tanner
Increase	Early, Ga	Leonard Lofter
Spring Creek	Early, Ga	R McCorquadate
Driver's Hill	Clinch, Ga	John L Morgan
Creek Stand	Macon, Ala	John W Foster
Caney	Washita, Ark	Jas Magness
Hadensville	Todd, Ky	Stephen Terry
Cropper's Depot	Shelby, Ky	Jas H Cropper
Falls of Rough	Grayson, Ky	Willis Green
Birmingham	Marshall, Ky	Laban S Locker
Mintonville	Casey, Ky	Jas Westley
Indian Creek	Washington, Tenn	Leroy W James
Cane Ridge	Clairberne P, La	Wash B Nicholson
Lisbon	Claiberne P, La	Seth Tatum
Sidney	Fremont, Iowa	Augustus Borchers
Amboy	Washington, Iowa	Robt Allen
Del Norte	Davis, Iowa	Ayres Taylor
Nebraska	Yell, Iowa	David B Spaulding
Fort Union	N Mex	J W Folger

Names Changed: 1-Lynford, Jefferson, Ky, changed to Saint Matthews.
2-Stewartsboro, Rutherford, Tenn, changed to Smyrna.
3-Andalusia, Rock Island, Ill, changed to Pleasant Ridge.

Died: on Sep 20, at Deep Falls, the residence of his grandmother, Mrs Eliza Thomas, Henry, aged 6 years & 6 months, son of Dr Jas & Ann M Waring, of Chaptico, St Mary's Co, Md.

WED OCT 8, 1851
Brick house for sale:3 stories with a basement. –H M Morfit, 4½ st.

Explosion of the steamer **Brilliant** on Sunday, about 6 miles from Plaquemine: Mr Levison, editor of the Baton Rouge Advocate was dangerously wounded; Mr Coteon, 1st clerk, Mr Cole, 2nd, all badly wounded; Mr McCarty, 2nd engineer, died at Plaquemine.

Three men who had been convicted of grand larceny were hung at Sacramento, Calif, on Aug 22. Their assumed names were John Thompson, Jas Gibson, & W B Robinson, & their real names Murphy, [or McDemott,] Hamilton, & Heppard. The 2 former were foreigners, & both had been transported to the English colonies for their crimes, & afterwards found their way to Calif. These were hung by the sheriff, pursuant to law. Robinson was hung by the mob. He had been duly convicted with the others. It is stated that he was a native of N Y C, & had been a soldier of the U S army during the Mexican war. He went to Oregon in the regt of Mounted Riflemen, &, having been transferred to the dragoon service, he deserted in May last from his company at Benicia.

Dwlg & valuable wharf property for sale: by decree of the Circuit Court of Alexandria Co, rendered at Jun term, 1851, in the suit of Briscoe & wife vs Slacum's heirs, the undersigned Com'rs will offer for sale, by auction, on Nov 8, the following:
1-Dwlg house & lot of ground at Wilkes & Fairfax sts: dwlg is 2 stories high.
2-A lot of ground on the east side of Union st, adjoining on the north the warehouse of Messrs McVeigh, Harper, & Chamberlain. A passage way 10 feet wide across Mr McVeigh's part of the wharf, into Prince st, secured to it forever by deed from John Harper in 1790. –Francis L Smith, W Arthur Taylor, Henry W Davis, Com'rs

Balt Patriot of Mon announces the death of the venerable Jas Beatty, at the advanced age of 81 years. Mr Beatty but a few short weeks since lost the companion of his youth & the soother of his old age, & now he too has gone to that bourn whence none return. There was no man nor merchant [says the Patriot] more highly esteemed in our city than Jas Beatty. He formerly, & for some time, filled the ofc of Navy Agent in Balt, & has long been the proprietor of extensive powder mills on Jones' Falls, & was perhaps the oldest merchant of Balt at his death. [Death date not given. Current item.]

Millard Fillmore, Pres of the U S A, recognizes: 1-Lewis Stanislaus, who has been appointed Counsul of Prussia, for Cincinnati, Ohio. 2-J W Jockusch, who has been appointed Consul of Prussia, for the port of Galveston, Texas. Oct 6, 1851

On Tue the ceremony of laying the corner stone of the new Church on the Island, Grace Church, took place, Rev Smith Pyne officiated in chief, with coadjutors Rev Alfred Holmead, the pastor, Revs Messrs French, Gilliss, Clarke, & others of the Episcopal communion. The Church will be located on D & 9th sts.

Mrd: on Oct 8, Wm G Temple, U S Navy, to Catlyna, 2nd daughter of Gen Totten.

Mrd: on Oct 2, by Rev F S Evans, Mr Edwin E Taue to Miss Mary Ellen Angel.

Mrd: on Oct 2, by Rev Mr Hodges, Jas M Robertson to Mgt Isabella Martin, all of Wash.

Students of Gtwn held a meeting to express their sorrow by the death of the late H Taney Diggs, of Chas Co, Md, Mr H W Brent, of Md, called to the chair, & Mr W B Fetterman, of Pa, chosen secretary. Cmte: Messrs E Lowe, R W Harper, W B Fetterman, J K Gleeson, & W J Boarman.

THU OCT 9, 1851

The Tuscaloosa [Ala] Monitor of Oct 2 states that John Kirby, an old & respected citizen, was shot in the court-house there on Sep 30. Kirby had indicted Fred'k P Hall for wounding him in April, & during the proceedings a quarrel ensued. Kirby drew a pistol, which a bystander named Whitfield attempted to take from him, & in the struggle, the gun went off, passing through Kirby's thigh, causing almost instant death. Kirby's son supposing Hall shot his father, fired at him, but missed.

Wash Corp: 1-The Mayor nominated Thompson Van Reswick as Com'r of the 5th & 6th Wards, in place of Jas Nokes, resigned: confirmed. 2-Ptn of Wm Martin, asking a settlement of his police account to Jun 30th last: referred to the Cmte on Police. 3-Ptn of Danl Rowland, for remission of a fine: referred to the Cmte of Claims. 4-Ptn of Clark Mills, for remission of a fine: referred to the Cmte of Claims. 5-Ptn of Jesse Sisson asking remuneration for the loss of tobacco in his cellar, which was inundated & caused by the improvement then being made on D st south: referred to the Cmte of Claims. 6-Cmte of Claims: asked to be discharged from the further consideration of the ptn of E Gannon: agreed to.

The invaders of Cuba. We learn from Havana the name of the last company sent to Spain. It will be seen that Geo Harrison, of Gtwn, who was supposed to have been killed, is still living, & is amongst the number sent to Spain. Sent to Spain by the brig **Ripa**:

C J Duffy, of New Orleans
Thos Little, Mobile
Michl Geiger, New Orleans
John D Brown, Cincinnati, Ohio
Geo S Berry, Cincinnati, Ohio
Thos Bryan, New Orleans
John Bachilder, New Orleans
John Brown, St Louis
Preston Essex, St Louis
John Cline, New Orleans
N Port, Prussia
John N Davis, New Orleans
J G Porter, Dublin
F Curvia, Havana
John Talbot, New Orleans
Jose Doubren, Cuba
Wm Losner, Saxony
Thos McNeill, Lumpkin Co, Ga
Wm Miller, Northampton, Eng
Jas B Weymouth, Nashville
John Robinson, England
Andraes Gonzales, Venezuela
Edw Conolly, Ireland
Louis Nagle, Missouri
Jas Myers, Ireland
Jos Myers, Ireland
John Seifer, Indiana
Michl Lyons, Ireland

John Doyle, England
Geo Harrison, Dist of Col
Wm Young, Ireland
John T Smith, Ireland
John Johnson, Ky
Eugene Cay, London, Eng
Geo Parr, Petersburg, Va
In the Hospital, all doing well:
Manuel Aragon
J B Rubira, Galicia
Jas Fiddles, Malta
G Richardson, New Orleans
M J Keenan, Mobile
Wilson A Rives, Miss
Jacob Jessert, Saxony

John A Sowers, Berryville, Va
Jos Stephens, N Y
Fred'k Hagan, Prussia
Augustin Montoro, Cuba
Isaac Freeborn, Ohio
Asher J Phillips, New Orleans

Henry Jasper, Saxony
L Palanka, Hungary
Geo Edgerton, Nachez
Col Blummenthal, N Y
David Gano, N Y
Chas J Hodge, England

Mrd: on Oct 8, by Rev F S Evans, Thos M Smith, of Columbia, Mo, to Miss Sallie M, daughter of Maj F F Kirby, of Wash City.

Lime, Wood, & Coal, fresh from the kiln, will be sold low. –Wm Warder, 12th & C.

FRI OCT 10, 1851
Dissolution of partnership existing between the subscribers, under the firm of Havenner & Bros, dissolved on Oct 1, by mutual consent. –Thos H Havenner, John F Havenner, Chas W Havenner. The subscribers will continue the business at the old stand under the firm of Havenenr & Bro. –Thos H Havenner, C W Havenner, C st, between 4½ & 6th sts.

American Institute's great Fair is now open in N Y; it was founded in 1828. Articles which have fallen today under my notice. 1-L T Boland, crest & ornament manufacturer, 186 Fulton st, N Y. 2-Yankee Clocks by F C Andrews, 3 Courtlandt st, N Y C. 3-C S Little, dealer in hardware, cutlery, & house builders ware, 34 Fulton st, N Y C. 4-Jonas R Knapp, 168 Read st, N Y C, samples of the patent premium hay, straw, & cornstalk cutter of J T Rich. 5-G H Swords, 116 Broadway, N Y C, magnificent chime of bells, manufactured by Andrew Meneely at West Troy, N Y, in the business for 20 years. 6-Geo Walker, 89½ Leonard st, N Y, manufacturers of hot-air furnaces, ventilators for vessels, & public bldgs. [Oct 11th newspaper: 1-Benj Myer, manufacturer of ploughs & agricultural instruments: 61 Broad st, Newark, N J. 2-Townsend Glover, of Fishkill Landing, N Y, exhibits cases of artificial plants, leaves, fruits & larvae, made by himself, of a composition of his own. 3-J B Tillinghast, Meigs Co,Ohio, exhibits a churn of novel construction, patented on Jun 18, 1849.]

Brick house, garden, & paddock for rent, to a permanent responsible family, who will engage to take the greatest care of the property. The furniture may be had at a valuation, & possession immediately. –Stephenson Scott

For rent: large double 2 story brick house on Pa ave, nearly opposite the Six Bldgs. Inquire of E G Brown, 3rd & Market sts, Gtwn, D C.

We learn by the late accounts from Havana that Robt H Breckenridge & Ransom Beach, both of Ky, & members of the late Cuban expedition, had been picked up at sea, 20 miles from land, by a Spanish coaster, & were about to be sent to Spain with the last company transported there as participants in the invasion. Their case having reach the ears of Capt Platt, of the ship **Albany**, & Mr Owen, the American Consul, who asked an interview. Since they were of Lopez's party, they were kept in Havana to await their trial, instead of being sent to Spain.

Millard Fillmore, Pres of the U S A, recognizes Carlos Morton Stewart, who has been appointed Consul of the Argentine Confederation for the port of Balt, Md. Oct 9, 1951

The American ship **Corsair**, from Boston, bound to Caldara, Peru, with railroad materials, put into Valparaiso, Aug 25, a serious mutiny having occurred on board. When the captain attempted to arrest the ringleader, a collision took place, in which the ofcrs were nearly overpowered & the capt & mate seriously wounded. A signal of distress being hoisted, relief was afforded them by the U S stcreship **Southampton**, lying at anchor near by, Lt Peter Turner, cmder, sending a boat with armed men, who soon captured the mutineers & put them in irons under a strong guard. The American Consul, Hon W Duer, had an examination on board the ship, & committed 6 of them to the Chilian prison, & will be sent to the U S by the first opportunity, to be dealt with according to law.

Va farm for sale: in Alexandria Co. near the farms of Messrs Hardin & Berryman, 2 miles from the Grwn Ferry. Apply to Colville Terrett, 6 Union Row, F st, or to the subscriber on the premises. –Alex H Terrett

Mrd: on Oct 5, at Louisville, Ky, in St Paul's Church, by Rev W T Rooker, the rector thereof, Geo Francis Train, of Boston, Mass, to Henrietta Wilhelmina Wilkinson, daughter of Col Geo T M Davis, of the former place.

Mrd: on Oct 7, at Balt, by Rev Dr Plumer, Dr Henry M Wilson & Eliza Kelso Hollingsworth, all of that city.

At a Meeting of the Columbia Fire Co, Oct 3, it was resolved that the thanks of this Company be tendered to Robt J Roche, for his liberal present of books in aid of the Library now forming for the use of the Company. –Jas McDermott, Sec'y pro tem.

Died: on Oct 8, Francis Dodge, in his 70th year. His funeral will take place on Oct 10, at 4 o'clock, from his late residence on Congress st, Gtwn. [Oct 13th newspaper: He leaves behind him a large & highly respectable family of both sexes, all well & wisely brought up. Mr Dodge was attached to the Presbyterian Church in Gtwn. He died in the 69th year of his age.]

SAT OCT 11, 1851
Elected to Congress from the State of Ga:

Jos W Jackson, Southern Rights	E W Chastain, Union
Jas Johnson, Union	Junius Hillyer, Union
David J Bailey, Southern Rights	A H Stephens, Union
Chas Murphy, Union	Robt Toombs, Union

The house of Mr John Goff, in Wirt Co, Va, was consumed by fire on Monday last. Three of his children perished in the flames. Mr Goff & his wife were out visiting at the time.

Potomac Savings Bank, 7th st, opposite the Post Ofc. –T M Hanson, Cashier

Monticello Watchman: trial of Wm R Palmer, charged with the murder of his brother, Timothy Palmer, in Mamakating, N Y, in May last: sentenced to be hung on Nov 20.

Accidental shooting on Thu on Fell's Point. Mr Elijah Linton, 2nd mate of the ship **William A Cooper**, went on board the ship **A Cheesborough**, which was about sailing, to take leave of a friend, the 2nd mate of the ship. His friend took up a pistol which he supposed to be unloaded, & playfully snapped it. The ball penetrated to the shoulder blade & the right lung is injured. The unfortunate man belongs to Wash, D C, & has relatives there. The man who fired the pistol was not retained, but sailed with his vessel. -Balt Clipper

On Mon two members of the press, Messrs J R S Van Vlet, of the N Y Day-Book, & S P Hanscom, late city editor of the Boston Commonwealth, came near losing their lives while standing upon the verge of one of the highest precipices, a short distance below the Falls. Mr Hanscom stepped upon a shelving point of earth, which he mistook for a projecting stone, when he suddenly felt the earth giving way. He succeeded in seizing a large tree. Mr Van Vleet seized a rail from the fence near by & saved his friend. Though this ended in a few scratches & bruises to Mr Hanscom, it was a heroic act by his friend. -Buffalo Express

At the last term of the Henry Circuit Court, Ky, a Jury rendered a verdict of $10,000 against Mastrom Roberts, for slandering a young lady of Shelby Co.

Gtwn, D C, Oct 9, 1851. Meeting of the merchants of Gtwn, D C, at the warehouse of Wm T Compton, on motion, Robt Read, called to the chair, & Chas H Brown, appt'd sec. Thos Brown made a few remarks regarding the late Francis Dodge. On Oct 10 they will attend the funeral as a body, & wear the badge of mourning for 30 days. –R Read, Chrmn

Household & kitchen furniture at auction: on Oct 14, on E st, the entire stock of Gen Geo A Davis, he being determined to relinquish business. -Dyer & McGuire, aucts

Died: on Oct 10, after a lingering illness of several weeks, Mrs Eliz H, wife of Mr Matthew McLeod, & daughter of Ignatius Manning, deceased, in her 43rd year, leaving 4 small children & a disconsolate husband to mourn their irreparable loss. Her funeral will be from her late residence, opposite the Convent, Gtwn, today, at 4 o'clock.

MON OCT 13, 1851
Cmdor Lewis Warrington, of the U S Navy, died at his residence in Wash City, yesterday, in his 69th year, after an illness of severe suffering. He was a native of Va, born in Nov, 1728, &, after passing his academic course at Wm & Mary College, entered the Navy in Jan, 1800; so that he had served nearly 52 years. He was almost the only one left of that noble roll of brave naval cmders who, in the war of 1812, achieved so much glory for their country by their brilliant victories against an enemy till then deemed invincible.

Col T F Johnson, late Superintendent of the Western Military Institute at Drennon, Ky, died on Oct 4, after a protracted illness.

By way of England, from Africa, we have advices from Cape Palmas to the 19th of Jul. Govn'r Russworm, of Cape Palmas, died on Jun 17. The U S ship **Germantown**, Capt Knight, & the ship **John Adams**, Cmder Barron, were at Cape Palmas.

Wm J Brown, the most extensive produce merchant west of N Y, has failed. His liabilities are very heavy.

Ebenezer T Andrews, formerly well known as a printer & bookseller of Boston, died on Monday at the advanced age of 84. He was one of the oldest practical printers in the U S, & has left a very large fortune.

Robt Wheaton, son of the late Hon Henry Wheaton, died at Providence, R I, on Wed last, of brain fever. He was recently admitted to the bar in Suffolk Co, Mass.

Balt College of Dental Surgery will be opened on the last Mon of Oct.
–W R Handy, Dean

Sale of pictures at the Hague, Sep 5: appears in the Journal des Debats: the day before yesterday the collection of pictures left by the late Baron A C W de Nagell was publicly sold. List of those pieces which were sold for 2,000f & upwards: a View of Italy, by J Both, 4,490f; Sea-piece, by J Cuyp, 18,000f; View of a Marsh, by J Van der Capelle, 3,100f; Meadow with Cattle, by A Cuyp, 5,000f; a Family Picture, by J Van der Hagen & A Vander Velde, 2,500f; Entrance of a Fortress, by J Van der Heyden & A Van der Velde, 11,000f; View of Elben on the Rhine, by the same, 4,300f; Scene in front of an Inn, by C Dujardin, 4,000f; Landscape in the form of a Panorama, by P de Konnick, 4,000f; Family group of Danish Peasants, by A Ostade, 7,300f; The Tippler, by the same, 2,000f; Lanscape, by J Ostade, 2,640f; Flock of Sheep in a Meadow, by P Potter, 10,000f; Portrait of a young Girl, by Rembrandt, 8,040f; Landscape, by Ruysdael, 3,500f; another Landscape, by the same, 6,000f; Landscape, by J Ruysdael & P Wouvermanns, 4,020f; a Flemish Kermesse, by Teniers the younger, 5,500f; Sea-piece, by Van der Welde, 3,100f; another Sea-piece, by the same, 2,020f; Landscape, by J Wynandis & A Van der Velde, 3,600f; Haymaking by P Wouvermanns, 17,600f; the Farrier, by the same, 4,400f; Sea-piece, by J C Schotel, 4,820f.

An affray took place near Gallatin, Tenn, on Oct 7, between Messrs McElrath & Robt P Peyton, brother of Hon Balie Peyton. Peyton struck McElrath with a cane, when the latter stabbed Peyton to the heart, causing instant death. McElrath has been arrested.

Navy Dept, Oct 13, 1851. The funeral of the late Cmdor Lewis Warrington will take place on Tue next, at 12 o'clock. The procession will form at St John's Church, & proceed to the Congressional Burial ground, the place of interment. –C M Conrad, Acting Sec of the Navy. Cmdor Henry E Ballard, Commandant U S Navy Yard, Wash.
+
Died: on Oct 12th, Cmdor Lewis Warrington, in his 69th year. His funeral will be from St John's Church on Oct 14, at 12 o'clock.

In consequence of the pressure in the money market North, the house of Freeman Rawdon, of N Y, largely interested in the coal trade, has been compelled to suspend payment. We know nothing of the liabilities of the house, but trust its assets will be sufficient to meet its liabilities. –Alexandria Gaz

Mrd: Oct 9, by Rev Mr Morgan, Mr John W Connell to Miss Eliz A M Dulaney, all of Wash City.

TUE OCT 14, 1851
Hon Thos C Hackett, member of the last Congress from Ga, died at Marietta, in Ga, on Oct 8.

In 1799, I think, or a year earlier, but not later, the mother, brother, & sister of Robt Fulton removed to Washington, in West Pa, the town wherein I was raised. The sister was the wife of David Morris, long a respected innkeeper of that borough, & where, I believe, the 3 persons found a final resting place. Robt Fulton was born at Little Britain, Lancaster Co, Pa, in 1765, & died in 1815, aged 55. Fulton gave millions to the world, & received perhaps not as many farthings in return.
—Wm Darby

Hon Wm Creighton, of Chillicothe, Ohio, one of the oldest subscribers to this paper, died in Chillicothe on Wed last. He was born in Berkeley Co, Va, on Oct 29, 1778, & was at his death nearly 73 years of age. He graduated with distinguished honor at Dickinson College, [Carlisle, Pa,] at a very early age. He studied law & was licensed to practice in Pa. In 1796, the season Chillicothe was laid out, he passed through this place on his way to Ky. Two years later he pitched his tent in Chillicothe.

The Bennington [Vt] Banner records the death on *Sep 11/14, of Mr Saml Safford, of Bennington, aged 90 years. He had just entered his 17th year when he volunteered to meet the veteran invaders under Col Baum, in the memorable Battle of Bennington; was one of the first to mount the Hessian breastwork, & is probably the last of that brave band of worthies. [*The print is light.]

The Cincinnati papers of Sep 5 mention the arrest there of a man calling himself John B Anderson alias Jas Irwin, charged with selling to one Wm B Hale 9 forged & counterfeit certificates of the U S, purporting to be land warrants. Mr Hale finding himself defrauded, followed & arrested Anderson, & recovered his money.

Horace B Conklin has been convicted at Utica, as the ringleader of a band of incendiaries, of arson in Feb last, & sentenced to be hung on Nov 21. A person named Orcutt was convicted of the same offence some time ago, & sentenced to the same punishment.

Mgt Garritt, the girl who, in Newark, N J, stabbed her lover in the street because he married another woman, had her trial last week for murder. The jury brought in a verdict of not guilty, the plea of insanity urged in her defence.

The new Archbishop of Balt: the Rt Rev Patrick Kenrick, D D, late Bishop of Phil, appointed successor to the late lamented Bishop Eccleston, arrived at Balt on Fri, has taken up his residence in the Archiepiscopal mansion adjoining the Cathedral. He was consecrated Bishop Jun 6, 1830. —Balt Sun

Home School for Young Ladies, Richmond, Va: will commence on the 1st Mon of Oct. -B B Minor, Atty at Law, Law Bldgs, Richmond, Va

Postmaster Gen has est'd the following new Post Ofcs for week ending Oct 11, 1851.

Ofc	County, State	Postmaster
Grantville	Norfolk, Mass	Wm H Adams
Laurel Fork	Carroll, Va	Hiram Bolt
Ivy Bend	Madison, N C	Harvey B Deaver
Beaumont	Chatham, N C	John M Green
Grove	Elbert, Ga	Jas A Rumsey
Quinfield	Muscogee, Ga	Allen O'Quin
Vineyard	Irwin, Ga	Thos Smith
Candleville	Coffee, Ala	Wm Thornton
Dobbin's Ranch	Yuba, Cal	Wm W Dobbins
Big Bar	Trinity, Cal	John T Weaver
Salmon Falls	El Dorado, Cal	Geo Coon
Chico	Butte, Cal	Alex H Barber
Park's Bar	Yuba, Cal	Jas Nash
Lassens	Butte, Cal	Chas W Pomeroy
Quartersburg	Mariposa, Cal	Thos Thorn
Agna Frio	Mariposa, Cal	Benj F Whitten
Goodyear's Bar	Yuba, Cal	David O Woodruff
Georgetown	El Dorado, Cal	Wm F Gibbs
Volcano	Calaverad, Cal	E W Gemmill
Downerville	Yuba, Cal	E W Haskell
Hall's Ranch	Colusi, Cal	Hewell Hall
Jacksonville	Tuolumna, Cal	Geo B Keys
Brick Church	Giles, Tenn	Jonatham Rothrock
Cottage Inn	Lafayette, Wis	Nathan Olmstead
Volga City	Clayton, Iowa	Wm H Gould
Scottsburg	Benton, Oregon	S F Chadwick

Names Changed: 1-Zebulon, Pike, Ark, changed to Murfreesborough.
2-Crooked Creek, Henry, Iowa, changed to Marshall.
3-Wiggin's Ferry, St Clair, Ill, changed to Illinoistown.

Mrd: on Oct 2, by Rev W H Foote, D D, at the residence of her father, C J Cummings, of Abingdon, Va, to Miss Eliza J A Gibson, daughter of Col David Gibson.

Died: on Oct 13, Mrs Aliey Spignul, in her 56th year. Her funeral is today at 3 o'clock, at the residence of her son, Wm Spignul, N Y ave & 7th st.

Died: on Sep 1, in Winchester, Ky, Wm Flanagan, in his 47th year. He was a graduate of the U S Military Academy. After his appointment to the Army, his health failing him, he resigned his position in the Army, & retired to the pursuits of private life.

Died: on Oct 8, in St Mary's Co, Md, the Rev Thos Cornelius, of the Balt Annual Conference, in his 28th year.

WED OCT 15, 1851
A State Medical Convention was held at Frankfort, Ky, last week, which organized the State Medical Society: Dr W L Sutten, of Gtwn, Pres; & Dr W S Cripley, of Lexington, Vice Pres.

$10 reward for return of strayed or stolen bay Mare Colt, from the common near the Twenty Bldgs. –Ann Bean, corner of 3rd st east, near Coombs' wharf.

Mrd: on Oct 7, by Rev Mr Alig, Mr Meinard Menke to Miss Eliz E Eichhorn, all of Wash City.

Mrd: on Sep 24, at the Thoroughfare, Prince Wm, Va, by Rev Mr Towles, Jos Horner, of Warrenton, Va, to Louisa, daughter of the late Geo Chapman, of the former place.

Mrd: on Oct 7, at Bowling Green, Ky, by Rev A C Dickerson, Jeanie, daughter of Hon J R Underwood, to Geo Clarke Rogers.

Mrd: on Oct 9, in Wash City, by Rev O B Brown, Mr Wm Moss to Miss Eliz Lomax.

Died: on Sep 5, in Livingston Co, N Y, Dr Chas Douglas, late Com'r of Public Bldgs in Wash City.

Land for sale: I will offer the farm on which I now reside, 2 miles from the Navy Yard, on the Piscataway road: contains 105 acres; improvements are new & spacious frame bldg & necessary outhouses. B P Smith, east wing of City Hall, is in possession of a plat of the farm, & can give all information relative to it.
–Jno E Dement

Copartnership: the undersigned have this day entered into a copartnership, having purchased the entire stock of Mr Edw Simms, they will carry on the Grocery, Wine & Liquor business at his old established stand, south side of Pa ave, opposite Jackson Hall. -Geo F Dyer, Saml Hamilton [Mr Edw Simms is retiring from the business.]

On Fri last John Blake, a non-resident of Washington, was fully committed by Capt Goddard for trial, on a charge of having set on fire the 2 stables which were burnt on Thu last, near 14th st & the canal. A bridle, the property of Messrs Ager & McLean, whose stable was one of those burnt, was found in his possession.

THU OCT 16, 1851
Lt J Findlay Schenck, Cmder of the U S mail steamship **Ohio**, has been presented by the passengers who were on board during the last passage from Chagres to N Y with an elegant silver pitcher, as a mark of their esteem.

U S ship **Cyane**: list of the ofcrs, which sailed from Norfolk, Va, bound to Havana, Oct 9, 1851: Cmder, John Stone Payne; Lts, Theodore P Green, H N Harrison, W D Hurst, A Wein; Passed Midshipman & Acting Master, Maurice Simmons; Passed Midshipman, N H Van Zandt; Surgeon, Solomon Sharp; Purser, G White; Assist Surgeon, G Peck; Midshipmen, E A Chapman, B E Hand, C L O Hammond, T P K Mygatt, N E Fitzhugh; Capt's Clerk, Jas B Hope; Boatswain, J Hulett; Gunner, R C Barnard; Carpenter, E W Barnicoat; Sailmaker, D C Drayton.

Valuable 3 story brick house & lot at auction: on Oct 29, belonging to J H Eberbach, at E & 8th sts, & the lot on which it stands, in square 407. The lower part of the house is used as a Restaurant, in which there is a large business done.
-A Green, auctioneer

The Desert News of Aug 19, published at Salt Lake City, announces the arrival there of Mr J Wesley Jones, superintendent of the grand panorama of the plains, Salt, Lake, & Calif, with his troupe of artists engaged upon the work. Mr Jones stated that a company of packers were attacked on Aug 9, about 7 miles n e of Steeple Rocks, on the **Fort Hall** road, by about 50 Indians, supposed to be Snakes & Half-breeds. The company was styled the Galena Co, from Ill. Those killed: Nathan Stewart, J R Garlinger, John Woods, John Burton, Jordan Underwood, Capt M Russell, of Galena; Louis Berry, of Shullsburg, & ___ Chamberlin, of Whiteoak Springs.

Died: on Tue last, at his residence in Wash City, after a brief illness, Moses Poor, in his 79th year. He was for many years a resident of Wash, & was much esteemed for his upright, exemplary & amiable character. He has left a large & respected family & numerous friends to lament his death. His funeral is this afternoon, at 3 o'clcok, from his late residence on F st.

Wash Corp: 1-Ptn from J A Wise, asking remuneration for damage done to a lot: referred to the Cmte on Improvements. 2-Ptn from T H Phillips for the remission of a fine: referred to the Cmte of Claims: passed. 3-Act for the relief of Thos Plumsill: passed. 4-Act for the relief of W B Mitchell: passed. 5-Act for the relief of Wm Martin: passed. 6-Ptn of J A M Duncanson & others for setting the curbstone & paving the footway in front of square 375: referred to the Cmte on Improvements. 7-Ptn of F S Evans for permission to retain a bldg, recently erected a little outside of the bldg line, in its present position: referred to the Cmte on Police. Also, ptn of F S Evans & others for grading & paving the alley in square 368: referred to the Cmte on Improvements. 8-Bill for the relief of Danl Rowland: referred to the Cmte of Claims.

After Mgt Garritt was acquitted of the murder of Edw Drum, on the ground of insanity, the Court appointed 6 physicians to examine her, & they reported they find at present no evidence of unsound mind, & the Court concurring in that opinion, the prisoner was released from custody.

Mrd: on Oct 14, by Rev Wm Hamilton, Mr R Laidler Hawkins to Miss Jane Eliz Wineberger, all of Wash City.

Mrd: on Oct 15, at St Paul's English Lutheran Church, by Rev Wm H Smith, of Pa, Rev J Geo Butler, Pastor of said Church, to Miss Clara E, daughter of Lewis Smith, of Gtwn, D C.

Mrd: on Sep 22, in St George's Church, Ramagate, England, Alfred Lowe, U S Consul at Civita Vecchia, Roman States, to Mary Ann, eldest daughter of Paul Balme, of Mile-end, Middlesex, & Romford, Essex.

Orphans Court of Wash Co, D C. Letters testamentary on the personal estate of Francis Dodge, late of said county, deceased. –Francis Dodge, jr; Robt P Dodge, excs

Sanderson's Hotel, corner of Franklin & Calvert sts, opposite the Calvert station, Balt, Md. -H S Sanderson

FRI OCT 17, 1851
Chas Gilpin, Whig, was re-elected Mayor of the city of Phil on Tues last.

Jas Buchanan, for many years the British Consul in N Y C, died while on a visit to his daughter in the vicinity of Montreal, on Sat last, suddenly, at age 81 years. –N Y Com Advertiser

Sale under decree: on Oct 30, 1851, before the Mayor's ofc, in the town of Alexandria, pursuant to a decree of the Circuit Court for said county, made Jun 14, 1851, in the suit of Jos Smith et al vs John West et al, will sell at public auction, the real estate of which the late Jos Mandeville died seized, & by his last will devised to the said John West, or so much as may be necessary to pay the debts & legacies, with interest thereon, expenses of sale, costs, provided for in said decree. Property on Queen & Pitts sts, with house & lot on Royal st. This is an entire half square, less the lot corner of Royal & Queen sts, occupied by the Misses Mandeville. House & lot on King st & store corner of King & Fairfax sts. House & shop on Fairfax st. Bldg & lot on Water st, [Soap Factory, fixtures, & implements.] Lots 2 thru 7, each fronting on Pitt st. Lot beginning on Queen st, at the n w corner of Mary & Julia Mandeville's lot. Lots 11, 12, & 13, in schedule A. Also, several other pieces of real estate, so described. -Jos Eaches, Com'r, Alexandria

The widow of Lopez is at present in Paris, having been separated from him for a long time. She belongs to a wealthy family in Cuba.

Mrd: on Oct 15, by Rev W T Eva, John B Riddlemoser, of Balt, to Hannah Melville Beveridge, of Wash City.

SAT OCT 18, 1851
$3 reward for runaway indented apprentice named Jas Robinson, a colored boy, between 17 & 18 years of age. —John Murphy, Butcher, living near the Navy Yard.

Lessons in Penmanship: $3 for 12 lessons: at his rooms in Duvall's Bldg, Pa ave, between 4½ & 6th sts. —W A Richardson

Furnished rooms for rent: one of the Six Bldgs on Pa ave. Apply to Chas Vinson, Treas Dept.

Biography of one of the earliest of the pioneers of the West: John Sevier, of Tenn, after his first coming to Congress, in 1811, was already far advanced in years. He was the first Govn'r of Tenn-[for 12 years;] his remains lie buried in a neighboring State, where he died more than 30 years ago in the service of his country, without a stone to mark the place, or an enclosure to protect them from unhallowed intrusion. He was descended from an ancient family in France whose name was Xavier; his father, Valentine Xavier, was born in London, & emigrated to America in the first part of the last century, settled on the Shenandoah, in Va, where John Sevier was born about 1740. When but a young man he married Miss Hawkins, by whom he had 6 children. Being delicate, she never moved from Eastern Virginia, but died there soon after the birth of her 6th child. His 2nd wife, Miss Catharine Sherrill, became the mother of 10 children. In 1778 it is probable that his first wife died, for in 1779, we believe, he was married to Miss Sherrill.

MON OCT 20, 1851
Court of Common Pleas at N Y on Sat, a verdict of $3,000 was awarded against the N Y & New Haven Railroad Co, for injury done Mr Hunt by a collision on that road, in which his step-daughter was killed.

Extensive sale of household furniture, mules, horses, colts, cows, oxen, hogs, wagons, carts, machinery, faming utensils, carriages & buggies at auction: on Nov 3, on the farm of Theodore Mosher, 2 miles from the Navy Yard, on the Piscataway road, adjoining the farms of Messrs Blagden, Young, & Jenkins. -A Green, auct

Orphans Court of Wash Co, D C. Letters of administration de bonis non on the personal estate of Lewis G Davidson, late of said county, deceased.
—W Redin, adm d b n

Orphans Court of Wash Co, D C. Letters of administration on the personal estate of Jas Stuart, late of the U S Army, deceased. –J W Stuart, adm

Orphans Court of Wash Co, D C. Letters of administration on the personal estate of Edw Holland, late of said county, deceased. –Jno E Holland, adm

Orphans Court of Wash Co, D C. Letters of administration on the personal estate of Eliza Davidson, late of said county, deceased. -W Redin, adm

The Augusta [Ga] Sentinel chronicles the death of Mr Henry Schultz, a German by birth, who emigrated to this country at an early age, & located in that city as a mechanic or common laborer, where, by his enterprise & industry, he amassed a fortune, which was wrecked in commercial reverses. For many years of the latter part of his life he carried on a fruitless litigation for the Augusta bridge, which he had built, & of which, at one time, he was part owner.

Mr Jas Castleman, tried at Berryville, Va, on the charge of so cruelly beating his slave as to cause his death, has been acquitted. A nolle prosequi was then entered in the case of his son, charged with the same offence.

Mrd: on Oct 2, at the Chapel of Grace, N Y C, by Rev Thos Gallaudet, Mr John W Compton, of Wash, to Miss Anna Mead, daughter of Chas Wayland, of the former place.

Died: on Oct 6, at his residence in New Geneva, Pa, Jas W Nicholson, in his 79th year. He was the only son of the late Cmdor Nicholson, was a Christian & a gentleman, beloved & respected by all who knew him.

Valuable improved property: a frame house, 2 stories, located on I st, between 9th & 10th sts. For terms apply to Wm Slade, Brown's Hotel.

Warning! The public are warned not to trust any body on my account, as I will not pay for any goods or money procured without my consent or knowledge.
–Leonard Zimmermaker

TUE OCT 21, 1851

Hon Jesse D Bright, U S Senator from Indiana, was struck by paralysis, at his residence in Madison, on Fri week, shortly after dinner. He was speechless for some moments, but by the aid of a medical attendant was restored to consciousness. [Oct 31st newspaper: The Indianopolis Sentinel says he was not afflicted with paralysis, but with a rush of blood to the head.]

Household & kitchen furniture at auction: on Oct 23, at the house of Maj Winder, on West st, near Congress: well-kept furniture. –Barnard & Buckey, Gtwn

Wm W Story, the son of the late Judge Story, sailed, with his family, on Oct 13, for Italy, where he intends to renew his residence & his studies in arts. He leaves the biography of his father, which he has been preparing, ready for immediate publication.

U S sloop-of-war **Vandalia**, at Acapulco, Sep 26, all well. List of her ofcrs: Cmder, Wm H Gardner; Lts, Robt E Johnson, Reed Werden, T Harman Patterson; Acting Lt, John P Bankhead; Acting Master, Walter V Gilliss; Surgeon, Jas C Palmer; Purser, John V B Bleecker; Lt of Marines, Jacob Reed; Assist Surgeon, Robt Carter; Passed Midshipmen, John B Stewart, Alex'r Habersham, Stephen B Luce, Henry St George Hunter; Midshipman, Chas H Cushman; Boatswain, Zachariah Whitmarsh; Gunner, John D Brandt; Carpenter, Robt M Bain; Sailmaker, John W North.

Household & kitchen furniture at auction: on Oct 27, at the residence of Philip Ennis, deceased, on 6th st, between F & G sts. Also, lots 12 thru 15 & #16, in square 673, on North Capitol st; also, a lot of hay. -Dyer & McGuire, aucts

Circuit Court of Wash Co, D C, in Chancery. Chas B Pratt, guardian of Sarah W Taylor & Rebecca Taylor, widow & administratrix of Geo W Taylor, deceased, vs Elise C D, sometimes called Eliza S; Martha M; Ella, sometimes called Hellen; & Catherine, sometimes called Kate, Voorhees, infants & heirs at law of Borden M & Sarah Voorhees, deceased, & Sarah W Taylor, infant & heir at law of Geo W Taylor, deceased. Chas S Wallach, the Trustee, reported to the Court that at a sale made by him of the property named & described in the above cause on Jul 17, 1851, John Greeves being the highest bidder for lot 30 in square 127, for the sum of $769.32; & John Potts became the purchaser of Lot 31 in square 127, for $1,073.96; & that Greeves & Potts have complied with the terms of the sale. -Jno A Smith, clerk

Chancery sale: by decree of the Circuit Court of Wash Co, D C, sitting as a Court of Chancery, made in the case of Dangerfield vs Mudd et al: #740: public auction on Nov 13: part of lot 13 in square 299, on Md ave. Also, part of lot 14 in square 299, on Md ave. The property is improved by 2 brick houses, & may be divided. –Walter S Cox, trustee -Dyer & McGuire, aucts

Died: on Oct 19, Mrs Mgt Slater, in her 47th year, wife of Wm Slater, & daughter of the late Isaac Cooper, of Wash City. Her funeral will be from her late residence on N J ave, at 2 p m.

WED OCT 22, 1851
Intelligence has been received at the Indian Bureau of the death, at San Antonio, of John H Rollins, Special Agent for the U S to the Texas Indians. Mr Rollins was a valuable ofcr, & his decease will be much regretted.

The Union copies from a private letter the following accurate list of the Hungarians now on their way to the U S with the patriot Kossuth: List of Hungarians embarked on board the U S steamer **Mississippi**, off the Dardanelles, Sep 10, 1851: Gov'n'r Louis Kossuth, wife, & 3 children; Instructor Ignatius Karody; Adrian Lemmi, Kossuth's private secretary, his wife, & 1 child; Col Nicholas Perczel & wife, Maj John Demeter & wife; Maj Adolphus Gzurman, wife, & 1 child; Maj Stephen Kovats & wife; Physician Louis Spacask, mother, wife, & 1 child; Mr Emanuel Luley, wife, & 5 children; Gen Jos Wysocsky, Col Julius Pryseinsky, Capt Lusakowsky, Lt Ladislas Kosak. Poles, Col Francis Huzman, Col Ladislas Bersensey, Lt Col Alex'r Asboth, Lt Col Danl Ihasz, Lt Col Edw Lerody, Maj Augustus Wagner, Capt Lewis Yorok, Capt Lewis Frater, Capt Wm Waigly, Capt Jos Meneth, Capt John Kalapsa, Capt Gideon Acs, Capt Anthony Serene, Capt Armin Miklosy, Lt Geo Gukenck, Lt Chas Lasio, Capt Merighy, & 6 soldiers.

Postmaster Gen has est'd the following new Post Ofcs for week ending Oct 18, 1851.

Ofc	County, State	Postmaster
Weathersfield Centre	Windsor, Vt	Jas W Goldsmith
Barre Plains	Worcester, Mass	Edw Denny
Dearmans	West Chester, N Y	Geo W Dearman
Portage Entry	Houghton, Mich	R Sheldon
Carp River	Marquette, Mich	Peter White
Casnovia	Ottawa, Mich	Danl Bennett
Big Otter	Braxton, Va	Wm Mollihons
Rock Camp	Braxton, Va	John S Taylor
Grass Lick	Jackson, Va	Jas Rollins
Tyler Mountain	Kanawha, Va	Wm A Howell
New Ports News	Warwick, Va	Robt E Bennett
Coon's Mill	Boone, Va	Andrew I Coon
Willow Spring	Russell, Va	John E C Easterby
Scotts Hill	New Hanover, N C	Jos M Foy
Blockers'	Cumberland, N C	S R Hawley
Fulton	Cobb, Ga	M L Harris
Newtown Academy	Monroe, Ala	Zephaniah Swift
Vidalia	Concordia P, La	Geo B Wailes
Arenosa	Victoria, Texas	Chesley D Strange
Caney Bridge	Chicot, Ark	Pryor P Bunch
Jefferson Mills	Jefferson, Mo	Jas Winn
Desmoinesville	Wapello, Iowa	Jas Nosler
Hammondsburg	Warren, Iowa	Robt G Hammond
Summum	Fulton, Ill	Jno S Gassaway
Rio	Vermillion, Ill	Wash H Carter
Steuben	Marshall, Ill	Aaron C Fosdick
Andersonville	Saline, Ill	A A Anderson

Midview	Henry, Ken	Robt H Ellis
Coytee	Monroe, Tenn	Jonathan Davis
Shop Spring	Wilson, Tenn	Young Grissom
Sampete	Utah	Isaac Morley

Names Changed: 1-Burnt Shop, Orange, N C, changed to Melville.
2-Hamilton, La Fayette, Wisc, changed to Darlington.
3-Ballinger's, Tipton, Indiana, changed to Sharpsville.
4-Kinklesburg, Oldham, Ky, changed to Cloves Depot.
5-Snoddyville, Jefferson, Tenn, changed to Wittville.

Mrd: on Oct 8, at Pensacola, by Rev P Donan, Gen David E Twiggs, of the U S Army, to Mrs Tabitha Hunt.

Died: on Oct 11, at New Orleans, Brevet Maj P W McDonald, U S Army. He graduated with distinction at the Military Academy in 1841, & was commissioned in the 2nd Dragoons, in which regt he saw much active service on the Western frontier & in Texas. Early in the Mexican war he was appointed aid-de-camp to Gen Twiggs, in whose staff he served with credit & efficiency throughout the war. He was present at nearly all the engagements on both lines, & was twice brevetted for gallantry & good conduct.

In Chancery. Antoni Marryett & Catharine his wife, against Saml Spencer & Asa M his wife, Thos Burrus & Susan his wife, Bennet Lucas, Wm Burrus & Jane his wife, Emily Lucas, & David Lucas. By order of the Circuit Court of Wash Co, D C, I am directed to inquire & report whether it will be to the advantage of the parties in the above suit to sell lot 3 in square 11, in Wash City, for the purpose of partition. Meeting on Oct 27 in the City Hall. –W Redin, auditor

THU OCT 23, 1851
Fatal affray at Aquia creek on Tue, in which Jas W Morrison stabbed John L Cantwell in 6 places in the back, & in the head, leaving some doubt of his recovery. Both the men were baggage masters, & quarreled about their business. Morrison has been arrested.

John Enders, an old, wealthy, & liberal merchant of Richmond, Va, was killed on Monday by falling from a ladder in a new warehouse he was erecting.

Wash Corp: 1-Ptn from Jas T Burns for a balance due him for grading I st north: referred to the Cmte of Claims. 2-Ptn from Trueman M Brush for remission of a fine: referred to the Cmte of Claims. 3-Cmte of Claims asked to be discharged from the further consideration of the ptn of Clark Mills; ordered to lie on the table. 4-Ptn from C Buckingham, captain of the Columbia Artl Co, asking that provision may be made for keeping in order 2 brass guns in his possession: referred to the Cmte on Finance.

For sale: a pair of black horses, perfectly sound. Also, 2 carriages, one open the other close, with harness. To be seen at Boteler's Stables, on G st, near the War Dept. For terms apply to Col Turnbull, F st.

Mrd: on Oct 21, in Phil, by Rev Mr Howe, J Munroe Chubb, of Wash City, to Caroline Augusta, daughter of Amos Leland, of the former city.

For rent: 2 parlors & 4 or 5 chambers, lighted with gas, over my Music & Stationery Store, Pa ave, between 11th & 12th sts. —Mrs Garret Anderson

For rent: newly erected frame house, fronting on N Y ave, near 12th st. —Wm Hunter

For rent: a large & desirable residence in the immediate neighborhood of the Pres' House. Apply to C St J Chubb, at the Banking House of Chubb, Schenck & Co.

$5 reward for return of strayed or stolen Cow. —Jos D Ward, 6th st, Island

Saddle horse for sale: I wish to sell my riding horse. Sold because I have no use for him. Can be seen at Thos Busk's Monument Livery Stable, on D, between 13½ & 14th sts. -Geo F Dyer

Wash City Ordinance: 1-Act for the relief of U B Mitchell: sum of $11 be paid to him for balance due in settlement of his police account to Jul 1, 1848.

Orphans Court of Wash Co, D C. Letters testamentary on the personal estate of Lewis Warrington, late of Wash Co, D C. —M R Warrington, C St J Chubb, excs

Valuable house & lot at public auction: deed of trust executed by Aloysius N Clements, on Sep 26, 1849, recorded in Liber J A S 6, folios 433 thru 436, Wash Co land records: sale of part of lot 9 in square 382, fronting on 9th st, with improvements, adjoining the large bldg on said lot erected by Mr R G Briscoe, & now occupied by Mr Starbuck as a hotel. -Dyer & McGuire, aucts

In Chancery: Re-petition of John Cox, trustee. The trustee reports he has sold the *Cedars* to A V Scott for $6,700; lots 209 & 211, in Threlkeld's addition to Gtwn, to Wm Jewell for $455; & part of lot 28, in old Gtwn, to *Bobert White for $10; & the purchasers have complied with the terms of the sale. —Jno A Smith, clerk [*Copied as written.]

Freestone Point Fishery for rent: at public auction: on Nov 20, before the Mayor's ofc, in Alexandria. —John W Fairfax, exc of Henry Fairfax, deceased.

$5 reward for recovery of strayed or stolen Buffalo Cow. —F W Benter, Wash Hall

Valuable real estate at auction: the subscriber, desirous of closing his mercantile affairs in Alexandria, with a view of devoting his whole time & attention to his business in Wash City, will sell on Oct 31, his 2 story brick fire proof Store & Dwlg, on Royal st, between King & Cameron sts. –Wm Egan

For rent: that desirable residence near 12th & N Y ave, occupied by the undersigned. –Wm Hunter

Stoves, Stoves, Stoves! Just received at the Stove Depot, s e corner of Pa ave & 10th st. –Jas Skirving, sole agent for Wash City.

Teachers wanted: the Trustees of the Marianna Male & Female Seminary are desirous to employing a competent Male & Female Teacher to take charge of the above institution, to open Jan 1 next. Salary of $800 for the male teacher, or $1,200 for male & female teachers per annum. –Fred'k R Pittman, Marianna Seminary, Jackson Co, Fla.

Sale of pews in Christ Church, Gtwn, at public auction on Oct 27. –Edw S Wright, auct

FRI OCT 24, 1851
Sharpshooters: Fourth Annual Ball on Nov 6. Managers:

Capt J Y Bryant
Lt M Birkhead
Lt W J McCullum
Lt J Ward
Ensign W Gallant
Serg H B Curtis
Serg P Harbin
Serg E C Eckloff

Serf J L Foxwell
Color Guard C J Queen
Color Guard O Collins
Corp W Pumphry
Corp E J Evans
Corp J Lewis
Corp N Kelly

Privates:
R Downing	J H Rightstine	W D Serrin
P Dowling	J E Phelps	C Klomann
W H Sommers	O Quigly	G Brenner
T Gallagher	E Maston	W Smith
C Kaugphman	M Ritter	R Birch
J H Glick	J Wilson	A Beedle
C Bell	D Barren	W Preston
F Dawson	W Ross	A M Caldwell
J H Kennan	J Houck	W Dawson
M Houck	C Stewart	W Tableman
W H Robertson	L Curtis	J Lasky
S P Robertson	B Hurst	R Simms
J Tretler	J Moran	T Brown

A F Forrest	G Myers	J H Goddard,
W Kinslo	C Edelin	Treasurer
W H Gorbett	L Hager	
J Kidwel	J Conklin	

Tickets $1, admitting a gentleman & laides, can be had at: R S Patterson's, W H Winter's, S Butt's, McIntyre's drug store, 7th & I sts; J Shillington's, Danl Kelly's, Navy Yard; J H Kidwell's drug store, Gtwn, or of either of the managers on the part of the company.

Phil, Oct 22. A young man named Cunningham, belonging to a wealthy family of Georgia, who has been confined in the Blockley Asylum, committed sucide this morning by hanging.

Rev Archibald Alexander, D D, of the Princeton Theological Seminary, died at Princeton on Wed, in his 81st year. He was one of the oldest & most distinguished clergymen of the Presbyterian Church in the U S. In 1811, when that Seminary was first established, he was elected a Professor, & continued in ofc up to the hour of his death.

Hon David Plant died suddenly at Stratford, Conn, on Sat last, from disease of the heart. In former days he occupied a prominent position as a politician in his State; was speaker of the Legislature, Lt Govn'r of the State, & member of Congress. He was 68 years of age.

Appointments by the Pres: 1-Jerome Fuller, of N Y, to be Chief Justice of the Supreme Court of the U S for the Territory of Minnesota, in place of Aaron Goodrich, removed. 2-Alex'r Wilkin, of Minnesota, to be Sec of the Territory of Minnesota, in place of Chas K Smith, removed. 3-Jos W Furbur, of Minnesota, to be Marshal of the U S for the Territory of Minnesota, in place of Henry L Tilden, removed.

Accident at Alexandria on Wed, at the dwlg of Mr John Paine, on Patrick st. His little son, more than a year old, in playing with a swing in the yard, got the rope coiled round his neck, & was strangled before assistance reached him. When found he was dead. -Gaz

Household & kitchen furniture at auction: on Oct 24, well kept furniture of Mrs Claudia Stewart, at her house on Gay st, between Green & Montgomery sts. -Barnard & Buckley, aucts, Gtwn.

Accident on the Orange & Alexandria Railroad on Wed, near Wheat's Mill, when the locomotive struck a raill & was precipitated down the embarkment. The engineer, Mr John Smith, & the fireman, Mr Geo H Butler, were severely injured. Mr Butler had his left leg almost entirely cut off near the ancle. -Gaz

Boston, Oct 22. Col John Mountford, of the U S Army, died suddenly at Mr Winthrop's house this morning. [Oct 27th newspaper: Col Mountford distinguished himself as an artillery ofcr during the war of 1812. He was in the engagements of Little York, [now Toronto,] Pittsburg, & at **Fort Niagara**. On Lake Ontario he volunteered & served his men as marines, & narrowly escaped death from a 42-pound shot. At Little York he received a severe wound from the explosion of the British fort, which was blown up by the enemy, & which caused the death of Gen Pike. He subsequently served in the Florida war.]

Mrd: on Oct 22, by Rev Mr Marks, Jas Hughes to Mrs Mary Downey.

Mrd: on Oct 22, by Rev Mr Marks, Wm Martin to Miss Jane Hooper, all of Wash City.

Mrd: on Oct 23, by Rev Mr Hodges, at the residence of her father, Miss Anne E Richards, of Wash, to Mr Elijah Wells, of Port Tobacco, Md.

Died: Oct 23, at her residence, in Wash City, after a most painful illness, Mrs Geo Ann Patterson, widow of the late Cmdor Danl T Patterson, of U S Navy, aged about 66 years. Her funeral will take place from her dwlg, at I & 21st st, Sat at 11 o'clock.

Died: at Thomaston, Me, Caroline F Holmes, widow of the late Hon John Holmes, & youngest daughter of Gen Knox, of Revolutionary memory. [No death date given-current item.]

Died: on Oct 11, at Fairfield, Me, Hon Jonathan G Huntoon, formerly Govn'r of the State of Maine, aged 70 years.

SAT OCT 25, 1851
Candidates for Justices of N Y Supreme Court, at the election to be held in Nov.
Whig:

Jas G King, jr	B F Roxford
Albert Lockwood	Saml Blatchford
Ira Harris	Jas Mullett
A B James	Moses Taggart
Danl Gott	Saml A Foot
J M Parker	

Democrat:

Jas J Rosevelt	Schuyler Crippen
Selah B Strong	Theron R Strong
Geo R Davis	Noah P Davis
Cornelius L Allen	Geo W Clinton
Danl Pratt	Alex'r S Johnson
Hiram Gray	

Wilson L Reeves, of the Lopez party, was released on Oct 19, & came passenger in the ship **Empire City**.

Appointment by the Pres: Ferdinand Coxe, of Pa, to be Sec of the U S Legation in Brazil, in place of Franklin H Clack, resigned.

In Chancery. Elias Travers & Jos Travers, cmplnts; & Jas Winne & Mary his wife, & others, dfndnts. The late Nicholas Travers devised to his son Nicholas, in fee simple, lots 4 thru 7 in square 36, with the dwlg house thereon; that said Nicholas, the son, survived his father & afterwards departed this life, unmarried & intestate, seized of the said lots & premises; that the cmplnts & dfndnts, the brothers & sisters of said Nicholas, the son, are entitled to the said lots as his heirs at law. The premises are not susceptible of partition, & that it will be to the advantage of all the heirs that the same should be sold for the purpose of division. That Jas Travers, one of the heirs, & one of the dfndnts, is a minor; & the object of the bill is to obtain a decree for the sale of said premises. The bill states that Jas Winne & Mary his wife reside out of this District & in Balt, Md. Same to appear in this Court, on or before the 4th Mon in Mar next. –John A Smith, clerk -Redin, for cmplnts

For rent: handsome frame bldg, just finished, on 13th st south. –Peter Hepburn, F & 9th sts, Wash.

Roslin for sale at auction: this beautiful & once highly cultivated estate, on the Appomattox river, in Chesterfield Co: sale on Nov 14. –Jas Alfred Jones, Atty for Miss Jane C Gamble -Jos E Cox, Agent for Ro Leslie.

On Sep 27, John N McKinley, sheriff of Smith Co, Texas, arrested at Canton Mr Jos Pierce with a warrant charged with assault with intent to commit a murder. After Pierce was arrested, Isaac Moore threatened to raise a crowd of Pierce's friends & rescue him. The sheriff summoned a guard to prevent the rescue. P M Moore, Robt Pierce, & Crawford, tried to rescue him. Robt Pierce, after receiving several shots, fell & expired. Isaac Moore was also shot dead. Crawford was severely wounded. On the sheriff's party, David Neil was killed, & Jas Holden & J W Patterson, both mortally wounded. Thos Brock was slightly wounded, & Sheriff McKinley severely wounded, but not considered mortal.

Md Agricultural Society: meeting at Balt on Thu, the following were elected ofcrs for the ensuing year: Chas B Calvert, of PG Co, Pres. Vice Presidents:

Balt City: John Glenn
St Mary's Co: H G S Key
Chas Co: J G Chapman
PG Co: Horace Capron
Calvert: Danl Kent
Anne Arundel: Thos S Ickelhart

Howard Dist: Chas Carroll
Montg: A Bowie Davis
Fred'k: John McPherson
Wash: Wm Dodge
Alleghany, Dr Saml P Smith
Carroll: Geo Patterson

Balt: Wilson M Carey
Harford: Alex Norris
Cecil: Rev Jas McIntyre
Kent: G S Holliday
Queen Anne's: Jas T Earle
Talbot: Col N Goldsborough
Caroline: T R Stewart
Dorchester: Dr Jos E Muse
Somerset: W H Jones

Worcester: J S Stevenson
D C: J H Bradley
Delaware: P C Holcomb
Va: J W Ware
Pa: Aaron Clement
Corr Sec: Geo W Dobbin
Rec Sec: Saml Sands
Treas: Wm P Lightner, Balt

Curators:
W W W Bowie, of PG Co
N B Washington, of Anne Arundel
J Carroll Walsh, of Harford

Jas Carroll, jr, of Balt Co
Ezra Whitman, of Balt Co
Martin Goldsborough, of Talbot

Died: Fri, Chas Richd Adams, infant son of John & America Wiley. His funeral is today at 3 o'clock, from the residence of his grandfather, Thos Adams, on 11th st, between O & H sts.

Died: on Oct 23, Harriet Rebecca, daughter of Jas M & Mary Rebecca Wright, aged 3 years. Her funeral is from the residence of her parents on 4th st west, today, at 2 o'clock.

The funeral of Mrs Com Patterson will be at St John's Church, at 11 o'clock, today.

Handsome bldg at auction: on Nov 4, by deed of trust from Wm W Stewart & Eliz Barron to the subscriber, dated Oct 28, 1847, recorded in Liber W B 138, folios 24 thru 27, of the land records of Wash Co, D C: sale of part of lot 8 in square 576, fronting on Md ave, near the corner of 1st st west. –Jos Bryan, trustee
-A Green, auctioneer

MON OCT 27, 1851
The Pres has appointed Jos Blunt, of N Y C, Com'r to China. He is a lawyer of high attainments & distinction in his profession. –Republic

Foreign items: among the deaths of the week may be mentioned that of the benevolent authoress, Mrs Sherwood, at age 77; & that of Count Reventhow, the Danish Ambassador to the Court of England, who died at Glasgow on Oct 6, of disease of the heart. Four English peers have also died, namely, Lords Calthrop, Liverpool, Stafford, & Bolingbroke; they were all of advanced in life.

Spain: the Queen has granted a pension to 20,000 reals to the widow of Gen Enna, in consideration of the recent services he rendered in Cuba.

We place no restraint upon our sorrow in recording the death of the large Shanghae cock of Mr Wm Stowe, our worthy postmaster & late chairman of the cmte on fowls. He died 3 days since while moulting. A rude grave was scooped in the ground, & he was buried. –Springfield Republican

In Chancery: in the cause of Fred A Wagler vs Jos C Wagler, Catherine M Wagler, Francis B Hilbus, Harriet Jane Hilbus, & Helen V & Mary S Wagner. Parties to appear before me, at the Auditor's room, City Hall, on Nov 1, to be heard touching the premises in regard to the real estate to be sold. –Walter S Cox, Special Auditor

In Chancery: in the cause of the petition of Jos R Underwood & Eliz C his wife, John T Cox, Richd S Cox, Watkins Addison & Mary Jane his wife, Thos C Cox, Robt M Cox & Ellen Mary Cox. The parties are to appear on Nov 6, at my ofc in the City Hall, Wash, in regard to the division of certain real property in Gtwn.
–W Redin, Auditor

Valuable Mill, brick dwg house, & 35 acres of rich Meadow Land attached, for sale: on Nov 7, at our auction rooms in Wash : sale of the above mentioned property on Four-Mile Creek, in Alexandria Co, Va, equidistant from Alexandria, Gtwn, & Wash City. To view the property, call on Dr R B Alexander, whose residence adjoins, or any information in relation to the same, can be obtained from Edw Swann, at his law ofc on 5th st, opposite the City Hall. -Dyer & McGuire, aucts

Mr Enos Stone, one of the founders of Rochester, died on Thu at the house of his son-in-law, in the city of Buffalo, aged 76 years. His name is widely known in the western parts of N Y in connexion with the earliest settlement in the region.

Four of the crew of the ship **Augusta**, of Gottemburg, lying in the North River, N Y, were drowned while endeavoring to get on board their vessel in a small boat. It appears they were intoxicated at the time. Their names were Anderson, Neilson, Peterson, & Berryson.

Died: on Oct 25, Edwin K, son of Dr S C & Emma Smoot, aged 15 months & 23 days. His funeral is today at 2 o'clock, from the residence of his father, Pa ave, between 19th & 20th.

Frank McGann, a plumber by trade, was detected on Sat attempting to rob the boarding house of Mrs Peyton, Pa ave & 4½ st. He was committed for trial by Justice Goddard.

Worthington G Snethen continues to practice law in the Supreme Court. Ofc at 5 Carroll Pl, Capitol Hill, Wash D C.

House with its furniture & stabling, for rent: on N J ave, south of the Capitol. Apply to J Bartram North.

TUE OCT 28, 1851
Railroad accident on Sat on the N Y & New Haven Railroad, at Mount Vernon: the fireman, a brakeman, & a Dr Sheldon, or Seldon, were killed instantly.

Postmaster Gen has est'd the following new Post Ofcs for week ending Oct 25, 1851.

Ofc	County, State	Postmaster
Bruce	Macomb, Mich	John Allen
Groton Centre	Erie, Ohio	Warstel Hastings
Hardeysville	Athens, Ohio	Martin Shaner
Happy Valley	Fairfax, Va	John H Murray
Cypress	Yazoo, Miss	Henry F Greer
Bryant's Station	Milam, Texas	Jas Anderson
Quitman	Wood, Texas	H Keys
Gilroy	Santa Clara, Calif	Jas Houck
Antioch	Contra Costa, Calif	Geo Kimball
Moon's Ranch	Colusi, Calif	Nathl Merrill
Yuba City	Sutter, Calif	Wm F Nelson
Staples' Ranch	San Josquin, Calif	David J Staples
Valley Forge	Jasper, Mo	Jesse Darrow
Spring Dale	Cedar, Iowa	Elia Heald
Cold Water	Delaware, Iowa	Jas Martin
Potato Hill	Benton, Iowa	Loyal F North
Kilmore	Clinton, Ia	Jas P Wright
Salisbury	Greene, Ia	Alex'r M Cole
Milo	Brown, Ia	David Beck
Walpole	Hancock, Ia	Cephas Fort
Olio	Hamilton, Ia	John Helms
Clear Lake	Sangamon, Ill	Rezin Judd

Names Changed: 1-Bainbridge, Macon Co, Ala, changed to Hernando.
2-Parkersburg, Jasper Co, Iowa, changed to Point Pleasant.
3-Young Hickory, Will Co, Ill, changed to New Lenox.

Wash City Ordinances: 1-Act for the relief of Wm Martin: sum of $137.13 be paid to him to settle his accounts, as police ofcr of the 4th Ward.

Desirable dwlg house & lots in Upper Marlboro for sale: on Nov 18, the commodious dwlg house & lots of which the late Dr Henry Brooke died possessed. The ofc upon the lot is now occupied by Dr Jas A Young. –C C Magruder, Trustee

Phil, Oct 26-A young man named McGarry was killed by a gang of fire rowdies. Jas McFadden has been committed on strong suspicion of being the murderer.

In Chancery: Virginia Semmes, Rice W Payne & America Ann his wife, & Wm B Fitzgerald & Clara his wife, against Sabina Semmes, Cora Semmes, & Ada Semmes, & Hugh Caperton, guardian ad lietam. By order of the Circuit Court of Wash Co, D C, it will be to the advantage of the parties, cmplnt & dfndnt, in the above suit, to sell lot 14 in square 457, in Wash City, for the purpose of partition.
—W Redin, Auditor

Died: on Oct 9, in the Parish of Avoyelles, La, Elenore Oneil, aged 51 years, consort of Capt Wm H Bassett, formerly of Wash.

Died: on Oct 27, Thos Macgill, in his 60th year. His funeral is today at 4 o'clock, from his late residence on 8th st, between G & H sts.

WED OCT 29, 1851
American Hotel, Superior st, Cleveland, Ohio. —Wm Milford

Phil, Oct 28. John Carroll, a custom-house broker, was picked up from the steps of a house in vicinity of 10th & Shipper sts on Sunday night. He had been struck on the head & his skull fractured, from the effects of which he died this morning.

In Chancery: Chas B Pratt, guardian of Sarah W Taylor, & Rebecca Taylor, widow of Geo W Taylor, against Eliz C D, Martha M Ella, & Catherine Voorhees, heirs of Borden M & Sarah Voorhees, & Sarah W Taylor, heir of Geo W Taylor. By an order of the Circuit Court of Wash Co, D C I am directed to state the Trustee's account in the above cause. Such order will be executed on Nov 7, at 10 o'clock, at my ofc in the City Hall, Wash. -W Redin, Auditor

THU OCT 30, 1851
Reps elected to Congress from the State of Va on Thu last:

John S Millson	Jas F Strother
Richd K Meade	Chas J Faulknew
Thos H Averett	John Letcher
Thos S Bocock	H Edmundson
Paulus Powell	Fayette McMullen
John S Caskie	J M H Beale
Thos H Bayly	Geo W Thompson
Alex R Holladay	

Hon Nathl W Howell died at his residence in Canandaigua, N Y, on Oct 10. He had nearly completed his 82nd year. Among the public stations that he held at different times was that of a member of Congress.

Appointment by the Pres: Thos L Kilby, Surveyor of Customs, Suffolk, Va, vice Thos W G Allen, deceased.

The Primary Dept of the Union Academy will be opened on Nov 7. Apply to the Principal, Z Richards, corner of 14th st & N Y ave.

Household & kitchen furniture at auction: on Nov 1, in the house over the Wine Store of Mr T F Simms, near Jackson Hall, on Pa ave, between 3rd & 4th sts.
–A Green, auctioneer

The Western Military Institute, Drennon Springs, Henry Co, Ky, is in full operation. For information apply to Col B R Johnson, Acting Superintendent, Drennon, Ky; O A Smith, Treasurer, Louisville, Ky. References:

Hon H Marshall, Henry Co, Ky	Dr E D Fenner, New Orleans
Adj Gen J M Harlan, Frankfort	R J Ward, Louisville
Gen Jno T Pratt, Gtwn, Ky	R S Hardaway, Columbus, Ga
Gen W O Butler, Carrolton, Ky	R Hazlett, Zanesville, Ohio
Hon T B Monroe, Frankfort	

Wash Corp: Oct 27: 1-Ptn of J D Hoover & others, for a flag footway across Pa ave, at 8th st: referred to the Cmte on Improvements.

The Rev Fr Yuny, from Ohio, will preach on Nov 2, in St Mary's Church, & a collection will be taken up for the orphans under the charge of the Sisters of Charity.

Excellent business stand for rent: on 11th st, near Pa ave. Apply to Geo A W Randall, 12th & Pa ave, south side.

FRI OCT 31, 1851
Pestilence at Cape de Verds: from a letter written by an ofcr on board the U S brig **Porpoise**, dated Teneriffe, Sep 4, 1851. Our Consul, Mr Torres, & his family, are all dead, except one child. He was a very worthy man, & had several handsome & interesting daughters, who were great favorites with the ofcrs of our ships that touched there. He sent them all into the interior upon the first appearance of the pestilence, but, hearing afterward that some of them were sick, he started off to join them, & on his arrival found them all dead, servants included, with the exception of the one child. In less than 5 hours after he himself was a corpse.

New Goods: Hardware & Cutlery, of both English & American manufacture.
–D English & Son, Gtwn, D C.

Affray on Oct 17, at East Point, 6 miles from Atlanta, Ga, between a young man, Leonard Raterree & Thos & John Connelly, in which Thomas received a fatal stab in the abdomen & has since died. His brother John was shot through the breast, but his wounds were not fatal. Raterree made his escape, & a $300 reward is offered for his apprehension.

I certify that Ignatius W Atchison brought before me as a stray trespassing upon his enclosures, a chestnut sorrel Horse. —Jas Crandall, J P. Owner of the above is to prove property, pay charges, & take him away. —Ignatius W Atchison, living 1st house to the right hand at the south end of the Navy Yard Bridge

Wash City Ordinance: 1-Act for the relief of Geo F Rider: to be paid the amount due him to settle his claim for bldg the iron bridge over the canal at 4½ st.
By writ of fieri facias: against the goods & chattels, lands & tenements of J M Smith, I have levied & taken sundry articles, property of said Smith, to sell on Nov 6, to pay a judgment in favor of Thos C Magruder & Jno Calvert, trading under the name of Magruder & Calvert. Terms cash. -Wm Cox, Constable

By writ of fieri facias, I have levied on sundry articles, property of Jas Lewis, to be sold to satisfy a claim due S S Noland: sale on Nov 6. —J A Ratcliff, Constable

By writ of fieri facias, I have levied on one chain with a Newfoundland dog attached to the end of it, as the property of Henry Dunlap, which, if not redeemed by Nov 6, I shall sell at public auction to satisfy a claim in favor of A Robinson.
—J A Ratcliff, Constable

Millard Fillmore, Pres of the U S, recognizes Henry Runge, who has been appointed Consul of the free & Hanseatic City of Hamburg, for Indianola, in the State of Texas.

OCT 30, 1851
Yesterday the Treasury Dept was the scene of the retirement by resignation of the Register of the Treasury, Townsend Haines, & his bidding an affectionate adieu to his fellow ofcrs and the clerks of the Dept, prior to assuming the duties of the District Judgeship in Pa, to which he had been appointed under the operation of the new constitution of that State. We hear that Michl Nourse has been appointed by the Pres Register ad interim.

Mrd: on Oct 30, by Rev Jas B Donelan, Jos Redfern to Josephine Vivans, all of Wash City.

Mrd: on Oct 28, by Rev Stephen P Hill, Henry Russell, of Loudoun Co, Va, to Joanna Louisa Hannan, of Wash.

Mrd: on Oct 9, in Cincinnati, by Rev P B Wilber, Electa V Mitchell, formerly of Mount Morris, Ill, & Andrew M Hilt, of Wash City.

Died: on Oct 21, at the residence of Robt Y Conrad, Winchester, Va, Mrs Betty Carr Harrison, aged 22 years, wife of Dr Edw Jaquelin Harrison, of Cumberland Co, Va, & eldest daughter of David Holmes Conrad, of Martinsburg.

Died: on Oct 29, suddenly, at her residence in Wash City, of a hemorrhage of the lungs, Miss Barbara Lowe, in her 85th year. She had been a resident of Wash for the last 40 years. She was the grand aunt of the present Govn'r of Md, the Hon E L Lowe. Her funeral will be today, at 2 o'clock, from her late residence, 4th & M sts.

Washington Seminary, D C: meeting on F st, next to St Patrick's Church, to organize the classes & fixing the hours of meeting in future. –Saml Barber, President

For rent: 3 story brick dwlg house on 6th st, recently vacated by F B Stockton. Apply to Thos Blagden.

SAT NOV 1, 1851
Candidates for Congress in Louisiana in this State are as follows. The election takes place on Monday:

Whigs:	Democrats:
Richd Hagan	Louis St Martin
J Artiste Landry	Van P Winder
E A Upton	Alex'r G Penn
John Moore	Isaac E Morse

Cleveland, Oct 31. The Jury yesterday found a verdict for murder in the 2nd degree against Horace L Brooks for causing the death of the Engineer of the Cleveland & Pittsburgh Railroad, by putting a stake on the track & throwing the engine off.

Private letters received at Charleston announce the death of Cmder Jas D Knight, of the U S Navy, while in command of the sloop-of-war **Germantown**, the flag ship of Cmder Lavalette, on the African station. This melancholy event occurred suddenly on Jul 19, in the harbor of Cape Palmas. The Charleston Mercury says: Capt Knight was a native of this city, about 60 years of age, & had been in the naval service upwards of 37 years.

The St Louis Union of Oct 17: Col Fremont has completed & confirmed the sale of his Mariposa tract of gold land in Calif. The sale was made to a company in London for one million of dollars, one hundred thousand of which [that being the 1st instalment] was to be paid to Col Fremont in N Y C on or about Oct 15. Col Fremont may now be considered among the wealthiest millionaires of the U S. He has, besides the *Mariposa* tract just sold, a vast amount of property in San Francisco.

Persons who have taken out licenses under the laws of the Corp of Wash during the months of Jul thru Sep, 1851.
Billards license: Bevans, Thos

Cart license:
Allen, Thos D-2
Barnes, Wm-2
Beom, W
Briddell, T
Beall, E
Boswell, Tubman
Burch, Wesly
Beckett, Geo
Cameron, G
Casparis, Jas
Connor, M
Davis, Henry
Davis, P C
Fink, C
Fowler, Alonzo R
Greeves & Smith
Hughes, Hugh-6
Hazel, Z
Hall, Worthington
Henderson, A
King, John
King, E
Linkin, Danl-2
Linkins, J W
Langley, Wm H
McCauley, John
Money, Edw
Mattingley, Geo ≡-2
Pegg, Wm
Pumphrey
Pribram, Solo
Ramsey, Wm
Richards, A-2
Stewart, Wm
Smith, Abner
Smoot, A E
Smith, Henry
Sheriff, G L
Welsh, D
Ward, Cato
Wallis, Jas

Concert license: Campbell Minstrels; Carncorss Family-2; Turner, R J

Dog license:
Adams, J M
Allen, thos D
Arthur, Robt
Bird, A
Brook, F J
Bryan, Saml
Bosse, M
Beckett, Geo
Bloomer, Wm
Burgess, T
Clark, W H
Clark, E M
Cluss, A
Claxton, John
Embro, David
French, A
Fleetwood, Isaac
Gill, C A
Goings, Sarah
Hellen, Johnson
Halloran, W E
Hickman, Jos
Hendley, J D
Hugner, Mrs
Johnson, Wm
Jackson, C V
Kembel, Chas
Keibel, John B
Kreuss, John
Lancaster, Cath'e
Larned, E K
McNamee, C
Mudd, Mary
Mills, Robt-2
Nokes, Jas
Nipple, Danl

459

Nugent, R
Patterson, W F
Pominelsky, A
Pendleton, A G
Robey, Thos
Ritter, John E
Staffin, Geo
Simms, Jeremiah
Smallwood, g F
Sandford, L

Smoot, Sanl C
Twim, D
Taylor, Thos B
Turner, H
Van Reswick, T
Watson, Jas
Waple, R L
Williams, Chas
Young, John

Hack license:
Lomax, E
Megee, R F

Pywell, R R

Hats, Caps, etc license:
Devin, Bernard
Grimes, M H
Morgan & Co, J B
Miller, Leonard
O'Dell, T T

Pumphrey, Saml
Rosewald, J
Scott, Thos A
Simmons, Geo T

Huckster license:
Avil, John
Beach, Nathl
Carter, Jas
Davis, Augustus
Denham, L J
Eichorn, E
Gross, Jas
Jones, J H
King & Weaver
Kidwell, J H
Miller, A
McElfresh, H B

O'Mears, W C
Robinson, R
Smith, Ann
Slater & Dyer
Simmons, g T
Sullivan, T
Scroggins, Geo W
Tilman, Rosa
Talbot, Thos
Thecker, Jas
Thorn, Jadson
Wilson, John L

Ins Agency:
Hickcox, Saml B
Lewis, J C

Morfitt, H M

Livery Stable license: Burk, Thos

Merchandise license:
Borremans, Chas

Blackison, Lewis

Burch, T M
Baird, D A
Davison, J
Demanel, Chas
Davis, Jas B
Drury, S T
Denham, L J
Evans, Travers
Eberbach, J H
Freidenwell & Co, M
Fowler & Shiles

Model Mt Vernon license:
Beecher, A T

Retail license:
Barker, Jno H
Barnes, Saml
Gibbon, Jas H S
Lauxman, M
Langley, Wm H
Meredith, Moses
O'Sullivan, David

Shop license:
Carney, Thos
Lehman, Anton
McNaughton, Geo

Slut license:
Malone, L
Thomas, Wm

Tavern license:
Coburn, John
Hendley, J D

Theatrical license:
Adams, A F

Wagon license:
Baldwin, W
Bower, John
Barrett, Thos J

Fowler, John L
Fowler, Solomon
Fowler, Alonzo R
Greeves & Smith
Lindsley & Beder
McCubbin, N O
Peirce, Danl
Simmons, Wm
Sheriff & Killmar
Stanford, W H
Talbert, Wm

Gull & Beeche

Pumphrey, Saml
Quinn, Danl
Sullivan, Timothy
Simmons, Geo T
Taylor, Nary
Williams, John H

Rupert, Eva
Scheide, Henry
Sullivan, John

Young, Wm

McCormick, Edw
Starbuck, N H

Glenn, S W

Bruce, Chas
Babb, J
Cameron, G

Conner, M
Choppin, W
Donn & Bro, J M
Fowler & Shiles
Hammon, E
Krafft & Co, G S-2
Killian, John

Lee, Josias
Mason, E
Simermacher, L
Taylor, Wm H
Taylor, John
Thomas, Letty

Persons fined during the months of Jul, Aug, & Sep, 1851:
Allen, Russell W: keeping open bar on Sunday
Barker, John: selling liquor less than a pint
Baltzer, Mary Ann: do
Burden, ___: do
Carter, Thos H: omnibus
Colburn, Jno: selling liquor
Carney, Thos: do
Dowling, Wm: do
Gensler, Henry: selling liquor without license
Gannon, Edmund: keeping open bar on Sunday
Hurley, Jas: omnibus
Klomane, Chas: selling liquor
Lauxman, Martin: selling liquor less than a pint
McNeill, Mark: open after hours
Middleton, Eliza: selling liquor
McLoman, Danl: keeping dog
Peg, Wm: selling liquor
Ragan, Jas: selling liquor less than a pint
Sinclair, Geo: selling liquor
Taylor, Hanson: wagon
Wormley, Andrew: dog

The celebration in honor of the completion of the monument at Acton, to the memory of Capt Isaac Davis, Abner Hormer, & Jas Haywood, the first victims of the Revolutionary battle of Concord, took place on Wed. A discourse was pronounced by Gov Boutwell; poem delivered by Rev John Pierpont; Rev Jas T Woodbury presided at the afternoon dinner; Hon R C Winthrop, Judge Hoar, Hon Benj Thompson, Hon Robt Rantoul, jr, Col Isaac H Wright, & others, expressed their sentiments. –Boston Courier

Hon John C Bucher died suddenly at Harrisburg on Sun last, from disease of the heart. He had been an Associate Judge for many years, & was formerly a member of Congress.

For rent: 2 story frame house, with high brick basement, on 14th st, above O st. Also, a large Brick House, N & 14th sts. Inquire of J Russell Barr, 11th & M sts.

Trustee's sale: by deed of trust from Wm Peters, recorded in Liber W B 44, folios 169, in the land records of D C: public auction on Nov 31, of lot 9 in square 558. –J H King -A Green, auct

Mrd: on Oct 28, in Boston, by Rt Rev Bishop Fitzpatrick, Capt L A B Walback, U S Ordance Corps, to Miss Penelope R, daughter of Saml K Williams.

MON NOV 3, 1851
Late from Calif: John Bigler, Democrat, is elected Govn'r by some 1,500 majority. The whole vote polled in the State is about 45,000.

Nathan Sargent has been appointed by the Pres, Register of the Treasury, in the place of Townsend Haines, resigned.

The sale advertised by A Green, auctioneer, of the property belonging to my mother, Mrs Eliz Ferrall, to take place on Oct 20th, is unauthorized by her. I therefore caution all persons not to purchase the same, as she left the property in my possession, & subject to my entire control during her absence. She is still absent in Ky. –D W Ferrall, Agent for Thos S Ferrall.

TUE NOV 4, 1851
Postmaster Gen has est'd the following new Post Ofcs for week ending Nov 1, 1851.

Ofc	County, State	Postmaster
Warwick Neck	Kent, R I	Geo A Willard
Cadiz	Cattaraugus, N Y	John H Aylworth
Bregens	Choctaw, Ala	J W Tippet
New Bethel	Benton, Ala	Benj N Page
Mill Creek	Bowie, Texas	E M Birdwell
Sisterdale	Cornal, Texas	Ottmar W Behr
Farmington	Sevier, Ark	John T Turrentine
Old Franklin	Howard, Mo	Edw H Dennis
Orrin Glen	Delaware, Iowa	Orrin S Boggess
Cobb	Jackson, Iowa	John B Cobb
Competine	Wapella, Iowa	G C Cowger
Campton	Kane, Ill	Eldridge Walker

Names Changed: 1-South Candor, Tioga Co, N Y, changed to Catatonk. 2-Russell's store, Boone Co, Ill, changed to Bonus.

Rev Dr Williams was consecrated Assist Bishop of Connecticut, in St John's Church, Hartford, on Oct 29.

Nat'l Medical College meeting on Nov 3; introductory lecture by Prof Johnston. The public are invited to attend. –Jno Fred May, Dean

A magnificent present of an illuminated & jeweled-studded missal was recently made by the Countee Montesquieu, of France, to the Chouteau family, of St Louis, for their kindness to her 2 sons, who were tried for murder some time since, & escaped under the plea of insanity.

Mr Gutzlaff, the famous Chinese missionary & scholar, died at Canton on Aug 9 last, in his 48th year. He was by birth a Pomeranian, & was sent to the east by the Netherlands Missionary Society in 1827, after spending 4 years in Batavia, Singapore, & Siam, he went to China in 1831.

Medical Dept of Gtwn College: Dr N Young will deliver a lecture in the Chemical Hall, College bldg, corner of F & 12th sts, Nov 3 on: Doctrine of Homoeopathy. The public are invited to attend. Flodoardo Howard, Dean

From Oregon. 1-Correspondent at Dallas states that the Snake Indians have been troublesome. Mr Hudson Clark, of Scott Co, Ill, who, with his mother, sister, & brother, had got ahead of his train, was attacked by about 30 Indians, near Raft river, about 40 miles west of **Fort Hall**, & his mother & brother were murdered. 2-A few days previous the same band of Indians attacked a wagon owned by Mr Miller, of Western Va, & killed his brother-in-law, Mr Jackson, & wounded a young lady, a daughter of Mr Miller. Mr Miller was seriously wounded, but it was thought he would recover.

New Orleans, Nov 2. The steamship **Fanny** has arrived from the Rio Grande, bringing dates to Oct 30. The attack on Matamoros by the Revolutionists commenced on the 21st, & on the 23rd Col Carvajal had possession of the city within 4 squares of the Plaza. The Revolutionists lost but 3 men, including Capt Ford, who commanded a company of Texas Rangers. Gen Avalos was wounded. Mr Langtree, doing business at Matamoros, had been killed. On the 25th Mr Devine's stores were set on fire & consumed, & the American Consul wounded.

WED NOV 5, 1851
Judge J P Scarburgh has been appointed Prof of Law in the Univ of Wm & Mary, in Va, to succeed Beverly Tucker.

Mrd: on Nov 4, by Rev Jas B Donelan, Mr Geo E Senseney, one of the Editors of the Winchester Republican, to Mary Helen, daughter of John S Gallaher, 3rd Auditor of the Treasury.

Millard Fillmore, Pres of the U S A, recognizes C H F Moering, who has been appointed Consul of the free & Hanseatic City of Lubeck, at Boston. –Nov 3, 1851

The case of Peltier S Towland vs Coleman & wife, in the Court of Common Pleas of Phil, was brought to a close on Sat. The verdict of the Jury on the main points at issue was, substantially, that John Rowland was indebted to his brother Peltier at the time of John's death, & that the release given by his widow to Peltier, on the day of her marriage to Coleman, for moneys remaining in his hands as executor of his brother's estate, was not freely & voluntarily given, but that it was obtained by taking unconscionable & inequitable advantage of her circumstances & condition. This verdict is virtually for the plntf, because, as the indebtedness of his brother is admitted, the release which is declared void could be of no practical value to him.

Died: on Tue, Mrs Mary H Wilson, in her 62nd year. Her funeral is on Thu, at 10 o'clock, from the residence of her daughter, Mrs Hill, Pa ave, between 9th & 10th sts.

Mrs Heaney informs her friends & customers that she will open this day, Nov 5, a beautiful assortment of Goods adapted to the season.

Desirable houses in the 1st Ward, well furnished, to let: 1-The house in *Gadsby's row*, near the West Market, lately occupied by the late Mrs Cmdor Patterson. 2-That house in the Six Bldgs at present in the occupancy of Capt David D Porter, U S Navy, with the furniture. For terms apply to Richd Smith.

Valuable bldg lot at auction: on Nov 8, by deed of trust from Chloe Ann Johnson, recorded in Liber W B, #140, folios 237 thru 239, of the land records for Wash Co, D C: sale of lot 11 in square 335, with a small frame tenement thereon. Property is on south C st, between 3rd & 4½ sts. –Nicholas Callan, Trustee -A Green, auct

Wash Corp: 1-Ptn from Wm Orme & others, to alter the pavement & pave the front on D st: referred to the Cmte on Improvements. 2-Cmte of Claims: act for the relief of Trueman M Brush: passed. Same cmte: asked to be discharged from the further consideration of the ptns of Jesse Sisson & Jas T Burns: discharged accordingly. 3-Ptn of Z Jones, praying remission of a fine: referred to the Cmte on Improvements. 4-Cmte of Claims: bill for the relief of Benj Bean: reported the same without amendment. 5-Cmte on Unfinished Business: act for the relief of John Bower: ordered to lie on the table. Same for the act for the relief of F B Poston. 6-Act for the relief of David Welsh: passed. 7-Cmte of Claims: act for the relief of Chas F McCarthy: passed.

The public are informed that the Trustee of the late Mrs Ann R Clarke, will sell, at the former residence of the family, on Lafayette Square, the whole of the rich, varied, & well preserved Furniture. -Dyer & McGuire, aucts

Mrs Spalding is prepared to accommodate a Congrssional mess of boarders during the ensuing session. Her house is pleasantly situated on C st, between 3rd & 4½ sts.

Michl Richardson, formerly of N Y C, [from the Alta California] died on Sep 18, from the effects of an attack of cholera. He was for many years in the employ of the late Mr Applegate, corner of Ann st & Theatre alley, & was at one time a pressman on the Mirror. -Mirror

Circuit Court of Wash Co, D C-in Chancery. Martha C Williams & others, against Ephraim, Mary Ann, Caroline Eliza, Rosetta, & Sarah Eliz Mullikin, heirs of John Mullikin. The trustee reports that John Robert became the purchaser of lot 11 in square 74, in Wash City, for $541, & he hath complied with the terms of the sale. –Jno A Smith, clk

St Louis, Mo: Nov 3. P G Glover, for many years Treasurer of the State of Missouri, died Oct 26.

On Monday, as Mr Peter Harvey, a young man in the employ of Mr John T Cassell, painter, on the Island, was turning the corner of 12th & D sts, he was surrounded by 3 men, who feigned intoxication. Two of them held him & he was dealt a murderous blow to his face from a colt or slung-shot by the 3rd man, which fractured his lower jawbone so as to divide it into 2 distinct parts at the chin. They failed to secure some $80 or $90 he had upon his person. Mr Harvey returned home & is now under the care of Dr Morgan.

THU NOV 6, 1851
Mortal remains of Gen Arthur St Clair's army at **Fort Recovery**, Mercer Co, Ohio. Disastrous defeat of St Clair's army in 1791: thrown into the wildest confusion by a surprise attack of the Indians of Western Ohio, on Nov 4. In Jan, 1792, Gen Harrison, it is supposed, buried the dead. Their burial place was found by merest accident. People were summoned to attend the funeral rites of those bones, upon the very ground, which 60 years before had drank their blood. Loud were their praises of the orator Hon Bellamy Storer, of Cincinnati, who spoke on the occasion. List of the killed & wounded ofcrs in the battle of Nov 4, 1791. Killed: Maj Gen Richd Butler; Col Oldham, Ky militia; Majors Ferguson, Clarke, & Hart; Capts Bradford, Phelan, Kirkwood, Price, Van Swearingen, Tipton, Smith, Purdy, Piatt, Guthrie, Cribbs, & Newman; Lts Spear, Warren, Boyd, MacMath, Burgess, Kelso, Read, Little, Happer, & Lickins; Ensigns Cobb, Balch, Chace, Turner, Wilson, Brooks, Beatty, & Purdy; Quartermasters Reynolds & Ward; adjt Anderson; Dr Grasson. Wounded: Lt Cols Gibson, Drake, & Sargent, adjt gen; Maj Butler; Capts Doyle, Trueman, Ford, Buchanan, Darke, & Slouth; Lts Greaton, Davidson, De Butts, Price, Morgan, McCrae, Lysle, & Thompson; Adjts Whistler & Crawford; Ensign Bines; the Viscount Malertie, volunteer aid-de-camp to Maj Gen St Clair.

Dr R N Hall, the Delegate from Henrico Co in the last Legislature of Va, committed suicide a day or 2 ago, in New Kent Co, by shooting himself with a pistol.

Union Hotel, Gtwn, D C at public sale on Nov 20, in front of the premises. Apply to J Humphreys, Gtwn, D C.

Chancery: Oct Term, 1851: Dillon vs Garretson. Trustee reported that he sold Lot 1 in square 324, in Wash City, to Geo R & Richd Adams for $860. –John A Smith, clk

Balt, Nov 5. Chas James, a notorious bully & gambler, was killed today at the 3rd Ward polls by a rowdy called Cutting Tobe. Tobe was arrested,& so severely wounded that he is likely to die.

Mrd: Tue, by Rev John C Smith, Mr Wm W S Kerr to Miss Mary Jane Bassett, all of Wash City.

Miss J A C Leach will open on Nov 8, at her store, on Bridge st, Gtwn, a rich & handsome stock of Paris Millinery.

FRI NOV 7, 1851
U S Patent Ofc, Nov 6, 1851. 1-Petition of Barnabas Langdon, of Buffalo, N Y, praying for the extension of a patent granted to him on Jan 9, 1838, for an improvement in machinery for planing shingles, for 7 years. Also, his petition for improvement for planing plank & other lumber, for 7 years, granted to him Jan 9, 1838. -Thos Ewbank, Com'r of Patents

Mr John Botts, living near Hall's Cross Roads, in Harford Co, Md, while tending his thrashing machine, on Fri week, had his right army caught therein, dreadfully lacerating & crushing it from the hand upwards toward the shoulder. Declining to submit to the necessary amputation, the foreit of his life was the consequence, on Tue last. Mr Botts leaves a wife & several children. –Sun

New residence for sale: beautiful 4 story brick, with observatory thereon, on North Capitol st, near C st. Apply to J Crutchett, at the Cottage, near the above.

Mrd: on Nov 4, by Rev David Kerr, Rector of Rock Creek Parish, Mr Alb't Charles, of D C, to Miss Anna Virginia Fay, of Wash City.

Chancery sale: by decree of the Circuit Court of Wash Co, D C: made in the cause of the petition of John Cox, trustee et al, dated Nov 4, 1851: sale at the corner of Fayette & 7th sts: 1-A meadow lot fronting on the line of 7th st, containing 3 1/3rd acres. 2-Parts of lots 193, 195, 197, 199, & 201, of Threlkeld's addition to Gtwn, fronting on Fayette st. 3-A lot of 24 acres, more or less, described in a deed from John Threlkeld to John Cox, trustee, dated Mar 30, 1824, & recorded in Liber W B #12, folios 165, of the land records of Wash Co. This lot in is the neighborhood of Mr John H King's farm. –Walter S Cox, trustee -Edw S Wright, auct

The 3 mutineers of the ship **Reindeer**, tried at Norfolk, have been acquitted, & a nolle prosequi entered in the case of Jas Henrick, one of the mutineers of the ship **Gov Arnold**. Geo Williams was convicted of mutiny, & sentenced to 60 days confinement.

Trustee's sale: by decree of the Circuit Court of Wash Co, D C, pronounced in a cause wherein Fred'k A Wagler is cmplnt, & Jos C Wagler, Francis B Hilbus & others are dfndnts, the following property, in Wash City, will be sold at auction on Dec 2: 1-East half of lot 24 in square 101, with brick house, now occupied by Nicholas Funk. 2-Part of lots 21 & 22 in square 101, fronting on H st, between 17th & 18th sts, with 2 frame houses. 3-Lots 1, 2, & 14 in square 255, with 2 frame houses on lots 1 & 2. 4-Lot 25 in square 462. 5-The fee simple in the south half of lot 10 in square 141, fronting on 19th st, subject to a lease, of which Saml S Duncan is the assignee, at an annual ground rent of $16.24, on which is a frame house. 6-The fee simple in the north half of lot 10, subject to a lease to B Random at $11.06 per annum, on which are 2 frame houses. 7-The fee simple of lot 9 in square 141, subject to a lease to Saml C Davison for 20 years from May 8, 1844, at the ground rent at $38.16 per annum, on which are 2 frame houses. 8-The fee simple of the west 22½ feet front on H st, part of lot 21 in square 166, subject to a lease for 99 years, at the annual ground rent of $23.08, on which is a frame house. -Wm Redin, trustee -Dyer & McGuire, aucts

Cmder Jas D Knight, of S C, who recently died on board the U S sloop-of-war **Germantown**, which he commanded on the coast of Africa, is represented as having been an excellent ofcr, & was about 60 years of age. Cmder Knight is numbered 53 on the list of cmders, the second grade; & at the time of his death he had been in the service of the U S 37 years. –Boston Journal

Wash Item: 1-Letter of resignation from Rev Wm T Eva, teacher of the Male Primary School of the 4th district, received & accepted. His resignation take place from Nov 17.

Died: on Oct 20, at Hancock, Delaware Co, N Y, Gen David Phelps, in his 83rd year. Gen P was born in Hebron, Conn, in 1768; graduated at Yale College in 1793; studied law in Sharon, in his native State, & in Poughkeepsie, N Y. In 1796 & 1797 he came into Colchester, & lived there more than 50 years. He moved, with his son, a little more than a year since, to Hancock.

$10 reward for 2 strayed black cows. Reward given on their delivery to Michl O'Brien, 2nd, between G & F sts.

For rent: residence near the corner of 12th st & N Y ave, occupied by the undersigned. Possession can be had at any time before Nov 25, on application to Wm Hunter.

SAT NOV 8, 1851

Appointment by the Pres: W L Sharkey, to be Consul of the U S, at Havana, in the Island of Cuba, in place of Allen F Owen, recalled.

In the Supreme Court of Mass, on Sat, in the case of Edwin Taylor vs W H Osgood & others, the jury awarded to the plntf $156 damages for being ejected from the Woburn branch train on Jul 4, 1850, not having purchased a ticket at the depot, he refused to pay the difference established by the by-laws of the company.

Died: on Nov 7, of consumption, Adolph Fornaro, draughtsman in the ofc of the U S Coast Survey, aged 37 years. He was a native of Switzerland, & held the rank of Major in the Corps of Topographical Engineers of that country. His funeral is Nov 9, from Mrs Langton's, Capitol Hill

In Chancery. W G W White & Brother, against Edw N Roach, administrator, & Ellen M Ellwood, widow, & Wm D Ellwood & others, heirs of Isaac T Ellwood. By an order of the Circuit Court of Wash Co, D C in the above cause, I am directed to state the account of the Trustee & the claims of the creditors upon the trust fund. Claims to be filed or or before Nov 20. –W Redin, Auditor

Circuit Court of Wash Co, D C-in Chancery. John Drake & Harriet his wife, against Francis Lambert, Thos Cissil & Eliza his wife, & Thos Wills & Jane his wife, heirs at law of Morris Lambert, deceased. Morris Lambert, of Wash Co, D C, was in his lifetime seized of certain real estate in said county, & died so seized in 1824, intestate, leaving 6 children, namely, Morris Lambert, Edw J Lambert, Francis Lambert, Eliza, [since intermarried with Thos Cissil,] Jane, [since intermarried with Thos Wills,] & Wm Lambert, besides his widow, who is since deceased; that the said Morris Lambert is since deceased, as is also the said Wm Lambert; that the said Edw J Lambert was the first husband of the said Harriet, & is also deceased, & that the said Harriet was afterwards intermarried with the said John Drake; that all & each of said deceased parties died without children & intestate; that, in consequence thereof, the said Harriet became entitled to her one-third or dower interest in the share or proportion of said real estate of which her said husband, Edw J Lambert, died seized; that, since 1832, said dfndnts have been in the enjoyment of the rents, issues, & profits of said real estate, without having even accounted with or paid over to the said Edw J Lambert, or to the said Harriet, or to the said cmplnts. any portion of the same, as they justly ought to have done. The bill prays for a partition of estate, an account of the rent, issues, & profits aforesaid, between the cmplnts & dfndnts. Francis Lambert is a non-resident of D C, & to appear on or before 1st day of the next March term. –John A Smith, clerk

Balt, Nov 7. Mrs Nancy W Hufford, who has been for some days on trial at Cumberland, Md, on a charge of having murdered Mrs Engle, by the administration of poison while she was sick, has been acquitted by the verdict of the jury.

MONDAY NOV 10, 1851
At a recent meeting of the Presbytery of White Water, in Lawrenceburg, Indiana, present were the father, brother, 4 sons, 1 son-in-law, & a nephew, all preaching the Gospel.
Father: Francis Monfort, at Concord, Indiana
Brother: David Monfort, D D, Indiana
Son: Jos G Monfort, Greensburgh, Indiana
Son: Francis P Monfort, Richmond, Indiana
Son: J W Monfort, Liberty, Indiana
Son: David Monfort, jr, Indiana
Son-in-law: J Gilchrist, Dunlapsville, Indiana
Nephew: John C King, Land Creek, Indiana
There are 2 or 3 more that claim relationship more distant, by marriage. They are all connected with the same Presbytery, making 10 or 11 in all. Father Monfort has another brother, who is a minister in the Associate Presbyterian Church.
–Presbyterian Herald

Third Ward Police: the subscriber, elected Police Magistrate, has removed his ofc to the s e corner of D & 9th sts. –Saml Grubb, Justice of the Peace

Cmdor Chas Morris has been appointed Chief of the Bureau of Ordnance & Hydrography, in place of Cmdor L Warrington, deceased. Cmdor Wm B Shubrick has been appointed Inspector of Ordnance, in place of Cmdor Morris, transferred to the Bureau.

The ship **Oregon**, Capt Thompson, of Boston, which sailed from N Y on Oct 23 for Kingston, Jam, with a crew of 9 men & 3 ofcrs, with 4 passengers on board, laden with coal, experienced a heavy gale at sea on Oct 27. She sunk that day. The crew & one passenger, Mr L K Fish, made their escape. Capt E R Wyman of the brig **Conductor**, of Yarmouth, N S, rendered assistance. The other 3 passengers were lost with the ship.

On Oct 31 in Iowa, near Ottumwa, Mr Robt Ralston, on the previous evening, had married the daughter of Mr Jos Woods. The next evening a party visited Mr Woods' house to charivari the newly married couple. A shot was fired in celebration, either by accident or design, & Mr Ralston was hit near the heart. He died on the following Monday. No evidence found to implicate any at the party, & they were discharged.

On Tue last, Caleb Damon, son of Arad Damon, of Hinckley, Medina Co, Ohio, was shot dead while hunting turkeys. Young Damon was creeping on his hands & knees, when Albert Spear, seeing a black object through the bushes, fired upon it, killing Damon instantly. –Cleveland Herald

Stock of Boots & Shoes & household furniture at auction: on Nov 13, at the Boot & Shoe Store of Mr P Emrich, on 7th st. –Dyer & McGuire, aucts

Md Election: known to have been elected by the whole State:
Comptroller of the Treasury:
P F Thomas
Lottery Com'r: T R Stewart
Com'r of the Land Ofc: Jas Murray
Elected by Districts: Court of Appeals
1st District: J Thompson Mason
2nd District: W H Tuck
3rd District: J C Legrand
4th District: J B Eccleston
Com'r of Public Works:
1st District: John S Gittings
2nd District: C R Stewart
3rd District: W P Pouder
4th District: John R Franklin
Judges in Balt City:
Superior Court: Wm Frick
Court of Common Pleas:
Wm L Marshall
Criminal Court: Henry Stump

An Arkansas paper of recent date announces the death, on Oct 14, in Arkansas Co, of M P J Julien de Visart, [Count de Bocarme,] an old & much esteemed citizen of that county. He was the father of the Count de Bocarme recently executed in France for the murder of his brother-in-law, & it is thought that his death was hastened by the wretched termination of the life of his son.

On Thu last John McDevitt, age about 20 years, was arrested on the oath of Mr Peter Harvey, as one of the persons that assaulted him on 12th st on Monday previous. Mr Harvey was unable to testify by word of mouth due to the yet painful condition of his jaw which was so severely injured, but gave evidence by writing. McDevitt was committed for trial. A second arrest was made of Danl Norris, a young man residing on the Island. He, too, in default of bail, was committed for trial. The third, & most prominent offender, Jas Selden, who inflicted the blow on Mr Harvey's face, was arrested on Sat.

Although my wines have been transferred to the rear & cellar of my house, all orders will be thankfully received at my front store, on the avenue. –Julius A Peters, Pa ave & 10th st.

Trustee's sale of valuable stock of groceries, liquors, wines, boots & shoes, standing casks, & store fixtures: by deed of trust, duly executed & recorded: public auction, on Nov 20, of the Grocery & Liquor store of E W Hall, on the corner of 7th & I sts. –Chas S Wallach, trustee -Dyer & McGuire, aucts

Orphans Court of Wash Co, D C. Letters testamentary on the personal estate of Catharine D Goldsborough, late of said county, deceased. –Louis M Goldsborough, executor

TUE NOV 11, 1851

Foreign Item-Oct 24: M Kossuth, his family & suite, arrived at Southampton, where his reception has been of the most enthusiastic kind. The Duchess d'Angouleme died at Frodshoff, in Lower Austria, on Oct 19, the anniversary of the execution of her mother, Marie Antoinette. The Duchess was 73.

We learn from the Churchman that at St Paul's Church, N Y, on Tue last, Rt Rev Bishop De Lancey pronounced the sentence of suspension for 1 year from the ministry of the Protestant Episcopal Church of Rev John Canfield Sterling, unless he should in the mean time engage to conform to the doctrine, discipline & worship of the Church. The Bishop also pronounced sentence of deposition from the ministry of the Protestant Episcopal Church upon Rev Wm Everett, who has connected himself with the Church of Rome.

Orphans Court of Wash Co, D C. Letters of administration on the personal estate of George Ann Patterson, late of said county, deceased. –Rd Smith, adm

The late Abraham G Thompson, of N Y, has left about $200,000 to charitable societies of that city. Among them are: $30,000 each to the American Bible Society & the American Tract Society. $20,000 each to the American Home M Society; N Y State Colonization; Central Board of Education; American B C F Mission; Deaf & Dumb Institution; & the Blind Institution.

Postmaster Gen has est'd the following new Post Ofcs for week ending Nov 8, 1851.

Ofc	County, State	Postmaster
East Caneadea	Alleghany, N Y	Anson Masters
Cottage	Cattaraugus, N Y	John H Blish
West Easton	Madison, N Y	Asa B Walden
Granby Centre	Oswego, N Y	Wm F Ensign
Algonquin	Houghton, Mich	Jos Coulter
Lindsey's Creek	Choctw, Miss	Wm J Shaw
Ouschita	Union P, La	Jas L Jones
Gainsville	Cook, Texas	Stephen D Brown
Johnson Station	Tarrant, Texas	Isaac Watson
Taos	Navarre, Texas	Rich C Donaldson
Birdsville	Tarrant, Texas	Francis Jordon
Union	Santa Clara, Cal	Benj F Bucknell
Murphy's	Calaveras, Cal	Lewis Berneand
Carson's Creek	Calaveras, Cal	Chas G Lake
Contra Costa	Contra Costa, Cal	Amedee Marier
Mud Spring	El Dorado, Cal	Darwin Chase
San Rafael	Maven, Cal	Moses Stoppard
Texas Hill	Sacramento, Cal	Jas A Crump
Cascade	Clark, Oregon	F A Chenoweth

Dalles	Oregon	W R Gibson
Winchester	Umpqua, Oregon	Addison R Flint
Sweet Home	Nodaway, Mo	Moses Stingley
Estell's Mills	Platte, Mo	Jas D Jones
Bell's Ridge	Madison, Iowa	Henry A Bell
Pisgah	Union, Iowa	Wm M Lock
Higginsport	Jackson, Iowa	John G Smith
Cotton Grove	Wapello, Iowa	Peter Goff
Western	Powesheik, Iowa	John McIntire
Westfield	Fayette, Iowa	Stephen H Ludlos
Hingham	Sheboygan, Wis	Lemuel Tibbets
Sargent	Waushara, Wis	Soward Lord
Lodi	Wabash, Ia	Elisha Bolin
Ashe's Creek	Spencer, Ky	Jacob J Lindle
Turkey Foot	Scott, Ky	Jas Fields
Monreath	Shelby, Tenn	Francis M Revis

Names Changed: 1-Anthony's Village, Kent, Rhode Island, changed to Anthony. 2-Upper Middletown, Middlesex, Conn, changed to Cromwell.

Independence, Nov. The Salt Lake mail arrived Oct 30. Passengers in the stage: Richd Phelps, from Salt Lake, Boyers & Forster, from **Fort Laramie**. By the Nov 4 stage, B D Harris, Secretary; G K Brandenburg, Chief Justice; P C Brocchus, Associate; H R Day, Indian Agent; & Moses Gillam & Young will be here. They have been forced to leave the territory in consequence of the secitious sentiments of Brigham Young, Govn'r. The $20,000 appropriated by Congress for public bldgs has been squandered by Young, & an attempt has been made to take $24,000 more from the Sec, but he would not comply, an injunction coming to his relief from the Court.

Scarlet fever prevails in the lower end of Hampshire Co, Va: between 25 & 30 children died from it during the last 4 or 5 weeks. Dr Kendall, near Pleasant Dale, within the last 10 days has buried all his children, three in number.

N Y, Nov 10. 1-Gardner Howland, of the firm of Howland & Aspinwall, in this city, died suddenly yesterday afternoon 2-The frig **Mississippi** has arrived, in 42 days from Gibraltar, bringing the Hungarian refugees attached to Kossuth's party.

In Chancery. John Tonnell, jr & Cecile his wife, Lawrent Salles, & N De Altaro & Josephine his wife, against Aaron Vail & Emilie L his wife, Lawrence Eugene Vail, Jules J Vail & Juliette Vail, Lispomard Stewart, Louisa L Stewart, & Sarah L Stewart. Decree of the Circuit Court of Wash Co, D C: to inquire & report whether lot 16 in square 221, in Wash City, & improvements thereon, are susceptible of division in specie. Report will be executed on Nov 19, at my ofc, in the City Hall, Wash, 10 o'clock. —W Redin, auditor

The Teacher of Male Primary School of the 4th District having resigned, the Board of Trustees will fill the vacancy on Nov 13. Salary $450 per annum. The undersigned will receive applications: G J Abbott, V Harbaugh, F S Walsh, & P M Pearson, Cmte of Examination.

In Chancery. Eliz Ford, against Peter Brady & John N Ford. By order of the Circuit Court of Wash Co, D C, the account of the Trustee to be stated. Creditors to file their claims at my ofc, City Hall, Wash, in the forenoon of Nov 20.
—W Redin, auditor

Sale this day of a lot of fine Hogs, 3 o'clock, at the Wash Asylum, near the Congressional Burying Ground, by order of the Com'rs.
—Ben E Gittings, Intendant Wash Asylum

For rent, pleasant rooms on Pa ave, in house occupied by Prof D E Groux, opposite Brown's Hotel.

WED NOV 12, 1851
N Y Home Journal: the fame & princely spirit & splendid hospitality of Geo Peabody has now gone abroad into all lands, & the distinction with which he caused the Jul 4th to be publicly honored in London, by a commemoration which involved an English tribute as well as an Amercian one to the dignity of the anniversary, has gained for him the respect & esteem of his countrymen in every part of the Union. Socially, though not politically, & at his own expense, not the nation's, he has long performed in London a ministerial function.

Columbia Statesman: Mr Geo C Bingham has just completed several beautiful works, the most striking of the collection are The day of Election; The Candidate Electioneer; the Chess Players, & a beautiful Scene on the Ohio.
—St Louis Intelligencer

Mr Gonder, well-known railroad contractor, died on Sat, at his residence in Lancaster, Pa, after an illness of several weeks. He has for years been extensively engaged in the construction of railroads in Pa & other States.

Brig Gen Francisco de Lavalette is, we learn by Madrid papers, to be sent to Cuba to occupy the post left vacant by the death of Gen Enna.

Wm Fontane, a Revolutionary soldier under Gen Marion, died on Oct 16, at the residence of Mr Jas Knoblock, in Florida. He was 105 years of age, & retained sufficient strength for out-door labor until about 3 days before his death.

A New Cap Store on Pa ave. Remember, we will not be outdone in low prices.
-J F Tirralla

The Duchess of Angouleme, daughter of Louis 16th, who died on Oct 19, leaves two millions of francs to her nephew, Comte de Chambord. [Nov 13th newspaper: The Duchess was born Dec 29, 1778, & had therefore nearly completed her 73rd year. She married her cousin, the son of Charles 10th, & has survived all her family of the elder branch of the Bourbons, except the 2 children of the Duke of Berri, the Count of Chambord [titular Henry 5th] & his sister the Duchess of Parma.
–Boston Traveller]

Mr Carey Thompson, of Harper's Ferry, received a letter from Prof Jackson, of Boston, in regard to the quartz taken from the Jefferson [Va] Silver Mine. Prof Jackson says that the white stone is milk-quartz or silex, & that does not contain any silver or ore of that metal.

Lumber for sale: just received from Albany, N Y. –J B Ward's Lumber Yard, 12th st, east side, & Canal wharf.

The New Orleans Picayune of Nov 4 gives particulars concerning the siege of Matamoros. Gen Twiggs gave orders for the 2 companies of the 1st artl, stationed at the barracks below New Orleans, to get in readiness to move to the seat of hostilities. They are under command of Bvt Lt Col Nauman. Brownsville, Oct 29, 1851. Tues Oct 28: names of the killed & wounded on Carvajal's side: Killed: Peter Culver, merchant in Brownsville; Alex'r Langstroth, by accident, while being upon the roof of his house. Wounded: Capt Alfred Norton, loss of right arm; F Gracesqui, loss of right arm; Col Ford, slightly wounded in the head; R Finley, wounded in the side, dangerously; T F Waddell, U S Consul, while engaged in saving people's goods from the fire. From the Rio Grande of Oct 29, printed at Brownsville: Lt Culver & Surgeon Finley are of the killed, & Col Ford, Capt Norton, & F R Gracesqui, the latter by accidental discharge of a gun-wounded.

Died: on Mon last, in Balt, Wm C Radcliff, son of Mr Jos Radcliff, of Wash City, after a short attack of congestive fever, succeeding an extreme nervous affection, in his 23rd year. His funeral will take place from the residence of his father, 6th & F sts, today at 2 o'clock.

Mrd: on Nov 6, by Rev L S Morgan, Wm D Serrin to Miss Sarah A Cumberland, all of Wash City.

Farmers living along the line of the Wash & Rockville Trunpike, within D C, held a meeting at the Emory Church, on Nov 7, to ascertain who, & how many of them, would be willing to aid in the construction of the contemplated plank road on the site of the present turnpike. Thos Fitnam was called to the chair, & Mr Archibald White was secretary. Cmte consisted of Fitnam, White, A C P Shoemaker, & Smith Thompson.

Death doings in N Y from the Commercial Advertiser of Monday. 1-Dr J Kearny Rodgers died yesterday, after a brief illness, a man universally esteemed. He was the son of the venerable Dr J R B Rodgers, of N Y, for many years the pastor of the first Presbyterian Church in this city. 2-Gardiner G Howland, one of our most eminent merchants, died suddenly yesterday. He was a member of the Rev Dr Pott's church, was in attendance at the morning service, & in a few moments after he reached his residence dropped down & instantly expired. He commenced business in this city in 1807, under the firm of G G & S Howland, & continued as until the partnership changed to Howland & Aspinwall. Mr Howland retired from active business about 14 years ago. [Rodgers & Howland both attended Dr Pott's church.] 3-On Sunday Mr Benj M Brown died at his residence in Westchester Co. He was for many years Pres of the Butchers' & Drovers' Bank in this city. 4-Rev Dr Wm Croswell, rector of the church of the Advent, [Protestant Episcopal,] was taken suddenly ill while in his pulpit yesterday. He was taken home & expired last evening. [Nov 15th newspaper: Dr J Kearny Rodgers was born in 1793, & therefore about 58 years of age: he was the grandson of Rev Dr Rodgers, the former pastor of the Wall st Presbyterian Church at the Revolutionary period.]

Wash Corp: 1-Ptn from Jas A Wise for the remission of sundry fines: referred to the Cmte of Claims. 2-Act for the relief of G Topham: passed. 3-Relief of David Welsh: passed. 4-Ptn of Michl Kelly, praying for the remission of a fine: referred to the Cmte of Claims. 5-Act for the relief of Thos Williamson: passed. 6-Relief of Trueman M Brush: referred to the Cmte of Claims.

Chancery Sale: by decree of Circuit Court of Wash Co, D C: in a cause wherein Antonie Manyett & Catharine his wife are cmplnts, & Saml Spencer & others are respondents: Public auction, on Dec 15, of lot 3 in square 11 in Wash City, improved by 2 substantial frame houses, in the vicinity of Easby's Ship Yard.
–Walter D Davidge, trustee -Dyer & McGuire, aucts

Jas Most, age 18, residing with his father near Cherry Hill, Cecil Co, came to his death on Mon, by the premature discharge of his gun, while he had his mouth to the muzzle, to blow in it, in order to ascertain if the touch-hold was free. At the time, being near a candle, the powder ignited, discharging the contents into his mouth, blowing out his front teeth, & severing some important blood vessel, by which he bled to death.

The Chesapeake & Ohio Canal is now in complete order, from end to end, & since Sunday has presented a busy aspect. Between 40 & 50 boats, laden with coal from Cumberland, have arrived, mainly for Alexandria, but a few for Wash City. The packets **Belle** & **Fashion** have been patronized so well, that a new boat **Delaware**, has been put on to run thrice a week between Gtwn & Harper's Ferry, A J Reeside, master.

The steamboat **Joseph Johnson** & the steamboat **Phenix** were sold at public auction on Mon, at Alexandria, & bought by Capt Peter Jones, the **Phenix** for $2,705, & the **Joseph Johnson** for $1,520-for Mr Geo Page, of Wash. We understand he intends to build 2 new boats of the latest models and put the engines of these boats in them.

THU NOV 13, 1851
A wife accidentally killed by her husband: the Warsaw New Yorker give particulars by which Mrs True, of Covington, wife of Wm True, was killed. He was driving a stake into the ground, & in the act of striking the stake with an axe he slipped & fell towards his wife, the axe striking her head as to cause immediate death. No one witnessed this unfortunate accident except the husband, who was thus made his wife's executioner. A coroner's jury rendered a verdict in accordance with the above statement.

Orphans Court of Wash Co, D C. The case of Henry C Matthews, adm of Henrietta Steptoe, deceased. The administrator & Court have appointed Dec 2 next for the payment & distribution of assets in the hands of the administrator.
–Ed N Roach, Reg/o wills

Circuit Court of Wash Co, D C-in Chancery. Lane vs Lane. Jas Adams, trustee reported he has sold the lots & pieces of ground described & contained in his report at the prices specified. [No other details.] -Jno A Smith, clerk

Mrd: on Nov 11, in Alexandria, Va, by Rev Geo King, Jos T Mitchell, of Kent Co, Md, to Miss Kate L, daughter of the late Gov Kent, of Md.

Died: on Nov 6, at his residence, in Wash Co, Robt L Beall, in his 95th year-one of the glorious band who fought to gain the liberties we now enjoy.

Died: on Oct 25, at Avondale, near St Charles, Missouri, aged 54 years & 21 days, Mrs Mary Ann Clough, wife of Mr Wm Clough, formerly instructor of the Mayhew school in the city of Boston, & more recently instructor of one of the State Normal schools of Mass. As a wife, a mother, a daughter, a sister, & a neighbor, the deceased had no superior.

For rent: with valuable servants included, a furnished Cottage in the 1st Ward. For terms & situation apply to B L Jackson & Bro.

FRI NOV 14, 1851
The dwlg house of E H Strangan, about 2 miles from Danville, Ind, was destroyed by fire last week, & a son about 4 years of age perished in the flames.

Among the distinguished arrivals in Wash City, in the past few days, is Gen R K Call, of Florida, in his early life an accomplished Aid-de-camp of Gen Jackson, & for many years since closely identified with the history of Florida.

The large flouring mill belonging to Messrs Worthington & Keller, on the Patapsco river, immediately at the Thomas Viaduct on the Wash Railroad, was entirely destroyed by fire on Wed. The fire is supposed to be the result of an accident.

Mrd: on Nov 11, in Wash City, by Rev Mr Slattery, Mr Alfred Rickerby to Miss Jane Teresa Rogers, both formerly of Baltimore.

Mrd: on Nov 11, by Rev Wm Hamilton, Mr M M Hitchcox, of Va, to Miss Columbia V Hawkins, of Wash City.

Mrd: on Thu, in Gtwn, by Rev John C Smith, Mr Thos E Reed to Miss Mgt Ellen, daughter of Mr Saml Cunningham, all of Gtwn.

Mrd: on Sabbath, by Rev John C Smith, Mr Wm Henry Temps to Miss Virginia Eliz Carroll, all of Wash City.

Mrs: on Nov 11, by Rev Nicholas D Young, Miss Sarah T Young to Mr John Carroll Brent, both of Wash City.

Died: on Nov 12, in Wash City, Dennis Higgins, a native of the county of Cork, Ireland, aged 78 years. His funeral will take place from the residence of his son-in-law, Mr Curry, on East Capitol st, Capitol Hill, this afternoon, at 3 o'clock.

Died: on Nov 8, Mrs Mgt Sutton, in her 63rd year.

Phil: disastrous fire on Nov 12 broke out in the large factory owned by Mr Jas P Bruner, at the s w corner of Nixon & Hamilton sts, near Fairmont. Several stories of the bldg were occupied by Messrs Faulkner & Lewis, machinists; David & Jas Donnelly, for spinning & carding wool; Bernard McNutt, manufacturer of cotton goods; & the 4th story by Mr Bruner, for the manufacture of cotton & woollen goods. Edw Crossley, Mary Ann Browning, & Agnes Morrow were burnt to death.

Orphans Court of Wash Co, D C. Letters of administration on the personal estate of Noah Hanson, late of Wash Co, deceased. –W Maria Hanson, admx

Millard Fillmore, Pres of the U S A, recognizes Wm Sleyden, who has been appointed Vice Consul of the Mexican Republic for the port of San Francisco, Calif. -Nov 12, 1851

The Wash Brewery. The extensive establishment near the Gtwn bridge, erected, & for many years previous to his death conducted by our friend Wm Hayman, is now owned & carried on by Mr Jos Davison. We found the brewery in full work, having commenced its season on Oct 28. Mr Davison has manufactured an article known as Brown Stout, which is found of so much utility in confirming convalescence from bilious & typhoid fevers.

The property of Mrs Eliz Ferral will be disposed of by Mr Green as auctioneer, the notion of D W Ferral to the contrary notwithstanding. She has ample legal authority to sell, convey, & settle up her mother's business. —Catherine V Ferral, Atty in fact for Eliz Ferral

SAT NOV 15, 1851
Distribution of Abraham G Thompson's estate: [the first statement of the bequests made by the late A G Thompson, of N Y, were erroneous.]
Funeral expenses: $1,000
Each child of is deceased brother Jonathan, $500: $2,000
To his half sister: $500
To his grand niece: $250
To his nephew: $250
To Mrs ___, a relative: $1,500
To a daughter of said relative: $500
To D F Cox, for claims: $1,000
To 2 young friends, $500 each; $1,000
To his nephew David: $3,000
To the one having care of the funeral $1,000, & for a monument $2,000: $3,000
To another nephew: $2,000
To grand daughter & daughter-in-law, $100 each: $200
To executors $200 cash: $1,400
To grandson Edw, son of Edw G Thompson, in trust, income of $15,000 for life, the principal to his children: $15,000
Pew in Dr Spring's Church, to Dr Spring for the poor: $400

Raleigh Register of Nov 12. Hon Richd Hines died in this city on Mon last, after a lingering illness of several weeks. The State has been deprived of one of its purest & most prominent citizens. He has gone to the grave in the ripeness of manhood, leaving his family the proud inheritance of an unblemished name. He was a native of Edgecombe Co, & represented, in the 19th Congress, the district which Edgecombe then comprised a part.

On Tue a little daughter of Jas E Williams, of New Bedford, Mass, was burnt to death by her clothes taking fire from the stove. She was 5 years of age.

Mr Wm P Byrd, a young lawyer of Richmond, on Tue was engaged in an exciting conversation with another person, when he fell back on a chair, & almost immediately expired. For some time past he had been afflicted with a disease of the heart. His death was occasioned by the rupture of a blood vessel.

Wash City Ordinances: 1-Act for the relief of David Welsh: the sum of $84.72 be paid him for grading on 15th st, & additional sum of $25.87 for gravelling H st. 2-Act for the relief of Jas B Greenwell & Lowrey & Stewart: the sum of $80.63 be paid to Jas B Greenwell for paving the culvert across F st; & $75 to Lowrey & Stewart, balance due them for extending the culvert across 10th st west.

Mrd: on Nov 13, by Rev C M Butler, Mr Benj Klopfer to Miss Sophia Hendley, all of Wash City.

Mrd: on Nov 11, at the Church of the Epiphany, in Wash City, by Rev J W French, Mr Reuben C Johnson, of Gorham, Maine, to Miss Caroline Alexander, of Phil.

Died: on Nov 9, at Petersburg, Va, Mrs Frances Maria Tracey, aged 49 years, formerly of Mount Erin, Fairfax Co, Va, the widow of the late Jas Francis Tracey, both natives of Dublin, Ireland. She was the only daughter of Matthew McDonald, of Dublin, Ireland.

Died: on Oct 18, at Corpus Christi, Texas, Capt S M Plummer, of the U S Army.

MON NOV 17, 1851
Jas B Bishop, jr, the son of J B Bishop, of Augusta, Geo, about 19 years of age, left his father's residence on Mon on a hunting excursion for the day, & was found dead the next afternoon with a gunshot wound passing up under his chin into the head, leaving no doubt that he was the victim of an accidental discharge of his gun.

As the widow of Dr Judson was embarking for the U S at Calcutta a number of noble-hearted & disinterest friends made her a present of 8,000 rupees, or nearly $1,500, as a testimonial of the reverence in which they held her lamented husband, & for the respect which they felt for his bereaved family. By providence she was preserved from taking passage on the ship **Buckinghamshire**, which was burnt in the Hoogly river.

On Sat 3 young men left Sheperdsville, Bullitt Co, Ky, on a hunting excursion. One of the guns accidentally discharged killing John Samuels, instantly. He was 17 years old, & the son of R F Samuels, & brother of Hon W J Samuels, present Rep in the Legislature from Hardin Co.

Mr Claiborne Rice, of Todd Co, Ky, had his tobacco house, with 30,000 lbs of tobacco, consumed by fire a few days ago, & suspecting his neighbor, Mr Riley, as the incendiary, he went to his residence & shot him dead. He then gave himself up.

Shocking accident in Ludlow, Vt, on Sat last week, by which 2 children of Cyrus Baker, one a girl of 7 years, & the other a boy of 4, were killed. They were playing near a cart body which had been left standing upon one end, when it fell upon them, killing the girl instantly, & injuring the boy so seriously that he died on Tue.

Explosion on Fri in the Bldg on Lafayette ave, Brooklyn, N Y, occupied by Hugh O'Rourke & John Morris, as a manufactory of fire-works. Of the inmates, Michl McCue & John Duffy were killed; Michl Conolly, Patrick Fitzgerald, & Peter S Kelley were horribly burnt. Kelley is about 40 years old, & has a family. The deceased were boys, about 16 years of age. Conolly & Fitzgerald were also boys. –N Y Com Adv

Circuit Court of Wash Co, D C-in Chancery. Benj Pollard against John G Robinson & the heirs of Wm Hewitt & Carey Selden. The bill states that on Jan 1, 1830, the above John G Robinson was indebted unto the above Benj Pollard in the sum of $1,500 current money, & to secure the payment of the same executed on that day a deed of trust on lot 8 in square 570, in Wash City. In this deed Wm Hewitt & Carey Selden were named trustees. The terms of the deed were that Robinson, his excs, adms, or assigns, should pay the money in said deed within 20 years to the said Pollard, his heirs, or assigns; the interest on said money was to have been paid quarterly; & also pay the taxes on said lot & the premium of the insurance on the bldgs which were to be erected thereon; & in case of the failure of Robinson or the person or persons legally claiming under him to perform either of these conditions, then the said lot became liable to be sold according to the terms of said deed. The 20 years has elapsed & no part of the principal of the money has been paid, but the whole of the $1,500 is due; & on Apr 1, 1850, the interest on the money then due & unpaid was $175.50; & the said lot, contrary to the terms of said deed of trust, was permitted by Robinson to be sold for taxes, & was redeemed by Pollard on Nov 11, 1850, for $82.77. Interest is due thereon. The bill states that Carey Selden & Wm Hewitt, trustees, are dead, & the object of the bill is to obtain a decree against their heirs & against Robinson for the purpose of selling the property mentioned in said deed to satisfy the debts & interests mentioned in this notice. The heirs at law of said Selden & Hewitt, namely, Rebecca Hewitt, Sarah E Graham, & Willoughby Selden reside beyond the jurisdiction of this Court. Same are to appear on or before the 1st Monday of Apr next. –J A Smith, clerk -E C Morgan, Solicitor

Judge Cole, of the U S District Court, died at Paris, Maine, on Wed.

New Orleans, Nov 8. Peter Conrey, jr, has failed, & presented his petition & schedule to the 2nd Dist Court. His assets are $1,072,294, & his liabilities $824,068.

The remains of Lt Richd M Bache, of the U S Navy, were on Sat borne to their last resting place in the Congressional Burial ground, attended by his relations & a few of his many army & navy friends, who chanced to be in Washington at the time. [He was drowned while on active service in Humboldt's Bay, of Upper Calif, when bravely striving to rescue a comrade from the breakers.]

Mr Littleberry Carrington, one of our oldest & most respected citizens, committed suicide yesterday. He was a perfectly upright gentleman, but had for some time past there was strong evidence of mental aberration. —Richmond Republican of Sat

Buffalo, Nov 14. The steam-boiler of White's edge-tool factory, in this city, exploded today. Scalded and lives despaired of, are Jas Kane, Peter Henderberger, & John Lorenz.

Mrd: on Nov 5, by Rev Mathias Alig, Wm Hannefin to Mary Donohough.

Mrd: on Nov 13, by Rev Mathias Alig, Mr Thos Fitzgerald to Miss Julia Connell.

Mrd: on Nov 12, by Rev Mr French, Saml V Niles to Mary Gordon, all of Wash City.

Died: on Nov 14, at the residence of his parents, Albert Morgan, aged 2 years, 11 months & 13 days, only son of Chas E & Mary Jane Walker.

TUE NOV 18, 1851
Fatal accident on the Worcester Railroad on Fri, at the Southboro Station: Miss Milly Morse, of Hopkinton, an elderly lady, had just crossed the track & mounted the platform whn she lost her balance & fell back on the track when the train was coming. It passed over her, mangling her body in a shocking manner. She breathed but a few times after. Miss Morse was a lady highly respected & beloved by all who knew her. —Boston Journal

Mrd: on Nov 4, at Bowling Green, Ky, by Rev Mr Tomes, Light Underood, daughter of Hon J R Underwood, to Arthur Middleton Rutledge, of Nashville, Tenn.

Mrd: on Nov 12, at Keene, N H, by Rt Rev Carleton Chase, Bishop of N H, John Sherwood, of N Y, to Miss Mary Eliz, eldest daughter of Hon Jas Wilson, of N H.

Mrd: on Nov 11, in Alexandria, Va, by Rev Geo King, Geo T Mitchell, of Kent Co, Md, to Kate L, daughter of the late Gov Kent, of Md.

Died: on Nov 16, Mrs Mary Virginia Mason, wife of Mr Maynardier Mason, of Fairfax Co, Va, aged 40 years. Her funeral is today at 2 o'clock, from the residence of her aunt, Miss Clark, on the Heights of Gtwn.

Died: on Aug 27, at the residence of his brother, Edw J Heard, on Lake Catahoula, in the parish of St Martin, La, Capt Jos Heard, in his 85th year.

Died: Nov 15, of pseudo-membranous croup, George, youngest son of Jos & Julia A Radcliff, in his 4th year.

On Fri residents of N Y presented to Henry Grinnell, through their reps, with a magnificent gold medal, in commenation of his philanthropic efforts to discover the missing navigator. It was manufactured by Peckham, Denis & Merill, of N Y. One side presents a view of the ships **Advance & Rescue** at a time when they were placed in the most imminent peril, surrounded on all sides by tremendous masses of ice. The reverse contains the following inscription:
The British Residents of New York to
Henry GRINNEL, Esq,
In grateful admiration of his noble effort to save
Sir John Franklin.
It is thine to heal another's wo,
And ours to mark the sacred glow
1851
Mr Grinnell was not present at the dinner, because he is averse to so public a display. The medal was quietly presented to him at his place of business. -Express

The estate of the late Jos Fowler, jr, of New Orleans, according to the inventory just made, is valued at $1,480,801.27, with very few liabilities. He had, however, never paid taxes on more than about ½ of his property. His real estate alone is valued at $328,900. The commission to each of his executors, at 2½ %, amounts to $32,803.40. Many of the heirs reside in the District of Columbia, & have already come in possession of a considerable share of these effects.

Military movements: the ship **Francis P Sage**, from N Y, arrived at New Orleans last week, with 260 U S troops, accompanied by ofcrs of the army, viz: Col Wm Chapman, Lt J H McArthur, Lt Garden Chapin, Lt Thos J C Amory, Lt H F Witter, Assist Surgeon A Taylor. Col Henry Wilson, of the 7th Infty, who had been promoted to the command of the 7th Military Dept-U S Army, [vice the late Gen Arbuckle,] arrived at Little Rock, Ark, on Oct 28, on his way to **Fort Smith**, the headquarters of that dept.

Died: on Nov 17, Jas Thomas, son of Jas & Mary E Frasier, aged 2 years & 5 months. His funeral is today at 3 P M, at the residence of his father, G st, near 7th st.

For rent: 2 parlors & 4 or 5 chambers, lighted with gas, over my Music & Stationery Store, 2 doors east of the Irving Hotel, Pa ave, between 11th & 12th sts.
-Mrs Garret Anderson

Postmaster Gen est'd the following new Post Ofcs for week ending Nov 15, 1851.

Ofc	County, State	Postmaster
Madawaska	Aroostook, Me	Baptiste Fourneag
Van Buren	Aroostook, Me	Michl Farrell
West Van Buren	Aroostook, Me	Moses Thibedeaux
West Madawaska	Aroostook, Me	Edw Guy
Morvin	Clark, Ala	Arch'd Campbell
Plum Grove	Fayette, Texas	Wm Scallorn
Pleasant Hill	Van Buren, Iowa	John Purdum
Gray's Creek	Monroe, Iowa	John C Church
Sweetland	Muscatine, Iowa	Jos N Harker
Panther Creek	Clayton, Iowa	Edw C Forbes
East Randolph	Dodge, Wis	John Converse
Turnersville	Lincoln, Ky	Geo A Bradley
Beach Point	Gibson, Tenn	Geo Akers
Fort Atkinson	Nebraska	Saml G Mason
Morganville	Hillsdale, Mich	Nile J Parrish

Names Changed: 1-Beckley Raleigh Co, Va, changed to Raleigh C H.
2-Shawnee Run, Mercer Co, Ky, changed to Pleasant Hill.
3-Van Buren, Ripley Co, Mo, changed to Wood's Mills.

For rent: a suite of rooms on the same floor & several other chambers, all neatly & comfortably furnished. Apply to Mrs Fleury, Pa ave, between 9th & 10th sts.

New Fashionable Tailoring Establishment. H F Loudon & Co, Men's Mercers & Tailors, Brown's Hotel, Pa ave.

Household & kitchen furniture at auction: on Nov 21, at the late residence of Mrs Barbary Lowe, deceased, at the conrer of 3rd st east & L st south.
-A Green, auctioneer

Furnished rooms for rent: in my house on 11th st, between E & F sts. C Gautier, a La Ville de Paris, corner of Pa ave & 11th st.

WED NOV 19, 1851
The Mormons have taken possession of the rancho of San Bernardina, near Los Angeles, for which they are to pay $102,000. $25,000 was paid down, & the remainder is to be paid in 2 equal annual payments.

Affray at Jackson, Caleveras Co, Calif, on Sep 14, between Wm F Smith, County Judge, & L A Collier, County Clerk. Collier struck Smith a blow in the face, when Smith drew a revolver & fired 4 times, 3 of his shots taking effect. Collier died soon after. Judge Smith was immediately arrested, & was honorably discharged: act of self-defence.

Gen Court Martial: Col Washington, Maj Anderson, Maj Williams, A D C to the Cmder-in-Chief; Maj Austine, Maj G P Andrews, Capt Shields, A D C to Brvt Maj Gen Wood, & Lt J S Mason, passed through Providence, R I, on Fri last for Portsmouth, N H, where the Sec of War ordered a Gen Court Martial to assemble.

U S Circuit Court at Savannah, Ga, on Nov 11: H L Kimbrough, of Columbus, Ga, was found guilty of embezzling $6,000 from the post ofc in Columbus in Dec.

Winter Millinery: Mrs M A Hill, Pa ave, between 9th & 10th sts.

Wm Tucker, Merchant Tailor, Lane & Tucker's bldg, Pa ave, between 4½ & 6th sts. All kinds of military garments made in the best manner, according to the late regulations.

For rent: new 3 story & attic house on 16th st west, near the residence of W W Corcoran, & opposite the residence of Cmdor Morris. —Jas Carrico, 10th st, between E & F sts.

For rent: Three of the 4 new three-story & attic houses, on the corner of 10th & H sts; the whole lighted with gas. Rent $400. Also a furnished house on Capitol Hill, lighted with gas, adjoining the public grounds, lately occupied by Hons S W Inge, & J A McClernand. —J F Brown

Orphans Court of Wash Co, D C. In the case of Elias Travers, administrator of Nicholas Travers, jr, deceased, the administrator & Court have appointed Dec 9 next, for the distribution of the assets in the hands of the administrator.
—Edw N Roach, Reg/o wills

Died: on Nov 18, Teresa Frances, in her 4th year, daughter of Francis & Mary Reilly. Her funeral is from their residence, 8th st, near the Navy Yard, this afternoon at 2 o'clock.

The headless body of a man named *McClure was found on Fri last, at the White Oak Bottom, about 22 miles east of Wash, by the Engineer of the passenger train from Balt to Wash. His head has not been found. The affair is certainly a very horrible one. [Nov 21: *MacClure's head was torn off when he was dragged about 2 miles, when caught in the cow-catcher of the train.] [*Two spellings.]

THU NOV 20, 1851
Marshal's sale: writ of fieri facias: sale of lots 9 & 10 in square 544, seized & levied upon as the property of Jos Martini, & will be sold to satisfy judicials 14 to Mar term, 1852; favor of John Purdy, use of Nathl Carusi. —B Wallach, Marshal D C

Orphans Court of Wash Co, D C. In the case of Maria G Devereux, admx of Wm Devereux, deceased: the Court & administrator have appointed Dec 9 next, for settlement of the estate with the assets in the hands of the admx.
–Ed N Roach, Reg/o wills

Orphans Court of Wash Co, D C. In the case of Mary McClelland & John McClelland, excs, of John McClelland, deceased: the Court & executors have appointed Dec 9 next, for settlement of the estate with the assets in the hands of the excs. –Ed N Roach, Reg/o wills

A laborer, Jas Mooney, was found dead at Pittsburg, Pa, on Fri, murdered by whom is unknown. He had only been in the city 2 or 3 days. Another man, Henry Hosack, was killed in a fight on Troy Hill on Tue. He attacked a man named Sweeny, while in a state of intoxication.

The Oregonian of Oct 4 publishes a letter from Col W G T Vault to Dr Dart, Superintendent of Indian Affairs, detailing the particulars of an attack by Indians on an exploring party employed in ascertaining the practicability of locating a road from Port Oxford to the upper Rouge river county. Those who were murdered are: A S Doherty, aged 30, Texas; Patrick Murphy, aged 22, N Y; John P Holland, aged 21, N H; Jeremiah Ryan, aged 25, Md; & J P Pepper, aged 28, Albany, N Y.

A fireman, Robt Baird, was accidentally killed at Brooklyn on Sun last, whilst in the discharge of his duty. He was leaning on one of the arms of the engine, when an order was given, Play away quick, which the men responded to before the deceased could move. He was thrown several feet into the air, & in falling struck his breast on part of the machine. He died in about 30 minutes.

Jos H Crane, of Ohio, died at Dayton on Nov 12, having fully accomplished his three score years & 10 with usefulness & honor. On the bench, in the halls of legislation, as a member of the bar, he was distinguished for honesty, ability, & dignity; as a man he was kind & generous; as a Christian, meek & charitable. –Dayton Gaz

Wash Corp: 1-Act for the relief of Richd Ballenger: ordered to lie on the table. 2-Ptn from Robt Earl, asking to be refunded certain money erroneously paid by him for a livery stable license: referred to the Cmte of Claims. 3-Ptn from Wm Greer, asking to be relieved, as surety, from the payment of a fine against Peter Johnson, now deceased: referred to the Cmte of Claims: passed. 4-Act for the relief of Caleb Buckingham. 5-Ptn of Jos M Padgett & others, praying a change in the grade of L st south, between 8th & 9th sts: referred to the Cmte on Improvements. 6-Bill for the relief of Thos Plumsill: passed.

Mr D W Quarles, son of Col Quarles, whose plantation is on Oyster Creek, in Brazoria Co, Texas, has made this season 400 bales of cotton on 160 acres of land, & with 12 hands.

In Caroline Co Court, as a Court of Equity, in the State of Md, Oct Term, 1851. Wm Turner & Mgt A Turner, vs Wm F Rich & Mary F Rich his wife, Caspar M Newman & Rebecca A Newman his wife, Saml Betts & Harriet E Betts, & Chas C Smith & Eliz A Smith. This suit is to procure a decree for ths sale of real estate in Caroline, Talbot, & Queen Anne Counties, belonging to the parties, cmplnts & dfndnts, subject to the dower interest & estate of a certain Harriet Turner therein, & for the distribution of the proceeds of sale between the parties in the proportion stated. Bill: Wm Turner & Mgt A Turner, the cmplnts, & Mary F Rich, wife of Wm H Rich, Rebecca A Newman, wife of Caspar M Newman, Saml Betts & Harriet E Betts, & Chas C Smith & Eliz A Smith, are seized as tenants in common in fee of certain real estate, lying in Caroline Co, subject to the dower interest & estate of Harriet Turner therein; that the five twenty-fourth parts of said real estate belong to your cmplnt, Wm Turner; the five twenty-fourths parts thereof belong to your cmplnt, Mgt A Turner; the five twenty-fourths parts thereof belong to the said Chas C Smith & Eliz A Smith jointly; the one-sixth part thereof belongs to the said Rebecca A Newman; & the one twenty-fourth part thereof belongs to the said Saml Betts & Harriet E Betts jointly; that it will be to the interest & advantage of all the parties entitled to sell the said real estate, subject to the dower interest aforesaid, & to divide the proceeds of sale between the parties in the proportion stated; but that the said Chas C Smith, Eliz A Smith, Saml Betts, & Harriet E Betts are infants under the age of 21 years, & that a sale cannot be had without the assistance of this Court, & that the said Wm H Rich resides out of the State of Md. Wm H Rich to appear in this Court on or before Dec 1 next. –Jas H Fountain, clerk

Mrd: on Nov 4, at Bowling Green, Ky, by Rev Chas Tomes, Arthur Middleton Rutledge to Miss Eliza, daughter of Hon Judge Underwood, U S Senator from Ky.

Mrd: on Nov 19, in Richmond, Alex'r F Taylor, of Culpeper Co, to Mrs Elvira M Higginbotham, daughter of John Henry, of Charlotte Co, Va.

Circuit Court of Wash Co, D C-in Chancery. Law vs Law. Jas Adams, the trustee in this cause, reported that he sold particular lots & pieces of ground contained in his report at the prices specified: ratify same. –Jno A Smith, Clerk [No other details.]

A young lady wishes to obtain a situation as Teacher in a private family. She will instruct in English branches, French, & Music, & can produce good references. Address M D, c/o J T Fracker, Zanesville, Ohio.

Mrd: on Nov 18, in Wash City, by Rev Mr Pyne, Dr Bernard M Byrne, U S Army, to Miss Louisa, daughter of Col J J Abert, Topographical Engineers, U S Army.

Mrd: on Nov 4, in Trinity Church, Pass Christian, Miss, by Rev Thos S Savage, D D, Prof Ruel Keith, U S Navy, to Miss Martha B Cleveland, daughter of Wm Cleveland.

In the Circuit Court of Wash Co, D C. In the matter of the petition of Bradley Dickson, for the partition of the real estate of which the late Thos Dickson died seized. The Com'rs appointed by the Circuit Court of the Dist of Columbia for Wash Co, to divide the said real estate, having made their return to the Court, & reported that the said property would not admit of division without loss & injury to the parties interested, & having returned the value thereof in current money: It is therefore, this 18th day of Nov, 1851, hereby ordered, adjudged, & decreed that unless the heirs at law of the said Thos Dickson, & all others who may have a right to elect, to take the said real estate at the valuation returned by the said Com'rs do, on or before the first Monday of Apr, 1851, so elect to take the said real estate will be sold by the said Com'rs; provided a copy of this order be published 3 times a week for 3 weeks; the first publication to be at least 4 months before the said first Monday of April next. By order of the Court. Test: -Jno A Smith, clerk
[Bradley Dickson/Dixon is the son of Thos Dickson/Dixon. Dixon is the proper spelling for this family-J M D.]

In Dorchester Co Court, as a court of Equity: Oct term 1851. Jos Caton vs Mary Caton & Thos E Caton, administrators C T A of Abel Caton, Mary Caton, Zachariah Caton, Aaron Wallace & Louisa his wife, Levin Caton, & Wm Caton. This suit is to procure a decree for a sale of the real estate of Abel Caton, late of said county, deceased, for the payment of his debts. Bill: Abel Caton in his life-time was indebted unto the said Jos Caton in the sum of $29.77, current money, on his certain bill obligatory, dated on or about Sep 8, 1841. That the said Abel Caton has lately died, leaving a last will & testament, of which he appointed Thos E Caton the executor, & thereby devised all his estate, both real & personal, to the said Mary Caton during her natural life, & at her death to be equally divided between all of his children, share & share alike. That the said Abel Caton left the following children, to wit: Zachariah Caton, Louisa Wallace, wife of Aaron Wallace, Levin Caton, & Wm Caton. That the said last will & testament was in due form admitted to probate, & the said Thos C Caton having renounced the execution thereof, letters of administration with the will annexed were granted by said Orphans' Court to Mary Caton & Thos E Caton aforesaid, who have, in virtue thereof, possessed themselves of the personal estate of the said deceased, & have applied the same to the discharge of other proper debts due by the deceased. That the personal estate of the said Abel Caton is insufficient for the payment of his debts, & that the said Jos Caton, & the other unsatisfied creditors of the said Abel Caton, are entitled to have their claims paid out of the real estate of the said deceased, in the hands of his heirs & devisees as aforesaid, & that the said Levin Caton & Wm Caton reside out of the State of Md. They are to appear in the Court on or before Apr 2 next. –Wm Jackson, clerk

FRI NOV 21, 1851
The U S frig **St Lawrence**, now at the Brooklyn navy yard, is to be the flag-ship of the Pacific squadron, & will shortly sail for her destination. Capt Bladen Dulany is to take command of her.

We learn by a letter from on board the U S ship **Susquehanna**, at Rio Janeiro, on Oct 23, that in consequence of some difference between Cmdor Aulick & Capt Inman, commanding the ship, the latter ofcr had been detached from the ship & ordered home. Some misunderstanding concerning rank or discipline, we presume.

Balt, Nov 20. The Fair of the Mechanics' Institute closes today. Joshua Vansant pronounces the valedictory address; after which the premiums will be distributed.

From Mexico: 1-The murderers of Gen Rea have been tried. Three were condemned to death; one to the galleys for 3 years; four to the galleys for 2 years; & two were acquitted. 2-The notorious Capt Parker H French has not been executed, but is in prison at Durango, with 11 companions, charged with highway robbery.

From Havana: Mr Robt H Breckenridge, of Ky, late of the Lopez Expedition, & who was one of the two picked up at sea in a boat by a Spanish coaster, has been released by the Capt Genr'l, & arrived at Charleston 2 or 3 days ago. His release is due to the exertions of Consul Owen, assisted by several other gentlemen. The ship **Isabella H** left Havana for old Spain on Nov 8, having on board the remains of the late Gen Enna, & the following prisoners belonging to the expedition: R Beach, of N Y; Geo Edgerton Richardson, of New Orleans; Hodges, of Texas; M J Keenan, of Mobile; Gano, of New Orleans; 2 Hungarians & a German, whose names are not recollected. There were only 3 persons attached to the expedition left in Havana, & they were in the hospital.

Fall & Winter Millinery: Mrs M A Eaton, at her residence, over Mr Eddy's Jewelry Store, a few doors east of the Nat'l Hotel.

Local: On Wed Henry Hunt Parker was arrested on the charge of being one of the party engaged in an outrage upon the police on last Fri night, & gave bail in $1,000 for his appearance at Court. He was clearly identified. Wm Crowley was also identified as another participant. He was bound over to appear for riot, in the sum of $266.

Wanted, a good Salesman, & to act as clerk in a furniture store. Inquire of C O Wall.

SAT NOV 22, 1851
Mr David Brumbaugh, of Hagerstown, Md, proposes to test his plough, the Washington County Regulator, against any plough in the U S of any foreign country, the ploughing to take place near Mason & Dixon's line, north of Hagerstown.

Terrible accident in N Y on Nov 20, at the new public school on Greenwich ave. Miss Harrison, teacher in primary school #26, fainted. A number of children ran to her side. Others became alarmed and raised the cry of FIRE. In panic they made a general rush down the stairway, & the press against the balustrade became so great that it gave way, precipitating to the floor below, with child after child being crushed & killed. The following is a list of the dead thus far ascertained:

Emma Gildersleeve	John Knapp	Amanda Hoff
Anna Slate	Anna M Hill	Anne Pike
Jacob Spinstead	John McMann	Geo Quackenbuss
Matthew Wood	Mary C Baxter	Margery Stephens
Edwin Glenroy	Sarah Boragdus	Harry Abbott
Sarah Bogart	Chas E Moore	Morris Waldron
John L Wooley	Geo Mills	Sarah Leny
Anne Wooley	Anna Van Dusen	Catharine Reynolds
Catharinee Doway	Geo Walden	Eliza O Neill
Julia Delano	Jan M De Voe	Mary Harper
A Von Tassel	Jane Elursa	Mary Teackard
Miss Brown	Delia Ackerman	
Lucy Carlow	Abby A Jacobs	

Many others were dreadfully injured. [Nov 24th newspaper: Miss Harrison was suddenly seized with a paralysis of the tongue while in the class. The contortions of her face alarmed her pupils. Three of the female teachers, Miss Barnes, Miss Smith, & Miss Traphagen, were much injured in the crush. Miss Harrison [the female principal,] was much better this morning.] [Nov 26 newspaper: Leititia, the youngest daughter of Mr Justice Bleakley, was a pupil in one of the small classes, & was extricated from the mass of children; injured by a piece of wood hitting her head. –Comm Adv of Monday]

Cmder Mattison, for some time past stationed at our Navy Yard, has resigned his commission in the Navy. He had been ordered by the Navy Dept to prepare the sloop-of-war **Portsmouth**, & take command of her & join the Pacific squadron; but he preferred a resignation of his commission to active service on so long a cruise. –Boston Traveller

Another Revolutionary patriot gone: Gilead Bradley, one of the heroes of Trenton in the winter of 1776, recently died at New Haven, Conn, in his 95th year.

The Most Rev Archbishop Kendrick, lately of Phil, has been invested with the Pallium, at Pontifical Mass, in the Balt Cathedral. It is simply a little garment placed upon the neck of the Bishop, & extending over the back & breast. The pallium is always buried with its possessor.

John Lorimer Graham recovered a verdict of $705,809, in the Circuit Court at Catskill recently, against the executors of O Day, deceased. The cause of action is not stated.

At Marion Court, on Sat week last, Col W W Avery, unarmed, was attacked by Saml Fleming, who had armed himself with a cow-hide, using a stone with stunning effect. The parties were separated. In Morgantown, on Tue last, Fleming, fully armed, appearing in Col Avery's presence, Avery rose & shot Fleming dead on the spot. Col Avery at once placed himself in the custody of the proper official.
–Lincolnton N C Republican

The copartnership existing under the firm of Morsell & Wilson was dissolved by mutual consent on Oct 10, 1851. –B P Morsell, J B Wilson. [Persons desiring to see me: I will be found at the ofc of R T Morsell, Atty at Law, City Hall. –B F Morsell]

For rent: 2 chambers, or a parlor & chamber on the 1st floor: F st. between 13th & 14th sts, next door east of Dr Lieberman's.

Millard Fillmore, Pres of the U S A, recognizes Alexandre de Carvalro Paes de Ardrade, who has been appointed Vice Consul of Brazil, for the State of Calif. Nov 20, 1851.

Mrd: on Nov 20, by Rev Mr Hill, Mr Wm G Brock, of Norfolk, Va, to Miss Mary F James, of Rockville, Md

Mrd: on Nov 18, in Camden, N J, by Rev Abel C Thomas, Lt Bayse Newcomb Westcott, U S Navy, to Mary, daughter of Saml Hart.

Died: on Nov 20, at Gtwn, John Pickrell, in his 69th year. His funeral will take place today at 3 o'clock, from his late residence on 1st st, Gtwn.

Died: on Nov 20, after a brief illness, at his father's residence, Francis King, eldest son of W W King, of Wash City. His funeral is this afternoon, at 4 o'clock.

Died: on Nov 10, at the residence of her husband, in Clarksville, Tenn, Mrs Eliz Johnson, wife of Hon Cave Johnson.

Valuable real estate for sale: by deed of trust by the late Richd B Mason, deceased, on Aug 28, 1841, & also a decree of the Circuit Superior Court of Law & Chancery of the County of Alexandria, Va, rendered at its Nov term, 1851: public auction of **Holmes' Island**, or more recently as **Jackson City**, in Alexandria Co, bordering upon the Potomac river, containing 338 acres 32 perches, by actual survey. Improvements consist of a comfortable dwlg house, with stables & out-bldgs, & a well of good water near the door. –R C Mason, truste

Pure Irish Whiskey: on hand. —Jno B Kibbey & Co, #5, opposite Centre Market.

Plenty of work for sober men. I wish to employ 4 long-boats to freight wood from the bluff below Alexandria to the Eastern Branch. I will give $1. per cord. Apply to me, Wm Clark, 14th st east, Pa ave, near the Navy Yard.

MON NOV 24, 1851
Orphans Court of Wash Co, D C. Letters testamentary on the personal estate of Barbara Lowe, late of Wash Co, deceased. —Geo Watterston, exc

Orphans Court of Wash Co, D C. Letters of administration on the personal estate of John Rowan, late of the U S Marine Corps, deceased. —Geo H Fulmer, adm

Dr Jas E De Kay died at Oyster Bay, where he has had his residence for some years past. He was a distinguished naturalist. His death happened in the 60th year of his age. To the names of Dr Kearney Rodgers, Dr Pattison, & Dr Manley, we must now add that of Dr De Kay, as the 4th eminent man of the medical profession who has fallen within the past fortnight. —N Y Evening Post [No death date given-current item.]

Orphans Court of Wash Co, D C. Letters of administration on the personal estate of Aaron McAlwee, late of Wash Co, deceased. —Jas Booth, adm

WILL-I, James Fennimore Cooper, declare & publish this to be may last Will & Testament: I give & bequeath to my wife, Susan Augusta, all my property now in possession, or to which I may have any claim, now or hereafter, whether real, or personal, or mixed; to be enjoyed by her, her heirs & assigns, forever. I make my said wife the executrix of this my will. Signed, Nov 8, 1849, & proved of record Sep 26, 1851.

Circuit Court of Wash Co, D C-in Chancery. John Marbury, adm of Francis Barklie, vs Mary Barklie & others. The trustee appointed to sell the real estate of Alex'r Dunlap in lot 89, & the north half part of lot 90, in Beatty & Hawkin's addition to Gtwn, reported he has sold the same, being an undivided half part thereof, jointly with Thos Luffeen, the owner of the other half of the same premises; that it was divided & sold in 8 lots, for the aggregate sum of $3,916.25, of which sum the estate of the said Alex'r Dunlap is entitled to $1958.12¼: the purchasers have complied with the terms of the sale. —Jno A Smith, clk

Cmder Thos A Dornin has been ordered to take command of the sloop-of-war **Portsmouth**. In justice to Cmder Mattison, he tendered his resignation in consequence of the severe illness of an only daughter, whom he could not leave in her present condition.

Mrd: on Nov 19, by Rev Jas P Donelan, Jas B French to Miss Amanda Jane Dant, all of Wash City.

Mrd: on Nov 20, by Rev W T Eva, John Lacey to Eliza Beagle, all of Wash City.

Mrd: on Nov 20, by Rev Mr Rogers, Mr Jas Medford, formerly of Annapolis, Md, to Miss Ann E Smith, of Alexandria.

Mrd: on Nov 18, at Aldie, by Rev Geo Adie, Richd S Cox, of Gtwn, D C, to Miss Mary L, daughter of Louis Berkley, of Loudoun Co, Va.

Died: on Nov 22, Mr Saml Walker, of Wash City, in his 49th year. His funeral is from his residence on 12th st, near F, this evening, at 3 o'clock.

Died: on Nov 19, in Wash City, Mr Joshua Higgins, [machinist,] of N Y, in his 27th year.

Furnished rooms for rent: on 10th st, south side of Pa ave. –Mrs A Best, on 10th st.

Died: on Nov 23, after a short illness, Mr Dana Miller, in his 34th year, formerly of Dummerstown, Vt, & at the time of his decease, & for the last 15 months, a clerk in the Census Ofc. He was much respected by those who knew him for intelligence & gentlemanly deportment.

Wanted, Teacher for a Primary School, midway of P G Co, Md. He must be of good moral character. –Wm Bryan, of Rd; Stanislaus Blandford, Local Trustees.

Situation wanted as wet nurse, by a married woman, who can come well recommended. She can be seen at Mr Wm G W White's, 4½ st, above C, until Nov 29th.

Wash City Ordinances: 1-Act for the relief of Caleb Buckingham: sum of $100.17 be paid to him for the balance due him for placing water-pipes on 13th st. 2-Act for the relief of Thos Plumsill: the sum of $75 to be paid him, being in full for services he rendered as acting police ofcr & Com'r of the 6th Ward, during the illness of Ignatius Howe, the regular ofcr. He is also to be paid $30.18 while acting police ofcr, as per certificate of Jos Radcliff, 1st clerk in the Mayor's ofc.

Accident on the railroad within 30 miles of Augusta, Ga, killed the engineer, Mr Philip Scholle, & 2 firemen, Fred'k Kruse & B Brother.

Local Item. The venerable & respectable John Davis, of Abel, master plumber in the Navy Yard, has resigned his place, & his son, Abel G Davis, is appointed in his stead.

On Sat last Danl F Hooe, of Alexandria, received the first load of flour ever carried to that town by railroad. It was sent down by Wm J Weir, of Prince Wm Co, via the Orange & Alexandria railroad, & was manufactured at Milford Mills.

Valuable farm near Wash at auction: on Dec 8, a handsome Farm, lying on the Piscataway road, belonging to Mr J E Dement, on which he resides, adjoining the farms of Messrs Young, Berry & Brent: contains 105 acres with a good new 2 story frame house. Mr Dement having purchased another farm, the above will be sold to the highest bidder. -A Green, auctioneer

Sale of valuable improved property on Pa ave: N Y Supreme Court-in Equity. Chas Yates, Wm K Fuller, & Geo K Fuller, acting executors & trustees, of John B Yates, deceased, vs Henry Yates, Ann Yates, Alex'r G Fonda, Susan Fonda, Mary Austin Fonda, Nathan N Whiting & Jane Helen his wife, John S Groot & Ann his wife, Anna Maria McDonell, Ann McDonell, Jos C Y Paige, John Delaney Watkins, & as Administrator of John Austin Yates, deceased, Jos C Y Watkins, John Watkins, Saml M Neill & Josepha his wife, Christopher Y Fonda, Ann Eliza Fonda, Jas Hooker Yates, Andrew J Yates, Anna E Yates, John R Stuyvesant & Mary A his wife, Ann Eliz Yates, Hannah Hooker Yates, Helen McDonell, Sarah L Fonda, Mary A Watkins, wife of John Delaney Watkins, John B Yates, Arthur R Yates, & Austin A Yates, children & heirs at law of John A Yates, deceased, & the Atty Gen of the State of N Y. Order in this cause, directs the Executors to sell & dispose of the real estate of John B Yates, deceased, of property in Wash City, D C, on Pa ave: being lot 18 in square B, with a 3 story brick dwlg & store & back bldgs thereon; 2nd parcel being lots 26 & 27 in square B, with 3 story brick dwlg, 2 stores, & back bldgs thereon; both parcels on the southerly side of Pa ave in the central business part of that city. Public auction in Wash City on Dec 23. Inquire of John W Maury, Pa ave. –Philo J Ruggles, Referee, N Y. R H Sherwood, Solicitor for Plntfs, 142 Broadway, N Y.

TUE NOV 25, 1851
Mrd: Nov 23, by Rev Mr Slattery, Mr Jas W Drane to Mrs Eliz A Jones, all of Wash City.

Mrd: on Nov 11, by Rev Mr Pendleton, of Fauquier, G Woodson Hansbrough to Virginia, daughter of Saml Chancellor, of Rappannock.

Instruction on the piano & singing, by Jos T Kepler. Apply at the Stationery Store of W Fischer, next door east of the Irving House.

For sale: desirable tract of land of Farm in Alexandria Co, Va, on Four-mile Creek, containing 230 acres: capable of being divided into 2 farms of 115 acres each. Refer to Edw Swann, Atty at Law, 5th st, or to Thos Swann, at Oakville, who will show the premises.

W H Standford, Merchant Tailor, north side of Pa ave, 4 doors west of 3rd st, under Gadsby's Hotel. I was employed in the establishment of P W Browning for 15 years, under his special charge in the most difficult branch of the Cutting Dept known to our trade. On hand I have a general assortment of necessary articles to complete a gentleman's wardrobe.

Handsome 2 story brick house & lot at auction: on north D between 9th & 10th sts, being part of lot 4 in square 378; adjoining the property of Mr T Donohoo.
-A Green, auctioneer

Furnished rooms for rent: one parlor & 4 chambers. Apply at the corner of 10th & C sts. —C Barry

Furnished house for rent: a gentleman, intending to pass the winter in the South, will rent for 6 months or more, the house he now occupies, a 3 story brick, well furnished, on F st. Apply to Mr Geo E French, at the Census Bureau, near the Genr'l Post Ofc.

Nat'l Hotel: remodeled & greatly improved: tables will be furnished with all the delicacies of the season. —M A Dexter

Strayed Cow broke into my lot: owner is come forward, prove property, pay charges, & take her away. —Wm Jenkins, 7th st, between P & Q sts.

Brick house, large garden, & paddock, within 250 yards of the Capitol garden, for rent. The paddock is 1 acre, & the bldgs adjoin the residence of the Minister from Spain. -Stephenson Scott, North B st, Capitol Hill.

Valuable mill, brick dwlg house, & 35 acres of rich meadow land attached, for sale: on Dec 22, at public auction. Persons wishing to view the property will call on Dr R B Alexander, whose residence adjoins the premises, or information can be obtained from Edw Swann, at his law ofc on 5th st. -Dyer & McGuire, aucts

WED NOV 26, 1851
Dr Granville Sharp Pattison, Prof of Anatomy in the Univ of N Y, died in N Y C, in his 60th year. He was a Scotchman by birth, & had been a resident of this country for many years. [No death date given-late item.]

Mrd: on Nov 17, by Rev Mathias Alig, in St Mary's Church, Mr Jos Bishop to Miss Gertrude Herbert.

Mrd: on Nov 22, by Rev Mathias Alig, in St Mary's Church, Mr Francis Rooney to Miss Eliz Connor, all of Wash City.

Died: on Nov 24, at the Navy Yard, Wash City, after an illness of 6 weeks, Thos Kelly, of Gtwn, D C, in his 40th year, leaving a wife & 6 children to mourn their loss. His funeral is today at 2 o'clock, from his late residence near Odd Fellows' Hall, Navy Yard.
+
I O O F: members of the Harmony Lodge, #9, to meet this day to attend the funeral of their late Brother, P G, Thomas Kelly. –John Grinder, N C

Died: yesterday, of consumption, Michl J Sheahan, in his 26th year. His funeral is this afternoon at half-past 3 o'clock, from the residence of his father on 1st st, near Pa ave.

Dog taken up, apparently astray, a yellow Setter Dog. Owner may recover him by applying to Jefferson Brown, [colored,] 6th st, north of G st.

For rent, to a punctual tenant, the 3 story brick dwlg on the n w corner of square 16, formerly occupied by Richd Rush, & recently by Mrs Geo Davis. Mrs Cummin will show the premises. Apply to Wm A Bradley.

Elegant parlor & bedroom for rent: opposite Selden, Withers & Co's Bank, 7th st.
-J Riggles

Mrs Richards, of Woodbury, daughter of the late John Osborn, of Naugatuck, while crossing the fields at the latter place, fell from a fence & broke her neck. Her daughter & brother were with her. She leaves a husband & 9 children. So says the Waterbury American.

THU NOV 27, 1851
Mrd: on Nov 19, in Richmond Va, by Rev C H Read, Jas D Bulloch, U S Navy, to Lizzie E, daughter of John Caskin, of Richmond.

Mrd: on Nov 25, by Rev John C Smith, Mr Noble D Larner to Miss Ann Mgt Keller, both of Wash City.

Died: on Nov 25, in Wash City, Mrs Mgt Watkins, in her 87th year. Her funeral will be from the residence of B F Beers, near the Navy Yard, today at 2 o'clock.

Died: on Nov 20, in Wash City, Mr Wilfred Smith, in his 43rd year.

Died: on Nov 24, at Harper's Ferry, Va, after a short illness, in his 34th year, Jas Walter Meem, oldest son of Geo A Meem, of Gtwn. His remains having been brought to town, his funeral will take place this morning, 10 o'clock, from the residence of his father-in-law, Mr Jas Murray, on High st.

Mrs Beveridge is prepared to accommodate a Congressional mess of Boarders during her ensuing session. Her house has been enlarged, & is on Pa ave, between 4½ & 3rd sts. -A F Beveridge -A Green, auct

Wash Corp: 1-Cmte on Improvements: bill for the relief of Wm Haggerty: passed. 2-Cmte of Claims: bill for the relief of Francis Holden: rejected. 3-Cmte on Police: bill for the relief of Chas McCarthy: passed. 4-Cmte of Claims: bill for the relief of Thos Williamson: passed. Same cmte: act for the relief of Robt Earl: passed. 5-Ptn of S A Peugh & others, for gravelling Delaware ave & N st: referred to the Cmte on Improvements. 6-Ptn of Anne R Dermott, praying permission to extend the steps of her bldg beyond the space allowed by law: referred to the Cmte on Improvement. 7-Cmte of Claims: asked to be discharged from the further consideration of the ptn of Washington Rawlings: which was agreed to. 8-Bill for the relief of Jas A Wise: passed. 9-Bill for the relief of M Holloran: passed.

Valuable farm, horses, cows, farming utensils, at auction: on Dec 10, on the premises, 150 acres on the Rockville Turnpike: the tract formerly belonged to the late Mr Burnett. Improvements consist of a new 2 story frame house with 7 rooms. -A Green, auct

The great Convention to nominate & present to the people of the U S the claims of the Hon Danl Webster for Presidency assembled on Nov 25 in Faneuil Hall, Boston.

The Union Academy, 14th st & N Y ave: Z Richards, Principal. Assistants: H Chase, H W McNeil. A C Richards, Teacher of the Primary Dept. A Zappoine, Teacher of Modern Languages. R Gibson, Teacher of Drawing & Painting.

SAT NOV 29, 1851
On Nov 4, the venerable & much esteemed poet, Jas Montgomery, completed his 80th year. In celebration, an oak tree was planted on the lawn of the Sheffield Infirmary. His name has been associated with the institution since it was projected in 1792. The ladies of Sheffield presented him with a friendship offering, a handsome beautifully carved easy chair. –London paper

Horses for sale: apply at Walley & Sutton's Livery Stable, on D. between 8th & 9th sts.

$25 reward for information that will lead to the conviction of the incendiary that set on fire the stable back of Jackson Hall last Thu, the property of the late Mrs D Galvin. -John P Pepper, J W Hicks, executors for the heirs.

Hardware, brushes & clocks: at the old established Variety Store, Pa ave, near 9th st. -Geo Savage

Appointment by the Pres: Nathl F Williams, Appraiser of Merchandise for the port of Balt, Md, vice Michl McBlair.

Dept of State, Wash, Nov 26, 1851. Information has been received from Jas F Waddell, U S Consul at Matamoros, of the murder by the Indians, high up on the Rio Grande river, of W C Frink, late a citizen of the U S. Mr Waddell has succeeded in recovering, & now has in his hands, a portion of the effects left by the deceased.

Mrs M France, 7th st, over the Nat'l Era ofc, will be pleased to accommodate gentlemen with board by the day, week, or month.

For rent: 2 handsomely furnished parlors, with bed chambers, on Pa ave, a few doors of the Nat'l Hotel. Inquire at the Jewelry store of the subscriber. –C W Haydon

Capt Wm E Dudley, aged about 77 years, was killed on Nov 21 by being thrown from his horse, while he was riding from his country residence to the city of Lexington, Ky. He was the eldest brother of Prof B W Dudley, & was esteemed for his high integrity.

Died: on Oct 20, at *Lapsley Hall*, his residence, near Bowling Green, Ky, Capt Thos Rogers, in his 86th year. He was a native of Caroline Co, Va; moved to Ky in 1811, & has since resided in this county. He was a brother of Capt John Rogers, of the cavalry, belonging to Gen Clark's expedition to the Illinois country, & maternal uncle of Hon J R Underwood, at present of the U S Senate from Ky. He died in the Christian's hope of a blessed immortality. [The Richmond Whig & Louisville Courier please copy.]

Five men drowned on Tue in Boston harbor by the swamping of a boat which was conveying three of them of them to the British steamer **Asia**. The names of 4 of them are known: Jas Hasket, John Sumner, David Watkins, & Alex'r Turnbull.

Died: on Nov 27, suddenly, John Augustus, son of Isaac & Johanah Hill, aged 6 years.

Summer Hill Farm, near the first mile-stone, adjoining the lands of A C Cazenove, on the Little River Turnpike, for sale. It contains 80 or 90 acres. Mr Padgett, at the toll-gate, will show the place. –Hugh Smith [For terms apply to Jas P Smith, Alexandria.]

Trustee's sale: by deed of trust from Wm Dowling, dated Jun 21, 1850, recorded in Liber J A S #15, folio 301, on Dec 29, lots 9, 10, & 11, in square 566, in Wash City. And by deed of trust from Wm Dowling, dated Aug 6, 1850, recorded in Liber J A S #16, folio 61, public sale for cash, part of lot 23 in square 254, in Wash City.
–E C Morgan, W E Howard, trustees -Dyer & McGuire, aucts

MON DEC 1, 1851

Hon John Ritter, formerly a Rep in Congress from Pa, died on Monday last, at his residence in Reading, from a stroke of apoplexy, under which he had been suffering since October last.

Cmder Wm M Armstrong has been ordered to the command of the ships in ordinary at the Gosport Navy Yard, in place of Cmder Dobnin.

At **Fort Wayne**, Indiana, on Nov 18, 2 young Germans, John Strung & Dedrick Reese, were found dead in their bed, while a third, a son of Mr Robt Armstrong, was barely alive. They had placed a small stove without a pipe, & put in some charcoal & lit it.

Millard Fillmore, Pres of the U S A, recognizes Henry A Shroeder, who has been appointed Consul of the Free & Hanseatic City of Hamburg, for Mobile, Ala. -Nov 25, 1851

Died: on Nov 30, Hannah Kettlewell, infant child S H & Hannah Ober. Relatives are invited to her funeral from F st, between 6th & 7th sts, at 3 o'clock, today.

TUE DEC 2, 1851

Organization of Congress. In the House of Reps: Hon Linn Boyd, of Ky, was, on the first trial, elected Speaker. John W Forney, of Pa, elected Clerk; A J Glossbrenner, of Pa, Sgt-at Arms; Z W McKnew, Doorkeeper, & John M Johnson, Postmaster of the House.

In the N Y Court of Oyer & Terminer on Sat, Antoine Lopez, a native of Spain, found guilty of the murder, by stabbing, of Michl Foster, policeman, 4th Ward, & Otto Grunzig, a native of Bavaria, found guilty of the murder, by poison, of his wife, were both sentenced to be hung

Mrd: on Nov 27, in Albemarle Co, Va, by Rev Chas E Ambler, Lt Henry H Bell, U S Navy, to Mgt C Henderson, daughter of the late Maj Richd Pollard.

Wash City Ordinances: 1-Act for the relief of Jas A Wise: to be paid $18.13, for fines paid by him on judgments rendered for keeping carts, the license on said carts having been paid in another person's name. 2-Act for the relief of Benj Bean: to be paid $70, in consideration of his horse being killed by a fall from the wing walls of the bridge across the canal at L st south, the same being broken & unsafe.

Died: on Nov 30, after a short illness, in her 22nd year, Mrs Eliz Chase, wife of Mr Wm Chase, of Wash City. Her funeral is today, 2 o'clock, from her late residence, 7th st & N Y ave & L st north.

Died: on Nov 24, at Annapolis, Md, Mrs Mary Ann Nelson, wife of Rev C K Nelson, & daughter of John Marbury, of Gtwn.

Died: on Nov 18, in Griffin, Ga, John C Mangham, jr, aged 28 years, late 2nd Lt & Adj of the 13th Regt of U S Infty.

Died: on Nov 15, at *Meadow Grove*, Fauquier Co, Va, the residence of his sister, Mrs Carter, Alex'r B Scott, in his 57th year.

Official: Gen Orders #60: War Dept, Adj Gen Ofc, Wash, Nov 29, 1851.
Promotions & appointment in the U S Army, made by the Pres, since the publication of Gen Orders, #39, Jul 19, 1851.
Promotions
Quartermaster's Dept:
Lt Col Thos F Hunt, Deputy Quartermaster Gen, to be Assist Quartermaster Gen, with rank of Colonel, Sep 16, 1851, vice Whiting, deceased.
Maj Danl D Tompkins, Quartermaster, to be Deputy Quartermaster Gen, with rank of Lt Col, Sep 16, 1851, vice Hunt, promoted.
Corps of Topographical Engineers: [Dated Aug 4, 1851.]
1st Lt John N Macomb, to be Capt, vice Hughes, resigned.
2nd Lt Geo Meade, to be 1st Lt, vice Macomb, promoted.
Bvt 2nd Lt Geo H Derby, to be 2nd Lt, vice Meade, promoted.
Ordnance Dept: [Dated Aug 31, 1851.]
2nd Lt Thos J Brereton, to be 1st Lt, vice Deshon, resigned.
Bvt 2nd Lt Silas Crispin, to be 2nd Lt, vice Brereton, promoted.
1st Regt of Dragoons: [Dated Oct 9, 1851.]
1st Lt John W T Gardiner, to be Capt, vice Kearny, resigned. [Co A]
2nd Lt John Adams, to be 1st Lt, vice Gardiner, promoted. [Co D]
2nd Lt Thos F Castor, to be 1st Lt, vice Couts, resigned. [Co A]
Bvt 2nd Lt Wm T Magruder, to be 2nd Lt, vice Castor, promoted. [Co B]
Bvt 2nd Lt Robt Ransom, jr, to be 2nd Lt, vice Adams, promoted. [Co I]
2nd Regt of Dragoons:
1st Lt Reuben P Campbell, to be Capt, Aug 8, 1851, vice Hamilton, deceased. [Assigned to Co E, vice May, transferred to Co A.]
1st Lt Wm Steele, to be Capt, Nov 10, 1851, vice Ker, resigned. [Co K]
2nd Lt Wm D Smith, to be 1st Lt, Aug 8, 1851, vice Campbell, promoted. [Co E]
2nd Lt Arthur D Tree, to be 1st Lt, Aug 11, 1851, vice McDonald, deceased. [Co B]
2nd Lt Saml H Starr, to be 1st Lt, Nov 10, 1851, vice Steele, promoted. [Co A]
Bvt 2nd Lt Lucius M Walker, to 2nd Lt, Aug 8, 1851, vice Smith, promoted. [Co H]
Bvt 2nd Lt John P Holiday, to be 2nd Lt, Oct 11, 1851, vice Tree, promoted. [Co B]
Bvt 2nd Lt Thos Bingham, to be 2nd Lt, Nov 10, 1851, vice Starr, promoted. [Co F]
Regt of Mounted Riflemen: Bvt 2nd Lt Alex'r McRae, to 2nd Lt, vice Stuart, dec'd, to date from Jul 1, 1851. [Co E]

1st Regt of Artl:
1st Lt Henry D Grafton, to be Capt, Sep 4, 1851, vice Fowler, deceased. [Co H]
2nd Lt Ambrose P Hill, to be 1st Lt, Sep 4, 1851, vice Grafton, promoted. [Co D]
Bvt 2nd Lt Caleb Huse, to be 2nd Lt, Sep 4, 1851, vice Hill, promoted. [Co A]
1st Regt of Artl: [Dated Oct 17, 1851.]
1st Lt Stephen D Carpenter, to be Capt, vice Plummer, deceased. [Co H]
2nd Lt Chas N Underwood, to be 1st Lt, vice Carpenter, promoted. [Co B]
Bvt 2nd Lt Saml H Reynolds, to be 2nd Lt, vice Underwood, promoted. [Co K]
3rd Regt of Infty:
2nd Lt Wm H Wood, to be 1st Lt, Sep 9, 1851, vice Williamson, resigned. [Co H]
Bvt 2nd Lt Martin P Parks, jr, to 2rc Lt, Jul 24, 1851, vice Brower, dismissed [Co F]
Bvt 2nd Lt Wm D Whipple, to be 2nd Lt, Sep 9, 1851, vice Wood, promoted. [Co C]
5th Regt of Infty: [Dated Aug 4, 1851.]
2nd Lt Edw F Abbott, to be 1st Lt, vice Farrelly, deceased. [Co B]
Bvt 2nd Lt Henry C Bankhead, to be 2nd Lt, vice Abbott, promoted. [Co A]
7th Regt of Infty: [Dated Aug 24, 1851.]
1st Lt Lafayette McLaws, to be Capt, vice Ross, deceased, & Page & Dana, Capts in the Staff, who vacate their regimental commissions. [Co D]
2nd Lt Matthew R Stevenson, to be 1st Lt, vice Page, Assist Adj, who vacates his regimental commission. [Co H]
2nd Lt Wm H Tyler, to be 1st Lt, vice Dana, Assist Quartermaster, who vacates his regimental commission. [Co C]
Bvt 2nd Lt Gurden Chapin, to be 2nd Lt, vice Stevenson, promoted. [Co K]
Bvt 2nd Lt Thos J C Amory, to be 2nd Lt, vice Tyler, promoted. [Co F]
Bvt 2nd Lt Edw A Palfrey, to be 2nd Lt, vice Wilcox, promoted. [Co I]
II-Appointments: Ordnance Dept:
Jas M McRea, of La, to be Military Storekeeper, Apr 28, 1851, vice Devall, declined.
Briscoe G Baldwin, jr, of Ala, to be Military Storekeeper, Oct 2, 1851, vice McRea, resigned.
III-Casualties: Resignations:
Bvt Lt Col Geo W Hughes, Capt Topographical Engineers, Aug 4, 1851.
Bvt Maj Philip Kearny, Capt 1st Dragoons, Oct 9, 1851.
Capt Crogan Ker, 2nd Dragoons, Nov 10, 1851.
Capt Arthur B Lansing, Assist Quartermaster, Sep 1, 1851.
1st Lt Andrew J Williamson, 3rd Infty, Sep 9, 1851.
1st Lt Cave J Couts, 1st Dragoons, Oct 9, 1851.
1st Lt Geo Deshon, Ordnance Dept, Oct 31, 1851.
Bvt 2nd Lt Jas H Wilson, 1st Infty, Sep 1, 1851.
Military Storekeeper Jas M McRea, Ordnance Dept, Jul 31, 1851.
Commissions vacated under provisions of the 7th section of the act of Jun 18, 1846.
1st Lt Francis N Page, *7th Infty, Aug 24, 1851, Assist Adj Gen.
1st Lt Napoleon J T Dana, *7th Infty, Aug 24, 1851, Assist Quartermaster.
Removed:
Military Storekeeper, John S Evans, Ordnance Dept, Nov 18, 1851.

Deaths:
Bvt Brig Gen Henry Whiting, Col Assist Quartermaster Gen, at St Louis, Mo, Sep 16, 1851.
Bvt Lt Col Richd H Ross, Capt 7th Infty, at Boston, Mass, Aug 24, 1851.
Bvt Maj Philip W McDonald, 1st Lt 2nd Dragoons, at New Orleans, La, Oct 11, 1851.
Capt Saml M Plummer, 1st Infty, at **Fort Merrill**, Texas, Oct 17, 1851.
* *Bvt Capt Jas Stuart, 2nd Lt, Mounted riflemen, Jun 18, 1851.
Capt Wm H Fowler, 1st Artl, at **Fort Myers**, Fla, Sep 4, 1851.
Capt Fowler Hamilton, 2nd Dragoons, on San Saba river, Texas, Aug 8, 1851.
1st Lt Patrick A Farrelly, 5th Infty, at Camp near **Fort Washita**, Ark, Aug 4, 1851.
Bvt 2nd Lt De Witt N Root, 3rd Artl, at Mohawk, N Y, Aug 4, 1851.
Dismissed:
2nd Lt Chas B Brower, 3rd Infty, Jul 24, 1851.
By order of the Sec of War: R Jones, Adj Gen
*-Regimental commission [only] vacated.
* *-Of wounds received, Jun 17, 1851, in affair with Indians on Rogue river, Oregon.

Died: on Nov 30, after a short illness, in her 22nd year, Mrs Eliz Chase, wife of Mr Wm Chase, of Wash City. Her funeral is today, 2 o'clock, from her late residence, 7th st & N Y ave & L st north.

Died: on Nov 24, at Annapolis, Md, Mrs Mary Ann Nelson, wife of Rev C K Nelson, & daughter of John Marbury, of Gtwn.

Died: on Nov 18, in Griffin, Ga, John C Mangham, jr, aged 28 years, late 2nd Lt & Adj of the 13th Regt of U S Infty.

Died: on Nov 15, at **Meadow Grove**, Fauquier Co, Va, the residence of his sister, Mrs Carter, Alex'r B Scott, in his 57th year.

WED DEC 3, 1851
Sale of land in Spottsylvania Co, Va: farm land within 3 miles of Fredericksburg, containing on or about 300 acres, with a neat & comfortable dwlg house, with all the necessary out houses. For particulars apply to Peyton Johnston, Richmond, Va.

Com'rs Ofc, Alexandria, Nov 26, 1851. Notice to stockholders named in the subjoined list to call upon Messrs A C Cazenove, E Hoffman, & Reuben Johnston, trustees, to receive their dividends declared. –Jos Eaches, Com
[List as of Jun 12, 1851.]

Adams, Austin L	Beverly, Robt
Adams, Susan W	Bennett, Chas, deceased
Auld, Colin	Beeler, Louis
Bartleman, Wm, estate	Burne, Andrew
Balmaine, Alex	Bierne, Geo

Boyd, John, estate
Cazenove, A C
Carter, Chas
Chapman, John
Cabell, Jos C
Cracroft, E O
Dulin, John, guardian of John A Somers' children
Dunbar, Jno R W
Fairfax, Thos, estate
Fairfax, A B
Fairfax, Orlan
Fire Ins Co of Alexandria
Fire Ins Co, of Balt
Foote, Fred'k
Fowle, Wm H, trustee of M S Turner
Fowle, Geo D, trustee of E T Fowle
Gardner, Wm C
Gernon, Richd
Griffith, Israel
Grubb, J B
Harrant, Jos
Harrison, B E
Hopkins, B & R Hull, trustees under the will of Jos Janney, deceased.
Howard, John B
Hoof, John, trustee for widows & orphans of deceased clergymen
Janney, Jn, deceased
Jamieson, Andrew
Janney, Jh, deceased
Janney, Jonathan, executor of I Taylor
Janney, Hannah
Jacobs, Presley
Kenworthy, Wm
Kennedy, Susannah
Keith, Jas
Lawson, John
Lewis, Lawrence
Leonard, Sophia
McKnight, Chas
McKenna, Nan R
Muncaster, J & E I Lee, Wardens of Christ Church
Nichols, Isaac
Nixon, Sarah
Norris, Wm H
Nichols, Wm S

Conway, Mary
Dixon, Turner
Dixion, Geo O
Dumbar, Laura
Dunbar, Eliz A
Hair, Mary
Harden, Ann E
Hewes, Deborah
Hewes, Eliza
Hewes, Sarah A
Hewes, Rachel
Hewes, Mary M
Herbert, J C, estate
Herbert, Alfred
Herbert, Mary V
Herbert, Eu F
Herbert, Julia
Herbert, Emma
Herbert, Lu, jr
Hewes, Cath
Hopkins, Saml
Marine Ins Co of Alexandria
Megrath, Owen F
Massie, J W, estate
Mason, R B, estate
Meschert, Hazzenga
Miller, Saml
Miller, Mordecai & son
Miller, Wm H
Miller, John S
Mills, John
Milburn, Ann
Minor, Smith
Muir, Jas, deceased
Norris, Edw
Norris, Eliza
Paton, Ann B
Paton, Rebecca

Peters, Geo
Peyton, Francis, trustee for Susanna G Gibson
Powell, Burr
Randolph, Peyton, trustee for R Singleton
Richards, John, deceased
Roberts, John
St Andrew's Society
Saunders, Robt
Stabler, Edw, estate
Sewell, W H B
W Jones
Semmes, Thos, deceased
Steer, Chas J
Steed, Juliana M
Smith, Lydia
Sommers, Eliza
Snowden, Edgar
Stuart, Sally J
Stuart, A C
Trustees Alexandria Academy
Tucker, St G, deceased
Trustees Bank of Potomac
Tucker, N F B
Van Havre, John Michl A
Van Bibber, Washington
Vowell, John C
Washington, J A, deceased
Washington, J C, executrix
Wash, G C, trustee of B Washington, jr
Washington, B, guardian of B W & N Herbert
Washington, B C
Walte, Obed, guardian
Weaver, Jacob
Whiting, Wm B
Whitmore, Saml
White, Eliz
Yeates, Wm
Waters, Wm, of Henry, Wm Waters, of Walter, & Danl Ruff Waters, of Harford Co, Md

Senate: 1-Memorial of Henry M Rice, praying for a grant of land for the construction of a railroad from the St Louis river of Lake Superior, via St Paul, in Minnesota Territory, to Dubuque, in the State of Iowa.

Virginia election: names of the candidates of both parties for State ofcrs, as follows:

	Whigs	Democrat
For Govn'r	Geo W Summers	Jos Johnson
Lt Govn'r	Saml Watts	Shelton F Leake
Atty Gen	Sidney S Baxter	Willie P Bocock

Fresh Family Groceries: La ave, opposite Bank of Wash. -E E White & Co

Naval: Capt John H Aulick has been recalled from the command of the East India squadron, for which station he recently sailed in the U S steamer **Susquehanna**, Capt Inman. Cmdor M C Perry has been designated as the successor of Capt Aulick. The reasons for the recall of Capt Aulick are said to be based upon reports made against him by Messrs Schenck & Todd, the present & late Ministers to Brazil; also by Capt Inman, whom Capt Aulick ordered home.

Shirts: to Members of Congress, Citizens, & Strangers. Wm H Faulkner, Shirt Manufacturer, south side of Pa ave, opposite the U S Hotel: at the Sign of the Shirt.

Dr John Richards, late of Alexandria, Va, has located himself in Washington: ofc on Pa ave, below 3rd st, near Adams' Express Ofc.

Notice to all whom it may concern. I have for sale the latest & most improved covered tilting or dumping Wagon now in use in the U S. —A V Cross, Wheelwright & Blacksmith, G st, between 6th & 7th sts.

Mrd: on Nov 27, by Rev David Kerr, Rector of Rock Creek Parish, at the residence of Geo W Riggs, Mr Tobias F Talbert to Miss Eliz Perry, all of the District of Columbia.

Mrd: on Dec 1, by Rev David Kerr, Rector of Rock Creek Parish, Mr Harvey M Newhouse to Miss Sarah Dawson, both of Fauquier Co, Va.

Died: on Dec 2, Wm Quigly, aged 20 months & 3 days, son of Wm & Mary Quigly. His funeral is at 2 o'clock.

THU DEC 4, 1851

Nat'l Theatre: management & corps dramatique are as follows: E A Marshall, sole lessee; W M Fleming, stage manager. Company Messrs W M Fleming, H C Jordan, Marchant, C Hill, C B Hill, H Tuthill, Harris, G B Vining, Owen, St Clair, Thorpe, Ryder, Walters, Hainer, Powellin, Chas Wood, Duremay. Prompter C Baker; scenic artist, C Lamb. Ladies of the company, Misses Heron, Raymond, Millington, Baker, Curry, & Hayes; Mesdames Hield, Hill, Thorpe, & Owen. Messrs Hilliard & Grain are also engaged for the scenery & decorations for the opening.

Rooms for rent. Apply to M A Stettinius, La ave, opposite City Hall.

The wife of Edmund Ray, of Norwich, on Tue last, had occasion for the use of morphine, but by mistake strychnine was sent her. She died in about an hour. She was an active member of the Baptist Church.

Mrd: on Mon, in Wash City, by Rev Mr Hill, Mr Wm H Scott to Miss Martha E Davison, daughter of Saml C Davis, all of Wash City.

Mrd: on Tue, by Rev Mr Wayman, Mr Saml Proctor, of Balt, to Miss Cassa Ann Martin, of Rockville, Md.

Mrd: on Nov 25, at the *Grove*, near Warrenton, Fauquier Co, Va, by Rev Geo Norton, Alfred B Carter, of Mississippi, to Bettie, daughter of Capt C C Randolph, of Va.

Died: on Tue last, in Wash City, Lydia Jane, wife of Mr David H Hanlon, of Balt, Md. Her funeral is today at 11 o'clock, from the residence of her brother, Jas F Haliday, 11th st west.

Died: on Dec 2, in Wash City, after a very short illness, Francis Barry, sr, in his 40th year. His funeral is from his late residence, 7th st east [Navy Yard,] today at 2 o'clock, & from St Peter's Church, Capitol Hill, at 3 o'clock.

Died: on Dec 2, after a short illness, in her 9th year, Amelia Elenora Little, daughter of Jas & Araminta Little. Her funeral is today at 2 o'clock, from her father's residence, on Va ave.

Orphans Court of Wash Co, D C. Letters testamentary on the personal estate of Frances Proctor, late of Wash Co, deceased. –Chas S Wallach, exec

FRI DEC 5, 1851
Senate: 1-Memorial from Foster B Pratt, asking compensation for the services & sufferings of his father in the war of the Revolution: ordered to lie on the table. 2-Memorial from J A Ragan, asking permission to execute a plan invented by him for draining the lands overflown by the Mississippi: ordered to lie on the table.

Original letter of Danl Boone to Gov Shelby. Feburey the 11th, 1796. Sir-after my Best Respts to your Excellency and family I wish to inform you that I have some intention of under-taking this New Rode that is to be Cut through the Wilderness and I think My Self intitled to the ofer of the Bisness as I first Marked out the Rode in March 1775 and Never Re'd any thing for trubel and Sepose I am no Statesman I am a Woodsman and think My Self as Capable of Marking & Cutting that Rode as any other man Sir if you think with Me I would thank you to wright mee a Line By the post the first opportunity and he Will Lodge it at Mr John Miler's on hinkstone fork as I wish to know When and Where it is to be Last [let] So that I many attend at the time I am Deer Sir your very omble sarvent. Daniel Boone To his Excellency governor Shelby.

Circuit Court of Wash Co, Md: a few days ago: C Hildebrand, the dfndnt in the case, was fined $2 & costs by a magistrate, for going round the toll-gate to avoid paying three cents toll, & the Circuit Court sustained his decision.

I certify that John B Wiltberger, of Wash Co, D C, brought before me as an estray trespassing on his enclosures in said county, a gray horse. –C H Wiltberger, J P [Owner can prove property, pay charges, & take him away. –John B Wiltberger, near Rock Creek Church]

Accident on the Cocheco [N H] Railroad on Fri, near Dover: killed instantly were Saml Troombley, engineer; Chas Young & Richd McCluskey, assist engineers. Troombley leaves a wife & 5 children.

For sale, a very superior cook, washer, & ironer, with one child. Inquire of Brooke Mackall, in Gtwn, or his ofc, F & 14th sts.

Marshal's sale: by writ of fieri facias: sale of part of lot 23 in square 254, in Wash City, near Geo Miller's & Nelson's property: seized & levied upon as the property of Wm Dowling, & will be sold on Dec 27, to satisfy #26 to Mar. 1852, in favor of Geo Cover, surviving administrator of Wm Hayman. –Richd Wallach, Marshal, D C

Mrd: on Thu, by Rev John C Smith, Peter Daggy to Miss Julia Lunt, all of Wash City.

Mrd: on Dec 3, at the U S Hotel, by Rev W T Eva, Wm O Johnson to Virginia A Harper, all of Louisa Co, Va.

Died: on Dec 3, suddenly, Patrick Dowling, in his 61st year, a native of the county Farmanagh, Ireland, but for the last 35 years a citizen of the District of Columbia. His funeral is from the residence of his brother, Wm Dowling, on F st, between 13th & 14th sts, tomorrow, at 3 o'clock.

SAT DEC 6, 1851

Died: on Dec 5, Isaac S Lauck, in his 59th year. Descended from a Revolutionary sire, the son, at an early age, in the war of 1812, marched as a volunteer from the same place [his native town of Winchester, Va,] whence his father had marched in the war of independence, to meet the enemies of his country, & to assist in driving them from the soil of his native State. His funeral is this afternoon at 3 o'clock, from his late residence on G st north, between 12th & 13th sts.

Household & kitchen furniture at auction: on Dec 11, at the residence of Mr Wm Chase, on 7th st, between K & L sts. -A Green, auctioneer

Danl Campbell, Saddle, Trunk, & Harness Maker. N B: Saddles made on the new style of trees imported from pairs, & Grimsby's equipment for army ofcrs. [Address not given.]

Desirable residence for rent, on the corner of 13th & H sts. Inquire of Mrs Knott, on the premises.

Horace B Conklin was executed at Utica, N Y, by hanging, a few days since, for house-burning.

Postmaster Gen est'd the following new Post Ofcs for week ending Nov 22, 1851.

Ofc	County, State	Postmaster
West Township	Albany, N Y	Stephen Van Etten
Clovesville	Delaware, N Y	Robt Humphrey
Sherretania	Erie, Pa	Andrew J Sterrett
Plum	Venango, Pa	Nathl Morse
Hemlock Grove	Meigs, Ohio	Byard McKinly
Deerlick	Mason, Va	Thos C Hill
Tumbling Greek	Tazeville, Va	Jas B Crabtree
Wilt's Spur	Patrick, Va	Jos H Edwards
Big Cedar Creek	Greenbrier, Va	Andrew H McClung
Scrabble	Beckley, Va	A R McQuilkin
Oak Grove	Union, N C	Saml W Rodgers
Elk Spur	Wilkes, N C	Jas Roberts
Indian Creek	Newbury, S C	Nathan F Johnson
Algooa	Stratanburg, S C	Willis Smith
Laffing Gal	Cherokee, Geo	Saml Hunt
Round Hill	Lumpskin, Geo	Dennis Hide
Bay Creek	Laurens, Geo	Michl Livinston
Camp Ground	Appling, Geo	Benien Hall
Piney Head	Appling, Geo	Neil Wilkinson
Hall	Appling, Geo	H J Smith
Cobbsville	Telfair, Geo	*Ddward J McDuffie
Emuckfair	Talapoosa, Ala	Benj Waller
Pilahatchee	Rankin, Miss	Edwin Lambreth
Magnolia	Anderson, Texas	Wm Haygood
Fairfield	Freestone, Texas	Dunbar Bragg
Cotton Gin	Freestone, Texas	Jas S Willis
Iverson	Bienville, La	Jno McDoual
Cork	Dearborn, Ia	Byant, Connally
Parker's Settlement	Posey, Ia	Wm J Deubler
Butlerville	Jennings, Ia	John Morris
Oakdam	Vanderburg, Ia	Edw Ingle
Irving	Noble, Ia	John Foster
Brocktown	Pike, Ark	Jackson Brock
Elon	Ashley, Ark	A B C Winfrey
Flag Pond	Washington, Tenn	John Woodard
Rushing's Creek	Benton, Tenn	Willis Rushing
Old Farm	*Wawrence, Ill	Aaron Beck
Cincinnati	Appanoose, Iowa	Jos Welsh

Names Changed: 1-Hobbieville, Alleghany Co, N Y, changed to Belvidere.
2-Clovesville, Delaware Co, N Y, changed to Griffin's Corners.
3-Wellsville, Newbury, N C, changed to Chappell's Bridge. [*Copied as written.]

Cigar Store for sale: corner of F & 11th sts. Subscriber desirous of relinquishing his business. –Wm Finly

$2 reward for lost purse: return to Mrs Dr J Green, C st, near 4½ st.

MON DEC 8, 1851

Letter from Paris, Nov 17, 1851. The frig **St Lawrence** was to bring to the U S the remains of Admiral Paul Jones. The remains are in the leaden coffin in which the Directory of France caused them to be interred; they remain covered by a bldg, & are now 15 feet below the surface. If our Congress choose to give some money to get them they can be soon in our Capitol Cemetery.

The St Louis Republican: disastrous collision on the Mississipi river between the steamer **Die Vernon** & the steamer **Archer**, by which the **Archer** sunk & lost all. This occurred on Nov 27, at Enterprise Island. Twenty-four passengers & 10 deck hands were drowned. Sarah Dick, a young woman, & a little boy, ___ Smyers, were saved. All the rest of their family were lost: Jas Smyers, sen, Jas Smyers, jr, Jane Smyers, Mary Smyers, Caroline Smyers, Mgt Ann Smyers, Sarah Smyers, & Ellen Smyers.

Criminal Court [Washington] met on Monday last, Judge Crawford presiding.

The Grand Jury:

Peter Force, foreman	Thos Brown	Jas C McGuire
Saml Drury	W T Dove	B W Reed
Andrew Rothwell	Geo W Riggs	Wm B Kibbey
Elexius Semmes	Geo Lowry	John G Robinson
Chas F Wood	Gotlieb C Grammer	Enos Ray
Harvey Cruttenden	John Van Riswick	Chas R Belt
Jonathan Prout	Peter F Bacon	
Judson Mitchell	Zach Walker	

The Petty Jury:

Danl Hauptman	Francis B Lord	Barton Hachney
Wm P McKelden	Robt M Harrison	Guy Graham
John W Delaware	Hugh Dougherty	Lincoln Chapin
Hudson Taylor	Anthony L Ray	Wm Burroughs
Thos P Morgan	Thos E Jacobs	John Wise
Jos Whitney	Wm Clarke	David Koones
Henry D Gunnell	Geo B Smith	Wm Lord
Benj F Morsell	Anthony Shoemaker	Geo T McGlue
Chas M Wright	Rickd Butt	Peter Magruder
Geo W Hopkins	Saml Perkins	Jos F Burke

1-First case was that of Jos & Hugh Dowling, for an assault on Thos Hunter, of Gtwn: convicted & fined $10 each & costs. 2-Ellen Frank tried for an assault on Catherine Davis, a small girl: case submitted to the Court: Ellen fined $1.

3-Jeremiah Toomey, indicted for an assault on Alex'r Dubant: fined $10. 4-Jeremiah & Timothy Toomey, for a riot, fined, the former $1, & the latter $5. 5-Dennis Toomey, indicted for assault & battery, with intent to kill, on Alex'r Dubant, fined $10 for assault, & for a riot, $1. 6-Jas Lyles, for assault on constable Wollard, sentenced to 4 months in the county jail, & fined $5. 7-Negro Robt Bruce, for assault & resisting constable Adams in the discharge of his duty: 3 months in jail, & fined $5. 8-Mary Sandford, indicted for an assault on Hester Mills, submitted her case to the Court: fined $5. 9-Benj Mortimer was acquitted on one indictment for larceny. On a second indictment for larceny, to the value of $4, on property in charge of Mrs Eliza Plant, as executrix, Mortimer was convicted. 10-Andrew McCabe, for an assault on his wife, submitted, & was fined. 11-Timothy & Honora Sullivan were indicted for keeping a disorderly house, & found guilty. They were also convicted of retailing liquor without a license, & fined $16. 12-Negro Jas Degges was convicted of stealing a dish belonging to the U S of the value of $1.50. This being his 4th or 5th offence, he was sentenced to the penitentiary for 3 years. 13-Saml Cooper, Saml Payne, Elias Sims, & Sunny Matthews were convicted of a riot. Matthews, being the youngest, was fined $1. The others were sentenced to 2 months in jail each, with a fine of $5 each. 14-The case of Augustus Kenny, for an assault on constable Wm Hickerson, was abandoned by the prosecuting atty, on account of a misfinding by the Grand Jury. 15-Phelim McKenna found guilty of an assault on Wm Hickerson: fined $8. 16-Robt Maud, indicted for an assault on Benedict Jost, submitted, & was fined $5. 17-Negro Wm Parker, alias Bill Johnston, was found guilty of stealing a vest worth $2.50, belonging to Geo Staffer: sentenced to 9 months in jail & fined $1.

Health Report, Wash, Dec 6, 1851. 53 interments during the month of Nov, 1851. -Thos Miller, M D, Pres of the Board of Health.

The Herald of the Union: is a new monthly newspaper just started in N Y, with C Edwards Lester, as Editor.

Nashville Whig: Gen Cullom was tried before the Gainsboro Circuit Court, for the killing of Davidson, & triumphantly acquitted: self-defence.

House of Reps: 1-Ptn of H J de Bruin & 43 others, citizens of Adams Co, Ohio, praying Congress to relieve Lindsey Gossett, as one of the securities of Isaac Prutzman, late postmaster at Scott, Adams Co, Ohio.

Lydia S Hall has recovered, in an action before the Supreme Court of Mass, $1,400 damages of the city of Lowell, for injuries received by her in falling upon the icy sidewalks of that city, by which her thigh bone was broken, & she was confined to her bed for several months.

Capt Kidd not a pirate. Meeting of the N Y Historical Society, on Tue, Judge Campbell, one of its members, delivered an address in vindication of Capt Kidd, in which he showed that Kidd had been an ofcr in the English Navy prior to 1691, when he married in this country, & took the command of a merchant ship owned by Mr Robt Livingston. About 1695 the coasts of New England were infested with pirates, & the Earl of Belmont, whom the King had sent out as Govn'r, proposed to the home Gov't to fit out a ship of 30 guns & 150 men, & commission Capt Kidd to command her in a cruise against the buccaneers. The Gov't was unable to furnish the vessel, but the Earl of Belmont, Lords Halifax, Somers, Romney, Orford, & others contributed, & entered into articles of agreement with Livingston & Kidd: filed on Dec 11, 1695. The **Adventure** galley was fitted out, & in Apr, Capt Kidd sailed to N Y, & commenced operation as a privateer. The Whig noblemen concerned in fitting out the ship **Adventure** were impeached. Rumors were spread that Capt Kidd had turned pirate, & when he entered Boston in Jun, 1699, he was seized & sent to England, where he was convicted of piracy, & executed in May, 1781. The impeached lords were afterwards acquitted.

Millard Fillmore, Pres of the U S A, recognizes C H F Moering, who has been appointed Consul of the Free & Hanseatic City of Bremen, at Boston, Mass. –Dec 5, 1851

Mrd: on Dec 4, in Gtwn, by Rev John Lanahan, Mr John H Meredith, of Wash City, to Miss Ellen G Wilson.

Died: on Nov 27, at Brownsville, N Y, suddenly, Mgt Lovel, wife of John E Brown, & daughter of the late Maj Gen Jacob Brown.

Household & kitchen furniture at auction: by order of the Orphans Court of Wash Co, D C: sale on Dec 11, at the residence of Frances Proctor, deceased, on Md ave, near the foot of the Capitol. –C W Boteler, auct

In Chancery. Thos Sewall, exec of Thos Sewall, W M Addison, & others, vs Jod T Costin, adm of Basil Simms & Sarah, Joshua, Caleb, David, & Mary Sims. The creditors of the late Basil Sims & the above named, are to attend at my ofc, in City Hall, Wash, on Jan 2, when I shall state an account of the personal estate of said Sims, the value of his real estate, & the debts owing by him. –W Redin, Auditor

TUE DEC 9, 1851
Miss E Gregg, of Balt, informs the ladies of Washington that she will open on Dec 11, a handsome assortment of French Millinery, over Geo F Allen's store, Pa ave, at 10th st.

Watch Repairing: I have re-established under the Nat'l Hotel. –Chauncey Warriner

Senate: 1-Ptn of Wm P Greene, on the files of the Senate: referred to the Cmte on Commerce. 2-Ptn & papers of the heirs of Wm Barton: referred to the Cmte on Pensions. 3-Ptn of Ira Day, on the files of the Senate: referred to the Cmte on Post Ofc & Post Roads. 4-Ptn of Azel Spalding: referred to the Cmte on Pensions. 5-Ptn of John H McGraw, on the files of the Senate: referred to the Cmte on Commerce. 6-Memorial of the heirs of Judith Worthen: referred to the Cmte on Pensions. 7-Memorial of Rufus Dwinnell: referred to the Cmte on the Post Ofc & Post Roads. 8-Memorial of Wm H Topping, on the files of the Senate: referred to the Cmte of Claims. 9-Ordered that Johnston Lykins have leave to withdraw his petition & papers. Same for Wm Rall. 10-Ordered that the petition & papers of W D Aiken be withdrawn, & referred to the Cmte on Naval Affairs. 11-Ptn of Sarah Bennett, widow of Ashael P Bennett, asking compensation for his services during the Revolutionary war: referred to the Cmte on Pensions. 12-Ptn of Hugh W Dobbin, asking compensation for his services as an ofcr in the last war with Great Britain: referred to the Cmte on Pensions. 13-Ptn of Hugh N Page & other ofcrs of the Navy, asking additional compensation in consideration of peculiar hardships & increased expenses to which they were subjected while in Calif: & of the petty ofcrs, seamen, & marines, who served in the frig **Savannah** during her cruise in the Pacific in 1849, asking addition pay: referred to the Cmte on Naval Affairs. 14-Bill introduced for the relief of Mrs E A McNeil, widow of the late Gen John McNeill. 15-Bill introduced for the relief of Mrs A M Dade, widow of the late Maj F L Dade, U S Army. 16-Memorial of E D Reynolds, a purser in the navy, asking compensation for his services as a naval storekeeper at San Francisco, & to be allowed the pay of a purser to a sloop-of-war for the time he performed the duties: referred to the Cmte on Naval Affairs. 17-Memorial of Wm Cranch, chief judge of the District Court of the U S for the District of Columbia, asking compensation for services in hearing & determining appeals from the decisions of the Com'r of Patents in certain cases: referred to the Cmte on the Judiciary. 18-Memorial of Winthrop Coffin, & Howard, Son & Co, proposing to establish a line of steamers between Boston & New Orleans, & asking that they may be authorized to contract for carrying the mail between those ports: referred to the Cmte on Naval Affairs. 19-Ptn of John Erwin, a settler on the Bastrop grant, asking to be allowed a section of land in lieu of a section he had been dispossessed of by the U S: referred to the Cmte on Private Land Claims. 20-Ptn of Thos J Durant, asking payment of a balance due him on a settlement of his accounts, & that he may be authorized to institute a suit against the U S for the purpose of obtaining a judicial decision of his claim: referred to the Cmte on the Judiciary 21-Memorial of Hezekiah Miller, a clerk in the Indian bureau, asking to be allowed certain arrears of pay: referred to the Cmte of Claims. 22-Ptn of David P Weeks, a pensioner of the U S, asking to be allowed arrears of pension: referred to the Cmte on Pensions. 23-Ptn of Jas Jeffries & P M Smith, asking to be released from a forfeiture incurred under a contract for carrying the mail: referred to the Cmte on the Post Ofc & Post Roads. 24-Ptn of Tarenor McKay & others, of Carson Valley, Calif, asking the grant of a certain tract of land in that State for the purpose of settlement & cultivation: referred to the Cmte on Public Lands. 25-Ordered that the papers of Wm

Hultzmann, on the files of the Senate, be referred to the Cmte on Military Affairs. 26-Ordered that the petition of John Moore White, on the files of the Senate, be referred to the Cmte on Revolutionary Claims. 27-Ordered that the petition & papers of the heirs of John Rice Jones, on the files of the Senate, be referred to the Cmte on Private Land Claims. 28-Ordered that the petition & papers, on the files of the Senate, of Saml F Butterworth, be referred to the Cmte on Post Ofcs & Post Roads.

The veteran Gen Walbach, who has served more than 50 years in the U S Army, is to reside at Baltimore as commandant of the 3rd military dept. He is now in his 86th year. He entered the army in 1799 as a lt & adj of cavalry, by invitation of Gen Washington, having come to this country on a visit after serving in the army of Louis XVI, until that monarch's imprisonment, & subsequently with the combined armies on the Rhine & in the Netherlands until 1797, when he covered the retreat of the Duke of York after the battle of Dunkirk.

The steamer **Baltimore** during the balance of the season, will make but one trip a week. Leave Wash on Monday at 7 a m & Balt on Thu at 4 p m. Apply to Chas Worthington, Balt; or Geo Mattingly, Agent, Wash. –B F Darricott, Capt

Highly valuable real estate for sale: decree of the Circuit Court of Fairfax Co, in the suit of Hannah B Terrett, etc, against Wm H Terrett & others, the undersigned Com'rs will sell, on Jan 3 next, the **Oaklands**, of which Geo H Terrett died seized, in said county, near **Cloud's Mill**: will be sold in 6 several parcels, as follows:
Lot 1-142 acres, 3 roods, & 4 poles.
Lot 2: 220 acres, 1 rood, & 11½ poles: with a frame dwlg house with 8 rooms.
Lot 3: 235 acres, 3 roods & 37½ poles.
Lot 4: 227 acres & 3 roods.
Lot 5: 182 acres & 35 poles.
Lot 6: 111 acres & 25½ poles, adjoining **Cloud's Mill**.
Also a small lot of 15 acres with a small log tenement thereon, near John Jackson's, on the road leading from the Columbia turnpike to the Theological Seminary. Tracts will be shown by Wm H Terrett, or N C Hunter, who reside on the premises, & who have a plat of the recent survey & division above referred to.
–Wm H Dulany, Com'r

Very desirable Farm for sale: by decree of the Circuit Court of Fairfax Co, in the case of Jas Sinclair & others, against Danl F Dulany & others, at Jun term, 1851: public auction on Jan 21, 1851, of the Farm belonging to Lt Danl F Dulany, U S Navy; adjoining the lands of Reid, McNerhany & others, containing 190 acres. Improvements consist of a new Frame dwlg house, barn, stable, & other outbldgs. Household & kitchen furniture at auction: at the same time & place.
–Wm H Dulany, Alfred Moss, Com'rs

For rent: 3 parlors with bedchambers attached, all furnished, at Jas McColgan's, Pa ave, opposite the Irving Hotel, between 12th & 13th sts.

Fatal accident occurred this morning, between K & L & 10th & 11th sts, in Wash City. A number of men were at work digging earth from the side of a hill when the embankment gave way. Patrick Lynch, an unmarried man, 33 or 34, was instantly killed. Thos Burns, age 40 years, had both bones of the left forearm broken; his chest & back much bruised. His is a serious case. He was taken to the Infirmary. J B McGill was injuried, & Jas Noland slightly. -Telegraph

Mrd: on Dec 3, at Goodwood, PG Co, Md, by Rev Mr Mackenheimer, Col Oden Bowie to Alice, 2nd daughter of Chas H Carter.

For rent: 2 fine parlors & 3 lodging rooms, furnished, on Capitol Hill. Inquire of Isaac Holland, Senate Chamber.

Died: on Sunday last, in Wash City, Mrs Beulah Stelle, relict of the late Pontius D Stelle, aged 84 years. Mrs Stelle was one of the oldest inhabitants of Wash, having come here from N J with the Gov't in 1800. She was one of the young ladies chosen to strew flowers in the path of Washington as he crossed tha bridge at Trenton, on his visiting N Y & the Eastern States while Pres of the U S. Her funeral is today at 2:30 p m, from the residence of her son, Mr E B Stelle.

Died: on Dec 8, in Wash City, Mrs Mary Douglas Stetson, formerly of Alexandria, Va, consort of the late Capt John Stetson, of Mass, in her 51st year. Her funeral is on Dec 10, at 11 o'clock, from her late residence on Pa ave, between 3rd & 4½ sts.

Died: yesterday, Caldwell, the youngest child of Chas W & Mary Jane Pairo, aged 2 years. The friends of the family are invited to the funeral services at 9:30 this morning, at the residence of the parents on Prospect st, Gtwn.

For rent: brick house, large garden, & paddock: within 250 yards of the Capitol garden: the house I now occupy, adjoining the residence of the Minister from Spain. –Stephenson Scott, North B st, Capitol Hill.

Leeches, Leeches, Leeches. Saml De Vaughan had just received a large supply of fresh Swedish Leeches. Residence on E st, near to Temperance Hall.

Cow strayed from the residence of the subscriber, near 14th st bridge: reward of $2.50 for recovery of the above Cow. Ann Frazier, 14th st, near the bridge.

WED DEC 10, 1851
Mrd: on Dec 9, at St John's Church, Wash, by Rev Dr Pyne, Goold Hoyt, of N Y, to Miss Camilla Scott, daughter of Gen Scott, of the U S Army.

Mrd: on Dec 4, by Rev Jas B Donelan, Wm E Dant to Miss Sarah J Beardsley, daughter of the late Jos Beardsley, all of Wash City.

The *Fort Smith* Herald of Nov 21 announces the death of Bvt Gen Wm G Belknap, of the Fifth Infty. He died on Nov 10, as he was returning from the Brasos, between Preston, in Texas, & *Fort Washita*. Gen Beklnaps' family was at *Fort Gibson*, to which post he was proceeding on sick leave. He was between 50 & 60 years of age, & has been a faithful & gallant ofcr. [Dec 24th newspaper: Bvt Brig Gen Wm G Belknap was born in the town of Newburgh, Orange Co, State of N Y, Sep 14, 1794, & at the time of his death had just attained his 57th year. During the war of 1812 he received, on Apr 5, 1813, a commission for the Pres of the U S as 3rd lt of 23rd Infty, & distinguished himself for gallantry & bravery before the enemy in the attack of the British on *Fort Erie*, Aug 15, 1814. He was promoted to Capt Feb 1, 1822. He was brevet, Feb 1, 1831, major, for 10 years' faithful service in this grade. In Jan, 1842, he was promoted major of the 8th Infty & on Mar 15, 1842, breveted lt col for gallant during the Florida war. He was awarded brevet of colonel, May 9, 1846, for his command of the 8th Infty, in the fields of Palo Alto & Rosaca de la Palma.]

Senate: 1-Mr Stockton presented a memorial signed by many of the citizens of the State of N J, asking the interference by the Gov't in behalf of Mr J S Thrasher, who [he said] is supposed to be now imprisoned in the Punta Castle at Havana, in the island of Cuba. 2-Ptn of Robt Jemmison & Benj Williamson: referred to the Cmte on the Post Ofc & Post Ofc Roads. 3-Ptn of Emily C P Thompson, widow of Capt C Thompson: referred to the Cmte on Naval Affairs. 4-Memorial of Henry Smith: referred to the Cmte on Indian Affairs. 5-Memorial of Mary W Thompson: referred to the Cmte on Pensions. 6-Memorial of A H Cole, the memorial of Isaac Varnes, sen, & the ptn of Allen G Johnson, on the files of the Senate: referred to the Cmte of Claims. 7-Documents on the files of the Senate relating to the claim of Capt Geo F McClelland's company of Florida volunteers: referred to the Cmte on Military Affairs. 8-Ptn of Eliz Arnold, only daughter of Jonathan Pitcher, deceased, an ofcr of the navy during the war of the Revolution, asking to be allowed a pension in consideration of the services of her father: referred to the Cmte on Naval Affairs. 9-Documents relating to the claims of Saml Crapin, a pensioner, asking increase of pension: presented. 10-Ptn of Leonard J Thomas, asking that pensioners under the act of Apr 14, 1816, may be entitled to draw pensions from the passage of said act: referred to the Cmte on Pensions. 11-Ptn of Geo C Paine & Polly Teall, heirs of Brinton Paine, an ofcr of the Revolution, asking to be allowed the back pay to which their ancestor was entitled, & also a pension: referred to the Cmte on Pensions. 12-Ptn of Adam Hays, asking to be allowed arrears of pension: referred to the Cmte on Pensions. 13-Ptn of Hiram Moore & John Hascall, asking an extension of their patent for a harvesting machine: referred to the Cmte on Patents. 14-Bill for the relief of Mark & Richd Bean: referred to the Cmte on Public Lands. 15-Bill for the relief of the widow of Gen Worth: referred to the Cmte on Pensions. 16-Memorial of Jas B Moore, Josiah Lawrence, & Henry H Goodman, of Ohio, & Jno H Diehl, of

Pa, & their associates, proposing, with the aid of the Gov't, to establish a regular line of mail steamers from Calif & Oregon to China: referred to the Cmte on Naval Affairs. 17-Memorial of H P Dorsey, of Calif, asking indemnity for loss by Indian depredations in consequence of want of adequate protection from the Gov't of the U S: referred to the Cmte of Claims. 18-Memorial of Frances Moore, legal rep of John Moore, deceased, asking payment of certain indents issued by the State of S C in the Revolutionary war: referred to the Cmte on Revolutionary Claims.

Obit-died: on Nov 30, in Greensboro, Ga, Mrs Signey Wingfield, widow of the late Thos Wingfield, of that place, & mother of the late Mrs Henrietta Dawson, so well known in this city as the amiable & accomplished consort of the Hon Wm C Dawson, of the U S Senate. Mrs Wingfield had attained the age of 73 years, & was in the enjoyment of usual health until a few days before her death.

House of Reps: 1-Ptn of Wm A Christian, praying to be allowed certain payments made to ofcrs on board the U S steamer **Princeton**. 2-Ptn of Danl S Anderson, praying an allowance of prize money due his father, Thos O Anderson, one of the captors of the frig **Philadelphia**. 3-Memorial of Jesse Godley, of Phil, atty for J H Polhemus, asking payment for money advanced by Capt Polhemus in the Revolutionary war; also, for payment of commutation. 4-Mr Chandler asked permission to withdraw from the Clerk's ofc the memorial & papers of the heirs & administrator of the late Rev Walter Colston, of Phil. Also, to withdraw the memorial & papers of the executor of the late John E Bisphan from the Clerk's ofc. 5-Memorial & papers of Mrs Susan Randall, of Phil, widow of the late Judge Archibald Randall: to be withdrawn. 6-Ptn of S B Phinney & others for a breakwater at Dennis, Mass. 7-Ptn of Andrew H Patterson, of Ohio, asking payment for certain mail bags made for the Post Ofc Dept. 8-Ptn of Alanson Grant, for 7 years' half-pay; of John S Gatewood, for pay for a horse; of Abigail Connell, for navy pension; of Thos Copeland, for renumeration for improvements in machinery; of John Pettibone, for claim of his father, Danl Pettibone; of J J Storer, for claim as acting purser. 9-Ptn of Wm Darby.

Local: 1-Incendiary fire on Mon in the wheelwright shop of Mr Jas Wise, between G & H sts. The fire communicated to Mr Wise's residence adjoining, which, with the shop, were entirely consumed. 2-Fire broke out in the stable of Mr David Desmond, F st south, on the Island, destroying it & a horse it contained. The fire started from the accidental dropping of a lighted candle amongst the hay in the stable.

Marshal's sale: by writ of fieri facias: public sale on Jan 6, 1852: of the east half of lot 6 in square 534, in Wash City, with a 2 story frame bldg, seized & levied upon as the property of John O'Leary, & will be sold to satisfy Judicials 9, to Mar, 1851, in favor of Jas McColgan. -Richd Wallach, Marshal D C

The undersigned wishes to employ a male Teacher, competent to instruct in Latin & French, & usual English branches, for ensuing year, to take charge of a small school in his own family. Address me at Reistertown, Fauquier Co, Va: Richd H Carter.

THU DEC 11, 1851
Senate: 1-Memorial of Wm L Meredith, who represents himself as the son & only heir of Col Wm Meredith by courtesy, & Major by actual rank. Mr Underwood said the memorialist availed himself of the precedent established by Congress in the case of Miss Charlotte Lynch. The Colonel was a soldier from its commencement to the close of the Revolution: he lived until 1833, a period which would have made his half-pay quadruple the amount received by commutation. The memorialist hopes that Congress will mete out to him the same justice meted to Miss Lynch. 2-Ptn of Avery Downer, a surgeon's mate in the Revolutionary army, asking to be allowed a pension: referred to the Cmte on Pensions. 3-Ptn of Sally T Floyd, widow of Geo R C Floyd, late a lt-col in the army of the U S, for a pension: referred to the Cmte on Pensions. 4-Memorial of Jos Mitchell, asking to be allowed arrears of pay & bounty land for services as a soldier in the late war with Great Britain: referred to the Cmte on Public Lands. 5-Additional documents submitted in relation to the claim of the heirs of Henry King: referred to the Cmte of Claims. 6-Additional documents relating to the claim of John S Devlin, administrator of E I Weed referred to the Cmte on Naval Affairs. 7-Memorial of Catherine B Turner, widow of Danl Turner, late a captain in the navy, praying reimbursement of expenses incurred by her husband in entertaining on board his vessel public functionaries of the U S & foreign countries in 1841 to 1844: referred to the Cmte on Foreign Relations. 8-Ptn of Lavinia Taylor, widow of a private in the army of the U S, asking to be allowed a pension: referred to the Cmte on Pensions. 9-Memorial of Anna De Neufville Evans, heirs of John De Neufville, asking repayment of advances made by said De Neufville in the Revolutionary war referred to the Cmte on Revolutionary Claims. PAPERS WITHDRAWN & REFERRED: 10-Of John T Sullivan: referred to the Cmte on the Post Ofc & the Post Roads. Of Wm C Easton: referred to the Cmte on Military Affairs. Of Hiram Paulding: referred to the Cmte on Naval Affairs. Of Horace Southmayd & Son: referred to the Cmte on Finance. Of Mary B Renner: referred to the Cmte of Claims. Of the heirs of Jos Watson: referred to the Cmte on Indian Affairs. Of W A Seely: referred to the Cmte on Foreign Relations. Of Alex'r Y P Garnet: referred to the Cmte of Claims. Of the heirs of Saml Prioleau: referred to the Cmte on Revolutionary Claims. Of Salvadora McLaughlin, widow of John T McLaughlin: referred to Cmte on Naval Affairs. Of a patent of Thos A Godman: referred to the Cmte on Patents & the Patent Ofc. Of Victor Morass: referred to the Cmte on Public Lands. Of the heirs of Wm Beatty: referred to the Cmte on Revolutionary Claims. Of Martha Gray, widow of Robt Gray: referred to the Cmte on Revolutionary Claims. Of A J Williamson: referred to the Cmte of Claims. Of the widow of the late Gen McNeil: referred to the Cmte on Pensions. Of Gerard Wood: referred to the Cmte on Revolutionary Claims.

Circuit Court of St Mary's Co, Court of Equity: Dec Term, 1851. John Greenwell, of Phil, & Catharine G his wife, vs John M Broome, administrator of Geo G Ashcom & others. This suit is to procure a decree for a sale of certain real estate in said county owned by John C Ashcom, deceased, late of said county. The bill states that John C Ashcom died in 1824 intestate, being seized & possessed of: ***Hammett's Discovery***-9 acres; ***Ashcom Land***-505 acres; ***Ridge, Legate, Haphazard, & Adams' Discovery***-141 acres; ***Part Parnassus & Punk Neck***-170 acres; ***Keeche's Folly, Locks' Meadows, & Best Land***-50 acres; ***Ashcom's Land***-250 acres; & leaving the following heirs, to wit: John Ashcom, Geo G Ashcom, Mgt C Bell, Catharine G Ashcom, Eliza C Ashcom, & that the said John Ashcom has since died leaving a widow, Ann Ashcom, & the following heirs at law, to wit: Catharine G, since married to Thos Gardiner, Eliza M, since married to Alex'r Martin, Geo H Ashcom, John C Ashcom, who are minors, under the age of 21 years, & that Mgt C Bell is a resident of the State of Texas, & that Eliza C Ashcom, afterwards intermarried with a certain Henry B Martin, & are now both residents of the State of Texas. Defendents to appear in this Court on the first Monday of Jun next. -Peter W Crain
-Jas T Blakistone, clk

Circuit Court of Wash Co, D C-in Chancery. Saml O Cunningham & Mary Cunningham his wife, Wm D Cunningham & Mgt M Cunningham his wife, Jas L Cunningham & Eliz S Cunningham his wife, & John Long & Mary E Long his wife, heirs at law of Jas Long, deceased, against John Withers & Sarah Payne, Edw F Tabb & Kitty Ann Tabb his wife, Allen C Hammond & Sarah Eliza Hammond his wife, John C Payne & Mary D Payne his wife, Jos E Payne & Sarah Ann Payne his wife, John M Payne & Mary D Payne his wife, Jas Anderson & Eliz Anderson his wife, Sarah Long, Abraham D Long, Geo Milligan & Mary Milligan his wife, Robt Merriett & ___ Merriett his wife, John W Milligan & Sarah Ann Milligan his wife, Saml Winning & Jas A Winning, heirs at law of Jas Long, deceased, dfndnts. The bill states that on Apr 20, 1844, the said dfndnt, John Withers, entered into & made & executed a certain instrument of writing or agreement, wherein he agreed, for & upon the payment of certain sums of money & the performance of certain conditions therein set forth, to sell & convey unto Jas Long lots E & F, of the subdivision of the east part of lots 1 & 6, in square 460, in Wash City, with the bldgs, improvements, rights, privileges, & appurtenances to the same belonging; & that the same Jas Long did, in his lifetime, pay to the said John Withers divers sums of money on account & in part payment of said sums of money in said instrument of writing mentioned & agreed to be paid for said lots & premises, with the appurtenances; that the said John Withers did since file his bill of cmplnt in the Circuit Court of D C against the said complainants & the then other heirs at law of the said Jas Long, deceased, & others, setting forth the said herein before mentioned instrument of writing, & a certain mortgage or deed of trust mentioned in said bill of cmplnt; whereupon the said Court did, on Apr 6, 1850, order, adjudge, & decree that the lands or property mentioned in said bill, or so much thereof as was necessary, be sold for the purpose, among others, of paying to the said John Withers the said sums of money in the said instrument of writing by said Jas Long agreed to be paid for the said lots & premises, with the appurtenances; & that the trustees appointed by said decree to make said sale did, on Nov 30, 1850, sell a part of said land & premises in said bill mentioned, & that the same produced a sufficient sum to pay the said John Withers the said sums of money, as well as all other sums of money then due & owing by the said Jas Long to the said John Withers; that the said sums of money, or so much thereof as was then due & owing, have been stated & allowed to him, the said John Withers, in the report made by the auditor of the Court, upon reference to him of the account of the said trustees; & it states that the said Jas Long died without having received or had made & executed to him any deed or conveyance of said lots & premises, with appurtenances; & that the fee simple title thereto still remains in the said dfndnt, the said John Withers; & that the said lots & premises, with appurtenances, are not susceptible of partition among the said cmplnts & the said dfndnts, the said heirs at law of the said Jas Long, deceased, & that a sale thereof would be greatly to the advantage of the said cmplnts & dfndnts, heirs at law of the said Jas Long, deceased; & that all the said dfndnts reside in the U S, & out of D C. The object of the bill is to procure a decree for the conveyance of the said lots & premises, with the appurtenances & the appointment of a trustee to make such sale, & a distribution of the proceeds of such sale among the said cmplnts & dfndnts, heirs at law of the said Jas Long, deceased, as they may be law be entitled thereto. Dfndnts to appear in Court in person or by solicitor on or before the 3rd Mon of Apr next. —Jas S Morsell, Assoc Judge of the Circuit Court -John A Smith, clerk -Chas S Wallace, Solicitor for cmplnts

Postmaster Gen has est'd the following new Post Ofcs for week ending Dec 6, 1851.

Ofc	County, State	Postmaster
Chesherville	Chenango, N Y	Leonard Foot
Greenspring Furnance	Washington, Md	B F Beman
Rothsville	Lancaster, Pa	Saml B Myers
Tomb's Run	Lycoming, Pa	Henry Tomb
Indian Orchard	Wayne, Pa	Calvin Y Lillir
Merlin	Falls, Texas	John W Jarvis
Colusa	Colusa, Cal	Benj Knight
Garrote	Tuolumne, Cal	Gage Tucker
Bonbrook	Franklin, Va	Griffin Bush
Langhorn's Tavern	Cumberland, Va	Wm R Coupland
Game Point	Stafford, Va	Wm W Dix
Torris	Hancock, Va	Wm Nicholson
State Line	Heard, Geo	Jackson Allen
Ewbank's Mills	Johnson, Ark	Jesse Dunlap
Whiteley's	Newton, Ark	Jesse Casey
Denton	Newton, Ark	Jas Stamps
Swingleville	Washington, Tenn	Benj Swingle

Post Ofc Names Changed: 1-Hall's Ranch, Colusi Co, Calif, changed to Tehoma. 2-Nebraska, Yell Co, Iowa, changed to Dekota, Risley Co. 3-Boonville, Boone Co, Iowa, changed bo Boonsboro'.

Lt Richd W Meade, who was ordered to the U S sloop of war **Portsmouth** as executive ofcr, has resigned his commission in the Navy. Lt Handy was detailed to fill the vacancy thus occasioned on board the **Portsmouth**, but had been detached on account of ill health, having been condemned by a Medical Board of Survey.

Died: on Tue last, Mrs Mary M, wife of D O Hare. Her funeral is today at 11 o'clock, from her late residence, 10th st, between L & M sts.

House of Reps: 1-Ptn of Robt Milligan, of Wash Co, Pa, a soldier of the war of 1812, for an increase of pension. 2-Ptn of Wm H Topping, for compensation as secretary to the commission appointed to investigate the affairs of the N Y custom-house. 3-Memorial of Horatio N Crabb, praying for allowances withheld by the accounting ofcrs of the Treasury. 4-Memorial of Bernard Henry, praying for the payment of a balance due him for the Gov't of the U S. 5-Ptn & memorial of Chas Foster, by Stewart Foster, his administrator, for a claim to indemnity against Mexico. 6-Ptn of Seth Crowell & others, for a breakwater at Dennis, Mass.

FRI DEC 12, 1851
Telegraphic dispatch from Phil informs that a verdict of acquittal was yesterday rendered by the Jury in the case of Castner Hanaway, on trial before the Circuit Court of the U S on a charge of treason, as one of the participants in the negro riot at Christiana in Sep last. Judge Grier charged the Jury that the crime of treason had not been sustained by the evidence.

Died: on Dec 11, Mrs Dorcas Walker, aged 80 years, for 60 years a resident of Wash City. Her funeral is from her residence on I st, between 18th & 19th sts, adjoining the Friends' meeting-house, 1st Ward, at 2 o'clock this afternoon.

Died: on Dec 11, Mrs Jane Lyon, widow of the late Jacob Lyon, in her 81st year. Her funeral is Dec 13, at 1 P M, from her late residence, N Y ave, between 9th & 10th sts.

Senate: 1-Memorial of Wm A Duer, adm of Wm Duer, asking payment of a balance due the estate on a contract for supplying rations to the army under Gen St Clair, in 1791: referred to the Cmte of Claims. 2-Memorial of Geo Talcott, late a colonel of ordnance & brig gen by brevet, complaining of injustice done him by the sentence of the court martial by which he was dismissed the service, & asking that an investigation may be made by the Senate. 3-Bill for the relief of M K Warrington & C S J Chubb, execs of Capt Lewis Warrington & others: referred to the Cmte on Naval Affairs. 4-Bill for the relief of Richd Chaney & others; also for the relief of Chas Melrose: referred to the Cmte on Public Lands. 5-Letter from Aaron H Palmer, with a description of the colonial dependencies of Japan, with a plan for opening commerce with the U S: which was read. 6-Ptn of Thos Pember, asking compensation for services rendered as purser in the navy: referred to the Cmte on Naval Affairs. 7-Memorial of Wm A Christian, a purser in the navy, asking certain payments made by him to ofcrs on board the U S steamer **Princeton** holding acting appointments: referred to the Cmte on Naval Affairs. 8-Memorial of Danl Anderson, heir of Thos O Anderson, late of the navy, asking payment of prize money due his father as one of the captors of the frig **Philadelphia**: referred to the Cmte on Naval Affairs. PAPERS WITHDRAWN & REFERRED. 9-Memorial of Robt M Hamilton: referred to the Cmte on Foreign Relations. 10-Memorial of T P McBlair: referred to the Cmte on Naval Affairs. 11-Memorial of Abraham L Knickerbocker: referred to the Cmte on Pensions. 12-Ptns of Barbara Riley & that of Thompson Hutchinson: referred to the Cmte on Pensions. 13-Memorial of Danl Winslow: referred to the Cmte of Claims. 14-Memorial of Thos M Taylor: referred to the Cmte on Naval Affairs. 15-Documents relating to the claim of Francis P Stockton, a purser in the navy: referred to the Cmte on Naval Affairs. 16-Ptns of Richd Mackall, Bryan Callaghan, & others, heirs of Robt Sewall: referred to the Cmte of Claims. 17-Memorial of the legal reps of Rinaldo Johnson & Ann E Johnson, of the legal reps of Wm Somerville, & the memorial of Hodges & Lansdale: referred to the Cmte on Pensions. 18-Memorial of Eliz Monroe: referred to the Cmte on Pensions. INTRODUCED. 19-Bill for the relief of John Develin: referred to the Cmte on Claims. 20-Bill for the relief of Wm Richardson & others: referred to the Cmte on Naval Affairs. 21-Rev Dr Butler having received 25 votes was declared duly elected Chaplain.

House of Reps: 1-Ptn of Thos M Newell, Capt in the U S Navy, for full pay during the period of his suspension from command. 2-Ptn off Jos Arnow & Peter Arnow, praying compensation for losses sustained from American troops in Florida in 1812 & 1813. 3-Ptn of Thos Ellis, of Platte Co, Mo, praying for a pension. 4-Memorial of David D Porter, a Lt in the U S Navy, praying for similar allowances as were granted to John Hogan, as diplomatic agent to the Island of St Domingo, having been employed upon similar service. 5-Ptn of T R Peal, asking for compensation for valuable articles lost by shipwreck while in the Exploring Expedition, & also for arrears of pay. 6-Ptn of Messrs Ferguson & Milhado, praying that their bond given for duties may be canceled. 7-Ptn of the heirs of Willis Riddick, asking compensation for losses sustained in the Revolutionary war. 8-Ptn of John G Wilkinson, praying compensation for his services as Navy Pension Agent. 9-Ptn of Robt B Storer, Pres of the Boston Marine Society, & others, praying that the money now in the U S Treasury unclaimed by deceased seamen as prize money in public & private vessels, & from contributions made by all seamen of twenty cents per month, be applied to the further relief of disabled seamen.

Millard Fillmore, Pres of the U S A, recognizes Leonetto Cipriani, who has been appointed Consul of Sardinia, for Calif, to reside in San Francisco. –Dec 9, 1851

Fire on Thursday in the dwlg & boarding-house of Mrs Riley, a widow lady, on Pa ave. The fire was kept within the walls where it originated. Mrs Riley was adequately insured.

Mrd: on Nov 19, at **Fort Snelling**, Minnesota Territory, T L Caster, 1st Lt U S Dragoons, to Mrs M C Whitehorn, daughter of Rev E G Gear, Chaplain U S Navy.

John Miller, Confectioner, between 10th & 11th sts, Pa ave, has on hand a choice assortment of almost every article in his line of business, for the Christmas Holydays.

SAT DEC 13, 1851
Senate: 1-Memorial of Lydia Ann Mills, widow of John Mills, late a boatswain in the navy of the U S, asking to be allowed a pension: referred to the Cmte on Naval Affairs. 2-Memorial of Jacob Cooper, asking to be allowed the 7 years' half-pay due his father as a lt in the army of the Revolution: referred to the Cmte on Revolutionary Claims. 3-Ptn of John Jackson, Jos Pineau, & Louis A S Smith, citizens of Port au Prince, Hayti, asking the payment of their travelling expenses in attending as witnesses for the U S in a criminal prosecution in the U S Circuit Court at Boston in 1849: referred to the Cmte on the Judiciary. PAPERS WITHDRAWN & REFERRED. 4-Memorial of Lewis Morris: referred to the Cmte on Military Affairs. 5-Documents relating to the claim of Jonathan Kearsley, & the petition of John Biddle: referred to the Cmte on Public Lands. 6-Eli Hobbs has leave to withdraw his petition & papers. 7-Ptn of Sydney S Alcott, with a bill for her relief: passed to a second reading. 8-Bill for the relief of Theodore Offutt: referred to the Cmte of Claims.

Wash Corp: 1-Nomination of H T L Wilson as a police ofcr for the 5th Ward, in place of Jas Lynch, resigned: was rejected. 2-Bill for the relief of Z Jones: to lie on the table. 3-Resolution authorizing Miss A R Dermot to extend the steps to her house 7 feet 6 inches from the bldg line: passed.

Stray cow came to the premises of the subscriber: owner is to come forward, prove property, pay charges, & take her away. –Wm Holmead, 1½ miles north of Wash City.

Wash City Ordinances: 1-Act for the relief of John Davis & others: sum of $20.25 to be paid for expenses of Davis & others, incurred by order of the Mayor. 2-Act for the relief of Wm Haggarty: sum of $627 be paid him for the balance due for work done on 8th st. 3-Act for the relief of M Holloran: sum of $47.80 to be paid Maurice Holloran for a balance due him for work done on 13th st. 4-Act for the relief of Chas J McCarthy: fine imposed for a violation in reference to the erecting of frame bldgs, is remitted: provided McCarthy pay the costs of prosecution.

Valuable business stand for rent in Wash: at the corner of 7th st west & Market space: built in the most modern style for the dry-goods business & with gas lights. Apply at the Potomac House, north side of Pa ave, between 3rd & 4½ sts.
—Anne R McDermott

In Chancery. John P King vs Henry May, trustee, Richd Wallach, administrator of John W Hunter, Henry D Hunter, Alex'r Hunter, Benj F Hunter, Isaac J Course, Richd B Mason, et al. Bill: Henry May, one of the dfndnts, was appointed by decree of the Circuit Court of Wash Co, D C, passed on Jun 4, 1844, a trustee to sell certain mortgaged premises, said premises having been mortgaged by John W Hunter, during his lifetime, to secure a debt due David E Twiggs; that said Henry May, trustee, proceeded to sell the premises, & that said sale was ratified; that the Auditor reported a balance in the hands of said trustee, after the payment of said debt, so as aforesaid secured by mortgage, of $2,474.73½ subject to the claims of the creditors of the said John W Hunter, deceased; that during his lifetime the said John W Hunter became & was indebted to the cmplnt in the above entitled cause, in the sum of $198.86; that letters of administration upon the personal estate of Hunter, deceased, were granted by the Orphans Court of Wash Co, D C, to Richd Wallach; that the personal estate of Hunter, deceased, was insufficient to pay the debts of said deceased; that the cmplnt was advised that the deficiency ought to be supplied by a sale of the real estate of said deceased; that said real estate has been sold, & the proceeds are in the hands of the trustee. All of the dfndnts, except Richd Wallach, the adm reside out of this District. Non-resident dfndnts are to appear in this Court, in person or by solicitor, on or before the 4th Mon in Mar next. —Jno A Smith, clk

By order of distrain for ground rent due to Jos Elgar from the estate of John Rully, deceased, & heirs, I will expose at public sale, in Wash City, on Dec 20, sundry goods & chattels. Also: public sale of lot 20 in square A, on Pa ave, between 3rd & 4½ sts, in Wash City. —H R Maryman, Bailiff

Hon John Freedley, an ex-member of Congress from the Montgomery [Pa] district, died in Phil on Dec 8.

Mrd: on Dec 11, by Rev Mr Hodges, Mr Saml E Arnold to Miss Sarah Ann Champion, all of Wash City.

Mrd: on Nov 5, in Wash City, by Rev C M Butler, Mr Alonzo R Fowler to Miss Frances A E Draper, 3rd daughter of the late Dr A C Draper, of Phil.

Mrd: on Dec 11, by Rev N P Tillinghurst, Passed Midshipman Leonard Paulding, U S Navy, to Miss Helen, daughter of the late John H Offley, of Gtwn.

Mrd: on Dec 11, in Balt, by Rev David Kerr, Rector of Rock Creek Parish, D C, Albert Troup Emory, of Queen Anne's Co, to Miss Sally R Winder, of Balt, Md.

Mrd: on Dec 9, at Norwich, Conn, by Rev Wm F Morgan, Wm P Williams, of N Y, to Julia Woodbridge, 2nd daughter of Chas Jas Lanman, of Norwich.

Died: yesterday, after a few days' illness, John A Donohoo, in his 55th year, leaving a large family to mourn their loss. His funeral is tomorrow at 1 o'clock.

Died: on Dec 10, in Gtwn, at the late residence of Henry H Chapman, Miss Mgt Davidson, formerly of Annapolis, Md, in her 77th year. Her funeral is today at 8 o'clock.

Situation wanted, as Coachman to a private family, by Thos McLaine, who is well acquainted in the city, & can give good references. Any gentlemen desiring his services is to address him through the Wash City Post Ofc.

MON DEC 15, 1851
The Grand Jury at New Orleans have found indictments against R O Smith, E F Arbell, St Leon Fazinde, Wm H Wilder, & J B Serapuru as participants in the Cuba riots in that city on Aug 21 last.

Guardians sale of valuable & desirable bldg lots: by decree of the Orphans Court of Wash Co, D C, confirmed by the Circuit Court of Wash Co, D C, the subscriber, guardian of the infant heirs of Cornelius Cox, deceased, will, on Jan 5, 1852, sell at public auction: lot 13 in square 165, on I st & Conn ave. Lots 15 & 16 in square 342, on Mass ave, between 10th & 11th sts. On Jan 6, 1852: lots 8 & 9 in square 530, on 4th st, between G & H sts. Lot 15 in square 532, on 3rd st, between Indiana ave & E st north. On Jan 7, 1852: lots 7, 8, & 9, in square 462, fronting south on Md ave, between 6th & 7th sts. Lot 19 in square 499, on I st, between 5th & 6th sts. Titles indisputable. -Caroline Cox, Guardian & trustee -Dyer & McGuire, aucts

Col Danl Kilgore, formerly a member of Congress from the State of Ohio, died on Fri at N Y, where he had been sick for 10 days with inflammation of the lungs.

Orphans Court of Wash Co, D C. Letters of administration on the personal estate of Jas Parsons, late of Wash Co, deceased. –P M Pearson, adm

The Boston Transcript announces the sudden death of Mr Alfred Richardson, an old & highly esteemed India merchant. He was in his usual health on Thu, attended to his business, & spent the evening with his family, & retired about 10:15 p m. Soon after he sprang up with a sensation of choking, fell back upon the pillow & died instantly: supposed to have been an affection of the heart. He was about 52 years of age & leaves a very large family.

The German Methodist Church, at the corner of Eutaw & Camden sts, Baltimore, was destroyed by fire yesterday. The lumber yard of Hiss & Austin was also consumed.

An insane man named Carrigan, living 7 miles from St John's, N B, on last Sun murdered his wife, 2 children, & aunt, & dangerously wounded 4 other persons, feared fatally. It appears he called his family to prayers, & then made the attack upon them, killing first his wife.

Mrd: yesterday, at St Peter's Church, by Rev Mr Lanahan, Mr Thomaso Prior, of Saratoga Co, N Y, to Miss Emily A Barrett, of Wash, D C.

Mrd: on Nov 19, at St Louis, by Rev Mr Gassaway, Maj D C Buell, of the Adj Gen's Dept U S Army, to Mrs Mgt Mason, of St Louis, Missouri.

Died: on Dec 12, in Wash City, Miss Ann Maria Doughty, daughter of Col Wm Doughty, of Gtwn, aged 52 years.

In Chancery. John W Ball & others, vs Geo M Oyster & Thos Parker, adms of Geo Oyster, D W Oyster, John H Oyster, W Godey, & Jane A Godey. Creditors of Geo Oyster are to appear before me to prove their claims on Dec 27, at the auditor's room, City Hall. -Walter S Cox, spec aud

To Western Travellers. Express Mail Line from Balt to Pittsburg, through in 22½ hours. This Line to Pittsburg over the Balt & Susquehanna & Pa Central Railroads is now in successful operation. This route is as reliable as any offered to the public. Fare through, either way, $11. -Alfred Gaither, Superintendent of Transportation.

Stray horse, on Dec 11, a small bay pony. Any person returning the same to the subscriber will be remunerated. –Evan Hughes, 13th & Pa ave.

Emigrants' Friend Society, Ofc 116 South Charles st, Balt, Md. Managers: His Honor Mayor Jerome, Dr J Hanson Thomas, Henry Mankin, J Harman Brown, J Thompson Graham, sec.

Valuable bldg lots at auction: by decree of the Circuit Court of Wash Co, D C, in Chancery, in the case wherein Isaac N Carey is trustee for Mary Jennings, alias Polly Jennings: sale of lots 1 & 2 in square 513, on one of which is a small frame tenement. The property fronts 140 feet 6 inches on north M st, & 50 feet on 4th st west, handsomely located. –Isaac N Cary, trustee -A Green, auct

Household, kitchen & hotel furniture at auction: on Dec 17, the entire furniture of the Empire [formerly King's Hotel,] on Pa ave, near 4½ st. -A Green, auctioneer

Mr Isaac Hoge, a highly respectable citizen of Loudoun Co, Va, died suddenly, at his residence near Hughesville, on Mon last. He had gone to attend to feeding his stock, but not returning, he was found lying senseless upon some fodder. He was taken home & died during the day.

TUE DEC 16, 1851
U S Patent Ofc, Dec 15, 1851. Ptn of Ira Wing, of Belfast, N Y, for the extension of a patent for improvement in the machine for sawing caves, troughs for conducting water from bldgs, etc: for 7 year from date of expiration which is Mar 17, 1852.
–Thos Ewbank, Com'r of Patents

Postmaster Gen est'd the following new Post Ofcs for week ending Dec 13, 1851.

Ofc	County, State	Postmaster
Randolph Center	Broome, N Y	David R Brown
Kenwood	Albany, N Y	Jas Condon
Clayton's Mills	Monumouth, N J	Saml Thompson
Francis' Mills	Ocean, N J	Chas Applegate
Glengary	Berkley, Va	Barak Behaven
Summers	Rockbridge, Va	Jonathan Shafer
Houston	Hancock, Ala	David Day
Jernigan	Barbour, Ala	Mortimer D Dewey
Coletta	Dewitt, Texas	Adolphus Zoble
Featherhoof's	Carroll, Ia	John Featherhoof
Welcher's Mill	Roane, Texas	Chas F Welcher
Loosahatchie	Shelby, Tenn	Saml Kennedy
Yuba	Hancock, Ill	Wm Kendall
Pleasant Hope	Polk, Mo	R D Smith
Adell	Sheboygan, Wis	Eliada Baldwin
Forest	Fen Du Lac, Wis	Newton Kellogg
Cobbsville	Johnson, Ark	Francis K Jones
Vista Ridge	Carroll, La	S C Floyd

Names Changed: 1-Corners, Windsor Co, Vt, changed to Ascutneyville.
2-Valina, Cas Co, Mich, changed to Picket's Corners.
3-South Nankin, Wayne Co, Mich, changed to Wayne.
4-Center Creek, Iron Co, Utah Territory, changed to Parovan.
5-Blentstown, Calhoun, Fla, changed to Winton.

Rev Saml Glover, formerly of Marshfield, Mass, died at Cambridge on Sat at the breakfast table, of disease of the heart.

For Hire: 3 negro boys aged 8, 10, & 12. For sale 2 horses, a black & a bay. One can be seen at the Capitol Stables; the other at the Stable of Robt Beall, Capitol Hill.
–Jas J Forbes

Senate: 1-Resolution for the relief of Louis Kossuth & his Associates, exiles from Hungary, now in the U S. 2-Memorial from Jos A Barelli, asking that the Sec of Treasury may be authorized to issue a register to the brig **Ada**, late the British brig **Josephine**: referred to the Cmte on Commerce. 3-Memorial from Jehiel Brooks, asking to be allowed to sue the U S for damages sustained by him in defending his title to certain land in a suit brought against him by the U S under false Representations: referred to the Cmte on the Judiciary. 4-Memorial of Geo Hervey, agent for the owners & consignees of the English ship **James Mitchell**, asking the payment of a sum of money due under an act of Congress & retained in the U S Treasury: referred to the Cmte on the Judiciary. 5-The petition & papers relating to the case of Mrs N E Cobb for a pension, in consideration of the services of her husband on Lake Erie, & afterwards on board of privateer **Paul Jones** & privateer **Teazer**, & subsequently a gunner in the U S navy, he having been twice wounded, & finally fell a victim to a disease contracted in the service: referred to the Cmte on Naval Affairs. 6-Ptn of Nancy Wright, widow of Jas Wright, late an ofcr in the navy, revenue cutter service, asking to be allowed a pension: referred to the Cmte on Pensions. 7-Memorial of May Walker, widow of Geo P Walker, late a paymaster in the marine corps, asking to be allowed the traveling expenses of her late husband in the settlement of his accounts: referred to the Cmte on the Military Affairs. 8-Memorial of Wm Butler, asking to be allowed a pension on account of injuries received in the naval service of the U S: referred to the Cmte on Pensions. 9-Memorial of Jno W Symonton & others, owners of the island of Key West, in Florida, asking indemnity in consequence of its occupancy by the U S: referred to the Cmte on Naval Affairs. 10-Memorial of the heirs-at-law of Herry Miller, asking compensation for the services of their ancestor during the Revolutionary war: referred to the Cmte on Revolutionary Claims. PAPERS WITHDRAWN & REFERRED. 11-Papers of Rodey Carter & Jennings: referred to the Cmte of Claims. 12-Ptn of Asenath M Elliot: referred to the Cmte on Pensions. 13-Ptn of Walter Colton: referred to the Cmte on the Judiciary. 14-Memorial of Ezra Williams: referred to the Cmte on the Judiciary. 15-Documents relating to the claims of Wm S Waller: referred to the Cmte of Claims. 16-Ptn of Robt Armstrong: referred to the Cmte on Pensions. 17-Memorials of Gen Roger Jones & Mgt Hetzel: referred to the Cmte on Military Affairs. 18-Ptn of Harriet R F Capron: referred to the Cmte on Pensions. 19-Ptn & papers relating to the claim of Thos Flanagan: referred to the Cmte on Pensions. REPORTS FROM CMTES. 20-Cmte on Pensions: ptn of the heirs of Richd Worthen: passed to a second reading. Same cmte: asked to be discharged from the further consideration of the ptn of citizens of Niagara Co, N Y, in favor of Stephen Warren.

Dissolution of partnership by mutual consent: all demands against the late firm are to be paid by Thos C Connolly. –Thos C Conolly, Jas Wimer, Thos McGill, Washington.

New residence for sale: 4 story brick with observatory thereon, on North Capitol st, near C st. For particulars apply to J Crutchett, at the Cottage, near the above.

Lawrence Reilly, convicted of a double murder in Brooklyn, sentenced to be hung on Jan 30.

The charge of false pretences against Hon Fernando Wood, of N Y, has been dismissed.

F Miller, a young printer, died at Pittsburg, on Thu, of lead fever, contracted by the practice of putting type in his mouth.

C F Babiana, convicted at New Orleans of defrauding the revenue, had been fiend $1,000, & imprisoned 5 days.

Dr Edw F Nicolls, of Donaldsonville, La, was killed a few days ago by a fall from his horse.

A horrid murder at Buffalo, N Y, on Dec 14: Benj Warner murdered his brother Christian Warner, after an altercation concerning some money transactions.

Rev Zane Bland, a highly esteemed member of the Baltimore Annual Conference, died of typhoid fever, in his 35th year, at Cumberland, Md, on Dec 12.

WED DEC 17, 1851
Criminal Court-Wash. 1-Capt Jas H Powell, of the schnr **Patrick Henry**, tried for the manslaughter of John Merinder on board said schnr, had been acquitted on the ground of self-defence 2-In the case of Saml Stettinius, tried for forging a signature to a power of atty in 1849, traverser was acquitted on the statute of 1795, limiting the period of liability for trial to 2 years after the commission of the crime.

Richd Cowling Taylor, our eminent Geologist & Mining Engineer, died at his residence in the city of Phil, on Nov 26, suddenly. Early educated in his own country, England, in 1881 Mr Taylor came to this country. –North American

Obit-died: on Dec 9, at Balt, Mrs Eliz T Arguelles, in her 65th year, a native of Boston, & for 26 years a resident of this city. A kind & affectionate mother, [which relation she bore to the writer of this;] beloved as a friend & respected on account of her charity.

House of Reps: 1-Bill to correct an error in the pension of Horace Crosby: objection was made.

Senate: 1-Ptn from E Parensted & F A Schumaker, asking the return of duties paid on goods which were lost at sea: referred to the Cmte of Claims. 2-Ptn from Saml Spalding, asking for arrears of pension: referred to the Cmte on Pensions. 3-Memorial of Isaac Bush, John Price, & Thos Suary, asking compensation for themselves & the ofcrs & men under their command during the Seminole war in Florida: referred to the Cmte on Military Affairs. PAPERS WITHDRAWN & REFERRED. 4-Documents relating to the claim of B Juan Domeroq, a Spanish subject: referred to the Cmte of Claims. 5-Memorial of Thos Howard: referred to the Cmte on Foreign Relations. 6-Ptn of Saml Crapin: referred to the Cmte on Pensions. 7-Memorial of L E L A Lawson, heir of Gen Wm Ripley: referred to the Cmte on the Judiciary. 8-Ptn of Phoebe Glove: referred to the Cmte on Pensions. BILL ON LEAVE: 9-Bill for the relief of Wm Darby. 10-Ptn from Eliza C Bache, widow of Geo M Bache, asking that she may receive the same amount that was paid to the widows of those ofcrs who were lost in the brig **Somers**: referred to the Cmte on Naval Affairs. 11-Ptn of Jos Hill & Sons, asking compensation for horses & mules stolen by the Indians: referred to the Cmte of Claims. 12-Ptn of Jas B Browning, asking indemnity for property stolen & destroyed in Calif during the war with Mexico: referred to the Cmte on Military Affairs. 13-Ptn from Jas C Cushing & others, representing that they had discovered a pass through the greater range of the Sierra Nevada, & proposing to open a wagon road upon certain conditions: referred to the Cmte on Public Lands. 14-Memorial of S H Duff, asking compensation for services in seizing spirituous liquors under an order of Gen Taylor during the war with Mexico: referred to the Cmte of Claims. 15-Ptn from Priscilla C Simonds, asking remuneration for the effects of her son, who died in service, which said effects were taken possession of by his superior ofcr & lost: referred to the Cmte of Claims. 16-Ptn from Gridley Bryant, proposing to enter into contract for the erection of a permanent lighthouse on Minot's Ledge, in Mass Bay: referred to the Cmte on Commerce. 17-Ptn from Isaac Lilly, asking compensation for a vessel & cargo sold by an agent of the Gov't under pretext of having on board timber cut from the live oak lands of the U S: referred to the Cmte on the Judiciary.

Foreign Item: Sickness has been prevalent here, says a Lisbon letter of Nov 19, & among the sudden deaths of the last few days I regret to report that of the amiable son of Hon C B Haddock, the American Minister.

Died: on Nov 18 last, at **Fort Gates**, Texas, Sally H, daughter of Dr John J Minge, & wife of Capt Geo E Pickett, U S Army.

Copartnership. C S Fowler has associated Mr John F Webb in his business, to be conducted under the firm of C S Fowler & Co. –C S Fowler, John F Webb

For rent: the Ice-house in the rear of **Gadsby's row**. Apply to J H McBlair, Pa ave.

R Finley Hunt, Dental Surgeon: in the mechanical dept, secured the assistance of Mr R B Donaldson. Ofc: Pa ave, between 9th & 10th sts.

New Orleans: In the First District Court of the U S an important suit has been commenced by the U S against John Kilty Smith, a broker of this city, & his son, John Chandler Smith, a resident of Baltimore. The plntf states that John Kilty Smith was a defaulter 30 years ago as navy agent, in the sum of $280,000, for which judgment was obtained in the District of Columbia in 1822. Since that time Mr Smith has been doing a heavy business under his son's name. The Court has granted a writ against the bank deposites & all other propery of the firm, to be held until the suit is decided. [Dec 25th newspaper: The Picayune says a writ of sequestration has been granted to seize the deposites in the Bank of La, the State Bank of La, the New Orleans Canal & Banking Co, & in the Mechanics' & Traders' Bank, made in the name of John Chandler Smith & John Kilty Smith. The interest will increase the claim to $700,000.]

House of Reps: 1-Ptn of Wm B Bingley & wife, asking compensation for lands sold to the U S as a site for the dry dock at Gosport. 2-Ptn of Mrs Harriet Saunders, admx of Capt Wm Davis, praying compensation for the services & reimbursement of the expenditures of said Davis while in command of the U S transport schnr **Eufala**. 3-Ptn of Maj E H Fitzgerald, U S Army, praying to be relieved from liability on account of the loss of $2,000 of the public funds. 4-Ptn of Thos H Baird, of Pa, for balance alleged to be due to Dr Absalom Baird for commutation of half pay. 5-Ptn of Seneca W Ely, present receiver of public moneys at Chillicothe, Ohio, John Hough, late receiver at the same place, Anthony Walker, present register of the land ofc, & Thos J Winship, late register of Chillicothe, praying Congress to allow the same compensation to land ofcrs for their services in case of each land warrant, already located, or hereafter to be located, as is at present allowed for a cash sale of the same quantity of land. 6-Ptn of Geo Elliott, formerly of Ky, now of Franklin Co, Mo, a soldier of the war of 1812, who was wounded & disabled while in discharge of his duty in the battle of **Fort Meigs**, on May 5, 1813, asking Congress for arrears of pension. 7-Ptn for the relief of Eliz Prewitt, widow of Robt Prewitt, deceased, of Lincoln Co, Mo, in regard to services rendered by said deceased under mail contract. 8-Ptn of Saml Gladney, of Lincoln Co, Mo, asking Congress to release to him any title the U S may have in a certain tract of land in said county, in said Gladney's possession for reasons set forth in said petition & accompanying papers. 9-Ptn for the relief of Jas W Campbell, of Pike Co, Mo. 10-Ptn of the heirs of Lt Richd Paulett, a Revolutionary soldier, praying for 5 years' full pay. 11-Ptn of Capt Thos Duer, praying for money advanced while in the service of the U S during the war with Great Britain. 12-The ptn & papers of Henry Johnson have been withdrawn & referred to the Cmte on Invalid Pensions. 13-The ptn & papers of the heirs of Lot Hall were taken from the files of the House & referred to the Cmte on Revolutionary Claims.

Died: on Dec 6, at Easton, Md, in his 87th year, Solomon Barrott, an aged & sentimental resident of that place. In 1781 he was in the Southern army under Gen Green, & participated in the battles of the Cowpens, Guilford Court-house, Camden, & Eutaw Springs, courageously fighting for those principles which he cherished to his dying day.

THU DEC 18, 1851

Mrd: on Dec 17, at the Methodist Episcopal Church South, by Rev Leonidas Rosser, Thos W Johnson to Charlotte Pinkney, daughter of Rev C A Davis, all of Wash City.

Mrd: in Oct, in Paris, at the Episcopal Church, by Rev Mr Chamier, Lorenzo Draper, U S Consul at Havre, to Mrs Ann Alecia Hawkins, of Balt, Md.

Senate: 1-John S Thrasher, a native born citizen of the U S, but for many years past a resident in Havana, & there lately tried for high treason or conspiracy, convicted, sentenced to 8 years' confinement to hard labor, & sent to Spain in execution of that sentence, has made no communication whatever to the Dept of State. His friends in this country seek the help of the Gov't of the U S. 2-Memorial of Zachariah Lawrence, asking compensation for the capture of the British sloop **Venture**, during the war with Great Britain: referred to the Cmte of Claims. 3-Memorial from Peter G Washington, J C F Solomon, & Wm Selden, proposing to enter into a contract with Gov't for supplying Washington & Gtwn with water from the Potomac River: referred to the Cmte on the District of Columbia. 4-Additional documents presented relating to the claims of Mariano G Vallejo to indemnity for property taken for the use of the U S troops under the command of Capt Fremont: referred to the Cmte on Military Affairs. 5-Ptn from Benj H Mooers & other heirs of a deceased ofcr in the Revolutionary army, asking to be allowed for the depreciation on the commutation of certificates issued to their ancestor: referred to the Cmte on Revolutionary Claims. PAPERS WITHDRAWN & REFERRED. 6-Memorial of Sylvester Churchill: referred to the Cmte on Military Affairs. 7-Ptn of the heirs of Chas Lewis: referred to the Cmte on Revolutionary Claims. 8-Ptn of Jno O Means: referred to the Cmte on Naval Affairs. 9-Ptn of Jas Durning: referred to the Cmte of Claims. 10-Documents presented relating to the renewal of a patent by Jno Shly to the Cmte on Patents; also, the ptn of Geo Talcott: referred to the Cmte of Claims. 11-Memorial of J K Rogers, legal rep of David Cordery: referred to the Cmte on Indian Affairs. FROM CMTE. 12-Cmte on Commerce: bill for the relief of John A McGaw, of N Y: to be printed. Same cmte: bill for the relief of W P Greene: to be printed. 13-Bill introduced for the relief of Chas A Kellett, & a bill for the relief of Enoch Baldwin: referred to the Cmte on Commerce. 14-Bill taken up for the relief of Mrs Mgt L Worth, speaking of the great merits of Gen Worth as an ofcr: bill passed the Senate at the last session with great unanimity, & did not get through the House from want of time.

To Machinists & Foundry Men: the Md Machine Manufacturing Co will positively sell at public auction, all their machinery, tools, fixtures, at the Factory, Ellicott's Mills, near Balt, on Jan 14, 1852. –Geo Poe, Agent, ***Ellicot's Mills***

Circuit Court of Wash Co, D C-in Chancery. Geo W P Mankin, by his next friend, against Geo C Bomford, Jas V Bomford, Geo W J Bomford, Richd C Derby & Louisa his wife, & John T Payne & Ruth his wife, & others. Bill: Ann Mary Parsons purchased from the late Benj L Lear, lot 14 in square 486, with the dwlg house thereon, in Wash City; that part of the purchase money remained unpaid at his death; that the legal title to said lot passed by his will to the late Geo Bomford, who hath died intestate, leaving the above named dfndnts his heirs at law, to whom such title is now vested, & that Ann Mary Parsons, not having fully paid said purchase money at the time of her death, by her will gave the said premises to the late John Boyle, in order that he might repay himself some advances he had made for her, & the residue of the said purchase money, & then apply said property, or the residue of the proceeds, to the said purchase money, & also all sums due to said John Boyle, were fully repaid to him in his lifetime; & the object of the said bill is to obtain a conveyance of the legal title in & to said lot & premises from the said heirs above named of said Geo Bomford, & an account of the rents of the said premises from the reps of the said John Boyle: it being made to appear that the said dfndnts above named do not reside within D C. Same are to appear either in person or by solicitor, on or before the first Mon of May next. –Jno A Smith, clk -Redin for cmplnt

Died: on Dec 17, in Wash City, Lt Col Danl Randall, Deputy Paymaster Gen U S Army, in his 60th year. He was a native of Annapolis, Md, & entered the army in Jul, 1818, as Paymaster of the 1st Regt of Infty. His body will be conveyed to Annapolis for interment. His funeral is at 10 o'clock on Dec 19, from the residence of Mrs Hagner, Pa ave.

Mrs Tilley is prepared to accommodate gentlemen & ladies with pleasant rooms & board: corner of Missouri ave & 3rd st.

Farmer & Gardner wanted on a small farm: apply to S W Handy & Co store opposite Willard's Hotel.

Dissolution of copartnership existing under the firm of Lindsley & Baden, by mutual consent. Persons indebted to make payment to H Lindsley. –H Lindsley, T E Baden

FRI DEC 19, 1851
Senate: 1-Memorial of Leslie Combs, of Ky, in which he states that the late republic of Texas was indebted to him $69,200, for which the memorialist held the bonds of the said republic for the payment of the interest semi-annually, for which the customs were solemnly pledged & set apart; said bonds had been regularly filed in the Treasury Dept. He petitioned Congress immediately on the annexation of the

republic to the U S to pay him the debt, with interest, but has never yet received either principal or interest: referred to the Cmte on Finance. 2-Memorial of Ashburn Regan, a native of Georgia, & a citizen of the parish of Natchitoches, La, stating that he had discovered a plan to prevent the overflowing of the Mississippi: referred to the Cmte on Roads & Canals. 3-Memorial of Caleb Dustin, asking that certain continental money issued to his grandfather in the Revolutionary war may be redeemed with interest: referred to the Cmte on Revolutionary Claims. 4-Memorial of Robt Mills, architect, asking to be allowed an opportunity to justify his acts as architect & superintendent of the wing of the Patent Ofc bldg against certain charges made against him by the Com'r of Public Bldgs in his report to the Sec of the Interior: referred to the Cmte on Public Bldgs. 5-Additional evidence presented in relation to the claim of the legal reps of Wm Somerville, deceased: referred to the Cmte of Claims. 6-Addition evidence presented relating to the claim of John Moore; & the ptn of Derrill H Darby, for himself & the heirs of Col W Johnson of the Revolutionary army, asking to be allowed commutation pay: referred to the Cmte on Revolutionary Claims. 7-Ptn of Francis Gardere, asking compensation for certain land claimed by him under a Spanish grant, & occupied by the U S for military purposes: referred to the Cmte on Private Land Claims. 8-Memorial of the administrator of Joshua B Smith, asking compensation for the use of a vessel employed under a contract with a Gov't ofcr in transporting troops during the Florida war; also of John H Patterson, asking compensation for his services as a Lt in the Florida war; also of C H Blood, asking compensation for supplies furnished a company of Florida volunteers; also of Sarah Flinn, asking for compensation for supplies furnished the troops of the U S during the Florida war; also of David Osburn, asking compensation for corn & fodder furnished the troops of the U S in Florida during the Seminole war; also of John W W Jackson, asking compensation for a horse killed in the service of the U S; also from Geo Baya, asking compensation for a horse lost in the military service of the U S: all of which several memorials & petitions were referred to the Cmte of Claims. 9-Memorial of Cadwalader Wallace: referred to the Cmte on Public Lands. 10-Memorial of the heirs of Wm Beatty: referred to the Cmte on Revolutionary Claims. 11-Cmte on Naval Affairs: memorial of Eliza C Bache: passed to a second reading. 12-Bill for the relief of the personal reps of Wm A Slacum: referred to the Cmte on Foreign Relations.

<u>Portrait painting</u>: J A Simpson, Artist, can be found at the room of the Cmte on Pensions, basement, north bldg in the Capitol, from 10 to 3½ o'clock daily.

Wash Corp: 1-Mayor nominates Dennis Callaghan as police ofcr for the 5th Ward: ordered to lie on the table. 2-Bill for the relief of Maurice Holbran: referred to the Cmte in Improvements. 3-Ptn of Jas Davis, praying to be released from certain fines: referred to the Cmte of Claims. 4-Cmte of Claims: Bill for the relief of Robt Earl: passed. 5-Cmte of Claims: bill for the relief of Trueman W Brush, reported the same without amendment. Same cmte: bill for the relief of Wm Greer, reported the same without amendment.

Dept of State, Wash, Dec 17, 1851. Letter to Mrs Ophella P Talbot, New Orleans, La. It gives me sincere pleasure to inform you that her Majesty the Queen of Spain, to whose Minister in this city a copy of your letter to the President of Sep 25 last had been communicated, with the request to intercede with his Govn't in behalf of your unfortunate son, Jas M Wilson, has not only graciously pardoned him, but has furnished him also from her own private purse the means to return speedily to his home. –Danl Webster

House of Reps: 1-Ptn of Edmund Rine, of the 2nd Regt of Pa volunteers in Mexico, praying for bounty land. 2-Ptn of John R Edie, heir of John Edie, praying for commutation pay & interest. 3-Ptn of W C Handley, grandson of Geo Handley, an ofcr of the Georgia continental line, praying commutation pay.

Stratham Church contains tombs of several families of distinction. Of Rebecca, the wife of Wm Lynes, the lamenting widower writes: Should I then thousand years enjoy my life, I could not praise enough so good a wife. On the south wall of a monument: Eliz, wife of Maj Gen Hamilton, who was married near 47 years, & never did one thing to displease her husband. An angry bachelor says: Perhaps she was never allowed.

Criminal Court-Wash. 1-Washington Rawlings was found not guilty of receiving stolen goods. 2-Patrick Carroll, for stealing said goods, also not guilty. 3-Thos Flinn, John Flinn, & John Barnes, guilty of a riot: fined $10 each. 4-Negro Susan Anderson, guilty of stealing clothing from Mrs Dr Busey: not yet sentenced. 5-Danl & Morris Sullivan guilty of an assault on Edmund Brooke: fined $10. 6-Danl Sullivan, tried for shooting & then stealing a chicken of Edmund Brooke, found not guilty. 7-Negro Geo Lee guilty of stealing a coat from Moses Leiblick: 2 years in the penitentiary. 8-Negro Geo Kendall guilty of stealing slippers: new trial moved on the ground of insanity. 9-Arthur Bradley, not guilty for assault & battery on John West. 10-Wm A Mulley, guilty for assault on Josh H March: fined $5. 11-Negro John Reed not guilty of an assault on Patrick McGhee. 12-John E Moody not guilty of an assault on J Dewdney. 13-Rosier Gibson, guilty of an assault on John Bohlayer: fine $10. For riot growing out of the same assault: fine $1. 14-Negro Bill Barns, not guilty for assault on Saml Ford. 15-Negro Jas Read guilty of stealing a box of candles from Messrs Bates: sentented to 9 months imprisonment. 16-Negro Moses Brown, guilty for stealing 2 hogs: 9 months in jail. 17-Negro Wm Mason, tried for the same, found not guilty. 18-Leonard Simmermecker, a boy, tried for stealing 2 cows from Josh B Hall, found guilty: not yet sentenced. 19-Negro Pug Slater, for an assault: fined $1. 20-Wm Baine guilty for stealing a coat from Thos Wall, gardener at the Pres' House: one year in the county jail. 21-Negro Geo Regalan, guilty of stealing $20 in small change from Jesse Brooks: 2 years in the penitentiary. 22-Jeremiah Higgins, guilty for a riot: fined $10. 23-Elias Matthews, not guilty with stealing servants' clothing of Mrs Ann S Hill. 24-Negro Richd Cruso, a boy, found not guilty of stealing a barrel of flour

Died: yesterday, in Wash City, John Francis, aged 6 months & 9 days, son of Wm F & Mary F E Purcell. His funeral is this evening at half past 2 o'clock, on Md ave between 6th & 7th sts.

Thos Swann, of Balt, has donated $3,000 to the Md Institute, to be appropriated in aid of the school of Applied Chemistry which it is proposed to organize in connexion with the Institute.

The extensive factory, grist mill, & cotton gin belonging to Abraham Ruddick, on Somerton creek, Nansemond Co, Va, was entirely consumed by fire on Sat last. Partially covered by insurance.

SAT DEC 20, 1851

Columbia Topographical Society meeting Sat at 7 o'clock, in the City Hall. —Wm E Nott, sec

Rev Jas Gallaher, of Missouri, will preach in the First Presbyterian Church, 4½ st, tomorrow at 11 a m & in the afternoon at 3:30 p m.

Mrs Fertig, on E st, offers to the public, at the cheapest prices, TOYS of all kinds, viz: Menageries, Mines, Furnished Rooms & Kitchens, Waterworks, Dolls, & Playing Musical Toys.

Senate: 1-Memorial of Thos J Page, lt in the U S Navy, asking compensation for services performed as purser: referred to the Cmte on Naval Affairs. 2-Memorial of Dr S Edwards & other medical ofcrs of the U S Navy, asking remuneration for extra expenses incurred in serving with a regt of marines in Mexico: referred to the Cmte on Naval Affairs. 3-Memorial of Jas P Lightburn, asking compensation for property destroyed while in the occupancy of the U S troops in 1849: referred to the Cmte of Claims. 4-Additional documents presented in the case of Jane Irwin, daughter of Jared Irwin, of the Revolutionary war: referred to the Cmte on Revolutionary Claims. 5-Additional documents presented in relation to the claim of Israel Ketchum for losses sustained as sub-contractor in the erection of fortifications on Dauphin Island: referred to the Cmte of Claims. 6-Ptn of Squire Moore, of Michigan, asking for an increase of pension: referred to the Cmte on Pensions. PAPERS WITHDRAWN & REFERRED. 7-Memorial of Clemens Bryan: referred to the Cmte of Claims. 8-Memorial of Noah Miller: referred to the Cmte on Commerce. 9-Memorial of the reps of Joshua Kennedy: referred to the Cmte on Military Affairs. 10-Bill introduced for the relief of the heirs & legal reps of Col Alex'r P Morgan: referred to the Cmte on Military Affairs.

Hon Joel R Poinsett, of S C, died at Stateburg, on Dec 12, in his 73rd year. He was born in Charleston on Mar 2, 1779. —Charleston Courier

Chancery sale of valuable property: by decree of the Circuit Court of Wash Co, D C, in a cause wherein Virginia Semmes & others are cmplnts, & Sabina Semmes & others are respondents, dated Dec 4, 1851: public auction, on Jan 19 next, of lot 14 & part of lot 15, in square 457, with the bldgs & the appurtenances.
–Walter D Davidge, B I Semmes, trustees -Dyer & McGuire, aucts

In the case of Beardsley et al vs Lewis Tappan, in the U S Circuit Court for the Southern Dist of N Y, the jury on Thursday rendered a verdict for the plntfs, assessing the damages at $10,000. The action was brought for a libel, alleged to have been published by the dfndnt affecting the credit of the plntfs, who are merchants in the State of Ohio.

Millard Fillmore, Pres of the U S A, recognizes Joaquin Jose Castillo, who has been appointed Consul of the Mexican Republic, at Brownsville, Texas. –Dec 19, 1851

The painting of the 8th & last historical picture for the Rotundo at Washington, fell on Wm H Powell, the choice of Congress. Nine years ago, at age 16, his works attracted the admiration of the visiters of the Academy of Design at N Y. The subject given him by Congress for his historical picture is The Discovery of the Mississippi by De Soto. [De Soto de Villenueva, Govn'r of Santiago de Cuba, takes possession in 1542, for his King & Emperor, Charles V, of the great Mississippi, its tributaries, & broad valley.] The picture is worthy to fill the vacant panel at the Rotundo.

Mrd: on Dec 16, in the M E Church, Winchester, Va, by Rev Wm Krebs, Rev John S Deale, of Cumberland, Md, to Miss Sallie, daughter of N Buckmaster, of Pittsburg, Pa.

Mrd: on Aug 20, 1851, at Salem, Ohio, by Rev Mr Henderson, J Gideon Crowley, of Wash, D C, to Miss Mary S Sproat, of the former place.

Died: on Fri, John Harrison Johnson, in his 23rd year. His funeral is today at 10 o'clock, from the residence of his uncle, Mr Wm Orme, on 11th st.

Died: on Dec 19, Mrs M Kirby, wife of Jas Kirby, & daughter of the late Raphael Boarman. Her funeral is Sunday, at 2 P M, corner of 16th & I sts west, near St John's Church.

MON DEC 22, 1851
On Fri last, at Newburyport, Col Abraham Williams, aged 65, for many years a leading merchant, slipped upon the ice in State street, striking heavily upon the back of his head, which caused his death in 5 minutes afterwards.

Mr Geo Blake, the oldest person in Springfield, so far as we know, the oldest in the county, died on Wed. He was in his 93rd year, & leaves behind him in Springfield but one Revolutionary pensioner, Mr John Edwards. Mr Blake has voted at every Presidential election since the formation of the Republic.
—Springfield [Mass] Republican

Real estate for sale: by decree of the Montgomery Co Court, [Md] as Court of Equity: in the case of Jedediah Gittings & others, vs Richd A Harding & wife, the subscriber, as trustee, will offer at public sale, on Jan 12, the following lots or parts of the real estate of which Thos Gittings, late of said county, died seized, in Montg Co: lot 4 contains 127½ acres, with a comfortable dwlg house. Lot 5 contains 66½ acres. Lot 6 contains 60½ acres, is separated from lots 4 & 5 by the public road.
—W Veirs Bouic, trustee

Mr Geo Ralston, of King's creek, Hancock Co, Va, purchased a keg of powder for blasting rocks. During his absence his little son, about 6 years old, applied a torch to the keg, & killed himself & another child, & 10 others were seriously injured.

Senate: 1-Memorial of Wm R Nevins, asking an extension of his patent of a machine for rolling & cutting crackers & biscuits: referred to the Cmte on Patents & the Patent Ofc. 2-Memorial of Chas Massey, jr, & other citizens of Phil, asking indemnity for French spoliations prior to 1800: referred to the Select Cmte on French Spoliations. 3-Memorial of Cmder Johnson, of the U S Navy, asking reimbursement of certain expenses to which he was subjected in obeying an order of the Sec of the Navy, & to be allowed the pay of captain for the time he discharged the duties of that position. PAPERS WITHDRAWN & REFERRED. 4-Ptn of Thos Rhodes: referred to the Cmte on the Post Ofc & the Post Roads. 5-Ptn of Mrs Maria M Alexander, of Ky: referred to the Cmte on Pensions. 6-John F Sheldon had leave to withdraw his memorial & papers REPORTS FROM CMTES. 6-Cmte on Foreign Relations: bill for the relief of the legal reps of Wm Slacum, deceased: recommended its passage. 7-Cmte on Foreign Relations: asked to be discharged from the further consideration of the memorial of Albert Fritz, & that the memorialist have leave to withdraw his papers: which was agreed to. 8-Joint resolution for the exiled Irish patriots, Smith O'Brien, Thos F Meagher, & their associates, was considered in Cmte of the Whole: ordered to lie on the table.

Circuit Court of Wash Co, D C-in Equity. JohnTonnele, jr et al, vs Aaron Vail et al. Public auction on Jan 5, 1852, of lot 16 in square 221, & premises, in Wash.
—Anthony Hyde, trustee

Died: on Dec 21, in Wash City, Mrs Eliz Waterman Leadbitter, daughter of the late Nathan Waterman, jr, of Providence, R I, & wife of Lt D Leadbitter, U S Corps of Engineers.

Died: on Dec 19, Chas Edw, son of Wm & Eliz A Hoover, aged 5 months & 12 days.

Stray horse taken up on the farm of Mrs Geo W Walker, on 16th st. Owner will please take him away & pay charges.

The creditors of John Pickrell, deceased, are notified to produce their claims for payment; all indebted to make early payment. —Ann Pickrell, excx of John Pickrell

TUE DEC 23, 1851
Senate: 1-Ptn of S Hempstead & others, asking that a pension may be granted to David L Davis, in consideration of an injury received while in the service of the U S as an assistant surveyor: referred to the Cmte on Pensions. 2-Memorial of Mary Robb, widow of a soldier in the late war with Great Britain, asking to be allowed a pension. 3-Additional documents in relation to the claim of Nathan Weston: referred to the Cmte on Military Affairs. 4-Memorial of Thos Mullett, asking compensation for his services as deputy surveyor of public lands in La: referred to the Cmte of Claims. 5-Ptn of John Ireland, now on the files of the Senate, be referred to the Cmte of Claims. 6-Cmte on Pensions: ptn of Eliz Arnold: passed to a second reading. BILLS INTRODUCED. 7-Bill for the relief of John R Bryan, adm of Isaac Garretson, deceased, late a purser in the U S Navy. 8-Bill for the relief of Thos H Leggett. 9-Joint resolution for the relief of Alex'r P Field, late Sec of Wisconsin Territory, & sureties.

Mrs Rilley, wife of Capt Jas Rilley, of the British merchant's service, was drowned in the James River & Kanawha Canal, about 3 miles from Richmond, on Dec 13. She had with her 2 boys, 6 & 3 years of age, &, under the protection of a lady & gentleman, on her way to join her husband, who had preceded her some months, in order to prepare an abiding home for his wife & family.

Geo W Boyd was choked to death in Phil on Thursday, by a piece of meat sticking in his throat while eating supper.

Fatal duel in Calif. Geo M Dibble, formerly a midshipman in the navy, was recently killed in a duel in Calif, by E B Lundy, a Canadian. J C Morehead & C E G Morse were the seconds, who, with the surviving principal, have been arrested. The parties used Colt's revolvers, at 15 paces.

Eaton Deyoe, a pretended Temperance Agent, has been sent to the penitentiary for 3 years for obtaining money from Hon Amos Lawrence, of Boston.

Died: on Sunday, in Wash City, after a short illness, Miss Mary Josephine Ladd. Her funeral is today, at 3 P M from Mr Boak's, corner of 4½ & Pa ave, south side.

Postmaster Gen est'd the following new Post Ofcs for week ending Dec 20, 1851.

Ofc	County, State	Postmaster
Mendon	Monroe, N Y	Willet Van Wagner
Coventry Centre	Kent, R I	Henry S Vaughan
Wauchussett Village	Worcester, Mass	Benj Wyman
South Action	Middlesex, Mass	Ezra C Radiman
Barden	Sciota, Ohio	Solomon Thompson
Yankeetown	Drake, Ohio	John B Witchell
Jackson's Mill	Davidson, N C	Peter D Swain
Mayfield	Jackson, Tenn	M A Bassham
Garriott't Landing	Trimble, Ky	Evan Garriott
Monterey	Allegan, Mich	Eli D Granger
Rowanter	Dinwiddie, Va	Williamson Perkins

Names Changed: 1-Brier Creek, Columbia, Pa, changed to Fowlersville.
2-Gold Mine, Chesterfield, S C, changed name & site to Jefferson.
3-Silo, Sullivan, Indiana, changed name & site to Busroen.

Ladies Union Benevolent & Employment Society: list of the ofcrs & managers for those who may need assistance: Directresses:

Mrs Mills, Capitol Hill
Mrs O B Brown, E st
Mrs Hammond, Sec
Mrs Eckard, N Y av
Mrs C S Fowler, F st
Mrs C Monroe, Treas

Managers:
Mrs W A Bradley, La av
Mrs Brawner, Island
Mrs J F Webb, 6th st
Mrs Wm Coxe, C st
Mrs L J Gilliss, N Y av
Mrs Duff Green, Capitol Hill
Mrs S P Hill, H st
Mrs Maher, 15th st
Mrs Capt Morris, Navy Yard
Mrs Wm Nourse, N st
Miss O'Neal, M st
Mrs Capt Powell, Navy Yard
Mrs Judge Platte, G st
Mrs D Ratcliffe, Franklin Row
Mrs Read, F st
Mrs A Steele, F st
Mrs Dr Smoot, near 7 Bldgs
Mrs C S Stewart, Capitol Hill
Mrs Rosalie Smith, Mass av
Mrs W B Todd, F st
Mrs Tucker
Mrs Walker, 15th st
Mrs Dr Young, Pa ave, near 4½ st

Mrd: on Sabbath evening, by Rev John C Smith, Mr John W Speaks to Miss Sarah Catharine Wilson, all of Wash City.

Died: on Dec 22, after a short illness, Mrs Bridget Nugent, a native of county of Westmeath, Ireland, aged 58 years. Her funeral is today, at 3 o'clock, from the residence of her son, corner of 13th & F sts.

Died: on Dec 22, suddenly, at the residence of Mrs A Sweeny, Thos O'Neill, of Phil, in his 39th year. His remains will be taken to the cars this evening at 4 o'clock.

Died: on Dec 21, after a brief illness of 6 days, from typhoid pneumonia, Edmund Brooke, in his 56th year, late a clerk in the Pension Ofc. His funeral is this morning at 10:30 o'clock, from his late residence on the Island, opposite the Smithsonian Institute. Friends & relatives are invited.

Died: Dec 21, Anna Catharine, daughter of Jno P & Sarah M White, aged 2 years & 4 months. Her funeral is today at 2 o'clock, from the residence of her father, N J ave, near D st.

Died: at her mother's residence in Rockville, Md, in her 21st year, Martha Hale Prout, daughter of the late Wm Prout, of Wash City.
[No death date given-current item.]

WED DEC 24, 1851
Senate: 1-Ptn of Catherine Elwes, widow of Dr Alfred W Elwes, late a Surgeon in the U S Army, claiming a pension on the ground of her husband having died of a brain fever contracted while attending the sick: referred to the Cmte on Pensions. 2-Additional documents in the case of Wm L Meredith, heir of Wm Meredith: referred to the Cmte on Revolutionary Claims. 3-Memorial of Jesse E Brown, in his own right, & also as administrator of Wm A Russell, for balance of a claim due him under an insufficient award of the Board on Mexican claims: referred to the Cmte on Foreign Relations. 4-Cmte on Military Affairs: bill for the relief of Mrs Mgt Hetzel, admx of A R Hetzel, late assistant quartermaster in the U S Army: passed to a second reading. 5-Cmte on Military Affairs: bill for the relief of Adj Gen Roger Jones: passed to a second reading. 6-Cmte on Military Affairs: asked to be discharged from the further consideration of the memorial of Richd W Johnson, of Ky: that it be referred to the Cmte on Naval Affairs. 7-Cmte on Military Affairs: asked to be discharged from the further consideration of the memorial of Preston Starrit, in relation to the appointment of a Board of Com'rs to investigate the Cherokeee claims, & the memorial of R W Hallett, asking compensation for property destroyed by Creek Indians, & that they be severally referred to the Cmte on Indian Affairs. PAPERS WITHDRAWN & REFERRED. 8-Memorial of Chas J Jackson: referred to the Cmte on Commerce. 9-Memorial of Chas Lee Jones: referred to the Cmte on Military Affairs. 10-Memorial of John W Whipple: referred to the Cmte of Claims. 11-Saml Colunn had leave to withdraw his petition & papers. 12-The heirs of Jas Bell had leave to withdraw their petition & papers.

On Thu in the neighborhood of Burkittsville, Md, the accidental burning of the dwlg house of Mr Feilder Thompson, who, besides losing his property & all his furniture & clothing, had 2 children, 6 & 8 years of age, consumed in the flames. Every effort was made to rescue them.

At N Y on Mon, a scaffolding erected about the steeple of the church in 6th st, on which 3 Swedish sailors, Henry Brown, John Henry, & Chas Moore, gave way, when Henry & Brown were precipitated to the ground, about 75 feet. Brown died & Henry is expected to live but a short time. Moore escaped by clinging to the window of the steeple.

Criminal Court-Wash-Thu: 1-Wm Colson, guilty of stealing shaving glasses & sundry articles at the recent fire on the premises of Mr Dennis Desmond, on the Island: sentenced to 6 months in the county jail. 2-Negro Jas Brown, alias Jas Bowie, not guilty of assault & battery on another negro, Hanson Steward. 3-Wm Umberfield, guilty for stealing a mule, wagon, & milk cans: 2 years in the penitentiary. 4-Owen Clark, guilty of stealing 50 empty gas tar barrels, property of Jos C Lewis: 4 months in jail.

Died: on Dec 22, in Gtwn, Eliz A, daughter of the late Henry H & Mary Chapman, aged 46 years. Her funeral is today at 3 o'clock.

Died: on Dec 23, Geo Peyton, son of Leonidas & Mary Bowen, in his 3rd year. His funeral is tomorrow at 2 o'clock.

Died: after a long & lingering illness, Nathl Herbert, long known as a faithful messenger in the Post Ofc Dept. He was appointed by Postmaster Gen Meigs, in 1812, 40 years since. As a husband, father, neighbor, & friend, he was kind, affectionate & charitable. His funeral is today at 2 o'clock.
[No death date given-current item.

THU DEC 25, 1851
Mrd: on Dec 23, at the E st Baptist Church, by Rev J D Anderson, Rev J Tilson, of Hingham, Mass, to Miss Martha D, daughter of Robt P Anderson, of Wash City.

Died: on Dec 24, in Wash City, Mrs Mary Dougherty, relict of the late Jos Dougherty, a native of Ireland, & a resident of Wash City for more than half a century, aged 86. Her funeral is on Fri, at 3 o'clock, from her residence on 6th st, beyond I.

On Nov 18, a difficulty occurred at Taylor's Bridge, Sampson Co, N C, between persons attached to John & Co's circus company & the citizens, in which Milton Matthias was killed. Johnson, the manager, & members of his company, were arrested.

I have a small farm of 63 acres, separated from Wash City by the Eastern Branch only, for sale. There is a comfortable house recently built on the land. Apply at my ofc, C & 3rd sts, D A Hall.

The Nat'l Library was destroyed by fire yesterday. The fire broke out in the Franklin Hotel, D & 8th sts, kept by Mr Thos Baker. The bldg was owned by Mr Patrick Kavanagh, & was insured. About 35,000 volumes of most choice & valuable books were destroyed, together with precious collections of manuscripts, painting, maps, charts, medals, statuary, the property of the Gov't & People of the U S. The fire was observed by Mr Jno W Jones, one of the guards in charge of the Capitol, & with Mr Hollohon, forced their way into the Library, & saw a large table & shelving & books on fire. The draught which their entrance produced lent vigor to the flames. Included in the destruction was Stuart's paintings of the first 5 Presidents; an original portrait of Columbus; a second portrait of Columbus; an original portrait of Peyton Randolph; a portrait of Bolivar; a portrait of Baron Steuben by Pyne, an English artist of merit; one of Baron De Kalb; one of Cortez; & one of *Judge Hanson, of Md, presented to the Library by his family. Of the statuary burnt: a statue of Jefferson; an Apollo in bronze by Mills; a very superior bronze likeness of Washington; a bust of Gen Taylor by an Italian artist; & a bust of Lafayette by David. [*Dec 27th newspaper: The portrait of John Hanson, who died in Phil in 1783 or 1784, while Pres of Congress, was never a Judge. The Portrait was presented to the joint Cmte on the Library by Pres John Hanson's descendant, Judge Chas W Hanson, of Md. –R H Weightman] [Dec 29th newspaper: one at least of Stuart's pictures of the first Presidents was saved: that of Pres Monroe, which received no damage except to its frame. It was removed to the house of Mr Carter, on Capitol Hill, where it probably remains.]

Mrd: on Dec 23, by Rev Mr Hodges, Saml Geo Cox to Miss Anna Maria Goddard, of D C.

SAT DEC 27, 1851
Wash City Ordinance: 1-Act for the relief of Dennis Drum: the sum of $5.25 to be paid him for blacksmith's work required in improving B st south: under Saml Gregg, superintendent. 2-Act for the relief of Robt Earl: sum of $10 be paid him for money erroneously paid in obtaining a license for keeping a livery stable. 3-Act for the relief of Wm E Stewart: sum of $18 be refunded him, in consideration of his inability to use the shop license granted to him Mar 1 to Jun 26, 1851.

The subscriber has resumed the Practice of the Law in Upper Marlboro, & will punctually attend to all professional business that may be entrusted to him.
–John B Brooke

Trustee's sale of real estate: by deed of trust executed by Jesse B Dow, recorded in Liber 143, pages 134 thru 137, of the land records of Wash Co, D C: public auction, to satisfy the claim secured by said deed of trust, on Feb 27, 1852: lot 4 in square 288; with a neat & comfortable 2 story brick house with basement. The property will be sold subject to a prior lien to the amount of about $700, more or less.
–John E Norris, trustee -Dyer & McGuire, aucts

Mr David Brister, of Trenton, was engaged with several men on Fri in cutting away the ice that obstructed the wheel of his mill. It suddenly began to turn, carrying him down through an aperture, crushing & killing him immediately. –Newark Daily Adv

Orphans Court of Wash Co, D C. Letters testamentary on the personal estate of Danl Randall, late of the U S Army, deceased. –A Randall, exc

Mrd: on Dec 24, by Rev Dr Butler, Dr Wm H Saunders to Hannah S, daughter of Jos H Bradley, all of Wash City.

Mrd: on Dec 25, in Gtwn, D C, by Rev Geo N Israel, Rev Saml Cornelius, of the Baltimore Annual Conference, to Virginia C Woodward.

Mrd: on Dec 23, in Wash City, by Rev J W Newton, Dr D N Mahon, of Carlisle, Pa, to Julia M, daughter of Capt J B Montgomery, of the U S Navy.

Mrd: on Dec 18, at Old Point Comfort, by Rev M L Chevers, Maj Henry J Hunt, U S Army, to Miss Emily C, daughter of Lt Col R E DeRussy, U S Corps Engineers.

Mrd: on Dec 23, in Anne Arundel Co, Md, by Rev Mr Nelson, Thos H Worthington, of Wash City, to Eliz M Williams, of the former place.

Died: on Dec 24, in her 82nd year, Mrs Nelly Wilson, a native of Somerset Co, Md, but for the last 28 years a resident of Wash City.

MON DEC 29, 1851
Mrd: on Dec 23, at the new Trinity Church, in Gtwn, by Rev P B O'Flanagan, Mr Jos Collins to Miss Mary A Hurdle.

Died: on Dec 22, in Wash City, Mrs Nancy King, consort of Wm King, of the Navy Dept. Mrs King was a native of Gettysburg, Pa, & had been only a short time a resident of Wash, long enough to have endeared her to her fellow worshippers in F st Presbyterian Church. –J L

Died: on Dec 21, in Raleigh, N C, Mrs Delia Haywood, aged 69 years, relict of the late Stephen Haywood, formerly of that place, & daughter of Col Philemon Hawkins, late of Warren Co, N C.

Died: on Dec 26, at his residence in Balt Co, Dennis A Smith, in his 71st year. A native of Calvert Co, he removed to Baltimore in 1795, & as early as 1813 had become not only the most prominent banker & shipper of that growing city, but enjoyed a high reputation through the country for his financial skill. The great financial depress after the war with England & the fall of Napoleon resulted in his embarrassment & ultimate failure; he never succeeded in retrieving his fortune.

Terrible conflagration at Phil on Dec 27. The heaviest losers are Dr Schenck, whose establishment was completely destroyed; T & T W Johnston, law booksellers; H Blakiston, & Getz & Buck, booksellers. Police Ofcr Johnson has been killed. W W Haley is missing & supposed to be killed. [Dec 31st newspaper: The remains of W W Haley & Mr Baker were recovered. Mr Haley a few months since married a daughter of Jacob Haldeman, of Harrisburg.]

Bookbindery to be sold low: in Alexandria, Va, with all the tools, nearly new. It is worth from $200 to $250. Apply to Robt Bell, Bookseller, Alexandria, Va.

Hon Benj Seaver was elected Mayor of the city of Boston on Wed last by a majority of one vote over all other competitors for the ofc. He was the regular Whig nominee. Lt Catesby Ap R Jones, U S Navy, who received severe wounds, writes a letter, dated Dec 5, to his father, Adj Gen Roger Jones, which confirms the account of the 2 wounds received. He states that he has the best medical attendance in Paris, & is doing well. In common with hundreds of others, [a friend who was in Paris the bloody days of Dec, writes,] Lt Jones was on the Boulevard listening to the cannonading of the Barricade at the Port St Denis, nearly ¾ mile distant, & apprehensive of no danger. The Boulevards were supposed to contain 50,000 troops. Orders were given to sweep with balls houses more than half a mile in extent, [in which were none but helpless females, or quiet families,] as well as to mow down all who happened to be in the street, without any notice given. The writer states that he & every American, as well as every intelligent Frenchmen with whom he conversed, regarded the affair on the Boulevards, a wanton act of Barbarity on the part of the military of Paris.

Terrible accident on Dec 12, near Prattsville, Ga, when the carriage of Mr R Winn, with his wife & 4 children came in contact with the Macon train, & was dashed to pieces. Two of the children & the driver, a negro, were instantly killed. Two other children are seriously injured. Mrs Winn was also very much hurt, but would probably survive. The driver is supposed to have been intoxicated.

The vacancy in the Tellership of the Bank of Wash, caused by the resignation of Hugh B Sweeny, will be filled by Wm E Howard.

Household & kitchen furniture at auction: on Dec 30, at the residence of Mr Westbrook, on Capitol Hill, on 2nd st, near East Capitol st. -A Green, auctioneer

TUE DEC 30, 1851
Obit-died: on Dec 9, in Phil, Madame Asigoigne, aged 81 years. Standing, as she did, in a relation almost maternal to at least 2 generations, grief for her is not limited to the domestic circle, but casts its shadow over a whole community.

By a late steamer from Europe we hear of the death of Vincent Priessnitz, the celebrated founder of the Hydropathic system of curing diseases. He died at Graefenburg on Nov 26, at age 52. He discovered the Water Cure system about 20 years ago, & established business at Graefenburg, Germany. His establishment has gained world wide celebrity.

The subscriber wishes to obtain a situation as a Carriage-driver with any Gentleman who may wish to give him a trial. He has been employed as a carriage-driver for the last 5 years with a respectable family in Wash City, & can give satisfactory references. –Benj Frazer

Died: on Dec 24, in Wash City, at the residence of his brother, on 9th st, Nathl W Adams, a Clerk in the Treasury Dept, formerly a resident of Buffalo, N Y, & a native of Conn, aged 29 years. His remains were interred on Fri in the Congressional Cemetery.

Senate: 1-Cmte on Naval Affairs: calling for the record of the Court of Inquiry convened on Board the U S ship **Cumberland**, in the bay of Naples, by order of Com Chas W Morgan, to investigate charges preferred against Capt Wm K Latimer. 2-Memorial of Jas Corrigan, asking an increase of pension: referred to the Cmte on Pensions. 3-Memorial of Amos Kendall & John E Kendall, asking compensation for their services in prosecuting the claims of the Western Cherokee Indians: referred to the Cmte on Indian Affairs. 4-Additional evidence in relation to the claim of Jas Jeffries & Jeremiah M Smith: referred to the Cmte on Indian Affairs. 5-Memorial of Santiago E Arguello, a capt in the Calif battalion, asking compensation for losses sustained during the war with Mexico: referred to the Cmte on Military Affairs. 6-Cmte on Indian Affairs: bill for the relief of the heirs of Jos Watson: ordered to a second reading. PAPERS WITHDRAWN & REFERRED. 7-Ptn of Willard Boynton: referred to the Cmte on Indian Affairs. 8-Ptn of Wm Russwurm: referred to the Cmte on Revolutionary Claims. 9-Ptns of Rhoda Frisbee & Wm Roberts: referred to the Cmte on Pensions.

Died: on Sunday, in Wash City, Reuben, son of Mr Henry & Mrs Catherine Walker, aged 5 years. His funeral is today at 3 o'clock, from the residence of his parents, on 16th st, near I st.

Died: on Monday, in Wash City, Mary Ann, daughter of Jas & Jane Lynch, aged 3 years & 4 days. Her funeral is today at 2 o'clock.

Died: at N Y, suddenly, in her 96th year, Mrs Jane Kip. [No death date given-current item.]

The copartnership between Berry & Beach is dissolved by mutual consent. –W O Berry, Wm E Beach

Died: recently, at Darien, Conn, Thaddeus Bell, aged 93. He was present at the burning of Danbury, during the Revolutionary war, & took part in the pursuit of the British. He was one of the congregation who, with their pastor, Dr Marthan, were seized during Divine worship by a band of Tories, & conveyed to the British headquarters at N Y.

WED DEC 31, 1851
Postmaster Gen est'd the following new Post Ofcs for week ending Dec 27, 1851.

Ofc	County, State	Postmaster
Troy Center	Waldo, Me	Lorenzo Garcelon
Davisville	Washington, R I	Jas M Davis
Vistal Center	Broome, N Y	Wm Gordon
North Copake	Columbia, N Y	Peter A Bain
Rensselaer Falls	St Lawrence, N Y	Archibald Shull
Phoenicia	Ulster, N Y	Isaac D Vandevort
Mansville	Perry, Pa	Wm Burd
West Mill Creek	Erie, Pa	Lewis H Mandaville
Long River	Perry, Miss	G K W Boulton
Sumpter	Trinity, Texas	T M Baily
Meyersville	Dewit, Texas	Adolph Meyer
Dorchester	La Fayette, Ark	Leonidas Morgan
Hazel Grove	Lawrence, Ark	Alex'r Campbell
Montengo	Drew, Ark	Isaac D Price
Terre Noir	Clark, Ark	Jas H Crow
Littleby	Audrain, Mo	Wiley Tully
Pineville	McDonald, Mo	John Starns
Austinville	Livingston, Mo	Andrew N Austin
Lactin	Cedar, Iowa	John Boydston
Hopeville	Clark, Iowa	David Newton
Oceola C H	Clark, Iowa	Percy Cowles
Littleport	Clayton, Iowa	Dennis Quigly
Londomills	Clayton, Iowa	Geo L Wheeler
Milton	Van Buren, Iowa	Robt Russell
Point Isabelle	Wapello, Iowa	Geo Thomas
Valley	Washington, Iowa	Robt Shaw
Fountain Prarie	Columbia, Wis	Smith Horton
Shoneaw	Columbia, Wis	W S Wherry
Logan	Edgar, Ill	Peter Igo
Rushaway	Menard, Ill	Jas W Simpson
Somerset	Saline, Ill	Handkerson Rude
Spring Rock	Whitley, Ky	Saml Beams
Carver's Ferry	Jassamine, Ky	Valentine Duncan
Godwinville	Bergen, N J	Cornelius Shurte

Morgantsville	Northampton, N C	Wm H Hays
Sill's Creek	New Hanover, N C	John A McInnis
Fillmore	Conecuch, Ala	Ira Road
Pine Apple	Wilcox, Ala	Elijah Linsor
Sanford	Jefferson, Fla	Wm H Cohn
Barclay's Fork	San Miguel, N Mex	Jos Doyle
American Ford	Utah T	L C Herrington
Corn Creek	Utah T	Anson Call
Payson	Utah, Utah T	Jas Pace
Salt Creek	Utah T	Timothy B Foot
Springville	Utah, Utah T	Aaron Johnson

Names Changed: 1-Cooksville, Caddo Parish. La, name & site changed to Central Spring, Harrison Co, Texas.
2-Martha's Mills, Flemming Co, Ky. name & site changed to Pin Hook.
3-Oak Forest, Wayne Co, Ky, name & site changed to Stubanville.
4-Culchote, Polk, Tenn, named & site changed to Hirassee Copper Mine.

Calif: 1-The Stockton Journal of Nov 29 records the execution of Frederic Salkmeyer & Noah E James for horse-stealing. 2-Henry Ogden, of N Y, Frank Wilson, a German, & Mr Conslaugh, a Swiss, were drowned in the bay of San Francisco on Nov 30 by the upsetting of a boat.

Mrd: on Dec 30, by Rev Dr Laurie, John S Maxwell to Miss Mary L Wilson, all of Wash City.

Died: on Dec 30, Mr John F Sweeny, aged 25 years. His funeral is on Jan 1, at 3 o'clock, at his mother's residence, Mrs A Sweeny, Capitol Hill.

Died: on Dec 28, suddenly, in Gtwn, D C, Mrs Alethea Burnett, aged 70 years, relict of the late Chas A Burnett. Her funeral is today at 3 o'clock, from her late residence on Bridge st.

I certify that Malachai B Farr brought before me, an estray, trespassing on his premises, a soreel Mare. —J W Beck, J P [Owner is to prove property, pay charges, & take her away-Malachi B Farr]

House of Reps: 1-Ptn of J W Bennett for payment of property lost in the destruction of Minot Ledge light-house. 2-Ptn of Chas Fletcher, of Lancaster, for a contract for carrying the mail in a line of steamers proposed to be established between Norfolk, Va, & Cadiz, Spain. 3-Memorial of Chas D Arfwedson, asking remuneration for his services as Charge d'Affaires & interim at the Court of Stockholm. 4-Ptn of Andrew Harwood, of Bristol Co, Mass, for a pension, on account of wounds received & services performed in the Mexican war.

By order of distrain from John Robinson, against the goods & chattels of Wm B Mitchell, I have this day distrained on Sundry goods, the property of said Mitchell, to satisfy rent due & in arrears to John Robinson: public sale on Jan 3, 1852.
–J A Ratcliff, Bailiff

New Year's Day: the President's Mansion will be open, as usual, tomorrow. Diplomatic Corps will be received at 11 o'clock, & other visiters from 12 to 2 P M.

A

Abbot, 98, 165, 177
Abbott, 54, 244, 279, 381, 474, 490, 501
Abell, 374
Abercrombie, 282
Abern, 186
Abernethy, 84
Abert, 162, 165, 248, 349, 487
Able, 8
Aborn, 331
Ackerman, 387, 490
Ackland, 87
Acs, 445
Acton, 165, 387, 462
Adae, 295
Adair, 53
Adam, 101, 108, 270
Adams, 2, 20, 21, 42, 46, 56, 61, 72, 73, 75, 104, 107, 124, 135, 138, 141, 150, 165, 170, 178, 186, 191, 199, 214, 256, 269, 279, 305, 306, 311, 322, 327, 331, 337, 341, 350, 362, 381, 383, 386, 403, 438, 452, 459, 461, 467, 477, 487, 500, 502, 510, 545
Adams' Discovery, 518
Adamses, 322
Adamson, 100, 268
Addams, 135
Addison, 21, 58, 84, 101, 314, 356, 381, 386, 421, 453, 511
addition to Fellowship, 48
Adellvig, 329
Adie, 493
Adler, 72, 241
Adriance, 270
Agassie, 47
Ager, 165, 319, 439
Aigler, 101
Aiken, 46, 115, 335, 354, 512
Aikin, 148

Ailer, 104, 165
Aitkin, 10
Ajtay, 394
Akers, 484
Alberti, 135
Albright, 41
Alby, 28, 60, 182
Alcock, 414
Alcom, 327
Alcott, 522
Alden, 39, 145, 321, 322
Alexander, 1, 101, 165, 212, 279, 331, 423, 449, 453, 480, 495, 537
Alfonso, 378, 409
Alford, 74, 179, 313, 346
Alfred, 179
Alig, 69, 192, 205, 320, 327, 363, 395, 399, 439, 482, 495
Allard, 62
Allem, 378
Allemander, 15
Allen, 3, 15, 55, 94, 101, 119, 121, 164, 165, 171, 183, 184, 220, 233, 236, 250, 309, 325, 326, 327, 331, 386, 403, 406, 407, 429, 450, 454, 455, 459, 511, 519
Allen's Fresh, 90
Allensworth, 179
Allern, 410
Alley, 127
Alliany, 410
Allison, 50, 191
Allmand, 346
Allmon, 370
Almonte, 57
Alsbourgh, 418
Alsop, 60
Althouse, 41
Alviso, 238
Ambler, 52, 499
Ambrose, 331
Ames, 393
Amitt, 74

Ammen, 260
Ammon, 98
Amory, 278, 290, 483, 501
Ampudia, 15
Analostan, 341, 426
ancient church, 79
Anderson, 10, 83, 101, 116, 127, 165, 191, 214, 331, 354, 366, 381, 437, 445, 447, 453, 454, 466, 483, 485, 516, 518, 521, 534, 541
Andrews, 4, 45, 116, 127, 181, 278, 289, 306, 402, 432, 435, 485
Andw, 382
Angel, 430
Angelbody, 233
Angell, 142
Angelrodt, 186
Angus, 151, 169, 182
Annable, 263
Anthony, 27
Anunally, 371
Applegate, 466, 526
Appleton, 301, 403
Aquelli, 378
Aragon, 378, 409, 432
Arbell, 524
Arbuckle, 159, 268, 276, 288, 303, 483
Archer, 28, 319
Archibald, 242, 338
Arden, 77
Arenas, 56, 181
Arfwedson, 547
Argenti, 309
Arghlir, 378
Arguelles, 528
Arguello, 545
Arista, 42, 123
Arlington House, 183
Armington, 236
Armistead, 72, 76, 92, 259, 264
Armstead, 101

Armstrong, 1, 37, 43, 49, 72, 74, 87, 174, 181, 233, 253, 357, 369, 385, 420, 499, 527
Arno, 378
Arnold, 5, 76, 101, 127, 207, 267, 287, 353, 359, 386, 411, 515, 523, 538
Arnow, 521
Arny, 47
Arrison, 338
Arrowsmith, 307
Art, 84
Arth, 165
Arthur, 256, 459
Asboth, 445
Ash Grove, 121
Ashbey, 257
Ashby, 257, 279
Ashcom, 518
Ashcom Land, 518
Ashcom's Land, 518
Ashdown, 165
Ashe, 254, 323
Ashford, 138, 275
Ashley, 10, 129, 179, 363, 396, 402, 418
Ashmead, 395
Ashton, 4, 6, 35, 257, 381
Asigoigne, 544
Aspinwall, 473, 476
Astor, 209
Atchinson, 400
Atchison, 457
Atkins, 165, 169, 315, 330
Atkinson, 3, 87, 175, 225, 266, 309, 383
AtLee, 279
Atocha, 123
Attridge, 295
Atwood, 248
Audubon, 44
Augustin, 31
Augustine, 331
Aukward, 129
Auld, 502

Aulick, 75, 215, 242, 489, 504
Austin, 212, 525, 546
Austine, 485
Austria, 112
Avalos, 464
Averett, 455
Averill, 396
Avery, 76, 239, 414, 491
Avil, 460
Ayler, 381
Aylmer, 104, 165, 383
Aylworth, 209, 463
Ayres, 325

B

Babb, 461
Babbitt, 259
Babcock, 194, 308
Babiana, 528
Bache, 165, 265, 306, 482, 529, 533
Bachilder, 408, 431
Backenstos, 287, 290
Bacon, 44, 104, 122, 177, 214, 225, 227, 302, 361, 385, 428, 509
Badalik, 394
Baden, 68, 95, 101, 107, 145, 358, 386, 532
Badger, 132, 280, 308, 341
Baeschlin, 386
Bagaley, 89
Baggett, 164
Baggitt, 423
Baggott, 383
Bague, 373
Bailey, 20, 130, 336, 372, 386, 387, 434
Baily, 396, 546
Bain, 444, 546
Bainbridge, 288
Baine, 534
Baird, 461, 486, 530
Baker, 1, 19, 39, 40, 41, 89, 98, 107, 115, 140, 157, 238, 250, 257, 258, 278, 283, 288, 289, 291, 309, 317, 318, 329, 352, 355, 356, 372, 378, 383, 407, 423, 481, 505, 542, 544
Bakers, 417
Bakes, 394
Balch, 289, 351, 466
Balderston, 17
Baldwin, 43, 136, 165, 179, 181, 206, 227, 230, 342, 344, 374, 428, 461, 501, 526, 531
Balier, 317
Ball, 104, 169, 235, 270, 338, 359, 413, 423, 525
Balla, 394
Ballard, 261, 281, 333, 436
Ballen, 3
Ballenger, 486
Ballentine, 328
Ballinger, 90, 386
Ballville, 423
Balmaine, 502
Balme, 441
Balogh, 393
Baltimore, 165
Baltzel, 395
Baltzell, 185
Baltzer, 387, 462
Ban, 394
Bandelier, 240
Bander, 378
Baneff, 57
Baney, 309
Bange, 9
Bangs, 1, 274
Bankard, 172
Bankhead, 444, 501
Banks, 46
Banta, 32, 77
Banton, 332
Bany, 383
Bar, 396
Baraclough, 362
Barber, 64, 101, 108, 165, 171, 194, 324, 353, 358, 386, 399, 438, 458
Barbour, 24, 60

Barcas, 393
Barclay, 195
Bardy, 393
Barelli, 527
Baring, 301
bark **Glen**, 315
Barker, 6, 12, 23, 28, 379, 426, 461, 462
Barkley, 12, 179
Barklie, 492
Barlow, 65, 414
Barmon, 32
Barmore, 312
Barnaclo, 12, 25, 44, 138
Barnard, 256, 338, 389, 440
Barnes, 18, 41, 101, 204, 236, 279, 284, 311, 318, 345, 352, 355, 381, 383, 459, 461, 490, 534
Barnett, 3
Barney, 119, 177
Barnhill, 256
Barnhouse, 379
Barnicoat, 440
Barns, 355, 534
Barnsley, 418
Barnum, 334, 414
barque **Glen**, 234
barque **Glenn**, 321
barque **Osmanli**, 97
barque **Victor**, 70
Barr, 98, 169, 381, 463
Barren, 448
Barrett, 54, 165, 208, 279, 381, 396, 461, 525
Barringer, 312
Barron, 189, 194, 198, 264, 435, 452
Barrott, 531
Barrow, 121, 171, 191
Barrows, 267
Barry, 131, 226, 242, 252, 298, 332, 383, 387, 421, 423, 495, 506
Barsochlin, 165
Bart, 104
Barth, 425

Barthels, 332
Bartholdt, 223
Bartholomew, 304
Bartle, 203
Bartleman, 502
Bartlett, 101, 152, 211, 312, 379
Bartley, 258
Bartol, 162
Barton, 33, 34, 46, 123, 132, 140, 157, 182, 512
Bartruff, 22
Bass, 10, 322
Bassett, 129, 306, 364, 455, 467
Bassham, 539
Bastianelli, 101, 174
Batchelder, 403
Batelle, 308
Bateman, 383
Bates, 54, 76, 98, 101, 165, 179, 232, 344, 400, 403, 407, 534
Bathyani, 420
Batman, 95
Battelle, 307
Bauder, 407
Baudouin, 27, 80, 82
Baughman, 111, 294
Baum, 74, 437
Baume, 260
Bautista, 378
Baxter, 185, 234, 490, 504
Baxton, 169
Bay, 394
Baya, 533
Bayard, 5, 112
Bayley, 63, 82, 88
Bayliss, 100, 169, 348, 387
Baylor, 183
Bayly, 101, 213, 381, 455
Bayne, 70, 99, 143, 367
Baynum, 151
Bays, 124
Beach, 285, 304, 319, 359, 433, 460, 489, 545
Beacham, 229

Bead, 165
Beagle, 493
Beale, 36, 245, 310, 315, 318, 332, 455
Beales, 134
Beall, 81, 105, 167, 174, 287, 332, 336, 356, 381, 385, 386, 395, 400, 401, 423, 459, 477
Beallsville, 401
Beams, 546
Bean, 101, 159, 247, 263, 269, 299, 381, 383, 411, 439, 465, 499, 515
Beans, 224
Bear, 99, 220
Bearder, 254
Beardsley, 64, 84, 212, 515, 536
Beasley, 98, 165
Beasly, 204
Beatley, 347
Beatty, 92, 182, 430, 466, 517, 533
Beaty, 355
Beauharnois, 366
Beaver Island Mormons, 295
Bechtold, 408
Beck, 17, 81, 239, 256, 454, 508, 547
Beckarshoerg, 341
Becker, 115
Becket, 99
Beckett, 165, 169, 267, 381, 459
Beckley, 165
Beckwith, 51, 126, 238, 287
Becser, 394
Becton, 329
Bedell, 427
Bedingfeld, 275
Bee, 127, 324
Beeche, 461
Beecher, 30, 224, 461
Beedle, 66, 448
Beelen, 27
Beeler, 53, 502
Beers, 70, 82, 496
Beeson, 244, 338
Beetley, 78

Begman, 252
Begnan, 99
Behaim, 198
Behaven, 526
Behr, 463
Beider, 151
Belch, 278
Belcher, 53
Belden, 119, 179, 182, 309
Belknap, 308, 515
Bell, 20, 31, 32, 44, 59, 64, 74, 98, 107, 113, 150, 165, 174, 272, 273, 278, 289, 318, 323, 329, 331, 371, 372, 408, 448, 473, 499, 518, 540, 544, 546
Belletti, 221
Bellinger, 323, 324
Belt, 21, 202, 269, 300, 509
Beltzhoover, 126
Beman, 519
Bend, 410
Bender, 25, 335, 393
Benedetti, 221
Benedict, 21
Benet, 317
Benguenel, 121
Benham, 191
Benix, 383
Benjamin, 325
Bennel, 254
Benner, 165
Bennet, 40, 47, 180
Bennett, 15, 115, 148, 165, 191, 208, 242, 249, 329, 352, 423, 445, 502, 512, 547
Benson, 51, 64, 94, 142, 189, 234, 282, 315, 321
Bent, 114
Benter, 107, 108, 171, 175, 447
Bentley, 94, 304
Bently, 334
Benton, 133, 203, 216
Bentz, 136, 142
Beom, 459

Bereton, 169
Berg, 38
Berger, 78
Bergh, 48, 66
Bergman, 101
Berkeley Springs, 258
Berkley, 361, 493
Berkmenn, 104
Bernard, 51
Berneand, 472
Bernhissel, 414
Beron, 319
Berrean, 397
Berry, 55, 79, 91, 101, 114, 154, 171, 190, 250, 264, 273, 284, 306, 327, 332, 359, 405, 408, 426, 427, 431, 440, 494
Berryman, 214, 357, 433
Berryson, 453
Bersensey, 445
Best, 493
Best Land, 518
Bethune, 210
Betout, 6
Better, 273
Betts, 487
Bevan, 25, 43, 104
Bevans, 355, 385
Beveridge, 442, 497
Beverly, 183, 502
Bewley, 157
Beyer, 214
Bibb, 261, 271
Bickelle, 169
Bierne, 502
Big Elk Lick Spring, 58
Bigel, 98
Biggs, 165, 170
Bigler, 374, 463
Bilkay, 394
Billing, 210
Billings, 5
Bines, 466
Bingham, 76, 474, 500

Bingley, 530
Binney, 176
Birch, 24, 25, 99, 165, 341, 448
Birckhead, 256
Bird, 91, 98, 101, 161, 194, 211, 459
Birdsall, 237
Birdwell, 463
Birkhead, 448
Birnie, 345
Biro, 373, 408
Birth, 104
Bishop, 5, 11, 13, 45, 88, 101, 108, 189, 219, 339, 480, 495
Bisphan, 516
Biss, 332
Bissey, 357
Bittinger, 121, 242, 383
Blache, 323, 324
Black, 17, 29, 165, 194, 258, 370, 418
Blackison, 460
Blackiston, 343
Blacksmith, 415
Blagden, 101, 107, 142, 171, 193, 216, 249, 256, 286, 335, 386, 421, 442, 458
Blair, 118, 145, 307, 363
Blair-Park, 302
Blake, 7, 14, 21, 72, 289, 309, 358, 411, 412, 413, 417, 426, 439, 537
Blakeslee, 30
Blakiston, 544
Blakistone, 219, 518
Blanc, 299
Blanchard, 269, 374
Blanche, 258
Bland, 528
Blandford, 493
Blaney, 135, 336
Blannerhasset, 45
Blanton, 313
Blatchford, 450
Blau, 352
Bleakley, 490
Bleecker, 444

Blish, 472
Bliss, 350
Blodget, 80, 82
Blodgett, 37, 313, 339
Blood, 533
Bloomer, 459
Blount, 176, 191, 365
Blox, 300, 324, 337
Blue, 5
Blume, 52
Blummenthal, 432
Blummmenthal, 372
Blunden, 427
Blunt, 6, 74, 452
Bluxome, 308
Boad, 278
Boak, 98, 165, 538
Boardman, 8, 40, 242
Boarman, 90, 92, 98, 165, 431, 536
boat **Ben West**, 274
boat **Delaware**, 476
boat **Nettle**, 90
boat **Peytone**, 55
boat **Thomas Collyer**, 252
Bochsa, 88
Bocock, 455, 504
Bodanek, 394
Bodisco, 325, 329
Boehm, 198
Bogan, 122, 146, 165
Bogart, 490
Boggess, 463
Boggs, 76, 257, 314
Bohlayer, 165, 534
Bohn, 101, 192, 383
Bohonyi, 394
Bohrer, 174, 256, 272
Bokee, 282
Boland, 432
Bolayer, 381, 386
Bolin, 473
Boling, 12
Bolingbroke, 452
Bolivar, 542

Bolles, 34, 75, 182
Bolling, 293
Bols, 199
Bolt, 438
Bomford, 65, 240, 241, 251, 253, 264, 532
Bonaparte, 336, 352
Bonce, 82
Bond, 290, 307, 402, 429
Bonham, 212
Bonner, 323
Bonnett, 206
Bonsell, 238
Bonte, 139
Bontila, 373
Bontilla, 408
Booker Gold Mine, 428
Booley, 5, 92
Boon, 101
Boone, 49, 115, 187, 198, 233, 319, 402, 506
Boos, 14
Bootes, 190
Booth, 78, 306, 321, 344, 411, 492
Boots, 62
Boragdus, 490
Borbely, 394
Borchand, 120
Borchers, 429
Borden, 281, 306, 362
Borders, 188
Bordley, 416, 417
Borie, 49
Borland, 373
Borondy, 394
Borremans, 323, 422, 460
Borrows, 240
Boscoe, 104
Bosque, 143, 182
Boss, 25, 91, 138, 211, 311
Bossard, 377
Bosse, 459
Boswell, 408, 459
Bosworth, 89

Boteler, 9, 12, 17, 50, 69, 87, 90, 101, 111, 115, 121, 162, 164, 185, 228, 231, 235, 266, 268, 286, 298, 321, 329, 447, 511
Both, 436
Bothcher, 308
Bott, 399
Botta, 394
Botts, 70, 394, 467
Boucher, 330, 338
Bouchke, 75
Boudouin, 37
Bouic, 537
Boulanger, 68, 106, 170
Bouldin, 180
Boulton, 546
Bourdel, 44
Boute, 85, 182
Bouther, 100
Bouton, 37, 49
Boutwell, 306, 462
Bowden, 56, 86
Bowdoin, 151
Bowen, 7, 27, 37, 39, 86, 98, 99, 128, 149, 165, 169, 174, 191, 193, 224, 259, 315, 319, 369, 381, 383, 541
Bower, 92, 101, 139, 461, 465
Bowers, 377
Bowey, 165
Bowie, 4, 7, 85, 135, 165, 169, 176, 249, 312, 318, 451, 452, 514, 541
Bowland, 267
Bowles, 389
Bowlin, 27
Bowman, 237, 418
Bown, 299
Box, 267
Boyce, 74, 96, 323
Boyd, 8, 26, 30, 74, 104, 125, 143, 176, 194, 298, 312, 368, 378, 408, 466, 499, 503, 538
Boydston, 546
Boyell, 339
Boyer, 188
Boyers, 473
Boyland, 175
Boyle, 6, 98, 104, 165, 246, 250, 353, 381, 383, 532
Boynton, 545
Boyts, 356
Bozeman, 141
Brace, 272
Brackett, 313
Braden, 175
Bradfield, 245
Bradford, 63, 153, 256, 311, 318, 337, 352, 403, 466
Bradlee, 402
Bradley, 25, 119, 138, 163, 165, 169, 191, 299, 311, 332, 370, 424, 426, 452, 484, 490, 496, 534, 539, 543
Bradstreet, 178
Bradwell, 385
Brady, 6, 94, 107, 122, 163, 165, 187, 277, 288, 291, 301, 378, 407, 474
Bragdon, 183
Bragg, 282
Braine, 40
Brame, 143, 181
Branch, 231, 324
Brandebury, 115
Brandenburg, 473
Brandon, 180
Brandt, 136, 142, 359, 367, 373, 444
Brank, 52
Brannan, 250, 307, 312
Brannegan, 165
Branson, 383
Brashear, 143
Brashears, 99, 104, 165, 423
Bratt, 291
Braun, 393
Brawner, 13, 99, 104, 415, 539
Braxton, 98
Bray, 386
Brazleton, 327
Breck, 149
Breckenridge, 433, 489

Breckridge, 233
Bredall, 137, 151, 182
Bredell, 60
Breedlove, 184
Breeze, 180
Brelenbridge, 372
Brelsford, 267
Brenan, 89
Brennan, 155
Brenner, 7, 101, 197, 448
Brent, 40, 66, 90, 91, 95, 114, 120, 165, 191, 207, 240, 261, 271, 293, 318, 323, 324, 342, 343, 351, 381, 402, 421, 431, 478, 494
Brenton, 32, 281, 355
Brereton, 101, 104, 165, 500
Brest, 269
Brewer, 130, 217, 279
Brewington, 237
Brewster, 234, 248, 309
Brice, 208, 359
Brick, 193, 393, 394
Brick Capitol, 269
Briddell, 459
Bridgman, 116
Bridwell, 21
Briel, 101, 165
Brien, 141, 232, 296, 385, 468, 537
brig **Ada**, 527
brig **Ada Eliza**, 24
brig **Ann**, 49
brig **Chatsworth**, 302
brig **Commerce**, 208
brig **Conductor**, 470
brig **Desire**, 374
brig **Eagle**, 90
brig **Englishman**, 353
brig **Foam**, 49
brig **Harriet**, 143
brig **Herman**, 116
brig **Josephine**, 527
brig **Lawrence**, 32
brig **Loriot**, 43
brig **Louisa**, 425

brig **Lowder**, 353
brig **Mary**, 9, 15
brig **Matador**, 57
brig **Nimrod**, 1
brig **Ophir**, 151
brig **Porpoise**, 79, 272, 456
brig **Ripa**, 431
brig **Shakespeare**, 90
brig **Somers**, 529
brig **Spy**, 9, 18, 20
Briggs, 74, 214
Brigham, 89, 372
Bright, 39, 77, 101, 234, 321, 443
Brightwell, 363
Brinley, 307
Brisbane, 233
Brisbin, 11
Briscoe, 87, 101, 138, 165, 300, 325, 334, 350, 386, 405, 430, 447
Brissette, 174
Brister, 543
Bristling, 306
Bristol, 299, 313
Bristow, 213
Britt, 149
Brittingham, 77, 142, 151, 173
Britton, 297
Brocchus, 473
Brock, 141, 451, 491, 508
Brockenbrough, 415
Brockle, 394
Brockway, 338
Brodbeck, 101, 165, 223
Broderick, 316
Bromley, 307
Bronaugh, 300, 391
Brook, 459
Brooke, 55, 73, 79, 81, 89, 110, 115, 133, 153, 177, 189, 191, 205, 224, 288, 291, 350, 395, 454, 534, 540, 542
Brooks, 33, 137, 165, 244, 265, 283, 313, 337, 370, 458, 466, 527, 534
Broom, 33

Broome, 76, 518
Brosnahan, 106
Brother, 493
Brothwick, 264
Brougham, 376
Brourke, 359
Brouwer, 181
Brow, 41
Brower, 321, 353, 501, 502
Brown, 2, 3, 6, 8, 15, 25, 30, 34, 37, 38, 39, 45, 57, 60, 62, 63, 64, 77, 80, 82, 98, 99, 101, 103, 104, 107, 108, 109, 113, 114, 119, 124, 126, 128, 130, 131, 137, 143, 145, 150, 153, 158, 159, 165, 169, 170, 171, 181, 191, 192, 206, 209, 217, 221, 227, 230, 243, 251, 265, 267, 279, 282, 297, 302, 309, 319, 331, 336, 340, 352, 356, 365, 370, 372, 373, 375, 378, 381, 383, 386, 408, 410, 414, 423, 431, 433, 435, 439, 448, 472, 476, 485, 490, 496, 509, 511, 525, 526, 534, 539, 540, 541
Brown's Hotel, 206
Browne, 82, 149, 263, 265, 307, 331
Browner, 137
Browning, 64, 91, 101, 165, 225, 377, 478, 495, 529
Brownlee, 79, 272
Brownson, 319
Broyle, 326
Bruce, 76, 83, 165, 359, 381, 461, 510
Brumbaugh, 489
Brundige, 89
Bruner, 478
Brunner, 165
Brunning, 12
Brush, 187, 385, 446, 465, 476, 533
Bryan, 29, 66, 91, 96, 230, 240, 287, 383, 386, 408, 431, 452, 459, 493, 535, 538
Bryant, 18, 114, 237, 307, 448, 529
Bryce, 372
Bryon, 97

Buchanan, 28, 204, 235, 441, 466
Bucher, 462
Buchman, 283
Buck, 266, 544
Buckey, 51, 338, 389
Buckingham, 6, 19, 37, 159, 170, 328, 446, 486, 493
Buckington, 4
Buckler, 200
Buckley, 106, 117, 165, 271, 302, 381, 386
Buckmaster, 536
Bucknell, 472
Buckner, 38, 127, 293, 371
Budwell, 302
Buel, 120, 127, 344, 398
Buell, 127, 128, 269, 374, 525
Buete, 140, 142
Buffington, 115
Buford, 319
Bugby, 423
Bukovite, 393
Bukovits, 394
Bulde, 38
Bulger, 9
Bull, 131, 148
Bullard, 185
Bullitt, 234
Bulloch, 496
Bullock, 132, 181, 308, 402
Bullwinkle, 94
Bully, 106, 165, 386
Bulwer, 428
Bulwinkle, 219
Bumstead, 301
Bunce, 31, 89, 132
Bunch, 248
Bunckley, 255
Bunge, 181
Bunting, 131, 210, 343
Bunton, 179
Burbank, 10
Burch, 23, 43, 98, 343, 383, 459, 461
Burche, 122, 228, 279, 286

Burd, 546
Burden, 462
Burdett, 75
Burdine, 383
Burford, 118
Burgess, 64, 276, 376, 381, 459, 466
Burgoyne, 233
Burgwin, 191
Burk, 196, 201, 379, 460
Burke, 324, 509
Burkhalter, 377
Burling, 308
Burman, 191
Burn, 181
Burnap, 200
Burne, 502
Burner, 370
Burneston, 157
Burnet, 191
Burnett, 43, 53, 60, 101, 131, 497, 547
Burnette, 36
Burnham, 199, 272
Burns, 25, 33, 39, 66, 99, 123, 155, 165, 169, 255, 302, 412, 421, 446, 465, 514
Burnside, 144, 201, 348
Burr, 138, 165, 174, 175, 296
Burrell, 108
Burrill, 98
Burrough, 39, 72, 92, 259
Burroughs, 36, 198, 509
Burrows, 174, 179
Burrus, 446
Burt, 374, 406
Burte, 106
Burton, 188, 440
Busey, 534
Bush, 5, 8, 46, 56, 98, 99, 171, 340, 372, 378, 383, 407, 519, 529
Bushell, 76
Busher, 160, 175
Busk, 447
Bustard, 207
Bute, 338

Butler, 4, 8, 11, 44, 54, 59, 72, 91, 98, 107, 108, 109, 121, 152, 165, 187, 192, 195, 213, 295, 332, 335, 343, 366, 381, 383, 336, 387, 398, 441, 449, 456, 466, 430, 521, 523, 527, 543
Butrick, 274
Butt, 48, 101, 214, 234, 317, 449, 509
Butterworth, 513
Buttman, 104
Butts, 82, 135, 323, 333, 397, 399, 411, 466
Buxet, 359
Buxton, 197
Byer, 104
Byers, 117
Byington, 45, 214, 237, 318
Byram, 178
Byrd, 480
Byrne, 52, 104, 165, 244, 318, 319, 487
Byron, 334, 360

C

Caballero, 123, 132
Cabell, 289, 503
Cabellero, 181
Cabet, 325, 348
Caden, 120, 165, 414
Cadun, 199
Cahal, 194, 248
Cain, 147, 225, 255
Calalane, 165
Calderwood, 406
Caldwell, 76, 126, 152, 166, 170, 239, 359, 368, 448
Calhoun, 18, 290, 326, 415
Califf, 313
Calkins, 212
Call, 478, 547
Callaghan, 38, 49, 521, 533
Callaghn, 132
Callahan, 101, 243, 370

Callan, 22, 42, 101, 117, 123, 142, 149, 193, 214, 216, 240, 274, 300, 335, 366, 465
Callaway, 360
Callen, 19
Callender, 145, 318
Calrus, 141
Calthrop, 452
Calvert, 45, 107, 165, 215, 273, 349, 387, 404, 451, 457
Calvin, 220
Calwell, 184, 415
Cameron, 137, 206, 223, 271, 378, 383, 408, 459, 461
Cammack, 22, 99, 159, 166, 183, 256, 266
Campbell, 19, 91, 98, 101, 104, 130, 170, 174, 186, 194, 236, 244, 279, 301, 364, 484, 500, 507, 511, 530, 546
Camper, 25, 214
Canales, 42, 123
Canby, 128, 288, 291
Candee, 211
Canfield, 188, 354
Cannaday, 130
Cannon, 64, 208, 345, 349, 381
Canterbury Tales, 360
Cantley, 359
Cantwell, 446
Caperton, 455
Capitol, 252
Capron, 4, 34, 243, 451, 527
Carbery, 164, 187, 202, 310, 329, 379
Carbonell, 247
Carder, 142
Carey, 229, 286, 452, 525
Carkaden, 199
Carl, 369
Carleton, 302
Carlin, 54, 56, 288
Carlisle, 195
Carlock, 130
Carlow, 490
Carlton, 231
Carman, 332
Carmichael, 362
Carnes, 314
Carney, 461, 462
Carothers, 217, 354
Carpenter, 158, 228, 234, 385, 501
Carpentier, 265
Carr, 35, 38, 40, 213, 281, 287, 332, 354, 457
Carrico, 240, 253, 485
Carrigan, 525
Carrill, 319
Carrington, 482
Carroll, 6, 30, 37, 68, 86, 135, 190, 191, 194, 323, 324, 373, 386, 451, 452, 455, 478, 534
Carrothers, 267
Carser, 8
Carson, 191, 383
Carter, 43, 55, 79, 82, 92, 101, 111, 135, 145, 155, 161, 166, 194, 207, 237, 241, 254, 257, 259, 316, 319, 346, 351, 383, 387, 408, 416, 444, 445, 460, 462, 500, 502, 503, 505, 514, 517, 527, 542
Carusi, 34, 67, 365, 391, 393, 420, 485
Caruthers, 258
Carvajal, 464, 475
Carvallo, 133, 140, 146, 300, 324
Carver, 5, 8, 10
Cary, 223
Casanave, 101
Casanova, 378, 407
Casanovia, 376
Case, 8, 159, 224, 309
Casey, 201, 395, 519
Cash, 165
Caskie, 455
Caskin, 496
Casneau, 308
Caspar, 370

Casparis, 107, 165, 214, 315, 377, 386, 400, 459
Casper, 341
Cassel, 114, 402
Cassell, 165, 234, 466
Cassilly, 418
Cassin, 358, 426
Casteel, 165
Castell, 104, 165, 166, 381
Castillo, 536
Castleman, 443
Castnor, 392
Castor, 500
Catchett, 359
Cathcart, 96
Cathey, 267
Caton, 101, 166, 329, 488
Catrick, 63
Caudle, 176
Caulk, 276
Caussans, 378
Causten, 140, 146, 242
Cavanton, 120, 137
Cavender, 221
Cay, 432
Cazanove, 381, 427
Cazenove, 303, 498, 502, 503
Cazonova, 193
Cedars, 255, 447
Center, 64
Central Academy, 369
Centre Market-House, 296
Chace, 466
Chadbourne, 414
Chaddendon, 113
Chadwick, 438
Chafin, 273
Chalfant, 203
Chamberlain, 58, 283, 430
Chamberlin, 405, 440
Chambers, 52, 201, 270
Chamier, 531
Champ, 38
Champion, 416, 523

Champlin, 416
Chancellor, 494
Chandler, 5, 8, 14, 118, 141, 147, 332, 429, 516, 530
Chaner, 78
Chaney, 520
Channing, 116
Chapell, 204
Chapin, 22, 91, 290, 381, 483, 501, 509
Chaplin, 399
Chaplinn, 399
Chapman, 25, 36, 45, 70, 83, 124, 255, 266, 355, 378, 407, 439, 440, 451, 483, 503, 524, 541
Chappell, 121
Charles, 467
Charlotte Hall, 425
Charlton, 175
Chasagne, 378
Chase, 4, 13, 98, 110, 182, 355, 385, 472, 482, 497, 499, 502, 507
Chassagne, 407
Chastain, 434
Chattanooga railroad company, 112
Chatton, 113
Chauncey, 125, 176, 179, 417
Chavis, 166
Cheatham, 180, 271
Cheever, 242, 305
Chenault, 121
Cheney, 63
Chenoweth, 472
Chenowith, 4, 6
Cherry, 146
Chesher, 228
Chester, 22
Cheti, 143, 181
Chevalier, 414
Chevers, 543
Chew, 2, 99, 165, 279, 332, 335, 381, 383, 424
Chiceri, 378
Chichester, 400

561

Child, 179, 403
Childs, 18, 101, 151, 248
Chilicote, 203
Chilling, 359
Chillum Castle Manor, 81, 187, 327
Chipman, 5, 8
Chiseltine, 165
Chism, 10
Choat, 234
Choate, 101, 352
Choppin, 95, 318, 383, 462
Choteau, 180, 464
Christ, 191
<u>Christ Church</u>, 448
Christian, 174, 182, 187, 516, 521
Christie, 336
Chubb, 166, 447, 520
Church, 37, 191, 399, 484
Churchill, 248, 531
Cipriani, 521
Cissel, 24
Cissil, 469
Clabaugh, 24, 358
Clack, 119, 451
Clafflin, 5
Claflin, 8, 46
Clagett, 8, 61, 101, 126, 224, 246, 356, 400
Claiborne, 61, 123, 181, 263
<u>Claims against Mexico</u>, 9, 12, 15, 18, 20, 24, 25, 28, 36, 42, 43, 44, 49, 53, 56, 57, 60, 67, 72, 79, 85, 96, 109, 113, 116, 123, 132, 134, 136, 137, 139, 143, 144, 146, 151, 152, 156, 158, 159, 161, 164, 173, 178, 320
Clair, 366
Clampett, 336
Clampitt, 72
Clapham, 64
Clapp, 73, 95, 331
Clare, 269, 323
Clark, 49, 53, 57, 63, 64, 70, 82, 87, 96, 99, 100, 105, 126, 127, 131, 138, 148, 150, 155, 156, 165, 166, 170, 182, 228, 242, 250, 267, 273, 275, 279, 292, 300, 306, 308, 321, 328, 339, 381, 383, 386, 387, 397, 402, 406, 416, 420, 423, 459, 464, 482, 492, 498, 541
Clarke, 3, 21, 91, 101, 104, 111, 152, 159, 169, 173, 181, 187, 193, 225, 233, 248, 255, 268, 292, 319, 329, 330, 336, 430, 465, 466, 509
Clarkson, 416
Clarvoe, 25, 101, 386
Clary, 194
Classen, 358
Clatterbuck, 152
Clavadetscher, 101
Claveloux, 165
Claxton, 459
Clay, 180, 291
Clayton, 31, 95, 97, 136, 254, 321, 396
Cleaveland, 313, 419
Clemens, 6, 71
Clement, 29, 452
Clements, 24, 45, 87, 98, 101, 107, 150, 166, 189, 212, 234, 269, 315, 321, 323, 379, 381, 425, 447
Clendendon, 113
Clendenin, 375
Clendennen, 359
Clephane, 256
Clermont, 218
Cleveland, 299, 488
Click, 5, 8
Clifford, 309
Clift, 63
Clifton, 261
Clifton Farm, 147, 238
Cline, 378, 409, 431
Clines, 178
Clinton, 450
Clitch, 101
Clitz, 127
Clokey, 91, 165

Close, 5, 8, 38, 162
Closson, 63
Cloud's Mill, 513
Clough, 292, 477
Clover, 141, 158
Clow, 12
Clower, 94
Clubb, 38
Cluskey, 139, 186, 285, 379
Clusky, 124, 305
Cluss, 459
Clymer, 311
Coal, 34
Coale, 34, 67, 420
Coates, 220
Coats, 5
Cobb, 37, 80, 82, 83, 141, 191, 282, 329, 463, 466, 527
Coburn, 108, 387, 461
Cochett, 359
Cochran, 84, 101, 155, 282, 410
Cochrane, 180, 310
Cock, 170
Cockrell, 41
Codrington, 213
Codwise, 343
Coffey, 121
Coffin, 313, 339, 512
Cogel, 306
Cohen, 99
Cohn, 547
Coke, 165
Colburn, 403, 462
Colby, 110
Colclazier, 269
Colcord, 288
Cole, 100, 148, 170, 175, 187, 244, 258, 308, 316, 362, 387, 429, 454, 481, 515
Coleman, 5, 81, 220, 308, 332, 407, 465
Coles, 88, 395
Colfax, 281
Colfer, 285

Collier, 10, 162, 484
Collins, 58, 69, 123, 126, 128, 131, 140, 171, 175, 179, 182, 184, 186, 208, 215, 282, 330, 332, 359, 381, 387, 423, 448, 543
Collison, 87, 91, 101
Colman, 22
Colmemeil, 259
Colmesnil, 36, 80, 92
Colquhoun, 99, 101
Colson, 541
Colston, 194, 197, 516
Coltman, 166, 277, 348, 360, 381
Colton, 10, 36, 330, 527
Columbus, 101, 542
Colunn, 540
Colvocoressis, 174, 272
Colwell, 37
Combs, 43, 95, 101, 165, 345, 361, 532
Compton, 73, 357, 435, 443
Comstock, 41, 73, 128, 307
Conch, 179
Concha, 395
Condon, 55, 155, 526
Conelly, 160
Congress burial ground, 413
Congressional Burial ground, 436, 482
Congressional Burying Ground, 125
Congressional Burying-ground, 60
Congressional Cemetery, 50, 140, 160, 292, 545
Conjurer's Defeat, 361
Conklin, 437, 449, 507
Conlan, 106, 166, 381
Conley, 26
Conlons, 369
Conly, 225
Connally, 508
Connaway, 188
Connell, 283, 381, 436, 482, 516
Connelly, 92, 300, 456
Conner, 25, 52, 107, 155, 166, 319, 462

Connick Farm, 135
Connick's Farm, 85
Connolly, 218, 527
Connor, 53, 166, 191, 298, 383, 386, 459, 495
Conolly, 431, 481
Conrad, 81, 266, 436, 457
Conrey, 481
Conroy, 273
Conslaugh, 547
Constantine, 276, 408
Contee, 383, 388
Converse, 187, 484
Conway, 131, 313, 339, 374, 503
Cook, 36, 39, 62, 152, 182, 230, 326, 328, 340, 359, 372, 378, 381, 383, 407, 418
Cooke, 9, 45, 145, 237, 306, 345
Cookson, 343, 349, 350
Coolbaugh, 333
Cooledge, 323
Cooley, 283, 309
Cooling, 20
Coomb, 285
Coombe, 50
Coombes, 350
Coombs, 108, 158, 171, 439
Coon, 74, 438, 445
Cooper, 32, 52, 83, 123, 124, 132, 134, 181, 182, 242, 274, 314, 339, 397, 405, 408, 418, 492, 510, 522
Copeland, 56, 79, 83, 516
Copp, 107, 166
Coquillard, 144
Corbin Hill, 73
Corcoran, 12, 99, 101, 142, 179, 182, 243, 251, 302, 319, 330, 392, 485
Cordery, 531
Corley, 288
Corliss, 109
Cornelius, 131, 439
Cornell, 158
corner stone, 275
Cornish, 166

Cornwallis, 44
Corridan, 69
Corrigan, 387, 545
Corrington, 166
Cortez, 542
Corwin, 161, 265, 416
Corwine, 33, 348
Cory, 19
Cosden, 93, 185, 228, 263, 264, 270, 342
Cossart, 109
Costigan, 171
Costin, 423, 511
Coston, 202
Coteon, 429
Cotton, 113
Cottrell, 180
Cottringer, 342
Cotzenberger, 106
Couch, 84, 344
Coughlin, 308
Coughtry, 362
Coulter, 472
Counselman, 416, 417
Counts, 19
Coupland, 519
Course, 523
Court House of Wellborn, 151
Courtney, 390
Cousans, 408
Cousins, 199
Couts, 500, 501
Cover, 315, 336, 507
Cowan, 28, 158, 383
Coward, 10
Cowdin, 402
Cowes, 66, 81
Cowger, 463
Cowgill, 326
Cowles, 546
Cowling, 98, 99, 166, 171, 348, 372
Cowman, 81
Cowper, 377

Cox, 1, 10, 12, 13, 25, 65, 101, 123, 156, 166, 175, 182, 200, 202, 214, 235, 250, 251, 255, 269, 300, 305, 309, 312, 377, 386, 405, 411, 444, 447, 451, 453, 457, 467, 479, 493, 524, 525, 542
Coxe, 49, 53, 242, 451, 539
Coy, 113
Coye, 332
Coyle, 16, 99, 101, 165, 166, 174, 195, 214, 247, 336, 363, 381, 386, 388, 392
Cozens, 123
Cozzen, 99
Crabb, 400, 520
Crabtree, 508
Cracroft, 503
Craft, 84, 372, 378, 407, 410
Cragin, 325
Craig, 25, 138, 152, 179, 196, 297, 302, 317, 318, 386
Crain, 14, 293, 518
Cranch, 512
Crandal, 237
Crandall, 14, 84, 169, 457
Crandell, 45, 138, 202, 214, 275
Crane, 106, 111, 248, 486
Crangle, 372
Crapin, 515, 529
Craven, 383
Crawford, 18, 128, 212, 284, 311, 314, 327, 337, 360, 396, 451, 466, 509
Crawley, 177
Crawson, 339
Cray, 193
Creamer, 311
Creasey, 80
Creighton, 282, 437
Crenshaw, 299, 314
Cressey, 37, 82
Cresson, 233
Cresswell, 368
Cribbs, 466
Cripley, 439

Crippe, 165
Crippen, 325, 450
Cripps, 398
Crispin, 500
Crissy, 408
Crittenden, 233, 263, 306, 365, 367, 369, 372, 375, 380, 419
Croff, 338
Croggan, 99
Croggon, 104, 166
Croghan, 277
Cronin, 300
Cronmiller, 81
Crooker, 327
Crooks, 188
Cropley, 43, 383
Cropper, 429
Crosby, 23, 40, 56, 149, 155, 242, 528
Crosdale, 225
Crosden, 89
Croskey, 66
Cross, 30, 165, 166, 201, 212, 229, 269, 381, 386, 505
Crossley, 478
Crossman, 100
Croswell, 7, 417, 476
Crotwell, 254
Crow, 129, 546
Crowel, 309
Crowell, 374, 520
Crowley, 381, 489, 536
Crown, 37, 120, 170
Crowninshield, 50
Crozgon, 170
Cruett, 413
Cruickshank, 75
Cruikshank, 358
Cruit, 22, 58, 101, 170
Cruitt, 48
Crump, 170, 171, 472
Crusat, 39
Cruso, 534
Crutchett, 34, 165, 223, 274, 303, 310, 315, 467, 528

565

Cruttenden, 381, 509
Cruzat, 36
Cryer, 383
Csermelyi, 373
Cuculla, 123
Cucullu, 314
Culbertson, 126
Culbreth, 396
Cull, 240
Cullom, 510
Cullum, 354, 365
Culver, 229, 279, 475
Culverwell, 241
Cumberland, 475
Cummin, 496
Cumming, 169, 423
Cummings, 387, 438
Cunningham, 151, 170, 199, 221, 309, 312, 326, 449, 478, 518
Curlett, 96
Curmeli, 408
Curry, 104, 282, 478, 505
Curson, 165
Curtis, 36, 71, 178, 191, 290, 306, 307, 308, 365, 370, 396, 448
Curvia, 409, 431
Curwen, 307
Cushing, 243, 313, 339, 403, 529
Cushman, 225, 268, 272, 444
Custace, 175
Custis, 183
Cuthbert, 106
Cutler, 327, 355
Cutter, 398
Cutts, 74, 129, 279, 318
Cuyler, 30
Cuyp, 436

D

D'Arusmont, 353
D'Hauterive, 29
d'Oremieuix, 126, 128
Dabbs, 236
Dabney, 192
Dacy, 108, 215, 336
Dade, 423, 512
Daggett, 173
Daggy, 507
Daguerre, 340
Daily, 281, 378, 407, 408
Dale, 40, 283
Daley, 317, 325
Dall, 308
Dallery, 364
Dallou, 317
Dalton, 64, 99, 160, 171
Daly, 381
Dameron, 37, 80, 82
Damewoor, 339
Damon, 470
Dana, 12, 20, 71, 292, 305, 308, 501
Danford, 427
Danforth, 42, 57, 181, 331
Dangerfield, 200, 444
Daniel, 27, 82, 237, 278, 290
Daniels, 226, 246, 399
Dankworth, 75, 166
Dant, 99, 379, 493, 515
Danton, 378
Darby, 24, 176, 195, 202, 437, 516, 529, 533
Darke, 466
Darling, 36, 39, 68, 250, 396
Darnall, 354
Darnes, 319
Darrell, 29
Darricott, 513
Darrow, 454
Dart, 486
Dashiel, 260
Dashiell, 203, 348
Daugherty, 80
Davenport, 142, 171, 294, 295
Davezac, 70
David, 67, 101, 166, 171, 191, 388, 542
Davidge, 476, 536

Davidson, 5, 8, 11, 27, 37, 39, 54, 65, 75, 91, 94, 122, 132, 234, 274, 385, 386, 442, 443, 466, 510, 524
Davies, 134
Davis, 12, 21, 37, 45, 48, 59, 67, 68, 71, 80, 82, 87, 91, 99, 101, 104, 106, 109, 112, 120, 122, 125, 133, 138, 139, 149, 159, 166, 170, 175, 177, 180, 200, 217, 218, 222, 262, 270, 277, 288, 296, 301, 307, 308, 309, 332, 335, 355, 356, 371, 381, 385, 386, 388, 401, 402, 404, 409, 414, 430, 431, 433, 435, 446, 450, 451, 459, 460, 461, 462, 493, 496, 505, 509, 522, 530, 531, 533, 538, 546
Davison, 28, 211, 423, 461, 468, 479, 505
Davy, 101
Dawes, 166, 273
Dawson, 16, 43, 53, 84, 87, 109, 410, 448, 505, 516
Day, 5, 36, 90, 108, 128, 141, 147, 203, 211, 214, 278, 289, 311, 317, 319, 321, 328, 337, 350, 473, 491, 512, 526
Dayly, 305
Dayton, 15, 266, 427
De Altaro, 473
de Ardrade, 491
De Borboulon, 197
De Bree, 71
de Bruin, 510
De Bruler, 281
De Camp, 231
de Fremery, 141
De Kalb, 36, 542
De Kay, 492
de Konnick, 436
De Koven, 309
De Lancey, 472
de Macedo, 409
De Maine, 177
de Masson, 264

de Miranda, 65
de Nagell, 436
De Neale, 381
De Neufeille, 259
De Neufville, 517
De Peyster, 410
De Russey, 21, 36
De Russy, 39, 46
De Rutte, 35
De Saules, 82, 165
De Selding, 385
De Soto, 536
de Vaudricourt, 324
De Vaughan, 514
De Vaugn, 166
de Visart, 471
De Voe, 490
de Walley, 151
De Wolk, 407
Dea, 332
Deacon, 272
Deagle, 383
Deakens, 58
Deal, 135
Deale, 363, 536
Deam, 129
Deamit, 5
Deammit, 8
Dean, 75, 84
Dearborn, 328, 331, 398
Dearman, 445
Dearmit, 23
Deaver, 438
Deblois, 307
DeBre, 71
Debreczenyi, 394
DeBree, 71
Decatur, 53, 241
Deck, 188
Decker, 333
Deckman, 171
Deeble, 320, 330
Deenrod, 37
Deevers, 381

Defalco, 388
Defalgo, 383
Deffner, 218
Degges, 510
Degraffenried, 340
DeKrafft, 92
del Hoyo, 181
del Hoys, 56
Del vechio, 309
Delaney, 99, 166, 494
Delano, 490
Delany, 198, 381
Delarue, 6, 101
Delaware, 509
Delaway, 91
Delon, 229
Deltro, 99
Demanel, 461
Demar, 192
Dembirh, 183
Deme, 394
Dement, 116, 439, 494
Demeter, 445
Demoss, 129
Dempsey, 245
Dempster, 164
Demsood, 410
DeNeale, 101, 104
Denham, 361, 460, 461
Denis, 483
Dennis, 99, 463
Denny, 44, 445
Dent, 111, 166, 261, 313, 339, 381, 385
Denton, 248, 378, 407, 408
Depew, 377
Derbis, 77
Derby, 241, 251, 307, 308, 378, 500, 532
Derlis, 58
Dermot, 522
Dermott, 166, 350, 363, 497
Derrick, 166
Derringer, 95

DeRussy, 128, 543
DeSaules, 107
Deshon, 317, 500, 501
Desmond, 106, 386, 516, 541
Desrayaux, 74
Detter, 166
Deubler, 508
Devalenger, 148
Devall, 340, 501
DeVaughan, 315
Develin, 521
Devens, 71
Deveny, 101
Devereux, 98, 486
Devier, 316
Devin, 460
Devine, 464
Devlin, 517
Devor, 161
Dewaw, 250
Dewdney, 138, 534
Dewey, 26, 526
Dexter, 5, 8, 107, 386, 495
Dey, 44
Deyoe, 538
Dhalgren, 278
Diamond, 129
Dias, 238
Diaz, 378
Dibble, 538
Dice, 131
Dick, 332, 381, 509
Dickens, 180
Dickenson, 110
Dickerson, 439
Dickinson, 158, 203, 338
Dickman, 172
Dickson, 243, 332, 488
Diehl, 515
Dier, 423
Dietz, 7, 232
Diffenderfer, 196
Digges, 2, 81, 187, 373
Diggs, 166, 431

Dike, 403
Dillon, 222, 329, 359, 383, 467
Dillow, 104
Dines, 219
Dinkle, 30
Dirbis, 143
Divan, 192
Dix, 34, 519
Dixion, 503
Dixon, 147, 157, 190, 192, 269, 483, 503
Doane, 140
Dobbin, 452, 512
Dobbins, 152, 438
Dobbyn, 120, 300
Dobbyns, 86
Dobezy, 394
Dobnin, 499
Dockman, 104
Dodd, 33, 70, 143, 423
Dodge, 30, 33, 46, 113, 263, 351, 383, 403, 434, 435, 441, 451
Dodson, 4, 42, 101, 166, 246
Doe, 166, 283, 388
Doherty, 486
Dolly, 263
Domercq, 40
Domeroq, 529
Don, 420
Donahoe, 332
Donaldson, 28, 100, 158, 170, 472, 530
Donan, 446
Donelan, 11, 70, 91, 96, 190, 191, 217, 270, 281, 284, 347, 367, 457, 464, 493, 515
Doniphan, 51, 383
Donn, 25, 101, 207, 327, 343, 411, 462
Donnell, 72
Donnelly, 5, 408, 478
Donoghue, 104, 168, 192
Donoho, 75, 177, 192, 205
Donohoo, 106, 166, 495, 524
Donohough, 482
Donohue, 363
Donovan, 104, 165, 386
Donues, 378
Dooley, 166, 300
Dorman, 82, 158, 415
Dornin, 46, 492
Dorsey, 2, 16, 166, 171, 206, 243, 298, 516
Doubren, 431
Dougal, 241
Dougals, 234
Dougherty, 49, 156, 182, 207, 509, 541
Doughty, 145, 525
Douglas, 74, 106, 164, 195, 439
Douglass, 23, 25, 101, 166, 182, 240, 308, 315, 321, 337
Douvren, 409
Dove, 19, 57, 62, 101, 117, 189, 240, 381, 407, 509
Dovilliers, 391
Dovren, 378
Dow, 150, 155, 351, 542
Doway, 490
Dowell, 381, 383
Dowlin, 66
Dowling, 66, 91, 229, 239, 381, 419, 448, 462, 498, 507, 509
Dowman, 372
Downer, 33, 240, 317, 338, 385, 407, 517
Downey, 450
Downing, 74, 319, 361, 377, 381, 448
Downs, 37, 80, 82, 85, 166, 181, 388
Dows, 309
Dowson, 22
Dowty, 393
Dox, 237
Doyle, 192, 194, 279, 416, 432, 466, 547
Dozer, 120
Dozier, 383
Drake, 30, 220, 466, 469

Drane, 494
Draper, 141, 267, 523, 531
Drayton, 81, 440
Dreher, 212
Drennen, 121
Dreschfelt, 307
Drew, 61
Dreyer, 182
Drill, 323
Drudge, 175
Drum, 340, 441, 542
Drumell, 166
Drummond, 76, 84, 177, 185, 228
Drune, 344
Drury, 14, 91, 124, 138, 202, 204, 214, 256, 275, 280, 300, 349, 374, 391, 461, 509
Du Barry, 36, 37
Dubamel, 58
Dubant, 82, 250, 300, 319, 510
Dube, 159
Ducachet, 389
Ducachey, 372
Duchess d'Angouleme, 472
Duchess of Angouleme, 475
Duckett, 154, 240, 383
Duckwall, 391
Duckworth, 101
Ducoing, 85
Dudley, 157, 179, 344, 498
Dudrey, 10
Duer, 76, 239, 324, 433, 520, 530
Duerson, 5, 8, 51
Duff, 206, 231, 309, 529
Duff Green's Row, 246
Duffey, 101, 103, 108
Duffield, 351
Duffy, 273, 305, 408, 431, 481
Dugill, 12
Duhamel, 143
Duhammel, 77
Dujardin, 436
Duke of Hamilton, 17
Duke of York, 513

Dulaney, 436
Dulany, 46, 170, 489, 513
Dulen, 305
Dulin, 166
Dumas, 66
Dumbar, 503
Dumberth, 243
Dunbar, 47, 503, 508
Duncan, 8, 41, 52, 141, 220, 227, 237, 254, 279, 302, 419, 468, 546
Duncanson, 440
Dundas, 126, 173
Dungan, 81
Dunham, 281, 355
Dunkin, 306, 327
Dunlap, 386, 457, 492, 519
Dunlevy, 149
Dunlop, 49, 247
Dunn, 38, 94, 185, 254, 340, 357, 372
Dunning, 13, 36, 531
Dunnington, 166
Dunond, 172
Dunscomb, 192
Duprat, 408
Dupuy, 332
Durant, 512
Durbin, 363
Duremay, 505
Durham, 91, 310, 325
Durkee, 129
Durkgrave, 34
Durrive, 92
Durvine, 39, 54
Durwin, 319
Dusenberry, 30
Dustin, 533
Duval, 179
Duvall, 40, 70, 95, 99, 101, 102, 104, 146, 165, 171, 175, 214, 291, 327, 332, 335, 353, 383, 388, 442
Dwen, 378
Dwight, 149
Dwin, 407
Dwinnell, 512

Dwyer, 165
Dyer, 13, 99, 101, 107, 125, 126, 142, 198, 214, 300, 306, 381, 383, 386, 439, 447, 460
Dygert, 32
Dyke, 301
Dykeman, 140
Dyson, 100, 166, 170, 228, 235, 381

E

Eaches, 441, 502
Eagan, 99, 101, 307
Eagen, 89
Eager, 417
Eagleson, 137, 175
Earl, 282, 423, 486, 497, 533, 542
Earl of Belmont, 511
Earl of Derby, 298
Earl of Dunmore, 17
Earl of Shaftsbury, 260
Earle, 99, 101, 166, 309, 452
Early, 377
Earp, 327, 390
Easby, 115, 154, 172, 174, 232, 240, 476
Easom, 406
East, 180
Easterby, 445
Easterline, 150
Eastman, 150, 406
Easton, 288, 291, 517
Easton Academy, 371, 372
Eaton, 9, 49, 181, 327, 336, 341, 489
Ebbett, 192
Eberbach, 107, 440, 461
Ebert, 415
Eccleston, 190, 194, 437, 471
Eckard, 366, 539
Eckardt, 101
Eckart, 385
Eckel, 72, 115, 341
Eckford, 247
Eckle, 7, 51
Eckloff, 448

Eddins, 142
Eddy, 94, 101, 307, 374, 489
Edelen, 219, 224, 240, 352
Edelin, 64, 143, 166, 324, 343, 449
Edes, 100, 255, 314, 358, 381
Edgar, 119, 282, 390
Edgecomb, 37
Edgerly, 86
Edgerton, 409, 432
Edie, 534
Edinger, 41
Edmands, 402
Edmonds, 201
Edmondson, 104
Edmonson, 270, 401
Edmonston, 99, 159
Edmundson, 455
Edred, 381
Edwards, 14, 36, 39, 42, 53, 59, 67, 68, 71, 104, 109, 121, 131, 188, 207, 212, 223, 229, 249, 274, 278, 287, 290, 300, 302, 313, 327, 333, 339, 360, 395, 396, 417, 508, 535, 537
Egan, 448
Egbert, 213
Egerton, 245
Eggleston, 212, 268
Ehle, 129
Ehler, 327
Ehmsel, 410
Ehramantrout, 107
Ehrmontrout, 166
Eichelberger, 157
Eichhorn, 439
Eichler, 373
Eichorn, 460
Eickorn, 166, 170
Elder, 73, 399
Eldridge, 79, 174, 213, 272
Eldward, 61
Elgar, 523
Eliot, 15, 79, 102
Elkins, 182, 381

571

Ellicot's Mills, 532
Ellicott, 186, 323, 383
Elliot, 68, 166, 273, 527
Elliott, 43, 75, 135, 220, 377, 530
Ellis, 29, 56, 71, 104, 268, 300, 308, 323, 359, 378, 409, 446, 521
Ellisi, 372
Ellsworth, 345
Ellwood, 469
Elmwood, 225
Elrod, 345
Elursa, 490
Elwell, 101
Elwes, 540
Ely, 18, 199, 530
Embray, 410
Embro, 459
Embrod, 98
Emerick, 99
Emerson, 386
Emert, 166
Emery, 1, 30, 63, 216, 381, 386
Emmert, 358
Emmons, 355
Emory, 287, 523
Emperor of Austria, 23, 27
Empress Josephine, 366
Emrich, 471
Enders, 446
Endicott, 403
Engle, 80, 150, 469
Englebach, 254
English, 20, 139, 323, 427, 456
English Hill, 17
Enna, 372, 452, 474, 489
Ennals, 229
Ennis, 4, 142, 160, 166, 185, 193, 216, 240, 262, 392, 444
Eno, 313
Enochs, 244
Ensign, 472
Entwisle, 101, 386
Entyminger, 19
Epting, 64

Erben, 76
Ergood, 166
Erney, 77
Erter, 192
Erwin, 150, 237, 282, 512
Eshelman, 175
Eskridge, 42
Eslin, 191, 381
Esperance Plantation, 6
Espey, 166, 300
Espy, 330
Essex, 431
Estes, 70, 158
Estis, 276
Etchison, 354
Etheridge, 413
Etting, 237
Eubank, 326
Eude, 58, 77, 143
Eustace, 270
Eustis, 71
Eva, 258, 357, 442, 468, 493
Evans, 26, 83, 98, 102, 119, 124, 126, 130, 131, 140, 166, 172, 201, 206, 242, 290, 307, 320, 361, 383, 402, 430, 432, 440, 448, 461, 501, 517
Eveleth, 273
Everett, 43, 47, 126, 166, 212, 281, 353, 356, 357, 404, 472
Evermay, 65, 234
Eversfield, 242
Everson, 309
Ewbank, 82, 122, 134, 173, 202, 246, 331, 365, 391, 428, 467, 526
Ewell, 169, 241, 317, 357
Ewing, 144, 371
Excelmans, 352
Ezzell, 282

F

Faces, 378
Fahs, 81, 242
Fair, 374
Fairbanks, 198

Fairchild, 314, 332, 339
Fairfax, 15, 42, 75, 79, 136, 166, 336, 447, 503
Fairfax's Pleasure, 136
Fairman, 70
Fairview, 377
Falbos, 378
Falconer, 164
Falkner, 403
Fallon, 309
Falls, 369
Fanning, 321
Fargandie, 309
Farkas, 393
Farley, 74, 423
Farmer, 281, 332, 402
Farmers' Hotel, 349
Farnham, 104, 177, 178, 416
Farns, 59
Farnsworth, 326
Farquhar, 184
Farr, 344, 407, 547
Farragut, 46
Farrall, 17
Farrar, 107, 193, 204, 235
Farrell, 421, 484
Farrelly, 375, 501, 502
Farthing, 370
Farwell, 308
Fast, 187
Faulk, 142
Faulkner, 104, 282, 370, 478, 505
Faulknew, 455
Faunce, 383
Faust, 100, 407
Favier, 183, 295, 386
Fay, 467
Fazinde, 524
Fearns, 188
Fearson, 159, 166, 170
Featherhoof, 526
Feathersby, 202
Fedray, 332
Feeney, 166

Feher, 393
Fekees, 394
Felch, 11
Felhiol, 34
Fell, 309
Feller, 8
Fellowship, 48
Fendall, 311
Fenner, 456
Fennimore, 267
Fenton, 24
Fenwick, 6, 65, 95, 164, 423
Ferguson, 26, 45, 91, 166, 212, 466, 521
Fernsly, 416
Ferral, 479
Ferrall, 381, 404, 463
Ferrie, 332
Ferrill, 383
Ferry, 205
Fertig, 535
Fesch, 336
Fesnot, 44
Fetterman, 319, 323, 431
Fickett, 262
Fiddes, 378, 409
Fiddles, 432
Field, 287, 538
Fields, 166, 185, 396, 473
Fill, 177
Fillebrown, 330
Filley, 416
Fillins, 53
Fillmore, 9, 19, 35, 83, 95, 116, 141, 148, 186, 207, 218, 233, 240, 243, 245, 280, 292, 295, 299, 430, 433, 457, 464, 478, 491, 499, 511, 521, 536
Filly, 416
Filton, 166
Finch, 8, 423
Fink, 166, 260, 459
Finkman, 107
Finlaw, 113

573

Finlay, 222
Finley, 428, 475
Finly, 509
Finn, 203, 377
Finnall, 374
Finne, 359
Fintay, 394
first steamboat, 78
Fischer, 494
Fish, 179, 470
Fisher, 10, 11, 37, 99, 100, 160, 166, 174, 192, 279, 308, 326, 333, 359, 381, 383, 423, 428
Fister, 166, 386
Fitch, 65, 106, 281, 355, 368, 416
Fithian, 242
Fitnam, 475
Fittz, 196
Fitz, 13
Fitzgerald, 36, 39, 69, 106, 107, 165, 166, 300, 381, 386, 455, 481, 482, 530
Fitzhugh, 83, 101, 133, 192, 283, 440
Fitzpatrick, 121, 320, 341, 463
Fitzsimmons, 373
Flagg, 402, 417
Flaherty, 363, 372
Flanagan, 26, 37, 80, 82, 140, 438, 527, 543
Flanaghan, 333
Flannagan, 395
Flarity, 225
Fleetwood, 459
Fleming, 2, 150, 156, 166, 182, 491, 505
Flemming, 24, 99, 169
Fletcher, 66, 91, 100, 106, 166, 174, 235, 284, 318, 332, 381, 383, 547
Fleury, 118, 190, 260, 408, 484
Flewellen, 287
Flinn, 533, 534
Flinn, Jno, 381
Flint, 108, 207, 381, 386, 388, 473
Flippo, 113
Flishman, 370
Flood, 385
Flournoy, 23, 31
Floyd, 46, 345, 517, 526
Focht, 3
Folansbee, 24
Foley, 70, 260
Folger, 182, 429
Follansbee, 104, 383
Follar, 169
Foller, 104, 222
Follins, 242
Fonda, 494
Fontane, 474
Fonts, 378
Foot, 450, 519, 547
Foote, 63, 77, 83, 97, 100, 145, 223, 323, 438, 503
Forbes, 12, 69, 423, 484, 526
Force, 277, 509
Ford, 4, 51, 76, 104, 166, 185, 189, 192, 208, 238, 283, 323, 377, 381, 464, 466, 474, 475, 534
Foreign Burial Ground, 265
Forest, 130
Forest Hill Cemetery, 365
Forestall, 217
Fornaro, 75, 469
Forney, 79, 499
Forrer, 177
Forrest, 6, 46, 166, 172, 196, 218, 226, 249, 376, 379, 449
Forrest Hall, 376, 426
Forrester, 83
Forshee, 386
Forst, 308
Forster, 378, 473
Forsyth, 75
Fort, 454
Fort Adams, 224
Fort Arbuckle, 159
Fort Atkinson, 484
Fort Brown, 425
Fort Duncan, 52

Fort Erie, 133, 153, 177, 515
Fort Gates, 529
Fort Gibson, 515
Fort Griffith, 146
Fort Hall, 440, 464
Fort Hamilton, 304, 336
Fort Independence, 11
Fort Lacey, 238
Fort Laramie, 473
Fort Leavenworth, 262, 274, 297, 311
Fort Meigs, 530
Fort Merrill, 502
Fort Monroe, 259, 318
Fort Myers, 502
Fort Niagara, 450
Fort Pitt, 44
Fort Recovery, 466
Fort Ripley, 396
Fort Scott, 262
Fort Smith, 204, 268, 276, 303, 335, 483, 515
Fort Snelling, 174, 275, 358, 522
Fort Taylor, 370
Fort Union, 429
Fort Washita, 375, 502, 515
Fort Wayne, 371, 499
Fort Wilkins, 338
Fortune, 334, 340
Forty Fort, 47
Fosdeck, 267
Fosdick, 445
Foster, 13, 64, 104, 166, 174, 179, 206, 255, 271, 305, 306, 352, 355, 383, 403, 407, 429, 499, 508, 520
Foulke, 52
Foulkes, 214
Fountain, 303, 309, 487
Fourgeaud, 307
Fourneag, 484
Fourney, 177
Foutz, 324
Fowke, 332
Fowle, 56, 89, 234, 303, 415, 503

Fowler, 44, 77, 104, 127, 170, 260, 269, 279, 363, 377, 379, 381, 403, 414, 422, 459, 461, 462, 483, 501, 502, 523, 529, 539
Fox, 140, 166, 180, 223, 244
Foxall, 139
Foxwell, 448
Foy, 107, 138, 202, 330, 344, 379, 445
Fracker, 487
Fraeler, 104, 166
Frailey, 142
Fraler, 104
Fraley, 328
France, 192, 209, 276, 498
Francis, 40, 113, 121, 166, 410, 422
Franconia, 112
Frank, 104, 509
Franklin, 91, 104, 170, 216, 239, 285, 286, 419, 471, 483
Franklin Row, 156, 348, 359
Franks, 71
Fraser, 117, 194, 364, 381
Frasier, 483
Frater, 445
Frazer, 40, 333, 545
Frazier, 6, 104, 423, 514
Frean, 123
Fredenburgh, 84
Free, 63, 298
Freeborn, 378, 432
Freedenrick, 99
Freedley, 214, 523
Freeland, 416
Freeman, 33, 37, 80, 82, 161, 179, 182, 205, 281, 352, 386
Freestone Point, 447
Freierson, 282
Fremont, 38, 109, 323, 458
French, 24, 47, 57, 137, 166, 190, 194, 205, 239, 275, 277, 316, 330, 361, 363, 368, 369, 383, 430, 459, 480, 482, 489, 493, 495
Frere, 269
Fretz, 166

Frick, 471
Friddel, 21
Fridell, 94
Fridley, 18, 121, 311, 317, 328
Friends' meeting-house, 520
frig **Chesapeake**, 189
frig **Columbia**, 366
frig **Dona Maria**, 11
frig **Dona Maria II**, 65
frig **Donna Maria II**, 75
frig **Hussar**, 316, 347
frig **Leopard**, 189
frig **Macedonian**, 275
frig **Marion**, 65
frig **Mississippi**, 473
frig **Philadelphia**, 176, 516, 521
frig **Saranac**, 270, 366
frig **Savannah**, 512
frig **St Lawrence**, 489, 509
Frink, 498
Frisbee, 545
Frisby, 135
Fritz, 537
Frost, 36, 299, 301
Frothingham, 308
Fry, 5, 47, 126
Frye, 45, 294
Fryrear, 370
Fugett, 171
Fugitt, 99, 104, 166, 335, 383, 386, 388
Fullalove, 178, 202
Fuller, 14, 26, 52, 108, 335, 339, 449, 494
Fullmer, 150
Fulmer, 125, 323, 492
Fulop, 393, 394
Fulton, 63, 212, 310, 420, 437
Funk, 104, 170, 468
Funnel, 306
Funsten, 341
Furbur, 449
Furley, 276
Furnage, 180

Furnell, 407
Furst, 140

G

Gadsby, 22, 107, 393, 394
Gadsby's row, 22, 465, 529
Gadsby's Row, 219
Gafin, 408
Gage, 1
Gaillard, 354
Gaines, 177, 425
Gaitan, 141
Gaither, 149, 266, 353, 525
Gal, 394
Galbraith, 180
Gale, 192, 416
Gales, 22, 316, 403
Gall, 113
Gallagher, 327
Gallaher, 337, 395, 464, 535
Gallahue, 227
Gallant, 225, 448
Gallary, 205
Gallaudet, 390, 443
Gallier, 120
Galligan, 100, 206
Gallup, 40, 179, 232
Galt, 26, 54, 60, 102, 126, 128, 166, 375
Galvez, 238
Galvin, 210, 397, 497
Gamble, 70, 192, 345, 451
Gambrill, 244, 353
Gannon, 3, 51, 384, 386, 431, 462
Gano, 432, 489
Gantt, 353, 384
Garcelon, 546
Garcia, 378
Gardenier, 34
Garder, 170
Gardere, 533
Gardiner, 15, 45, 50, 149, 182, 303, 320, 328, 343, 500, 518

Gardner, 91, 102, 117, 160, 222, 231, 388, 444, 503
Gardnier, 327
Garlinger, 440
Garlock, 36, 39, 56
Garner, 102, 381, 382, 383
Garnet, 517
Garnett, 9, 234, 255, 288
Garnier, 415
Garrard, 278
Garraty, 340
Garret, 170
Garretson, 329, 420, 467, 538
Garrett, 91, 166, 282, 346, 384
Garrettson, 102
Garriott, 539
Garrison, 73, 326, 362
Garritt, 437, 441
Garrott, 410
Gartland, 395
Garwood, 307
Gary, 152, 182, 206
Gas Establishment, 337
Gassaway, 155, 274, 445, 525
Gates, 102, 118, 152, 170, 308, 381, 385
Gatewood, 179, 317, 396, 516
Gatlin, 429
Gattenson, 102
Gatton, 18
Gattrell, 174
Gautier, 6, 102, 384, 484
Gay, 368
Gayer, 166
Gaylord, 50
Gear, 522
Gedney, 257
Gee, 254, 388
Geiger, 408, 431
Geisinger, 46, 156
Gelation, 304
Gellaly, 374
Gelston, 56
Gemmill, 41, 438

Gengenback, 104
Gennaty, 386
Gensler, 106, 172, 462
Gentry, 299, 354
George IV, 145
Gerard, 352
Gere, 388
German Methodist Church, 525
German Roman Catholic, 37
Gernon, 503
Geron, 38
Gerrard, 290
Gerzso, 394
Getty, 344
Getz, 544
Gevelot, 31
Gewin, 336
Gibb, 283, 374
Gibbard, 3
Gibbon, 461
Gibbs, 18, 108, 128, 438
Giblin, 408
Gibson, 28, 35, 94, 99, 107, 132, 166, 192, 222, 248, 271, 287, 294, 354, 384, 386, 417, 430, 438, 466, 473, 497, 504, 534
Giddings, 39
Gideon, 91, 214, 240, 253, 279
Gier, 386
Giesboro, 286
Gilbert, 63, 75, 86, 122, 292
Gilchrist, 19, 470
Gildermeister, 166
Gildermester, 381, 386
Gildermiester, 309
Gildersleeve, 490
Gilkey, 314, 339
Gill, 92, 126, 145, 259, 384, 459
Gill, 382
Gillam, 473
Gillem, 289
Gillen, 278
Gillespie, 297
Gillet, 270

Gilliland, 84
Gillis, 95
Gilliss, 22, 69, 99, 156, 189, 203, 262, 430, 444, 539
Gilman, 41, 102, 141, 148, 183, 271, 294, 304, 344, 408, 428
Gilmer, 18
Gilmore, 21, 338
Gilpin, 135, 403, 441
Ginger, 276
Girard, 17, 416
Girdes, 74
Girdon, 174
Gisner, 180
Gist, 236
Gittings, 471, 474, 537
Given, 217
Givney, 166
Gladman, 226
Gladmon, 166
Gladney, 176, 530
Glasco, 44
Glasgow, 19
Glassell, 76, 238
Glasvar, 90
Gleason, 196, 197
Gleek, 112
Gleeson, 431
Glendy, 65, 76
Glenn, 451, 461
Glenroy, 490
Glick, 166, 448
Glore, 20
Glorious, 166
Gloss, 393
Glossbrenner, 499
Glove, 529
Glover, 48, 327, 432, 466, 526
Gluck, 75
Goddard, 42, 104, 166, 247, 269, 283, 286, 311, 320, 343, 388, 399, 439, 449, 453, 542
Goder, 396
Godey, 525

Godfrey, 113, 384
Godley, 516
Godman, 517
Godon, 242
Godwin, 57, 181
Goff, 434, 473
Goings, 98, 382, 459
Golday, 372
Goldborough, 243
Golden, 273
Goldin, 172
Golding, 91, 99, 107, 355
Goldsborough, 42, 208, 214, 452, 471
Goldsmith, 326, 333, 445
Golembiowski, 245
Gonder, 474
Gondin, 242
Gonsalves, 50
Gonzales, 31, 431
Gonzalez, 378, 409
Gooch, 102, 207
Good, 80
Goodall, 166
Gooden, 269
Goodhue, 402
Goodloe, 277
Goodman, 140, 515
Goodrich, 63, 119, 449
Goodridge, 130
Goodsil, 220
Goodwin, 114, 119, 202, 301
Goodwood, 241
Goodyear, 68, 269
Goolrick, 166
Gorbett, 449
Gorden, 193
Gordon, 7, 11, 88, 127, 166, 192, 240, 263, 278, 400, 422, 482, 546
Gore, 13, 127, 324, 418
Gorham, 10, 208
Gorman, 281, 355
Gormley, 373, 382
Gorsuch, 6, 131, 183, 249, 327, 391, 395

Gosett, 40
Gosler, 91
Goss, 384
Gossage, 22
Goszler, 324
Gott, 307, 450
Gould, 113, 130, 420, 423, 438
Gouverneur, 373
Gove, 37, 80, 82
Gowen, 302
Gower, 299
<u>Grace Church</u>, 430
Gracesqui, 475
Gracia, 238
Graesbeck, 428
Graeter, 244
Graff, 63
Grafton, 501
Graham, 11, 18, 98, 155, 161, 166, 175, 176, 182, 184, 256, 308, 309, 348, 372, 382, 384, 392, 413, 423, 481, 491, 509, 525
Grahan, 306
Grain, 505
Gramlich, 327
Grammer, 45, 91, 97, 136, 174, 292, 509
Grandin, 131
Granenger, 340
Granger, 113, 149, 539
Granner, 402
Grant, 89, 94, 128, 178, 269, 317, 516
Grantt, 166
Grasson, 466
Grathard, 99
Gratiot, 405
Graves, 176, 313
Gray, 14, 19, 54, 71, 72, 78, 86, 92, 102, 158, 166, 182, 220, 259, 328, 372, 384, 395, 450, 517
Grayson, 207
Greason, 106, 114, 166, 382
Greaton, 466

Green, 6, 9, 26, 34, 35, 36, 39, 49, 56, 59, 68, 88, 98, 102, 104, 131, 136, 137, 138, 141, 147, 150, 151, 164, 166, 177, 181, 207, 229, 242, 278, 296, 298, 331, 338, 342, 344, 345, 346, 349, 359, 375, 380, 381, 382, 384, 386, 390, 410, 412, 424, 429, 438, 440, 497, 509, 525, 531, 539
<u>Green Turtle soup</u>, 226
Green's Row, 229, 310
Greenbann, 258
Greene, 31, 38, 235, 290, 402, 512, 531
Greenfield, 104, 172
Greenhow, 323
Greenleaf's Point, 229
Greenough, 275
Greenwell, 38, 75, 286, 315, 348, 390, 480, 518
Greer, 102, 331, 338, 382, 486, 533
Greeves, 26, 222, 384, 444, 459, 461
Gregg, 87, 213, 354, 381, 511, 542
Gregoire, 32
Gregory, 174, 272, 403
Greig, 175
Greiner, 121, 213
Grey, 100
Grider, 407
Gridley, 344
Grier, 520
Griffin, 4, 29, 99, 100, 102, 113, 212, 315, 361, 384
Griffith, 69, 96, 126, 135, 166, 197, 220, 221, 284, 384, 398, 503
Griggs, 199
Grignon, 46, 86
Grimes, 11, 79, 99, 166, 228, 277, 386, 410, 460
Grimsley, 228
Grinder, 104, 138, 382, 384, 496
Grinnell, 483
Gripton, 362
Grissom, 446
Griswold, 49, 307

Grizzard, 220
Groat, 344
Groff, 312
Grogan, 175
Groot, 494
Grosh, 162
Gross, 107, 388, 460
Grosvenor, 207
Groux, 354, 474
Grove, 41, 320, 505
Grubb, 175, 470, 503
Grun, 394
Grundy, 388
Grunzig, 499
Grupe, 102, 329
Grymes, 183
Gtwn College, 368, 464
Guenet, 182
Guerin, 424
Guerra, 378
Guest, 131
Guidziorowesky, 299
Guild, 418
Guildford, 134
Gukenck, 445
Gull, 461
Gunn, 166, 368
Gunnell, 39, 42, 190, 302, 384, 509
Gunning, 188
Gunst, 408
Gunter, 158
Gunton, 171, 255, 292
Gurley, 270
Guthrie, 23, 28, 30, 312, 466
Guttridge, 166
Gutzlaff, 464
Guy, 133, 302, 484
Guyton, 102
Gwathmey, 415
Gwin, 204, 272, 323, 324
Gwinn, 52
Gzurman, 445

H

Ha_ley, 19
Habersham, 444
Hachney, 509
Hackel, 408
Hackett, 83, 436
Haddock, 239, 529
Haden, 141
Hades, 334
Haff, 308
Hagan, 432, 458
Hagar, 384
Hager, 300, 386, 449
Hagerman, 171
<u>Hagerstown Academy</u>, 375
Hagerty, 104, 382
Haggarty, 522
Haggerty, 12, 49, 104, 382, 497
Hagner, 194, 317, 318, 532
Hahan, 175
Haight, 307
Haigue, 327
Haile, 288
Hainer, 505
Haines, 71, 175, 395, 457, 463
Hair, 503
Haislip, 102, 136, 382
Haldeman, 403
Hale, 30, 41, 68, 129, 234, 327, 340, 437, 540
Halehran, 192
Haley, 19, 179, 544
Haliday, 166, 177, 255, 312, 506
Hall, 3, 7, 8, 10, 37, 39, 40, 45, 50, 57, 82, 92, 100, 102, 105, 108, 124, 129, 167, 192, 212, 213, 241, 252, 265, 274, 279, 285, 306, 329, 332, 359, 382, 385, 386, 403, 417, 431, 438, 459, 466, 471, 508, 510, 530, 534, 541
Hallet, 54, 181
Hallett, 540
Halloran, 459
Halloway, 11, 156

Hallowell, 351
Halpin, 408
Halstead, 83
Haman, 308
Hambleton, 119, 371, 372
Hamersley, 102, 386
Hamersly, 186
Hamilton, 29, 32, 33, 39, 131, 132, 193, 197, 210, 251, 296, 312, 318, 319, 332, 344, 348, 386, 424, 430, 439, 441, 478, 500, 502, 521, 534
Hammack, 51, 102
Hammel, 399
Hammersley, 167
Hammett's Discovery, 518
Hammon, 462
Hammond, 100, 287, 290, 291, 440, 445, 518, 539
Hamner, 214
Hampton, 242, 377
Hanagan, 191
Hanaway, 520
Hancock, 77, 107, 167, 322
Hand, 37, 220, 252, 440
Handay, 166
Handley, 102, 159, 534
Hands, 147
Handy, 25, 50, 104, 138, 167, 175, 228, 235, 399, 435, 520, 532
Hangya, 394
Hank, 105, 131
Hanki, 372
Hankins, 39
Hanlon, 347, 506
Hanly, 166
Hanna, 364, 407
Hannahan, 277
Hannan, 457
Hannaway, 392, 416
Hannefin, 482
Hannigan, 326
Hannum, 84
Hanrahan, 282
Hansbrough, 494

Hanscom, 434
Hanson, 19, 110, 123, 131, 167, 214, 221, 246, 256, 350, 366, 381, 382, 384, 434, 478, 542
Haphazard, 518
Happe, 314
Happer, 466
Harbaugh, 102, 145, 167, 177, 279, 474
Harbele, 408
Harbin, 448
Hardaway, 456
Hardcastle, 404
Harden, 503
Hardenbergh, 411
Hardie, 131
Hardin, 23, 39, 92. 130, 259, 278, 433
Harding, 19, 161, 180, 317, 318, 377, 537
Hardington, 341
Hardman, 326
Hardy, 223
Hare, 335, 520
Harford Co Academy, 411
Hargerty, 99
Hargous, 53, 85, 161, 173, 182
Hargrove, 64
Harker, 484
Harkness, 91, 167, 372
Harlan, 121, 456
Harley, 384
Harlitt, 217
Harman, 192
Harmar, 44
Harmer, 314, 339
Harmony, 298
Harney, 309
Harnot, 359
Harper, 1, 67, 102, 121, 318, 430, 431, 490, 507
Harrant, 503
Harrer, 378
Harrington, 88, 104, 107, 145, 212, 279, 360, 369, 371, 385, 390, 391

Harris, 2, 81, 90, 94, 97, 102, 111, 119, 129, 130, 141, 166, 174, 177, 188, 282, 352, 353, 354, 384, 400, 404, 424, 445, 450, 473, 505
Harrison, 25, 27, 44, 54, 59, 75, 76, 81, 98, 106, 113, 122, 130, 138, 192, 213, 218, 248, 267, 293, 352, 408, 431, 432, 440, 457, 466, 490, 503, 509
Harroer, 206
Harrover, 108, 393
Harrow, 365, 391
Harry, 129, 169, 374, 384
Harshman, 91, 382
Hart, 5, 8, 19, 38, 83, 84, 204, 233, 267, 307, 308, 327, 378, 407, 466, 491
Hartford, 426
Hartman, 268
Hartshorn, 99, 180
Hartzell, 242
Harvey, 91, 100, 102, 104, 158, 382, 466, 471
Harvy, 237
Harwood, 547
Hascall, 515
Haskell, 438
Hasket, 498
Haskin, 126, 128
Haskins, 126
Hass, 2
Hassan, 123
Hassand, 181
Hassler, 75
Haste, 308
Hastings, 227, 374, 426, 454
Hatch, 85, 102, 144, 182, 244, 256, 287
Hatfield, 131
Hathaway, 74, 179, 311
Haukey, 212
Haunchild, 91
Hauptman, 509
Hausenpflute, 132

Haven, 302
Havener, 337
Havenner, 240, 255, 386, 432
Havens, 234
Haviland, 206
Haw, 255
Hawes, 414
Hawkins, 31, 36, 139, 154, 167, 170, 263, 287, 338, 441, 442, 478, 531, 543
Hawks, 375
Hawley, 150, 242, 445
Haworth, 103
Hawthorne, 185
Hay, 75
Hayden, 31, 123, 283, 311
Haydon, 498
Hayes, 59, 179, 505
Haygood, 508
Hayman, 424, 479, 507
Haymond, 401
Hayne, 380, 395
Haynes, 170, 188, 283, 372, 409
Hays, 207, 256, 515, 547
Hayward, 355
Haywood, 352, 355, 462, 543
Hayworth, 52, 370
Hazard, 25, 102, 384
Hazel, 172, 398, 405, 419, 459
Hazeltine, 308
Hazlett, 456
Hazlup, 219
Head, 300, 404
Headley, 291
Headly, 307
Heaggard, 11
Heald, 454
Healey, 319, 380
Heaney, 122, 365, 465
Heard, 102, 147, 196, 386, 483
Hearn, 52
Hearsey, 359, 408
Heath, 121, 180, 237, 279, 344
Hebard, 242, 318

Hedges, 64
Hedgman, 210
Hedrick, 279
Heeler, 332
Hefren, 378
Hefron, 407
Heildman, 327
Heileman, 272
Heilman, 79
Hein, 75, 391
Heisler, 106
Heiss, 40, 413
Heitmiller, 104, 166, 386
Helfer, 364
Hellen, 267, 419, 459
Hellyer, 338
Helm, 289
Helms, 454
Heltmiller, 382
Hempler, 300
Hempstead, 538
Henderberger, 482
Hendershot, 52, 84
Henderson, 20, 31, 125, 139, 142, 212, 233, 242, 279, 302, 305, 374, 401, 417, 418, 459, 499, 536
Hendley, 385, 459, 461, 480
Hendrick, 396
Hendricks, 281, 355
Hendrickson, 358
Hening, 426
Henke, 386
Henkle, 2
Hennessey, 324
Henning, 102, 167
Henrick, 468
Henry, 49, 57, 59, 94, 100, 104, 108, 113, 128, 141, 161, 182, 258, 306, 347, 376, 385, 395, 408, 487, 520, 541
Hensey, 382
Henshaw, 12
Hensley, 380
Henton, 152

Hepburn, 25, 91, 167, 451
Heppard, 430
Heptinstall, 396
Herb, 299
Herbert, 121, 174, 176, 319, 495, 503, 541
Hercus, 104
Hereford, 257
Hernandez, 359, 373, 378, 407
Herndon, 114
Herold, 166
Heron, 505
Herrell, 347
Herren, 409
Herrera, 151, 173, 234
Herrick, 46, 56
Herring, 37, 80, 82, 84
Herrington, 10, 547
Herrlich, 218
Herron, 374
Herst, 47
Hess, 94, 166, 211
Hesser, 83
Hetzel, 56, 527, 540
Hevner, 63
Hewes, 503
Hewett, 290
Hewit, 289
Hewitt, 481
Heydenfeldt, 374
Heyward, 207
Hezekiah, 179
Hibbard, 10, 371
Hibbert, 242
Hickcox, 460
Hickerson, 269, 510
Hickey, 65
Hickman, 142, 166, 167, 228, 384, 459
Hicks, 167, 210, 255, 339, 382, 397, 426, 497
Hide, 508
Hield, 505
Hieskell, 280

Higbee, 150
Higginbotham, 41, 179, 487
Higgins, 71, 194, 205, 375, 478, 493, 534
High, 196
Highlands, 132
Hilbus, 116, 385, 453, 468
Hildebrand, 506
Hill, 38, 70, 78, 98, 102, 130, 132, 136, 151, 166, 170, 181, 217, 223, 239, 240, 269, 280, 306, 308, 309, 333, 349, 382, 384, 424, 457, 465, 485, 490, 491, 498, 501, 505, 508, 529, 534, 539
Hill Serene, 334
Hillary, 12, 16
Hilleary, 95
Hillegas, 112
Hilliard, 105, 307, 505
Hills, 200
Hillyer, 434
Hilt, 457
Hilton, 65, 113, 242, 308, 378, 407, 422
Hilyard, 75
Hinblink, 40
Hinchman, 94
Hines, 104, 122, 262, 281, 479
Hinnahan, 282
Hinton, 58, 102
Hirst, 149
Hiss, 166, 525
Hitchcock, 9, 127, 287, 288, 289, 414
Hitchcox, 478
Hittle, 52
Hitz, 102, 104, 166
Hixson, 267
Hlasco, 28
Hoar, 462
Hoban, 17, 142, 216, 332
Hobbie, 166
Hobbins, 122
Hobbs, 77, 522
Hobson, 308

Hocker, 59, 370
Hockley, 294
Hodgden, 113
Hodge, 66, 105, 112, 309, 321, 432
Hodges, 14, 57, 66, 79, 218, 234, 278, 290, 327, 411, 431, 450, 489, 521, 523, 542
Hodgkins, 100, 102, 382
Hodgson, 25, 158
Hoe, 311
Hoeke, 4
Hoff, 490
Hoffar, 139
Hoffman, 106, 115, 139, 167, 175, 180, 288, 315, 317, 502
Hogan, 37, 359, 521
Hoge, 301, 332, 526
Holbrook, 94, 179, 402
Holcomb, 452
Holden, 211, 263, 275, 377, 385, 451, 497
Holdship, 408
Holeman, 64, 121
Holiday, 500
Holladay, 271, 455
Holland, 44, 208, 212, 342, 384, 443, 486, 514
Holliday, 225, 452
Hollidge, 19, 167, 397
Hollingsworth, 375, 433
Hollison, 175
Hollister, 369
Hollohon, 542
Holloran, 497, 522, 533
Holman, 3, 188
Holmead, 102, 105, 122, 263, 291, 302, 384, 430, 522
Holmes, 39, 90, 162, 245, 248, 378, 450
Holmes' Hole, 329
Holmes' Island, 491
Holoran, 382
Holroyd, 118
Holt, 244

Homan, 179
Homans, 11
Homes, 115
Homewood, 195
Homola, 394
Hone, 216, 282
Honeywood, 197
Honschild, 91, 142
Hood, 19, 40, 410
Hooe, 46, 102, 185, 279, 303, 494
Hoof, 503
Hooks, 64
Hooper, 106, 450
Hoover, 100, 172, 255, 279, 382, 387, 456, 538
Hope, 25, 31, 45, 62, 440
Hopeton, 195
Hopkins, 27, 36, 37, 39, 72, 80, 81, 92, 121, 195, 212, 256, 259, 348, 355, 382, 384, 503, 509
Hopp, 411
Hormer, 462
Horn, 43
Horne, 77
Horner, 81, 439
Horning, 102, 167, 386
Hornor, 232
Horr, 313, 339
Horschamp, 277
Horsey, 202
Horskamp, 269
Horsthamp, 104, 167
Horsthump, 382
Horstkamp, 363
Hort, 424
Hortin, 308
Horton, 212
Horwqath, 393
Hosack, 486
Hottinger, 253
Houck, 448, 454
Hough, 33, 170, 407, 530
Houghton, 400
Hourly, 193

House, 57, 129, 278
Houseman, 367
Houston, 176, 294, 300
Hovey, 333
How, 94
Howain, 372
Howard, 63, 107, 122, 166, 167, 279, 301, 304, 307, 311, 319, 342, 370, 373, 382, 384, 386, 464, 498, 503, 512, 529, 544
Howder, 372
Howe, 30, 108, 169, 213, 237, 316, 355, 447, 493
Howel, 170
Howell, 30, 89, 100, 104, 108, 226, 323, 350, 382, 445, 455
Howes, 359
Howie, 166
Howison, 32, 97, 107, 131
Howland, 263, 287, 473, 476
Howle, 67, 324, 373
Howlett, 300, 312, 326, 382, 397
Howling, 171
Hoye, 58
Hoyt, 406, 514
Hubbard, 212, 220, 231, 269, 282
Hubbi, 372
Huddleson, 332
Huddleston, 42
Hudnall, 372, 408
Hudson, 316, 340
Huff, 44
Hufford, 469
Hugenots, 210
Huger, 166, 318
Huggins, 91, 102, 104, 384
Hughart, 362
Hughes, 22, 59, 61, 67, 105, 150, 170, 180, 192, 286, 370, 377, 378, 386, 407, 450, 459, 500, 501, 525
Hugner, 459
Huguenot, 335
Hugunan, 170
Huie, 307

Hulett, 440
Hull, 22, 85, 113, 179, 329, 345, 375, 503
Hulseman, 307
Hultzmann, 513
Hume, 167
Hume, 192, 320
Humphrey, 508
Humphreys, 385, 467
Hungerford, 52, 104, 162, 194
Hunnicutt, 136
Hunsberger, 382, 385
Hunt, 31, 223, 244, 248, 299, 301, 377, 410, 418, 424, 442, 446, 500, 508, 530, 543
Hunter, 42, 66, 76, 84, 113, 121, 220, 229, 231, 242, 279, 330, 363, 370, 372, 374, 413, 416, 444, 447, 448, 468, 509, 513, 523
Huntington, 149
Hunton, 110
Huntoon, 450
Huntt, 167
Hurd, 396, 408
Hurdle, 543
Hurley, 379, 462
Hurse, 147
Hurst, 70, 220, 426, 440, 448
Hurt, 62
Huse, 289, 501
Hussey, 89, 222
Husten, 372
Huston, 367, 380
Hustus, 194
Huszak, 394
Hutchingson, 240, 384
Hutchins, 12, 44, 68, 71, 391
Hutchinson, 7, 18, 44, 82, 214, 521
Hutchison, 35, 38, 235, 332, 371
Hutter, 39, 45
Hutton, 167, 308, 424
Hutxthal, 52
Huxley, 308
Huzman, 445

Hyatt, 100, 102, 278, 289, 307
Hyde, 30, 84, 85, 96, 113, 194, 353, 382, 537

I

Iardella, 9, 102, 275, 319
Ibera, 422
Ickelhart, 451
Iddings, 385
Idemanar, 167
Igo, 546
Igon, 220
Ihasz, 445
Iken, 308
Iler, 148
Imlay, 246
Incze, 393
Ingall, 390
Inge, 282, 485
Ingersol, 14
Ingersoll, 37, 121
Ingle, 110, 167, 214, 269, 286, 336, 345, 413, 508
Ingraham, 118
Ingram, 120, 384
Inman, 129, 242, 489, 504
Innis, 233
Inslee, 407
Ireland, 131, 538
Irvine, 290
Irving, 341
Irwin, 45, 63, 77, 155, 194, 219, 291, 437, 535
Isaac, 387
Israel, 215
Ivey, 385

J

Jabe, 334
Jack, 32, 53, 58
Jackson, 10, 13, 21, 36, 40, 49, 52, 72, 89, 97, 105, 121, 124, 143, 167, 181, 196, 225, 260, 268, 274, 291, 297, 302, 308, 372, 385, 386, 388,

413, 434, 459, 464, 475, 477, 478, 488, 522, 533, 540
Jackson City, 491
Jacob, 100, 167
Jacobs, 192, 226, 237, 255, 312, 338, 490, 503, 509
Jagiello, 347
Jakab, 394
Jamaison, 192
James, 183, 214, 359, 364, 372, 429, 450, 467, 491, 547
Jameson, 20, 266, 274, 277
Jamesson, 413
Jamieson, 167, 384, 503
Jamison, 29, 99
Janney, 100, 312, 503
Jansen, 162
Janson, 205
Jarboe, 14, 216
Jardello, 72
Jardin, 295
Jarnagin, 270
Jarrero, 151
Jarvis, 519
Jasper, 39, 59, 99, 432
Jay, 237
Jaycox, 156
Jefcoart, 326
Jefferson, 73, 80, 167, 253, 322, 321, 398, 424, 542
Jeffrey, 370
Jeffries, 512, 545
Jemmison, 515
Jeney, 394
Jenifer, 354
Jenkins, 76, 117, 167, 170, 213, 307, 316, 392, 421, 442, 495
Jenks, 29, 141
Jennings, 334, 390, 525, 527
Jerome, 525
Jessert, 408, 432
Jesup, 201, 217, 384
Jett, 114, 238
Jetton, 10

Jewell, 176, 199, 447
Jewett, 345
Jillard, 102
Jobson, 85, 181
Jockusch, 430
John, 355, 522
Johns, 15, 70, 317
Johnson, 5, 7, 8, 14, 24, 29, 45, 47, 48, 50, 62, 73, 98, 100, 102, 105, 116, 124, 127, 129, 149, 167, 170, 180, 205, 208, 238, 240, 247, 253, 258, 267, 274, 280, 283, 284, 288, 301, 304, 305, 311, 337, 345, 354, 363, 365, 372, 379, 384, 385, 393, 396, 406, 410, 416, 417, 418, 424, 427, 432, 434, 435, 444, 450, 456, 459, 465, 480, 486, 491, 499, 504, 507, 508, 515, 521, 530, 531, 533, 536, 537, 540, 541, 544, 547
Johnston, 10, 115, 159, 178, 195, 201, 239, 358, 464, 502, 510, 544
JohnTonnele, 537
Jolly, 102, 217, 382
Jones, 9, 10, 23, 25, 35, 38, 40, 41, 43, 55, 69, 76, 84, 94, 100, 102, 105, 107, 108, 119, 128, 133, 140, 147, 150, 161, 167, 170, 171, 181, 188, 192, 201, 211, 213, 214, 225, 236, 248, 254, 263, 264, 266, 267, 269, 270, 271, 274, 278, 282, 289, 291, 295, 304, 307, 312, 318, 320, 323, 324, 326, 335, 337, 346, 354, 359, 360, 372, 382, 383, 385, 387, 406, 417, 418, 419, 423, 427, 428, 440, 451, 452, 460, 465, 472, 473, 477, 494, 502, 504, 509, 513, 522, 526, 527, 540, 542, 544
Jordan, 127, 128, 289, 505
Jordon, 167, 270, 472
Josetti, 284
Jost, 106, 510
Jouguo, 309
Jourdan, 167
Jourden, 240

Joy, 308
Joyce, 105, 384, 415
Judd, 454
Judson, 16, 100, 362, 480
Julian, 281
June, 98
Juneman, 171
Junot, 145
Justice, 297
Justus, 176

K

Kailing, 393
Kalapsa, 445
Kanalay, 87, 154
Kane, 244, 385, 482
Kantner, 394
Karody, 445
Karppe, 356
Kauffman, 167, 385
Kaufman, 46, 48, 50, 384
Kaugphman, 448
Kavanagh, 542
Kealey, 167
Kean, 124, 424
Kearns, 155
Kearny, 500, 501
Kearsley, 522
Keath, 182
Keating, 260
Keavy, 371
Keck, 376
<u>Kedge Anchor</u>, 122
Kedglie, 34
Keech, 111
Keeche's Folly, 518
Keefe, 250
Keenan, 409, 432, 489
Keener, 211
Keese, 25, 148, 175, 214, 235
Kehl, 384
Keibel, 459
Keisler, 220
Keith, 113, 488, 503

Keithley, 230
Keithly, 384
Keizer, 99
Kelcher, 99, 388
Keleher, 284
Kelemen, 394
Keley, 105
Kell, 242
Kelleher, 167
Kellen, 223
Keller, 5, 120, 426, 478, 496
Kellett, 531
Kelley, 155, 171, 209, 213, 481
Kellogg, 30, 73, 526
Kelly, 5, 8, 18, 30, 38, 102, 175, 180,
    181, 209, 214, 220, 225, 227, 240,
    268, 286, 358, 372, 382, 384, 388,
    395, 409, 448, 449, 476, 496
Kelso, 466
Kelton, 278, 290
Kembel, 459
Kemble, 277
Kemp, 308
Kemper, 84
Kempton, 372
Kenally, 139
Kendall, 3, 68, 77, 117, 179, 229, 263,
    473, 526, 534, 545
Kendig, 313
Kendrick, 21, 97, 490
Kenerly, 100
Kennan, 448
Kennedy, 3, 35, 60, 115, 179, 187,
    214, 226, 262, 286, 289, 291, 338,
    362, 395, 414, 503, 526, 535
Kennet, 89
Kenny, 207, 510
Kenrick, 437
Kent, 155, 255, 262, 353, 451, 477,
    482
Kenwick, 355
Kenworthy, 503
Kepler, 131, 167, 387, 494
Ker, 500, 501

Kerby, 171
Kercker, 408
Kerr, 25, 30, 62, 82, 119, 137, 181, 227, 286, 302, 359, 365, 367, 373, 380, 467, 505, 523
Kerry, 388
Kershaw, 279
Kerskes, 373
Kessler, 52, 335
Ketchum, 78, 207, 232, 344, 535
Kettlewell, 499
Kevan, 144
Kewen, 374
Key, 219, 224, 451
Keys, 424, 438, 454
Keyworth, 102, 167, 262, 279, 300
Khen, 410
Kibbal, 387
Kibbey, 91, 102, 105, 183, 492, 505
Kibble, 384
Kibby, 29, 70, 167
Kidd, 244, 511
Kidder, 72, 114, 180, 181
Kidwel, 449
Kidwell, 57, 62, 167, 449, 460
Kieckhoefer, 300
Kierman, 169
Kiernan, 410
Kilby, 455
Kilgore, 524
Killeher, 174
Killen, 238
Killian, 102, 167, 384, 462
Killman, 461
Killmon, 105, 376
Kilroy, 323
Kimball, 239, 306, 454
Kimber, 413
Kimberton Farm, 413
Kimbrough, 226, 485
Kimmell, 170
Kinder, 53
King, 8, 24, 25, 29, 35, 38, 46, 60, 61, 63, 91, 98, 100, 102, 105, 107, 108, 109, 115, 119, 121, 129, 134, 167, 172, 174, 188, 192, 196, 201, 203, 227, 231, 269, 300, 307, 309, 317, 318, 319, 330, 358, 360, 382, 384, 387, 402, 450, 459, 460, 463, 467, 470, 477, 482, 491, 517, 523, 525, 543
King of Hanover, 242
Kingman, 167
Kingsbury, 307, 318
Kingsland, 11
Kingston, 159
Kinney, 38, 86, 294
Kinnsey, 214
Kinsil, 338
Kinsley, 99, 248
Kinslo, 449
Kirby, 56, 256, 300, 377, 431, 432, 536
Kirk, 174
Kirkham, 127
Kirkpatrick, 14, 300, 384
Kirkwood, 466
Kirtus, 307
Klein, 209
Kleindienst, 105, 384
Kleipstein, 292
Kliendienst, 167
Klingle, 302
Klomane, 462
Klomann, 107, 108, 167, 448
Klopfer, 214, 480
Klopper, 167
Klutts, 370
Knapp, 51, 432, 490
Kneady, 98
Knickerbocker, 59, 202, 521
Knight, 22, 67, 74, 75, 174, 179, 272, 435, 458, 468, 519
Knoblock, 224, 474
Knoll, 378
Knott, 98, 100, 102, 105, 108, 167, 316, 387, 507
Knowles, 94, 221, 266, 268, 279

Knox, 23, 119, 232, 309, 371, 450
Kolembeski, 245
Kolle, 75
Koones, 509
Kosak, 445
Kosciusko, 240, 253
Kossuth, 71, 109, 420, 445, 472, 473, 527
Koszta, 393
Kough, 105
Kovach, 394
Kovats, 445
Kowach, 394
Krabb, 19
Krafft, 102, 167, 171, 387, 462
Krauss, 77
Krebs, 536
Kresge, 73
Kretschmar, 250
Kreuss, 459
Kroeber, 167
Krouse, 49
Krucsanyi, 394
Kruse, 493
Kuhl, 106, 112, 167, 228
Kuhland, 280
Kuhn, 394
Kulnman, 308
Kuns, 410
Kunsten, 29
Kurtz, 208, 215, 251, 256
Kyger, 371
Kyle, 212

L

La Fort, 352
La Reintree, 5
La Truite, 424
Labbe, 412, 422
Labruere, 123, 181
Labucere, 132
Lacey, 279, 493
Lachance, 5
Lackland, 395
Lacoste, 378, 407
Lacy, 273
Lacy, 382
Laczko, 393
Ladd, 77, 398, 538
Lafayette, 18, 542
Laffler, 137, 182
Lafler, 28, 151, 173
Laframboise, 174
Lagow, 174
Laguerenna, 44
Laguerenne, 49
Lahuzan, 372
Laidlaw, 260
Laine, 408
Lair, 64
Laird, 274
Lajos, 394
Lake, 48, 472
Lakey, 154
Lallande, 323
Lamar, 401
Lamb, 44, 379, 402, 505
Lambell, 167, 190, 286, 382
Lambert, 64, 75, 308, 348, 365, 384, 469
Lambreth, 508
Lamoree, 237
Lamson, 63
Lanahan, 6, 13, 44, 131, 241, 245, 511, 525
Lancaster, 52, 107, 387, 459
Lancey, 120
Landie, 332
Landingham, 372
Landis, 209, 283
<u>Landon Female Seminary</u>, 349
Landrick, 167
Landry, 137, 458
Landsdale, 192
Lane, 47, 102, 169, 178, 235, 263, 371, 382, 396, 424, 477, 485
Lanegan, 140
Laneghan, 395

Lang, 103, 282
Langdon, 243, 282, 467
Langerman, 308
Langhery, 327
Langley, 25, 216, 425, 459, 461
Langstroth, 475
Langton, 75, 469
Langtree, 464
Lanham, 191
Lanier, 15
Lanman, 524
Lanphier, 170, 210
Lansdale, 521
Lansdown, 129
Lansing, 128, 287, 290, 501
Lapadar, 394
Lapolt, 327
Laporte, 256, 311
Lapreux, 384
Lapsley Hall, 498
Larabee, 30
Lardner, 79, 272
Large, 10
Larkin, 9, 49, 181
Larkins, 370, 410
Larmon, 62
Larned, 140, 368, 369, 459
Larner, 496
Larrier, 258
Larsh, 84
Lashler, 410
Lasio, 445
Laskey, 200, 279
Lasky, 448
Lastrapes, 121, 319
Laszlo, 394
Latham, 50, 53, 305, 384, 385
Lathan, 50, 363
Lathrie, 355
Lathrop, 83, 149
Latimer, 203, 320, 545
Latty, 196
Laub, 105, 167, 270, 323, 324
Lauck, 94, 507

Laudvaigt, 384
Laughlin, 76, 267, 338
Laughton, 384
Lauman, 167
Launders, 388
Laurel Farm, 208
Laurence, 47
Laurie, 29, 327, 391, 547
Lauxman, 167, 461, 462
Lavalette, 174, 458, 474
Lavallette, 272
Lavender, 167
Law, 167, 228, 344, 345
Lawrason, 191
Lawrence, 10, 68, 102, 171, 139, 219, 239, 242, 247, 261, 338, 340, 414, 503, 515, 531, 538
Lawrenson, 198
Lawrey, 74
Lawrie, 25, 206
Laws, 229, 339
Lawson, 21, 75, 140, 141, 167, 382, 503, 529
Lay, 74, 288
Layton, 196
Lazarus, 354
Lazenby, 60, 229
Le Roy, 389
Lea, 121, 274, 297
Leach, 467
Leadbitter, 537
Leakins, 363
Lear, 253
Leary, 276
Leasure, 244
Leavenworth, 307
Leavitt, 344
Lebby, 354
Leddy, 3, 51, 105, 167, 268
Lederer, 167, 387
Ledlie, 323
Lee, 23, 37, 39, 51, 54, 62, 75, 99, 167, 178, 181, 184, 237, 238, 246, 248, 258, 263, 279, 288, 306, 360,

373, 378, 384, 388, 407, 424, 462,
  503, 534
Leehy, 69
Leery, 159
Leese, 308
Leeswitzet, 384
Lefever, 417
Leftwich, 179
Legare, 424
Legate, 518
Leggett, 156, 182, 247, 326, 538
Legrand, 223, 471
Lehman, 105, 106, 461
Lehmann, 167
Leib, 304
Leiblick, 534
Leigh, 64
Leisberger, 107
Leland, 119, 447
Leming, 221
Lemmi, 445
Lemmon, 353
Lemnan, 387
Lemot, 307
Lenaghan, 239
Lenahan, 9
Lendrum, 128
Lenman, 34, 102
Lenox, 25, 239, 269, 328
Leny, 490
Leonard, 503
LePreux, 105
Lerody, 445
Lesberger, 384
Lesher, 52
Lesirur, 130
Leslie, 89, 314, 339
Lester, 163, 510
Lesure, 403
Letcher, 29, 455
Letitia, 336
Letmate, 102
Leve, 378
Levely, 45

Levison, 429
Levy, 116, 181, 265, 407
Lewis, 8, 52, 96, 99, 102, 118, 167,
  178, 183, 192, 195, 206, 212, 250,
  269, 279, 309, 337, 377, 382, 384,
  388, 389, 396, 416, 421, 448, 457,
  460, 478, 531, 541
Lewohl, 372
Leyman, 326
Leypoldt, 167
Libbey, 15, 120, 178, 279
Lichtenstein, 393, 394
Lickins, 466
Lieberman, 491
Lieblick, 169
Lieger, 378
Liesberger, 100, 102
Liggert, 81
Light, 10, 59
Lightburn, 535
Lightner, 452
Ligon, 370
Lillir, 519
Lilly, 529
Limehouse, 343
Lincoln, 227, 403
Lind, 98, 221, 341, 414
Lindauer, 198
Lindenberger, 91
Linder, 212
Lindle, 473
Lindner, 115
Lindsay, 287, 411
Lindsey, 102, 263
Lindsley, 2, 20, 42, 89, 137, 167, 358,
  461, 532
Lingard, 336
Linkin, 459
Linkins, 87, 114, 167, 239, 277, 284,
  336, 382, 384, 390, 422, 459
Linn, 56
Linnard, 193, 201, 287, 291
Linnean Hill, 140, 195
Linsor, 547

Linthicum, 427
Linton, 434
Liomim, 384
Liphard, 105
Lippett, 284
List, 40, 71, 263
Little, 55, 67, 98, 117, 167, 235, 269, 279, 328, 359, 378, 384, 388, 405, 408, 431, 432, 466, 506
Livermore, 238, 313, 339
Liverpool, 452
Livingston, 6, 14, 76, 370, 415, 420, 511
Livingstons, 310
Livinston, 508
Llewellyn, 197
Lloyd, 105, 157, 167, 293, 361, 406, 407
Locheny, 105
Lock, 473
Locker, 429
Lockett, 379
Lockhart, 281, 355
Locks' Meadows, 518
Lockwood, 6, 15, 76, 194, 220, 306, 332, 450
Locust Grove, 154
Locust Hill, 224
Lofter, 429
Lofton, 418
Logan, 27, 203, 233
Logen, 392
Lokey, 112, 154, 206
Lomax, 382, 388, 391, 439, 460
Lomex, 172
Lomix, 384
London, 167
Long, 16, 65, 76, 172, 287, 294, 326, 406, 518
Longstreet, 140
Longstreeth, 319
Longuemare, 318
Longwell, 417
Loobey, 106

Looby, 99
Looker, 82
Loomis, 288
Looper, 74
Lopez, 31, 365, 369, 372, 373, 375, 380, 407, 408, 409, 433, 442, 451, 489, 499
Lorant, 394
Lord, 44, 105, 112, 123, 167, 179, 330, 350, 403, 410, 473, 509
Lorenz, 482
Loring, 71, 150, 263, 329
Lorintz, 394
Loron, 212
Losner, 378, 409, 431
Lott, 351
Loudon, 311, 484
Lougee, 403
Loughborough, 6, 374
Louis XVI, 223, 513
Lounda, 332
Lounds, 201
Lovatt, 374
Love, 163, 180, 362, 370
Lovejoy, 122, 345, 384
Lovel, 511
Lovelace, 141
Loveless, 382
Lovell, 60
Low, 36, 39, 66
Lowder, 178
Lowe, 6, 66, 93, 167, 192, 249, 270, 431, 441, 458, 484, 492
Lowell, 306
Lower Teddington, 293
Lowndes, 99, 274
Lowrey, 311, 480
Lowrie, 345
Lowry, 148, 335, 509
Loxmann, 57
Lucas, 277, 308, 311, 382, 446
Luce, 75, 209, 444
Lucy, 98
Ludlos, 473

Ludlow, 258, 424
Ludwig, 117, 408
Luffeen, 492
Lukacs, 394
Luley, 445
Lumpkin, 233
Lunceford, 175
Lundy, 538
Lunt, 507
Lusakowsky, 445
Lusby, 102, 146, 167
Luster, 364
Lutz, 28, 102, 178, 207, 275
Luxen, 82
Luxon, 384
Lykins, 512
Lyles, 404, 510
Lyman, 342
Lynch, 37, 71, 78, 80, 82, 92, 105, 140, 174, 197, 198, 259, 332, 514, 517, 522, 545
Lyndall, 364
Lyne, 140
Lynes, 534
Lynn, 400
Lyon, 203, 288, 324, 338, 416, 520
Lyons, 91, 126, 175, 268, 279, 281, 431
Lysle, 466
Lyvus, 382

M

Maach, 386
Mac Gregor, 158
MacAllister, 277
Macauley, 76, 279
Maccoun, 81
Macdaniel, 162
Macduel, 65
Mace, 355
Macedo, 242
MacElfresh, 423
Macghee, 39, 51
Macgill, 455

Macgregor, 28
Mack, 126
Mackabee, 330
Mackall, 51, 82, 83, 139, 190, 507, 521
Mackay, 1, 14, 134
Mackenheimer, 241, 514
Mackey, 372
Mackinney, 378
Macleod, 197
MacMath, 466
MacNeill, 417
Macomb, 142, 500
Macpherson, 256, 307
Macrae, 15, 194
MacRae, 173
Maddison, 332
Maddox, 2, 14
Madison, 1, 47, 50, 64, 73, 168, 232, 382, 420
Maffitt, 174, 428
Magar, 120
Magee, 105, 155, 305, 387
Magness, 21, 53, 429
Magnus, 384
Magruder, 7, 67, 81, 85, 100, 102, 132, 167, 193, 240, 271, 279, 303, 375, 382, 400, 454, 457, 500, 509
Maguire, 100, 335
Mahan, 408
Maher, 539
Mahon, 45, 75, 91, 543
Mahoney, 194, 307
Mahony, 404
Mahorney, 347
Mains, 37, 80, 82
Major, 204
Malcolm, 345
Malertie, 466
Malett, 145
Malkey, 415
Mallory, 64, 179
Malone, 171, 461
Maltby, 59

Malthy, 39
Malumpy, 248
Malvin, 424
Manahan, 315
Mandaville, 546
Mandeville, 32, 441
Mangham, 500, 502
Mangnus, 171
Manion, 229
Mankin, 525, 532
Mankins, 137, 167, 170
Manley, 492
Manly, 109
Mann, 100, 256, 270, 299, 311, 313, 337, 350
Manning, 231, 310, 435
Mansfield, 167, 264, 365, 384
Manville, 359
Manyett, 476
Mapes, 40, 52
Maple Hill, 266
Marbury, 91, 134, 248, 341, 349, 358, 360, 381, 427, 492, 500, 502
Marcello, 76
Marcellus, 256
Marceron, 105, 303, 384, 395
March, 534
Marchant, 208, 505
Marcus, 71
Marden, 267, 382
Marechal, 194
Mareschal, 190
Marianna Seminary, 448
Marie Antoinette, 472
Marier, 472
Maril, 157
Marion, 474
Mariposa, 458
Mark, 308
Markland, 37, 252, 361
Markoe, 199
Marks, 40, 42, 64, 118, 123, 161, 157, 182, 220, 279, 324, 363, 384, 417, 450

Markus, 394
Markwald, 341
Marlow, 36, 39, 51
Marquise de Livry, 223
Marr, 167
Marriott, 215
Marron, 254
Marryett, 446
Marsh, 158, 238, 399
Marshall, 24, 35, 60, 96, 127, 164, 167, 169, 170, 188, 190, 274, 285, 288, 307, 333, 374, 396, 410, 424, 456, 471, 505
Marshall Hall, 409
Marsi, 167
Marston, 46, 70
Martan, 378
Martell, 192
Marteni, 68
Marthan, 546
Martin, 16, 20, 49, 82, 98, 99, 103, 105, 108, 122, 131, 167, 170, 204, 206, 248, 260, 280, 281, 293, 315, 328, 371, 387, 404, 415, 431, 440, 450, 454, 505, 518
Martinez, 57, 123, 339, 378, 408
Martini, 34, 67, 420, 485
Marye, 419
Maryman, 2, 33, 51, 78, 197, 200, 217, 246, 405, 419, 523
Masi, 99, 102, 153, 300
Mason, 17, 23, 99, 131, 167, 203, 214, 215, 217, 218, 238, 311, 335, 351, 382, 384, 387, 426, 462, 471, 482, 484, 485, 491, 503, 523, 525, 534
Mason's Island, 426
Massey, 218, 413, 537
Massi, 384
Massie, 503
Massoletti, 234
Masters, 472
Masterson, 191, 299
Maston, 448
Mathews, 16, 37, 82, 318, 319, 357

Mathieu, 309
Mathiot, 385
Matlack, 29
Mattaponi, 85, 135
Matthews, 67, 132, 149, 206, 236, 242, 297, 327, 424, 425, 477, 510, 534
Matthias, 192, 541
Mattingley, 459
Mattingly, 69, 82, 100, 139, 168, 281, 393, 513
Mattison, 490, 492
Maud, 510
Maulsbey, 179
Maupin, 27, 371
Maury, 122, 240, 301, 427, 494
Maxwell, 21, 102, 127, 267, 319, 547
May, 12, 40, 79, 92, 180, 183, 196, 217, 226, 230, 242, 263, 276, 323, 325, 340, 375, 422, 426, 464, 500, 523
Mayer, 161
Mayes, 109
Mayfield, 375
Maynadier, 278, 289, 347
Maynard, 134, 384
Mayo, 81, 321, 345
Mc Colcock, 110
McAfee, 237
McAlister, 96
McAllister, 221
McAlwe, 397
McAlwee, 492
McArann, 272
McArthur, 12, 15, 48, 483
McAtee, 323
McAvoy, 62
McBain, 423
McBlair, 85, 219, 498, 521, 529
McBride, 3
McCabe, 408, 510
McCafferty, 102
McCahill, 258, 308
McCaleb, 31

McCall, 9, 18, 339
McCalla, 260
McCann, 339
McCannon, 90
McCanplin, 172
McCardle, 28
McCarthy, 102, 269, 363, 412, 465, 497, 522
McCarty, 178, 248, 305, 325, 429
McCauley, 332, 384, 459
McCaullay, 303
McCauly, 162
McCawley, 418
McCeney, 266
McChesney, 105
McClasky, 247
McClellan, 152
McClelland, 9, 18, 408, 486, 515
McClennen, 324
McClernand, 485
McClery, 75, 82, 108, 167, 199
McClintock, 43, 92, 135, 145, 259
McClung, 508
McClure, 6, 371, 485
McCluskey, 507
McColgan, 514, 516
McCollam, 17
McCollum, 53, 336
McComb, 79, 374
McConchie, 112, 217
McConnell, 34, 128
McCook, 384
McCorckle, 410
McCorcle, 329
McCord, 267
McCorkle, 159, 196, 235, 374
McCormick, 4, 17, 67, 177, 205, 233, 245, 285, 286, 291, 300, 345, 364, 420, 461
McCorquadate, 429
McCorrie, 361
McCown, 126, 344
McCoy, 75, 167, 424
McCrackin, 339

McCrae, 466
McCrea, 174
McCready, 30
McCreery, 225
McCrone, 41
McCubbin, 227, 358, 461
McCue, 481
McCullar, 370
McCullough, 129
McCullum, 448
McCurdy, 239, 272, 326
McCutchen, 102
McDanald, 141
McDaniel, 196, 209
McDellans, 378
McDemott, 430
McDermott, 137, 168, 256, 385, 433, 523
McDevitt, 17, 51, 102, 170, 387, 471
McDonald, 127, 332, 372, 378, 407, 446, 480, 500, 502
McDonell, 494
McDonnel, 75
McDonogh, 30
McDoual, 508
McDougald, 317
McDowell, 126, 128, 192, 252, 258, 305, 314, 339, 345, 364, 421
McDuell, 82
***McDuell's Row*, 189**
McDuffie, 122, 307, 508
McElfresh, 90, 100, 131, 167, 375, 460
McElhany, 43
McElrath, 94, 436
McElroy, 369
McElvoy, 41
McEmon, 410
McEnery, 34
McEntire, 220
McEvers, 333
McFadden, 58, 135, 188, 410, 454
McFaden, 89
McFarland, 187, 324

McGann, 453
McGarry, 454
McGarvey, 387
McGaughey, 281, 286
McGaw, 531
McGee, 134, 329
McGehee, 283
McGermy, 332
McGhee, 36, 534
McGill, 43, 63, 233, 254, 351, 514, 527
McGirr, 19
McGlue, 284, 356, 382, 509
McGough, 330
McGovern, 299
McGowen, 374
McGrann, 296
McGrath, 378, 407
McGraun, 106
McGraw, 512
McGreary, 196
McGreevy, 168
McGregor, 103, 108, 198, 335, 387
McGrier, 378
McGuffey, 373
McGuffy, 423
McGuire, 13, 73, 107, 232, 325, 381, 383, 386, 509
McGunnegle, 274
McHallon, 410
McHargues, 41
McHarvey, 332
McHaughten, 167
McHenry, 94, 205, 408
McIlcer, 359
McIleer, 359
McIlton, 262
McInnis, 547
McIntire, 28, 102, 473
McIntosh, 223, 279, 289
McIntyre, 283, 449, 452
McKan, 332
McKaraher, 308
McKay, 512

McKean, 44, 118, 170, 171
McKee, 89, 236, 257, 355
McKelden, 204, 242, 363, 387, 509
McKelyutth, 320
McKenna, 217, 366, 374, 503, 510
McKenney, 123, 139, 156, 347, 382
McKennon, 85
McKenzie, 303, 428
McKeune, 180
McKim, 51, 167, 177
McKinger, 50
McKinley, 9, 18, 20, 32, 451
McKinly, 508
McKinney, 299, 313, 413
McKinnis, 408
McKinnon, 351
McKinny, 43
McKinsey, 407
McKinstry, 154
McKneiss, 408
McKnew, 188, 499
McKnight, 503
McLain, 169, 170, 319, 424
McLaine, 524
McLanahan, 13
McLane, 197, 265
McLaughlin, 103, 108, 111, 206, 244, 296, 517
McLaws, 501
McLean, 33, 102, 121, 167, 305, 314, 439
McLees, 52
McLeod, 117, 212, 237, 264, 377, 435
McLoman, 462
McMachen, 63
McMagee, 332
McMahon, 248, 384
McMann, 490
McManus, 15
McMaster, 417
McMichael, 339
McMinn, 19, 204, 210
McMullen, 408, 455
McMullin, 25

McMurray, 360, 378, 407
McNair, 36, 39, 41, 92, 259
McNamara, 207, 249
McNamee, 16, 459
McNaney, 407
McNaughton, 411, 461
McNeal, 106, 396
McNeil, 409, 497, 512, 517
McNeill, 431, 462, 512
McNeily, 299
McNerhany, 513
McNew, 382
McNiell, 424
McNier, 279
McNulty, 327
McNutt, 478
McOuran, 90
McPhail, 210, 280
McPherson, 70, 91, 102, 105, 167, 218, 224, 451
McQuay, 167, 170
McQuilkin, 508
McRae, 182, 220, 278, 289, 405, 500
McRea, 501
McRee, 264
McRoddy, 158
McSherry, 81
McTeer, 244
McVay, 231
McVean, 125, 190, 396
McVeigh, 303, 430
McVickan, 264
McWhir, 61
McWinn, 11
Meacham, 402
Mead, 82, 332, 388, 443
Meade, 31, 178, 242, 271, 373, 384, 455, 500, 520
Meadow Grove, 500, 502
Meagher, 537
Means, 32, 181, 283, 531
Meany, 371
Mears, 53, 139, 303, 328, 403, 460
Mebane, 287

Mechlin, 349
Mecklin, 167
Medford, 493
Mediperis, 2, 256
Medleshall, 278
Medley, 120, 122
Meehan, 33
Meek, 40
Meem, 324, 496
Megee, 460
Megrath, 503
Meier, 5, 8
Meiere, 277
Meigs, 268, 432, 541
Melesimo, 378
Mellus, 307
Melrose, 1, 201, 267, 520
Melvin, 83, 370
men for smoking, 138
Mendenhall, 289
Meneely, 432
Meneth, 445
Menke, 439
Mercer, 3, 99, 382
Meredith, 74, 102, 300, 315, 511, 517, 540
Merefield, 65
Merighy, 445
Merill, 483
Merinder, 218
Meriwether, 196
Merrian, 402
Merrick, 29, 74, 90, 347
Merrill, 129, 196, 454
Merriman, 129
Merring, 331
Merritt, 160
Merry, 196
Meschert, 503
Messervey, 25, 259
Messinger, 267
Metcalf, 234, 407
Metcalfe, 155, 378
Metman, 73

Mexwell, 84
Meyer, 69, 146, 182, 263, 308, 546
Mezchase, 145
Michaels, 396
Michon, 192
Mickle, 68
Middleton, 105, 167, 255, 279, 337, 382, 384, 385, 424, 462
Mignot, 324
Miklosy, 445
Milan, 225
Milburn, 18, 34, 167, 503
Mileman, 378
Miles, 115, 184, 238, 388
Milestone, 370
Milford, 455
Milhado, 336, 521
Milhau, 289
Millard, 83
Mille, 107, 167
Miller, 5, 45, 56, 86, 92, 97, 102, 119, 161, 164, 167, 169, 175, 180, 228, 240, 244, 254, 274, 291, 293, 302, 303, 306, 309, 327, 332, 338, 342, 345, 354, 357, 378, 382, 384, 387, 406, 409, 422, 428, 431, 460, 464, 493, 503, 507, 510, 512, 522, 527, 528, 535
Milligan, 47, 518, 520
Milliken, 71
Millington, 505
Millins, 99
Mills, 51, 92, 100, 105, 124, 135, 141, 159, 167, 168, 171, 172, 214, 259, 296, 346, 359, 382, 387, 431, 446, 459, 490, 503, 510, 522, 533, 539, 542
Millson, 455
Milner, 188, 196
Milnor, 406
Milstead, 105, 384, 385, 386
Miltenberger, 335
Mina, 146
Miner, 192

Minge, 529
Minitree, 249
Minor, 117, 167, 437
Minturn, 308, 309
Miskimins, 196
Miss Heaney's Academy, 365
Misservy, 181
Missouri Mills, 355
Mister, 382
Mitchel, 80, 296
Mitchell, 54, 82, 101, 111, 121, 138, 144, 149, 150, 167, 234, 249, 279, 293, 306, 321, 334, 382, 395, 398, 402, 410, 421, 440, 447, 457, 477, 482, 509, 517, 548
Mittag, 331
Mix, 154
Mocaby, 382
Mockbee, 269
Mockebee, 210, 229
Mockobee, 384
Mockoby, 382
Moering, 464, 511
Moffatt, 352
Moffett, 102, 249
Moffit, 355
Moffitt, 83
Mohun, 13, 154, 203, 240, 300, 382
Molinard, 278, 290
Mollihons, 445
Molnar, 394
Money, 459
Monfort, 470
Monly, 394
Monroe, 35, 52, 73, 76, 396, 428, 456, 521, 539, 542
Montandon, 29, 218, 268
Monteith, 267
Montesquieu, 464
Montgomery, 2, 403, 420, 497, 543
Montmorenci Falls, 264
Montoro, 432
Mony, 283
Moodisbang, 309

Moody, 396, 429, 534
Moody Farm, 93
Mooers, 531
Mooney, 424, 486
Moor, 109, 264, 424
Moore, 16, 21, 36, 38, 39, 46, 58, 61, 98, 100, 102, 107, 108, 121, 155, 167, 168, 170, 171, 175, 179, 196, 201, 220, 238, 246, 250, 255, 256, 276, 278, 288, 289, 306, 309, 314, 326, 329, 332, 335, 362, 374, 382, 402, 416, 420, 425, 451, 458, 490, 515, 516, 533, 535, 541
Moorhead, 226
Moorman, 15
Moran, 25, 122, 382, 407, 448
Morass, 517
More, 212
Morehead, 150, 538
Moreland, 302
Moreno, 238
Morey, 20
Morfit, 320, 429
Morfitt, 460
Morgan, 13, 25, 53, 74, 95, 102, 111, 131, 164, 174, 179, 187, 198, 223, 240, 262, 279, 284, 310, 311, 351, 361, 384, 404, 406, 410, 416, 421, 423, 424, 429, 436, 460, 466, 475, 481, 482, 498, 509, 524, 535, 545, 546
Moriarty, 140
Morley, 103, 150, 446
Mormons, 484
Morrill, 220
Morris, 10, 14, 61, 71, 95, 144, 176, 202, 216, 278, 279, 280, 290, 329, 339, 342, 379, 384, 428, 437, 470, 481, 485, 508, 522, 539
Morrison, 36, 39, 55, 56, 102, 103, 142, 279, 308, 330, 354, 427, 446
Morriss, 133
Morrow, 121, 127, 128, 478
Morse, 78, 98, 106, 458, 482, 508, 538

Morsel, 261
Morsell, 24, 25, 51, 79, 91, 105, 124, 135, 138, 193, 202, 204, 257, 275, 279, 297, 491, 509, 519
Mortimer, 102, 510
Morton, 51, 220, 278, 289, 300
Moseley, 121, 428
Mosely, 262
Moses, 3, 11, 41, 82, 84, 96, 119, 386, 461
Mosher, 421, 442
Moss, 75, 309, 332, 439, 513
Mossman, 356
Most, 476
Mothershead, 102, 382
Mott, 347
Moulden, 94
Moulton, 212
Moultrie, 141, 207
Mount, 7, 215, 416
Mount Airy, 354
Mount Alban Institute, 393
Mount Crawford House, 314
Mount Hope, 149, 412
Mount Oak, 7
Mount Pleasant, 11, 18
Mount Vernon, 61, 205, 330, 389
Mount Wollaston, 322
Mountain View Farm, 195
Mounted Rifles, 263
Mountford, 450
Mountz, 96
Mourou, 378
Mower, 115, 121
Mowers, 30
Moyer, 83, 406
Mozier, 144
MrAlig, 320
Mudd, 50, 90, 114, 115, 200, 282, 382, 384, 411, 444, 459
Muir, 503
Mulford, 129, 196
Mullanphy, 258, 264, 270
Mullay, 198, 204, 210, 310, 427

Mulledy, 17
Mullen, 25, 167, 169, 407
Muller, 372, 373
Mullett, 450, 538
Mulley, 534
Mulliken, 239, 404
Mullikin, 7, 170, 466
Mullin, 78, 326
Mullins, 321
Mullone, 281
Mullowny, 205
Mulloy, 138, 175, 216, 240, 258
Mulrey, 200
Mulvey, 416
Muncaster, 426, 503
Munch, 103, 167
Munday, 377
Mundell, 399, 400
Munford, 213
Munger, 187
Munroe, 214, 349, 408
Munson, 237, 338
Murdock, 58
Murphy, 90, 91, 123, 137, 157, 167, 181, 185, 192, 228, 229, 264, 270, 282, 342, 363, 370, 382, 385, 399, 408, 430, 434, 442, 486
Murray, 17, 24, 25, 39, 46, 57, 61, 89, 98, 105, 114, 121, 167, 170, 233, 241, 248, 268, 323, 361, 365, 385, 386, 417, 454, 471, 496
Murtagh, 102
Murter, 205
Murtigh, 408
Muse, 88, 167, 452
Mussey, 367
Mustin, 116, 167, 266
Myer, 103, 432
Myerle, 36
Myers, 15, 47, 91, 103, 105, 127, 131, 157, 158, 159, 162, 167, 168, 213, 223, 248, 326, 372, 382, 385, 431, 449, 519
Mygatt, 440

Myrick, 371

N

N H Gazette, 234
Nafton, 345
Nagle, 321, 431
Naglee, 308
Nagy, 393, 394
Nailor, 105, 262, 286, 384
Nairo, 103
Napoleon, 336, 366, 543
Narris, 283
Nash, 69, 91, 438
Nason, 306
Nat'l Library, 542
National Greys, 89
Naudaine, 14
Naughton, 205
Nauman, 475
Naylor, 26, 99, 103, 104, 149, 168, 202, 348, 354, 381
Neal, 332
Neale, 25, 114, 155, 168, 177, 194, 281, 309, 322, 323, 324, 388
Neale, 382
Near, 211, 232
Needham, 158, 400
Neek, 293
Neil, 58, 451
Neill, 494
Neilson, 453
Neims, 19
Neins, 23
Nelson, 18, 29, 108, 115, 168, 248, 301, 328, 391, 408, 454, 500, 502, 507, 543
Nemes, 394
Nemethy, 394
Nepp, 168
Nesbaum, 258
Nesbit, 146
Neumeyer, 137
Neville, 13
Nevin, 58

Nevins, 537
new addition, 48
New Counties in Va, 184
Newall, 299
Newell, 19, 42, 119, 123, 521
Newhouse, 505
Newman, 121, 466, 487
Newmyer, 170
Newton, 168, 171, 263, 387, 415, 543, 546
Newy, 237
Ngikos, 408
Nichol, 81
Nicholas, 107, 233
Nicholls, 168, 310
Nichols, 64, 279, 402, 503
Nicholson, 42, 74, 194, 322, 353, 364, 372, 429, 443, 519
Nickerson, 33, 150
Nicks, 418
Nicol, 293
Nicoll, 217
Nicolls, 370, 528
Niegler, 105
Night, 370
Niles, 279, 482
Ninelist, 150
Nipple, 459
Nisbet, 216
Niseman, 359
Nixon, 503
Noah, 140, 201
Noble, 168, 237, 382, 424
Noel, 312
Noell, 103
Noerr, 168, 382, 387
Noguens, 56
Nokes, 168, 382, 431, 459
Nolan, 159, 179
Noland, 105, 323, 404, 457, 514
Nolen, 193
Noll, 407
Norbeck, 103
Norborne Hall School, 343

Normon, 384
Norris, 16, 70, 188, 218, 263, 278, 289, 388, 452, 471, 503, 542
Norriss, 407
North, 73, 155, 174, 272, 425, 444, 454
Northrup, 129
Norton, 10, 62, 67, 221, 412, 475, 505
Nosler, 445
Nott, 294, 371, 535
Nottingham, 103
Nourse, 103, 132, 135, 162, 226, 249, 369, 457, 539
Novakovich, 394
Novelle, 88
Nowes, 378
Nowland, 151
Nowlin, 231
Noyce, 316
Noyes, 100
Nuckolls, 203
Nugent, 117, 168, 314, 386, 460, 539
Nulty, 75
Nutt, 305
Nutting, 314, 339
Nutwell, 14
Nye, 5, 329
Nyilas, 394
Nyircgyjazy, 394
Nyiregyhazy, 394
Nyiri, 394

O

O, 490
O'Bryan, 92
O'Conner, 69
O'Dell, 103, 460
O'Donnel, 191
O'Donnoghue, 323, 324, 385
O'Ferrall, 294
O'Flaherty, 179
O'Flannigan, 42
O'Hara, 31, 215
O'hare, 105
O'Hare, 382
O'Keennen, 378
O'Leary, 105, 165, 330, 388, 516
O'Meara, 103, 281
O'Neal, 213, 539
O'Neale, 100, 154, 168, 170, 382
O'Neill, 540
O'Quin, 438
O'Regan, 131
O'Reilly, 110
O'Rourke, 481
O'Sullivan, 31, 451
Oak Grove, 164, 284
Oak Hill Cemetery, 215, 427
Oakes, 287, 307
Oaklands, 513
Oakley, 324
Oakwood, 357
Ober, 75, 105, 268, 327, 385, 499
Oberto, 373
Oceanic House, 185
Odell, 43, 255
Oelricks, 292
Offenstein, 175, 268
Offley, 22, 523
Offutt, 65, 249, 323, 332, 522
Ogden, 284, 371, 421, 424, 547
Ogilvie, 347
Oglevie, 408
Olcott, 312
Old Braintree, 322
oldest woman, 216
Oldfield, 279
Oldham, 466
Olenstein, 168
Olin, 353
Oliphant, 94
Olive, 105
Oliver, 242, 301
Olmstead, 438
Olyphant, 303
Omeara, 172
Onacker, 362
Oneil, 455

Oppenheimer, 104
Orcutt, 246, 437
Ore, 172
Orem, 100, 168
Ormand, 168
Orme, 105, 300, 358, 465, 536
<u>Orphan Asylum</u>, 292
Orr, 53, 108
Orrison, 382
Osborn, 149, 197, 206, 427, 496
Osborne, 139, 192
Osburn, 344, 533
Osgood, 308, 469
Ostade, 436
Ostermeyer, 100
Ostrander, 9, 15, 180
Oszlany, 394
Otis, 20, 81, 308, 378
Ott, 146, 326, 344
Ottenheimer, 307
Otterback, 105, 168, 172, 387
Otterson, 421
Otts, 407
Ould, 87, 214
Ousley, 348
Overweg, 425
Owen, 3, 7, 51, 85, 97, 100, 105, 115, 121, 160, 181, 273, 329, 396, 418, 433, 469, 489, 505
Owens, 168, 194, 302, 382
Owings' Mills, 322
Owner, 110, 168
Ownes, 372
Oxby, 98
Oxley, 98
Oyster, 170, 525
Oyuster, 382
Ozias, 37

P

Pace, 547
Pacheco, 56
Pack, 370
Packard, 315

packets **Belle & Fashion**, 476
Padgett, 486, 498
Padownowsky, 168
Page, 53, 98, 99, 103, 107, 114, 138, 165, 168, 190, 213, 232, 240, 265, 382, 387, 409, 412, 463, 477, 501, 512, 535
Paige, 494
Paine, 67, 117, 168, 241, 320, 371, 428, 449, 515
Pairo, 385, 514
Palank, 373
Palanka, 409, 432
Palatinate, 112
Palfrey, 278, 290, 393, 501
Palmer, 98, 124, 128, 168, 263, 324, 355, 377, 382, 384, 426, 434, 444, 520
Palts, 237
Parcell, 190
Pardon, 198
Pardy, 374
Paredes, 234
Parensted, 529
Paris, 279
Parish, 19, 406
Park, 103, 212
Parke, 168
Parkenham, 220
Parker, 12, 40, 44, 51, 62, 91, 94, 105, 108, 168, 206, 213, 225, 242, 256, 262, 281, 292, 315, 332, 339, 348, 355, 366, 370, 375, 379, 382, 385, 387, 402, 415, 450, 489, 510, 525
Parkhurst, 187, 256
Parks, 40, 176, 278, 283, 290, 313, 339, 418, 501
Paroles, 28
Parr, 372, 432
Parriott, 276
Parris, 226, 304, 367, 384
Parrish, 484
Parrot, 76, 182
Parrott, 18, 57, 151, 173, 182, 239

Parsons, 9, 40, 45, 105, 151, 384, 524, 532
Part Parnassus, 518
Partnership, 136
Parton, 168
Partridge, 264
Patan, 378
Patapsco Female Institute, 355
Paton, 503
Patrick, 137, 528
Patsy, 394
Patten, 317, 318, 365
Patterson, 36, 103, 179, 196, 238, 264, 278, 290, 326, 327, 345, 384, 398, 444, 449, 450, 451, 452, 460, 465, 472, 516, 533
Pattison, 492, 495
Patton, 176, 212, 272, 368
Paul, 170
Paulding, 26, 131, 517, 523
Paulett, 530
Payne, 8, 62, 119, 147, 165, 168, 170, 195, 209, 215, 251, 279, 328, 382, 387, 440, 455, 510, 518, 532
Payran, 307
Peabody, 474
Peaco, 103
Peake, 129, 308
Peal, 521
pear tree, 206
Pearce, 59, 127, 129, 140
Pearson, 36, 37, 103, 109, 177, 256, 279, 346, 377, 387, 474, 524
Pearson's Mill, 193
Pease, 209
Pecht, 88
Peck, 52, 81, 168, 192, 316, 360, 383, 387, 440
Peckham, 483
Peddicord, 170, 384
Pedersen, 389
Pedraza, 239
Peebles, 370
Peel, 168

Peerce, 171
Peg, 462
Pegg, 196, 222, 235, 382, 459
Peirce, 48, 92, 202, 225, 228, 310, 391, 400, 461
Pelham, 176
Pelom, 209
Peltier, 5
Pember, 521
Pemberton, 249
Pendegrast, 366
Pendergrast, 270
Pendleton, 90, 115, 119, 242, 376, 397, 460, 494
Penfield, 427
Penn, 323, 336, 458
Pennell, 393
Pennock, 76
Penrose, 151
Pepin, 137
Pepper, 210, 240, 362, 397, 486, 497
Perchment, 369
Perczel, 445
Perdue, 118
Perkins, 23, 159, 168, 202, 236, 382, 397, 509, 539
Perret, 114
Perrie, 56
Perry, 32, 103, 188, 211, 267, 278, 289, 293, 356, 400, 504, 505
Persey, 325
Pertzel, 420
Peter, 43, 48
Peter's Mill Seat, 48
Peteri, 373
Peters, 97, 105, 158, 171, 276, 382, 463, 471, 504
Petersham, 145
Peterson, 453
Petinon, 382
Petrenyi, 394
Petrie, 408
Pett, 105

605

Pettibone, 103, 146, 154, 168, 217, 235, 382, 387, 516
Pettingall, 110
Pettingell, 330
Pettit, 10, 75, 100, 149, 168, 175, 193
Peugh, 497
Peusye, 195
pew #67, 393
Peyton, 227, 281, 303, 322, 436, 453, 504
Pharaoh, 368
Pharoah, 70
Phelan, 466
Phelps, 28, 57, 280, 312, 355, 448, 468, 473
Philippe, 325
Philips, 84
Philliber, 83
Phillippis, 388
Phillips, 33, 88, 100, 103, 115, 121, 149, 168, 172, 176, 177, 230, 239, 249, 303, 309, 349, 359, 366, 408, 432, 440
Phinney, 516
Pianos, 373
Pianos & Music, 222
Piatt, 37, 466
Pickard, 158
Pickens, 83
Pickett, 31, 128, 206, 529
Pickrell, 91, 255, 384, 491, 538
Pierce, 13, 58, 78, 164, 195, 255, 271, 329, 374, 403, 451
Pierpont, 462
Piggford, 221
Piggott, 269, 342
Pike, 5, 8, 34, 450, 490
Pilcher, 36, 39
Piles, 279
Pilling, 103, 105
Pin, 27
Pinckney, 40
Pine Grove, 406
Pineau, 522

Pinkney, 531
Pinnell, 41, 84
Piper, 98, 168, 278, 289, 421
Pitcher, 515
Pittingill, 93
Pittman, 448
Pitts, 342
Pix, 37, 39, 43
Placosio, 373
Plant, 121, 168, 240, 246, 256, 282, 382, 384, 449, 510
Plater, 28, 318
Platt, 37, 80, 82, 192, 395, 409, 433
Platte, 539
Pleasants, 184
Pleasonton, 168, 184, 195
Plumb, 306
Plumbe, 83
Plumer, 179, 403, 433
Plummer, 338, 420, 480, 501, 502
Plumnkitt, 347
Plumsell, 168
Plumsill, 172, 421, 440, 486, 493
Plunkett, 90
Plympton, 248
Poe, 5, 8, 256, 323, 360, 532
Pogeis, 336
Poinsett, 535
Polacaek, 393
Poletti, 168
Polhemus, 516
Polizzi, 168
Polk, 171, 202
Pollard, 78, 80, 101, 192, 314, 339, 481, 499
Pollock, 1, 24, 249, 334, 340
Polock, 181
Polowaski, 245
Pomeroy, 438
Pominelsky, 460
Pomona, 400
Pond, 3, 396
Pontalis, 75
Pool, 37, 39, 56, 62, 267

Poole, 170, 366
Poor, 105
Pope, 158, 402
Pope's Creek, 183
Poplar Hill, 300
Porcher, 354
Port, 378, 409, 431
Porter, 26, 39, 43, 164, 171, 263, 300, 310, 327, 346, 351, 352, 365, 378, 409, 431, 465, 521
Portrait painting, 533
Posey, 171, 355, 372, 384
Post, 309
Post Ofcs, 3, 10, 19, 30, 41, 46, 52, 63, 73, 83, 94, 113, 129, 140, 149, 158, 175, 187, 196, 203, 211, 220, 228, 237, 244, 254, 267, 276, 283, 299, 312, 326, 338, 344, 356, 362, 369, 377, 396, 406, 417, 428, 438, 445, 454, 463, 472, 484, 508, 513, 519, 526, 539, 546
Postlethwaite, 74
Poston, 189, 304, 465
Potosi, 53, 320
Pott, 476
Potter, 63, 165, 171, 203, 239, 350, 386, 436
Potts, 64, 114, 279, 316, 415, 444
Pouder, 471
Powell, 30, 49, 99, 152, 163, 172, 182, 184, 218, 227, 246, 260, 280, 305, 313, 421, 427, 455, 504, 528, 535, 539
Powellin, 505
Power, 82, 319, 335
Powers, 79, 83, 90, 103, 151, 243, 382
Powhatan Hill, 354
Pragay, 372, 397
Prather, 348, 382
Pratt, 59, 308, 316, 444, 450, 455, 456, 506
Preble, 6, 76, 125, 230, 239
Prebram, 170
Prenell, 378

Prenit, 378
Prentiss, 13, 233
Prescott, 362
Presidential Mansion, 85
Pressey, 34
Preston, 6, 137, 409, 448
Preswick, 23
Prettyman, 131, 312
Prevost, 18, 90
Prewitt, 530
Pribram, 459
Price, 18, 27, 37, 39, 56, 148, 339, 416, 466, 529, 546
Priessnitz, 545
Prigmore, 196
Primus, 234
Prince, 403
Princess Sidonia, 23
Printz, 187
Prioleau, 39, 517
Prior, 525
Pritchard, 46, 158
privateer **Paul Jones**, 527
privateer **Teazer**, 527
Prizzini, 323
Proctor, 2, 505, 506, 511
Prospect Hill, 147, 342
Prother, 150
Prout, 509, 540
Provest, 16, 376
Pruitt, 407
Prutzman, 510
Prymus, 51
Pryor, 53, 445
Pryseinsky, 445
Puckett, 362
Pudorowsky, 172
Pugh, 174
Pulis, 344
Pulizzi, 382
Pullen, 219
Pulliam, 267
Pullin, 168
Pulsifer, 402

Pumphrey, 80, 98, 105, 168, 170, 171, 172, 239, 246, 385, 390, 397, 459, 460, 461
Pumphry, 448
Pumroy, 424
Punk Neck, 518
Purcell, 36, 103, 328, 535
Purdum, 484
Purdy, 22, 23, 103, 358, 372, 382, 387, 466, 485
Purgit, 406
Purnell, 18, 334, 408
Purrington, 62
Purse, 330
Pursell, 168
Putnam, 187
Pyne, 36, 146, 194, 197, 243, 487, 514, 542
Pywell, 99, 387, 460

Q

Quackenbush, 357
Quackenbuss, 490
Quackinbush, 211
Quail, 321
Quantirl, 256
Quarles, 487
Queen, 100, 105, 214, 269, 275, 332, 356, 382, 390, 391, 448
Queen Isabella, 227
Queen of Portugal, 11
Queen Victoria, 239
Quick, 385, 408
Quiggin, 191
Quigley, 105, 106, 384
Quigly, 448, 505, 546
Quincy, 359
Quinn, 40, 255, 332, 388, 461
Quintana, 341
Quintmen, 31
Quisenberry, 118, 125
Quitman, 1, 404

R

Rabathy, 394
Rabina, 378
Rabitaille, 141
Radcliff, 24, 79, 103, 170, 181, 218, 332, 417, 421, 475, 483, 493
Radcliffe, 34, 176
Radford, 330
Radiman, 539
Radnitz, 408
Radrich, 372
Rady, 65, 97, 109, 111, 120, 131
Ragan, 25, 34, 171, 214, 382, 399, 462, 506
Raidy, 382
Raiford, 121
Railroad Depot, 63
Railroad Jubilee, 402
Raily, 168
Rainer, 255
Rains, 127, 288
Ralston, 426, 470, 537
Ramos, 219
Ramsay, 318, 323
Ramsey, 326, 459
Rance, 410
Randall, 5, 32, 100, 105, 125, 149, 168, 298, 307, 313, 318, 456, 516, 532, 543
Randolph, 19, 22, 45, 86, 91, 177, 242, 302, 504, 505, 542
Random, 468
Randon, 43
Rankert, 44
Ranlett, 292
Ransom, 338, 500
Ranson, 36, 70
Rantoul, 462
Rapole, 17
Rappetti, 103, 168
Ratcliff, 34, 78, 428, 457, 548
Ratcliffe, 34, 67, 300, 365, 404, 420, 539
Raterree, 456

Rathburn, 94
Raub, 168
Raukert, 132
Ravenel, 39
Rawdon, 436
Rawleigh, 63
Rawlings, 4, 168, 387, 396, 497, 534
Ray, 43, 89, 91, 168, 194, 231, 255, 340, 505, 509
Rayland, 316
Raymond, 8, 46, 138, 505
Rayner, 424
Raynes, 308
Raynolds, 307
razee **Independence**, 413
Rea, 358, 489
Read, 6, 86, 281, 286, 350, 358, 363, 371, 389, 435, 466, 496, 534, 539
Reading, 374
Ready, 106, 168
Reagor, 255
Reardon, 40
Rearich, 19
Rector, 335
Red Hook, 420
Reddick, 250
Reddin, 388
Redding, 309
Redfern, 105, 168, 262, 382, 457
Redin, 65, 95, 121, 149, 443, 451, 455, 468, 473
Redpath, 276
Redstrake, 100, 105
Reed, 5, 16, 49, 66, 72, 91, 105, 113, 134, 157, 168, 179, 180, 181, 185, 254, 332, 346, 359, 369, 412, 444, 478, 509, 534
Reeder, 136
Reese, 34, 76, 282, 332, 403, 499
Reeside, 104, 214, 388, 476
Reeves, 52, 84, 105, 126, 128, 237, 351, 451
Regalan, 534
Regan, 281, 533

Reid, 4, 100, 319, 382, 385, 425, 513
Reigart, 416
Reille, 352
Reilly, 273, 372, 485, 528
Rekendorf, 372
Rembrandt, 436
Remer, 180
Remond, 192
Remsburg, 418
Renner, 517
Renzanterger, 418
Resurvey on Cor's Basket, 161
Reventhow, 452
Revis, 473
Revsurvey on Plantire, 161
Reyan, 112
Reynes, 71
Reyninger, 58
Reynolds, 30, 141, 192, 216, 300, 307, 312, 336, 357, 406, 466, 490, 501, 512
Rhea, 97, 112
Rhiselin, 135
Rhoades, 306, 344
Rhodes, 35, 38, 100, 168, 257, 382, 384, 387, 537
Ricard, 428
Ricardi, 123
Rice, 105, 158, 165, 172, 252, 319, 354, 382, 481, 504
Rich, 73, 150, 432, 487
Richards, 31, 43, 111, 114, 194, 197, 258, 298, 354, 382, 388, 450, 456, 459, 496, 497, 504, 505
Richardson, 4, 9, 15, 66, 100, 121, 127, 149, 168, 170, 175, 180, 237, 313, 378, 382, 395, 409, 425, 432, 442, 466, 489, 521, 524
Richey, 412
Richland, 258
Richmond, 11, 13
Richstein, 332
Rickerby, 478
Rickets, 75

Ricketts, 200
Rickey, 42
Rickman, 12
Riddick, 521
Riddle, 119, 414
Riddlemoser, 442
Ridemour, 63
Rider, 8, 73, 300, 387, 457
Ridge, 518
Ridgely, 87, 96, 103, 160, 204, 214, 289, 300, 315, 358
Riechard, 64
Rielly, 323
Rieves, 378, 409
Rigdon, 105
Riggles, 170, 282, 496
Riggs, 94, 123, 130, 132, 168, 181, 192, 195, 418, 424, 505, 509
Rightstine, 448
Rigsbey, 382
Rigsby, 230
Riker, 350
Riley, 45, 71, 100, 103, 106, 122, 127, 132, 168, 190, 199, 243, 248, 319, 358, 382, 387, 424, 481, 521, 522
Rilley, 538
Rine, 534
Ring, 169, 338
Ringgold, 87, 393
Ringland, 27
Ringold, 153
Riordan, 168
Ripley, 10, 301, 529
Rishley, 410
Rison, 228, 235, 340, 382
Ritchey, 103
Ritchie, 21, 387
Rittenhouse Academy, 354
Ritter, 103, 106, 122, 165, 448, 460, 499
Rives, 78, 204, 302, 326, 350, 377, 432
Roach, 4, 286, 379, 385, 389, 397, 469, 477
Road, 547
Roallons, 398
Roane, 9, 15, 376
Roback, 160
Robards, 68
Robb, 161, 382, 384, 538
Robbins, 77, 355, 398
Roberson, 10
Robert, 466
Roberts, 25, 27, 37, 41, 42, 52, 67, 80, 82, 105, 168, 201, 206, 297, 370, 434, 504, 508, 545
Robertson, 1, 13, 71, 277, 284, 376, 386, 431, 448
Robey, 382, 460
Robinett, 50
Robins, 41
Robinson, 8, 12, 14, 17, 24, 30, 39, 40, 49, 51, 98, 103, 156, 168, 170, 180, 182, 192, 212, 214, 220, 228, 279, 281, 307, 330, 355, 359, 374, 381, 409, 412, 430, 431, 442, 457, 460, 481, 509, 548
Robiou, 306
Robison, 36, 63, 213
Roby, 332, 335
Rochant, 105
Rochat, 168, 280
Roche, 30, 233, 285, 323, 412, 433
Rock Creek, 271
Rodburn, 257
Roddey, 111
Rodgers, 131, 272, 476, 492, 508
Roe, 320, 355
Roemmell, 105
Roemmelle, 398
Roers/Rogers, 181
Roger, 19
Rogers, 29, 41, 43, 97, 98, 118, 132, 146, 168, 174, 180, 181, 185, 207, 283, 285, 286, 396, 418, 439, 478, 493, 498, 531
Rolando, 200
Rollins, 106, 257, 444, 445

Roman, 374
Romero, 378
Romley, 391
Ronaldson, 92
Ronke, 359
Rooker, 91, 361, 433
Rooney, 495
Root, 59, 248, 267, 278, 289, 311, 502
Rosberry, 267
Rosbury, 8, 46
Rose, 338, 384
Rose Farm, 195
Rosenstock, 100
Rosenthal, 258
Rosevelt, 450
Rosewald, 460
Roslin, 451
Ross, 39, 43, 87, 99, 112, 116, 129, 142, 230, 235, 269, 284, 359, 361, 365, 384, 415, 425, 448, 501, 502
Rossberry, 29
Rosser, 531
Roszel, 131
Roszell, 56
Roth, 168
Rothrock, 438
Rothwell, 58, 115, 206, 285, 381, 393, 509
Rousseau, 372, 378, 407
Roussel, 173
Roux, 168, 328, 387
Rowan, 40, 275, 492
Rowe, 162
Rowell, 19
Rowland, 154, 222, 348, 431, 440, 465
Rowle, 171
Rowles, 216, 382
Rowzee, 210
Roxford, 450
Rozier, 332
Rozsa, 394
Rubira, 432
Ruckingham, 175

Rudd, 86
Ruddick, 535
Rude, 546
Rudolph, 9, 60, 181
Ruff, 168, 186, 256, 263, 311, 376, 504
Rugg, 100
Ruggles, 494
Ruledge, 418
Rully, 523
Rulman, 359
Rumford Academy, 342
Rumpf, 75, 172, 294
Rumsey, 256, 438
Runge, 457
Runkel, 267
Runkle, 306
Rupert, 461
Rupp, 107, 168
Ruppel, 106
Ruppert, 230
Rurira, 409
Rush, 338, 496
Rushing, 508
Rushton, 192
Rushworth, 155
Russell, 3, 20, 119, 137, 158, 181, 211, 263, 283, 314, 339, 367, 440, 457, 462, 540, 546
Russels, 220
Russworm, 435
Russwurn, 545
Rust, 156, 314, 396
Rustic, 76
Rutherford, 88
Rutledge, 199, 482, 487
Rutter, 168
Ruysdael, 436
Ryan, 242, 248, 259, 307, 388, 486
Ryant, 362
Ryckman, 307
Ryder, 5, 178, 223, 308, 505
Ryland, 131, 345
Ryle, 23

Rynd, 229
Ryon, 105, 231, 385
Ryther, 104, 169

S

Saddler, 103
Sadler, 10
Safford, 437
Sage, 22, 143, 424
Saile, 408
Salamon, 394
Sale of pictures, 436
Sales, 135, 345
Saleyman Bey, 420
Salkmeyer, 547
Sallarue, 227
Salles, 473
Sallus, 162
Salmon, 307, 359
Salter, 155
Saltsman, 175
Salvi, 221
Sample, 396
Sampson, 383
Samuels, 480
San Francisco, 254
Sanburn, 110
Sanders, 66, 168, 372
Sanderson, 103, 245, 441
Sandford, 41, 100, 168, 460, 510
Sandifer, 255
Sandoval, 238
Sands, 73, 76, 239, 300, 306, 452
Sandy, 224
Sandy Point, 293
Sanford, 383
Sanger, 403
Sanks, 359
Sansbury, 279
Santangelo, 132
Santer, 139
Sargent, 288, 463, 466
Sasscer, 384
Satchwell, 283

Satterlee, 406
Sauer, 19, 38, 159, 186
Saul, 332
Saulnier, 161
Saunders, 5, 8, 18, 24, 46, 54, 157, 215, 241, 287, 290, 311, 325, 345, 390, 402, 403, 504, 530, 543
Saur, 168, 186
Sauter, 124
Savage, 36, 49, 103, 300, 397, 406, 488, 497
Savory, 402
Sawson, 248
Sawyer, 180, 215, 220, 276, 390
Sawyers, 364
Saxony, 112
Saxton, 178
Saylor, 338
Scallorn, 484
Scarburgh, 464
Scarlet fever, 473
Scarlett, 143, 212
Schad, 103, 168, 386, 404
Schadd, 25, 103, 106
Schaefer, 69
Schatzell, 180
Scheel, 116
Scheide, 461
Scheifele, 393
Scheifner, 388
Schenck, 119, 177, 242, 308, 440, 447, 504, 544
Schermerhorn, 143
Scheuber, 237
Schlab, 168
Schlatmann, 320
Schlattman, 69
Schlegel, 103
Schlessinger, 407
Schley, 186
Schlezinger, 372
Schlicht, 373
Schmid, 77
Schmidt, 95, 103, 309, 407, 408

Schmielt, 394
Schneck, 408
Schneider, 206
schnr **Alert**, 109, 137
schnr **Ann**, 36, 427
schnr **Brazoria**, 123
schnr **Caroline**, 9, 137
schnr **Columbia**, 85, 173
schnr **Constitution**, 143
schnr **David Carter**, 177
schnr **Escambia**, 260
schnr **Escambria**, 152
schnr **Eufala**, 530
schnr **Ewing**, 309
schnr **Fairy**, 367
schnr **Fraternitie**, 143
schnr **Hannah Elizabeth**, 123, 137
schnr **Hylas**, 96
schnr **Isaac McKim**, 124
schnr **John B Lindsay**, 425
schnr **Juliet**, 161
schnr **Julius Caesar**, 9, 143
schnr **Lewellyn**, 190
schnr **Lodi**, 60, 137, 151
schnr **Louisiana**, 49, 53, 123, 156, 260
schnr **Martha**, 9
schnr **Martha Greene**, 398
schnr **Mary Ann**, 116
schnr **Merchantman**, 78
schnr **Montezuma**, 136
schnr **Mott Bedell**, 427
schnr **Nolson**, 132
schnr **Oregon**, 343
schnr **Pampero**, 427
schnr **Patrick Henry**, 218, 528
schnr **Patuxent**, 59, 67
schnr **Rebecca Eliza**, 49
schnr **S Marvin**, 248
schnr **Scott**, 72
schnr **St Croix**, 146
schnr **Susan**, 54, 72
schnr **Susannah**, 152
schnr **Sussanah**, 85

schnr **Townsend Jones**, 427
schnr **Vigilant**, 25, 43
schnr **Volant**, 427
schnr **Wanderer**, 58
schnr **Wm A Graham**, 47
schnr **Wm C Beale**, 374
Scholfield, 26
Scholle, 493
Schotel, 436
Schott, 75
Schouler, 402
Schroth, 220
Schuermann, 368
Schultz, 443
Schumaker, 529
Schureman, 384
Schutz, 408
Schuyler, 310
Schwartze, 99, 103, 106, 108, 168, 216, 385
Schwarz, 232
Schwearing, 106
Scifferle, 168
Scotoozsler, 327
Scott, 26, 42, 100, 128, 130, 134, 136, 140, 143, 147, 148, 150, 168, 174, 216, 233, 238, 276, 283, 305, 317, 346, 347, 365, 378, 383, 384, 385, 386, 403, 407, 425, 433, 447, 460, 495, 500, 502, 505, 514
Scovell, 64
Scowell, 256
Screven, 151, 289, 291
Scribner, 291
Scrivener, 76, 91, 170, 256, 311, 337
Scroggin, 424
Scroggins, 460
Scully, 408
Seabrook, 237, 354
Seagur, 151
Seaman, 165, 383
Sears, 102, 321, 356, 361
Seaton, 158, 395
Seaver, 25, 29, 375, 544

Seay, 378, 407
Sebastiani, 352
Sebring, 408
Secor, 273
Sedam, 129
Seeger, 223
Seelust, 378
Seely, 237, 517
Segrest, 184
Segur, 74
Seib, 75
Seibel, 284
Seibert, 388
Seifer, 431
Seigfried, 246
Selby, 355, 382
Selden, 17, 255, 260, 323, 324, 333, 363, 366, 471, 481, 496, 531
Seldiner, 100, 124
Seldner, 100
Seldon, 454
Seley, 418
Selfridge, 236
Seligman, 308
Sellman, 301, 353
Selthausen, 103
Seltzer, 283
Semmes, 105, 106, 122, 132, 167, 168, 224, 324, 385, 455, 504, 509, 536
Semoice, 36, 39, 51
Senepli, 378
Sengstack, 100, 105, 137, 168, 319
Senical, 362
Senseney, 464
Sensheimer, 100
Serapuru, 524
Serene, 445
Sergeant, 26, 174
Serrin, 346, 448, 475
Server, 359
Sessford, 168, 317
Sessions, 187
Settle, 4

Seufferle, 47
Seven Gables, 185
Sevier, 442
Sewall, 21, 31, 40, 111, 125, 175, 382, 511, 521
Sewell, 168, 504
Sewer, 359
Seymour, 306, 361
Shackelford, 218
Shackleford, 410
Shadd, 108, 226, 384, 389
Shadrack, 71
Shaeff, 290
Shaeffer, 171
Shafer, 103, 526
Shaff, 278
Shaffner, 68
Shalcross, 55
Shall, 299, 313
Shamrock Hill, 250
Shaner, 454
Shanks, 91
Shannon, 134, 223, 276
Shannondale Springs, 395
Sharff, 290
Sharkey, 469
Sharman, 312
Sharp, 141, 440
Sharpe, 43, 180
Sharpless, 70, 368
Sharps, 134
Shaw, 7, 94, 143, 215, 228, 244, 307, 345, 366, 472, 546
Shea, 277, 383
Sheahan, 91, 204, 214, 250, 312, 496
Sheckell, 153
Sheckells, 105
Shed, 168
Shedd, 387
Sheets, 99
Sheffield, 175
Sheid, 100
Sheil, 260
Shelby, 233, 506

614

Sheldon, 228, 445, 454, 537
Shellady, 196
Shelley, 41
Shelton, 10, 94, 228, 270, 342, 356, 504
Shepherd, 3, 272, 299, 313, 371, 383, 384, 411
Shepherd's Hill, 355
Sheppard, 216
Sherburne, 254, 270
Sheriff, 165, 459, 461
Sherman, 7, 53, 76, 128, 162, 270, 279, 428
Sherrard, 424
Sherrill, 442
Sherry, 170, 283
Sherwell, 221
Sherwood, 170, 179, 180, 308, 348, 452, 482, 494
Sheweetzer, 170
Shield, 339
Shields, 30, 74, 118, 168, 178, 485
Shiles, 126, 461, 462
Shillington, 82, 103, 336, 449
Shindler, 307
Shinn, 67, 303
ship **A Cheesborough**, 434
ship **Adams**, 37
ship **Adventure**, 511
ship **Albany**, 192, 433
ship **Augusta**, 453
ship **Boxer**, 272
ship **Buckinghamshire**, 480
ship **Challenge**, 248
ship **Chandler Price**, 5, 8
ship **Columbia**, 5, 8, 297
ship **Commodore Preble**, 261
ship **Corsair**, 433
ship **Cumberland**, 545
ship **Cyane**, 440
ship **Devonshire**, 333
ship **Empire City**, 239, 451
ship **Enterprise**, 272
ship **Francis P Sage**, 483

ship **Franconia**, 55
ship **Franklin**, 410
ship **Germantown**, 272, 435
ship **Gov Arnold**, 468
ship **Hindostan**, 398
ship **Isabella H**, 439
ship **Ivanhoe**, 155
ship **James**, 29
ship **James Mitchell**, 527
ship **John Adams**, 435
ship **Joseph Walker**, 155
ship **Marion**, 11, 65, 75
ship **Mayflower**, 234
ship **Minerva**, 208
ship of war **Esperanza**, 380
ship **Oregon**, 470
ship **Pennsylvania**, 46, 325
ship **Portsmouth**, 174, 272
ship **Primera de Gautemala**, 407
ship **Reindeer**, 463
ship **Serapis**, 304
ship **Shannon**, 96
ship **Silas Leonard**, 11
ship **St Lawrence**, 76, 306
ship **St Louis**, 249
ship **Sterling**, 9
ship **Susquehanna**, 489
ship **Transit**, 137, 151
ship **Venus**, 407
ship **William**, 374
ship **William A Cooper**, 434
Shipley, 383
ships **Advance & Rescue**, 483
Shiras, 335
Shly, 531
Shoemake, 314
Shoemaker, 32, 62, 89, 97, 159, 232, 339, 475, 509
Shograsby, 155
Sholly, 122
Shook, 242
Shorey, 354
Short, 331
Shover, 31

Shrader, 63
Shreeve, 243
Shreeves, 154, 188
Shreve, 87, 105, 124, 168, 170
Shreves, 183
Shrieve, 170
Shriver, 81
Shroeder, 499
Shubrick, 142, 470
Shucking, 315, 372
Shuler, 406
Shull, 546
Shultz, 168, 308
Shumate, 429
Shurlock, 313
Shurte, 546
Shuster, 103, 160, 417
Shuts, 168
Shyne, 92
Sibley, 103, 178, 371, 383, 387, 426
Sicard, 237
Sickner, 331
Siddons, 277
Siebel, 265
Sigur, 31, 413
Silesia, 112
Sill, 403
Silliman, 344, 395
Sills, 185
Silney, 410
Simermacher, 462
Simison, 74
Simmermecker, 534
Simmes, 410
Simmons, 45, 121, 136, 185, 290, 331, 383, 440, 460, 461
Simms, 61, 106, 165, 168, 174, 214, 255, 269, 272, 304, 337, 361, 382, 383, 384, 386, 387, 439, 448, 456, 460, 511
Simon, 100
Simonds, 269, 277, 284, 298, 318, 529
Simons, 37, 368, 417
Simonson, 51, 263

Simonton, 180
Simpson, 27, 168, 258, 303, 353, 365, 372, 378, 391, 407, 418, 533, 546
Simpton, 307
Sims, 258, 384, 416, 510
Sinclair, 194, 246, 268, 336, 348, 462, 513
Singleton, 99, 122, 504
Sinon, 383
Sinsheimer, 114, 155
Sioussa, 168, 206, 300
Sipess, 394
Sirbert, 75
Sis, 170
Sisson, 294, 431, 465
Sister M de Sales, 292
Sisters of Charity, 368
Siter, 294
Skeen, 277
Skidmore, 330
Skilling, 421
Skinner, 18, 134, 207
Skirving, 103, 387, 448
Sky, 352
Slack, 179, 242, 410
Slacum, 79, 430, 533, 537
Slade, 443
Slamm, 297
Slate, 490
Slater, 301, 444, 460, 534
Slatterly, 92
Slattery, 15, 67, 140, 319, 478, 494
Slavin, 5
Slayter, 30
Slayton, 344
Slemmer, 126
Sleyden, 478
Slezinger, 408
Slicer, 346
Slight, 168
Slingerland, 233
Sloan, 96, 237, 308
Slocum, 34, 221
sloop **Meridian**, 202

sloop of war **Albany**, 395
sloop of war **Portsmouth**, 520
sloop of war **Preble**, 321
sloop of war **Vincennes**, 316
sloop **Rebecca Ford**, 325
sloop **Venture**, 531
sloop **Wm J J Murray**, 374
sloop-of-war **Germantown**, 174, 458, 468
sloop-of-war **John Adams**, 194
sloop-of-war **Plymouth**, 366
sloop-of-war **Portsmouth**, 490, 492
sloop-of-war **Vandalia**, 444
sloop-of-war **Warren**, 205
sloop-of-war **Yorktown**, 46, 70
Slouth, 466
Small, 25, 73, 155, 276
Smalls, 300
Smallwood, 99, 168, 172, 383, 460
Smart, 129
Smead, 317
Smeaton, 315
Smith, 5, 9, 15, 19, 31, 34, 36, 37, 38, 39, 40, 42, 43, 51, 55, 70, 75, 76, 77, 80, 95, 98, 99, 106, 115, 117, 123, 129, 130, 131, 138, 139, 140, 142, 144, 149, 150, 155, 156, 160, 162, 163, 168, 179, 180, 182, 183, 189, 192, 194, 198, 200, 203, 206, 208, 209, 211, 216, 217, 219, 223, 228, 230, 231, 234, 236, 238, 240, 241, 243, 245, 247, 248, 251, 253, 254, 257, 258, 261, 262, 263, 265, 268, 269, 274, 277, 278, 279, 281, 282, 286, 288, 289, 290, 296, 309, 313, 314, 319, 320, 322, 323, 325, 335, 337, 339, 342, 345, 348, 352, 359, 363, 366, 370, 371, 376, 377, 378, 384, 395, 404, 406, 408, 416, 418, 419, 430, 432, 438, 439, 441, 444, 447, 448, 449, 451, 456, 457, 459, 460, 461, 465, 466, 467, 469, 472, 473, 477, 478, 481, 484, 487, 488, 490, 492, 493, 496, 498, 500,
503, 504, 507, 508, 509, 512, 515, 519, 522, 523, 524, 526, 530, 532, 533, 539, 543, 545, 546
Smithia, 399
Smithson, 99
Smoot, 21, 28, 70, 112, 168, 323, 332, 348, 351, 383, 400, 453, 459, 460, 539
Smyers, 509
Smyth, 105
Smythe, 137
Smythie, 120
Snape, 164
Sneary, 331
Snedlak, 393
Snell, 30
Snelling, 283
Snethen, 453
Sniffin, 54, 206
Snively, 230
Snook, 196
Snow, 1, 46, 309
Snowden, 419, 504
Snuffin, 74
Snyder, 40, 132, 171, 229, 355, 384
Society of Friends, 376
Solan, 90
Solomon, 531
Solona, 162
Somers, 409
Somerville, 382, 521, 533
Sommers, 448, 504
Sommerville, 347
Sopher, 41
Sorel, 428
Sorin, 20
Sothorn, 106
Sothoron, 91
Sothroron, 358
Soule, 143, 175, 309
Soult, 352
Southall, 271
Southam, 307
Southard, 40, 158

Southerland, 52
Southmayd, 9, 181, 517
Southorn, 386
Southworth, 406
Sowers, 432
Spacask, 445
Spalding, 159, 206, 292, 308, 323, 465, 512, 529
Spang, 417
Sparkman, 62, 362
Sparks, 5, 8, 46
Spaulding, 47, 429
Speake, 168
Speaks, 172, 539
Spear, 470
Speer, 368
Speiden, 37, 168
Speir, 210
Spencer, 59, 65, 129, 148, 190, 231, 266, 326, 348, 446, 476
Spicer, 40, 107, 168, 387
Spignall, 168, 170
Spignul, 438
Spinstead, 490
Spore, 30
Sporn, 394
Sprague, 211
Sprig, 214
Sprigg, 7, 14, 18, 200, 248
Spring, 307, 479
Spring Tavern, 86
Springer, 192, 211, 323
Springman, 168
Sproat, 536
Sproston, 76
Sprout, 73
Spurling, 384
St Angelo, 49
St Clair, 27, 30, 44, 86, 107, 120, 193, 233, 466, 505, 520
St John, 123
St Martin, 458
St Matthew's Church, 54
St Patrick's Burial-Ground, 392

St Vrain, 86
St Vraine, 188
Stabler, 308, 504
Staffan, 413
Staffer, 510
Staffin, 460
Stafford, 276, 358, 452
Staggers, 10
Stalford, 333
Stamford, 359
Stamps, 519
Standford, 495
Standish, 321
Stanford, 260, 359, 365, 372, 380, 394, 461
Stanhope, 18, 145
Stanislaus, 245, 430
Stanley, 82, 209, 298
Stanly, 247
Stanmyre, 408
Stansbury, 14, 69, 76, 239, 245
Stanton, 142, 354, 359
Staples, 454
Starbuck, 447, 461
Stark, 19, 179
Starke, 261
Starkweather, 418
Starns, 546
Starr, 10, 114, 500
Starrit, 540
Staufer, 344
steamboat **John Adams**, 46
steamboat **Joseph Johnson**, 291, 477
steamboat **Penobscot**, 328, 375
steamboat **Phenix**, 67, 477
steamboat **Rough & Ready**, 347
steamboat **Yanke**, 174
steamer **Alleghany**, 92
steamer **Archer**, 509
steamer **Asia**, 498
steamer **Atlantic**, 46
steamer **Baltimore**, 513
steamer **Bolivia**, 164
steamer **Boston**, 331

steamer **Brilliant**, 429
steamer **California**, 204
steamer **Champion**, 138
steamer **Columbia**, 292
steamer **Comet**, 191
steamer **Commodore Stockton**, 222
steamer **Dacotah**, 352
steamer **Dakotah**, 355
steamer **Die Vernon**, 509
steamer **Duroc**, 334
steamer **Fremont**, 265
steamer **Fulton**, 272
steamer **Governor**, 331
steamer **Habanero**, 359, 380
steamer **Haberno**, 419
steamer **Isael la Catollca**, 407
steamer **James Jackson**, 410
steamer **Jefferson**, 357
steamer **John Adams**, 55
steamer **Michigan**, 232
steamer **Mississippi**, 445
steamer **Missouri**, 302
steamer **Ohio**, 222
steamer **Pacific**, 395
steamer **Pampero**, 413
steamer **Princeton**, 516, 521
steamer **Roselia of Washington**, 154
steamer **Saranac**, 40
steamer **Sea Gull**, 261
steamer **Spitfire**, 125
steamer **Star**, 325
steamer **Susquehanna**, 134, 242, 504
steamer **Union**, 148
steamship **Arctic**, 159
steamship **Fanny**, 464
steamship **Georgia**, 164
steamship **McLane**, 1
steamship **North America**, 109
steamship **Ohio**, 440
Stearns, 41, 196
Stebbins, 187, 306
Steed, 19, 504
Steedman, 92
Steele, 30, 124, 137, 177, 500, 539

Steen, 363
Steenroad, 27
Steer, 103, 504
Steffan, 100
Stegall, 64
Steiger, 168
Steil, 292
Stelle, 514
Stem, 340
Stember, 73
Stephens, 94, 196, 354, 396, 399, 432, 434, 490
Stephenson, 383, 385, 387
Stepper, 168
Steptoe, 477
Sterling, 84, 472
Sterrett, 508
Stetinius, 192
Stetler, 297
Stetson, 250, 423, 514
Stettinius, 168, 172, 207, 414, 505, 528
Steuart, 81
Steuben, 542
Stevens, 41, 56, 91, 100, 103, 170, 181, 237, 264, 301, 308, 341, 351, 372, 419
Stevenson, 19, 40, 180, 307, 452, 501
Steward, 356, 541
Stewart, 12, 41, 42, 63, 103, 106, 108, 130, 168, 170, 192, 204, 206, 210, 235, 242, 257, 257, 326, 332, 338, 344, 360, 370, 372, 382, 383, 384, 387, 390, 410, 424, 433, 440, 444, 448, 449, 452, 459, 471, 473, 480, 539, 542
Stillman, 15, 180
Stilwell, 173
Stinger, 192, 332
Stingley, 473
Stipes, 132
Stith, 122
Stivers, 362
Stock, 168

Stockett, 353
Stocking, 76
Stockton, 40, 203, 238, 241, 242, 414, 458, 515, 521
Stoddard, 32, 97, 132, 138, 168
Stoddart, 34, 256
Stolp, 20
Stone, 7, 25, 37, 73, 89, 92, 103, 168, 203, 218, 261, 311, 334, 354, 383, 384, 422, 424, 453
Stoner, 331
Stonestreet, 168, 368
Stony Arbor Farm, 240
Stony Harbor, 352
Stoops, 91, 105, 300, 323
Stoppard, 472
Storer, 164, 360, 366, 466, 516, 521
storeship **Charlotte**, 374
storeship **Fredonia**, 13
storeship **Lexington**, 275, 330
storeship **Southampton**, 433
Storm, 105
Story, 398, 444
Stott, 103, 199, 240, 253, 303, 383
Stout, 203, 220, 330, 341, 479
Stover, 10, 241
Stow, 41
Stowe, 340, 453
Straber, 32
Strain, 194
Strang, 232, 295
Strangan, 477
Strange, 48, 169, 445
Strasbinger, 100
Stratham Church, 534
Stratton, 326
Straub, 387
Straudberg, 138
Strawhun, 318
Streeter, 28
Stregle, 188
Strickland, 183
Strider, 271
Striker, 203

Stringfellow, 411
Strong, 53, 87, 283, 338, 450
Strother, 180, 258, 411, 455
Stroud, 25
Strung, 499
Stuart, 47, 73, 162, 205, 300, 330, 443, 500, 502, 504, 542
Stubbs, 212, 344, 359, 362
Stukey, 201
Stull, 84, 309
Stump, 471
Stutz, 105, 107
Stutze, 168
Stuyvesant, 494
Suarez, 56
Suary, 529
Sucit, 378
Suddards, 330
Suddreth, 74
Sudulph, 64
Suit, 384
Sujliorit, 378
Sullivan, 55, 57, 108, 171, 199, 314, 320, 339, 383, 385, 386, 388, 416, 460, 461, 510, 517, 534
Sulyok, 394
Summer Hill, 66
Summer Hill Farm, 498
Summers, 317, 504
Summy, 283
Sumner, 36, 43, 64, 197, 202, 498
Sunderlin, 73
Sutherland, 10
Sutliff, 8
Suto, 394
Sutten, 439
Sutton, 127, 128, 141, 242, 308, 478, 497
Suydam, 143, 144
Suzeneau, 180
Swabia, 112
Swaggert, 170
Swain, 220, 539

Swann, 135, 215, 319, 453, 494, 495, 535
Swartz, 275
Swartzeman, 422
Swazey, 178
Swearingen, 158, 344
Sweater, 168
Sweats, 404
Sweeney, 237
Sweeny, 97, 168, 216, 288, 300, 485, 540, 544, 547
Sweet, 73, 150
Sweeting, 107
Sweetland, 226
Sweitzer, 148
Swift, 52, 149, 264, 445
Swigert, 387
Swingle, 519
Swords, 432
Sxucs, 394
Sykes, 211
Symington, 318
Symonton, 527
Sypes, 334, 340
Szabo, 393, 394
Szatmaty, 393
Szekely, 394
Szoboszlay, 394
Sztacho, 394

T

Tabb, 46, 518
Taber, 308
Tableman, 366, 448
Tabler, 169, 266, 284
Taft, 52, 83
Taggart, 73, 384, 450
Tailor, 407
Tainter, 283
Takacs, 393
Talbert, 106, 383, 384, 461, 505
Talbot, 4, 169, 256, 409, 431, 460, 534

Talcott, 76, 248, 256, 295, 317, 318, 520, 531
Talley, 47
Tallmadge, 330, 414
Talty, 107, 174, 196, 239
Taney, 301
Taneyhill, 230
Tanner, 169, 429
Tansell, 106
Tansill, 98, 192, 424
Tappan, 110, 536
Tarbel, 198
Tarlton, 169
Tarrant, 33
Tarring, 354
Tassel, 426
Tassey, 186
Tastett, 169
Tate, 25, 46, 82, 106, 321
Tatham, 246
Tatnall, 40
Tator, 428
Tatum, 429
Taue, 430
Tayloe, 255
Taylor, 18, 22, 45, 53, 64, 77, 87, 92, 94, 96, 97, 106, 122, 140, 141, 154, 169, 183, 185, 195, 201, 209, 218, 222, 228, 244, 263, 269, 270, 272, 279, 287, 292, 297, 299, 301, 306, 310, 311, 321, 332, 336, 342, 345, 354, 356, 362, 378, 384, 387, 390, 395, 409, 418, 425, 427, 429, 430, 444, 445, 455, 460, 461, 462, 469, 483, 487, 503, 509, 517, 521, 528, 529, 541, 542
Tayor, 374
Teachemacher, 176
Teackard, 490
Teagle, 20
Teall, 515
Tebes, 394
Teed, 362
Tegyveressy, 394

Tekete, 394
Telfair, 262
Temple, 430
Templeton, 340, 406
Temps, 478
Ten Broeck, 110, 393
Ten Eyck, 5, 8
Tenan, 209
Tench, 106, 199, 256, 379, 384
Teniers, 436
Tennant, 75
Tenney, 169, 200, 387
Tenny, 426
Terrett, 357, 419, 433, 513
Terry, 20, 151, 182, 241, 429
Teschemacher, 308
Teschmaker, 307
Teusdale, 383
Thackara, 7
Tharp, 340
Thayer, 24, 79, 181, 264, 306, 323
The Hive, 133
Thecker, 47, 100, 109, 460
Thibedeaux, 484
Thing, 129
Thoma, 106
Thomas, 11, 18, 25, 36, 39, 43, 44, 68, 80, 94, 106, 107, 111, 112, 119, 140, 169, 176, 190, 194, 212, 246, 255, 269, 298, 300, 308, 319, 335, 344, 354, 364, 383, 384, 386, 387, 388, 410, 429, 456, 461, 462, 471, 491, 515, 525, 546
Thomason, 378, 407
Thomasson, 129
Thompson, 9, 37, 43, 49, 53, 55, 68, 74, 83, 86, 100, 106, 108, 133, 135, 138, 141, 169, 170, 174, 181, 192, 197, 205, 218, 234, 236, 237, 258, 275, 277, 278, 279, 289, 299, 307, 308, 329, 332, 334, 343, 345, 355, 357, 364, 379, 384, 387, 397, 402, 418, 426, 430, 455, 462, 466, 470, 472, 475, 479, 515, 526, 539, 540

Thoms, 387
Thomson, 272
Thorn, 100, 106, 438, 460
Thornley, 79, 91, 106
Thornton, 318, 422, 438
Thorp, 334
Thorpe, 505
Thrall, 3
Thrasher, 515, 531
Three Cent Coin, 209
three cent pieces, 152
Threlkeld, 467
Throckmorton, 320
Throop, 234
Thruston, 68, 163, 178
Thumb, 12
Thurman, 131
Thurston, 204
Thyson, 104, 165, 381
Tibball, 169
Tibbets, 473
Tiber, 252, 402
Tiber creek, 410
Tiber Creek, 315
Tiber Mill, 109
Tice, 73
Ticknor, 83, 185, 261
Tidball, 350
Tiffany, 247
Tiffe, 76
Tilden, 115, 275, 449
Tilford, 278, 289
Tilghman, 169, 265, 323
Tilip, 394
Tilley, 300, 532
Tillinghast, 126, 164, 270, 287, 308, 432
Tillinghurst, 523
Tillotson, 420
Tillou, 247
Tilman, 384, 460
Tilson, 302, 541
Tilton, 87
Timberlake, 271

Tingle, 184
Tingley, 289
Tinkle, 47
Tinkler, 44
Tippet, 463
Tipton, 466
Tirralla, 474
Titcomb, 202, 302
Tittle, 314
Titus, 340
Tobe, 467
Tobias, 361
Toby, 173
Tochman, 240, 253, 347, 393
Todd, 3, 5, 8, 29, 34, 65, 76, 100, 120, 129, 156, 274, 283, 285, 296, 353, 504, 539
Todschinder, 106
Todschnider, 169, 384
Togno, 54, 158, 182
Tokes, 394
Tolson, 171, 278, 332
Tomb, 519
Tomes, 28, 482, 487
Tomics, 394
Tomlin, 88
Tompkins, 52, 73, 169, 500
Tonge, 96
Tonkaways, 159
Tonnell, 473
Toombs, 399, 434
Toomey, 510
Toon, 174, 272
Toothaker, 222
Topa, 418
Topham, 107, 476
Toping, 169
Topliff, 396, 406
Topping, 512, 520
Toreyson, 157
Torres, 456
Toth, 394
Totten, 63, 248, 317, 430
Touquignet, 359

Tournique, 372
Tourniquet, 359
Towers, 300
Towland, 465
Towles, 439
Towndraw, 276
Townley, 244
Townsend, 55, 57, 232, 345, 370
Tracey, 480
Tracy, 225
Trail, 90
Train, 403, 433
Trammell, 74
Traphagen, 490
Travals, 36
Travers, 106, 153, 169, 218, 241, 268, 308, 383, 451, 485
Traverse, 106
Traxlar, 176
Treadwell, 308, 313
Treat, 79, 181, 273, 361
Tree, 500
Treese, 283
Trenholm, 190
Trent, 377
Trest, 24
Tretler, 249, 448
Trimble, 106, 298
Trinity [Catholic] Church, 247
Trinity Church, 109
Triplett, 170
Troombley, 507
Trott, 169
Trousdale, 92
True, 477
Trueman, 466
Trumball, 47
Trumbull, 73
Trundle, 424
Trunnell, 114
Truss, 176
Tubbs, 288, 290, 308
Tuck, 85, 471

Tucker, 47, 58, 61, 68, 74, 82, 91, 98, 100, 106, 169, 170, 216, 256, 287, 290, 317, 374, 383, 384, 402, 422, 464, 485, 504, 519, 539
Tully, 546
Tump, 374
Tump Farm, 374
Tunion, 165, 169
Turk, 235, 307
Turley, 177, 241, 248
Turnage, 9, 15
Turnbull, 209, 379, 447, 498
Turner, 20, 41, 99, 119, 131, 138, 196, 231, 311, 314, 323, 332, 339, 433, 460, 466, 487, 503, 517
Turney, 387
Turon, 98
Turpin, 169, 205, 221
Turrell, 268
Turrentine, 125, 463
Turtin, 25
Turtohn, 169
Turton, 321
Tusa, 394
Tuthill, 56, 140, 505
Tuxton, 383
Tweedy, 144
Twiggs, 248, 266, 295, 446, 475, 523
Twim, 460
Tylden, 302
Tyler, 25, 50, 332, 383, 424, 501
Tyng, 67, 70, 306
Tyrell, 389
Tyrill, 387
Tysdell, 73
Tyson, 48, 106

U

Udall, 182
Ujhazi, 10
Ulerich, 250
Ulrick, 57, 181, 320
Ultdorfar, 384
Umberfield, 541

Underhill, 9, 18, 20, 181, 248
Underood, 482
Underwood, 76, 91, 392, 439, 440, 453, 482, 487, 498, 501, 517
Uniacke, 338
Union Row, 50, 57
Unisck, 165, 383
University of Georgia, 375
Upper Quarter, 293
Upper Teddington, 293
Upperman, 106, 171, 172, 420
Upshaw, 342
Upshur, 46
Upton, 458
Urquhart, 424
Usher, 107, 384
Uzzell, 150

V

Vail, 84, 308, 473, 537
Valazco, 408
Valdejo, 188
Valentine, 99
Valeton, 314
Vallejo, 314, 531
Van Alen, 239
Van Benschoten, 339
Van Bibber, 504
Van Bockkelin, 309
Van Buren, 124, 355
Van der Hagen, 436
Van der Velde, 436
Van der Welde, 436
Van Derveer, 124
Van Dusen, 490
Van Etten, 508
Van Havre, 504
Van Hise, 41
Van Ness, 52, 180
Van Patten, 78, 216, 285
Van Rensselaer, 26
Van Rensselaers, 310
Van Reswick, 25, 103, 169, 214, 240, 431, 460

Van Riswick, 383, 509
Van Stavoren, 15, 67, 72, 151, 180, 181
Van Swearingen, 466
Van Sykle, 352
Van Tilbauth, 309
Van Vechten, 372, 378, 395, 409
Van Vlet, 434
Van Windle, 182
Van Winkle, 355
Van Zandt, 24, 440
VanBenchoten, 313
Vance, 38
Vanderbilt, 26
Vanderlyn, 73
Vanderwerken, 104, 388
Vandevort, 546
Vandiver, 276
Vanesson, 239
Vangale, 378
Vanhooser, 31
Vanhorsigh, 4, 186
Vanmeter, 370
Vann, 235
Vansant, 489
Vantine, 80
Vanvallenburg, 190
VanWick, 279
Varden, 291
Vargies, 394
Varnel, 362
Varner, 362
Varnes, 515
Vaskovich, 394
Vaughan, 539
Vaughn, 396, 407
Vault, 486
Vaunum's Row, 190
Veacy, 359
Vegh, 394
Vehlein, 36, 43, 53
Velker, 394
Venable, 41, 64, 73, 82, 170, 386

Vermillion, 16, 133, 185, 246, 256, 385
Vernon, 384
vessel **Ann**, 66
vessel **Atlantic**, 118
vessel **Lady of the Lake**, 183
vessel **Loriot**, 236
vessel of war **General Bravo**, 123
Vest, 113
Viaduct, 478
Victoria, 173
Vidal, 169
Viedt, 384
Vienne, 373
Vigne, 314
Vigo, 69
Villard, 198, 202
Vincent, 145
Vining, 505
Vinne, 359
Vinson, 243, 442
Vinton, 151
Viosg, 408
Vise, 345
Visser, 103, 169, 387
Vivans, 457
Von Essen, 99
Von Lengerk, 308
von Lengerke, 295
Von Schlicht, 408
Von Tassel, 490
Von Weissenfels, 32
Vonderlehr, 399
Vonderlick, 169, 387
Voorhees, 444, 455
Vosbrugh, 202
Vose, 89
Voss, 103, 270
Vowell, 504
Vroman, 53
Vrooman, 29

W

Waddell, 326, 475, 498

Waddy, 313
Wade, 152, 159, 169, 192
Wadsworth, 10, 17, 46, 75, 155, 156, 160, 169, 215, 231, 279, 307, 389, 390, 410
Wagaman, 169
Waganer, 387
Wagler, 385, 453, 468
Wagner, 169, 170, 445, 453, 539
Waif, 378
Waigly, 445
Wailes, 3, 72, 117, 445
Wainwright, 25, 75, 318, 353
Wait, 89
Waite, 423
Waite, 169
Wakefield, 327
Wakeman, 152, 307, 308, 316
Walbach, 248, 513
Walback, 463
Walbridge, 171, 387
Walden, 472, 490
Waldo, 71, 87
Waldron, 490
Wales, 129
Walker, 4, 75, 78, 81, 89, 91, 103, 108, 169, 170, 187, 192, 212, 225, 226, 230, 268, 282, 283, 287, 308, 319, 323, 324, 367, 371, 373, 383, 385, 387, 389, 405, 410, 432, 463, 482, 493, 500, 509, 520, 527, 530, 538, 539, 545
Wall, 81, 100, 103, 201, 371, 387, 489, 534
Wallace, 55, 83, 95, 147, 169, 170, 171, 178, 237, 244, 281, 322, 327, 332, 418, 488, 519, 533
Wallace, Saml, 387
Wallach, 12, 17, 34, 48, 124, 138, 158, 193, 214, 279, 285, 372, 385, 444, 471, 485, 506, 507, 516, 523
Waller, 172, 292, 361, 508, 527
Walley, 28, 151, 497
Wallingsford, 118, 170, 300

Wallis, 169, 459
Walls, 220
Wally, 28, 158, 182
Walsh, 40, 95, 103, 119, 134, 177, 280, 343, 452, 474
Walte, 504
Walter, 205, 262
Walters, 232, 315, 364, 505
Walton, 94, 129, 228, 242, 429
Waltz, 130
Wampler, 75
Wannall, 89, 106, 240
Waple, 460
Ward, 2, 10, 21, 69, 103, 107, 119, 127, 135, 136, 146, 149, 174, 182, 193, 200, 212, 238, 240, 253, 272, 276, 307, 348, 364, 374, 383, 385, 426, 447, 448, 456, 459, 466, 475
Ward, 383
Wardell, 256, 311, 337, 350
Warden, 353
Warder, 103, 383, 432
Wardwell, 308
Ware, 238, 452
Warfield, 157, 328
Warford, 267
Waring, 11, 61, 277, 324, 429
Warley, 354
Warner, 75, 82, 161, 169, 332, 344, 383, 385, 410, 414, 528
Warren, 8, 17, 59, 83, 104, 207, 212, 322, 402, 411, 466, 527
Warriner, 103, 140, 511
Warring, 42
Warrington, 37, 169, 193, 207, 385, 435, 436, 447, 470, 520
Warson, 355
Warthen, 264
Warwick, 10, 215
<u>Wash Nat'l Monument</u>, 422
Washburn, 94, 189, 315
Washington, 31, 61, 73, 80, 89, 121, 183, 188, 205, 233, 252, 254, 300, 317, 328, 332, 353, 383, 385, 389,

395, 420, 452, 485, 504, 513, 531, 542
Washington Monument, 111, 353, 371
Washington Nat'l Monument, 294
Washington Seminary, 358
Wasson, 269
Watchman, 291
Waterman, 411, 537
Waters, 2, 23, 41, 103, 106, 143, 171, 172, 229, 239, 256, 332, 376, 383, 417, 504
Watkins, 17, 192, 324, 354, 494, 496, 498
Watrous, 121
Watson, 35, 61, 151, 169, 182, 192, 271, 302, 307, 308, 323, 419, 460, 472, 517, 545
Watsson, 271
Wattenbe, 267
Watterson, 169
Watterston, 34, 285, 354, 492
Watts, 9, 115, 281, 385, 504
Waugh, 147
Way, 312, 370
Wayland, 443
Wayman, 505
Wayne, 9, 24, 44, 126, 233
Weaver, 200, 221, 313, 315, 361, 385, 412, 424, 438, 504
Webb, 66, 97, 169, 170, 231, 256, 304, 365, 529, 539
Webber, 188, 402
Weber, 169
Webster, 79, 93, 110, 116, 149, 169, 180, 211, 228, 307, 380, 383, 419, 497, 534
Weed, 170, 224, 263, 421, 517
Weeden, 169, 389
Weeks, 29, 301, 313, 404, 512
Weichmann, 100
Weiden, 171
Weidig, 142
Weightman, 86, 121, 162, 269, 312, 366, 542

Wein, 440
Weir, 494
Weiss, 408
Welch, 69, 75, 258, 389
Welcher, 278, 525
Welcker, 289
Weld, 52
Wellford, 207
Wellman, 222
Wells, 40, 69, 99, 307, 400, 416, 418, 450
Welply, 385
Welsh, 99, 165, 172, 323, 383, 386, 459, 465, 480, 508
Wendell, 149, 369
Wendt, 116
Werd, 30
Werden, 444
Werner, 169, 235, 360, 369
Wert, 107
West, 6, 119, 149, 169, 192, 308, 336, 360, 383, 385, 408, 441, 534
Westbrook, 544
Westcott, 76, 491
Westerfield, 103, 160, 169, 175, 189, 214, 219, 270, 385
Western Military Institute, 456
Western Travellers, 525
Westley, 429
Weston, 538
Wethered, 123, 132, 162, 181
Wetherell, 123
Wethers, 163
Wetmore, 123, 144
Wetsell, 338
Wever, 169
Weymouth, 409, 431
Weyrick, 387
Whaley, 40, 162, 170
Wharton, 65, 120
Wheat, 31, 51, 159, 258, 303
Wheatley, 106, 385
Wheaton, 375, 435
Wheelan, 413

Wheeler, 2, 8, 103, 125, 150, 169, 240, 245, 255, 297, 309, 338, 377, 419, 546
Wheelock, 403
Wheelwright, 307
Wherry, 546
Whetmore, 59, 328
Whipple, 45, 188, 278, 287, 290, 501, 540
Whistler, 151, 466
Whiston, 403
Whitaker, 244, 370
Whitall, 303
Whitcomb, 69, 424
White, 6, 24, 25, 42, 64, 73, 75, 76, 78, 80, 84, 91, 103, 109, 155, 169, 188, 202, 211, 278, 282, 296, 299, 300, 303, 306, 323, 324, 332, 340, 341, 344, 376, 383, 385, 386, 387, 403, 440, 445, 447, 469, 475, 482, 493, 504, 513, 540
Whitehead, 207, 348
Whitehorn, 522
Whitehouse, 52
Whitely, 318
Whitener, 53
Whitesides, 359
Whitfield, 103, 190, 194, 302, 387, 431
Whiting, 7, 74, 76, 81, 410, 412, 423, 494, 500, 502, 504
Whitlock, 347
Whitman, 299, 452
Whitmarsh, 444
Whitmore, 178, 210, 229, 256, 330, 504
Whitney, 49, 83, 321, 383, 509
Whittaker, 428
Whittelsey, 404
Whittemore, 63
Whitten, 429, 438
Whittingham, 82, 83
Whittlesey, 97, 103
Whitwell, 169, 379, 422

Whyte, 75, 264
Wickard, 71
Wickliffe, 185
Wiensenfeld, 100
Wier, 339, 378, 407
Wiggins, 306
Wight, 258
Wightman, 403
Wigton, 23
Wilban, 212
Wilbanks, 396
Wilber, 457
Wilcox, 3, 169, 208, 385, 501
Wilder, 524
Wildman, 323
Wildred, 162, 205
Wiley, 192, 385, 452
Wilhelm, 347
Wilhite, 255
Wilkes, 66, 75
Wilkin, 449
Wilkins, 10, 36, 71, 76, 103, 178, 383
Wilkinson, 36, 39, 84, 169, 192, 233, 378, 385, 407, 433, 508, 521
Willard, 53, 95, 104, 107, 463
Willcox, 11
Willell, 171
Willett, 138, 169, 255
Willey, 186, 302, 425
Williams, 1, 3, 6, 10, 12, 25, 33, 36, 39, 48, 52, 70, 73, 75, 78, 82, 87, 100, 103, 107, 113, 118, 148, 151, 159, 169, 170, 175, 179, 188, 192, 194, 213, 215, 246, 257, 269, 275, 278, 280, 289, 300, 311, 313, 317, 319, 323, 324, 332, 339, 341, 345, 353, 354, 372, 378, 383, 385, 396, 404, 408, 411, 416, 460, 461, 463, 466, 468, 479, 485, 498, 524, 527, 536, 543
Williamson, 5, 7, 29, 66, 98, 269, 315, 383, 406, 476, 497, 501, 515, 517
Williford, 176
Willis, 76, 114, 508

Willow Glen, 415
Wills, 222, 319, 469
Willson, 387
Wilmot, 362
Wilner, 103
Wilson, 2, 13, 14, 30, 43, 45, 55, 57, 59, 61, 67, 92, 94, 100, 103, 105. 106, 111, 112, 119, 121, 124, 131, 136, 154, 169, 170, 172, 177, 186, 192, 207, 215, 222, 237, 240, 251, 258, 279, 288, 298, 307, 324, 325, 332, 338, 354, 360, 363, 378, 383, 385, 389, 402, 407, 408, 433, 448, 460, 465, 466, 482, 483, 491, 501, 511, 522, 534, 539, 543, 547
Wiltberger, 91, 147, 202, 506
Wimer, 527
Wimsatt, 16, 106, 197
Wimsett, 171
Winborn, 408
Winchester, 169, 319, 383
Winder, 120, 128, 317, 443, 458, 523
Winders, 4
Windsor, 189
Wineberger, 441
Winfrey, 508
Wing, 41, 64, 526
Wingate, 148
Wingenroth, 107, 171
Wingerd, 164
Wingfield, 121, 516
Winkley, 129
Winn, 37, 268, 279, 445, 544
Winne, 451
Winney, 21
Winning, 518
Winship, 127, 287, 403, 530
Winslow, 31, 37, 142, 150, 521
Winston, 282, 376
Winter, 103, 169, 279, 307, 332, 449
Winters, 52
Winterson, 353
Winthrop, 97, 402, 450, 462
Wircott, 106

Wirt, 28, 60, 106, 107, 131, 169, 240
Wise, 30, 75, 222, 246, 255, 267, 383, 421, 440, 476, 497, 499, 509, 516
Wiseman, 359
Wishart, 5
Wisse, 378
Wiswell, 19
Witchell, 539
Withers, 91, 363, 496, 518
Witter, 119, 278, 290, 483
Wm & Mary, 464
Wm & Mary College, 317, 331, 398
Wolf, 179
Wolfe, 51, 119
Wolland, 356
Wollard, 25, 50, 122, 138, 175, 214, 222, 235, 320, 510
Wondulick, 103
Wood, 19, 30, 37, 40, 58, 62, 82, 98, 103, 174, 192, 222, 272, 287, 309, 321, 332, 389, 398, 406, 485, 490, 501, 505, 509, 517, 528
Woodard, 508
Woodbery, 19
Woodbridge, 5, 8, 51, 68, 524
Woodbury, 43, 367, 373, 418, 462
Woodcock, 109, 122
Woodfin, 84
Woodhouse, 322
Woodhull, 56
Woodle, 418
Woodley, 140
Woodman, 403
Woodruff, 113, 438
Woods, 126, 357, 383, 416, 440, 470
Woodward, 25, 59, 67, 75, 91, 103, 202, 212, 218, 232, 279, 302, 305, 311, 543
Woodworth, 144, 307, 352
Woody, 385
Wool, 140, 248
Woolard, 323
Wooley, 272, 490
Woolfolk, 355

Woolington tract, 305
Woolley, 79, 86, 121
Woolsey, 178
Woolworth, 355
Worden, 383
Workman, 326
Worley, 362
Wormley, 169, 306, 385, 389, 462
Wormsley, 14
Worn, 308
Worth, 390, 515, 531
Worthen, 310, 512, 527
Worthington, 36, 60, 148, 155, 187, 250, 256, 353, 379, 385, 478, 513, 543
Worthinton, 192
Wouvermanns, 436
Wregy, 359
Wren, 107
Wright, 1, 9, 11, 37, 45, 65, 99, 130, 132, 169, 170, 171, 172, 178, 180, 202, 229, 255, 262, 276, 283, 311, 326, 353, 354, 389, 391, 402, 418, 425, 426, 448, 452, 454, 462, 467, 509, 527
Wrist, 283
Wroe, 95, 106, 158, 321
Wroughton, 238
Wurner, 169
WWayne, 128
Wyatt, 286
Wyeth, 391
Wylie, 128, 136, 181, 206
Wyman, 107, 470, 539
Wynandis, 436
Wyse, 9, 365
Wysham, 81
Wysocsky, 445
Wysowski, 420

X

Xavier, 442

Y

Yadon, 212
Yarborough, 326
Yates, 10, 328, 345, 395, 494
Yeatman, 170, 218
Yeaton, 351
Yenny, 212
Yerby, 73, 88, 103, 176, 279, 281, 323, 332, 357, 366, 428
Yerkees, 302
Yokely, 230
Yokum, 141
Yorger, 83
York, 149
Yorok, 445
Youder, 140
Young, 2, 6, 25, 42, 45, 67, 71, 81, 100, 117, 134, 135, 145, 152, 187, 223, 244, 250, 255, 256, 280, 283, 346, 363, 379, 385, 387, 411, 421, 432, 442, 454, 460, 461, 464, 473, 478, 494, 507, 539
Youngman, 52
Youngs, 224
Yulee, 252
Yunganz, 399
Yuny, 456

Z

Zac, 186
Zacharie, 54, 72, 137, 143, 151, 181, 182
Zamora, 378
Zander, 85
Zantzinger, 414
Zappoine, 497
Zappone, 116, 219
Zavala, 43, 53, 123
Zeltner, 253
Zigler, 418
Zimmermaker, 443
Zimmerman, 375
Zoble, 526
Zoeller, 264

Zoka, 393
Zollickoffer, 33

Zrimbo, 394

Other Heritage Books by the author:

National Intelligencer *Newspaper Abstracts Special Edition: The Civil War Years Volume 1: January 1, 1861-June 30, 1863*

National Intelligencer *Newspaper Abstracts Special Edition: The Civil War Years Volume 2: July 1, 1863-December 31, 1865*

National Intelligencer *Newspaper Abstracts 1852*

National Intelligencer *Newspaper Abstracts 1851*

National Intelligencer *Newspaper Abstracts 1850*

National Intelligencer *Newspaper Abstracts 1849*

National Intelligencer *Newspaper Abstracts 1848*

National Intelligencer *Newspaper Abstracts 1847*

National Intelligencer *Newspaper Abstracts 1846*

National Intelligencer *Newspaper Abstracts 1845*

National Intelligencer *Newspaper Abstracts 1844*

National Intelligencer *Newspaper Abstracts 1843*

National Intelligencer *Newspaper Abstracts 1842*

National Intelligencer *Newspaper Abstracts 1841*

National Intelligencer *Newspaper Abstracts 1840*

National Intelligencer *Newspaper Abstracts, 1838-1839*

National Intelligencer *Newspaper Abstracts, 1836-1837*

National Intelligencer *Newspaper Abstracts, 1834-1835*

National Intelligencer *Newspaper Abstracts, 1832-1833*

National Intelligencer *Newspaper Abstracts, 1830-1831*

National Intelligencer *Newspaper Abstracts, 1827-1829*

National Intelligencer *Newspaper Abstracts, 1824-1826*

National Intelligencer *Newspaper Abstracts, 1821-1823*

National Intelligencer *Newspaper Abstracts, 1818-1820*

National Intelligencer *Newspaper Abstracts, 1814-1817*

National Intelligencer *Newspaper Abstracts, 1811-1813*

National Intelligencer *Newspaper Abstracts, 1806-1810*

National Intelligencer *Newspaper Abstracts, 1800-1805*

www.ingramcontent.com/pod-product-compliance
Lightning Source LLC
Chambersburg PA
CBHW070905300426
44113CB00008B/938